FOURTH EDITION

CULTURE COUNTS

A Concise Introduction to Cultural Anthropology

Serena Nanda
John Jay College of Criminal Justice, City University of New York

Richard L. Warms
Texas State University

CENGAGE
Learning·

Australia • Brazil • Mexico • Singapore • United Kingdom • United States

Culture Counts: A Concise Introduction to Cultural Anthropology, Fourth Edition
Serena Nanda and Richard L. Warms

Product Director: Marta Lee-Perriard

Product Manager: Elizabeth Beiting-Lipps

Content Developer: Julie Anderson, Lumina Datamatics, Inc.

Product Assistant: Timothy Kappler

Senior Content Project Manager: Cheri Palmer

Art Director: Michael Cook

Manufacturing Planner: Judy Inouye

Production Service: Jill Traut, MPS Limited

Photo Researcher: Lumina Datamatics, Inc.

Text Researcher: Lumina Datamatics, Inc.

Text Designer: Lisa Buckley

Cover Designer: Michael Cook

Cover Image: Subir Basak/Getty Images

Compositor: MPS Limited

For product information and technology assistance, contact us at **Cengage Learning Customer & Sales Support, 1-800-354-9706.**

For permission to use material from this text or product, submit all requests online at **www.cengage.com/permissions**. Further permissions questions can be e-mailed to **permissionrequest@cengage.com.**

Library of Congress Control Number: 2016947235

Student Edition:
ISBN: 978-1-337-10968-0

Loose-leaf Edition:
ISBN: 978-1-337-11615-2

Cengage Learning
20 Channel Center Street
Boston, MA 02210
USA

Cengage Learning is a leading provider of customized learning solutions with employees residing in nearly 40 different countries and sales in more than 125 countries around the world. Find your local representative at **www.cengage.com**.

Cengage Learning products are represented in Canada by Nelson Education, Ltd.

To learn more about Cengage Learning Solutions, visit **www.cengage.com**.

Purchase any of our products at your local college store or at our preferred online store **www.cengagebrain.com**.

Printed in the United States of America
Print Number: 01   Print Year: 2017

Dedication

To the grandchildren:
Alexander, Adriana,
Charlotte, Kai, and Waverly.
—SN—

To the students of Texas State University,
whose questions, comments, and
occasional howls of outrage have,
since 1988, made being an anthropology
professor the best job I can imagine.
—RW—

BRIEF CONTENTS

FEATURES CONTENTS

DETAILED CONTENTS

CHAPTER 10

SEX AND GENDER   245

PREFACE

ANTHROPOLOGY is the study of all people, in all places, and at all times. Students and scholars alike are drawn to anthropology as part of the realization that our lives and experiences are limited, but human possibilities are virtually endless. We are drawn to anthropology by the incredible variability of human society and our desire to experience and understand it. We are drawn by the beauty of other lives and sometimes by the horror as well. We wrote this fourth edition of *Culture Counts* to transmit some of our sense of wonder at the endless variety of the world and to show how anthropologists have come to understand, analyze, and engage with human culture and society.

Culture Counts, fourth edition, is a brief introduction to anthropology written particularly for students in their first two years of college but is appropriate for other audiences as well. Our goal has been to write in a clean, crisp, jargon-free style that speaks to readers without speaking down to them. Each chapter is relatively brief but is packed with ethnographic examples and discussions that keep readers involved and focused. Although it is written in an extremely accessible style, *Culture Counts* sacrifices none of the intellectual rigor or sophistication of our longer work, *Cultural Anthropology,* now in its 11th edition.

We have retained the same chapters as the third edition and the internal organization of the chapters is the same as well. Each chapter begins with clearly stated student learning objectives. These are followed with an opening ethnographic situation, circumstance, history, or survey designed to engage the readers' interest and focus their attention on the central issues of the chapter. These chapter opening essays raise questions about the anthropological experience, the nature of culture, and the ways in which anthropologists understand society. Much of what follows in each chapter indicates the ways in which the themes of the opening stories are illuminated by anthropological thinking.

Each chapter includes a section called "Using Anthropology," which provides an example of the ways in which anthropologists are engaged in applying anthropology to solve practical human problems. "Using Anthropology" is designed to bring anthropology into the lives of students and to show them how anthropological knowledge and the work of anthropologists is an active force in the social, political, and economic lives of people around the world.

At the end of each chapter, a feature entitled "Bringing It Back Home" explores a current controversy, issue, or debate from an anthropological perspective. Each example is followed by critical thinking questions entitled "You Decide." The questions encourage students to apply anthropological understanding as well as their own life experiences and studies to the issue under discussion. Through these exercises, students learn to use anthropological ideas to grapple with important issues facing our own and other cultures. They learn to apply anthropology to the realities of the world.

Finally, each chapter concludes with a summary written in question-and-answer form. This helps students actively review the chapter material and encourages them to think about anthropological information and part of the solution to problems.

Design is an important feature of *Culture Counts*. One of our goals is to present students with a clear, easy-to-follow text that is uncluttered and that highlights the main source of anthropology—ethnographic data. To address the visual orientation of contemporary students, we have taken considerable care to choose visually compelling photographs and to include high-quality maps and charts that provide visual cues for content and help students remember what they have read. Each image and its accompanying explanatory caption reflects specific passages and themes in the text. Extended ethnographic examples are accompanied by maps that provide the specific geographical location of the group under discussion.

PERSPECTIVE AND THEMES

As with *Cultural Anthropology,* our main perspective in *Culture Counts* is ethnographic, and our theoretical approach is eclectic. Ethnography is the fundamental source of anthropological data, and the interest in ethnography is one of the principal reasons students take anthropology courses. Ethnographic examples have the power to engage students and encourage them to think about other cultures as well as to analyze and question their own. Ethnographic examples that illuminate cultures, situations, and histories, both past and present, are used extensively in every chapter. *Culture Counts* describes the major issues and theoretical approaches in anthropology in a balanced manner, drawing analysis, information, and insight from many different perspectives. It takes a broad, optimistic, enthusiastic approach and promotes the idea that debates within the field are signs of anthropology's continued relevance rather than problems it must overcome.

In addition, we believe that issues of power, stratification, gender, ethnicity, globalization, and change are central to understanding contemporary cultures. These topics are given chapters of their own as well as integrated in appropriate places throughout the text.

Each chapter is organized so that the main ideas, secondary ideas, important terms and definitions, and ethnographic material stand out clearly. Although we have a deep appreciation for classic ethnography and cite it frequently, each chapter also presents current work in anthropology and includes many references to books and essays published in the past five years.

Culture Counts, fourth edition, continues the collaboration between Serena Nanda and Richard Warms. Warms's specialties in West Africa, anthropological theory, and social and economic anthropology complement Nanda's specialties in India, gender, law, and cultural anthropology. The results are synergistic. Our experiences, readings, discussions, and debates, as well as feedback from reviewers and professors who have adopted our books, have led to the production of a book that reflects the energy and passion of anthropology.

Both Nanda and Warms have extensive experience in writing textbooks for university audiences. In addition to *Cultural Anthropology,* now in its 11th edition, Nanda, with Jill Norgren, is the author of *American Cultural Pluralism and Law,* now in its third edition, and *Gender Diversity: Cross-cultural Variations,* now in its second edition. Nanda is also the editor of the gender section of the new *International Encyclopedia of Human Sexuality* (ed. By Anne Bolin and Patricia Whelehan). Warms, with R. Jon McGee, is author of

Anthropological Theory: An Introductory History, now in its sixth edition. Warms and McGee are also the editors of *Theory in Social and Cultural Anthropology: An Encyclopedia.* Warms, McGee, and James Garber have also written *Sacred Realms: Readings in the Anthropology of Religion,* second edition. Collaborative writing continues to be an exciting intellectual adventure for us, and we believe that the ethnographic storytelling approach of this book will promote students' growth as well.

▋▊ NEW IN THIS EDITION

We have made a number of significant changes and additions to this fourth edition, based partly on recent developments in the field of anthropology and partly on the valuable feedback we have received from our adopters and reviewers. Some substantial changes include:

△ A greater number of photos, directly tied to the text narrative, as well as an increased number of maps, tables, charts, and graphs.

△ New chapter opening stories, including "Working with Young Offenders in Brazil," "Arctic Cultures and Climate Change," "Wealth and Power of the Ashanti State," "Wealth and Poverty: Global Perspectives," and "The Contradictions of Globalization."

△ New Bringing It Home chapter features include "UX (User Experience)," "Discrimination Against Trans People in the United States," "Fundamentalism and Religious Change," and "Religion, Art, and Censorship."

▋▊ CHAPTER OVERVIEWS

Chapter 1, "What is Anthropology and Why Should I Care?" has substantial updates in the "Biological Anthropology" section. The "Linguistic Anthropology" section has been updated to include new technology. The "Using Anthropology: Forensic Anthropology" section has been updated to include examples of mass murder and genocide. The organization of the section discussing the reasons for studying anthropology has been improved and new archaeological data about human violence has been added.

In Chapter 2, "Culture Counts," has increased coverage of medical anthropology, focusing on the differentiation of disease and illness. The coverage of the legalization of marijuana has been updated and the photography program has been expanded and revised.

Chapter 3, "Doing Cultural Anthropology," has a new opening ethnography about working with young offenders in Brazil. New information has been added to emphasize the distinction between cultural and moral relativism and the section on power and voice in anthropology has been rewritten. An updated and expanded "Using Anthropology" section focuses on Polly Wiessner and her work with the Enga in Papua New Guinea. The "Bringing It Back Home" section has been updated to include the Islamic State and Boko Haram.

Chapter 4, "Communication," has been revised to increase coverage of political speech and of the "Northern Cities Shift." The "Bringing It Back Home: English Only" section has been substantially updated and now includes new coverage of the "three-generation rule."

Chapter 5, "Making a Living," has an edited and revised chapter opening story, which is now called "Arctic Cultures and Climate Change." The "Human Adaptation and Environment" section has been substantially rewritten and reorganized. There is additional coverage of pastoralism and the case study of "Musha: A Peasant Agricultural Village in Egypt" has been expanded.

Chapter 6, "Economics," includes improvements to the organization of the section "Organizing Labor," and a new subsection on households and kin groups in small-scale society. There has been a significant rewrite of the section "Specialization in Complex Societies" (with a new quote from Adam Smith), and there is a new "Using Anthropology" section about Ukraine, which includes events of the past three years. All statistics in the chapter are updated, and there is a new "Bringing It Back Home" section about UX (User Experience).

Chapter 7, "Political Organization," begins with a new feature about wealth and power in the Ashanti State. It includes an updated section on chieftainships, reflecting the ways these were changed by globalization. There are also updates to the "State and Social Stratification" section that reflect the current refugee crisis and problems of the denial of citizenship. The "Bringing It Back Home" section on the U.S./Mexico border fence has been substantially revised.

Although the structure of Chapter 8, "Stratification: Class, Caste, Race, and Ethnicity" remains unchanged, large sections of the chapter have been thoroughly rewritten. There is a new opening story: "Wealth and Poverty: Global Perspectives." The section on "The American Class System" is almost entirely new. There has been a major revision of "Using Anthropology: Homelessness and Social Activism" and a thorough rewrite of "Race and Racial Stratification in the United States." The section on "Ethnic Stratification in the United States" has been thoroughly updated.

Chapter 9 on "Marriage, Family, and Kinship" includes a new "Using Anthropology" section examining domestic violence and the culture defense. The section on arranged marriage has been expanded to incorporate changes taking place among female Indian garment workers. The "Bringing It Back Home: Caring for the Elderly" section has been expanded.

Chapter 10, "Sex and Gender," includes a new section on gender hierarchies in wealthy nations and a new "Bringing It Back Home" essay about discrimination against trans people in the United States.

Chapter 11, "Religion," has been slightly scaled down to match the size of the other chapters. It includes significant revisions of the section on "Shamans" and the section on "Witches and Sorcerers." There is a new ethnography that features the work of Charles Price on the Rastafarians and a new "Bringing It Back Home" section that explores fundamentalism and religious change.

Chapter 12, "Creative Expression: Anthropology and the Arts," includes several new features. There is a new section on Frida Khalo that highlights the relationship between art and politics. Another new section focuses on marketing indigenous arts, and a new "Bringing It Back Home" examines the connections between art, religion and censorship.

Chapter 13, "Power, Conquest, and a World System," has been updated to provide more emphasis on the Americas. There is new information on the role of disease in the colonization of the Americas. A new passage examines the historic role of the United Nations in relation to national self-determination. The "Bringing It Back Home" on the limits of tolerance has been updated to include information about the refugee and terror crises of 2015–2016.

Chapter 14, "Culture, Change, and Globalization," has been updated and expanded to provide more information on the great contemporary migrations now taking place throughout the Middle East and Europe. There is a new opening ethnography about the contradictions of globalization. There is a new section on families adapting to globalization as well as substantial updates to the sections on sweatshop labor and political instability. All of the statistical information has been updated to the most recent available.

▌▌▌ TEACHING FEATURES AND STUDY AIDS

Each chapter includes outstanding pedagogical features to help students identify, learn, and remember key concepts and data. Several learning aids help students better understand and retain the chapter's information, as follows:

△ Full-color opening photos with captions placed at the beginning of each chapter.

△ Student Learning Objectives provide clearly stated, measurable goals for student learning.

△ Each chapter opens with an essay that focuses on an ethnographic situation, circumstance, or history designed to capture students' interest and launch them into the chapter.

△ Each chapter concludes with a brief essay ("Bringing It Back Home") and questions ("You Decide") that encourage the application of anthropological thinking to a current controversy, issue, or debate. The questions can be used as assignments or to promote classroom discussion.

△ Summaries are arranged as numbered questions and answers at the end of each chapter and recap critical ideas to aid with study and review.

△ Key terms are listed alphabetically at the end of each chapter, for quick review.

△ A running glossary of key terms is found in the margins of the pages where the terms are introduced.

△ References for every source cited within the text are listed alphabetically at the end of the book.

▌▌▌ SUPPLEMENTS

▌▌▌ Instructor Resources

△ **Online Instructor's Manual with Lesson Plans.** The manual includes learning objectives, a detailed chapter outline, key terms, film and media suggestions, discussion questions, in-class activities, and Anthropology Connections.

△ **Downloadable Word Test Bank.** The enhanced test bank includes a variety of questions per chapter—a combination of multiple-choice, true-false, completion, essay, and critical thinking formats, with a full answer key. The test bank is coded to the learning objectives that appear in the main text, and identifies where in the text (by section) the answer appears. Finally, each question in the test bank has been carefully reviewed by experienced anthropology instructors for quality, accuracy, and content coverage so instructors can be sure they are working with an assessment and grading resource of the highest caliber.

△ **Cengage Learning Testing.** Powered by Cognero, the accompanying assessment tool is a flexible, online system that allows you to:

- import, edit, and manipulate test bank content from the text's test bank or elsewhere, including your own favorite test questions;
- create ideal assessments with your choice of 15 question types (including true/false, multiple-choice, opinion scale/Likert, and essay);
- create multiple test versions in an instant using drop-down menus and familiar, intuitive tools that take you through content creation and management with ease;
- deliver tests from your LMS, your classroom, or wherever you want—plus, import and export content into other systems as needed.

△ **Online PowerPoint Lectures.** Helping you make your lectures more engaging while effectively reaching your visually oriented students, these handy Microsoft PowerPoint® slides outline the chapters of the main text in a classroom-ready presentation. The PowerPoint slides reflect the content and organization of the new edition of the text and feature some additional examples and Quick Quizzes.

Student Resources

△ *Globalization and Change in Fifteen Cultures: Born in One World, Living in Another,* **edited by George Spindler and Janice E. Stockard.** In this volume, 15 case study authors write about culture change in today's diverse settings around the world. Each original article provides insight into the dynamics and meanings of change, as well as the effects of globalization at the local level. (978-0-534-63648-7)

△ *Case Studies in Cultural Anthropology,* **edited by George Spindler and Janice E. Stockard.** Select from more than 60 classic and contemporary ethnographies representing geographic and topical diversity. Newer case studies focus on culture change and culture continuity, reflecting the globalization of the world, and include a legacy edition of Napoleon Chagnon's *Ynomamö,* and a fourth edition of Richard Lee's *The Dobe Ju/'hoansi.* Recent publications include *Shadowed Lives,* by Leo Chavez.

△ *Case Studies on Contemporary Social Issues,* **edited by John A. Young.** Framed around social issues, these new contemporary case studies are globally comparative and represent the cutting-edge work of anthropologists today. Recent publications include *Slaughterhouse Blues,* by Donald Stull and Michael Broadway, and *Seeking Food Rights: Nation, Inequality and Repression in Uzbekistan,* by Nancy Rosenberger.

ACKNOWLEDGMENTS

It gives us great pleasure to thank the many people who have been associated with this book. We are most appreciative of the helpful comments made by our reviewers: Karen Kapusta-Pofahl, *Washburn University;* Leilani Declue, *Casper College;* Rebecka Daye, *Oregon State University;* Shahna Arps, *University of Toledo;* Anthony Conard, *Sinclair Community College;* Melony Stambaugh, *Gateway|NKU|Art Academy of Cincinnati;* Erin Kenny, *Drury University;* Cynthia Klink, *SUNY-Oneonta;* Katherine Nelson, *Inver Hills Community College;* Christine Dixon, *Green River College;* Angela McArdle, *Sandhills Community College;* Angela Montague, *University of Oregon;* Mark Mansperger, *Washington State University–Tri-Cities;* Benjamin Augustyn, *Miami Dade College;* Karen Danner, *Pierce College;* Cynthia Reeves, *Richmond Community College;* Linda Scott, *Cuesta College|Allan Hancock College;* Jennifer Zovar, *Whatcom Community College;* Bruce Sanchez, *Lane Community College|Linn-Benton Community College;* and Paris Adkins, *Los Angeles Southwest College.*

We gratefully acknowledge the support of our universities and the help of the staffs of our departments at John Jay College of Criminal Justice and Texas State University. In addition, many of our students have contributed ideas, reflections, and labor to this project. Serena Nanda would particularly like to thank her former student, Carolann Riccardi for her many comments and information on the American family and professor Niko Besnier for his ongoing interest, help, and superb research, particularly in sports, gender, and gender diversity.

Our families continue to form an important cheering section for our work, and we thank them for their patience and endurance and for just plain putting up with us.

We are deeply grateful to the people at Cengage Learning, particularly our Product Manager, Elizabeth Beiting-Lipps, for her support, encouragement, and insight. In addition, we thank Julie Anderson, content developer, and Cheri Palmer, content production manager. We are also grateful to Jill Traut of MPS Limited who shepherded us through the production process.

The knowledge, editing skills, and superb suggestions made by the many people involved in the production of this book have greatly contributed to it.

ABOUT THE AUTHORS

Serena Nanda is professor emeritus of anthropology at John Jay College of Criminal Justice, City University of New York. In addition to *Cultural Anthropology,* now in its 11th edition, her published works include *Neither Man nor Woman: The Hijras of India,* winner of the 1990 Ruth Benedict Prize; *American Cultural Pluralism and Law;* and *Gender Diversity: Cross Cultural Variations, now in its second edition.* She most recently was the associate editor of the gender section of the international encyclopedia of sexuality. Nanda is also the author of two anthropological murder mysteries: *The Gift of a Bride: A Tale of Anthropology, Matrimony and Murder,* set in an Indian immigrant community in New York City, and *Assisted Dying: An Ethnographic Murder Mystery on Florida's Gold Coast.* She has also authored many journal and encyclopedia articles on arranged marriage, gender pluralism, and teaching anthropology. She has always been captivated by the stories people tell and by the tapestry of human diversity. Anthropology was the perfect way for her to immerse herself in these passions, and, through teaching and writing, to spread the word about the importance of understanding both human differences and human similarities. Students and faculty are invited to contact her with their comments, suggestions, and questions at snanda@jjay.cuny.edu.

Richard L. Warms is professor of anthropology at Texas State University in San Marcos, Texas. In addition to *Cultural Anthropology,* now in its 11th edition, his books include *Anthropological Theory: An Introductory History,* now in its 6th edition, and *Sacred Realms: Essays in Religion, Belief, and Society.* Warms is co-editor of the SAGE *Encyclopedia of Theory in Social and Cultural Anthropology* as well as the author of articles in journals and edited volumes on commerce, religion, and ethnic identity in West Africa; African exploration and romanticism; African veterans of the French colonial armed forces; kinship and friendship in Africa; as well as essays on the history of anthropology. Warms's interests in anthropology were kindled by college courses and by his experiences as a Peace Corps volunteer in West Africa. He has traveled extensively in Africa, Europe, Asia, and Latin America. He continues to teach Introduction to Cultural Anthropology each year and also teaches classes on the history of anthropological theory, economic anthropology, the anthropology of religion, and the anthropology of film and media at both the graduate and undergraduate levels. Students and faculty are invited to contact him with their comments, suggestions, and questions at r.warms@txstate.edu.

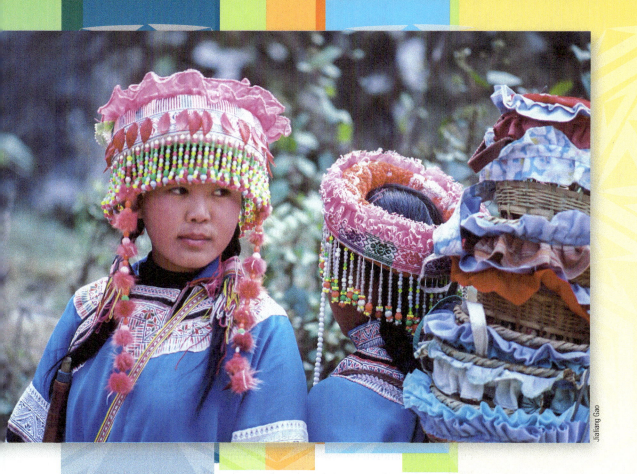

Jialiang Gao

Although most anthro-
pologists study a single
problem, together they
are interested in the total
range of human activity.
Here, colorfully dressed
women from the Miao
ethnic minority pose on
a narrow mountain trail
in Guizhou, China. What
questions would you ask
about them?

1

WHAT IS ANTHROPOLOGY AND WHY SHOULD I CARE?

AFTER YOU HAVE READ THIS CHAPTER, YOU WILL BE ABLE TO:

△ Define anthropology and explain how it differs from other academic disciplines.

△ List the major subdisciplines of anthropology.

△ Explain some of the ways that anthropology is applied both for careers and for general understanding.

△ Discuss and explain the ideas of cultural relativism and ethnocentrism.

△ Describe anthropology's position on race.

△ Describe some of the key reasons for studying anthropology.

THE NACIREMA

NTHROPOLOGISTS have become so familiar with the diversity of ways different peoples behave in similar situations that they are not surprised by even the most exotic customs. However, the magical beliefs and practices of the Nacirema are so unusual that it seems desirable to describe them as an example of the extremes to which human behavior can go. The Nacirema are a North American group living in the territory between the Canadian Cree, the Yaqui and Tarahumare of Mexico, and the Carib and Arawak of the Antilles. Little is known of their origin, although tradition states that they came from the east.

Nacirema culture is characterized by a highly developed market economy, but Naciremans spend a considerable portion of the day in ritual activity. The focus of this activity is the human body, the appearance and health of which loom as dominant concerns in the ethos of the people.

The fundamental belief underlying the whole system appears to be that the human body is ugly and has a natural tendency to debility and disease. People's only hope is to avert these through the use of ritual and ceremony, and every household has one or more shrines devoted to this purpose. The rituals associated with the shrine are secret and are discussed with children only when they are being initiated into these mysteries. I was able, however, to establish sufficient rapport with the natives to examine these shrines and to have the rituals described to me.

The focal point of the shrine is a box or chest built into the wall in which are kept the many charms and magical potions no native believes he could live without. Beneath the charm box is a small fountain. Each day, every member of the family, in succession, enters the shrine room, bows his head before the charm box, mingles different sorts of holy water in the fountain, and proceeds with a brief rite of purification. The holy waters are secured from the Water Temple of the community, where the priests conduct elaborate ceremonies to make the liquid ritually pure.

The Nacirema have an almost pathological horror of and fascination with the mouth, the condition of which is believed to have a supernatural influence on all social relationships. Each day, Naciremans perform a complex set of rituals devoted to the mouth. Were it not for these rituals, they believe that their teeth would fall out, their gums bleed, their jaws shrink, their friends desert them, and their lovers reject them.

In addition to daily mouth rites, the people seek out a holy-mouth-man once or twice a year. These practitioners have an impressive set of paraphernalia, consisting of a variety of augers, awls, probes, and prods. The use of these objects in the exorcism of the evils of the mouth involves almost unbelievable ritual torture of the client. The holy-mouth-man uses these tools to scrape, prod, and cut particularly sensitive areas of the mouth. Magical materials believed to arrest decay and draw friends are inserted in the mouth. The extremely sacred and traditional character of the rite is evident in the fact that the natives return to the holy-mouth-men year after year, despite the fact that their teeth continue to decay. One has but to watch the gleam in the eye of a holy-mouth-man, as he jabs an awl into an exposed nerve, to suspect that a certain amount of sadism is involved in these practices. And indeed much of the population shows definite masochistic tendencies. For example, a portion of the daily body ritual performed only by men involves scraping and lacerating the surface of the face with a sharp instrument.

Nacirema medicine men have an imposing temple, or *latipsoh,* in every community of any size. The more elaborate ceremonies required to treat very sick patients can be performed only at this temple. These ceremonies involve not only the priests who perform miracles but also a permanent group of vestal maidens who move sedately about the temple chambers in distinctive costume.

The *latipsoh* ceremonies are so harsh that it is surprising that sick adults are not only willing but also eager to undergo the protracted ritual purification, if they can afford to do so. No matter how ill the supplicant or how grave the emergency, the guardians of the temple will not admit a client if he cannot give a rich gift to the custodian. Even after one has gained admission and survived the ceremonies, the guardians continue to demand gifts, sometimes pursuing clients to their homes and businesses.

Supplicants entering the temple are first stripped of all their clothes. Psychological shock results from the fact that body secrecy is suddenly lost. A man whose own wife has never seen him in an excretory act suddenly finds himself naked and assisted by a vestal maiden while he performs his natural functions into a sacred vessel. Female clients find their naked bodies are subjected to the scrutiny, manipulation, and prodding of the medicine men. The fact that these temple ceremonies may not cure, and may even kill the patients, in no way decreases the people's faith in the medicine men.

In conclusion, mention must be made of certain practices of the Nacirema that have their base in native esthetics but depend on the pervasive aversion to the natural body and its functions. There are ritual fasts to make fat people thin and ceremonial feasts to make thin people fat. Other rites are used to make women's breasts larger if they are small, and smaller if they are large. General dissatisfaction with breast shape is symbolized by the fact that the ideal form is virtually outside the range of human variation. A few women afflicted with almost inhuman hyper-mammary development are so idolized that they make a handsome living by simply going from village to village and permitting the natives to stare at them for a fee.

Our review of the ritual life of the Nacirema has shown them to be a magic-ridden people. It is hard to understand how they have managed to exist so long under the burdens they have imposed upon themselves. But even exotic customs such as these take on real meaning when they are viewed with the insight that Bronislaw Malinowski, one of the most important 20th-century anthropologists, provided when he wrote: "Looking from far and above, from our high places of safety in civilization, it is easy to see all the crudity and irrelevance of magic. But without its power and guidance early man could not have mastered his practical difficulties as he has done, nor could man have advanced to the higher stages of civilization."

The essay you've just read is adapted from a classic piece of American anthropology by Horace Miner (1912–1993). Despite being more than half a century old, it has lost none of its bite. The essay is good because it plays upon two critical themes that continue to draw people to anthropology: our quest to gain knowledge and to understand people who are vastly different from ourselves and our desire to know ourselves and our own culture better.

Miner's essay draws you in as you read about the strange and bizarre customs of people who at first appear utterly different from yourself. You're not only titillated by the details of exotic practices but also comforted by the scientific writing style that seems to assure you that somehow this all makes sense. At some point in your reading, you probably realized that Miner is, in fact, describing American customs as they might be seen from the point of view of an unknowing but perhaps quite perceptive observer. Your first reaction might be to chuckle at the narrator's misunderstandings and treat the essay as an example of just how wrong an outside observer might be about a culture. But if you're a reflective person, you might have also wondered if the narrator hadn't turned up some fairly penetrating insights about the nature of our society. Clearly, the narrator has misunderstood some of the ways Americans think about bathrooms, dentists, and hospitals. But is the narrator so far off in describing the American attitude toward disease, decay, and death? Finally, if you caught the joke early enough, you might have pondered the meaning of the quote that ends the essay: Have we really "advanced to the higher stages of civilization?" What does that mean anyway?

Miner's essay deals with some of the critical questions and desires at the heart of anthropology: How do we understand other people and actions that seem different, odd, or strange? Why do people do what they do? And, perhaps more profoundly, how do we go about describing other people's cultural worlds, and how do we know if these descriptions are accurate? We will return to these issues in many places in this book. But first, a brief definition and description of anthropology: **Anthropology** is the scientific and humanistic study of human beings. It encompasses the evolutionary history of humanity, physical variation among humans, the study of past societies, and the comparative study of current-day human societies and cultures.

A **society** is a group of people who depend on one another for survival or well-being. **Culture** is the way members of a society adapt to their environment and give meaning to their lives. It includes ideas, beliefs, and values as well as behaviors.

Some critical goals of anthropology are to describe, analyze, and explain different cultures, to show how groups live in different physical, economic, and social environments, and to show how their members give meaning to their lives. Anthropology attempts to comprehend the entire human experience. Through human paleontology, it describes the evolutionary development of our species. Through archaeology, it reaches from current-day societies to those of the distant past. Through primatology, it extends beyond humans to encompass the animals most closely related to us.

Human beings almost everywhere are **ethnocentric** (see Figure 1.1). That is, they consider their own behavior not only right but also natural. We often want other people to behave just like we do, and we feel troubled, insulted, or outraged when they do not. Indeed, part of our reaction to the Nacirema essay stems from the fact that the Naciremans seem to

Anthropology: The scientific and humanistic study of human beings encompassing the evolutionary history of humanity, physical variation among humans, the study of past societies, and the comparative study of current-day human societies and cultures.

Society: A group of people who depend on one another for survival or well-being as well as the relationships among such people, including their statuses and roles.

Culture: The learned behaviors and symbols that allow people to live in groups; the primary means by which humans adapt to their environment; the ways of life characteristic of a particular human society.

Ethnocentrism (ethnocentric): Judging other cultures from the perspective of one's own culture. The notion that one's own culture is more beautiful, rational, and nearer to perfection than any other.

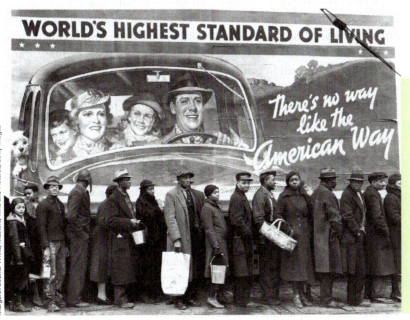

Margaret Bourke-White/Masters/Time Life Pictures/Getty Images

Figure 1.1 Ethnocentrism is the belief that one's own culture is superior to any other. This famous photograph, taken in 1937 by Margaret Bourke-White, draws attention to the contrast between the sentiment on the billboard and the people waiting in a bread line beneath. Note that the passengers in the car are white but all the people waiting for food are black.

do things that, to us, seem neither right nor natural. However, as the essay suggests, the range of human behavior is truly enormous. For example, should you give your infant bottled formula, or should you breast-feed not only your own child but, like the Efe of Zaire, those of your friends and neighbors as well (Peacock 1991:352)? Is it right that emotional love should precede sexual relations? Or should sexual relations precede love, as is normal for the Mangaian of the Pacific (Marshall 1971)? If a child dies, should we bury it, or, as Wari' elders say was proper, should it be eaten (Conklin 1995)? And what about sex? Are boys naturally made into men through receipt of semen from older men, as the Sambia claim (Herdt 1987)? For anthropologists, these examples suggest that what is right or natural for human beings is not easily determined and that attempts to understand human nature and theories of human behavior cannot be based simply on our own cultural assumptions. To accurately reflect humanity, they also must be based on studies of human groups whose goals, values, views of reality, and environmental adaptations are very different from our own. We can achieve an accurate understanding of humanity only by realizing that other groups of people who behave differently from us and have different understandings also consider the things they do and the ways they understand the world to be normal and natural.

One job of anthropology is to understand what actions and ideas mean within their contexts and to place these within the broader framework of human society, environment, and history. Anthropologists refer to the practice of attempting to understand cultures within their contexts as **cultural relativism**. It is important to understand that practicing cultural relativism does not mean that anthropologists believe all cultural traditions to be good or to be of equal worth. Anthropologists do not believe that all cultural traditions should be honored or preserved. People around the world, and indeed in our own society, do terrible things. Slavery, human sacrifice, and torture are all cultural practices. Anthropologists do not defend such customs on the basis of cultural relativism. However, anthropologists do believe that we need to understand even those practices that horrify us. Anthropologists study how they developed, how they work in society, and how they are experienced by the people who live them. And, sometimes, how they might be changed. Both ethnocentrism and cultural relativism are examined in greater detail in Chapter 3.

Anthropologists bring a holistic approach to understanding and explaining. To say anthropology is **holistic** means that it combines the study of human biology, history, and the learned and shared patterns of human behavior and thought we call *culture* in order to analyze human groups. Holism separates anthropology from other academic disciplines, which generally focus on one factor—biology, psychology, physiology, or society—as the explanation for human behavior.

Cultural relativism: The idea that cultures should be analyzed with reference to their own histories and values rather than according to the values of another culture.

Holism (holistic): In anthropology, an approach that considers the study of culture, history, language, and biology essential to a complete understanding of human society.

Because anthropologists use this holistic approach, they are interested in the total range of human activity. Most anthropologists specialize in a single field and a single problem, but together, they study the small dramas of daily living as well as spectacular social events. They study the ways in which mothers hold their babies or sons address their fathers. They want to know not only how a group gets its food but also the rules for eating it. Anthropologists are interested in how people in human societies think about time and space and how they see and name colors. They are interested in health and illness and the significance of physical variation as well as many other things. Anthropologists study these things not only in other societies but in our own as well. Anthropologists maintain that culture, social organization, history, and human biology are tightly interrelated. Although we can never know absolutely everything about any group of people, the more we know about the many different facets of a society, the clearer the picture we are able to draw and the greater the depth of our understanding.

SPECIALIZATION IN ANTHROPOLOGY

In the United States, anthropology has traditionally included four separate subdisciplines: biological (or physical) anthropology, linguistic anthropology, archaeology, and cultural anthropology. In this section, we briefly describe each of them.

Biological or Physical Anthropology

People live in a broad range of ecological and social conditions. Our ability to survive and prosper in many different circumstances is based on the enormous flexibility of cultural behavior. The capacity for culture, however, is grounded in the biological history and physical makeup of our species. Humans are biocultural beings; that is, our lives involve both biological and cultural dimensions. Therefore, to understand fully what it is to be human, we need a sense of how the biological aspects of human adaptation came about and how they both influence and are influenced by human cultural behavior.

Biological (or physical) anthropology is the study of humankind from a biological perspective. It focuses primarily on the aspects of humanity that are genetically inherited. Biological anthropology includes numerous subfields, such as the analysis of skeletons; the study of human nutrition; the statistical study of human populations; the study of patterns of disease; and the study of primates, animals that are closely related to humans.

Biological (or physical) anthropology: The subdiscipline of anthropology that focuses on the study of people from a biological perspective, primarily on aspects of humankind that are genetically inherited.

Biological anthropology is probably best known for the study of human evolution. Paleoanthropologists search for the origins of humanity, using the fossil record to trace the history of human evolution. They study the remains of the earliest human forms, as well as those ancestral to humans and related to humans.

Another subspecialty of biological anthropology, called human variation, is concerned with physiological differences among humans. Anthropologists who study human variation map physiological differences among modern human groups and attempt to explain the sources of this diversity.

Our unique evolutionary history resulted in the development of a biological structure, the human brain, capable of inventing, learning, and using cultural adaptations. Cultural adaptation, in turn has affected human biology. For example, in *Catching Fire* (2009), Richard Wrangham argues that an aspect of culture, the ability to control fire and use it to cook food, led to dramatic biological and social changes in human ancestors. Cooked food was more digestible than raw, and this resulted in changes in human anatomy (far shorter digestive tracts than our closest primate relations). Cooking food required changes in social organization that led to much greater cooperation between males and females than is found among nonhuman primates. Wrangham thus shows that human beings are not simply social and cultural "software" running on biological "hardware." Rather, the cultural and the biological are intimately related and ultimately inseparable. Human evolution is both a biological and a cultural process.

In addition to studying humans and their ancestors, biological anthropologists study nonhuman primates as well. These are members of the biological order that includes monkeys, apes, and humans. We study monkeys and apes for the clues that their chemistry, physiology, morphology (physical structure), and behavior provide about our own species. At one time, primates were studied mainly in the artificial settings of laboratories and zoos, but now much of the work of biological anthropologists involves studying these animals in the wild. Jane Goodall, who works with chimpanzees in Tanzania is among the best known anthropologists. Other well-known primatologists include Sarah Hrdy and Jill Preutz.

▌▌▌ Linguistic Anthropology

Language is the primary means by which people communicate with one another. Although most creatures communicate, human speech is more complex and creative, and it is used more extensively than the communication systems of other animals. Language is an essential part of what it means to be human and a basic part of all cultures. **Linguistic anthropology** is concerned with understanding language and its relation to culture.

Linguistic anthropology:
The study of language and its relation to culture.

Language is an amazing thing we take for granted. When we speak, we use our bodies—our lungs, vocal cords, mouth, tongue, and lips—to produce noise of varying tones and pitches. And, somehow, when we do this, if we speak the same language, we are able to communicate with one another. Linguistic anthropologists want to understand how language is structured, how it is learned, and how this communication takes place.

Language is a key way that we transmit culture. Thus, studying language helps us understand culture. For example, people generally talk about the people, places, and objects that are important to them. Therefore, the vocabularies of spoken language may give us clues to important aspects of culture. Knowing the words that people use for things may help us to glimpse how they understand the world.

Language involves much more than words. When we speak, we perform. If we tell a story, we don't simply recite the words. We emphasize some things. We add inflection that can turn a serious phrase comic or a comic phrase serious. We give our own special tilt to a story, even if we are just reading a book out loud. Linguistic anthropologists are interested in the ways in which people perform language—in the ways they change and modify the meanings of their words.

All languages change. Historical linguists work to discover the ways in which languages have changed and the ways in which languages are related to each other. Understanding linguistic change and the relationships between languages helps us to work out the past of the people who speak them. Knowing, for example, the relationships among various Native American languages give us insight into the histories and migrations of those who speak them.

The technological changes of the past two decades have opened a new world of communications. The widespread use of cell phones, email, texting, and social networking sites such as Facebook create entirely new ways of communicating, changing both the occasions on which people communicate and the language they use. For example, 50 years ago, people who lived at great distances from each other communicated relatively rarely. The mail was often slow, and phone calls were expensive. Now, such people may communicate many times daily, texting each other, speaking on the phone and interacting with each other using tools such as Facebook, Instagram, and Snapchat. Online and mobile games such as Warcraft, Minecraft, Words with Friends, and many others allow real-time interaction across vast distances. Cell phones in particular have become extremely important in poorer nations. For example, in 1998, there were no cell phones in Botswana. But by 2006, there were more than 800,000, enough for half the total population and more than six times the number of landlines. By 2008, virtually the entire population had cell phones (Aker and Mbiti 2010). A 2014 Pew Research Center survey of seven African nations showed that two-thirds or more of the population owned cell phones (Pew Research Center 2015a). Studying these changes in communication is an exciting new challenge for linguistic anthropologists.

Understanding language is a critical task for people interested in developing new technology as well. We live in a world where computers talk to us and listen to us. We will be able to build machines that use language effectively only if we understand how humans structure and use language.

▮▮▮ Archaeology

Archaeology: The subdiscipline of anthropology that focuses on the study of past cultures based primarily on their material remains.

Archaeology is the study of past cultures through their material remains (archaeologists don't dig up dinosaurs or other ancient fossils; that is the job of paleontologists). Archaeologists add a vital time dimension to our understanding of cultures.

Many archaeologists study prehistoric societies—those for which no written records have been found or no writing systems have been deciphered. However, even when an extensive written record is available, as in the case of ancient Greece or Colonial America, archaeology can help increase our understanding of the cultures and lifeways of those who came before us.

Archaeologists' goal is to reconstruct past culture from material remains or artifacts. An artifact is any object that human beings have made, used, or altered. Artifacts include pottery, tools, garbage, and whatever else a society has left behind.

In the popular media, archaeology is mainly identified with spectacular discoveries of artifacts from prehistoric and ancient cultures, such as the tomb of the Egyptian king Tutankhamun. As a result, people often think of archaeologists primarily as collectors. But contemporary archaeologists are much more interested in using their findings to understand and explain past cultural behavior than in creating collections. Their principal task is to explain how people lived in the past based on the nature and the patterns of the artifacts such people have left behind. Archaeologists work like detectives, slowly sifting through and interpreting evidence. The context in which things are found, the location of an archaeological site, and the precise position of an artifact within that site are critical to interpretation. In fact, these may be more important than the artifact itself.

There are many different specialties within archaeology. Urban archaeology is a good example. Urban archaeologists delve into the recent and distant past of current-day cities. In doing so, they uncover knowledge of the people often left out of the history books, making our understanding of the past far richer than it was. For example, Elizabeth Scott's work at Nina Plantation in Louisiana (2001) adds to our understanding of the lives of slaves and free laborers from the 1820s to the 1890s, and the discovery of an African Burial Ground in New York City in 1991 provides us with insight into the lives of free and enslaved Africans in the 17th and 18th centuries.

Another important archeology subfield is cultural resource management, or CRM. Archaeologists working in CRM are concerned with the protection and management of archaeological, archival, and architectural resources. They are often employed by federal, state, and local agencies to develop and implement plans for the protection and management of such cultural resources.

▌▌▌ Cultural Anthropology

The study of human society and culture is known as **cultural anthropology**. Anthropologists define society as a group of people persisting through time and the social relationships among these people: their statuses and roles. Traditionally, societies are thought of as occupying a specific geographic location, but modern transportation and electronic communication have made specific locales less important. Societies are increasingly global rather than local phenomena.

As Chapter 2 will show, culture is an extremely complex phenomenon. Culture is the major way in which human beings adapt to their environments and give meaning to their lives. It includes human behavior and ideas that are learned rather than genetically transmitted, as well as the material objects a group of people produces.

Cultural anthropologists attempt to understand culture both as a universal human phenomenon and as a characteristic of a group of people. They use many different research strategies to examine the dynamics of particular cultures and to search for general principles that underlie all cultures. They may explore the ways in which different societies adapt to their environments, the means by which they produce or acquire food, the structure of their economy, how their members understand the world and their place in it, or how members of different cultures interact with and change one another (see Figure 1.2). Anthropologists are often particularly interested in the effects of differences of power both among cultures and within individual cultures. Research in cultural anthropology is almost always based on participant observation, long-term fieldwork gathering data by observing and participating in people's lives.

Ethnography and ethnology are two important aspects of cultural anthropology. **Ethnography** is the description of society or culture. An ethnographer attempts to describe an entire society or a particular set of

Cultural anthropology: The study of human thought, behavior, and lifeways that are learned rather than genetically transmitted and that are typical of groups of people.

Ethnography: The major research tool of cultural anthropology, including both fieldwork among people in a society and the written results of such fieldwork.

Figure 1.2 Cultural anthropologists describe and analyze current-day cultures. Their studies often focus on culture change. Here, young Buddhist monks in Bagan, Myanmar study their smartphones. Before 2012, cell phones were rare in Myanmar. Now more than one in three Myanmarese have them.

Prasit Chansareekorn/Getty Images

Emic: Examination of societies using concepts, categories, and distinctions that are meaningful to members of those societies.

Etic: Examination of societies using concepts, categories, and rules derived from science; an outsider's perspective.

Ethnology: The attempt to find general principles or laws that govern cultural phenomena through the comparison of cultures.

cultural institutions or practices. Ethnographies may be either emic, or etic, or may combine the two. An **emic** ethnography attempts to capture what ideas and practices mean to members of a culture. It attempts to give readers a sense of what it feels like to be a member of the culture it describes. An **etic** ethnography describes and analyzes culture according to principles and theories drawn from Western scientific traditions such as ecology, economy, or psychology. **Ethnology** is the attempt to find general principles or laws that govern cultural phenomena. Ethnologists compare and contrast practices in different cultures to find regularities.

Cultural anthropology is a complex field with many different subfields. One index of this complexity is the more than 50 different sections and interest groups of the American Anthropological Association; the vast majority of these are concerned with cultural anthropology. Some examples include political and legal anthropology, which is concerned with issues of nationalism, citizenship, the state, colonialism, and globalism; humanistic anthropology, which is focused on the personal, ethical, and political choices humans face; and visual anthropology, which is the study of visual representation and the media.

Cultural anthropologists are often particularly interested in documenting and understanding the ways in which cultures change. They examine the roles that power and coercion play in change, as well as humans' ability to invent new technologies and social forms and modify old ones. Studies of culture change are important because rapid shifts in society, economy, and technology are basic characteristics of the contemporary world. Understanding the dynamics of change is critical for individuals, governments, and corporations. One goal of cultural anthropology is to be able to contribute productively to public debate about promotion of and reaction to change, both in our own society and elsewhere.

▮▮▮ Applied Anthropology

Although anthropology is mainly concerned with basic research—that is, trying to answer the big questions about the origins of our species, the nature of culture, and the meanings and functions of human social institutions—from the start, anthropologists have been interested in the application of their studies. Anthropologists such as Franz Boas contributed to debates on race and foreign policy at the turn of the 20th century. Margaret Mead, Ruth Benedict, and others did studies aimed at helping America's efforts during World War II. However, throughout much of the 20th century, almost all anthropologists worked in universities. In the past 50 years, however, anthropology has increasingly become a full-time profession for people outside of academe. **Applied anthropology** is the use of cultural anthropology, linguistics, archaeology, and biological anthropology to solve practical problems in business, politics, delivery of services, and land management. There are anthropologists who analyze factory floors and decision-making structures for large corporations. There are those who try to determine the best ways to sell products or deliver services. There are anthropologists who work for hospitals and health care organizations, improving the ability of these agencies to serve their patients. Some anthropologists work in politics, performing foreign and domestic policy analysis for governmental agencies. Some are employed in trying to find effective ways to deliver aid to people in poor nations. Other anthropologists work in museums or on public lands, uncovering our archaeological heritage and both preserving it and making it available to the public.

Applied anthropology: The application of anthropological knowledge to the solution of human problems.

▮▮▮ Using Anthropology: Forensic Anthropology

Every chapter in this book has a section called "Using Anthropology," in which we describe some of the different ways that anthropologists use their skills in effecting action in the world. Among other topics, we explore examples of how engaged anthropologists work for the communities they study (Chapter 3), linguistic anthropologists help solve crimes (Chapter 4), and nutritional anthropologists help stop hunger (Chapter 5). Our first section is about forensic anthropologists.

Popularized in television shows such as *Bones* and documentaries such as *The Decrypters*, forensic anthropology is a well-known example of applied biological anthropology. Forensic anthropologists use their

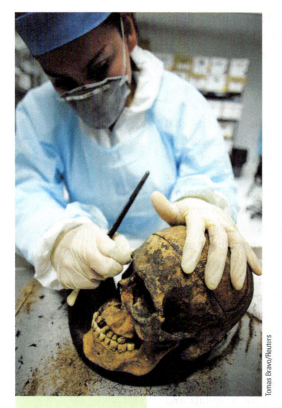

Tomas Bravo/Reuters

Figure 1.3 Forensic anthropologists advise law enforcement agencies and other organizations about the identity of victims of crime, political violence, and natural disaster. Here, a forensic anthropologist cleans a skull exhumed from a mass grave near Juarez, Mexico.

Source: Tomas Bravo/ Reuters/Landov

anthropological training to identify skeletal or badly decomposed human remains (see Figure 1.3). Their goal is to discover information that can assist in the detection of crime and the prosecution of those responsible.

A case begins when a law enforcement agency or medical examiner's office calls for help in discovering the identity and cause of death of an individual whose remains have recently been found. Sometimes, the remains are nonhuman or very old. However, in many cases they are from a recent violent crime.

The next step is the recovery of the body. Anthropologists are frequently called upon to assist law enforcement personnel and supervise the procedure. Sometimes bodies are found well preserved, but often they are burned, fragmentary, or in various stages of decomposition. Michelle Hamilton, a forensic anthropologist at Texas State University, has recovered bodies in caves, on mountaintops, in forests, down wells, under water, from burned homes, and in many other environments. In one tricky case, Hamilton was called in to excavate underneath a house. A family member who lived in this house had disappeared seven years previously. When she found the body, it was still fully fleshed and recognizable. Therefore, Hamilton concluded that it could not have been buried the entire time since the individual first disappeared. The mystery was solved when family members confessed that the individual had been killed seven years ago, but they had stored the body in a freezer and had only buried it that week.

After a body has been recovered, the anthropologist's job is to establish the individual's identity and to help interpret the events surrounding death. To do this, anthropologists analyze bones and other remains. They search for unique identifying marks. They also analyze trauma and fracture patterns that can provide information about how the person died. In some cases, facial reconstructions are made to provide a likeness of the deceased and to further aid in identification.

In every case, forensic anthropologists are required to produce a report of their findings. Law enforcement agencies use these reports to match bodies with missing persons reports and, if foul play is suspected, to prosecute the individuals believed to be responsible. Usually the anthropologist's work ends with the delivery of the report, but on occasion, a forensic anthropologist is required to testify as an expert witness in a criminal trial.

In addition to working on individual criminal cases, forensic anthropologists have also played very important roles in identifying the dead in cases of political mass murder or genocide (Fondebrider and Wilson 2015). Some examples are excavations to find and determine the identity of those who "disappeared" during the "dirty war" in Argentina (1974–1983) and those who were murdered during the Bosnian genocide (1992–1995).

Everyday Anthropology

Although there are many careers in anthropology, it is our conviction that applied anthropology consists of more than just people earning their living with the skills they gained through training in anthropology. Perhaps the most important aspect of anthropology (and the primary justification for its existence) is the way an anthropological perspective demands that we open our eyes and experience the world in new ways. In a sense, learning anthropology is like a fish coming to understand the meaning of water. How could a fish understand water? Water is all a fish knows, and it knows it so well it cannot distinguish it from the nature of life and reality itself. Similarly, all humans live in cultures, and our experiences are normally bounded by our cultures. We often mistake the realities and truths of our culture for reality and truth itself, thinking that the ways we understand and do things are the only appropriate ways of understanding and doing.

The fish understands the meaning of water only when it is removed from the water (usually with fatal consequences). If anthropology is not exactly about removing people from their culture, it is, in a sense, the conscious attempt to allow people to see beyond its bounds. Through learning about other cultures, we become increasingly aware of the variety of different understandings present in the world and of the social dynamics that underlie culture. This promotes awareness of the meanings and dynamics of our own and other cultures and encourages us to think creatively.

Applied anthropology doesn't just mean that you get paid to use your anthropological training. All of us do applied anthropology when we bring anthropological understandings and insight to bear on problems of inequality, education, war, violence, and peace. We don't apply anthropology only when we write a report. We apply anthropology when we go to the voting booth and to the grocery store, when we discuss issues with our friends and, if we're religious, when we pray. Anthropology provides no simple answers. There is no correct anthropological way to vote, shop, or pray. However, anthropology does inform our decisions about these things. Our attempt to understand other cultures and our own lets us look on our own with new eyes.

❚❚❚ ANTHROPOLOGY AND "RACE"

One thing that anthropology can help us understand is "race." In the United States, most people see humanity as composed of biological "races." Census forms, applications, and other documents ask us to indicate our "race." Although "race" is clearly an important social and historical fact in the United States, most anthropologists believe that "race" is not a scientifically valid system of classification. Despite more than a century of attempts, biological anthropologists have never found an agreed-on, consistent system of "racial" classification. We have put the word *race* in quotation marks in this paragraph to begin to focus your attention on these problems. To make reading easier, we dispense with the quotation marks for the remainder of the book.

There are many problems in developing a scientifically valid racial classification scheme. First, most Americans understand race as a bundle of traits: light skin, light hair, light eyes, and so on. But, if this is so, the races you create are the result of the traits you choose. For example, races based on blood type would be very different than races based on skin color. Skin color strikes most Americans as a "natural" way to identify race, but there is no biological reason to think that skin color is more important than blood type. Almost all traits we use to assign people to a race are facial traits. It is hard to imagine a biological reason why the shape of one's eye or nose should be more important than the characteristics of one's gallbladder or liver. However, it is easy to find a social reason: Traits easily visible on the face enable us to rapidly assign individuals to a racial group. This is a good clue that race is about society, not biology.

There are many other problems with racial classifications. For example, if race is biological, members of one race should be genetically closer to one another than to members of different races. But measurement reveals that people are as different from others classified in their same race as they are from those in different races. Or consider people from Central Africa, Melanesia (islands in the western Pacific), and France. Most Central Africans and most Melanesians have dark-colored skin (see Figure 1.4). Most French are light. However, Africans are more closely related to the French than either is to Melanesians. This isn't surprising considering the geographical distances involved (it's about 3,200 miles from Bangui in Central Africa to Paris but about 10,000 miles from Bangui to Vanuatu in Melanesia), but it suggests that traits like skin color have arisen at many times and many places in the past. Furthermore, although the characteristics of our species, *Homo sapiens,* were fully present 35,000 to 40,000 years ago, a 2004 study by Rohde, Olson, and Chang argues that all current-day humans have common ancestors who lived only 2,000 to 5,000 years ago. At a time depth of more than 5,000 years, all people alive today have exactly the same ancestors. Rohde, Olson, and Chang write: "no matter the languages we speak or the color of our skin, we share ancestors who planted rice on the banks of the Yangtze, who first domesticated horses on the steppes of the Ukraine, who hunted giant sloths in the forests of North and South America, and who labored to build the Great Pyramid of Khufu" (2004: 565).

Anthropology teaches us that the big differences among human groups result from culture, not biology. Adaptation through culture, the potential for cultural richness, and creativity are universal. They override physical variation among human groups. We explore issues surrounding race and ethnicity many places in this book, particularly in Chapter 8.

WHY STUDY ANTHROPOLOGY

If you're reading this book for a course at a college or university, and particularly if you are considering a major in anthropology, you've probably faced some strong questioning from friends and family members. Some may have known about anthropology and applauded your wisdom in taking this course. Others may have had no idea what anthropology is. Still others probably asked you what anthropology is good for and what you hope to do with it. You might have told them that you want to work in one of the many aspects of applied anthropology or to become a college professor, but we think there are other good answers as well.

Some Honest Talk about College Majors and Jobs

Anthropology is, in most places, part of a liberal arts curriculum, which also generally includes English, geography, history, modern languages, philosophy, political science, psychology, and sociology, as well as

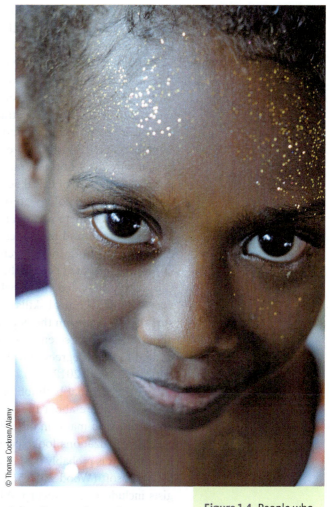

© Thomas Cockrem/Alamy

Figure 1.4 People who appear similar might have very different ancestries. The girl in this photo might look African but is from Vanuatu in the South Pacific Ocean, over 8,000 miles from the closest point on the African continent.

other departments and programs. Some liberal arts departments have teacher-training programs. If you want to teach middle school English, in most places, you will probably need a degree in English. Some liberal arts programs involve training in highly technical skills that are directly applicable to jobs. For example, geography departments may offer training in remote sensing, the acquisition and analysis of aerial photography, and multispectral and infrared imagery and radar imagery for use by government and business. However, the vast majority of liberal arts programs produce generalists. An undergraduate degree in psychology does not generally get you a job as a psychologist. Most people who study political science do not go on to be politicians, and few who study sociology go on to work as sociologists. In fact, survey data show that there is often little connection between people's undergraduate major and their eventual career. For example, in a survey of 3,000 alumni from the University of Virginia School of Arts and Sciences, 70 percent reported that there was little such connection. And this survey included many who had majored in subjects that taught very specific technical skills (University of Virginia 2008). Even more surprising, data from the National Science Foundation show that only about a quarter of science and engineering graduates hold jobs that are related to their degrees and that require at least a bachelor's degree to perform (*Science* 2012:275).

The fact is that both job prospects and the careers that people eventually pursue are about the same for students who study anthropology and those who major in other liberal arts disciplines. Many private and public organizations look specifically to hire anthropologists. The U.S. government is probably the largest employer of anthropologists, followed by Microsoft (Wood 2013:51). Companies that have hired anthropologists include Intel, Citicorp, AT&T, Kodak, Disney, and General Mills, and many others. In a 2015 article in the business magazine *Forbes* titled "That 'Useless' Liberal Arts Degree Has Become Tech's Hottest Ticket," the chief information officer at a major tech firm argues that technological brilliance is not enough, firms need people who understand arts and processes (Anders 2015).

In addition, there are numerous jobs for anthropologists in the public and nonprofit sectors, including positions in international development, social services, museums, national parks, and governmental organizations concerned with national security. However, like students with other majors, most anthropology graduates go on to more general positions in government, business, and the professions. Some become executives at large corporations, some are restaurateurs, some are lawyers, some are doctors, some are social service workers, some sell insurance, some are government officials, some are diplomats, and yes, no doubt, some still live with their parents and might even ask, "Do you want fries with that?" And you could say the same of the vast majority of majors in most subjects at every university.

▌▌▌ Asking Better Questions

To refocus our question, we might ask: What are the particular ways of thought that anthropology courses develop and that are applicable to the very broad range of occupations that anthropologists follow? How is anthropology different from other social science disciplines? Although there are certainly many ways to answer these questions, it seems to us that three are of particular importance.

First, anthropology is the university discipline that focuses on understanding different groups of people. This focus on culture is one of the most valuable contributions anthropology can make to our ability to understand our world. Understanding cultures and approaching cultural differences from the perspective of cultural relativism helps us to develop the critical thinking skills that aid in analyzing and solving problems.

Although the United States has always been an ethnically and culturally diverse place, for most of its history, white Protestant men of northern European ancestry have held the reins of wealth and power. This isn't to say that all such men were rich and powerful. Most certainly were not. However, even if they were poor, they had an advantage: They were members of the dominant culture. If members of other cultural groups wanted to speak to them, do business with them, participate in public and civic affairs with them, they had to learn to speak the proper style of English. They had to learn the forms of address, body language, clothing, and manners appropriate to their role in U.S. culture. Because others had to do the work of changing their behavior, white Protestant men were often unaware of this disparity and accepted it simply as the way things were. *Miami Herald* columnist Leonard Pitts has pointed out that "if affirmative action is defined as giving preferential treatment on the basis of gender or race, then no one in this country has received more than white men" (2007). This is true whether or not such men wanted preference or even realized they were getting it. Many, focusing on their own hard work and very real struggles, bristled at the notion that they were privileged, but this didn't make it any less true.

The white, Protestant, northern European male is hardly an extinct species in the United States (such people still today control most of the nation's wealth). However, by the late 20th century, their virtual monopoly on power had begun to break up. Women and men from a great diversity of religious, ethnic, and racial backgrounds have moved to stronger economic and political positions. Moreover, the United States increasingly exists in a world filled with other powerful nations with very different histories and traditions. It is less and less a world in which everyone wants to do business with the United States and is willing to do so on American terms. Instead, it is a rapidly globalizing world characterized by corporations with headquarters and workforces spread throughout the globe and by capital and information flows that cross cultural boundaries in milliseconds. Americans who wish to understand and operate effectively in such a world must learn other cultures and other ways; failure to do so puts them at a distinct disadvantage.

At home, the United States is once again a nation of immigrants (see Figure 1.5). Until the late 20th century, most immigrants were cut off from their homelands by politics and by the expense and difficulty of communication. Under these conditions, assimilation to the dominant culture was essential. Although politics will always be an issue, today's immigrants can, in most cases, communicate freely and inexpensively with family and friends in their homelands and may be able to travel back and forth on a regular basis. Thus, complete assimilation is far less necessary or desirable.

Some people may applaud multiculturalism; others may bemoan what they feel is the passing of the "American" way of life. What no one can really dispute is that the world of today is vastly different from the

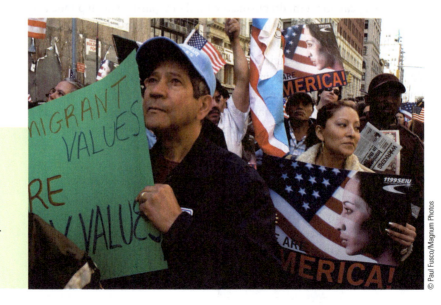

Figure 1.5 The United States is once again a nation of immigrants. In 2015 almost 14 percent of the U.S. population was foreign-born. This picture shows a 2006 demonstration in New York City against changes in immigration laws.

© Paul Fusco/Magnum Photos

world of 1950. Given the increasing integration of economic systems, declining costs of communication and transportation, and the rising economic power of China and other nations, we can be sure that people of different ethnic, racial, and cultural backgrounds will meet more and more frequently in arenas where none has clear economic and cultural dominance. Thus, an understanding of the nature of culture, and knowledge of the basic tools scholars have devised to analyze it are essential, and anthropology is the place to get them.

In addition to this first, very practical application, there is a second, more philosophical concern of anthropologists. Like scholars in many other disciplines, anthropologists grapple with the question of what it means to be a human being. However, anthropologists bring some unique tools to bear upon this issue. Within anthropology, we can look for the answer to this question in two seemingly mutually exclusive ways. We can look at culture as simply the sum total of everything that humans have done, thought, created, and believed. In a sense, as individual humans, we are heirs to the totality of human cultural practices and experiences. Anthropology is the discipline that attempts to observe, collect, record, and understand the full range of human cultural experience. Through anthropology, we know the great variety of forms that cultures can take. We know the huge variation in social organization, belief systems, production, and family structure that is found in human society. This gives us insight into the plasticity of human society as well as the limits to that plasticity.

Alternatively, we can answer the question by ignoring the variability of human culture and focusing on the characteristics that all cultures share. In the 1940s, George Murdock listed 77 characteristics that he believed were common to all cultures. These included such things as dream interpretation, incest taboos, inheritance rules, and religious ritual. More recently, authors (Antweiler 2016; Brown 1991; Cleaveland, Craven, and Danfelser 1979) have developed other lists and analysis. Brown (1991:143) notes that human universals are very diverse, and there is likely no single explanation for them. However, thinking about such commonalities among cultures may guide us in our attempt to understand human nature.

Finally, a third interest of anthropologists is in creating new and useful ways to think about culture. One particularly effective way to understand culture is to think of it as a set of answers to a particular problem: How does a group of human beings survive together in the world? In other words, culture is a set of behaviors, beliefs, understandings, objects, and ways of interacting that enable a group to survive with greater or lesser success and greater or lesser longevity. At some level, all human societies must answer this critical question, and to some degree, each culture is a different answer to it.

In the world today and in our own society, we face extraordinary problems: hunger, poverty, inequality, violence between groups, violence within families, drug addiction, pollution, crime. The list is long. However, we are not the only people in the world ever to have faced problems. At some level, all of these problems are the result of our attempt to live together as a group on this planet. Learning how other peoples in other places, and other times, solved or failed to solve their problems may give us the insight to solve our own; we might learn lessons, both positive and negative, from their cultural experiences.

In some ways, the cultures of today are unique. Societies have never been as large and interconnected as they are now. They have never had the wealth that many societies have today. They have never had the levels of technology, abilities to communicate, and abilities to destroy that our current society has. These characteristics make it naive to imagine that we can simply observe a different culture, adopt their ways as our own, and live happily ever after. We can no more recreate tribal culture or ancient culture or even the culture of industrialized nations of 50 years ago than we can walk through walls. But it does not therefore follow that the answers of others are useless to us.

In Greek drama, the notion of hubris is critical. Hubris is probably best understood as excessive pride or confidence that leads to both arrogance and insolence toward others. In Greek tragedy, the hubris of characters is often their fatal flaw and leads to their downfall. Heroes such as Oedipus and Creon were doomed by their hubris.

We surely won't find that the members of other cultures have provided ready-made answers to all the problems that confront us. But to imagine ourselves as unique, to imagine that the experiences of other peoples and other cultures have nothing to teach us, is a form of hubris, and as in tragedy, could well lead to our downfall.

The ancient Greeks contrasted hubris with *arete*. This characteristic implies a humble striving for perfection, along with the realization that such perfection cannot be reached. With the notion of *arete* in mind, we approach the study of anthropology cheerfully and with a degree of optimism. From anthropology, we hope to learn new ways of analyzing, understanding, celebrating, and coming to terms with the enormous variations in human cultural behavior. We hope to be able to think creatively about what it means to be human beings and to use what we learn to provide insight into the issues, problems, and possibilities of our own culture. We hope that, with the help of such understanding, we will leave the world a better place than we found it.

BRINGING IT BACK HOME
THE ANTHROPOLOGY OF VIOLENCE

The holistic approach of anthropology can help us understand violence. To what extent is violence simply an ineradicable part of human nature and to what extent is it a product of certain kinds of cultures? Have human beings always been violent, or was there an age when people lived in societies without violence? Can we hope for a future without violence or are we condemned to ever-increasing cycles of violence?

There are no simple answers to these questions. Anthropologists, political philosophers, and others have sometimes imagined that people in early human societies led a peaceful, almost utopian existence. At other times, they have imagined such societies as a struggle of all against all: constant battle for survival in which violence against nonfamily and non-group members was the rule rather than the exception. Neither of these ideas seems to hold much validity.

There is no doubt that humans have often lived in societies characterized by high levels of violence. Further, violence is ancient: a recent analysis of skulls at a 430,000-year-old archaeological site in Spain shows evidence of humans killing other humans (Sala et al. 2015). But Dr. Nohema Sala, the lead author of the study also notes that finds at the same site also show that human ancestors cared for the sick and the dead (Gill 2015).

Cultural anthropologists have often documented violence, and sometimes warfare, in many different societies. However, anthropologists have documented societies that have extremely low levels of violence as well. Some of these include the Chewong of the Malaysian peninsula (Howell 1989), the G/wi of central Botswana (Silberbauer 1982), and the Yandi of the Indian state of Andhra Pradesh (Kumar 1995). The Semai, a gardening society in the central Malay Peninsula, are one of the best-documented peaceful societies. Clayton and Carole Robarchek, anthropologists who have studied the Semai for more than 30 years, report that worldview is a key factor in Semai peacefulness. Semai see themselves as "essentially helpless in a hostile and malevolent universe" and believe that virtually all activities, even the most innocuous, are fraught with danger (1992:201). In this frightening world, they depend vitally on one another, and anything that threatens discord or violence is understood as a threat to their survival itself. Thus, although their society is peaceful, theirs is not a worldview that many would like to share.

More recently, Steven Pinker in *The Better Angels of Our Nature* (2011) argues that humanity as a whole is becoming less violent. He claims that acts of violence, torture, and cruelty of all types that were common in humanity's past are far less present today. Pinker argues that the decline in violence is the result of a combination of factors including the political dominance of large state societies whose governments monopolize the use of force, the emergence of humanitarian thinking in 17th- and 18th-century Europe, and the spread of commerce. Using a phrase from philosopher Peter Singer, Pinker talks of an "escalator of reason" that we use to discover that our interests are similar to those of other people and thus, we develop empathy with them.

Many anthropologists will be deeply skeptical of Pinker's claims. It is probably true that the routine cruelty of the relatively recent Western past has greatly diminished. However, much of this has happened quite recently and clearly the use of torture is still an important political issue in our society. There is little doubt that, in terms of total numbers of people killed, the 20th century was the most violent in the history of humanity. Much of this death occurred in various forms of state-sponsored violence, from warfare to famines caused by political actions. Even when physical violence is not present, state society includes the pervasive violence of inequality and, in many cases, outright oppression.

Anthropology does not provide any easy answers on violence. Instead, it shows that both violence and reconciliation are very basic aspects of human and indeed nonhuman primate behavior. The sources of both peace and violence may ultimately lie in human nature. However, the expression of violence is clearly an aspect of culture. The ways in which our cultures are structured and the worldviews we hold deeply affect the degree to which violence is present in any given society. Humans will probably always have violent thoughts and desires. But we can hope to create societies in which violence is rare or, perhaps, even entirely absent.

YOU DECIDE

1. Do you believe that humankind is getting more or less violent and cruel? What evidence can you bring to support your position?
2. The Robarcheks' analysis of the Semai shows that their peaceful lifestyle is a product of both the way their society is structured and the worldviews they hold. What kind of social structures and worldviews do you think promote peace?
3. Do you believe in the possibility of a society and a world without violence? What do you think is the relationship between physical violence and less obvious forms of violence such as discrimination, inequality, and oppression?

CHAPTER SUMMARY

1. What critical themes presented in Horace Miner's essay "Body Ritual among the Nacirema" continue to draw people to anthropology? Miner's essay encourages us to think about our quest to gain knowledge and understanding of people who are different from ourselves, and our desire to know ourselves and our own culture better.

2. What is anthropology? Anthropology is a comparative study of humankind. Anthropologists study human beings in the past and in the present and in every corner of the world.

3. What does it mean to say that anthropology is holistic? Anthropologists study the entire range of humans' biological, social, political, economic, and religious behavior as well as the relationships among the different aspects of human behavior in the past and present.

4. What are the main subfields of anthropology? Cultural anthropology, linguistic anthropology, archaeology, biological (physical) anthropology, and applied anthropology.

5. Does anthropology stress biological or cultural adaptation? Anthropology stresses the importance of culture in human adaptation. It asserts that critical differences among individuals are cultural rather than biological.

6. What is the anthropological position on race? Anthropology demonstrates that race is not a valid scientific category but rather is a social and cultural construct.

7. What sorts of jobs do anthropology majors usually get? Anthropology is part of the liberal arts curriculum. Both the job prospects and the careers of those who study anthropology are similar to those who study other liberal arts disciplines.

8. What critical problems and ways of thinking do anthropology courses address? Anthropology courses develop three important ways of thought that are applicable to the broad range of occupations followed by anthropologists: (1) Anthropology focuses on understanding other groups of people within their own historical and cultural context; (2) anthropologists grapple with the question of what it means to be human by observing, collecting, recording, and attempting to understand the full range of human cultural experience; and (3) anthropology encourages us to use our understanding of other cultures to think about our own.

9. What does anthropology tell us about humans and violence? Anthropology tells us that violence is ancient and part of our human heritage. However, peacemaking and reconciliation are also part of that heritage. Nonviolent societies do exist and we can hope to build societies with low levels of violence.

KEY TERMS

Anthropology	Emic
Applied anthropology	Ethnocentrism
Archaeology	Ethnography
Biological (or physical)	Ethnology
anthropology	Etic
Cultural anthropology	Holism (holistic)
Cultural relativism	Linguistic anthropology
Culture	Society

Many dimensions of culture are expressed in the ritual dress of these Maasai men participating in an initiation ritual. They are dressed in styles and patterns that the Maasai have used for many years, but each wears a wristwatch as well.

2

CULTURE COUNTS

AFTER YOU HAVE READ THIS CHAPTER, YOU WILL BE ABLE TO:

△ List the major characteristics of culture.

△ Describe the role that child-rearing practices play in culture.

△ Explain the relationship between culture and the ways in which people classify the world.

△ Give some examples of the way in which symbols create meaning for people in particular cultures.

△ Explain the ways in which culture can be considered a system and the ways in which it is not like a system.

△ Tell some of the ways in which culture is and is not shared.

△ Compare and contrast cultural and biological adaptation.

△ List some of the ways in which culture changes and describe the role of conflict and consensus in change.

FERAL CHILDREN

EUROPEANS, as well as members of many other cultures have often been fascinated by tales of feral or wild children, human children who are alleged to have grown up by themselves in the wild, apart from human civilization. Accounts of such children date to antiquity, and a website that appeared in the early 2000s claimed to document more than 80 cases between 250 and 2002 c.e. (Benzaquén 2006). Frequently, feral children are popularly supposed to have been raised by members of other animal species, often wolves or bears.

There is no reliable evidence that any human child has ever actually been raised by members of another species. Some of the many accounts of feral children seem to be outright fraud, but many others are probably stories about children who were abandoned because of a physical or mental disability and who survived by scavenging and begging around the edges of human settlements. Many of the most famous of these cases would, if they were alive today, probably be diagnosed with autism.

Two of the most famous feral children were Peter the Wild Boy, and Victor the Wild Boy of Aveyron (Newton 2002). Peter was found in 1725, in what is today northern Germany. Brought to the court of King George I in England, he was a well-known curiosity for the rest of his long life. Given to the care of court physician John Arbuthnot, who tried to educate him, Peter acquired the ability to use a few simple words and perform a few tasks but made little progress beyond that. He disappeared for more than three months in the summer of 1751 and, after he was found, was forced to wear a brass collar engraved with his name and address.

Victor lived in the forests around Aveyron in southern France in the last years of the 1790s. Like Peter, Victor's inability to speak and his bizarre behavior garnered much attention, first in Aveyron and later in Paris. Like Peter, Victor was given to the care of a physician, Jean Marc Gaspard Itard, who attempted to teach him to speak and to perform rudimentary tasks. And like Arbuthnot, Itard's attempts at instruction were largely ineffective.

Peter and Victor were famous in their own day and to some degree in ours as well. Some of the most important intellectuals of the era wrote about Peter, including Jonathan Swift (author of *Gulliver's Travels*), Daniel Defoe (author of *Robinson Crusoe* and many other works), and the Scottish jurist and early evolutionist James Burnett, Lord Monboddo. Victor was also the subject of extensive commentary during his lifetime, and his fame has continued into modern times. His life in both realistic and fictionalized form appears in many novels and films, particularly Francois Truffaut's 1970 film *L'enfant sauvage* (*The Wild Child*).

So, what is it about feral children that fascinated people in the 17th and 18th centuries and continues to fascinate today? Swift, Defoe, and Monboddo provided different answers: Swift's work is a critique of the culture of his era. Swift imagined Peter, who in reality was mute, trying to comprehend the alien social customs of the British aristocracy. Thus, through Peter, the culture of his era was made visible, and through his eyes, it was shown to be corrupt and absurd.

Defoe (1726) approached Peter from a more challenging angle. He wondered about the degree to which Peter really was a human being. Did he have a soul? Peter was human in form, but he could neither speak nor participate in human society in any meaningful way. Unable to speak, he was perhaps unable to think as well. Without culture, Peter's existence was a horribly lonely burden.

For Monboddo, Peter and other wild children proved that little or nothing was natural to humanity: Speech, upright posture, walking on two feet are all capacities that people had to be taught through a process of civilization. Monboddo used this idea to argue that orangutans were humans too; they had the capacities for human characteristics but had not learned to use them (Benzaquén 2006:131).

Victor (Figure 2.1) was captured and displayed in the era immediately following the French Revolution and The Terror. In this context, he too raised important questions. The philosophers of the French Revolution wanted to make humanity over. Many, following the philosopher Jean-Jacques Rousseau, believed that humans, in their natural form, free of the constraints of (European) culture, lacked morals but were essentially noble. Was Victor a "noble savage" without culture? Could proper education make him into a new and better type of person? Did Itard's failure to educate Victor mean that humans without society were so degraded that they could not be brought into society?

Figure 2.1 Victor, the Wild Boy of Aveyron, lived in France in the late 18th and early 19th centuries. Victor was probably autistic, but his "discovery" and the failure of attempts to educate him led to intense debate about human nature and culture. This romantic image was published in 1807.

Because Peter and Victor were almost certainly individuals with profound autism (and in Peter's case, perhaps a rare chromosomal disorder as well [Kennedy 2011]), observations of them could not have answered questions about humanity without culture. However, the writings and questions that surrounded them and the continued interest in cases of feral children today draw our attention to the nature of culture and the relationship between culture and human nature. Cases of wild children seem to make it clear that, without the constraints, assumptions, and patterns imposed by culture, it is extraordinarily difficult to express our human qualities and abilities. But what is culture?

Although coming up with a useful, brief definition of culture is difficult, an anthropologist from Mars observing the many different human cultures might discover six characteristics shared by all cultures:

1. Cultures are made up of learned behaviors. People are not born knowing their culture. They learn it through a process called enculturation.

2. Cultures all involve classification systems and symbols. A **symbol** is simply something that stands for something else. People use cultural symbols to create meaning.

3. Cultures are patterned and integrated. Thus, changes in one aspect of culture affect other aspects. However, elements of culture do not necessarily work smoothly with one another.

4. Cultures are shared. Although there may be disagreement about many aspects of a culture, there must be considerable consensus as well.

5. Cultures are adaptive and include information about how to survive in the world, but cultures can contain much that is maladaptive.

6. Cultures are subject to change. Whether propelled by their internal dynamics or acted upon by outside forces, cultures are always in flux.

Based on this list, we might define culture as the learned, symbolic, at least partially adaptive, and ever-changing patterns of behavior and meaning shared by members of a group.

Although anthropologists agree on the basic characteristics of culture, they disagree on their relative importance, how to study them, and indeed the goals of anthropology itself. For example, some anthropologists are deeply concerned with observable behavior. Other anthropologists wish to comprehend the ways in which other people understand their world. Some anthropologists hope to find general laws of human culture. Others are more concerned with describing specific aspects of particular cultures. These disagreements reflect different theoretical positions within anthropology. For our purposes, an **anthropological theory** is a set of propositions about which aspects of culture are critical, how they should be studied, and what the goal of studying them should be. Although those who hold different theoretical perspectives may insist that there is a right way and a wrong way to do anthropology, we suggest that theoretical perspectives are more like different windows through which one may view culture. Just as two windows may have views that overlap or views that show totally different scenes, perspectives on culture may overlap or reveal totally different aspects. Some of the major theoretical perspectives in anthropology are summarized in Table 2.1.

Symbol: Something that stands for something else. Central to language and culture.

Anthropological theory: A set of propositions about which aspects of culture are critical, how they should be studied, and what the goal of studying them should be.

Table 2.1 Some Major Anthropological Schools of Thought and Their Understanding of Culture.

Theory Name	Understanding of Culture	Critical Thinkers
Nineteenth-century evolution	A universal human culture is shared, in different degrees, by all societies.	E. B. Taylor (1832–1917) L. H. Morgan (1818–1881)
Turn-of-the-century sociology	Groups of people share sets of symbols and practices that bind them into societies.	Emile Durkheim (1858–1917) Marcel Mauss (1872–1950)
American historical particularism	Cultures are the result of the specific histories of the people who share them.	Franz Boas (1858–1942) A. L. Kroeber (1876–1960)
Functionalism	Social practices support society's structure or fill the needs of individuals.	Bronislaw Malinowski (1884–1942) A. R. Radcliffe Brown (1881–1995)
Culture and personality	Culture is personality writ large. It both shapes and is shaped by the personalities of its members.	Ruth Benedict (1887–1948) Margaret Mead (1901–1978)
Cultural ecology and neo-evolutionism	Culture is the way in which humans adapt to the environment and make their lives secure.	Julian Steward (1902–1972) Leslie White (1900–1975)
Ecological materialism	Physical and economic causes give rise to cultures and explain changes within them.	Morton Fried (1923–1986) Marvin Harris (1927–2001)
Ethnoscience and cognitive anthropology	Culture is a mental template that determines how members of a society understand their world.	Harold Conklin (1926–2016) Stephen Tyler (1932–)
Structural anthropology	Universal original human culture can be discovered through analysis and comparison of the myths and customs of many cultures.	Claude Lévi-Strauss (1908– 2009)
Sociobiology	Culture is the visible expression of underlying genetic coding.	E. O. Wilson (1929–) Jerome Barkow (1944–)
Anthropology and gender	The ways societies understand sexuality are central to understanding culture.	Michelle Rosaldo (1944–1981) Don Kullick (1960–)
Symbolic and interpretive anthropology	Culture is the way in which members of a society understand who they are and give lives meaning.	Mary Douglas (1921–2007) Clifford Geertz (1926–2006)
Practice theory	Culture emerges from the dynamic relationship between social structure and individual choice.	Pierre Bourdieu (1930–2002) Sherry Ortner (1941–)
Postmodernism	Because understanding of cultures most reflect the observer's biases, culture can never be completely or accurately described.	Renato Rosaldo (1941–) James Clifford (1945–)
Globalization	Culture is best analyzed as the global flow of identity, symbolism, money, and information.	Arjun Appadurai (1949–) David Harvey (1935–)

Note: Theoretical positions in anthropology represent sophisticated thinking and cannot be summed up in a single line. There are many outstanding books about anthropological theory, including McGee and Warms (2012), *Anthropological Theory: An Introductory History*.

In this chapter, we examine each element of our definition of culture. Each is a common characteristic of all human groups. However, each also raises questions, problems, and contradictions. Through examining these elements, we come to a keener appreciation of the nature of culture and, ultimately, what it means to be human.

CULTURE IS MADE UP OF LEARNED BEHAVIORS

Just about everything that is animate learns. Your dog, your cat, even your fish show some learned behavior. But, as far as we know, no other creature has as much learned behavior as human beings. Almost every aspect of our lives is layered with learning. Our heart beats, our eyes blink, and our knees respond reflexively to a doctor's rubber mallet, but to get much beyond that, we need learning. Food is a good example. Humans must eat; that much is determined biologically. However, we do not just eat; our culture teaches us what is edible and what is not. We decline many things that are nutritious as not being food. Many insects, for example, are perfectly edible. The philosopher Aristotle was particularly fond of eating cicadas, and northern Europeans ate some species of beetles well into the 19th century. Yet, most Americans have learned that insects are not food, and they will go hungry, to the point of starvation, before knowingly eating them (though we are perfectly willing to eat them if we are unaware we are doing so. For example, Natural Red #4, a common food dye is made from cochineal, a type of beetle). Further, we eat particular things at particular times, in particular places, and with particular people. For example, although it is acceptable to eat popcorn at the movies, you would be unlikely to have lamb chops and asparagus or a nice stir-fry at most movie theaters.

We sometimes think of learning as an aspect of childhood, but in every society, human beings learn their culture continuously. We are socialized from the moment of our births to the time of our deaths.

Although large demands for labor and responsible behavior may be placed on children in many societies, all humans remain physically, emotionally, and intellectually immature well into their teen years and perhaps into their early 20s. This lengthy period of immaturity has profound implications. First, it allows time for an enormous amount of childhood learning. This means that very few specific behaviors need be under direct genetic or biological control. Second, it demands that human cultures be designed to provide relatively stable environments that protect the young for long periods of time. Child-rearing practices in all cultures are designed to produce adults who know the skills, norms, and behavior patterns of their society—the cultural content. But the transmission of this content also involves shaping children's attitudes, motivations, values, perceptions, and beliefs so that they can function in their society. The process of learning to be a member of a particular cultural group is called **enculturation**.

As an example, consider child rearing among the Inuit, a hunting people of the Arctic. The Inuit teach their children to deal with a world that is a dangerously problematic place, in which making wrong decisions might well mean death (Briggs 1991). To survive in this harsh environment, Inuit must learn to maintain a "constant state of alertness" and an "experimental way of living." Therefore, developing skills for solving problems quickly and spontaneously is central to Inuit child rearing. Children are brought up to constantly test their physical skills to extend them and to learn their own capacity for pain and endurance (Stern 1999).

The Inuit.

Enculturation: The process of learning to be a member of a particular group.

Inuit children learn largely through observing their elders. Children are discouraged from asking questions. Rather, when confronted with a problem situation, they are expected to observe closely, to reason, and to find solutions independently. They watch, practice, and then are tested, frequently by adults asking them questions based on the idea of *isummaksaiyuq*, a northern Baffin Island Inuit term meaning to "cause (or cause to increase) thought." Some questions are very practical. For example, as they travel on the featureless, snow-covered tundra, an adult may ask a child, "Where are we?" or "Have you ever been here before?" Others are existentially challenging. Adults may ask children "Why don't you kill your baby brother?" or "Your mother's going to die—look, she's cut her finger—do you want to come live with me?" Such questions are not considered cruel. Rather, they force children to grapple with issues of grave consequence (Briggs 2005:161).

Play is a critical part of Inuit child rearing. Inuit games prepare children for the rigors of the arctic environment by stressing hand–eye coordination, problem solving, and physical strength and endurance. Some games involve learning by taking objects apart and trying to put them back together. This process develops careful attention to details and relationships, patient trial and error, and mental recording of results for future reference. Many games stress the body and test the limits of the individual's psychological and physical endurance (Nelson 1983). For example, in the ear pull game (see Figure 2.2), a thin loop of leather is positioned behind the ears of each of two competitors, who then pull away from each other until one gives up in pain (World Eskimo Indian Olympics 2016).

In addition to being physically adept and independent, Inuit children must learn to be cooperative and emotionally restrained. Under the

Figure 2.2 The Inuit ear pull game is a harsh test of physical endurance. Contestants pull against one another until one can no longer endure the pain. Here, Jacey Brave Heart, age 12, pulls against Drew Dewberry at the 2007 World Eskimo Indian Olympics in Anchorage, Alaska.

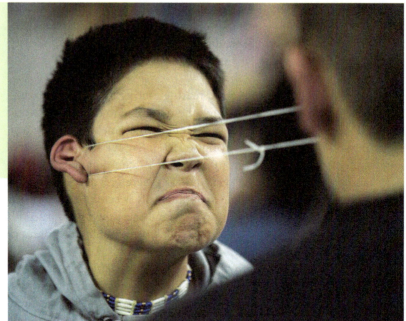

conditions of their closely knit and often isolated camp life, expressions of anger or aggression are avoided. The Inuit prize reason, judgment, and emotional control, and they believe that these characteristics grow naturally as children grow.

The Inuit believe that children have both the ability and the wish to learn. Thus, educating a child consists of providing the necessary information, which the child will remember sooner or later. Scolding is seen as futile. Children will learn when they are ready; there is no point in forcing children to learn something before they are ready to remember it. Inuit elders believe that frequent scolding makes children hostile, rebellious, and impervious to the opinions of others.

The study of enculturation has a central place in the history of anthropology and gave rise to some of its classic works. Margaret Mead's 1928 book, *Coming of Age in Samoa,* was a popular best seller and a landmark work that changed how Americans looked at childhood and culture (Mead 1971/1928). Mead and others who studied childhood learning are known as **culture and personality** theorists. They held that cultures could best be understood by examining the patterns of child rearing and considering their effect on adult lives and social institutions. Culture and personality theory was extremely influential from the 1920s to the 1950s. In more recent times, Practice Theorists and some Marxist anthropologists have focused on the ways in which education and child-rearing practices help societies reproduce through time. Enculturation remains an important topic of anthropological research.

Culture and personality:
A theoretical position in anthropology that held that cultures could best be understood by examining the patterns of child rearing and considering their effect on social institutions and adult lives.

CULTURE IS THE WAY HUMANS ORGANIZE THE WORLD AND USE SYMBOLS TO GIVE IT MEANING

Consider this: Can you really see your environment? For example, when you walk into a classroom, you notice some things but not others. You see your friends and other students, the professor, the video equipment, and so on. You might spend an entire semester without ever seeing the cracks in the ceiling, the pattern of the carpeting, or the color of the walls. Yet these things are as physically present as the chairs and your friends.

You see certain things in the classroom and overlook others because you mentally organize the contents of the classroom with respect to your role as a student. It is virtually impossible to see things without organizing and evaluating them in some manner. If you paid as much attention to the cracks in the wall, the patterns on the floor, and the humming of the ventilation system as you did to the professor's lecture, not only would you likely fail the class, but you would also live in a world that was overwhelming and impossibly confusing. Only through fitting our perceptions and experiences into systems of organization and classification can we comprehend our lives and act in the world. A human without this ability would be paralyzed, frozen by an overwhelming bombardment of sensations.

Methods of organizing and classifying are typical of groups. You are not the only one who thinks that the students and professors in a classroom are more important than the ceiling tiles; all students and professors probably share that perception.

Anthropologists have long proposed that culture is a shared mental model that people use to organize, to classify, and ultimately to understand their world. A key way in which this model is expressed is through language, a symbolic system.

Different cultures have different models for understanding and speaking about the world. For instance, in English, the verb *smoke* describes the action of ingesting a cigarette and the verb *drink* describes the action of consuming a liquid. However, in the Bamana language (also known as Bambara), spoken by the Bambara of Mali, the verb *min* is used both for smoking and for drinking. Americans classify rainbows as objects of beauty and frequently point them out to one another. However, Lacandon Maya in southern Mexico classify rainbows as dangerous and frightening, and pointing them out to other people is highly inappropriate. For them, rainbows are unlucky because they hold back the rain. Snakes, rather than a pot of gold, are found under them, and they are associated with particular types of ghosts.

Anthropologists who are particularly interested in describing the systems of organization and classification different cultures use often use a theoretical perspective called **ethnoscience**. Generally, these anthropologists are interested in capturing the understanding of members of a culture. Ethnoscience is one position or technique within a broader perspective called **cognitive anthropology**, which focuses on the relationship between the mind and society.

Ethnoscience: A theoretical position in anthropology that focuses on recording and examining the ways in which members of a culture use language to classify and organize their cognitive world.

Cognitive anthropology: A theoretical position in anthropology that focuses on the relationship between the mind and society.

▌▌ Using Anthropology: Culturally Specific Diseases—The Case of Lia Lee

Because all human beings are extremely similar biologically, all are subject to the same biologically based diseases. However, the ways in which people classify, experience, and understand health and illness differ dramatically among cultures. Anthropologist Arthur Kleinman (1988) differentiates between "disease," a patient's biological problem, and "illness," the social and cultural context in which the disease is experienced and the ways in which it is classified.

Anthropologists have identified many culturally bound syndromes, illnesses that are identified in only one or a small number of cultures. Fan death, the commonly held Korean belief that running a fan overnight in a room with the windows and doors closed can lead to the death of those sleeping in the room, is one example (Jennings 2013). *Bangungot*, the name for another culturally specific syndrome, is a term originating from the Tagalog word for "bad dream" and is found in the Philippines and elsewhere in Southeast Asia. Bangungot is diagnosed when young people, particularly adolescent and young adult men, die suddenly in their sleep. Eating disorders such as anorexia nervosa are culturally bound syndromes particular to rapidly industrializing societies, particularly in western Europe, the United States, and Asia.

Different ways of classifying and understanding illness and of treating disease present enormous challenges to health care around the world, particularly in multicultural societies such as the United States. The case of Lia Lee, described in Anne Fadiman's now classic 1997 *The Sprit Catches You and You Fall Down*, presents a powerful example and a cautionary tale. Lia Lee (see Figure 2.3) was the 14th child born to Foua Yang and Nao Kao Lee,

Figure 2.3 Foua Yang, Lia Lee's mother, holds Lia Lee's picture in 2012.

Sacramento Bee/Getty Images

Hmong refugees from Laos living in California. When she was 3 months old she began to experience seizures. However, the Lees were unable to explain Lia's condition to health care workers who spoke no Hmong and had no experience of Hmong culture. For them, the seizures were evidence that Lia's soul was being touched or taken by something from a different realm. Health care workers could not understand this, and it took a long time to diagnose Lia with epilepsy. However, this was the beginning of the problem, not the end. For the doctors, epilepsy was a disease to be treated with medicines, and they demanded that the Lees comply with their prescriptions, some of which were quite difficult and unpleasant to administer to a toddler. For the Lees, Lia's symptoms showed that she had *qaug dab peg*, an illness caused when a person's soul becomes separated from her body. Though Lia's condition needed a cure, it also meant that she could have spiritual powers and might become a shaman.

Doctors, social workers, and the Lee family fought bitterly over Lia's treatment. At one point, she was placed in foster care for a year because her parents refused to administer her medications, treating her instead with herbs and shamanic ritual. In 1986, when she was 4 years old, Lia suffered a profound seizure, followed by an infection. She lost most brain function, and was expected to die, but didn't. Although doctors and medical personnel at hospitals that treated her often spoke of her as if she were dead, she lived for another 26 years, never regaining consciousness but both cared for by her family and central to their lives. Though Fadiman (2012) acknowledges that it's not a medical explanation, she feels that Lia was kept alive by the constant love of her family.

Fadiman's account of Lia's story and the role of different cultural understandings in health care is required reading in many medical and social work programs. It was one of many cases that led to greater sensitivity regarding issues of language and culture in health care delivery in the United States. In an interview after Lia's death in the summer of 2012, Fadiman said that one of the key lessons of Lia's case was that Western medical personnel must try to understand illness from the point of view of their patients, particularly when they have patients from cultures that have different conceptions of health and illness. Doctors must understand that treatment is not something they can dictate but something that must be created through collaboration between patients and health care providers (Fadiman 2012; Fox 2012).

Symbols and Meaning

Human beings not only classify the world, but they also fill it with meaning. A key way that they do this is through the use of symbols. The simplest definition of a symbol is something that stands for something else. Words, both

Chris Sattlberger/Getty Images

Figure 2.4 Symbols do not have a single meaning but stand for large numbers of ideas and feelings. For many people in the United States, patriotic symbols such as the flag have deep intellectual and emotional content.

Symbolic anthropology: A theoretical position in anthropology that focuses on understanding cultures by discovering and analyzing the symbols that are most important to their members.

Interpretive anthropology: A theoretical position in anthropology that focuses on using humanistic methods, such as those found in the analysis of literature, to analyze cultures and discover the meanings of culture to its participants.

spoken and written, objects, and ideas can all be symbols. Symbols enable us to store information. For example, the book you are currently holding contains a huge amount of information all stored symbolically. Nonhuman animals must learn through experience or imitation and, therefore, the amount they can learn is relatively small. Humans can store information symbolically, as stories and teachings passed from generation to generation or as written words, thus human cultures can be endlessly large.

Symbols also have the ability to condense meaning (see Figure 2.4). People may take a single symbol and make it stand for an entire constellation of ideas and emotions. Religious symbols and national symbols often have this characteristic. The meaning of a national flag or a symbol such as the cross cannot be summed up in a word or two. These symbols stand for vast complexes of history, ideas, and emotions. People are often literally willing to fight and die for them.

Symbolic anthropologists try to understand a culture by discovering and analyzing the symbols that are most important to its members. These often reflect the deep concerns that are difficult for culture members to articulate. For example, according to Victor Turner (1967), among the Ndembu of East Africa, the mudyi tree is a central symbol and plays an important role in girls' puberty rites. The tree has a white, milky sap that symbolizes breast-feeding, the relationship between mother and child, the inheritance through the mother's family line, and, at the most abstract level, the unity and continuity of Ndembu society itself. It is unlikely that all Ndembu think deeply about all of these meanings during the puberty rites of their girls. However, Turner argues that this complex symbolism helps hold Ndembu society together by reaffirming its central tenets. For anthropologists, to understand the meaning of the mudyi tree and the role it plays in Ndembu society is to have penetrated deeply into the Ndembu view of the world.

Culture can also be analyzed using the tools of literature, and this is the job of **interpretive anthropology**. Clifford Geertz, one of the best-known interpretive anthropologists, said that, in a sense, culture is like a novel. It is an "ensemble of texts . . . which the anthropologist strains to read over the shoulders of those to whom they properly belong" (Geertz 2008/1973a:531). He meant that culture is a story people tell themselves about themselves. Like all good stories, culture engrosses us and helps us understand the nature and meaning of life. It comments on who we are and how we should act in the world. Interpretive anthropologists often find these cultural texts in public events, celebrations, and rituals. Analyzing them gives us clues and insights into the meaning of culture for its participants.

Consider the American fascination with football. American football has little appeal outside the United States, but here it draws more fans than any other sport. Football has lots of excitement and action, but so do many less popular sports. Some anthropologists argue that football's popularity is related to its symbolic meanings, that is, the unique ways in which it presents and manipulates important American cultural themes. Football attracts us because, more than other sports, it displays and manipulates ideas about the violence and sexuality underlying competition between men, the relationship of the individual to the group, racial character (Oriard 1993:18), as well as themes of national identity, particularly competitive opportunity and homeland security (Lindquist 2006:445). Football is just a game, but so is checkers. Millions watch football because it is meaningful to them in ways that checkers is not. For interpretive anthropologists, football's meaning derives from the ways in which it explores and comments on critical themes in American culture. Those who wish to understand American culture would do well to consider the meanings of football.

Interpretive and symbolic anthropologists use methods drawn from the humanities rather than from the sciences to uncover and interpret the deep emotional and psychological structure of societies. Their goal is to understand the experience of being a member of a culture and to make that experience available to their readers (Marcus and Fischer 1986).

||| CULTURE IS AN INTEGRATED SYSTEM—OR IS IT?

Consider a biological organism. The heart pumps blood, the lungs supply the blood with oxygen, the liver purifies the blood, and so on. The various organs work together to create a properly functioning whole. An early insight in anthropology was the usefulness of comparing societies to organisms. The subsistence system provides food, the economic and political systems determine how the food is distributed, religion provides the justification for the distribution system, and so on. Societies, like bodies, are integrated systems.

This **organic analogy** has strengths and weaknesses. It allows us to think about society as being composed of different elements (such as subsistence, politics, and religion), and it implies that anthropologists should describe the shape and role of such elements as well as the ways in which changes in one affect the others. For example, subsistence and

Organic analogy: The comparison of cultures to living organisms.

social structure are two identifiable social elements and are related to each other. Foraging is an activity most often done in small groups and requires little direction or coordination. People who forage for their food will probably have relatively loosely defined social groups with changing membership. Farming requires more coordination than foraging; therefore, people who farm will likely have a society with a more rigid structure and a more stable membership. If a group were to move from foraging to farming, we would expect it to develop an increasingly well-defined social structure.

However, the organic analogy also implies that properly functioning societies should be stable and conflict-free. The parts of a biological organism work together to keep the entire being alive and well. The lungs do not declare war on the liver. The result of conflict between the parts of a living thing is usually sickness or death. If such conflict occurs (an autoimmune disease, for example), we understand that the organism is not functioning properly, and steps should be taken to restore the system. Thinking of cultures as systems may similarly suggest that their parts should work in harmony and that conflict and struggle are deviations from normality. But are cultures really like that? Do their elements really fit well together?

Consider, for example, whether the American family system fits well with the demands made by most American jobs. Most Americans want to maintain long-term marriage commitments, raise families, and live middle-class lifestyles. Most jobs in the United States provide inadequate income for this purpose. Many require mobility, long hours, and flexibility, which come at the expense of the family. Americans must negotiate the contradictions between the lifestyle they desire, the demands of their families, and the requirements of their jobs.

Consider that, in socially stratified societies, different groups have different interests, and this creates conflict. For example, in capitalist societies, both workers and owners want their companies to do well, but within this context, the owners hope to maximize their profit and the workers want to maximize their pay. However, increases in workers' pay come at some expense to owners' profits. Therefore, there is a structural conflict between the owners and the workers. This conflict does not occur because society is not working properly. Rather, it is a fundamental condition of a capitalist society.

There is nothing uniquely American or modern about contradiction and conflict within culture. People in nonindustrialized societies must also handle conflicting commitments to their families and other social groups such as secret societies or religious associations. Even in societies that lack social groups beyond the family, the interests of men and women, or those of the old and the young, may differ. Thus, in all societies, social life is characterized by conflict as well as concord. Although culture certainly is patterned and surely is a system, often the parts may rub, chafe, and grind against each other.

Anthropologists who are drawn to the study of the relationships among different aspects of culture have often sought to find laws of cultural behavior. In the first half of the 20th century, **functionalists** such as A. R. Radcliffe-Brown and Bronislaw Malinowski searched for such laws in the mutually supportive relationships among kinship, religion, and politics. For example, Radcliffe-Brown (1965/1952:176) argued that religion supports social structure by giving individuals a sense of dependence on their society.

More recently, **ecological functionalists** have focused on the relationship between environment and society. These anthropologists view social institutions and practices as elements in broader ecological systems. They are particularly concerned with ways in which cultural practices both alter and are altered by the ecosystem in which they occur. For example, Marvin Harris's (1966) classic explanation of the Hindu taboo on eating beef focused on the effect of cattle in the Indian environment rather than on the Hindu belief system (see Figure 2.5). Harris noted that despite widespread poverty and periodic famine in India, Hindus refuse to eat their cattle. Although superficially this seems unreasonable, it makes good ecological sense. Cows are important in India because they provide dung for fertilizer and cooking fuel, and they give birth to bullocks, the draft animals that pull the plows and carts essential to agriculture. If a family ate its cows during a famine, it would deprive itself of

Functionalism: A theoretical position in anthropology that focuses on finding general laws that identify different elements of society, showing how they relate to each other, and demonstrating their role in maintaining social order.

Ecological functionalism: A theoretical position in anthropology that focuses on the relationship between environment and society.

Noah Seelam/Getty Images

Figure 2.5 A Hindu devotee offers prayers to a cow on the eve of a festival. Some anthropologists argue that Hindu reverence for cattle and the taboo on their slaughter serve practical, ecological functions.

the source of bullocks and could not continue farming. Thus, the Hindu religious taboo on eating beef is part of a larger ecological pattern that includes the subsistence system.

Many anthropologists today choose to focus on conflicts within cultural systems. This often reflects the deep influence of the work of Karl Marx and the early 20th-century sociologist Max Weber. Both Marx and Weber saw conflict in society as a key factor driving social change. For example, Marx understood society to be made up of different social groups, such as factory owners and workers, who had opposing interests. Marx believed that, over time, these opposing interests inevitably would lead to both conflict and social change.

Norms: Shared ideas about the way things ought to be done; rules of behavior that reflect and enforce culture.
Values: Shared ideas about what is true, right, and beautiful.

CULTURE IS A SHARED SYSTEM OF NORMS AND VALUES—OR IS IT?

What would a person with his own private culture be like? Perhaps he would be like Peter or Victor in the introduction to this chapter, unable to meaningfully participate in the society around him. Alternatively, such a person might live in a world in which everything has one set of meanings to her but different meanings to everyone else. People with certain forms of schizophrenia seem to have just this problem; they live in a world rich in symbols that have meaning only to them. In either case, it would be very difficult for such people to interact with others; they would probably be isolated and, in some cases, considered insane. Clearly, then, at some level, members of a culture must share ways of thinking and behaving. Often, we refer to these as *norms* and *values*.

Norms are shared ideas about the way things ought to be done—rules of behavior that reflect and enforce culture. **Values** are shared ideas about what is true, right, and beautiful. For example, shaking hands rather than bowing when introduced to a stranger is an American norm. The notion that advances in technology are good is an American value.

Human behavior is not always consistent with cultural norms or values (see Figure 2.6). People do not necessarily do what they say they should do. Norms may be contradictory and manipulated

Roger Spooner/Getty Images

Figure 2.6 Not everyone in a culture must conform. Although cultures demand a certain amount of consensus, members often show great variability in knowledge, style, and beliefs.

for personal and group ends. For example, people in India believe that women should stay in their homes rather than go out with their friends. They also believe that women should spend a lot of time in religious activities. Modern Indian women use the second of these ideals to get around the first. By forming clubs whose activities are religious, they have an excuse to get out of the house, to which their elders cannot object too strongly.

This example raises important questions. How do we determine the norms and values of a society? Do all people in society agree on these things? How many people must agree on something before it is considered a norm or a value? Research shows that, even in small societies, norms are not always followed and values are not universal. Individuals differ in their knowledge, understanding, and beliefs. For example, one might expect that all members in a small fishing society would agree on the proper names for different kinds of fish, but on Pukapuka, the small Pacific atoll Robert Borofsky (1994) studied, even experienced fishermen disagreed much of the time.

The degree to which people do not simply share a single culture is even more obvious in large societies. Sometimes the term **subculture** is used to designate groups within a single society that share norms and values significantly different from those of the **dominant culture**. The terms *dominant culture* and *subculture* do not refer to superior and inferior but rather to the idea that the dominant culture, because it controls greater wealth and power, is more able to impose its understanding of the world on subcultures than the reverse.

Dominant cultures retain their power partly through control of institutions, like the legal system, criminalizing practices that conflict with their own (Norgren and Nanda 1996). In contemporary society, public schools help maintain the values of the dominant culture, and the media play an important role in encouraging people to perceive subcultures in stereotypical (and usually negative) ways. For example, in a study that focused on television news and reality shows, Oliver (2003) found that images of race and crime systematically overrepresented African Americans as criminal. Furthermore, such shows tended to portray black men as particularly dangerous and presented information about black suspects that assumed their guilt. By contrast, many portrayals of African Americans in the 1990s and early 2000s focused on the "magical Negro," "a lower-class, uneducated black person who possesses supernatural or magical powers" (Hughey 2009:544). The "magical Negro" appears in films such as *The Green Mile* (1999), *Bruce Almighty* (2003), and all three films of the *Dark Knight Rises* trilogy (*Batman Begins* [2005], *The Dark Knight* [2008], and *The Dark Knight Rises* [2012]). Hughey argues that, although such

Subculture: A group within a society that shares norms and values significantly different from those of the dominant culture.

Dominant culture: The culture with the greatest wealth and power in a society that consists of many subcultures.

characters are an improvement over earlier stereotypes, they capitalize on traditional stereotypes of African Americans, such as poverty, cultural deficiency, and folk wisdom. They treat whiteness as normal, and allow important black characters only when they are placed in subservient positions.

Although domination of one group by another is sometimes extreme, rarely is it complete. People contest their subjugation and protect their subcultures through political, economic, and military means. Sometimes, when domination is intense, minorities can protect themselves only through religious faith or by building cultural tales in which they hold positions of power and their oppressors are weak (Scott 1992).

Ideas we sometimes think of as timeless and consensual are constantly changing and being renegotiated. This involves conflict and subjugation as well as consensus. Which norms and values are promoted and which are rejected is particularly important because such cultural ideas influence and are influenced by wealth, power, and status. For example, what are American norms and values about using drugs to alter one's state of consciousness? Should the use of such drugs be legal? Clearly, these are difficult questions. In the past, Americans considered alcohol to be a dangerous mind-altering substance. Its manufacture, sale, and transport were prohibited in the United States between 1920 and 1933. Even today, substantial numbers of Americans oppose alcohol. In 2006, the Southern Baptist Convention, which represents about 16 million church members, passed a resolution expressing "total opposition to the manufacturing, advertising, distributing, and consuming of alcoholic beverages" (Southern Baptist Convention 2006). Marijuana, on the other hand, has been illegal in the United States since 1937, but a Quinnipiac University poll in December 2012 showed that about 51 percent of American voters favored its legalization, substantially up from the one-third who favored legalization in the early 2000s (Carroll 2005). This norm is clearly changing rapidly. The second edition of this book noted that 14 states had legalized medical marijuana. By the time the third edition came out, 16 states and the District of Columbia had legalized medical marijuana and two states, Colorado and Washington, had legalized recreational marijuana as well. By 2016, 23 states and Washington, D.C., had legalized medical marijuana, four had legalized recreational marijuana, and three additional states had decriminalized possession of small amounts of marijuana.

Believing that people should consume or not consume either alcohol or marijuana clearly does not make one more or less "American." However, which of these notions is held by those in power is critical. It influences the laws and social policies that shape our lives and history.

The focus on culture as a shared set of norms and values is often associated with the American anthropologists of the first half of the 20th century, particularly Franz Boas and his students, members of a school of thought referred to as **historical particularism**. These anthropologists were interested in presenting objective descriptions of cultures within their historical and environmental context. Their emphasis on norms and values was designed to show that, although other cultures were very different from our own, they were coherent, rational, and indeed often beautiful. In contrast to the logical coherence seen by the historical particularists, some contemporary anthropologists, particularly **postmodernists**, believe that culture is a context in which norms and values are contested and negotiated. Rather than assuming a cultural core of shared beliefs and values, these anthropologists see culture and society as battlegrounds where individuals and groups fight for power and the right to determine what is accepted as true.

Historical particularism: A theoretical position in anthropology associated with American anthropologists of the early 20th century that focuses on providing objective descriptions of cultures within their historical and environmental contexts.

Postmodernism: A theoretical position in anthropology that focuses on issues of power and voice. Postmodernists hold that anthropological accounts are partial truths reflecting the backgrounds, training, and social positions of their authors.

CULTURE IS THE WAY HUMAN BEINGS ADAPT TO THE WORLD

All animals, including human beings, have biologically based needs. All need habitat and food, and each species must reproduce. All creatures are adapted to meet these needs. **Adaptation** is a change in the biological structure or lifeways of an individual or population by which it becomes better fitted to survive and reproduce in its environment. Nonhuman animals fill their needs primarily through biological adaptation. Lions, for example, have a series of biologically based adaptations that are superbly designed to enable them to feed themselves and their mates. They have large muscles for speed as well as sharp teeth and claws to capture and eat their prey.

Humans are different. We lack offensive biological weaponry, and, if left to get our food like the lion, we would surely starve. There is little evidence that we have an instinct to hunt or consume any particular kind of food, to build any particular sort of structure, or to have a single fixed social arrangement. Instead, human beings, in groups, develop forms of knowledge and technologies that enable them to feed themselves and to survive in their environments. They pass this knowledge from generation to generation and from group to group. In other words, human beings develop and use culture to adapt to the world.

Most of a lion's adaptation to the world is set biologically. The growth of its teeth and claws, its instinct to hunt, and the social arrangement of a pride are largely expressions of the lion's genetic code. Humans have a biological adaptation to the world: learning culture. All humans, except

Adaptation: A change in the biological structure or lifeways of an individual or population by which it becomes better fitted to survive and reproduce in its environment.

Figure 2.7 At Inle Lake in Myanmar, people adapt to the humid and wet environment by building houses on stilts. The light weight and loose weave of the building materials allows for ventilation that helps keep the residents relatively comfortable.

James Strachan/robertharding/Getty Images

those with profound biologically based differences (such as autism) automatically learn the culture of their social group. This strongly suggests that such learning is a manifestation of our genetic code. Thus, our biology compels us to learn culture. But it does not compel us to learn a particular culture. The range of human beliefs and practices is enormous. However, people everywhere learn to fill their basic needs, such as food and shelter, through cultural practices. Culture everywhere must, to some extent, be adaptive (see Figure 2.7).

Cultural adaptation has some distinct advantages over biological adaptation. Because humans adapt through learned behavior, they can change their approach to solving problems quickly and more easily than creatures whose adaptations are primarily biological. Lions hunt and eat today in much the same way as they have for tens of thousands of years. The vast majority of human beings today do not live like humans of even three or four generations ago, let alone like our distant ancestors. Our means of feeding ourselves, our culture, have changed. **Plasticity**—the ability to change behavior—has allowed human beings to thrive under a wide variety of social and ecological conditions.

Cultural adaptation has some disadvantages too. Misinformation, leading to cultural practices that hinder rather than aid survival, may creep into human behavior. Cultural practices, such as unrestrained logging, mining, or fishing that encourage destruction of the environment, may lead to short-term success but long-term disaster. Furthermore, many human practices are clearly not adaptive, even in the short run. Political policies of ethnic cleansing and genocide that urge people

Plasticity (in anthropology): The ability of humans to change their behavior in response to a wide range of environmental and social demands.

to murder their neighbors may benefit the leaders of a society, but it is hard to see any meaningful way in which these practices are adaptive. A normal lion will always inherit the muscle, tooth, and claw that, given a relatively stable environment, let it survive. Normal humans, on the other hand, may inherit a great deal of cultural misinformation that hinders their survival.

Historically, a focus on the adaptive aspect of culture is associated with a theoretical position called **cultural ecology**, first proposed in the 1930s. Although many of our ideas have changed since then, investigating the adaptive (and maladaptive) aspects of culture continues to be an important aspect of anthropology. Anthropologists who view culture as an adaptation tend to be concerned with people's behavior, particularly as it relates to their physical well-being or the relationship of cultural practices to ecosystems. They investigate the ways in which cultures adapt to specific environments and the ways in which cultures have changed in response to new physical and social conditions.

Cultural ecology: A theoretical position in anthropology that focuses on the adaptive dimensions of culture.

▌▌▌ CULTURE IS CONSTANTLY CHANGING

Did you ever want to visit a culture where people were untouched by the outside world, living just the same way they have been living for thousands of years? Well, you are out of luck. One of the most romantic notions of anthropology presented in the media is that there are "Stone Age" cultures waiting to be discovered. But this is false. No culture has ever been stuck in time or isolated from others for very long. Cultures are constantly changing. They change because of conflict among different elements within them. They change because of contact with outsiders. Population growth, disease, climate change, and natural disaster all drive culture change. However, cultures do not always change at the same speed. Cultural change may happen in small increments, or it may happen in revolutionary bursts. Historically, in most places and at most times, culture change has been a relatively slow process. However, the pace of change has been increasing for the past several hundred years and has become extremely rapid in the past century.

Since the 16th century, the most important source of culture change has been the development of a world economic system based primarily in the wealthy nations of Europe and Asia. This has involved invasions, revolutions, and epidemic diseases. These historic processes and the resultant global economic system are the primary foci of Chapters 13 and 14. Here, we focus on some of the more traditional ways in which anthropologists have examined culture change.

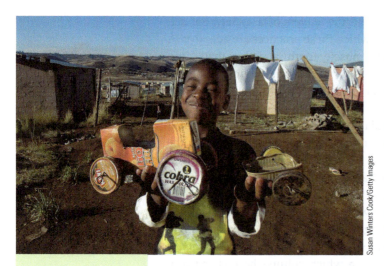

Susan Winters Cook/Getty Images

Figure 2.8 Innovation often involves repurposing materials to create something new. Here, a child in Transkei, South Africa shows off toy cars he has made from discarded tins and cartons.

Innovation: An object or way of thinking that is based upon but is qualitatively different from existing forms.

Diffusion: The spread of cultural elements from one society to another.

Anthropologists sometimes discuss cultural change in terms of innovation and diffusion. An **innovation** is an object, a way of thinking, or a way of behaving that is new because it is qualitatively different from existing forms (Barnett 1953:7). Although we often think of innovations as technological, they are not limited to the material aspects of culture. New art forms and new ideas are also innovations (see Figure 2.8).

New practices, tools, or principles may emerge from within a society and gain wide acceptance. Anthropologists sometimes call these *primary innovations,* and they are frequently chance discoveries and accidents. In our own society, some examples of accidental discovery include penicillin, found when British researcher Alexander Fleming noticed that bacteria samples he had left by a window were contaminated by mold spores, and Teflon, discovered by Roy Plunkett, who was trying to find new substances to use in refrigeration. All such innovations are based on building blocks provided by culture. For example, although Fleming is justly famous for the discovery of penicillin, this innovation also illustrates the importance of context and incremental discovery. Fleming was not a random person who woke up one morning thinking about mold and bacteria. He was a trained bacteriologist who had been looking for a substance to fight infection for more than a decade. He was very aware of the work of other scientists studying the problem of infection. It does not diminish his achievement to point out that he, like every other inventor or discoverer, did not create something totally new. He realized the critical importance of new combinations of things that already existed. His culture provided him with the training, tools, and context in which his discovery could be made.

Innovations tend to move from one culture to another, a process known as **diffusion**. Diffusion can happen in many ways; trade, travel, and warfare all promote it. Direct contact among cultures generally results in the most far-reaching changes, and cultures located on major trade routes tend to change more rapidly than do those in more isolated places. However, because no human society has ever been isolated for a long time, diffusion has always been an important factor in culture. This implies that "pure" cultures, free from outside influences, have never existed.

Innovation and diffusion are not simple processes. People do not "naturally" realize that one way of doing things is better than another or that one style of dress, religion, or behavior is superior. For innovation and diffusion to occur, new ideas must be accepted, and even when the desirability of an innovation seems clear, its integration into a culture is a very complex process. Again, the discovery of penicillin provides a good example. Although Fleming understood some of the importance of his discovery in 1928, human trials did not take place until World War II, and the drug was not widely prescribed until the mid- to late 1950s (Sheehan 1982; Williams 1984).

People may not accept an idea because they do not fully understand it, but other factors are usually involved as well. For psychological reasons, individuals may vary in their willingness to adopt change. Far more importantly, changes rarely provide equal benefits to everyone. For example, new agricultural techniques were introduced in Latin America and Asia from the 1940s to the 1960s (an era known as the "Green Revolution"). The new techniques did radically improve crop yields, but large landowners received the greater part of the benefit. Laborers, many of whom were landless, were often impoverished by the change and, as a result, were very resistant to it (Das 1998).

Change is often promoted or resisted by powerful interests. Innovations that have strong political, economic, or moral forces behind them may be rapidly accepted. But, when those forces are arrayed against an innovation, acceptance can be delayed. New technologies may face resistance from those who have invested heavily in older ones. For example, FM radio broadcasting is clearly superior to AM broadcasting; it has greater fidelity and is much less susceptible to static and interference. Although it was invented in 1933, the opposition of CBS, NBC, and RCA, powerful corporations heavily invested in AM technology, prevented FM from gaining popularity until the late 1960s (Lewis 1991).

Like innovation, diffusion is often accompanied by conflict. People who are colonized or captured by others are often forced to assume new cultural practices. New rulers may require that older traditions be abandoned. Economic demands by governments or creditors often compel the adoption of new technologies and practices. Although these processes happen in most places where cultures have confronted one another, they have been particularly important in the past 500 years. During this time, cultures have been increasingly tied together in an economic system controlled largely in northern Europe, North America, and Japan, a process we explore further in Chapters 13 and 14.

The rapid pace of cultural change and diffusion, particularly in the past 100 years, raises the question of cultural homogenization. Are cultural differences being erased? Are we all being submerged in a single global culture? There are no simple answers to these questions. On the one hand, modern technological culture now penetrates virtually every place on earth. On the other hand, this penetration is uneven. The wealthy have far greater access to and ability to control technology than the poor.

The world dominance of industrialized nations has affected cultures everywhere, but rather than annihilating local culture, cultural traits are transformed as they are adopted, and new cultural forms result. Radio, television, and video recording are good examples. Developed by industrialized societies, these technologies have spread around the world. However, they do not necessarily promote the values and practices of the societies that created them. Insurgents and revolutionaries around the world use cell phones, Twitter accounts, and other technologies to pursue political and social goals vastly different than those of most members of the societies that created these products.

Anthropologists have traditionally worked in tribal and peasant societies. Because such cultures have been profoundly affected by their contact with industrial societies, most anthropologists today, whatever their theoretical orientations, are interested in change. The study of cultural change has special interest for applied anthropologists, particularly those who investigate issues related to the economic development of poor nations.

▌▐ CULTURE COUNTS

Culture is many different things. It is learning, symbolism and meaning, patterns of thought and behavior, the things we share with those around us, the ways in which we survive in our world, and dynamism and change. It is both consensus and conflict. Culture makes us human and ties us to others everywhere. Ultimately, because all societies are based around fundamental patterns of culture, no society can be utterly incomprehensible to members of another. On the other hand, enormous variability is built into these patterns. The fact that human lifeways are shared, learned, and symbolic, the fact that we don't simply adapt to our environment but fill it with meaning, results in extraordinary differences in human cultures.

Naked mole rats are a highly social species found in the Horn of Africa. Their behavior is extremely complex, but they lack culture in a human sense. Each colony is more or less identical to every other. Imaginary mole rat explorers visiting each colony would understand everything they saw or heard. But the history of human exploration is one of miscomprehension. Because cultures are so different and count for so much in human life, we need tools to help us understand them. One job of anthropology is to provide these tools. In Chapter 3, we examine the methods anthropologists have used to investigate culture.

BRINGING IT BACK HOME
IS THERE AN AMERICAN CULTURE?

Throughout this chapter, we have identified culture as something shared by a group of people. This is a necessary aspect of culture. However, it is also problematic. We often think of groups as neat, bounded collections of individuals or families. But think for a moment: How many groups do you belong to? You almost certainly have a nationality, a place where you grew up, a school (or perhaps more than one), perhaps an ethnic identity, perhaps a religious identity, maybe you were a member of a group like the military, and, of course, you certainly had some kind of family identity. These identities overlap, but are different. All of them have characteristics of culture such as processes of enculturation and symbolism. Now, which of these is your culture? There is no one on the planet who shares precisely your cultural experience. Even identical twins don't end up with identical lives. So, are you then a culture of one?

The problem of culture is particularly acute when we talk about very large and complex groups. The United States is a nation of more than 318 million people. They have different geographical origins, ethnicities, beliefs, sexualities, and so on. New immigrants and visitors from other cultures may have a very different view of American culture too (see Chapter 14, pp. 371–374). In a vast, diverse country, can there really be anything such as American culture?

If the question is "Are there things upon which 100 percent of Americans agree?" then the answer is almost certainly no. It's difficult if not impossible to find that kind of consensus even in a very small community. However, as we have seen in this chapter, discord, argument, even violence are not aberrations; they are common parts of all cultures. To have a culture, we don't need to agree but we do need to share some things, not in the sense that we all partake of them equally, but rather that, overwhelmingly, we have some significant connection with them.

So what kinds of things do Americans share? There's no definitive list, but here are some ideas. We share and are shaped to some degree by the critical institutions of our society: the federal government, court system, and education system. Although many languages are spoken in the United States, we are overwhelmingly an English-speaking nation, and historically, virtually all grandchildren of non–English-speaking immigrants are monolingual English speakers.

Anthropologists and other social scientists have proposed a variety of other American characteristics. Anthropologist Clyde Kluckhohn (Kluckhohn and Kluckhohn 1947) described American culture as characterized by "effort optimism": the belief that if a person tries hard enough at anything, he or she will succeed. Sociologist Robert Bellah and his colleagues (1985) say that the dominant elements of American culture are utilitarian individualism and expressive individualism. Utilitarian individualism is the claim that humans have a right to behave in their self-interest, pursuing the satisfaction of their goals, appetites, and fears. Bellah sees this as countered and moderated by expressive individualism, the belief that each person has the right to express a unique core of creativity and individuality. Bellah and others have also noted that ideas such as utilitarian and expressive individualism are reinforced constantly in schools, films, and television. They also work well with American capitalism.

Numerous other attributes have been proposed. A typical list includes things such as the belief that the environment can and should be controlled for the benefit of people, belief that progress is good and that things in the future will probably be better, a strong sense of good and bad (combined with a belief that we can know what is morally good and we should act upon it), the notion that there should be a schedule and that people should stick rigorously to it, a fundamental belief in human equality (often combined with a deep prejudice toward particular groups of people), and the idea that people should be friendly and open. However, we're sure that you can think of many cases where you and people you know do not behave in ways this list suggests they should. Does this mean that American culture is a fiction, or that American culture contains much friction?

YOU DECIDE:

1. Do you believe there is such a thing as American culture? Support your position with at least three examples.
2. Briefly explain the connections between values such as effort optimism, utilitarian individualism, and the American economic system.
3. To how many cultures do you think you belong? Describe some of the critical differences between different cultures to which you belong.

CHAPTER SUMMARY

1. Give a definition of *culture*. Culture is the learned, symbolic, at least partially adaptive, and ever-changing patterns of behavior and meaning shared by members of a group. Humans are vitally dependent on culture for their existence.

2. Describe the importance of learning in culture. Almost all human behavior is learned. Humans learn throughout their entire life span. The example of the Inuit shows how children are taught to survive in a harsh environment.

3. Describe the importance of symbols in culture. Humans understand the world by classifying it and using symbols to give it meaning. Different cultures use different systems of classification. People use symbols to give meaning to their lives. Anthropologists analyze and interpret symbols and rituals to understand cultural meanings.

4. How does the case of Lia Lee illustrate differences in cultural classification systems? Doctors understood Lia Lee as having epilepsy, members of her family believed her soul had separated from her body. The results of this difference in understanding were tragic.

5. In what ways are cultures like biological organisms, and what are the problems with this organic analogy? Like biological organisms, cultures are systems of related elements working together. However, unlike biological organisms, cultural systems include contradictions that lead to conflict.

6. What are norms and values? Do people within a culture agree on them? Norms are shared ideas about the way things ought to be done. Values are shared ideas about what is true, right, and beautiful. Typically, people within a culture do not fully agree on norms and values. Some amount of conflict is the rule, not the exception.

7. How is culture similar to the biological adaptations of nonhuman animals? Culture is the way that humans adapt to their world. Unlike other species, humans adapt primarily through cultural learning. This enables people to respond to change rapidly but can, in some cases, also be maladaptive.

8. Are cultures typically static, or do they change? All cultures change. Innovation and diffusion are two sources of change. Many factors determine the acceptance or rejection of a culture change.

9. What role does anthropology play in coping with cultural differences? Culture makes humans unique, but the vast differences between human cultures make cultural understanding a challenge. Anthropology supplies tools to meet that challenge.

10. Is there such a thing as American culture? Although every individual's experience is different, Americans are bound together by legal and institutional frameworks. Anthropologists have proposed many characteristics of American culture. However, these are not necessarily shared by all Americans.

KEY TERMS

Adaptation
Anthropological theory
Cognitive anthropology
Cultural ecology
Culture and personality
Diffusion
Dominant culture
Ecological functionalism
Enculturation
Ethnoscience
Functionalism

Historical particularism
Innovation
Interpretive anthropology
Norms
Organic analogy
Plasticity
Postmodernism
Subculture
Symbol
Symbolic anthropology
Values

Courtesy of Greg Simon

Anthropologist Gregory Simon joins friends at a Minangkabou wedding feast in Bukittinggi, West Sumatra. Simon notes that he had left home that day not intending to go to a wedding feast. Had he known, he would have dressed differently. However, he also points out that anthropologists are often cultural participants who may be a bit out of place.

3

DOING CULTURAL ANTHROPOLOGY

AFTER YOU HAVE READ THIS CHAPTER, YOU WILL BE ABLE TO:

△ Explain who Boas and Malinowski were and what their importance to the development of anthropology was.

△ Define *participant observation* and explain its importance in anthropology.

△ Describe some of the techniques that anthropologists use during their fieldwork.

△ Analyze the role of cross-cultural research in anthropology and describe some of the tools used to conduct it.

△ Summarize the importance of feminism and postmodernism in the development of anthropology.

△ Describe collaborative and engaged anthropology and give examples of them.

△ Discuss the advantages and difficulties of doing fieldwork in one's own society.

△ Give some examples of ethical dilemmas facing anthropologists.

WORKING AMONG YOUNG OFFENDERS IN BRAZIL

OING fieldwork is a fundamental part of anthropology, but is often a deeply challenging experience as well. Kristen Drybread (2006) set off to study adults who work with "at risk" youth in Northeastern Brazil but soon found herself working with juvenile male prisoners. Her work brought her into conflict with prison officials and other local elites but brought rich rewards in rapport with her young research subjects.

The first issue Drybread confronted was that elites and prison administrators did not understand the techniques of anthropology. Although they were well acquainted with survey research and brief fact-finding missions, they had no experience of the patient, long-term daily involvement that doing cultural anthropology requires. They neither understood it as research nor respected it. In time, their disrespect would turn to outright hostility. She found this surprising in light of her desire to portray her subjects in an honest and sympathetic manner.

Drybread soon found out that although the guards used both physical and verbal abuse against the boys, it was the prisoners' "codes of honor, respect, and silence that determined the status and security of each inmate." Rebellions, fights, even murders were common means of social control within the prison. Prisoners rebelled to exact vengeance against informers, to scare the guards and administrators, and because they were bored.

The inmates' boredom made Drybread's job easier. Talking with her provided novelty and distraction and they were often glad to do it. She was also helped by two "fortuitous" events. First, on a preliminary visit to the prison, she had accidentally left a pen in the hands of a prisoner. In a prison, a pen can be a lethal weapon and Drybread had mistakenly broken an important prison rule in leaving it. However, it helped build her credibility among the prisoners. In a second incident that happened outside the prison, Drybread had an accident that left her hospitalized with a three-inch knife wound. The inmates assumed that she had received the wound through a violent confrontation and that she had shown herself strong enough and smart enough to survive. This (false) assumption gave her legitimacy with the prisoners.

Early in her research, Drybread was given a small office and prison officials requested that she interview her subjects there. However, after her knife wound, the administration increasingly treated her like a prisoner. She stayed outside in the prison yard, shared the prisoner's food, and witnessed their frequently illegal activities including "drug deals, prostitution, and the hatching of escape plans." Drybread was constantly

Brazil.

tested by the prisoners. They made sure she saw relatively minor crimes to see if she would report them to the guards. When she did not, she earned a reputation as a person who could be trusted. She also built trust by bringing her bag into the prison yard and allowing the boys to examine it, something no one else did. Drybread let it be known that she could not witness violence without reporting it. As a result, even though the prison had a reputation as one of the most violent juvenile detention centers in the nation, and even though violence occurred during the time she was researching the prison, she personally witnessed almost none of it. Thus, working with the prisoners changed Drybread, and her presence changed the culture of the prison yard, making it less violent while she was present.

After nine months of work in the prison yard, Drybread was suddenly forbidden to work there. The administration claimed that the yard was dangerous and that she faced the possibility of violence or rape. Drybread, confident of her own safety, appealed to the judge of the local juvenile court to be allowed to continue to work. He agreed to permit her work to continue but gave the prison administrators the right to impose "intimate search" on her. Thus, she had to face a cavity search each time she wished to enter the prison. The search did nothing to improve her safety but was a strong technique of intimidation. Reflecting on the events, Drybread noted that after promising the prisoners that she would keep their recorded life histories private, she had refused the prison's psychologists and social workers access to them. This was her punishment, designed to teach her that going back on promises to respect the privacy of the powerless is much easier than having her own privacy destroyed by those more powerful than her.

As Drybread's work continued, the administration's hostility grew. After the cavity search incident, they restricted her to interviewing prisoners in an office and falsely told her that those she wished to interview either were busy or refused to meet her. Eventually she discovered ways to continue meeting with the prisoners but continued to face strong hostility from the administration. She found herself become more hostile and disrespectful of them as well.

Drybread writes that her experiences changed her ideas about violence. Before she went to Brazil, she believed that violence was never "a viable solution to conflict." However, she is now convinced that nonviolence is unlikely to work in Brazil. In Northeast Brazil, murder is used as a tool of power by rich and poor alike. Murder and blood vengeance are common among the inmates with whom Drybread worked. However, they murdered not out of "inveterate criminality" but to seek vengeance and justice. For the powerless in Brazil, violence is a "last ditch attempt to be reckoned with, to be treated with at least a modicum of respect." By the end of her research, Drybread was receiving death threats herself. Her subjects urged her to take them seriously and she reports that like them, she has "taken to sleeping with one eye open."

Drybread's experiences are extreme; relatively few anthropologists work with violent offenders and probably even fewer are able to work with the active opposition of local officials. However, she faced many problems common to all anthropologists: how to gain access to the people you wish to study, how to establish rapport, the limits of the anthropologist's responsibility to those with whom they work, and other issues as well.

If you have any picture of anthropologists at all, you probably think of men and women who share the lives of people who are different from themselves. Indeed, although anthropologists also work in their own cultures, one of the fundamental ways in which anthropologists work is by spending time in other cultures. Psychologists or sociologists may be able to do research without leaving the college campus. They conduct surveys using the telephone, the Internet, or the postal service, or they may bring students into a laboratory and ask them questions or observe their reactions. Philosophers or scholars of literature may work by reading, observing, and pondering. Anthropologists do these things too, but, in addition, they must go into the field.

For more than 100 years, anthropologists have gone into other cultures. They have lived among small isolated groups that forage for their food, have joined with societies that travel with their herds, and have spent time in agricultural villages and in bustling modern cities. They have lived among farmers, craftsmen, thieves, and crack cocaine dealers. If you enjoy anthropology, fieldwork is probably one of the key reasons you are attracted to it. There is something profoundly romantic about the idea of living with members of another culture, learning their way of life, and attempting to understand the world in a new and different manner. However, as Drybread's description of her experiences show, there are also challenges, ethical dilemmas, alienation, and sometimes even danger. Fieldwork is a wonderful experience. It is essential to the ways in which anthropology is done. However, it can also be intensely lonely and disturbing. It changes almost everyone who undertakes it, often in unexpected ways. In this chapter, we explore some of the history and practice of fieldwork. We examine fieldwork techniques and different trends in anthropological data collection and discuss some of the ethical issues raised by the practice of anthropology.

▌▌▌ A LITTLE HISTORY

Anthropology was not always based around fieldwork. The first scholars who called themselves anthropologists worked in the second half of the 19th century. Among the most famous of them were Sir Edward Burnett Tylor and Lewis Henry Morgan. Both saw themselves as compilers and analysts of ethnographic accounts rather than as field researchers. They relied largely upon the writings of amateurs—travelers, explorers, missionaries, and colonial officers—who had recorded their experiences in remote areas of the world. Because of this, critics of Tylor and Morgan sometimes referred to them as "armchair anthropologists."

Morgan and Tylor were deeply influenced by the evolutionary theories of their era. They assumed that such theories could be applied to human society. Thus, as they analyzed societies, they used type of technology and social institutions, such as family and religion, to place each society on an evolutionary scale of increasing complexity. Their scale began with simple, small-scale societies (classified as "savages"), passed through various chiefdoms (usually classified as "barbarians"), and ended with societies such as their own (classified as "civilization"). Although Morgan and Tylor were extremely critical of many aspects of their own societies, they were also convinced that they lived in the most highly evolved society that had ever existed.

There were numerous problems with Morgan and Tylor's evolutionary anthropology. Explorers, colonial officials, and missionaries had particular interests in playing up the most exotic aspects of the societies they described. Doing so increased the fame of explorers (and the number of books they were able to sell). It made the natives more in need of the "good government" or salvation that colonial officials and missionaries claimed they could provide. Perhaps more importantly, the evolutionists were so sure that they had properly formulated the general evolutionary history of society that they twisted and contorted their data to fit their theories.

▌▌▌ Franz Boas and American Anthropology

The problems implicit in Morgan and Tylor's evolutionary approach led to a radical reappraisal of evolutionary anthropology at the end of the 19th century. The most important critic of evolutionism was Franz Boas (see Figure 3.1). Born in Minden, Germany, Boas came to the United States after completing his doctorate in geography and living among the Inuit on Baffin Island. In the late 1890s, he became the first professor of anthropology at Columbia University in New York City. From there, he trained many students who became the leading anthropologists of the

Science Source

Figure 3.1 In the early 20th century, Franz Boas was the most influential anthropologist in the United States. He emphasized fieldwork and cultural relativism. In this picture, taken in a photography studio in Germany, he dresses as an Inuit awaiting the return of a seal to its blowhole.

Ethnocentrism: Judging other cultures from the perspective on one's own culture. The notion that one's own culture is more beautiful, rational, and nearer to perfection than any other.

first half of the 20th century. As a result, Boas's ideas had a profound impact on the development of anthropology in the United States.

Boas's studies and his experiences among the Inuit convinced him that evolutionary anthropology was both intellectually flawed and, because it treated other people and other societies as inferior to Europeans, morally defective. Boas argued that anthropologists should not be collectors of tales and spinners of theories but should devote themselves to objective data collection through fieldwork. Anthropologists must live among the people they study, both observing their activities and collecting stories and information from the most knowledgeable members of society. They should record as much information about the group's culture as possible. This was particularly important because Boas believed that many of the lifeways of the societies he and his students studied (most often Native American societies) were disappearing.

One of Boas's core beliefs was that cultures are the products of their own histories. He argued that a culture's standards of beauty and morality as well as many other aspects of behavior could be understood only in light of that culture's historical development. Because our own ideas are also the products of history, they should not be used as standards to judge other cultures. Evolutionists failed partly because they assumed, incorrectly, that the most evolved cultures are those that have values most similar to their own. In other words, the evolutionists failed because of their own ethnocentrism. In one sense, **ethnocentrism** is simply the belief that one's own culture is better than any other. In a deeper sense, it is precisely the application of the historical standards of beauty, worth, and morality developed in one culture to all other cultures.

An American tourist who asks "How much is this in real money?" when presented with a handful of Mexican pesos is being ethnocentric. He or she thinks of the money of their own country as real but that of others as "play money." But there is nothing uniquely American or Western about ethnocentrism. People all over the world tend to see things from their own culturally patterned point of view. For example, when the people living in Highland New Guinea first saw European outsiders in the 1930s, they believed them to be the ghosts of their ancestors. It was the only way they could initially make sense of what they were seeing (Connolly and Anderson 1987).

Although most people are ethnocentric, the ethnocentrism of Western societies has had greater consequences than that of smaller, less technologically advanced and more geographically isolated peoples. Wealth and military technology have given Westerners the ability to impose their beliefs and practices on others. It may matter little, for example, to the average Frenchman if the Dogon (an ethnic group in Mali) believe their way of life to be superior. The Dogon have little ability to affect events in France. However, French ethnocentrism mattered a great deal to the Dogon. The French colonized Mali and imposed their beliefs and institutions on its people.

Some ethnocentrism seems necessary. A group's belief in the superiority of its own way of life binds its members together and helps them to perpetuate their values. However, to the extent that ethnocentrism prevents building bridges between cultures and leads members of one culture to force their ways of life on another, it is maladaptive. It is but a short step from this kind of ethnocentrism to **racism**—beliefs, actions, and patterns of social organization that exclude individuals and groups from the equal exercise of human rights and fundamental freedoms.

Boas insisted that anthropologists free themselves, as much as possible, from ethnocentrism and approach each culture on its own terms. This position came to be known as **cultural relativism** and is one of the hallmarks of anthropology. Boas and his followers maintained that anthropologists must understand and accurately report the logic and dynamics of other cultures. It is important to understand that cultural relativism is not moral relativism. Anthropologists do not argue that all cultural practices are good simply because they are cultural practices. Instead they argue that all practices need to be understood within their cultural and historical context. Understanding something and approving of it are vastly different. Anthropology pushes us to really understand cultural practices before we critique them.

Boas was a tireless campaigner for human rights and justice. He argued that all human beings have equal capacities for culture and that although human actions might be considered morally right or wrong, no culture was more evolved or of greater value than another. He was an unwavering supporter of racial equality. His work and that of his students, notably Ruth Benedict and Margaret Mead, were widely used by Americans who argued for the equality of men and women and for the rights of African Americans, immigrants, and Native Americans (Baker 2007). Today, virtually all anthropologists rely on Boas's basic insights.

Racism: The belief that some human populations are superior to others because of inherited, genetically transmitted characteristics.

Cultural relativism: The idea that cultures should be analyzed with reference to their own histories and values rather than according to the values of another culture.

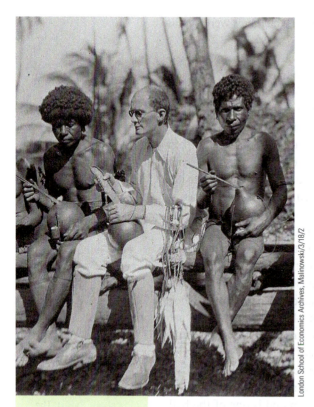

London School of Economics Archives, Malinowski/3/18/2

Figure 3.2 Bronislaw Malinowski, one of the pioneers of participant observation, worked in the Trobriand Islands between 1915 and 1918.

Ethnography: The major research tool of cultural anthropology, including both fieldwork among people in a society and the written results of such fieldwork.

Participant observation: The fieldwork technique that involves gathering cultural data by observing people's behavior and participating in their lives.

From Haddon to Malinowski in England and the Commonwealth

While Boas was forming his ideas in the United States, a separate fieldwork tradition was developing in Britain. In the late 19th century, Alfred Cort Haddon mounted two expeditions to the Torres Straits (between New Guinea and Australia). Haddon originally was a biologist, but his travels turned his interest to **ethnography**, the gathering and interpretation of information based on intensive firsthand study. Haddon and his colleagues became professors at Cambridge and the London School of Economics, where they trained the next generation of British Commonwealth anthropologists. Like Boas, their understandings were based in fieldwork, and they made it a basic part of their students' training.

Bronislaw Malinowski was one of the most prominent students of the Torres Straits scholars. Malinowski grew up in Krakow, then part of the Austro-Hungarian Empire (now in Poland). He came to England to study ethnography, and his mentor, Charles Seligman, sent him to do fieldwork on the Trobriand Islands (in the Torres Straits) (see Figure 3.2). Malinowski arrived in the Trobriands in 1914, as World War I broke out. Because Australia governed the Trobriands and Malinowski was a subject of the Austro-Hungarian Empire, he was considered an enemy national. As a result, he was unable to leave the islands until the end of the war. Thus, what he had intended as a relatively short fieldwork expedition became an extremely long one.

Malinowski's time on the Trobriands was a signal moment in British Commonwealth anthropology. A diary he kept during those years shows that he was frequently lonely, frustrated, and angry. Despite his problems, he revolutionized fieldwork. The Torres Straits scholars had studied culture at a distance, observing and describing it for a short time. Malinowski spent years with native Trobrianders, learning their language, their patterns of thought, and their cultural ways. He not only observed the culture, but to the extent that it was possible he also participated in it, joining in many Trobriand activities. Malinowski's style of fieldwork became known as **participant observation** and has become central to the practice of anthropology. Malinowski also centered his research on empathic understandings of native lifeways and on analyzing culture by describing social institutions and showing the cultural and psychological functions they performed.

In an era when non-Europeans were often considered incomprehensible and illogical, Malinowski forcefully promoted the idea that native cultural ways were logical. For example, in a famous essay on science and magic, he argued that natives used magic only for goals, such as controlling the weather, which they were unable to attain by more rational means (Malinowski 1948).

The anthropologies of Malinowski and Boas were quite different. Boas and his students focused on understanding cultures with respect to their context and histories. Malinowski and his students emphasized the notion of function: the contribution made by social practices and institutions to the maintenance and stability of society. However, both developed traditions of fieldwork and participant observation. Both traditions have strong histories of opposition to racism. Both see other cultures as fully rational and as neither superior nor inferior to Western culture. Despite the great many new approaches in anthropology since the days of Boas and Malinowski, their fundamental insights remain basic to the discipline.

The Trobriand Islands.

■I■ ANTHROPOLOGICAL TECHNIQUES

Today, anthropologists work in a wide variety of settings. They work for universities, for businesses, for government, and for nongovernmental organizations. They work on a variety of projects from investigating the relations among kin to researching topics such as shopping behavior and the ways in which people relate to their computers. Because of the multiplicity of anthropologies, it would be impossible to describe all of the different ways that anthropologists go about their work. Therefore, we will focus on the ways in which fieldwork is done in small communities.

Most anthropologists begin to do fieldwork as part of their graduate training and continue fieldwork as a basic element of their careers. Fieldwork is often funded by grants given by universities, government agencies, and nonprofit organizations that promote social science research. Decisions about which communities anthropologists investigate are based on factors including personal history, geographical preferences, political stability, cost, physical danger, and connections their professors and other mentors may have. However, the most critical aspect of choosing a location has to do with the particular research questions that anthropologists wish to answer.

In the early 20th century, anthropologists studying relatively small groups often attempted to write complete descriptions of societies. Their books, with titles such as *The Tiwi of North Australia* (Hart and Pilling 1960),

The Sebei (Goldschmidt 1986), and *The Cheyennes* (Hoebel 1960), had chapters on subjects such as family, religion, farming, and legal affairs. In a sense, it did not matter much where anthropologists chose to work; any small-scale community or society could be described.

Today, few anthropologists attempt to write such descriptions. This is partly because most feel that societies are so complex that they cannot be adequately described in a single work. But, more importantly, although societies never were really isolated, they are so interconnected today and so changed by these connections that they must be seen in regional and global contexts. Current ethnographies focus on specific situations, individuals, events, and, frequently, on culture change. For example, recent ethnographies describe the ways in which people in Jamaica use cell phones (Horst and Miller 2006), the survival techniques of drug addicts on the streets of San Francisco (Bourgois and Schonberg 2009), and sexuality, femininity, and black magic in Brazil (Hays 2011). As research has narrowed, both the questions anthropologists ask and the conditions and locations where they can be answered have become more specific.

After they have identified an area of interest, anthropologists spend time reading the existing research on their subject. It is no exaggeration to say that most researchers spend several hours reading for each hour they spend doing active field research. From their studies, they gain an understanding of the geography, history, and culture of their chosen area. They find out what is known and what remains to be learned about the subjects of their interest. They then try to design projects that help close the gaps in existing knowledge. It is a bit like filling in pieces of a jigsaw puzzle, with one important exception: You can finish a puzzle, but good research leads to more interesting questions and, thus, more research.

Arriving at a field location can be a disorienting experience. For most people, living in another culture and trying to learn its ways are difficult. Anthropologists are objects of curiosity and sometimes, like Kristen Drybread in the passage that opens this chapter, hostility. Perhaps more importantly, culture is learned behavior, and we have been learning our culture since the moment of our births. When we move to a radically different culture, much of that learning is no longer relevant.

Anthropologists arriving in new cultures are in many ways like children. Their language skills are often weak, and their speech is sometimes babyish. Their social skills are undeveloped. They are ignorant of many aspects of their environment and their new culture. One almost universal result of this situation is the syndrome called **culture shock**—the feelings of alienation, loneliness, and isolation common to one who has been placed in a new culture. For graduate students, sometimes the journey stops there. You can be an outstanding scholar—well versed in literature and able to think and write creatively—yet be unable to do fieldwork.

Culture shock: Feelings of alienation and helplessness that result from rapid immersion in a new and different culture.

Getting past culture shock is a process of learning the language, customs, and social organization, of gaining the fundamental grounding knowledge that it takes to be an adult in a different culture. Most anthropologists never truly become members of the cultures they study. They are separated from their subjects by their backgrounds, educations, and sometimes by the color of their skin (see Figure 3.3). Anthropologists are also separated by the knowledge that their time in the field is temporary and that they will leave to rejoin their other lives. However, in our best moments, anthropologists do come close to acting and feeling like members of the cultures they study.

Figure 3.3 In field-work, anthropologists both observe culture and participate in it, as with this anthropologist living with the Mentawai in Sumatra, Indonesia. Such tattoos are usually incised with needles and vegetable dye, but these are being done with washable pigments.

In most cases, as anthropologists begin to adapt to new cultures, they develop networks of friends and contacts who both guide them in their new surroundings and offer insights into the culture. Traditionally in anthropology, these people are called **informants**. They may also be called **respondents**, **interlocutors**, **consultants**, and sometimes **partners**. These terms emphasize the collaborative nature of fieldwork and suggest that the people who work with anthropologists are active and empowered. Much of what anthropologists know they learn from such people, who frequently become enduring friends. In some cases, anthropologists work with a few individuals whom they believe to be well informed and eager to talk with them (called "key informants"). Alternatively, they may construct statistical models and use techniques such as random sampling to choose their consultants. Sometimes, they are able to interview all members of a community.

Working with consultants is often informal, but anthropologists also use an arsenal of more formal tools, depending on their theoretical interests. Much of anthropology is done by interviewing, using many different techniques. Some anthropologists prepare exhaustive inventories and questionnaires; however, more frequently, they design a series of open-ended questions that allow their subjects to talk freely and extensively on a topic. Sometimes they use interview techniques drawn from ethnoscience and designed to help identify the objects and ideas their consultants think are important. Because kinship structures are important in many societies, anthropologists become adept at gathering genealogical information. Table 3.1 details some specific types of interviews. Almost

Consultant/informant/interlocutor/respondent/partner: A person from whom anthropologists gather data.
Partner: See consultant.

Judith Pearson

Table 3.1 Interviewing Techniques

Informal Interviews	Researchers engage in, overhear, remember, and write down conversations from their daily experience.
Unstructured Interviews	Researchers engage with another in a scheduled conversation. Researchers may have a plan but informants are allowed to express themselves as they choose.
Semistructured Interviews	Similar to an unstructured interview but based on the use of a written list of questions or topics that the researchers intend to cover in a specific order.
Structured Interviews	Researchers ask different subjects to respond to a set of questions as nearly identical as possible; often involves the use of very explicit instructions.

all anthropologists use informal, unstructured, and semistructured interviews. Structured interviews are less common.

In addition to interviewing, anthropological data gathering includes participating in activities with culture members, mapping, photographing, carefully observing activities, measuring various kinds of production, and, occasionally, serving apprenticeships. It all depends on the nature of the problem the anthropologists are investigating. For example, an anthropologist studying nutrition might need to observe food gathering and preparation techniques, weigh and measure all food consumed, and analyze it for nutritional value. An anthropologist studying religious ritual would be unlikely to use any of these techniques.

As with the techniques used, analysis of data also depends on the questions asked and the theoretical perspective of the researcher. Anthropological data generally come in the form of extensive field notes, tape recordings, and photographs. In most cases, organizing data presents substantial challenges. Notes have to be indexed, recordings transcribed, and data entered in spreadsheets. Successful anthropologists often spend more time working with their data than they did collecting it in the first place. Recording an interview may take only an hour or two. Transcribing and indexing that recording may take several days.

▮▮▮ Ethnographic Data and Cross-Cultural Comparisons

Boas and his students were interested in describing cultures in their contexts. Because they understood each culture as the product of its unique history, they did not attempt systematic comparison of one culture to another, and they were not very interested in discovering laws or principles of cultural behavior. However, some comparison has always been implicit in anthropology. For example, one goal of the Boasians was to use their research to cause Europeans and Americans to see their own societies in a new light.

British and European anthropologists were more explicitly interested in **ethnology**, the attempt to find general principles or laws that govern cultural phenomena. They compared societies in the hope of finding such laws and principles. Starting in the 1860s, Herbert Spencer began to develop a systematic way of organizing, tabulating, and correlating information on a large number of societies, a project he called *Descriptive Sociology.* The American scholar William Graham Sumner, his student Albert Keller, and Keller's student George Murdock brought this idea to the United States. In the late 1930s, Murdock and Keller created a large, indexed ethnographic database at Yale University. First called the *"Cross Cultural Survey,"* in the late 1940s, the project was expanded and its name was changed to the **Human Relations Area Files (HRAF)**.

> **Ethnology:** The attempt to find general principles or laws that govern cultural phenomena through the comparison of cultures.

The HRAF is an attempt to facilitate cross-cultural analysis. It provides a single index to ethnographic reports and other sources on 710 numbered subject categories. Some examples of categories are 294 (techniques of clothing manufacture) and 628 (traditional friendships and rivalries within communities). Using the HRAF, researchers can find information on these and many other topics for a wide range of current and historic societies.

> **Human Relations Area Files (HRAF):** An ethnographic database that includes cultural descriptions of more than 300 societies.

The HRAF frequently comes under fire as critics charge that the project takes cultural data out of context and therefore corrupts it. They correctly note that the works indexed in the HRAF were written from different perspectives, for different purposes, and in different eras. In consequence, the indexing is often inconsistent and analyses based on it are suspect. Despite these problems, work based on the HRAF is often both interesting and insightful. For example, in the 1950s, the rising divorce rate in the United States was causing alarm. Was divorce truly something new and different, a product of modernity? Murdock used the HRAF to show that almost all societies had some form of divorce and that the divorce rate in the United States (in the 1950s) was lower than average. Thus, his use of the HRAF allowed people to think about divorce in a comparative context. In recent years, the HRAF, now available online, has been used to consider a wide variety of issues, including family violence (Levinson 1989), patterns of cultural evolution (Peregrine, Ember, and Ember 2004), the relationship between production and beliefs about the afterlife (Dickson et al. 2005), and patterns of warfare and violence (Younger 2012).

▌▌▌ CHANGING DIRECTIONS AND CRITICAL ISSUES IN ETHNOGRAPHY

In the past several decades, new trends and issues in anthropological research have emerged. These include anthropology and gender, postmodernism, engaged and collaborative anthropology, and issues surrounding studying one's own culture.

▌▌▌ Anthropology and Gender

By the 1960s, the role of fieldwork in anthropology was extremely well established. In addition, the position of women within academic anthropology was relatively good, particularly in comparison to other areas of universities. Franz Boas had trained several female anthropologists who had gone on to become well known within the discipline. One, Margaret Mead, had become a household name outside of anthropology as well. Despite this (or perhaps because of it), the political movements of the 1960s, particularly the civil rights movement and the feminist movement, caused anthropologists to begin thinking about gender and their discipline in new ways.

Feminists soon discovered that the presence of some very-high-profile women within anthropology did little to counteract the fact that the overwhelming majority of anthropologists were men and that their areas of interest tended to focus on the social roles, activities, and beliefs of men in the societies they studied. There were several reasons why anthropologists had focused on men. First, in many societies, men and women live quite segregated lives. Because they were men, most anthropologists had little access to the lives of women. Second, anthropologists tended to assume that men's activities were political and therefore important, whereas women's activities were domestic and therefore of less importance. Third, in most societies, men's activities were far more public than women's activities. Anthropologists tended to assume that what was public and visible was more important than what was more behind the scenes and less visible. However, this clearly is not always (or even often) the case.

The result of taking men more seriously than women was a systematic bias in anthropological data and understandings. Anthropologists had often reported with great detail and accuracy about men's social and cultural worlds, but they had barely scratched the surface of women's worlds. Furthermore, the assumption frequently implicit in ethnographies that men spoke for all of society often made cultures appear more harmonious and homogeneous than they actually were.

Starting in the 1970s, increasing numbers of women joined university anthropology faculties. By the late 1990s, more than 50 percent of new

Aroon Thaewchatturat/Alamy

Figure 3.4 Anthropologist Narumon Hinshiranan of Chulalongkorn University, Bangkok, interviews a Moken woman in Kuraburi, Thailand. The Moken are a nomadic people who depend on ocean resources for their livelihood. Their way of life is threatened by economic changes and development in Thailand.

anthropology PhDs and more than 40 percent of all anthropology professors were women (Levine and Wright 1999). They began paying greater attention to women's lives (see Figure 3.4). By the 2000s, lesbian, gay, bisexual, transgender, and questioning (LGBTQ) people also found increasing representation on university faculties, leading to the emergence of LGBTQ studies as an academic field. As this happened, anthropologists turned from the study of women to more general considerations of the nature and role of gender in our own and other societies. We will address these issues more fully in Chapter 9.

▌▌▌ Postmodernism

Ultimately, the issue of gender in anthropology focused on ways of knowing. Feminists argued persuasively that male anthropologists had missed vital dimensions of society because their gender and their academic interests predisposed them to see certain things and not others. These ideas dovetailed well with **postmodernism**, a critique of both natural and social sciences that gained prominence in the 1980s. Postmodernists hold that all knowledge is influenced by the observer's culture and social position. They claim fieldworkers cannot discover and describe an objective reality because such a thing does not exist (or exists but cannot be discovered or comprehended by human beings). Instead, postmodernists propose that there are many partial truths or cultural constructions, which depend on frame of reference, power, and history.

Postmodernists urged anthropologists to examine the ways they understood both fieldwork and writing. They demanded that anthropology

Postmodernism: A theoretical position in anthropology that focuses on issues of power and voice. Postmodernists hold that anthropological accounts are partial truths reflecting the backgrounds, training, and social positions of their authors.

become sensitive to issues of history and power. Some postmodernists challenged the ethnographer's role in interpreting culture, claiming that anthropological ethnographies were just one story about experienced reality and the ethnographer's voice was only one of many possible representations.

During the 1990s, reflection on the nature of fieldwork and the anthropological enterprise became a central focus of writing in anthropology. Works such as *Writing Culture* (Clifford and Marcus 1986) and *Women Writing Culture* (Behar and Gordon 1995) encouraged anthropologists to think about the ways in which their own status, goals, and the techniques of academic writing shaped the work they produced. In many cases, anthropologists turned from writing about culture to writing about anthropology itself, and critical analyses of earlier anthropological literature became common. In other cases, rather than trying to describe culture or to find principles underlying cultural practices, anthropologists wrote about their own experience of living in other cultures.

The claims of postmodernists were a subject of intense debate in anthropology. Few anthropologists accepted the postmodern critique in its entirety. However, some of the ideas of postmodernism have become part of the mainstream. The issues of power and voice (who gets to tell a story, who is believed) have become basic aspects of current anthropology. Most ethnographers spend time reflecting critically on their positions as observers, considering the way their background and interests affect their work. And most think far more about the moral and political consequences of their work than they did before the postmodern critique.

▌▌▌ Engaged and Collaborative Ethnography

Collaborative ethnography: Anthropological work that gives priority to desires and interests of cultural consultants on the topic, methodology, and written results of fieldwork.

Engaged and **collaborative ethnography** reflect some of the concerns just noted. Collaboration is the process of working closely with other people and in a sense describes all anthropological research. Collaborative anthropologists highlight this aspect of their work. They consult with their subjects about shaping their studies and writing their reports. They attempt to displace the anthropologist as the sole author representing a group, turning research into a joint process between researcher and subject. The work of James Spradley (1934–1982) is an important contribution to collaborative, engaged anthropology. His classic ethnography, *You Owe Yourself a Drunk* (1970), was aimed at getting the public to understand and help the homeless alcoholics who were the subject of the book.

Eric Lassiter, an anthropologist inspired by Spradley, has done collaborative work with the Kiowa Indians in Oklahoma. The Kiowa were particularly interested in an ethnography of Kiowa song. They stipulated that it be written so that it could be read and understood by the Kiowa people themselves and that they would be acknowledged for their contributions. Lassiter emphasizes that a critical aspect of his collaboration with the Kiowa was to give the highest priority to representing the Kiowa cultural consultants as they wished to be represented, even if this meant adding or changing information or changing his interpretations. For Lassiter (2004), collaborative ethnography is not just eliciting the comments of the cultural consultants but, even more importantly, integrating these comments into the text.

Although many anthropologists practice some elements of collaborative anthropology, there are deep problems with the notion that anthropologists' primary job is to write and say what their consultants want. First, most probably would agree that anthropologists have an obligation to accurately report what people actually say and do rather than what people want said of them. Furthermore, communities are rarely so homogeneous that they speak with a single voice. Collaborative anthropology may give voice and legitimacy to one element of a community over another. Often, writing what consultants want really means choosing their side in a political contest.

▮▮▮ Using Anthropology: A Life in Engaged Anthropology

Anthropology has a long history of engagement with the societies that anthropologists study and political activism in anthropologists' own societies. Franz Boas, for example, wrote and spoke frequently on the major political and social issues of his day. He was deeply involved with the National Association for the Advancement of Colored People (NAACP) and contributed to its journal, *The Crisis* (Lewis 2001). His work was fundamental to the Supreme Court's *Brown v. Board of Education* decision ending legal segregation (Baker 2000). Many other anthropologists have followed Boas's example of engagement.

Pauline Wiessner has been a working anthropologist since the early 1970s. Though she trained in archaeology, her interests shifted to working with current-day people during research for her doctoral thesis among the Ju/'hoansi bushmen in Botswana and Namibia. In Botswana, she documented the gift giving and exchange patterns that tied people together and helped them survive in difficult times by giving them broad access to resources. However, Wiessner's academic interests soon led to deeper and more active engagement in the community. As the Ju/'hoansi lost access to their historic lands and were forced to move from nomadic to sedentary lifestyles, Wiessner became concerned with their ability to feed themselves. She established a nonprofit organization, the Tradition

Courtesy of Pauline Wiessner

Figure 3.5 Anthropologist Polly Wiessner and an Enga elder return from a trip to the highland forests.

and Transition Fund, to help the Ju/'hoansi protect their water sources and gardens from animals and develop new sources of food (see Figure 3.5).

Wiessner's involvement with the Enga of Papua New Guinea (PNG) has been even more dramatic. She began working with the Enga in the 1980s. As with the Ju/'hoansi, her initial interest was in documenting exchange patterns and social networks across both space and time. However, by the 1990s, it turned to warfare. The Enga, like many PNG groups, had a long history of warfare. Though these wars were serious, they were fought with bow, arrow, and spear, and the number of people killed was small, usually less than five. This changed in the 1990s, when young Enga men became increasingly impoverished and hopeless, but had growing access to weaponry such as M16 rifles. Previously small, contained wars erupted in large-scale violence that claimed hundreds of lives and turned large areas of Enga territory into wastelands.

Wiessner's studies have shown that the violence came to an end after more than a decade as the result of three factors: the exhaustion of the majority of the population, the influence of the Christian church that provided an alternative ideology of peace to the Enga ideology of war, and the presence of a traditional justice system that could be used to mediate disputes (Wiessner and Pupu 2012; Culotta 2012). Wiessner used the results of her research to lobby with both Enga leaders and local government officials to gain support for the use of the traditional justice system.

In the past decade, Wiessner and the Enga Provincial Government have become increasingly concerned with the rapid loss of Enga culture. The justice system is an area of particular concern. Customary law courts handle 80 to 90 percent of all Enga disputes. If young people do not know the customs, principles, and values of their own society, these courts will struggle.

Beginning in 2005, Wiessner used her own funds along with money she and her Enga colleagues raised to open the Enga Take Anda, a community center and museum located in the capital of Enga Province that both preserves Enga culture and provides a neutral place where members of different groups could come together (Balter 2010).

More recently, with the support of the Enga Provincial Government, Wiessner has developed a curriculum for schools, grades 6 to 12, which integrates culture into every subject and encourages students to do cultural research in their own communities. Starting in 2017 cultural education will be taught in all Enga schools.

▌▐▌ Studying One's Own Society

When most people think of anthropologists, they imagine researchers who study others in exotic locations, but, since the early 20th century, anthropologists have also studied their own societies. W. Lloyd Warner, Solon T. Kimball, Margaret Mead, Zora Neale Hurston, and Hortense Powdermaker were all American anthropologists who wrote about American culture. Kenyan anthropologist (as well as freedom fighter and first president of Kenya) Jomo Kenyatta wrote about the Gikuyu of Kenya in 1936, and Chinese anthropologist Francis Hsu wrote extensively on Chinese society. In recent years, writing about one's own culture has become even more common. This trend is driven by many factors, including the training of more anthropologists from more different cultures, the increasing total number of anthropologists, the rise of interest in ethnicity in the United States and Europe, as well as the dangers of violence in some areas where anthropologists have studied in the past.

The emphasis on more reflective fieldwork and ethnography affects all anthropologists but particularly those who study their own societies. Traditionally, anthropologists doing fieldwork try hard to learn the culture of the people with whom they are working. In a sense, anthropologists working in their own culture have the opposite problem: They must attempt to see their culture as an outsider might. This is challenging because it is easy to take cultural knowledge for granted. In addition, it may be as difficult to maintain a neutral stand in one's own culture as it is in a different one. As Margaret Mead once noted, it may be easier to remain culturally relativistic when we confront patterns, such as cannibalism or infanticide, in other cultures than when we confront problematic situations such as child neglect, corporate greed, or armed conflict in our own.

Some of the problems and the rewards of studying one's own culture can be seen in Barbara Myerhoff's books and films. Myerhoff contrasted her work with the Huichol of northern Mexico (1974) with her work among elderly Jewish people in California (1978). She notes that, in the first case, doing anthropology was "an act of imagination, a means for discovering what one is not and will never be." In the second case, fieldwork was a glimpse into her possible future, as she knew that someday she would be a "little old Jewish lady." Her work was a personal way to understand that condition and to contemplate her own future. Tragically, it was a future that never arrived. Myerhoff died of cancer when she was only 49.

More recently, Darren Ranco, an anthropologist and member of the Penobscot American Indian Nation, has considered the problems and issues native anthropologists face. Ranco notes that in his earliest anthropological projects, he had trouble trying to do work that seemed anthropological to him and at the same time treat his family and friends in respectful ways. For Ranco, one way out of this dilemma was to try to do work that the Penobscots themselves would find interesting and important. He decided that the criteria for such work included empowering people, involving members of the community, making the finished products of research available to the community, and focusing on research that provides direct benefits to the community. Ranco writes that when he considers a project, he asks himself how the project will "endorse, elaborate, or enhance tribal sovereignty" (2006: 74), and he will not undertake the research if he cannot answer the question.

We can all empathize with Ranco's desire to benefit our own community. However, we can also see the complications it may create. How can one be sure of the outcome of a project at its beginning? What should anthropologists do if project results turn out not to enhance tribal sovereignty? Should any anthropologist refrain from asking questions for fear that the answer might be displeasing? Is enhanced tribal sovereignty always beneficial to all members of the Penobscot Nation?

Anthropologists should certainly investigate groups to which they belong and may indeed have particularly useful insights into those groups. However, the very concept of a native anthropologist is problematic. Groups are almost never homogeneous, and individuals have many identities. Being a native in one identity does not make one a native in all one's identities (Cerroni-Long 1995; Narayan 1993).

ETHICAL CONSIDERATIONS IN FIELDWORK

As questions about native anthropologists show, ethical issues frequently arise in anthropological research. Anthropologists have obligations to the standards of their discipline, to their sponsors, to their own and their host governments, and to the public. However, their first ethical obligations are usually to the people they study and to the people with whom they work. These obligations can supersede the goal of seeking new knowledge. According to the American Anthropological Association *Code of Ethics* (2009), "Anthropological researchers must ensure that they do not harm the safety, dignity, or privacy of the people with whom they work. ..." This includes safeguarding the rights, interests, and sensitivities of those studied, explaining the aims of the investigation as clearly as possible to the people involved; respecting anonymity of informants; not exploiting individual informants for personal gain; and giving "fair return" for all services. It also includes the responsibility to communicate the results of the research to the individuals and groups likely to be affected, as well as to the general public.

Informed consent is a critical aspect of anthropological ethics. Generally, this requires anthropologists to take part in ongoing discussion with their consultants about the nature of study as well as the risks and benefits of participation in it (Clark and Kingsolver n.d.). In particular, informed consent means that study participants should understand the ways in which release of the research data are likely to affect them and that they must be free to decide whether or not they will participate in the study (and, if they begin to participate, they must always be free to stop).

Anthropologists also have obligations to the discipline of anthropology. Two of these obligations seem particularly important. First, anthropologists should conduct themselves in ways that do not endanger the research prospects or lives of other anthropologists. Anthropologists who violate the mores and ethics of the communities where they work make it unlikely that those communities will accept other anthropologists in the future. Anthropologists who become involved with and identified with governments, military forces, or political platforms may endanger not only their own safety but also the work and lives of others. People may come to believe that because some anthropologists are identified with specific political actors, all are.

Most anthropologists also believe that the primary purpose of research is to add to the general store of anthropological knowledge. Thus, they have an obligation to publish their findings in forms that are available to other anthropologists and to the general public. Publishing usually involves review of the work by other anthropologists to help ensure the validity and quality of research. Anthropologists acknowledge that certain forms of secrecy are acceptable, and, on occasion, even required. For example, to protect both the communities where they work and the individuals with whom they work, anthropologists may decide to not reveal the precise location of their research or the actual names of the individuals they discuss. However, research in which the methods and findings are secret is a far greater problem. Not only does such research not contribute to general anthropological knowledge, but the scientific community also has no way of assessing its validity.

The obligations to protect other anthropologists and to publish research findings both pose dilemmas. The engaged anthropologists described in this chapter believe that anthropologists must work for the communities they study. However, this may make it impossible for future anthropologists to work at all. Governments may not grant anthropologists research visas, and organizations may not allow research if they believe anthropologists will promote political action against them. For example, Kristen Drybread's work, described in the opening of this chapter, is fascinating and important. However, it is hard to believe that officials at the prison where she worked will ever allow another anthropologist in the door. Applied anthropologists wish to work for businesses and governments. Often anthropological findings have greatest value for these entities when they are not shared with other businesses or the general public. There may be very few jobs available for applied anthropologists who insist on the right to publish all of the results of their research.

Numerous projects have tested the boundaries of ethics in anthropology, both with regard to the people anthropologists study and to the discipline itself. One early example was "Project Camelot," a mid-1960s attempt by the U.S. Army and Department of Defense to enlist anthropologists and other social scientists in achieving American foreign policy goals. Project Camelot's purpose was to create a model for predicting civil wars, but it was also implicated in fighting insurgency movements and propping up friendly governments (Horowitz 1967). When Project Camelot was made public in 1965, the United States had recently invaded the Dominican Republic and was escalating the war in Vietnam.

Project Camelot created controversy both inside and outside of anthropology. In countries where anthropologists worked, people began to see them as spies whose presence presaged a U.S. invasion. At the American Anthropological Association, Project Camelot led to vitriolic debate, where members raised concerns for the integrity of research, the safety of anthropologists in the field, and the purposes to which anthropological knowledge might be put. These concerns eventually led to the issuing of the first official statement on anthropological ethics in 1971.

Marco Di Lauro/Getty Images

Figure 3.6 Anthropologists and other social scientists working for the military raise important ethical concerns. Here, Ted Callahan talks to Afghan villagers in 2009. Callahan spent 18 months working for the U.S. Army's Human Terrain System program.

▌▐▐ Anthropology and the Military

In the past decade, concerns similar to those raised by Project Camelot have reemerged over the engagement of some anthropologists with the U.S. military (see Figure 3.6). Anthropologists have worked at military colleges and bases, providing anthropological training for officers or analyses of the culture of the military itself. They and other social scientists have also worked on the ground collecting data in zones of active conflict as part of a program called the Human Terrain System (HTS).

Between early 2007 and September 2014, the Pentagon employed HTS teams to help its combat brigades. According to some, the program achieved early success (Fondacaro and McFate 2008). For example, the obituary of Michael Bhatia, an HTS member killed in active duty in 2008, reports that his work helped save the lives of both U.S. soldiers and Afghan civilians. However, the use of anthropologists in such circumstances is extremely problematic.

It is indeed difficult to see how many of anthropology's ethical requirements can be met under conditions of warfare. How, for example, are participants to give coercion-free consent while being subject to military occupation? How can anthropologists honestly inform participants about the ways the research data will be used and are likely to affect them? Are individuals in a conflict ever really free to decide whether or not they will participate in a study? Can anthropologists working under such circumstances ensure, within reason, that the information they supply will not harm the safety, dignity, or privacy of the people with whom they work? Isn't the point of their work sometimes just the opposite of that? What about anthropologists' obligation to publish their research? Aren't the results of this sort of research necessarily secret? Historically, anthropologists have been concerned with protecting the rights and safety of the people they study. The primary concern of anthropologists working in HTS must be the safety, security, and goals of their employers instead.

Given all of the problems with programs such as HTS, it is probably safe to say that a strong majority of anthropologists oppose this use of anthropology. In fact, the American Anthropological Association has issued an official statement disapproving of it (AAA 2007).

Ultimately, ethical behavior is the responsibility of each individual anthropologist. The members of the AAA are supposed to subscribe to its code of ethics. Universities and some other research organizations have institutional review boards (IRBs) that examine all research involving human subjects for ethical violations. However, not all anthropologists are subject to the AAA or to IRBs. Lawyers who behave unethically can be disbarred. Doctors can have their medical licenses revoked. In both cases, they violate laws and can be punished if they continue to practice. There is no comparable sanction for anthropologists (and, indeed, for members of most disciplines). Therefore, there will always be a great diversity of anthropological practice.

▌▌▌ NEW ROLES FOR ETHNOGRAPHERS

Although there have been native anthropologists for a long time, until the 1970s, the prevailing model of fieldwork was a European or North American ethnographer visiting a relatively isolated and bounded society and then reporting on that society to other Europeans and North Americans. In some cases, anthropologists may have overstated the degree to which the societies they studied were isolated. Societies have always been connected with each other. However, in the past several decades, inexpensive communication, relatively cheap airfare, and immigration have greatly increased the scale of these connections.

Whether they work in cities, villages, or with tribal groups, anthropologists nowadays have to take regional and global connections into account. Research may mean following consultants from villages to their workplaces in cities, collecting genealogies that spread over countries or even continents, and following cash and information flows around the world. In addition to expanding the research site, contemporary ethnographers must often use techniques such as questionnaires, social surveys, archival material, government documents, and court records in addition to participant observation. The deep connections among cultures and the global movement of individuals mean that we must constantly reevaluate the nature of the cultures we are studying, their geographical spread, their economic and political position, and their relation to one another.

Today, not only are native anthropologists much more common, but the people anthropologists study also generally have far greater knowledge of the world than they did in earlier times. They are likely to understand what anthropology is and what anthropologists do, something not true in the past. In some cases, this has led to difficulties as people struggle over the question of who has the right to speak for a group. In other cases, people from the groups that anthropologists have described have publicly taken issue with their analysis. For example, in the early 2000s, a fierce controversy broke out over anthropological descriptions of the Yanomamo, an often studied Amazonian group. Had their primary ethnographer, Napoleon Chagnon, portrayed them accurately? Was the research team that he was part of responsible for spreading disease and decimating Yanomamo villages? Anthropologists, journalists, and Yanomamo tribe members debated these questions at meetings and in the popular press (for a review of the debate, see Borofsky 2005).

Despite controversies, for the most part, natives' increased knowledge of the outside world has resulted in closer relations among anthropologists and the people they study as well as more accurate ethnography. Ethnographic data are often useful to a society. Sometimes they serve as the basis for the revitalization of cultural identities that have been nearly effaced by Western impact (Feinberg 1994). Sometimes they play important roles in establishing group claims to "authenticity" and are useful in local political and economic contexts. For example, when Kathleen Adams (1995) carried out her fieldwork among the Toraja of Sulawesi, Indonesia, she became a featured event on tourist itineraries in the region.

Toraja tour guides led their groups to the home of her host, both validating his importance in the village and bolstering the tourists' experience of the Toraja as a group sufficiently "authentic" and important to be studied by anthropologists.

In the past, anthropologists sometimes worried about their subject disappearing. They argued that the main thing anthropology was designed to study was small-scale, relatively isolated "primitive" societies. They worried that, as economic development spread around the world, such societies would go out of existence and anthropology would essentially be done. In a small sense they were right, but in the larger sense they were wrong. Any anthropologist today looking to study a society untouched by the outside world would be out of luck. No such societies have existed for a long time. On the other hand, the forces of globalization have been as productive of diversity as they have been of homogeneity. Economic, political, and social forces bring groups of people together in new ways, in conflict and in cooperation. New cultural forms are created and old ones modified. Human cultural diversity, imagination, and adaptability show no signs of dying out, so anthropologists will always have material to study. Wherever human cultures exist and however they change, anthropologists will be there, devising means to study, understand, and think about them.

BRINGING IT BACK HOME
ANTHROPOLOGISTS AND HUMAN RIGHTS

What could be more obvious than that anthropologists should support human rights and be actively engaged in their promotion? For most Americans, doubting the value of human rights is unthinkable, like arguing against freedom of speech or claiming that children are not important. Yet, human rights pose ethical dilemmas for anthropologists. Almost all anthropologists believe firmly in their duty to promote human rights in their own society. Many also believe that they have an obligation to promote the interests of those they study. For example, Laura R. Graham (2006:5) writes that "[o]ur privileged position, specialized training, and unique skills . . . carry with them specific ethical obligations to promote the well-being of the people who are collaborators in our anthropological research and in the production of anthropological knowledge." Ida Nicolaisen points out that standing for human rights is often a matter of life and death. For example, she notes that in the Philippines between 2005 and late summer 2006, at least 73 indigenous people were "subjected to extra-judicial killings" and concludes that "[w]e owe it to indigenous peoples and other marginalized groups to stand up for their basic human rights when needed" (Nicolaisen 2006:6).

But there often are difficulties determining what the rights are and whether or not we should stand up for them. Laura Nader (2006:6) writes that ideas about human rights were developed in a largely western European context and are often conceived of as "something Euro-Americans take to others." Promoting Western notions of human rights may mean denying people in other societies what they consider to be their rights to pursue individual and cultural choices.

Consider Islamic hadd ("to the limit") punishments, such as stoning for adultery, amputation of limbs for theft, and flogging for moral offenses like consumption of alcohol. Hadd punishments deeply offend many people (including many Muslims), yet they form a core component of ethical belief and practice for many people in some Islamic nations. Courts in Saudi Arabia, Northern Nigeria, Iran, and numerous other nations hand down sentences involving punishments such as amputations of hands and feet for robbery and floggings for lesser crimes. It is important to note, however, that such sentences are often (but not always) commuted. Recently, groups such as Islamic State and Boko Haram, citing Islamic law, have implemented executions, floggings, and amputation.

Anthropologist Carolyn Fluehr-Lobban (2005) interviewed attorneys, judges, social scientists, and journalists in Sudan, a country that has practiced hadd punishments. She notes that most Sudanese Muslims oppose the use of hadd, and see it as an abuse of religion by the state. However, they also think that Western interest in eliminating such punishment is unwarranted interference in their right to determine their own culture. They point to a double standard: Westerners, particularly Americans, see hadd punishments as "barbaric" while they ignore their own abuses of human rights, such as the death penalty, waterboarding, the torture and abuse of prisoners that took place at the Abu Ghraib prison and elsewhere during the Iraq War, and the detention of prisoners without trial at Guantanamo Bay.

In 1990, Richard Schwartz wrote: "Every culture will have its distinctive ways of formulating and supporting human rights. Every society can learn from other societies more effective ways to implement human rights. While honoring the diversity of cultures, we can also build toward common principles that all can support." A noble idea indeed, but are we any closer to fulfilling it than we were a quarter century ago?

YOU DECIDE:

1. Given the diversity of culture and the anthropological importance of cultural relativism, can there be such a thing as universal human rights?
2. If anthropologists have moral obligations to the people with whom they work, should they ever work with people whose beliefs and practices they disapprove of? If yes, then what obligations do they have to such people? If no, how are we to accurately represent such people?
3. What sorts of things do you consider to be universal human rights? How good is our society at ensuring the rights you have identified? Do you think there is a core set of universal rights upon which most people could or should agree?

CHAPTER SUMMARY

1. Describe the research style and goals of early anthropologists. Anthropology began in the 19th century. In that era, anthropologists did not go into the field. They were compilers of data, and their goal was to describe and document the evolutionary history of human society. There were numerous problems with their data and methods.
2. Explain Franz Boas's role in founding modern American anthropology. In the United States, Franz Boas established a style of anthropology that rejected evolutionism. Boas insisted that anthropologists collect data through fieldwork. He argued that cultures were the result of their own history and could not be compared to one another, a position now called *cultural relativism*.
3. How did Bronislaw Malinowski and other British Commonwealth anthropologists contribute to the development of modern anthropology? Malinowski and others in Britain developed a tradition of fieldwork that emphasized participant observation. Although their focus was different than Boas's, they also saw members of other cultures as fully rational and worthy of respect.
4. Where do current-day anthropologists work and what are their techniques? Almost all anthropologists today do fieldwork. Although many continue to work in small communities, others work in large industrial and postindustrial societies. Most focus on answering specific questions rather than describing entire societies. Anthropological techniques include participant observation, interviews, questionnaires, and mapping.

5. **What is the role of cross-cultural comparison in anthropology?** Cross-cultural comparison has always been an aspect of anthropology. The Human Relations Area File (HRAF) is a large database that facilitates cross-cultural research.

6. **How has the role of gender as an anthropological subject changed over the past century?** Despite the presence of important women in early-20th-century anthropology, women were historically underrepresented in anthropological writing. This situation began to be redressed in the late 1960s, as increasing numbers of women became anthropologists and as anthropologists increasingly studied women. In the past 25 years, anthropologists have increasingly seen gender roles as central to social analysis, and anthropology based around LGBTQ issues has become more important.

7. **What was the influence of postmodernism on anthropology?** In the 1980s, postmodernists urged anthropologists to become more sensitive to issues of voice, history, and power. Postmodernists' insistence that the objective world was unknowable and that the anthropologist's voice was uncertain created intense debate but ultimately enriched ethnography.

8. **What are collaborative and engaged anthropology?** One response to postmodernism was collaborative and engaged anthropology. Some anthropologists placed special emphasis on the political dimensions of their work. They often took great pains to involve members of the group being studied in the production of ethnographic knowledge. Engaged anthropologists also promote social change in the communities where they work.

9. **What are native anthropologists and what advantages and disadvantages do they face?** Native anthropologists are those who study their own society. Although native anthropologists may have advantages of access and rapport in some cases, they also experience special burdens more intensely, such as whether to expose aspects of the culture that outsiders may receive unfavorably.

10. **What ethical issues are raised by anthropology and how are they addressed?** Anthropological ethics require protecting the dignity, privacy, and often the anonymity of the people whom anthropologists study. However, anthropological ethics are rarely simple. The use of anthropologists in pursuit of foreign relations goals is sometimes extremely problematic.

11. **How has globalization changed anthropological practice?** Anthropologists are increasingly enmeshed in a global society. Those they study are rarely isolated and are often quite knowledgeable about anthropology. Anthropological knowledge is often important in the

ways people understand their identity and, as such, is increasingly political.

12. Do anthropologists support human rights? Yes, but they are also aware that what constitutes human rights varies from culture to culture. Support for universal human rights may sometimes conflict with people's desire to determine their own cultural practices.

KEY TERMS

Collaborative ethnography

Consultant

Cultural relativism

Culture shock

Ethnocentrism

Ethnography

Ethnology

Human Relations Area
   Files (HRAF)

Informant

Interlocutor

Participant observation

Partner

Postmodernism

Racism

Respondents

AP Images/Sergei Grits

4

COMMUNICATION

Human language consists of words and gestures, as illustrated by this interaction between two Tajik men in a square on the outskirts of Dushanbe, the capital of Tajikistan.

AFTER YOU HAVE READ THIS CHAPTER, YOU WILL BE ABLE TO:

Δ List some of the characteristics of human languages, and explain how humans learn language.

Δ Summarize the meanings of phonology, morphology, syntax, and semantics.

Δ Illustrate the relationship between language and culture.

Δ Explain the ways in which language is related to social structure, and give examples.

Δ Summarize the Sapir-Whorf hypothesis, and debate the relationship between language and thought.

Δ List several forms of nonverbal communication.

Δ Compare different ways in which language changes, and discuss the implications of globalization for language change.

WHY DON'T YOU SPEAK GOOD?

IN'T ain't a word. .... Or is it? Language is full of different styles of speaking. Different individuals and different communities express themselves in different ways. Are any of these ways of speaking better or worse than any others? Do any of them have important implications for the ability of their speakers to think logically? For example, is it better, more logical, more beautiful to ask "Why don't you speak well?" instead of "Why don't you speak good?"?

It has certainly often been proposed that speaking "properly" and thinking logically are linked. For example, from the 1950s to the 1970s, a group of linguists, psychologists, and educators called *cultural deficit theorists* argued that children who spoke African American Vernacular English (AAVE), a variety of English common in many (but not all) African American communities, did poorly in school because of the way they spoke English. The theorists argued that the poor speech of these children, which they characterized as coarse, simple, and irrational, was due to a culturally deprived home environment (Ammon and Ammon 1971). They proposed that if children could be taught to speak "proper" English, they would be able to think more logically, and this would help lift them from poverty (Bereiter and Engelmann 1966; Engelmann and Engelmann 1966).

The work of linguists such as William Labov has disproved these ideas. Labov and his colleagues analyzed the speech of African American teens and demonstrated that it was neither logically nor structurally inferior to any other sort of speech; it just used rules that were somewhat different from the language of most white upper-middle-class Americans (called Standard American English, or SAE). For example, whereas speakers of SAE use words such as *usually* and *always* to express habitual action (I am usually in my office by 7:30), speakers of AAVE use the verb *be* to express the same thing (I be in my office by 7:30) (Green 2002:48). The AAVE usage is concise, logical, and consistent. AAVE is just a different way of speaking and, from a linguistic point of view, neither better nor worse than any other.

So, what is good English? Consider the double negative. Almost everyone reading this book has heard someone (perhaps a teacher) claim that a double negative is really a positive. Thus, saying "I don't want no" is really saying "I want some." This is simply incorrect. When Mick Jagger sings, "I can't get no satisfaction," no native English speaker believes he is saying how satisfied he is. And no one imagines that the kids singing in Pink Floyd's "The Wall" are telling us how much they want to go to school.

But sometimes, two negatives do make a positive, as when a child who refuses to do her homework says: "I won't not do my homework if you buy me some ice cream." And two or more positives can sometimes make a negative, as in:

Speaker A: "Yes, I will do it."

Speaker B: "Yeah, yeah, yeah, sure you will."

The point is that, from a linguistic perspective, one way of speaking is as good as the next. There is no reason to prefer "I don't have any money" to "I ain't got no money," and there is no reason that saying "I'm about to go get lunch" is better than saying "I'm fixin' to get me some lunch." All the statements are fully logical, comprehensible, and communicate the information the speaker desires.

So why does society act as if one way of speaking is good and the other bad? Different ways of speaking often identify the speakers' ethnic background, social class, level of education, geographical location, and other aspects of their life. Our judgments are really about people, not about the speech itself. "I ain't got no money," is "wrong" not because it is logically or intellectually inferior but rather because it identifies the speaker as likely having a lower educational and social class position than the person who says: "I don't have any money."

Communication in general and language in particular are great examples of the ways in which human biology and human culture are intimately entangled. Language is a biological aspect of human beings. All humans who are physically able to do so communicate through language. Deaf communities create sign languages that are as complex and sophisticated as spoken languages. However, speech is not just an aspect of biology. The language we speak, the style of our speaking, to whom we speak, and how we speak to them are all aspects of culture. In this chapter, we briefly explore some of the biological and structural elements of language and communication and then turn to their social and cultural aspects.

▌▎▎ THE ORIGINS AND CHARACTERISTICS OF HUMAN LANGUAGE

Although passing information is critical to the survival of most living things, members of other species communicate very differently from humans. No member of any other species can make up a story and tell it to another, understand a piece of poetry, or discuss what it would like to eat tomorrow, yet these are things that people in all human cultures do regularly.

Animal vocalizations are referred to as *calls,* and animal **call systems** may be very sophisticated. However, even large call systems are restricted to a fixed number of signals generally uttered in response to specific events. Human language, on the other hand, is capable of re-creating complex thought patterns and experiences in words (see Figure 4.1).

Patrick Gijsbers/Getty Images

Figure 4.1 Howler monkeys, found in South America, have calls that include vocalizations that primatologists refer to as the "incipient roar" the "male woof" and the "oodel."

So, when did humans first begin to speak? Anthropologists offer several answers to this question. Certainly our distant ancestors communicated, but they probably used call systems similar to modern-day primates. Some believe that language might have begun as early as two million years ago, when the genus *Homo* emerged (Schepartz 1993:119), but most anthropologists think that language like our own has been limited to members of our own species. The earliest *Homo sapiens* date from about 200,000 years ago, so language may well have emerged at that time. A third position (Bickerton 1998) holds that modern human language emerged about 50,000 years ago, in connection with a big jump in the sophistication of human toolmaking and symbolic expression. Work in biology suggests a relationship between language and a gene called FOXP2. Although the ability to acquire and use language is controlled by many genes, FOXP2 is the only one that has been clearly identified (Dominguez and Rakic 2009). Interestingly, the human form of FOXP2 has also been found in Neanderthals (Krause et al. 2007).

Call system: The form of communication among nonhuman primates composed of a limited number of sounds that are tied to specific stimuli in the environment.

Regardless of when humans acquired language, anthropologists generally agree that language is part of our biological adaptation. Although in any culture, some people talk with greater or lesser artistry than others, all physiologically normal individuals in all cultures develop adequate language skills.

Language is more than simply a human capacity or ability. For example, people have the capacity to learn algebra or ice-skating, but they may or may not do it, as their culture and their individual choices dictate. Language is different. Unless prevented by total social isolation or physical incapacity, all humans learn a first language as part of the developmental process of childhood. All go through the same stages of language learning in the same sequence and at roughly the same speed regardless of the language being learned. Language is an innate property of the mind.

Humans have what Steven Pinker (1994) calls a "language instinct." Pinker points out that the language instinct in humans is very different from instinctive communication in other animals. Among animals, the instinct for communication means that dogs do not *learn* to wag their tails when they are content and growl when they are angry: They do these things as an expression of their underlying genetic code. Dog behavior is specieswide. A growl means the same thing to a dog in Vladivostok as it does to a dog in Manhattan. But language is not instinctual in this way. The human instinct is to learn the language of the group into which the individual is socialized. There is no biological basis for learning one language over another. For example, an infant born to French-speaking parents but raised in an English-speaking family has no predisposition to speak French.

The universality of the process of learning a first language as well as the underlying similarities that unite all human languages led Noam Chomsky (1975) and many others to propose that there is a **universal grammar**—a basic set of principles, conditions, and rules that form the foundation of all languages. Children learn language by applying this unconscious universal grammar to the sounds they hear.

The social element of language learning is critical. To learn language, we must be able to interact verbally with others. There is a particularly important period from our birth until about 6 years of age. Children deprived of contact during these years never learn to speak like other members of their community. This is illustrated by the case of Genie, a child discovered by social workers in the 1970s in California. Genie had been locked in an attic for the first 12 years of her life. With training and good living conditions, she acquired a large vocabulary, but she was never able to master English syntax; she created sentences like "Genie have momma have baby grow up" (Pinker 1994:292). Children like Genie demonstrate that although language is a biological capacity, it can only be activated within a social group. Thus, language provides an outstanding example of the interrelation of biology and culture.

Human language is first and foremost a system of symbols. A **symbol** is just something that stands for something else. Words are symbols, and they stand for things, actions, and ideas because speakers of a language agree that they do, a feature of human language called **conventionality**. An animal is no more a dog than it is a *chien* (French), a *perro* (Spanish), or a *kutta* (Hindi).

This seemingly trivial fact is critical for two reasons. First, because the relationship between a series of sounds (a word) and their meaning is symbolic, relatively few sounds can be used to refer to an infinitely large number of meanings. For nonhuman animals, there is a direct connection between a sound and its meaning; 60 sounds equal 60 meanings.

Universal grammar: A basic set of principles, conditions, and rules that form the foundation of all languages.

Symbol: Something that stands for something else. Central to language and culture.

Conventionality: The notion that, in human language, words are only arbitrarily or conventionally connected to the things for which they stand.

Most human languages have only 30 to 40 sounds. However, used in combination, these sounds can produce an endless variety of words and meanings. There is no maximum number of words or sentences in any human language. People constantly create new ones, a characteristic known as **productivity**.

Second, symbols enable humans to transmit and store information, a capacity that makes our cultures possible. If humans had to learn everything they know by trial and error or by watching others, our lives would be vastly different and much simpler than they are. Human beings do learn by these methods, but they also learn by talking. We tell each other our experiences and the stories passed down to us. We discuss the past and plan for the future using words. This human ability to speak about different times and places is called **displacement**.

In cultures with writing, the information stored symbolically is truly vast. Consider, for example, that no one individual could possibly know everything written in the books in even a relatively small university library. However, because we can store our knowledge symbolically as words, we can have access to everything that is there. And with the Internet ... well, you get the point!

▌▌▌ THE STRUCTURE OF LANGUAGE

Although there are enormous differences among languages, there are also some compelling similarities. Every language has a structure: an internal logic and a particular relationship among its parts. Descriptive, or structural, linguistics is the study of the internal workings of language. A basic insight of structural linguistics is that all languages are composed of four subsystems: **phonology** (a system of sounds), **morphology** (a system for creating words from sounds), **semantics** (a system that relates words to meanings), and **syntax** (a system of rules for combining words into meaningful sentences).

At a very basic level, all language is made up of sounds. Humans use a vast array of sounds in their languages. For example, the International Phonetic Alphabet (IPA), a system designed to represent the sounds of all human languages in writing, has more than 100 base symbols, which can be altered by about 55 modifiers. A sound found in human language is called a **phone** of language. No individual language uses more than a small subset of this huge number of possible sounds. A sound that is used in any individual language is called a **phoneme** of that language. Thus, phones are universal: any young child can learn to make the sounds used in any human language. However, phonemes belong to particular languages, and an adult who speaks one language may have difficulty learning the phonemes of another.

Productivity (linguistics): The idea that humans can combine words and sounds into new, meaningful utterances they have never before heard.

Displacement: The capacity of all human languages to describe things not happening in the present.

Phonology: The sound system of a language.
Morphology: A system for creating words from sounds.
Semantics: The subsystem of a language that relates words to meaning.
Syntax: A system of rules for combining words into meaningful sentences.
Phone: Smallest identifiable unit of sound made by humans and used in any language.

Phoneme: The smallest unit of sound that serves to distinguish between meanings of words within a language.

At some level, almost everyone is aware of the phonemic differences among languages. For example, the "rolled r" common in Spanish is not found in most varieties of English, and many English speakers find the sound difficult to make. On the other hand, the "/th/" sound (as in the word *the*) is common in most varieties of English but does not exist in French or Japanese (as well as many other languages). Different languages have different phonemes, and within a language, different geographical, ethnic, and social groups use somewhat different sets of phonemes. We experience these different sets of phonemes as accents (though accents may also include word choice). Because everyone speaks their own language with a particular set of phonemes not shared by all speakers, everyone always speaks with an accent!

Morpheme: The smallest unit of language that has a meaning.

All languages are made up of units that have meaning called **morphemes**. Morphemes can be composed of any number of phonemes. Some are as simple as a single phoneme (the English morphemes "a" and "–s," for example), and most are relatively brief. Words are composed of any number of morphemes. Some are extremely simple: "A" is a phoneme, a morpheme, and a word. Some more complex: "–s" is a phoneme, a morpheme (it means make the thing before it plural), but not a word. The word *teacher* has two morphemes: "teach" and "–er" (here, "–er" refers to someone who does what came before it). Long words, such as antidisestablishmentarianism, for example, are simply strings of morphemes.

Lexicon: The total stock of words in a language.

The total stock of words in a language is known as its **lexicon**. A lexicon often provides clues to culture because it tends to reflect the objects and ideas that members of that culture consider important. For example, the average American can name 50 to 100 types of plants, but members of foraging societies can often name 500 to 1,000 types (Harris 1989:72). Germans in Munich have a vocabulary of more than 70 words to describe the strength, color, fizziness, clarity, and age of beer because it is so central to their culture (Hage 1972, cited in Salzmann 1993:256) (see Figure 4.2). Americans have large numbers of words to describe cars or money but have far fewer to describe bicycles.

William Perugini/Shutterstock

Figure 4.2 Languages build vocabularies around ideas and things important to their speakers. Germans in Munich have more than 70 words to describe beer.

Anthropologists sometimes use vocabulary as a clue to understanding different cultures. For example, the words people use for their kin tell us something of the nature of their families. In English, a woman uses the term *brother-in-law* to speak about her sister's husband, her husband's brother, and the husbands of all her husband's sisters. The use of a single term for all of these relations reflects the similarity of a woman's behavior toward the men in these kinship statuses. In Hindi, a language of North India, a woman uses separate terms for her sister's husband (*behnoi*), her husband's elder brother (*jait*), her husband's younger brother (*deva*), and her husband's sisters' husbands (*nandoya*). The variety of words in Hindi reflects the fact that a woman treats the members of each of these categories differently.

Sounds and words alone do not make up a language. To convey meaning, every language has syntax, rules that structure the combination of words into meaningful utterances. Languages differ in their syntactic structures. In English, word order is a basic element of syntax, so statements such as "The dog bit the man" and "The man bit the dog" have very different meanings. Word order is not equally important in all languages. In Japanese, the subject and object of a sentence are indicated by word endings, and order is less important. For example, John gave Mary the book is translated *John-san ga Mary-san ni hon o ageta*. The same word order, with the word endings "ga" and "ni" reversed *(John-san ni Mary-san ga hon o ageta)* would be "Mary gave John the book."

Parts of speech (nouns, verbs, and so on) are a critical aspect of syntax. All languages have a word class of nouns, but different languages have different subclasses of nouns, frequently referred to as *genders*. (Although masculine and feminine are common linguistic genders, the word *gender* in linguistics refers to the category or "class of a word," not its sex-related connotation or characteristics.) For example, Papago, a Native American language, divides all the features of the world into two genders: "living things" and "growing things." Living things include all animated objects; growing things refer to inanimate objects. Some languages have many more subclasses. Kivunjo, a language spoken in East Africa, has 16 of them (Corbett 2008; Pinker 1994:27).

Applying the rules of grammar turns meaningless sequences of words into meaningful utterances, but we can recognize a sentence as grammatical even if it makes no sense. To use a now classic example (Chomsky 1965), consider the following sentences: "Colorless green ideas sleep furiously," and "Furiously sleep ideas green colorless." Both sentences are meaningless in English, but English speakers easily recognize the first as grammatical, whereas the second is both meaningless and ungrammatical.

▌▌ Using Anthropology: Forensic Linguistics

Everyone speaks with an accent. That is, they speak their language with a particular set of phonemes. Most native speakers of American English can use these accents to guess at some of the characteristics of the speaker: their geographical origin, perhaps their ethnic background. In addition to marking group membership, our speech and our writing contain mannerisms that are particular to ourselves alone. We may favor certain words or combinations of words. We may even use particular forms of punctuation. Forensic linguistic anthropologists use the details of speech and writing to provide legal evidence in a wide variety of situations.

Immigration and customs officials often make use of linguistics experts to find out whether the accent, slang, and idiomatic expressions used by asylum seekers are the same as those of the countries they claim to be from. Information identifying the regional origin of an individual can play an important role in criminal investigation as well. For example, forensic linguist Roger Shuy helped solve a kidnapping in Illinois. In this case, the kidnapper had left a ransom note that instructed that money be left in a trash can on the "devil's strip" at a particular street corner. Shuy knew that there is only one place in the United States where the term *devil's strip* is used to identify the small grass area sometimes found between a sidewalk and the street: Akron, Ohio. There was only one suspect from Akron and, when confronted with this evidence, he confessed (Dahl 2008; Hitt 2012).

In some cases, forensic linguists may be able to identify a particular individual rather than just the region a person comes from. For example, in 2006, Garry Weddell, a police inspector who lived near London, claimed he came home to find that his wife Sandra, a nurse, had committed suicide, leaving a typed suicide note. However, police were suspicious about the cause of death. A forensic linguist examined the suicide note and compared the wording and, in particular, the sentence structure, to diaries and other writings by Sandra and Garry Weddell. The linguist concluded that it was extremely unlikely that Sandra Weddell could have written the suicide note but that the writing was a good match for her husband (Narayanaswami 2010; Wright 2008), and he was arrested for the murder of his wife.

Forensic linguistics is often extremely important in determining what is said in voice recordings. Such recordings are problematic because a lot of meaning in conversation is carried in visual expression, hand gestures, and other nonverbal aspects of communication. These are missing in such recordings. In addition, we tend to hear what we want to hear: Our existing ideas and prejudices can deeply affect how we interpret what is said. In this circumstance, forensic linguists' close attention to the specifics of phonetics can often clarify meaning, sometimes reversing what people think they hear (Hitt 2012).

Forensic linguistics is a powerful tool, but it needs to be used cautiously. Attempts at detection based on writing can sometimes fail spectacularly. For example, in 2003, English professor Donald Foster, who had used a literary forensics technique to reveal the author of an anonymously published popular book claimed to use the same technique to discover the person who sent anthrax spores to the offices of politicians and news media in 2001, killing five and infecting 17 others (Foster 2003). However, Steven Hatfill, the man he identified, was innocent and later sued both Foster and the magazines that published the article (Freed 2010). It may be fine for amateurs to speculate on the authorship of literary works, but court cases really demand careful work by highly trained professionals.

▮▮▮ LANGUAGE AND CULTURE

Phonemes, morphemes, syntax . . . these are essentially elements of the biology of language, but language is much more than just its structure. Consider the following exchange:

> *Scene: It's a clear, hot evening in July. J and K have finished their meal. The children are sitting nearby. There is a knock at the door. J rises, answers the knock, and finds L standing outside.*

J: Hello, my friend! How're you doing? How are you feeling, L? You feeling good? *(J now turns in the direction of K and addresses her.)*

J: Look who here, everybody! Look who just come in. Sure, it's my Indian friend, L. Pretty good, all right. *(J slaps L on the shoulder and, looking him directly in the eyes, seizes his hand and pumps it wildly up and down.)*

J: Come right in, my friend! Don't stay outside in the rain. Better you come in right now. *(J now drapes his arm around L's shoulder and moves him in the direction of a chair.)*

J: Sit down! Sit right down! Take your loads off you ass. You hungry? You want crackers? Maybe you want some beer? You want some wine? Bread? You want some sandwich? How about it? You hungry? I don't know. Maybe you sick. Maybe you don't eat again long time. *(K has now stopped what she is doing and is looking on with amusement. L has seated himself and has a look of bemused resignation on his face.)*

J: You sure looking good to me, L. You looking pretty fat! Pretty good all right! You got new boots? Where you buy them? Sure pretty good boots! I glad. . . . *(At this point, J breaks into laughter. K joins in. L shakes his head and smiles. The joke is over).*

The joke is over. So what was the joke? This joke, from the Western Apache, recorded by Keith Basso (1979), is about how the Apache see white people as communicating with them and with each other. In the

The Western Apache.

joke, *J* pretends he is a white man. The joke is that white speech, as *J* presents it, is highly inappropriate and offensive to the Apache. For starters, you do not publicly call someone a friend or ask how he or she is feeling. For the Western Apache, these are very personal statements and questions. To use them in a highly public way as *J* does here conveys insincerity. The Apache believe that one should enter and leave a room as unobtrusively as possible, so *J* making a big to-do about *L* coming into the room is inappropriate as well. Actions such as putting an arm around another man's shoulder or asking repeatedly if he wants something to eat are understood as both violations of individual dignity and overwhelming bossiness. To the Apache, such actions suggest that the speaker thinks the person he or she is talking to is of no account and that his wishes can be safely ignored. Perhaps worst of all is suggesting that another might be sick. Not only is this a violation of privacy, the Apache fear that talking about misfortune may well bring it on.

Knowing only the technical grammatical aspects of language would not help much in understanding J's and L's speech. Their speech embeds critical cultural concepts and values. Without understanding their culture, an observer cannot possibly get the joke.

Language is so heavily freighted with culture that understanding one is almost always a key to understanding the other. One way anthropologists analyze this relationship is to think in terms of speech performance. Such performance includes what people are saying as well as what they are communicating beyond the actual words. **Sociolinguistics** is the study of the relationship between language and culture. Sociolinguists study speech performances and attempt to identify, describe, and understand the ways in which language is used in different social contexts.

The ways in which people actually speak are highly dependent on the context of their speech as well as issues such as class, gender, ethnicity, and geography. A public political speech has different purposes and is limited by different norms than a political discussion among friends. For example, American Presidents since Ronald Reagan have almost always ended their annual State of the Union address with the "God bless America" or similar wording. However, it would be strange if you ended a political discussion with friends with these words. And different cultures have different norms regarding political speeches: who can participate as speaker and audience, the appropriate topics and cultural themes for such a speech, where such speeches can take place, the relationship between the speaker and hearer, the language used in a multilingual community, and so forth.

Speech is critical in the construction of identity. Penelope Eckert (2000) has studied the way children and adolescents in American schools use language to create and enforce social roles and identities. This process

Sociolinguistics: The study of the relationship between language and culture and the ways language is used in varying social contexts.

starts with teasing in elementary and junior high schools. It continues for girls in the form of both true and false compliments that "establish and enforce social hierarchies and boundaries" (Eckert 2004), and for boys with increased use of language styles specifically opposed by teachers and other powerful adults, including sexual references and obscenities. In high schools, verbal labels indicate social terrain and frequently physical location within the school. In the Detroit high school Eckert studied, the critical labels were jocks and burnouts. Jocks identified with the institution, with adolescence, and with the white suburban middle class. Burnouts saw themselves as opposed to the institution, wanting to be adults, and identified with the urban working class. Jock and burnout groups used language differently: Jock girls were the most standard speakers, and burnout girls used the most vernacular language. Boys' language was between these two groups. Burnout girls made frequent use of multiple negatives and other stigmatized speech forms. These differences involved not only the use of different vocabularies but changes in the sounds of the languages they used as well (Eckert 1989).

In some cultures, different speech forms are used depending on whether the speaker and hearer are intimate friends, acquaintances on equal footing, or people of distinctly different social statuses. French, German, and Yoruba, among many other languages, have formal and informal pronouns that are not found in English. The rules for their use vary among cultures. In France, parents use the informal term to address their children, but children use the formal term to address their parents. In the Spanish spoken in Costa Rica, many people use three forms: the informal *tú* is used by an adult speaking to a child (or lover), the formal *usted* is used among strangers, and the intermediate term *vos* can be used among friends. In India, the status of a husband is higher than that of a wife, and among most Hindi speakers, a wife never addresses her husband by his name (certainly not in public) but uses a roundabout expression that would translate into English as something like "I am speaking to you, sir."

▮▮▮ Language and Social Stratification

From a linguistic perspective, all languages are equally sophisticated and serve the needs of their speakers equally well, and every human being speaks with equal grammatical sophistication. Despite this, as we saw in the opening of this chapter, in complex stratified societies such as the United States, some speech is considered "correct" and other speech is judged inferior.

In hierarchical societies, the most powerful group generally determines what is "proper" in language. Indeed, the grammatical constructions used by the social elites are considered *language,* whereas deviations from them are often called *dialects.* Because the power of the speaker rather than any inherent qualities of a speech form determines its acceptability, linguists sometimes say that a language is "a dialect with an army and a navy" (see Language in Society 1997:469).

The relation of language usage to social class and power is reflected in the speech of different social classes in the United States. In a classic study, sociolinguist William Labov (1972) noted that elites and working-class people have different vocabularies and pronounce words differently. The forms associated with higher socioeconomic status are considered "proper," whereas forms spoken by those in lower socioeconomic statuses are considered incorrect and are stigmatized.

Labov found that speakers often vary their vocabulary and pronunciation in different contexts and that the degree of such variation is related to their social class. At the top and bottom of the social hierarchy, there is little variation. Elites use privileged forms of speech, and the poor use stigmatized forms. However, members of the lower middle class often use stigmatized forms in casual speech but privileged forms in careful speech. One interpretation is that people at the bottom and top of the social hierarchy do not vary their speech because their social position is stable. The very poor do not believe they have much chance to rise, and the wealthy are secure in their positions. Members of the lower middle class, however, are concerned with raising their social position and, in consequence, copy the speech patterns of the wealthy in some social situations. However, they are also concerned with maintaining connections to family and friends and therefore use stigmatized speech with them. Labov's study makes clear what many of us know but do not like to admit: We do judge a person's social status by the way he or she speaks. What we say and how we say it are ways of telling people who we are socially or, perhaps, who we would like to be.

The development of D4 accents in Ireland (Moore 2011) shows an interesting parallel to Labov's observations and shows the complexity of the relationship between language and social stratification. D4 is the postal code of a prosperous area of Dublin. In the 1990s, as the economy of Ireland grew, D4 became associated with a way of speaking that differentiated those who used it from Irish who spoke with rural or Dublin working-class accents. D4—sometimes called "DORTspeak" after the way its users pronounce DART, the name of the Dublin public transportation system—identified its users with the rising, globalized, urbanized elite (see Figure 4.3). It rapidly spread from Dublin to other areas of the country. However, D4 also came under brutal criticism as being pretentious and inauthentic. Authors of newspaper editorials tied the use of D4 to what they imagined was the rejection of Irish identity. Moore (2011:59)

Dublin, Ireland.

notes that for many, particularly after the Irish economic crash of 2008, the D4 became associated with the worst excesses of the era of Irish growth and the (supposed) disintegration of Irish society. This changed its meaning and led to a decline in its use.

Although there are many stigmatized variants of American English, including Appalachian English, Dutchified Pennsylvania English, Hawaiian Creole, Gullah, and emergent Hispanic Englishes, the most stigmatized is African American Vernacular English (AAVE). As we noted earlier, AAVE is simply a variant of Standard English, neither better nor worse than any other. Further, from Mark Twain and William Faulkner to Toni Morrison and Maya Angelou, from George Gershwin to Usher and The Weekend, AAVE has had deep influences on American art, speech, fiction, and music.

Figure 4.3 The Dublin Area Rapid Transport (DART) lent its name to DORTspeak, an accent associated with the Irish globalized elite of the 2000s.

Individuals who speak only AAVE are at a disadvantage in the larger society, and most realize that AAVE is stigmatized as symbolizing ignorance, whereas Standard American English (SAE) is considered "normal" and symbolizes intelligence. Fordham (1999) found that successful students at a predominantly black high school in Washington, DC, learned to switch rapidly between using SAE in the classroom and AAVE with friends and in social settings. Often, they attempted to hide their proficiency in SAE from their friends. In fact, most AAVE speakers do become effective speakers of several varieties of English. AAVE and SAE have similar capacities to deliver both "formal and informal knowledge as well as local knowledge and wisdom" (Morgan 2004), but speakers of AAVE, like others who are bilingual, must learn **code-switching**, to move seamlessly between two languages, and this ability is often central to their identities and their interactions inside and outside of their communities.

Code-switching: Moving seamlessly and appropriately between two different languages.

The Sapir–Whorf Hypothesis

The close relationship between culture and language raises interesting questions about the connections between language and thought. At the opening of the chapter, we pointed out that some social scientists in the 1950s and 1960s believed, incorrectly, that AAVE was less logical than SAE and that, as a result, AAVE speakers thought illogically. In believing this, they assumed a strong relationship between speaking and thinking. The existence of such a relationship is an old and controversial idea in anthropology. It is often associated with the work of Boas's student Edward Sapir and Sapir's student Benjamin Lee Whorf.

In the early 20th century, Sapir and Whorf argued that, because language played a critical role in determining the way people understand the world, then people who spoke different languages must understand the world in different ways. They proposed that people's ability to think about things such as time, space, and matter are conditioned by the structure of the languages they speak. They argued that we perceive the world in certain ways because we talk about the world in certain ways. This idea has come to be known as the **Sapir-Whorf hypothesis**.

Sapir-Whorf hypothesis: The hypothesis that perceptions and understandings of time, space, and matter are conditioned by the structure of a language.

We clearly choose our words to guide and direct the thoughts of others. Politicians, for example, routinely search for derogatory words and phrases to characterize their opponents. Or consider the term *side effect*. A side effect is an unwanted consequence of something such as a drug. However, the phrase *side effect* encourages us to think of it as off to the side and therefore less important than the *"central" effect* of the drug. But is it less important? In the late 1950s and early 1960s, thalidomide was prescribed to calm the stomachs of pregnant mothers. The drug was effective but had the horrible side effect of causing severe malformations in babies born to those mothers. Clearly, there was nothing "off to the side" about these effects.

Calling the deformities *side effects* did not prevent people from thinking that they were more important than the drug's effect. In fact, the thalidomide case led to special testing of drugs prescribed during pregnancy. This makes an important point: Word choice can encourage people to think certain ways. However, words cannot force people to think in one way or another. Even a government that controlled all the words people used could not control their thoughts. People merely invent new words or give the old ones new and ironic meanings (for example, if something is "sick," is that good or bad?).

Sapir and Whorf also argued that the grammatical structure of languages compelled their speakers to think and behave in certain ways. For example, Whorf (1941) claimed that because tenses in the Hopi language were very different from tenses in English, Hopi speakers necessarily understood time in ways very different from English speakers. This position is sometimes called "strong determinism," and it has some deep problems. For example, consider the differences in the way we speak about missing a person in English and in French. In English, we say "I miss you." "I," the person doing the missing, is the subject; "you," the person being missed, is the object. In French, however, the order is reversed: You say "Tu me manques." The person being missed is the subject, and the person doing the missing is the object. Literally translated, the French sentence appears to mean "you miss me." A strong determinist would expect this structural difference to indicate that speakers of French and English have different understandings of missing a person. However, no evidence suggests that this is so.

This is not to say that language structure and thought are completely unrelated. For example Gordon (2004) reports that members of the Piraha, a Brazilian tribe he studied, have difficulty understanding and recalling numbers for which they have no words. Experiments done by Gilbert et al. (2006) suggest that language affects color perception in the right visual field, but not the left. This corresponds to the fact that language processing is located primarily on the left side of the brain. Casasanto (2008) conducted studies on the way that Greek and English speakers estimate time. He notes that all languages use space and the accumulation of material as metaphors for time. For example, in English we talk about a long time, or visualize time as sand in an hourglass. However, languages use these metaphors unequally. For example, English uses mostly distance metaphors whereas Greek uses mostly material metaphors. Casasanto showed that, in an experimental situation, Greek and English speakers estimated time differently because of this. However, a brief training session caused these differences to disappear. Casasanto's work, like that of Gilbert et al., shows the complexity of the relationship between language and perception. But, it also shows that the relationship between the two is fairly weak and the effect of language on perception is easily overcome.

▌▌▌ NONVERBAL COMMUNICATION

Before returning to our discussion of spoken language, it is important to note that anthropologists also study the nonverbal ways in which humans communicate. Our use of our bodies, interpersonal space, physical objects, and even time can communicate worlds of information. As Edward T. Hall, one of the founders of the study of nonverbal communication said, "Time talks" and "space speaks" (1959). Nonverbal communication includes artifacts, haptics, chronemics, proxemics, and kinesics.

In the context of nonverbal communication, **artifacts** such as clothing, jewelry, tattoos, piercings, and other visible body modifications send messages. For example, among the Tuareg, a people of the Sahara, men often wear veils and use their position as an important part of nonverbal communication (Murphy 1964). A Tuareg man lowers his veil only among intimates and people of lower social status. He raises it high when he wishes to appear noncommittal. The use of artifacts to send messages is familiar to every American. Tattoos, piercings, and jewelry all provide information about those who wear them.

Artifacts (in communications studies): Communication by clothing, jewelry, tattoos, piercings, and other visible body modifications.

Haptics: The analysis and study of touch.

Haptics refers to the study and analysis of touch. Handshakes, pats on the back or head, kisses, and hugs are all ways we communicate by touch. Many American males, for example, believe that the quality of a handshake communicates important information. Firm handshakes are taken to indicate self-confidence and strength of character, whereas limp handshakes often suggest indecisiveness or effeminacy.

Some anthropologists suggest that societies can be divided into "contact" cultures, in which people tend to interact at close distances and touch one another frequently, and "noncontact" cultures, in which people interact at greater distance and avoid touching (Hall 1966; Montagu 1978). Contact cultures are common in the Middle East, India, and Latin America. Noncontact cultures include those of northern Europe, North America, and Japan. But this dichotomy is simplistic. In India, for example, social equals may touch, but nonequals almost never do. In the United States, equality and inequality also play an important role in touch. Your boss may pat you on the back, but you will rarely pat your boss (Leathers 1997:126).

Chronemics: The study of the different ways that cultures understand time and use it to communicate.

Chronemics refers to the study of cultural understandings of time. For example, in North American culture, what does it say when a person shows up for an appointment 40 minutes late? Does it mean something different if he or she shows up 10 minutes early? Is a Latin American who shows up late for an appointment saying the same thing?

Hall (1983) divided cultures into those with monochronic time (M-time), such as the United States and northern European countries, and those with polychronic time (P-time) such as Brazil and India. Hall argued that in M-time cultures, time is perceived as inflexible and people organize their lives according to schedules. In P-time cultures, time is understood as fluid. The emphasis is on social interaction, and activities are not expected to proceed like clockwork. Thus, being late for a meeting in P-time cultures does not convey the unspoken messages that it conveys in an M-time culture (Victor 1992).

Like the contact/noncontact dichotomy, M-time and P-time seem to capture a basic truth about cultural variation but fail to account for the enormous variability within cultures. How long an individual is kept waiting for an appointment may have more to do with power than with cultural perceptions of time. People are likely to be on time for their superiors but may keep their subordinates waiting.

Proxemics: The study of the cultural use of interpersonal space.

Proxemics is the social use of space. Hall (1968) identified three different ranges of personal communicative space (see Figure 4.4). *Intimate distance,* from 1 to 18 inches, is typical among intimates. *Personal distance,* from 18 inches to 4 feet, characterizes relationships among friends. *Social distance,* from 4 to 12 feet, is common among relative strangers. These distances are affected by circumstances, culture, gender, and individual

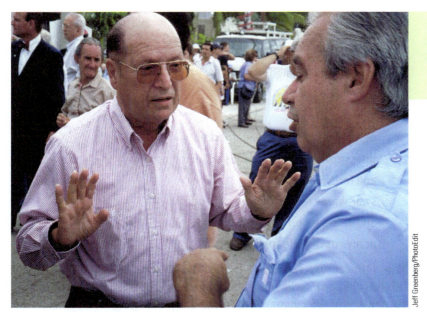

Jeff Greenberg/PhotoEdit

Figure 4.4 In addition to speaking, people use hands and facial expressions as well as interpersonal space to communicate.

personality. We speak to strangers at a much closer distance in a movie or a classroom than in an unconfined space. In the United States, women and mixed-gender pairs talk at closer distances than do men. In Turkey, on the other hand, men and women talk at close distances with members of their own sex but at very large distances with members of the opposite sex (Leathers 1997).

Finally, **kinesics** refers to body position, movement, facial expressions, and gaze. We use our posture, visual expression, eye contact, and other body movements to communicate interest, boredom, and much else. Smiling and some other facial expressions likely are biologically based human universals. There are no societies in which people do not smile. In all societies, social interactions are more likely to have a positive outcome if people are smiling than if they are frowning or scowling. Smiling is also found in chimpanzees and gorillas, our nearest nonhuman relations.

Smiling also shows the powerful effects of culture on biology. A smile does not mean the same thing in all cultures. Americans generally equate smiling with happiness, but people in many cultures smile when they experience surprise, wonder, or embarrassment (Ferraro 1994). A guidebook on international business advises American managers that the Japanese often smile to make their guests feel comfortable rather than because they are happy (Lewis 1996:267). Despite this, Japanese and Americans agree that smiling faces are more sociable than neutral faces (Matsumoto and Kudoh 1993), and that they most often interpret smiles in the same way (Nagashima and Schellenberg 1997).

Kinesics: The study of body position, movement, facial expressions, and gaze.

▌▌▌ LANGUAGE CHANGE

> Fæder ure þu þe eart on heofonum
>
> Si þin nama gehalgod
>
> to becume þin rice
>
> gewurþe ðin willa
>
> on eorðan swa swa on heofonum.
>
> urne gedæghwamlican hlaf syle us todæg
>
> and forgyf us ure gyltas
>
> swa swa we forgyfað urum gyltendum
>
> and ne gelæd þu us on costnunge
>
> ac alys us of yfele soþlice[1]

This 11th-century version of the Lord's Prayer shows how much English has changed in the past thousand years. The sounds, structures, and vocabulary of all languages are constantly changing, and some of this change happens in patterned ways.

Consider sound. When we imagine people speaking English hundreds of years ago, we often think of them using different words than we do but otherwise sounding pretty much like us. But English spoken in the 14th century sounded very different from the English of today. Between 1400 and 1600, there was a change in sound of English called the **great vowel shift** (see Table 4.1). A correct reading aloud of the Lord's Prayer at the beginning of this section would involve speaking the words using the sounds of 11th-century English. For example, the fifth word of the last line, *yfele*, gives us the modern English word *evil*. The medieval pronunciation is close to "oo-vah-la." Shifting sounds are not just something out of the past. Language sounds are constantly changing. For example, since about 1950, some vowel sounds in U.S. cities around the Great Lakes have been changing, a process linguists call the "northern cities shift" (Labov, Ash, and Boburg 2005). For example, if you pronounce the word "cot" more or less the same way you pronounce the word "cat," you probably grew up in the Great Lakes region of the United States.

Great vowel shift: A change in the pronunciation of English language that took place between 1400 and 1600.

---

[1]In Modern English, the Lord's Prayer is: "Our father who art in heaven, hallowed be thy name. Thy kingdom come, thy will be done on earth as is in heaven. Give us this day our daily bread and forgive us our trespasses as we forgive those who trespass against us; and lead us not into temptation but deliver us from evil, amen." You can hear how the 11th-century version printed here probably sounded at http://bit.ly/1T8E82U. The nonstandard symbols are from the International Phonetic Alphabet mentioned on page 84. You can find additional information on the International Phonetic Alphabet at http://internationalphoneticalalphabet.org or http://bit.ly/1UBuN2Y.

Table 4.1   The Great Vowel Shift

Middle English Vowel	Shifts to	Modern English Vowel	Middle English Word	Is Pronounced to Rhyme with	Modern Word	Becomes	Modern Word
i	aj		mis	piece			mice
u	aw		mus	moose			mouse
e	i		ges	place			geese
o	u		gos	close			goose
ɛ	e		brɛk	trek			break
ɔ	o		brɔk	squawk			broke
a	e		name	comma			name

The grammatical structures of a language (its syntax) also change. For example, as we have seen, meaning in modern English is tightly tied to word order. But in Old English, as in Latin, the endings of nouns indicated whether they were subjects or objects, making word order within sentences less important. Thus, in Old English, "The dog bit the child" and "The dog the child bit" would have the same meaning and be equally grammatical.

Vocabulary, particularly slang, is the most noticeable aspect of language change. Consider slang terms from the 1950s and 1960s, such as *boss* to mean "great" (as in "The new Little Richard album is really boss") or *bag* to mean something that an individual likes (as in "What's your bag?"). We may still understand slang from the 1960s, but terms from the 19th century and early 20th century are almost entirely lost: Would you know what *ramstuginous* or *kafooster* means?

New words are constantly added to language. In the past few decades, an entire vocabulary has grown up around computers and the Internet. Words such as *software, dot-com, gigabyte,* and *email* would have been unintelligible to most people in 1980. *Wi-Fi, spyware, domain name, texting,* and many others would have been meaningless to people in the mid-1990s. Until quite recently "the cloud" was where rain came from.

Language and Culture Contact

The meeting of cultures through travel, trade, war, and conquest is a fundamental force in linguistic change. Languages thus reflect the histories of their speakers. Current-day English has French words such as *reason, joy, mutton,* and *liberty,* which came into the language after the Norman Conquest of England in the 11th century. Other words speak of more recent political events. For example, *cot, pajamas, avatar,* and *jungle* come from Hindi and reflect the British colonization of India. *Gumbo, funky, goober,* and *zebra* come from Kongo and reflect the slave trade. Nahuatl, a language spoken in Mexico and Central America, gives us *tomato, coyote, shack,* and *avocado.* Most Americans in 1970 probably did not know the meanings of words such as *Sunni, jihad,* or *ayatollah.* Today, we do.

When people from societies where different languages are spoken meet, they often develop a new language that combines features of each of the original languages. Such languages are called *pidgins* (see Figure 4.5). No one speaks a pidgin as a first language, and the vocabulary of pidgin languages is often limited to the words appropriate to the sorts of interactions shared by the people speaking it.

As culture contact deepens and time passes, pidgins are sometimes lost, and people speak only the language of the dominant power. Or pidgin languages may become creoles. A *creole* is a language composed of elements of two or more different languages. But some people do speak creoles as their first languages, unlike with pidgins, and the vocabulary of these languages is as complex and rich as any other.

Many creoles were formed as Europeans expanded into Asia and the Americas. Often, in countries that were colonized, upper classes speak the language of the colonizing power, while the lower classes speak creoles. For example, in Haiti, 70 to 90 percent of the population speaks only Creole, but almost all governmental and administrative functions are performed in French, the language of the elite.

Figure 4.5 Pidgin languages develop when people who speak different languages come together. This church banner in Papua New Guinea, where people speak more than 750 different languages, means "Jesus is Lord."

Fredrick Atwood

▌▌▌ Tracing Relationships among Languages

Comparative linguistics is a field of study that traces the relationships of different languages by searching for similarities among them. When such similarities are numerous, regular, and basic, it is likely that the languages are derived from the same ancestral language. Linguists use a statistical technique called glottochronology to estimate the date of separation of related languages, to discover historic relationships among languages, and to group languages into families.

Considering the history of language raises two interesting questions. First, at any point was there a single original human language? Second, in the future will there be a world with one language? Neither of these questions is fully answerable, but we can speculate about each of them.

We do not know if there was a single original human language. However, the development of language almost certainly involved specific genetic changes. Such changes probably happened in a single small group. If this is the case, an original language probably did exist. What might it have been like? Well, again, we cannot say with any confidence. There are no established techniques for discovering the patterns and content of language that can reach back tens of thousands of years.

The question of whether a single world language is emerging is provocative. We are certainly moving toward a world of linguistic homogenization. The number of languages in the world has clearly declined. About 10,000 years ago, there may have been as many as 15,000 different languages. Today, there are only about 6,500, and half of these are under threat of extinction in the next 50 to 100 years (Krauss 1992). Today, 95 percent of the world's languages are spoken by only 5 percent of the world's population. Almost one-third of the world's languages are spoken by fewer than 1,000 people. At the same time, more than half of the world's population speaks one of the 20 most common languages (Table 4.2) (Gibbs 2002).

Languages may disappear for various reasons: All their speakers may be killed by disease or genocide. Government policies may deliberately seek to eliminate certain languages. For example, in 1885, the U.S. government explicitly forbade the use of Indian languages in Bureau of Indian Affairs schools. Children were beaten and otherwise punished for speaking their tribal languages (Coleman 1999).

Nation-states often try to suppress linguistic diversity within their borders, insisting that government, the court system, and other aspects of public life be conducted in the language of the most numerous and politically powerful groups. Global trade favors people who speak the languages of the wealthiest and most populous nations. Similarly, the vast majority of television and radio broadcasts, as well as the Internet, are in a very few languages. In the face of such forces, people who are members

Comparative linguistics: The science of documenting the relationships between languages and grouping them into language families.

Table 4.2   Most Common Languages by Country

Number	Language	Primary Country	Number of First-Language Speakers in Millions
0	Chinese (all types)	China	1,302
1	Chinese (Mandarin)	China	897
2	Spanish	Spain	427
3	English	United Kingdom	339
4	Arabic (all types)	Saudi Arabia	267
5	Hindi	India	260
6	Portuguese	Portugal	202
7	Bengali	Bangladesh	189
8	Russian	Russian Federation	171
9	Japanese	Japan	128
10	Lahnda	Pakistan	117

Source: Ethnologue, Summary by Language Size. Retrieved October 17, 2016, from https://www.ethnologue.com/statistics/size.

of linguistic minorities often abandon their languages because they find it more convenient, prestigious, or profitable to speak the languages of wealth and power.

In some ways, linguistic homogenization is a positive development. Today, more people are able to speak to one another than ever before. In the future, this may be true to an even greater extent. However, the global movement toward fewer languages is troubling. There is generally a strong connection between language and ethnic identity. Language often is rooted in culture and is entwined with it. As language is lost, so are important elements of cultural identity. In addition, the disappearance of languages reduces our ability to understand the underlying structures of all language and the range of variability they enable.

Not all global forces lead toward language homogenization. First, there is no language spoken by the majority of the world's people. Mandarin Chinese, with more than a billion speakers, is by far the most commonly spoken language, while hundreds of millions of people speak English, Spanish, Russian, French, Hindi/Urdu, Arabic, Portuguese, and several other languages. None of these languages seems likely to disappear in the foreseeable future. Second, although the number of languages spoken in the world has diminished, the diversity within each language has increased. People in New York City; Kingston, Jamaica; Glasgow,

Scotland; and Mumbai, India may all speak English, but that does not necessarily mean they can understand what each other says. Perhaps more importantly, the nature of language, the human ability to create new meanings, new words, and new grammatical structures, means that language adapts to the needs, interests, and environments of its speakers. Thus, even as globalizing forces move humans toward cultural and linguistic homogeneity, spaces are created in which diversity can flourish.

BRINGING IT BACK HOME:
ENGLISH ONLY

Language has become an important political issue in the United States. As of spring 2016, a total of 31 states have enacted legislation to make English their state's official language. No federal bill making English the national language has yet passed both chambers of Congress, but the House and the Senate have, at different times, both voted to make English the national language or to require the federal government to conduct all of its official business in English. A recent survey suggests that 83 percent of Americans believe English should be the official national language (Rasmussen Reports 2014).

U.S. English, Inc., a lobbying group that promotes legislation to make English the official language of every state, claims to have 1.8 million members. According to U.S. English, Inc., "Official English benefits every resident of this wonderful melting pot called America. The melting pot works—because we have a common language. English is the key to opportunity in this country. It empowers immigrants and makes us truly united as a people. . . . (U.S. English 2012).

Most social scientists see groups like U.S. English as trying to solve a problem that doesn't really exist. Mary Waters (2011:239) notes that "the United States has always been very efficient at stamping out other languages and quickly assimilating the children of immigrants linguistically." Linguists often think of assimilation in terms of a "three-generation rule." The first generation (those who immigrated as adults), speak their native language and have only minimal language skills in the language of their new country. Their children (the second generation) understand their parents' language but primarily speak the dominant language of the country in which they were born. The third generation (the grandchildren of immigrants) may understand a few words and phrases of their grandparents' language but speak only the dominant language of the country of their birth.

The three-generation rule seems to apply well to Spanish-speaking immigrants to the United States. A Pew Center report showed that although only 23% of Hispanic immigrants spoke English well, 88% of their (adult) children did and by the third generation, almost all spoke English. By the third generation, only 6% spoke exclusively Spanish at home (Hakimzadeh and Cohn 2007).

Anthropologists also suspect that when people talk about language, they really are talking about race. Laura Graham and her collaborators (2007) note that "People in positions of social advantage feel free to say things about the language of stigmatized groups that they would never say about [their] race or ethnicity." Finally, critics of English-only efforts say that the idea that requiring official English will unify the nation and help provide answers to the problems of racism is backward. The underlying problem is not language; it is inequality. Official English, in the name of promoting unity and opportunity, actually disadvantages the poor and the powerless, making it harder for them to gain access to education and public services.

YOU DECIDE:

1. Do you speak a language other than English as a first language? If so, do you want your children and grandchildren to speak that language? If English is your first language, did your parents or grandparents speak a different first language? How do you feel about your abilities (or lack of ability) in that language?
2. In the United States, how closely is language linked both to American identity and to ethnic identity? To what degree can a person be a full citizen of the United States without speaking English as a primary language?
3. Multiple languages are great assets in the global economy. Should the United States mandate increase training in second languages rather than mandate the use of English?

CHAPTER SUMMARY

1. Are some ways of speaking a language better than others? Is there any correct way of speaking a language? From a scientific point of view, no way of speaking is better or worse than any other.
2. How does human language differ from animal communication? Human language is far more complex than animal call systems. It is

symbolic, and it is able to describe abstract times, places, and ideas in ways that animal communications are not.

3. What are the principal components of all human language? Despite great variability, all human languages show deep similarities. All are composed of a phonology (a system of sounds), morphology (a system for creating words from sounds), semantics (a system that relates words to meanings), and syntax (a system of rules for combining words into meaningful sentences).

4. What is the relationship between the rules of language and the performance of language? Language can be described by rules, but actually speaking and understanding language requires a deep understanding of culture. Environment, cultural ideas, values, and beliefs are encoded in the way people speak. The meaning of conversation is usually much more than simply the words that are spoken.

5. What is the relationship between language and social stratification? Cultural aspects of language are heavily influenced by wealth and identity. Privileged and stigmatized ways of speaking reflect the power dynamics of different groups. Individuals who move between social groups must often learn multiple forms of speech and the correct times and places to use them.

6. What is the relationship between speech and thought? Speakers choose words to encourage others to think in certain ways. Early-20th-century theorists Sapir and Whorf believed that the structure of language had a critical influence on culture, but this does not seem to be the case. Because language can be changed rapidly, it can neither force people to think in one way nor prevent them from thinking in others.

7. What forms of nonverbal communication are used in human societies? In addition to speaking, people communicate through touch, the use of time, the use of space, and the use of body position. There is substantial variability in nonverbal aspects of communication, both within and between cultures.

8. Does language change? The sounds, words, and structures of language all are subject to change. Comparative linguists study the ways language changes and are able to describe the historical relationships among different languages. However, no agreed-upon technique has been found to determine or describe very early human language.

9. Are we moving toward a world with only a single language? Linguistic diversity has decreased dramatically, and many languages face extinction. However, many languages also have millions of speakers and are unlikely to disappear. In addition, as languages expand, the diversity within them increases; people who speak the same language may not understand one another.

10. Should English be the official language of the United States? This is a political question that anthropology cannot resolve. Those who favor official English say that it will help unify the nation. Those who oppose argue that it is unnecessary since research shows that English is overwhelmingly dominant by the second and third generation. They note that talk about language often encodes talk about race and that official English is likely to disadvantage those who are already poor.

KEY TERMS

Artifacts	Morphology
Call system	Phone
Code-switching	Phoneme
Chronemics	Phonology
Comparative linguistics	Productivity
Conventionality	Proxemics
Displacement	Sapir-Whorf hypothesis
Great vowel shift	Semantics
Haptics	Sociolinguistics
Kinesics	Symbol
Lexicon	Syntax
Morpheme	Universal grammar

© Stuart Franklin/Magnum Photos

People in different societies use many different strategies to make their livelihoods. Subsistence patterns develop in response to seasonal variation, long-term environmental changes, demographic changes, and the presence of other groups. Here, llamas are herded in Peru.

5

MAKING A LIVING

AFTER YOU HAVE READ THIS CHAPTER, YOU WILL BE ABLE TO:

△ Explain the relationship between environment and subsistence strategy.

△ Summarize the major characteristics of foraging, pastoralism, and horticulture, and give an example of each.

△ Analyze the differences between horticulture and agriculture, and discuss the environmental impact of each.

△ Explain the role of landlords, peasants, and the state in agricultural systems.

△ Differentiate between agriculture and industrialism, and assess the advantages and disadvantages of each.

ARCTIC CULTURES AND CLIMATE CHANGE

 WICH'IN elders long ago predicted that a day would come when the world would warm and things would not be the same with the animals. That time is now ..." says Matthew Gilbert of the Gwich'in, an Athabascan people of northeastern Alaska and northwest Canada. "The lakes, the rivers, the waterfowl and, most of all, the caribou that we depend on are under threat" (Gilbert 2007).

The subsistence strategies of Arctic populations such as the Gwich'in are well adapted to their harsh environment. Their knowledge and ingenious technology enabled them to be successful hunters. For thousands of years, the Gwich'in, the Inuit, and other peoples of the Arctic hunted large land and sea animals, including caribou, polar bear, seal, walrus, and whales. They devised technologies that effectively utilized the materials of their environment for survival, building shelters of snow, which hold the heat and keep out the wind, and expertly fashioning layered clothing that keeps out the cold yet prevents overheating.

Their culture and social organization are also adapted to their environment and foraging strategy. Their values emphasize cooperation and mutual aid; their religious rituals provide effective outlets for the isolation and tension of the long dark winters; and their flexible kinship organization allows local populations to expand and contract in response to the seasonal variation in resources. For the Inuit of Baffin Island, this involves a set of economic practices called *ningiqtuq*, best translated as "sharing." *Ningiqtuq* orders the flow of goods and food across individuals, families, and entire communities. Among the Inuit, no one need go without food or shelter. Inuit subsistence isn't just about food. It is also about practices that provide individuals with security (Wenzel 2009:92–93).

As with many other foragers, however, the Arctic peoples and their subsistence strategies have been significantly changed by 20th-century contact and the global economy (Chance 1990; Condon et al. 1996). Most now base their livelihoods on a combination of cash income and foraging. Commercial trapping and fur sales became dependable sources of income, providing cash, which they used to buy guns and ammunition, food, tobacco, tea, canvas tents, and clothing. Other sources of income today are handicrafts, tourism, work for oil corporations, various kinds of government subsidies, and, for the Alaska natives, payments from the Alaska Native Claims Settlement Act.

Subsistence hunting and use of wild foods still provide at least half of the diet for Arctic peoples, and current-day foraging techniques make use of modern technology, such as snowmobiles, gasoline, fishing nets, and sleeping bags. Many Arctic households also enjoy modern conveniences, and this requires that household members work full time or seasonally in the cash economy (Kofinas 2007).

However, Arctic lifestyles are threatened by global warming. Gideon James, a Gwich'in Elder notes that "30 years ago the permafrost was solid so the land was flat. Now there's dents everywhere" (Gilbert 2012). These dents make travel and hunting far more difficult. Sea ice is critical to the adaptations of animals such as polar bear, seals, and walrus and to the Arctic populations that depend on hunting them, but it is disappearing. Although there are year-to-year variations, satellite data show an Arctic sea ice decline of more than 13 percent per decade (NASA 2016) (see Figure 5.1). The 2015 ice minimum (the measurement in September before waters begin to freeze again) was almost 30 percent less than the 1981–2000 average (Perovich et al. 2015). As the climate warms and ice melts, hunting becomes more difficult and the cultural patterns it sustains more fragile.

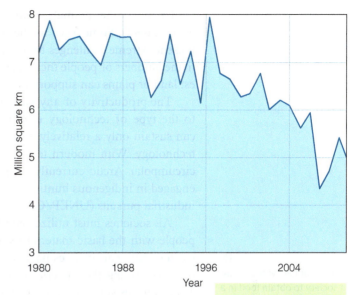

Figure 5.1 The average Arctic sea ice minimum, reached every year in September, has declined steadily since 1980.

Source: NASA 2016.

In addition to climatic changes, Arctic peoples also face challenges to their subsistence from drilling for oil in the Arctic. Some (but not all) of them have become locally active in resisting the exploitation of oil reserves in the Arctic National Wildlife Refuge and other areas where oil companies now have access to offshore energy resources revealed by global warming (Matthiessen 2007).

It is not clear how Arctic peoples will cope with the challenges that confront them. On the one hand, people regret the changes in hunting patterns that will inevitably happen as the earth warms. One Canadian Inuit said: "The next generation . . . is not going to experience what we did. . . . We can't pass the traditions on as our ancestors passed on to us" (Myers et al. 2005). On the other hand, Arctic peoples have faced climate changes before and it is worth remembering that they collectively have thousands of years of experience adapting to an extremely difficult environment. Arctic peoples have shown great flexibility in the past. Although global warming will lead to the disappearance of some species, it is also likely to lead to abundance in others, and Arctic hunters will likely adapt (Ford, Smit, and Wandel 2006).

Unlike most other animals, humans live in an extremely broad range of environments. Some, such as the Arctic or the Great Australian Desert, present extreme challenges to human existence and are relatively limited in the numbers of people they can support. Others, such as temperate forest land or plains can support large populations.

The productivity of any particular environment, however, is related to the type of technology used to exploit it. For example, the Arctic can sustain only a relatively small population with the traditional Inuit technology. With modern technology and transportation, however, the circumpolar Arctic currently supports more than four million people, engaged in indigenous hunting and herding strategies as well as modern industrial pursuits (UNEP/GRID-Arendal 2008).

Subsistence strategies: The pattern of behavior used by a society to obtain food in a particular environment.

All societies must utilize the physical environment to provide their people with the basic material requirements of life: food, clothing, and shelter. Different societies have different **subsistence strategies**, or ways of transforming the material resources of the environment into food. These various subsistence strategies are, in turn, related to differences in economic systems and forms of social organization. However, as environments change, so must subsistence strategies, and hence, other aspects of culture as well.

▌▌▌ HUMAN ADAPTATION, THE ENVIRONMENT AND TECHNOLOGY

Foraging (hunting and gathering): Fishing, hunting, and collecting vegetable foods.

For most of the history of our species, humans and our ancestors lived by **foraging**—fishing, hunting, and collecting vegetable foods. As populations increased, foragers spread out into many environments, creating new tools, and developing diverse cultures. By 16,000 to 12,500 years ago, humans had spread to every continent except Antarctica (see Stanyon, Sazzini, and Luiselli 2009). However, foraging sets significant limits on population growth and density and, consequently, on the complexity of social organization.

About 11,000 to 10,000 years ago, human groups in the Old World began to domesticate plants and animals, a change that occurred about 1,000 years later in the New World (Bryant 2003; Temple University 2009). Called the "agricultural revolution" or sometimes the "neolithic revolution" the transition to food production was really a gradual process that happened over centuries, although it was revolutionary in the possibilities it opened up for the development of complex social organization.

Sedentary: Settled, living in one place.

The domestication of plants and animals supported increased populations, and **sedentary** village life became widespread. Over time, means of applying more technology to farming and animal management were developed. This led not only to increased productivity but also to greater control of human labor, and, eventually, to complex social forms such as the state.

In general, humans have historically used technology to produce greater quantities of food. At the same time, societies have tended to increase in both size and complexity. However, this did not happen everywhere and happened in different ways in different places.

The question of why cultivation did not arise everywhere—and why some populations, such as the aboriginal peoples of Australia or the Inuit, never made the transition from foraging to food production—has several answers. First, many environments make cultivation difficult or impossible. The climate in the Arctic or in some deserts may preclude agriculture. Alternatively, some climates, such as the fertile valleys of California, are so productive that there was little pressure for people to make the transition to food production.

Second, foraging is often far less work than cultivation. Farming requires field preparation, weeding and tending, harvesting, and storage of the harvest. Foraging does not. Farming requires long-term commitment to living in a single place and this may not be possible in all places at all times. Lack of year-round water or political conditions such as raiding and warfare may make permanent residence impossible.

Third, sometimes foraging strategies actually were more dependable than cultivation or animal husbandry. For example, with the introduction of the horse by the Spaniards in the 16th century, some Native American Plains cultures, such as the Cheyenne, did so well with bison hunting that they gave up farming and returned to foraging. Even today, many foraging and pastoral populations resist abandoning these occupations for cultivation.

The Industrial Revolution of the late 18th and early 19th centuries was another dramatic change in human subsistence strategies. The Industrial Revolution involved the replacement of human and animal energy by machines. It was truly revolutionary, both in the speed with which it developed and in its effects on society.

Industrialism greatly increased human productivity: In a typical nonindustrial society, more than 80 percent of the population is directly involved in food production; in industrial societies, this number declines dramatically. In addition, industrialization has produced a relatively high standard of living for enormous numbers of people.

However, the price of industrialization has been high. Industrial societies have high levels of inequality, and industry itself is a major source of environmental degradation and climate change. The energy and production needs of business and the consumer desires of the world's people have had a devastating effect on the environment. The U.S. Environmental Protection Agency controls over 180 hazardous air pollutants alone

VCG/Getty Images

Figure 5.2 High levels of pollution are often one effect of industrialization. Here a policeman and two women wear masks to provide some protection against the smog in Tiananmen Square, in Beijing during a smog alert on December 22, 2015.

Pastoralism: A food-getting strategy that depends on the care of domesticated herd animals.

Horticulture: Production of plants using a simple, nonmechanized technology and where the fertility of gardens and fields is maintained through long periods of fallow.

Agriculture: A form of food production in which fields are in permanent cultivation using plows, animals, and techniques of soil and water control.

(U.S. Environmental Protection Agency n.d.). Oil and gas exploration, logging, mining, dams, and many other large-scale projects fundamentally change the environment.

Although consumers in wealthy nations are responsible for most of the world's pollution, populations in China, India, and many other nations contribute increasing amounts and will contribute even more in the future. In mid-January 2013, the Air Quality Index for Beijing climbed to 755. Any reading over 400 is considered hazardous (*Economist* 2013). In December 2015, the Chinese Government issued a "red alert," closing schools and limiting outdoor construction for several days as a result of high air pollution levels (see Figure 5.2) (BBC 2015).

The environmental problems resulting from industrial and postindustrial society have reawakened interest in and respect for the subsistence adaptations of nonindustrial people. Through detailed knowledge of their environment and using ingenious, if simple, technology, many nonindustrial societies live in ways that are sustainable and that create fewer environmental problems than industrialization. However, it is important to recall that current world population levels cannot be maintained by nonindustrial subsistence techniques. We have much to learn from understanding nonindustrial subsistence patterns, but we cannot simply copy them.

MAJOR TYPES OF SUBSISTENCE STRATEGIES

Anthropologists identify five basic types of subsistence strategies: foraging, pastoralism, horticulture, agriculture, and industrialism (Cohen 1971). Foraging depends on the use of plant and animal resources naturally available in the environment. **Pastoralism** primarily involves the care of domesticated herd animals, whose dairy and meat products are a major part of the pastoralist diet. **Horticulture** is the production of plants using a simple, nonmechanized technology. **Agriculture** is food production that involves more complex technology that may include draft animals, the plow, and sophisticated techniques of water management, soil fertility, and erosion control. In agriculture much of the land is under permanent cultivation. Finally, **industrialism** involves the use of machine technology and chemical processes for the production of food and other goods.

Within these basic types of subsistence strategies there is much diversity. Furthermore, many societies combine strategies to meet their material needs. Today, no society, however seemingly remote, remains unaffected by industrialism and the global economy.

Each subsistence strategy generally supports a characteristic level of **population density** (number of people per unit of land), **productivity** (yield per person per unit of land), and **efficiency** (yield per person per hour of labor invested). These criteria, in turn, tend to be associated with characteristic forms of social organization and certain cultural patterns. For example, in most environments, societies that use a foraging subsistence strategy have relatively low productivity and efficiency (compared with other subsistence strategies). As a result, they cannot support large populations. To limit population growth, they are likely to use cultural practices such as sexual abstinence, abortion, infanticide, late weaning, and prohibitions on sexual intercourse after the birth of a child.

In the sections that follow we will describe and provide example of each of the five subsistence strategies, focusing on the relationships between technologies, the structures of society, and cultural practices.

Industrialism: The process of the mechanization of production.

Population density: The number of people inhabiting a unit of land (usually given as people per square mile or kilometer).
Productivity (food production): Yield per person per unit of land.
Efficiency (in food production): Yield per person per hour of labor invested.

🔲🔳 Foraging

Foraging is a diverse strategy that includes hunting large and small game, fishing, and collecting various plant foods. Foragers do not produce food, either directly by planting or indirectly by keeping domestic animals. In most cases, foragers use simple tools including digging sticks, spatulas, spears, and bows and arrows. However, in some places, such as the Arctic, foraging technology can be quite complex. Because foragers do not consciously alter their surroundings to produce food, in most cases they have less impact on the environment than people following other subsistence strategies.

Foragers use a variety of strategies. In some extreme environments, like that of the Arctic peoples described in the chapter opening, they may depend almost entirely on hunting. However, in most cases, they rely primarily on gathered vegetable foods. In most (but not all) foraging societies, women are responsible for gathering and men for hunting. Successful foraging requires extensive and highly detailed knowledge of the environment. Studies among Ju/'hoansi foragers of Botswana and Namibia show that women can identify over 150 species of edible plants, and men recognize over 40 species of edible animals (Lee 2003).

In most cases, foraging can support only a low population density. Foragers generally live in communities of between 20 and 50 individuals.

Even at this low density, few of the marginal areas where current-day foragers are found can support a year-round human population. Therefore, foraging almost always involves seasonal movement to gain access to water or food. Thus, foraging requires independence and mobility. For this reason, foraging bands tend to have highly flexible social arrangements, and values like *ningiqtuq* (see the chapter opening) are common. Seasonal movement is also a strong disincentive for the accumulation of material goods. Because they must frequently transport everything they own, their material possessions tend to be limited to items essential to their survival.

In some environments, foraging is unquestionably a harsh and dangerous way of life. However, in less demanding places, foragers often live in relative abundance. Further, the extreme flexibility of forager social arrangements means that there is very little hierarchy in foraging societies.

At one time, all human beings lived by foraging, and foragers occupied fertile plains and river valleys. However, as other forms of production developed, the number of foragers declined. Today, they constitute only a very small proportion of the world's population and are mostly found in marginal areas such as deserts and arctic tundra into which they have been pushed by the expansion of militarily superior agricultural peoples and states.

▮▮▮ The Pintupi: A Foraging Society in Australia

The Pintupi people of the Gibson Desert of Australia were more typical of foraging than the Inuit described in the opening of this chapter. The key to their adaptation was the use of a wide variety of seasonally available plant and animal foods and their detailed knowledge of their environment. Even with simple technology, this made foraging a reliable strategy, though a very difficult way of life in certain seasons.

The Pintupi recognize and can name 126 plants serving 138 different social, economic, and medicinal functions. They use more than 75 different plants for edible seeds. Their diet also includes tubers, fruits, nectars, sap, and edible insects, as well as birds, bird eggs, lizards, and small mammals (see Figure 5.3). The main constraint on them is the scarcity of water during the driest and hottest months, which influences the distance they travel, the places they stay, and how much time they spend in each place. Thus, the Western Desert societies consist of small, isolated family groups, and have population densities as low as one person per 150 to 200 square miles.

Climatic changes are extreme. Summer temperatures reach 120 degrees, and winter temperatures average around 72 degrees. Rainfall is very low, unpredictable, and evaporates quickly. In the wet season, December through February, water is available but food is scarce, limited mainly to

Gibson Desert, Australia.

that left over from the previous year's growing season. Men and women gather lizards and edible toads, which are relatively easy to collect. Families spread across the desert, moving great distances to search for food and to attend ceremonies.

At the end of the wet season, when temperatures moderate, families move near the large surface water holes. June and July bring the greatest material prosperity, as tubers, fruits, and grass seeds are all abundantly available. Edible fruits are collected from 12 different plants and stored for the "hungry time" in November, when temperatures will rise to reach 120 degrees. People live

Figure 5.3 A wide variety of plant foods and small animals allow people to survive in the harsh environment of the Gibson Desert. Here, Pintupi women hold goanna lizards.

around the water holes until August, when food availability decreases and temperatures rise. As the landscape dries out, people fall back to large rock holes where there is water. They set fires on the plains to attract game and to stimulate the growth of new grass seeds and tubers for the following year. Both men and women spend most of the day in the food quest, hunting monitor lizards and kangaroos and gathering fruits, bulbs, tubers, and grass seeds, which are both eaten and stored.

November is the harshest time of year. The heat is intense and families travel to the largest rock holes for water, but even these occasionally run dry. Food becomes less available, and many seeds and tubers run out completely. If the rain has not come by December, foraging ceases almost entirely. People try to take it easy to conserve food and water. Women remain in camp, looking after the children and the elderly while the men search for food, sometimes traveling as far from camp as 12 miles a day. Average daily intake may be reduced to 800 calories per person. Heat stress and the shortage of water prevent the whole camp from moving to areas where food might be more available, and people are thus "trapped" in the areas around the larger water holes. Under these conditions, weak individuals may be fed blood from healthier people to get them through the worst times.

The Pintupi and other Australian foragers demonstrate the extraordinary ability of human beings to adapt to the most extreme environments. Though constrained by their simple technology, foragers' detailed knowledge of their environment has permitted them to survive for thousands of years, as well as to develop highly complex ceremonial, religious, kinship, and artistic cultural patterns.

Tribes such as the Pintupi survived using foraging strategies until the mid-20th century. Beginning in the 1920s, because of prolonged drought, the Pintupi began moving to mission stations, cattle stations, government settlements, and towns around the desert fringe. The last Pintupi left the Western Desert in 1984 (Adam 2007; Myers 1986). Though they often visit the desert and continue to do some foraging, they no longer depend on it for all their needs. From their point of view, food was easier to get elsewhere.

The Pintupi subsistence strategy demonstrates that foraging in extreme environments can be a harsh existence with periods of desperation. However, in less extreme environments where predictable vegetal foods can be supplemented by hunting, foragers may experience abundant leisure time and generally good health. For example, Richard Lee estimated that an adult Dobe Ju/'hoansi of the Kalahari Desert in southern Africa spends an average of only two and a half six-hour days per week in subsistence activities, and a woman can gather enough in one day to feed her family for three days (1984:50–53).

Today, like the Pintupi, most foragers have moved to permanent settlements, either by choice or as the result of government pressure. Old trading relationships between foragers and nonforaging people have, in most places, disappeared or become greatly diminished. Although people throughout the world continue to forage when they can, members of contemporary foraging bands rely on markets for much of their food.

▌▌▌ Pastoralism

Pastoralists depend primarily on the products of domesticated herd animals. They are found mostly in environments that, because of hilly terrain, dry climate, or unsuitable soil, cannot support a large human population through agriculture. However, these places can support herd animals if they are allowed to range over a large area. Because human beings cannot digest grass, raising animals that can live on grasses makes pastoralism an efficient way to exploit grasslands. Unlike ranching (commercial animal husbandry), in which livestock are fed grain that could be used to feed humans, pastoralism does not require that animals and humans compete for the same resources (Barfield 1993:13).

Pastoralists may herd cattle, sheep, goats, yaks, or camels, all of which produce meat, milk, and blood (see Figure 5.4). The major areas of pastoralism are found in East Africa (cattle), North Africa (camels), southwestern Asia (sheep and goats), central Asia (yaks), and the subarctic (caribou and reindeer). Before the arrival of Europeans, and with the exception of llama and alpaca, North and South America did not have animals that could be herded, so pastoralism was much less common there.

Pastoralism is either transhumant or nomadic. In **transhumant pastoralism**, found mostly in East Africa, men and boys move the animals regularly throughout the year to different areas as pastures become available at different altitudes or in different climatic zones, while women and children and some men remain at a permanent village site. In **nomadic pastoralism**, the whole population moves with the herds throughout the year, and there are no permanent villages.

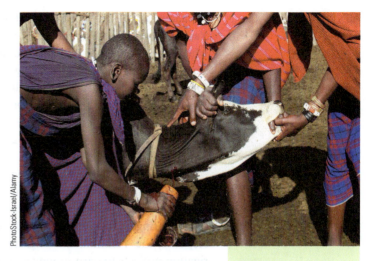

PhotoStock-Israel/Alamy

Figure 5.4 In East African cattle cultures, like the Maasai, the blood and milk of cattle are the major dietary elements. Cattle are killed for meat only on very special ceremonial occasions.

Pastoralism involves a complex interaction among animals, land, and people. With domestication, animals became dependent on their human keepers for pasture, water, breeding, shelter, salt, and protection from predators. Pastoralists must be highly knowledgeable about the needs of their animals, the carrying capacity of the land, and the subsistence demands of the human population.

The key to the pastoralist economy is herd growth. The number of animals needed to support a family is a constant concern for pastoralists. Eating or selling too many animals in a single year may lead to insolvency, so pastoralists must always balance their present needs against future herd production. However, animals are also a source of wealth and prestige among pastoralists so they may also keep herd sizes well above any immediate need. Pastoralism is a risky business; weather disasters such as drought or storms, disease, or theft can easily decimate a herd.

Although there are some groups, such as the indigenous people of Chukotka (far northeast Siberia, near Alaska) who eat diets almost entirely composed of meat and fish (Berezovikova and Mamleeva 2001), most pastoralists also need access to grains and other agricultural products. They acquire these by trading animal products with other people and, sometimes, spend part of the year working in other occupations. The Yarahmadzai, described below, are a good example of this.

Transhumant pastoralism: A form of pastoralism in which herd animals are moved regularly throughout the year to different areas as pasture becomes available.

Nomadic pastoralism: A form of pastoralism in which the whole social group (men, women, children) and their animals move in search of pasture.

The Yarahmadzai: A Nomadic Pastoralist Society in Iran

The Yarahmadzai, who live in the southeastern corner of Iran known as Baluchistan, are an example of a mixed pastoralist adaptation that has undergone changes due to both a global economy and the restraints

Baluchistan, Iran.

of adapting to the control of the national state (Salzman 2000). Yarahmadzai territory occupies a plateau at 5,000 feet above sea level, where adequate water and pasture are available only part of the year. They solve this problem by moving to seek pasture according to the seasons. The Yarahmadzai live in small camps of between 5 and 20 families. When they receive information about the location of good pasture, the whole Yarahmadzai camp migrates. Because even good pasturage can be quickly exhausted, the camp migrates constantly, anywhere from 5 to 25 miles in each move.

Most of the maximum-six-inch annual rainfall occurs in winter. This means that there is good pasturage on the Yarahmadzai's high plateau in the spring. However, by June or July, the animals have eaten all of the spring growth and the weather has turned very dry and hot. In response, the Yarahmadzai migrate to areas served by government irrigation projects to earn money by harvesting grain. They remain there until the harvest ends in early autumn. Then they migrate to the lowland desert where there are groves of date palms, leaving their tents, as well as their goats and sheep on the plateau in the care of young boys. They harvest dates and prepare date preserves for the return journey to their winter camps. At this time, the Yarahmadzai plateau is almost completely barren, with very little for the animals to eat. Animals must live on their accumulated fat and the small quantities of roots, grains, dates, and processed date pits their keepers provide. The people depend on food stores from the previous year, but because winter is the rainy season, water is normally available.

Milk is the staple food of the Yarahmadzai and is consumed in many different forms and preserved as dried milk solids and butter. Milk and milk products are also sold and exchanged for grain. Milk is the main source of protein, fat, calcium, and other nutrients; the Yarahmadzai, like most other pastoral peoples, do not eat much meat. Their herds are their capital, and the Yarahmadzai hope to increase their size. Because killing animals for food works against this objective, the Yarahmadzai rarely do it (Salzman 1999:24).

As we have seen, although the Yarahmadzai continue to herd animals, their activities engage them in larger economic spheres. Many pastoralists have adapted their production to the often challenging and unstable demands of local and even global markets (Gertel and Le Heron 2011). Nomads in Afghanistan and Iran, for example, are highly integrated into national and international trade networks. They specialize in selling meat animals to local markets, lambskin to international buyers, and sheep intestines to meet the huge German demand for natural sausage casings (Barfield 1993:211). In eastern Tibet, pastoralism persists, but pastoralists depend on harvesting caterpillar fungus, which is highly valued in China, Japan, and in Southeast Asia for its medicinal uses. Fungus trading now accounts for 50 to 80 percent of household incomes among Eastern Tibet's pastoralists (Gruschike 2011).

Pastoralism cannot support an indefinitely increasing population. Further, since it is difficult to provide services to mobile populations or to control them, nations often design policies to encourage or force pastoralists to become sedentary. However, because the products of pastoralism are in high demand and because pastoralism is a powerful strategy for survival on lands where agriculture is difficult, pastoralism, in some form, has a strong future.

▮▮▮ Horticulture

Horticultural societies depend primarily on the production of plants using simple, nonmechanized technology such as hoes or digging sticks, but not draft animals, irrigation techniques, or plows. Gardens are used for a number of years and then allowed to recover their fertility over a long fallow period, sometimes lasting decades.

Horticulturalists usually grow enough food in their fields or gardens to support the local group, but they do not produce surpluses that involve the group in a wider market system. Population densities among horticultural peoples are generally low, usually not exceeding 150 people per square mile (Netting 1977). Despite this, horticultural villages may be quite large, ranging from 100 to 1,000 people.

Horticulture may be practiced in dry lands—such as northeastern Arizona, where the Hopi Indians cultivate maize, beans, and squash—but is typically a tropical forest adaptation. In these environments, people practice **swidden** (slash-and-burn) cultivation, clearing fields by felling trees and burning the brush. The burned vegetation is allowed to remain on the soil, which prevents it from drying out. The resulting bed of ash also acts as a fertilizer, returning nutrients to the soil. Fields are used for a few (1 to 5) years and then allowed to lie fallow for a longer period (up to 20 years or longer) so that the forest cover can be rebuilt and soil fertility restored. Swidden cultivators require five to six times as much fallow land as they are actually cultivating.

Swidden cultivation *can* have a debilitating effect on the environment if fields are cultivated before they have lain fallow long enough to recover their forest growth. Eventually, the forest will not grow back, and grasslands will replace the tree cover. Because of this, governments often consider swidden cultivation both inefficient and destructive. However, modern industrial strategies such as logging and agribusiness, not swidden cultivation, are mainly responsible for the deterioration and disappearance of tropical forests (Sponsel 1995). Recent studies report that

Swidden (slash-and-burn) cultivation: A form of cultivation in which a field is cleared by felling trees and burning the brush.

soil fertility is better preserved using long-fallow swidden agriculture than using annual cropping or tree plantations (Bruun et al. 2009), and that replacing swidden with intensified agriculture can lead to swift environmental deterioration (Rerkasem et al. 2009).

Horticulture is also a mixed subsistence strategy. Most swidden cultivators grow several crops. They may also hunt, fish, or raise some domestic animals. In New Guinea, for example, domestic pigs are an important source of protein, and the Yanomamo of the Amazon rain forest hunt monkeys and other forest animals. The Kofyar of Nigeria practice a wide range of strategies including swidden, agriculture, keeping domesticated animals, and participating in the global economy (Stone 1998).

The Lua': A Horticultural Society in Southeast Asia

The Lua' of northern Thailand are swidden cultivators (see Figure 5.5). Swidden gardens are cultivated in a regular rotational sequence. After using a block of land for one or two years, villagers allow it to lie fallow for about nine years before planting again.

In January, village elders inspect the gardens they expect to use the following year to confirm that the forest regrowth is adequate for cultivation. Using long steel-bladed knives, the men clear their fields by felling

Figure 5.5 Swidden, or slash-and-burn, horticulture, as practiced traditionally in northern Thailand, is based on a deep understanding of the forest environment. All the features of the landscape are taken into account as Lua' build their houses and plant their fields.

F. Jack Jackson/Bruce Coleman Inc./PhotoShot

small trees. They leave strips of trees along watercourses and at the tops of ridges to prevent erosion and provide seed sources for forest regrowth during the fallow period. They leave taller trees standing, but trim their branches so they will not shade the crops. Such Lua' practices encourage ecosystem diversity (Rerkasem et al. 2009).

The fields cleared in January and February dry until the end of March when a day is chosen to burn them. First, a firebreak is cleared around the field so that fire does not accidentally spread into the forest. Then the swidden is burned.

The cultivators plant cotton and corn on the slopes of the fields, and yams on the lower, wetter portions. By mid-April, they begin to plant the main subsistence crop, upland rice, jabbing the earth loose with ten-foot iron-tipped planting poles. They hope the rice will take root and sprout before the heavy monsoon rains come.

Different types of rice are sown in different areas of the field. Quick-ripening rice is planted near the field shelter, where it can be easily watched. Drought-resistant varieties are planted on the drier, sandier tops of the slopes, along with millet. In addition, there are gardens with mustard greens, peppers, beans, and other vegetables. Vine plants are grown in places particularly susceptible to erosion.

By May, weeding begins, with mainly women and older children using a short-handled tool to scrape and hack at the weeds on the surface; weeds are not dug or pulled out by the roots.

Both men and women harvest the rice, using small, handheld sickles, cutting the stems of each bunch of rice close to the ground. The stalks are spread out to dry for a few days, and then young men beat them against a threshing mat to knock the rice grains loose, separating them as completely as possible. After a second winnowing, the cleaned rice is loaded into baskets and kept in a temporary barn near the field shelter.

After the harvest, swiddens are allowed to lie fallow. However, the Lua' also keep pigs, water buffalo, cattle, and chickens, and these animals use the plants that grow on the fallow gardens. The Lua' also forage for medicinal plants and during times of food shortage. In earlier times, the Lua' hunted and fished, but environmental changes and increased population in the past 50 years has greatly reduced these activities.

By the mid-20th century, many newcomers had begun to settle in Lua' territory. They were less careful about their swidden practices than the Lua', and the quality of the land began to deteriorate. In addition, through environmental regulations and the promotion of development projects, the government pressured the Lua' to limit their use of swiddens (Delcore 2007:96). The result has been an increase in intensive agriculture and cattle herding. Many crops such as sorghum and cotton have been severely reduced or eliminated. Cattle now graze the fallow

The Lua' of northwestern Thailand.

swiddens, leaving few plants for human use. The increase of cash cropping in soybeans has transformed the previously clear and free-flowing
streams to muddy, polluted pools, which the Lua' consider too dirty to
wash their clothes in, and year-round irrigation has brought in year-round
mosquitoes.

The changes in swidden practices among the Lua' are typical of trends
in Southeast Asia, and perhaps, worldwide. Rising population, pressure
toward industrial agriculture from governments and corporations, and
the desire of farmers to raise and sell cash crops all work against swidden
agriculture. A recent analysis shows that other agricultural systems are
replacing swidden farming in Southeast Asia, and that fallow times are
growing shorter where it is still being practiced. The authors note, however, that farmers maintain short fallow swidden farming alongside other
agricultural practices so it is unlikely to disappear entirely (Schmidt-Vogt
et al. 2009). Despite this, the move away from swidden farming will have
profound cultural consequences for the Lua' and other groups.

■■|■ Using Anthropology: Anthropologists and Nutrition

Anthropologists have long been involved in trying to understand the foods
that people eat and their effect on health and nutrition. Some nutritional
anthropologists are concerned with trying to improve the nutritional status of people. Others are more concerned to discover what we can or
cannot learn from the diets of various groups.

The work of the husband and wife team of Nevin Scrimshaw (1918–
2013) and Mary Goodrich (1920–2014) is a good example of the first.
Scrimshaw, was one of the world's most important nutrition scientists
and was trained in biology, physiology, medicine, and public health.
Goodrich, his wife, was trained in nutritional anthropology. As a doctor
working in Central America after World War II, he was struck by the
large number of young children who suffered from protein malnutrition.
He designed a cheap protein source based on cottonseed meal that was
both culturally acceptable and extremely inexpensive. He did the same
with a peanut-based product in India in the 1960s. He also worked to
find ways to add goiter-preventing iodine to the types of salt available
in Central America. Scrimshaw traveled with his wife, who introduced
anthropological data into his studies. They worked together in Guatemala, Indonesia, and many other places (Martin 2013; Scrimshaw 2012).
When he helped found the Institute of Nutrition of Central America and
Panama, a direct aid and research organization that works to provide
food security in seven Central American countries, he sought advice from
well-known anthropologists including Margaret Mead. As the institute's

first director, he brought in anthropologists, including Richard Adams and Nancy Solien de Gonzalez, to help guide the institute's policies, particularly toward native Mayan populations (Scrimshaw 2012).

James Howe's work among the Kuna is an example of anthropologists learning from the diets of different societies. The Kuna are a large ethnic group living mostly in Panama. In the past decade, they have received a lot of attention because of claims that their high level of cocoa consumption was linked to lower rates of cardiovascular disease. Norman Hollenberg, the lead researcher of many of the studies, claimed that the high consumption of locally grown chocolate by rural Kuna explained the fact that they had far lower levels of hypertension and heart disease than Kuna living in urban areas such as Panama City. According to Hollenberg, the rural Kuna consumed a minimum of 35 cups of chocolate drink a week and that this was associated with their good health (2006). Unfortunately for the chocolate lovers among us, Howe's work shows that Hollenberg's assertions about Kuna chocolate consumption are simply incorrect (2012:45). Although the Kuna do drink chocolate, they consume very much less than Hollenberg states, and much of that is commercial powdered chocolate. They do use cacao beans in religious ceremonies—but by burning them rather than drinking chocolate. Howe notes that the rural Kuna diet is low in fat and higher in fruit and fish than that of urban dwellers in general and that this is far more likely to explain their better health than is chocolate consumption. He argues that Hollenberg makes the mistake of basing health claims for chocolate on the Kuna because he neither spent sufficient time with the Kuna nor devoted effort to examining the rich anthropological literature about them (2012:50).

Agriculture

In agriculture, the same piece of land is repeatedly cultivated with plows, draft animals, and more complex techniques of water and soil control than horticulturalists use. Plows are more efficient at loosening the soil than are digging sticks or hoes, and turning the soil brings nutrients to the surface. Irrigation is often important in agriculture and may require elaborate terracing in hilly areas and sophisticated systems of water control. Preindustrial agriculture also uses techniques of natural fertilization, selective breeding of livestock and crops, and crop rotation, all of which increase productivity.

Intensive cultivation generally supports higher population densities than horticulture. In Indonesia, for example, the island of Java, with 9 percent of the nation's land area, is able to support more than two-thirds of the Indonesian population through intensive rice cultivation using elaborate irrigation terraces. The Javanese population density of well over 2,000 people per square mile (Republic of Indonesia 1997) contrasts sharply with the maximum population density of swidden areas in Indonesia, which is about 145 people per square mile.

The greater productivity of agriculture also results from more intensive use of labor. Farmers must work long and hard to make the land productive. For example, growing rice in an irrigated paddy requires about 233 person-days of labor per year for each hectare (Barker, Herdt, and Rose 1985:128) (a hectare is about 2.5 acres). In addition to human labor, agriculture requires more capital investment than horticulture. Plows must be bought and draft animals raised and cared for. Although agriculturalists may have more control over food production than horticulturalists, they are more vulnerable to the environment. When people depend on the intensive cultivation of one or two crops, one crop failure or a disease that strikes draft animals may become an economic disaster.

Agriculture is generally associated with sedentary villages, the rise of cities and states, occupational diversity, social stratification, and other complex forms of social organization. In contrast to horticulturalists, who grow food primarily for the subsistence of their households, most agriculturalists are **peasants**. They produce for their own family but are also integrated into large, complex state societies. Part of their food production is taken from them through markets, rents, and taxes. This supports non-food-producing occupational specialists, such as religious and political elites, trade and craft people, and a variety of other professionals.

Peasants: Rural cultivators who produce for the subsistence of their households but are also integrated into larger, complex state societies.

Robert Caputo/Aurora Photos

Figure 5.6 In peasant villages in Egypt, farmers make important decisions about allocating labor, buying products for home and farm, scheduling machinery, and dealing with the government.

Musha: A Peasant Agricultural Village in Egypt

Musha is an agricultural village about 250 miles south of Cairo in the Nile Valley. Musha's farmers practice a two-year crop rotation system based on both summer and winter crops (see Figure 5.6). The cycle begins with cotton in the first summer, followed by wheat in the first winter. Maize or sorghum follows in the second summer, or the land may be left fallow. The cycle is completed in the second winter with millet, lentils, and chickpeas. In addition, farmers grow grapes and pomegranates and raise a variety of vegetables for home consumption. They also depend on the milk, cheese, and butter from water buffalo, cows, sheep, and goats. A portion of the production must be used to pay taxes (currently about 14 percent of the value of the land) or for rent if farmers do not own all of the land they plant. Far more must be used to acquire other things the household needs.

The household is central in Musha cultivation, with extra laborers hired as needed. Women do not work in the fields, but keep house, care for animals, and make cheese. Children, who often work both for their own families and are hired by others, cut clover for animals and help harvest cotton. The head of the household plays a key managerial role supervising others, making agricultural purchases, hiring labor, and managing the household budget.

Egypt.

Historically, Musha farmers relied on either animal power or human effort and a few basic wooden tools. Shallow plows and threshing sleds were pulled by oxen. Winnowing relied on the wind and a winnowing fork and sieves for the final cleaning. Donkeys and camels were also used to haul crops, people, and equipment.

Starting in the 1950s, Musha farmers began to move to mechanized agriculture. By 1980, almost all farmers used machines at least some of the time. They also came to depend on chemical fertilizers and pesticides as well as animal manure.

In the 1960s, when the completion of the Aswan High Dam brought an end to the flooding of the Nile, the government constructed feed canals, and these became the main source of water for the fields. The government maintains the canals, and farmers must raise water from them to the level of the fields. The gasoline-powered pumps that perform this task are generally owned by several people who share the work involved in their maintenance and operation. After arranging for the distribution of water to his fields, the farmer must hire a driver and tractor to plow the fields if he, like many small farmers, does not own one. Fertilizer and seed are hauled from the village bank to his home and from his home to the field. The fertilizer is then spread by hand.

Wheat is one of the most important crops in Musha. It is planted in November and harvested in May and June. Hired laborers usually harvest wheat using a small sickle. The reaped wheat is bundled into sheaves, which are transported by camel or wagon to the threshing ground, where it is fed into a threshing machine. The threshed grain is winnowed and sifted by specialists who are paid piece rates. Finally, the grain and straw are hauled from the threshing ground back to the farmer's storeroom.

In deciding on their strategies for making a living, Musha farmers must adapt to government policies. At one time, the government controlled prices for key crops such as wheat and cotton. However, direct government intervention was greatly reduced or eliminated in the 1980s and 1990s. Despite this, the government is still heavily involved in agriculture. Government organizations make loans to farmers, distribute agricultural inputs such as seed and fertilizer, subsidize the production of particular agricultural products, and buy some of the farmers' crops. State policies such as importing wheat from the United States affect the prices that farmers receive. The state sets land-ownership laws, makes rules governing land tenancy, and affects the labor market through policies that encourage migration.

Profits from farming are uncertain, and most families have several sources of income. Sales of animals, fruits and vegetables, and handicrafts supplement household income. In fact, 70 percent of village households derive their major income from activities other than farming: day labor, government jobs, craft trades, specialist agricultural work, as well as remittances from family members who have migrated, or from rents and pensions.

Farmers today must know the skills of farming as well as how to manage a wide range of other activities. They must interact with family members and government officials and negotiate with the owners of tractors, day laborers, and many others. They supervise agricultural work and manage a wide range of activities, making important decisions at every step. Farmers are affected by global prices for the commodities they produce as well as the policies of their own national government and foreign governments. All over the world, farmers are increasingly part of a globalized, industrialized economy.

Industrialism

In industrialism, the focus of production moves away from food to the production of other goods and services. Investments in machinery and technologies of communication and information become increasingly important. In foraging, pastoralism, horticulture, and agriculture, most of the population is involved in producing food. Although the food industry is very large in industrial societies, only a very small percentage of the population is directly involved in food production. In the United States, in the early 1900s, more than one-third of families lived on farms (Lobao and Meyer 2001). In 2012, there were 2.1 million farms in the United States but only one million people, less than one-half of one percent of the population, listed farming as their primary occupation. Further, 75 percent of U.S. farms had sales of $50,000 or less (U.S Department of Agriculture [USDA] 2014). This means that more than 80 percent of total U.S. agriculture comes from the remaining 25 percent of U.S. farms.

Industrialism has an explosive effect on many aspects of economy, society, and culture. It has led to vastly increased population growth, expanded consumption of resources (especially energy), increased occupational specialization, and a shift from working for subsistence and selling the products of one's labor to selling the labor itself for hourly or yearly wages. In every industrialized society, most people work for wages that they use to purchase food, goods, and services. Although cash transactions are found in other production systems, almost all transactions in industrial economies involve money.

Industrial economies are based on the principles that consumption must constantly expand, and material standards of living must always rise. This contrasts with economies created by the production systems previously discussed, which put various limits on both production and consumption and thus make lighter demands on their environments. Industrialism today has vastly outgrown national boundaries. The result has been great movement of resources, capital, and labor, as the whole world has gradually been drawn into the global economy, a process called **globalization**.

Globalization: The integration of resources, labor, and capital into a global network.

Contemporary industrial and postindustrial societies are characterized by well-coordinated specialized labor forces that produce goods and services and by much smaller elite and managerial classes that oversee the day-to-day operations of the workplace and control what is produced and how it is distributed. Increasingly, mobility, specific skills, and education are required for success.

Because industrialized societies generate much higher levels of inequality than societies based on foraging, pastoralism, or horticulture and because industrial systems require continued expansion, wealth and poverty become critical social issues. Unequal distributions of opportunity, economic failure, illness, and misfortune limit the life chances of vast numbers of people in industrialized societies. Conversely, economic success creates lifestyles well above poverty for large numbers, and conditions of truly extraordinary wealth for a very small number.

Inequalities characterize relations among as well as within nations. The creation of complex global systems of exchange between those who supply raw materials and those who use them in manufacturing, as well as between manufacturers and consumers, has resulted in increasing disparities of wealth around the world.

The Beef Industry: Industrialized Agriculture in the United States

The American beef industry is a good if disturbing example of industrialism. Americans have long had a love affair with beef. Because meat was expensive for the average family during much of America's past, in the 20th century, beef became both the symbol and the substance

David Clynch/Alamy

Figure 5.7 In industrial agriculture, food is processed using techniques similar to those of other manufacturing processes.

of having made it into the middle class. For Americans, steak is symbolic of manliness, and "meat and potatoes" make up the iconic American meal.

As the standard of living in the United States rose after World War II, so did the demand for inexpensive beef. The postwar era brought the rise of the suburbs and the entry of large numbers of women into the workforce. This increased the complexity of American family life and reduced the amount of time available for cooking and dining together, thus favoring packaged convenience foods and meat that could be rapidly prepared. In addition, beginning in the 1960s, the expansion of fast-food industries greatly increased American consumption of hamburgers and the demand for beef. In 2007, McDonald's purchased close to one billion pounds of beef in the United States alone (Roybal 2007).

Until the mid-20th century, American dinner tables had been supplied with meat that came through a production chain that started on a family farm and ended in the neighborhood retail butcher shop. However, this system of production could not generate the levels of supply that families and fast-food chains now demanded. Only large corporations employing mass production technologies could meet this high level of demand (see Figure 5.7). By the late 1980s, most family farms were no longer economically viable, and many small farmers lost their land. Rural America became dominated by large farming operations, tied to multinational corporations (see Figure 5.8).

The cost of labor is a significant factor in the production of meat. Through the 1970s and 1980s, meat processors succeeded in driving down the wages paid to workers. The key to this was their use of nonunion workers, frequently immigrants from Latin America and Southeast Asia. In many cases, these workers were undocumented. For example, when Immigration and Customs agents raided Agriprocessors in

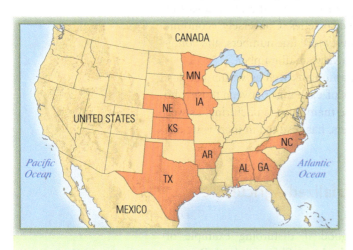

Figure 5.8 Top livestock and poultry slaughtering states.

Source: American Meat Institute 2011.

Postville, Iowa, in 2008, more than a third of its workers were found to be undocumented (Jones 2012). Such workers were not easily (or very willingly) absorbed into tightly knit farm communities and small towns. As the rural economy declined, resentment of immigrants and social problems increased. There were strains on health care, schools, and social services (Artz, Orazem, and Otto 2007). Binge drinking is far more common among rural than among urban children (ages 12 to 17). Use of methamphetamine and OxyContin among young adults (ages 18 to 25) in rural areas is about twice as high as the use of these drugs among their urban counterparts (Main Rural Health Research Center 2007).

In many cases, large-scale meatpacking had disastrous environmental impacts. U.S. livestock production creates about 900 million tons of waste annually. In Iowa, hog farming alone produces 50 million tons of manure annually. This waste often seeps into local streams and groundwater supplies, polluting critical resources (Bittman 2008). Although some rural regions experienced short-term job increases from the meatpacking industries, this pollution created a hidden cost and a long-term downside for rural communities (Stull and Broadway 2004).

The efficiency of assembly-line beef processing has high human costs as well. The meatpacking industry has a long history of horrific working conditions. In 1906, Upton Sinclair described the deeply impoverished lives, terrible working conditions, and hopelessness of workers in Chicago's slaughterhouses. Although the meatpacking industry today is vastly different from the industry of the early 20th century, working conditions at America's 6,278 meat and poultry slaughtering and processing plants are still deeply disturbing in many cases.

The low costs and high availability of American meat is made possible by cheap labor and getting the maximum product out the door. "On the floor," this translates into a large proportion of unskilled, poorly trained, low-paid hourly workers; a sped-up "disassembly" line; and few break periods for workers.

Work in the meatpacking industry is difficult and dangerous even in the best plants. The processing operations involve thousands of moving animals being stun-gunned by a "knocker," axed in half by "splitters" on moving platforms, and deboned and cut up with sharp knives wielded by an assortment of specialists such as "stickers," "gutters," "tail rippers," and "head droppers" (Broadway and Stull 2008). The working conditions of this sector of American agribusiness are so severe that Human Rights Watch has deemed them in violation of international standards and basic human rights (Human Rights Watch 2004). These conditions affect not only the health of the workers, but also the quality of the product. This was dramatically demonstrated in early 2008, when the Westland/Hallmark Meat Packing Company recalled 143 million pounds

of contaminated meat, some of which was used in school lunch programs; it was the largest meat recall in U.S. history. Smaller recalls are
frequent; for example, there were 150 meat recalls in 2015, together total-
ing more than 21.1 million pounds (USDA 2016a). Despite this, demand
for inexpensive beef remains high, and meaningful reform of the industry
does not seem likely in the near future.

The Global Marketplace

The contemporary world is characterized by connectedness and change
of a magnitude greater than anything seen in earlier times. For some
people, the expansion of the global economy has meant new and more
satisfying means of making a living. However, these opportunities are not
equally available to all peoples or to all individuals within a culture. For
many people, the promise of prosperity offered by the global economy
has yet to be fulfilled.

Anthropology is particularly sensitive to the complex linkages among
local, regional, national, and global contexts that structure the modern
world. Anthropologists today can play an important role in shaping government and global economic policies that take into account the environmental impact of different ways of making a living, the values and
practices of local cultures, international plant and animal conservation
efforts, and corporate- and state-driven efforts to participate in global
markets. In the postindustrial globalized society, individuals, governments, and businesses must find new ways to adapt to significant changes
in the production and distribution of goods. We explore some of these
changes in Chapter 6 on economics.

BRINGING IT BACK HOME:
GLOBALIZATION AND FOOD CHOICE

In the relatively recent past, much of the food on American tables was
locally produced and seasonally available. Today, our food is produced
on large farms located in rich agricultural regions thousands of miles
away from the populations they serve. For example, more than half of
all fruit produced in the United States comes from California, which, together with Washington and Florida, accounts for 80 percent of U.S. fruit
production (USDA 2012). However, our culinary net spreads far wider
than the United States. In fiscal year 2014, the United States imported
$111.7 billion worth of agricultural products (USDA 2016b).

The presence of so much food from distant places is one of the great triumphs of globalization. Fruits and vegetables are available all year long. We dine on frozen Indian meals actually prepared in India and accompany them with water from Fiji and fruit from Chile. However, this global food network also extracts a high price. Although determining the carbon footprint of individual products is extremely difficult (*Economist* 2008), moving food around the world may have high environmental costs. For example, the average tomato imported into Canada has traveled almost 3,000 miles and, in so doing, results more than three times more carbon dioxide than a locally grown tomato (Brandt 2008:26). As our dependence on imported food increases, so does our reliance on the fuel necessary to move it. This means that changes in the price of oil can result in large jumps in the price of food, making our food supply more vulnerable than ever to global economics and politics (Figure 5.9).

Dependence on food shipped long distances also favors foods that look pretty and are easy to ship. Along with this comes the loss of indigenous and traditional varieties. Although estimates about the percentage of plant species that have disappeared vary, one study found that 97 percent of the vegetable varieties on a U.S. Department of Agriculture list from the early 20th century are extinct today (Brandt 2008:56).

The varieties that are extensively grown, along with the fertilizers and pesticides necessary to grow them, are produced by large multinational corporations such as Monsanto, ADM, Cargill, DuPont, and Bayer. These companies make huge profits, sometimes at the expense of workers. According to the World Health Organization (2004), there are about three million cases of pesticide poisoning each year, resulting in a quarter million deaths. Poor nations account for only 25 percent of the world's pesticide use but 99 percent of the deaths from pesticide poisoning (World Health Organization 2008). Buying globally does provide jobs

Figure 5.9 World food index versus Brent oil prices.

Source: United Nations Food and Agriculture Organization (FAO) and U.S. Energy Information Agency (EIA).

for agricultural workers around the world, but working conditions in such jobs are often very harsh, and the key beneficiaries are the corporations that organize food production and transportation.

In recent years, food alternatives have become more mainstream. These include vegetarianism, the slow food movement, and community-supported and local agriculture. All of these are probably healthier for both individuals and the environment than large-scale globalized food production (Wilk 2006). However, thus far, they affect relatively few people in wealthy nations, often cost more than alternatives, and increasing their use involves the difficult task of changing culturally ingrained food habits.

YOU DECIDE:

1. What are the cultural patterns and values that underlie food choices in the United States, and how do they affect what you eat?
2. Locavores are people who eat only food grown within a relatively short distance of their home. Would you become a locavore? Why, or why not?
3. Do you believe movements in favor of local agriculture, organic foods, and slow foods are likely to have success in the United States? What factors might favor or retard their success?

CHAPTER SUMMARY

1. What is the relationship between the environment and the subsistence (food-getting) pattern of a society? All societies must adapt to their physical environments, which present different problems, opportunities, and limitations to human populations. The subsistence pattern of a society develops in response to seasonal variations in the environment and environmental variations over the long run, such as drought, flood, animal diseases, climate, demographic changes, and the presence of other groups.
2. What are the five major subsistence strategies of human populations? The five major patterns of using the environment to support human populations are foraging (gathering, fishing, hunting), pastoralism, horticulture, agriculture, and industrialism.
3. What is foraging? Give an example of a foraging society and explain how foraging has been affected by climate change. In foraging, people rely on food, most often plants, naturally available in the environment. Climate change threatens foragers' livelihood, particularly in the Arctic. The Pintupi people of the Gibson Desert of Australia were a foraging culture.

4. What is pastoralism? Give an example of a pastoralist society and comment on the relationship between pastoralism and more sedentary lifestyles. Pastoralism is subsistence based primarily on the care of domesticated herd animals. Because it is difficult to live on animal products alone, pastoralism either is found along with cultivation (transhumance) or involves trading relations with food cultivators. The Yarahmadzai are an example of a nomadic mixed pastoralist economy.

5. What is horticulture? Give an example of a horticulturalist society. Horticulture typically is a tropical forest adaptation based around planting gardens or small fields. It uses simple technology and requires the cutting and burning of jungle to clear fields for cultivation. Fields are not used permanently but are allowed to lie fallow after several years of productivity. The Lua' are swidden cultivators in Thailand.

6. What is agriculture and how is it related to larger societies and states? Agriculture is the use of large areas that are permanently cultivated, usually in grain. It often involves more complex technology than horticulture, often including plows and irrigation. Agriculture generally supports high population densities and is associated with sedentary village life. Agricultural societies are stratified and farmers constitute only one element of them. Governments often intervene in agriculture. Musha, an Egyptian village, is an example of peasant agriculture.

7. What is industrialism and how is it related to wealth and environment? In industrialism, machines and chemical processes are used for the production of goods. Food production constitutes only a small percentage of total production and occupies little of the population. Industrialism creates great material prosperity of many people, but at a cost of high levels of inequality and environmental destruction.

KEY TERMS

Agriculture	Peasants
Efficiency	Population density
Foraging (hunting and gathering)	Productivity
Globalization	Sedentary
Horticulture	Subsistence strategies
Industrialism	Swidden (slash-and-burn) cultivation
Nomadic pastoralism	Transhumant pastoralism
Pastoralism	

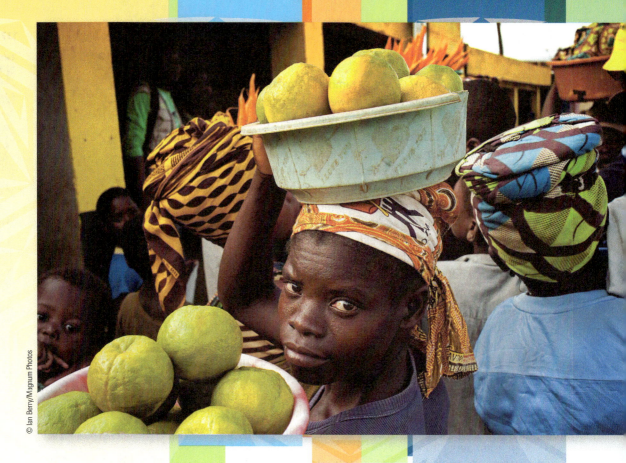

© Ian Berry/Magnum Photos

6

ECONOMICS

AFTER YOU HAVE READ THIS CHAPTER, YOU WILL BE ABLE TO:

△ Define economic behavior, and give examples of situations in which people use it and when they do not.

△ Summarize the ways in which people in foraging, pastoral, horticultural, and agricultural societies generally allocate resources.

△ Differentiate between generalized, balanced, and negative reciprocity, and give an example of each.

△ Discuss the differences between redistribution and reciprocity using examples of the potlatch and kula trade.

△ Define market exchange, and analyze the ways in which it differs from other systems of distribution.

△ Summarize the key characteristics of capitalism.

△ Describe the ways in which people in wealthy nations both participate in and resist capitalism. Debate the advantages of each.

ULTIMATE DICTATOR

THE notion that human beings are rational, individual economic actors underlies much of Western economic theory. Economists assume that people are capable of assessing the economic choices facing them, and, when they do so, they make decisions that maximize their wealth and minimize their labor. There is certainly some truth to this idea, and all of us can think of cases in which we behave precisely this way. But economic choices do not occur in a vacuum. Real economic decisions are made in a cultural context and are influenced by ideas about what is right, valuable, and moral, not just about how much we can profit. However, as we have seen in the previous chapters of this book, what is right, valuable, and moral are not the same for everyone.

Economists and anthropologists have developed interesting tools to test the degree to which people in different cultures really behave the way that theories say they are supposed to. Two examples are the dictator game and the ultimatum game (Ensminger and Henrich 2014).

In the dictator game, there are two individuals: a "proposer" and a "responder." The proposer is given a sum of money, say the equivalent of one day of wages, and is told to split it with the responder. The proposer and the responder are unknown to each other and they play the game only once, so there is no chance that generosity will be reciprocated. If people simply try to maximize their wealth and minimize their work, we would expect that the proposer would keep the entire sum, offering nothing to the responder. In fact, that doesn't always happen. In the United States and other wealthy nations, about 30 to 40 percent of the players take the whole pot. However, most proposers leave between 20 and 30 percent for the responders. Jean Ensminger (2002) found that among the Orma, a group of cattle pastoralists living in Kenya, far fewer people, only 9 percent, took the whole pot; the others gave an average of 31 percent to the responders.

The ultimatum game is also played with a proposer and a responder. However, in this case, the proposer offers to split a sum of money, and the responder may either accept or reject the split. If the responder accepts the split, the money is divided and the game is over. If the responder rejects the split, neither player receives any money and the game ends. As in the dictator game, players are anonymous and play only once, so generosity cannot be returned. In the ultimatum game, respondents who behaved simply as rational maximizers would always accept the proposer's offer because accepting the offer involves no financial cost, and even a very low offer is greater than nothing. But real people do not play this way.

In the past 15 years, anthropologists and economists have played the ultimatum game with members of many different cultures. The results show that there are no cultures in which everyone is willing to accept whatever is offered . . . and they show a great deal of variation in how much people are willing to offer. For example, among the Machiguenga of the Peruvian Amazon, proposers rarely offered more than 15 percent, and offers were almost never rejected (Henrich et al. 2004). American college students, on the other hand, offered 42 to 48 percent of the pot to their responders, and responders tended to reject offers of less than 30 percent.

Some of the results may seem counterintuitive. For example, in foraging groups, there is a high degree of equality, but foragers were not generous game players. The Hadza, foragers who live in Tanzania, made some of the lowest proposals of any groups tested. On the other hand, industrialized economies are highly stratified and unequal, but their members are likely to offer almost half the pot to responders. In fact, the results show an interesting trend. The greater the degree to which a group is involved in a market economy, the more likely proposers were to give a larger share of the money to responders. Later in this chapter, we will explore some of the reasons why this is the case.

The results of the dictator and ultimatum games demonstrate the social and cultural dimensions of economic decision making. The fact that, cross-culturally, a strong majority of proposers give responders something may show that all people have a bias toward at least a little generosity. However, the systematic differences among cultures demonstrate that decisions are set in cultural contexts that determine moral and appropriate behavior, and that these are different in different economic systems.

Economics: The study of the ways in which the choices people make combine to determine how their society uses its scarce resources to produce and distribute goods and services.

Economic system: The norms governing production, distribution, and consumption of goods and services within a society.

Economics is the study of the ways in which the choices people make as individuals and as members of societies combine to determine how their society uses its resources to produce and distribute goods and services. But, as our example shows, this process is always set within a cultural context. How we make these decisions depends on the values we give to both goods and ideas. And that depends upon culture.

Every society must have an **economic system** in the sense that each group of people must produce, distribute, and consume. However, cultural context determines the ways in which goods and services are produced and distributed as well as the meanings of consumption.

▌▌▌ ECONOMIC BEHAVIOR

Economists assume that because human wants are unlimited and the means for achieving them are not, organizations and individuals must make decisions about the best way to apply their limited means to meet

Scott Olson/Getty Images News/Getty Images

Figure 6.1 Decisions these traders at the Chicago Board of Trade make are based almost entirely on profit and loss. However, most of the time, our decisions are motivated by other considerations as well. We may prefer relaxation and free time to financial return.

their unlimited desires. As we saw in the opening story, one way of understanding economic decisions is to assume that decision makers will always maximize their financial benefit and minimize their work. Will a business firm cut down or expand its production? Will it purchase a new machine or hire more laborers? Such decisions are assumed to be motivated by the desire to maximize profit (see Figure 6.1).

However, the opening story also shows us that this understanding misses critical factors. As human beings, we have only so much time and energy to expend in meeting our desires. But, we do not always allocate these to maximize our financial wealth. Consider a choice you may make today. After you finish reading this chapter, you might confront a series of decisions: Should you reread it for better comprehension? Should you study for another course? Call and get a pizza delivered? Play with your kids? Socialize with your friends? Hang out online? You will make your choice based on some calculation of benefit. However, that benefit probably cannot be reduced to financial profit. You may believe that you will make more money if you study and get higher grades. However, your choice is set in a context in which money is unlikely to be the most important element of value; we value our friends, our children, our leisure time, and many other things as well. If you choose to socialize instead of hitting the books, your choice is not irrational, even though it does not necessarily lead to greater profit. We cannot assume that you will always act to increase your material well-being. Rather, we need to find out what motivates you.

Just as you might value an evening spent with friends over an "A" in this class, members of other cultures might value family connections, cultural tradition, social prestige, leisure time, or other things over monetary profit. For example, the Hadza, mentioned earlier, live in an area of Tanzania with an abundance of animal and vegetable food. They have considerable leisure time but make no attempt to use it to increase their wealth. Although they know how to farm, they don't do so. They say it would require too much work (Woodburn 1968). Thus, they value their leisure (and the socializing they use it for) over what they could produce farming.

Leisure time is only one of the ends toward which people expend effort. They may also direct their energies toward increasing social status or respect. In Western society, **prestige** is primarily tied to increased consumption and display of goods and services, but this is not universal. In many societies, prestige is associated with giving goods away. Conspicuous consumers and stingy people become objects of scorn and may be shunned or accused of witchcraft (for examples, see Danfulani 1999; Offiong 1983). The notion that prestige can be gained through giving is well established in our own society. Universities have buildings bearing the names of their most generous donors. Bill Gates is not only the chairman of Microsoft, but, with his wife and father, he also co-chairs the world's largest charitable foundation. The Bill and Melinda Gates Foundation had over $39 billion in assets in 2016, and in 2015, gave more than $4.2 billion in grants (Bill and Melinda Gates Foundation n.d.).

To understand the economies of various cultures, anthropologists face two related problems. First, they must analyze the broad institutional and social contexts within which people make decisions, and second, they must determine and evaluate the factors that motivate individual decision making.

One way we can think about any given economic system is to consider a series of fundamental issues that all societies must face. Because all societies must acquire the food and other materials necessary to their lives, all must engage in production. To do so, all societies must acquire resources, such as land and water, and all must have some system through which the rights to use such resources are allocated.

However, resources in and of themselves do nothing. Rather, people must be organized in specific ways to use resources in the production of goods and services. Thus, each society has a **division of labor**: a pattern by which different tasks are given to different members of a society. For example, foragers rely on the plants and animals in their environment. But, foragers never simply gather and eat the plants and animals randomly. In each group, specific groups of people do specific tasks. Most often, men hunt and women gather. Thus, they are organized to produce.

In addition, people in all societies exchange and consume the products of production. Thus, each society has a system of distribution, and

Prestige: Social honor or respect.

Division of labor: The pattern of apportioning different tasks to different members of a society.

in each, there are distinct styles and patterns of consumption. In the remainder of this chapter, we will explore how different societies tackle the problems of allocating resources, organizing labor, and distributing and consuming the results of production.

ALLOCATING RESOURCES

Productive resources are the things that members of a society need to create goods and services and to participate in the economy. How people access these is basic to every culture. The most obvious productive resources are tools, labor, and, in some economic systems, money. However, knowledge is also a critical productive resource. We can see the effects of access to knowledge in current-day society by looking at the relationship between university degrees and income. According to the U.S. Bureau of Labor Statistics (2016), the median income for high school graduates in 2015 was about $35,256. The median income for those with a bachelor degree was almost $59,124. The median for those with master's and doctoral degrees was substantially higher (see Figure 6.2). Of course, the university is not the only source of knowledge in our society.

An important point of contrast between economic systems is the extent to which the members of a society have access to productive resources. In general, differential access to resources develops as population

Productive resources: Material goods, natural resources, or information used to create other goods or information.

Unemployment rate in 2015 (%)   Median weekly earnings in 2015 ($)

	Unemployment rate	Median weekly earnings
Doctoral degree	1.7	1,623
Professional degree	1.5	1,730
Master's degree	2.4	1,341
Bachelor's degree	2.8	1,137
Associate's degree	3.8	798
Some college, no degree	5.0	738
High school diploma	5.4	678
Less than a high school diploma	8.0	493

All workers: 4.3%   All workers: $860

Note: Data are for persons age 25 and over. Earnings are for full-time wage and salary workers.

Figure 6.2 The relationship between education and earnings in the United States.

Source: U.S. Bureau of Labor Statistics, 2016.

and social complexity increase. Most small-scale societies use a relatively small number of productive resources, and most everyone has access to them. Large-scale societies have a great many more resources, but access to them is limited. Again, considering differential access to knowledge in the United States, we see that only 3 percent of the students at the most selective U.S. universities come from households in the lowest 25 percent of the income scale, but 72 percent of students come from the wealthiest 25 percent of American families (Giancola and Kahlenberg 2016). Thus, family wealth plays a critical role in accessing knowledge and is a powerful predictor of future wealth and social position.

Access to the knowledge that allows one to make and use tools plays an important role in all societies. There may be additional important forms of knowledge that can be controlled as well, such as the knowledge of healing or of religious rituals. In preindustrial societies, however, the most basic resources are land and sometimes water. Examining the ways in which people access these particular resources can give us insight into the social organization and other aspects of a culture.

In foraging societies, naturally occurring abundance and scarcity shape people's relationship to land. Where resources are scarce and large areas are needed to support the population, boundaries usually are not defended. Where resources are more abundant and people move less, groups may be more inclined to fight outsiders who try to use their territory (Cashdan 1989:42). In most cases, boundaries are flexible so that they can be adjusted as the availability of resources change.

Among pastoralists, the most critical resources are livestock and land. Livestock are owned and managed by individual heads of households. Animals, in turn, produce goods that are directly consumed, such as milk and blood. They are also kept as a form of wealth, to produce other animals, and to exchange for goods and services. Land and water are generally not owned. In many cases, during the summer or the rainy season, cattle graze in deserts and highland areas unsuitable for farming. In the winter or dry season, they move to areas that are occupied by settled farmers. There, agreements with landowners and village leaders allow animals to graze on crop waste and the stubble from harvested fields. Most such agreements specify rights, payments, and schedules for all parties.

In most societies characterized by horticulture, land is communally owned by an extended kin group. Designated elders or officials of the group allocate the rights to use land to individuals or heads of households. But such land may not be sold. Because almost everyone belongs to some land-controlling kin group, few people are deprived of access to this basic resource. Thus, control over land is not a means by which one group can exploit or exert permanent control over another.

Horticulture often involves investing a great deal of labor in clearing, cultivating, and maintaining land, and the rights to cleared land and its products are vested in those who work it. Because such individuals may die while the land is still productive, some system of inheritance of use rights is usually provided. Among the Lacandon Maya, for example, individuals can farm any unused piece of land. However, clearing virgin land is difficult, so people retain rights to land they have cleared even if it is not currently in production. Maya who migrate may lose their land rights, but their families retain ownership of any fruit trees that they have planted. Should a man die after investing time and labor in clearing and planting land, his wife and children retain rights to use the land (McGee 1990).

In more politically and technologically complex societies, agriculture dominates production. Enormous amounts of labor are invested in the land and very large quantities of food are produced (see Figure 6.3). When this happens, control of the land becomes an important source of wealth and power. Land ownership moves from the kin group to the individual or family. Within the limits of law or custom, an owner has the right to keep others off the land and to dispose of it as he or she wishes.

In agricultural societies, land and other productive resources are often owned by an elite group and those who own the land usually do not work it themselves. Most fieldwork is done by laborers who often are referred to as *peasants*. Today, peasants typically pay cash rent to their landlords, but in the past, they also provided goods and services, including a portion of their agricultural production, labor, finished craft goods such as cloth, and raw material such as lumber. As a result, landowners enjoy relatively high standards of living but peasants do not.

jochem wijnands/Horizons WWP/Alamy

Figure 6.3 In complex societies, enormous amounts of labor are often invested in land, as is evident in these rice paddies in Bali. High investment in land results in high levels of production, and land ownership becomes an important source of wealth and power.

Many current-day societies rely on industrialized agriculture. But in these cases, as we saw in Chapter 5, only a minuscule percentage of the population is directly involved in farming. Therefore, access to productive land is not important for most people in these societies. In industrialized economies, most people earn their livelihood by working for wages for businesses and other organizations that provide goods and services. These usually are organized as capitalist enterprises. We will discuss capitalism at some length later in this chapter.

ORGANIZING LABOR

Resources by themselves are simply physical objects. In order to become useful to society, people must be organized to use them. Different societies use different patterns of social organization to access and use resources.

Households and Kin Groups in Small-Scale Societies

In many small-scale economies, the household or some extended kin group is the basic unit of economic organization (White 1980). Rather than working for wages, people labor for their households or kin groups. The labor they perform is an important aspect of their social identity. It situates them with respect to others in their household or kin group and gives them a sense of meaning and identity.

Household: A group of people united by kinship or other links who share a residence and organize production, consumption, and distribution among themselves.

Kin group: a group of people who understand themselves to be related by either blood or marriage.

The **household** is an economic unit—a group of people united by kinship or other links who share a residence and organize production, consumption, and distribution of goods among themselves. A household is different from a family because it may include lodgers, servants, and others. A **kin group** is a group of people who understand themselves to be related by either blood or marriage. Households and kin groups do sometimes seek financial gain, but this is not their primary purpose. Their goals are often social or religious rather than monetary.

In economies in which households or kin groups are the units of production, there is often great stability but little economic change. They cannot easily fire their members or acquire new ones. Thus, it is difficult for households and kin groups to respond to economic opportunities or contract during difficult times.

In large-scale industrial and postindustrial societies, work also has very important social implications. Of course, people work to put food on their table and a roof over their head. But, as anthropologist Pamela Crespin notes, in the United States, an individual's self-image and social status is bound up with work. Joblessness or the inability to earn a living wage diminishes an adult's identity and status (Crespin 2005:20). This is an important issue in a nation such as the United States, where in 2011, about one-third of working families earned less than twice the official poverty rate (DeNavas-Walt and Proctor 2015).

Gender also plays an important role in organizing labor. In all human societies, some tasks are considered appropriate for women and others appropriate for men. At some level, the sexual division of labor is biological because only women can bear and nurse children. However, beyond this, the specific tasks defined as men's or women's work vary widely from group to group. For example, in Aztec Mexico, weaving was a female task. Newborn girls were presented with tools for weaving, and weaving equipment was placed with women when they died (Brumfiel 1991, 2006:866). However, in most West African societies, weaving is considered men's work. The tight connections between gender and the organization of society are explored at length in Chapter 9.

▌▐ Specialization in Complex Societies

The division of labor in society becomes more specialized and complex as the population increases and agricultural production intensifies. This is particularly the case in which a society is dependent on grain agriculture. Grains are hard, durable, and storable. People who are able to control them have access to wealth and power in new and important ways. They often become landowners and rulers. Such people are able to use their access to food to support others who are not directly engaged in food production. These are likely to include specialists such as soldiers, government officials and members of the priesthood. Occupational specialization spreads through society as individuals are increasingly able to exchange their services or the products they produce for food and other forms of wealth.

Traditional areas of contemporary India provide an excellent example of occupational specialization. There, only people belonging to particular hereditary kinship groups can perform certain services or produce certain kinds of goods. Literally thousands of specialized activities—washing clothes, drumming at festivals, presiding over religious ceremonies, making pots, and painting pictures—are performed by specific named hereditary groups.

Much of the world's population today lives in industrial or postindustrial societies, and almost everyone is a specialist of one kind or another. In the United States, the Department of Labor recognizes 840 numbered occupational categories and divides each of these into many subspecialties (SOCPC 2010).

Specialization undoubtedly has advantages in terms of efficiency and the ability to produce large quantities of goods, however, it can take

Figure 6.4 In the past 200 years, jobs have become increasingly specialized. Repetitive monotonous factory labor, such as work at this electronic appliance factory in Taizhou, China, has altered people's lives and led to new understandings of identity.

© PeerPoint/Alamy

a physical and emotional toll on members of a society. Since the beginnings of the industrial age, many factory jobs involved repetitious and mind-numbing labor (see Figure 6.4). Adam Smith, generally considered the founder of modern economics, recognized this. In 1776, in *The Wealth of Nations* he wrote that "a man whose whole life is spent in performing a few simple operations ... general becomes as stupid and ignorant as it is possible for a human creature to become" (Smith Book V, Ch 1, part 3, article 2).

Although American automobile workers certainly were not stupid, the automobile plants of the early 20th century were examples of extreme mechanization. Workers simply inserted pieces into machines, turned a switch and waited until the machine completed its task, removed the finished pieces, and passed them on to the next worker. The machinery determined the pace of work and the tasks performed. In the 1920s, one worker said simply, "The machine is my boss" (Meyer 2004).

Factory labor often led to new notions of identity. For example, before the advent of factory labor and assembly lines, many American workers associated masculinity with skilled labor, independence, and decision-making power at work. However, on factory assembly lines labor was boring and monotonous, and workers had little decision-making ability. Companies such as Ford Motors, through public speeches, company policies, and employment practices, sought to redefine masculinity, associating it with "working hard in the company of other men, on a useful product, and being paid well for it" (Lewchuk 1993:852), rather than with skill and independence.

DISTRIBUTION: SYSTEMS OF EXCHANGE AND CONSUMPTION

In all societies, goods and services are exchanged. In fact, some anthropologists have long thought that the exchange of goods is one of the fundamental bases of culture. The great French anthropologist Marcel Mauss (1990/1924) theorized that societies were held together by patterns of giving and receiving. He pointed out that, because gifts invariably must be repaid, we are obligated to each other through exchange. Such obligations help to hold societies together.

The three main patterns of exchange are reciprocity, redistribution, and the market. Although more than one kind of exchange system exists in most societies, each system is predominantly associated with a certain kind of political and social organization (Polyani 1944). Let us look first at reciprocity.

Reciprocity

Reciprocity is the mutual give-and-take among people of similar status. Three types of reciprocity can be distinguished from one another by the degree of social distance between the exchanging partners (Sahlins 1972).

Generalized reciprocity usually is carried out among close kin and carries a high moral obligation. It involves a distribution of goods in which no overt account is kept of what is given, and no immediate or specific return is expected. In our culture, the relationship between mother and child is usually a good example. Ideally, such transactions are without any thought of self-interest.

Generalized reciprocity involving food is an important social mechanism among foraging peoples. In these societies, hunters distribute meat among members of the kin group or camp. Each person or family gets an equal share or a share dependent on its kinship relationship to the hunter. We might wonder what the hunter gets out of this arrangement. Aren't some people always in the position of providing more than others? Part of the answer is that because all people in the society are bound by the same rules, the system provides everyone with the opportunity to give and receive, although this does not necessarily mean that people do so equally. Particularly good hunters also gain satisfaction and a degree of prestige from accomplishing a highly skilled and difficult task (Woodburn 1998).

Balanced reciprocity involves greater social distance than generalized reciprocity and entails a clear obligation to return, within a reasonable time limit, goods of nearly equal value to those given. In the United States, we participate in balanced reciprocity when we give gifts at weddings or birthdays, exchange invitations, or buy a round of drinks for friends. The

Reciprocity: A mutual give-and-take among people of equal status.

Generalized reciprocity: Giving and receiving goods with no immediate or specific return expected.

Balanced reciprocity: The giving and receiving of goods of nearly equal value with a clear obligation of a return gift within a specified time limit.

economic aspect of these exchanges is repressed; we say it is the spirit of the gift that is important. However, we also know that accepting a gift involves the obligation to return a gift of approximately the same value. If we fail to do so, our relationship with the gift giver is unlikely to last very long.

Balanced reciprocity is often characteristic of trading relations among nonindustrialized peoples without market economies. Such trade is frequently carried out over long distances and between different tribes or villages. It is often in the hands of trading partners, men or women who have a long-standing and personalized relationship with one another.

Kula ring: A pattern of exchange among trading partners in the South Pacific Islands.

Bronislaw Malinowski's (1984/1922) analysis of the **kula ring**, an extensive system of intertribal trade among the inhabitants of a ring of islands off New Guinea, is one of the most famous anthropological studies of reciprocal trading. The kula trade moves two types of prestige goods, necklaces and bracelets, from island to island around the kula circle. *Soulava*, long necklaces of red shell, always move in a clockwise direction. *Mwali*, bracelets of white shell, move counterclockwise (see Figure 6.5). Participants receive the necklaces or bracelets from their trading partners. Although kula items can be permanently owned and can be taken out of circulation (Weiner 1976), people generally hold them for a while and then pass them on. Kula valuables are not simple objects. Each item is known by its history and associations, and some are much more valuable and important (and famous) than others. The gift or receipt of an important *soulava* or *mwali* is an action heavily loaded with prestige and politics. Kula exchanges can carry a deep emotional importance, and issues of jealousy, anger, sickness, and witchcraft are sometimes involved (Munn 1990).

Although the central drama of trading involves the gift or receipt of a kula valuable, *mwali* are never simply exchanged for *soulava*. A visiting trader hoping to receive an important kula valuable instead brings goods that may include canoes, axe blades, pottery, and pigs well as other items. Traders are likely to bring things not found on the island where the trading is taking place, because these are likely to be of greater value to their recipients. The presentation of goods by a visiting trader, as well as declarations of alliance and support, encourages a kula partner to give particularly good *mwali* or *soulava* to the visitor. Such gifts (especially gifts of important or famous valuables) demonstrate and confirm the political importance and allegiances of both giver and recipient. Critically, the receipt of such a gift also implies the obligation to present gifts of equal or greater importance to the kula partner when he or she comes as a visiting trader.

Kula exchanges thus have economic, social, and political functions. They bring kula partners into systems of balanced reciprocity and, in so

Figure 6.5 The kula trade binds people in the South Pacific in a network of reciprocal trading relationships.

doing, create alliances that are critical in settling disputes and maintaining peace. This is particularly important because there is no formal government incorporating the different groups that take active roles in the kula. In addition, by moving products from island to island, kula exchanges increase the islanders' consumption of a wide range of goods, especially those they do not produce, thus raising their standard of living.

Negative reciprocity is the unsociable extreme in exchange. It happens when trade is conducted for the purpose of material advantage and is based on the desire to get the better of a bargain. Negative reciprocity is characteristic of both impersonal and unfriendly transactions.

Negative reciprocity: Exchange conducted for the purpose of material advantage or the desire to get something for nothing.

Tribal and peasant societies often distinguish between the insider, whom it is morally wrong to cheat, and the outsider, from whom every advantage may be gained. Anthropologist Clyde Kluckhohn, who studied the Navajo in the 1940s and 1950s, reported that their rules for interaction varied with the situation; to deceive when trading with outsiders is a morally accepted practice. Even witchcraft techniques are considered permissible in trading with members of foreign tribes (Kluckhohn 1959).

Negative reciprocity helps explain some of the findings from the ultimatum game described in the opening of this chapter. Recall that in ultimatum, one person splits a quantity of money, offering a portion to another. If the second person accepts the split, they divide the money. If the second person rejects the offer, neither gets any money. Researchers found that the results of the game varied from society to society. In many kin-based societies, the first person was likely to offer only a small percentage of the money and the second person usually accepted it, whereas in market-based societies, the first person offered much larger percentages and the second was likely to reject small offers (Chibnik 2005; Henrich et al. 2004).

A key aspect of the ultimatum game is that the players are anonymous. In kin-based societies, negative reciprocity often characterizes anonymous transactions. For players from such societies, offering little or nothing to an anonymous partner is both expected and proper. Because the second player does not expect to receive much from an anonymous person, he or she is likely to accept very small offers. Polly Wiessner (2009) found that although Ju/'hoan foragers were very stingy game players, in real-life situations, in which there was no anonymity, they were far more generous.

▌▐▌ Using Anthropology: Gifts, Bribes, and Social Networks

Many classic anthropological studies have focused on gift exchange in relatively small societies without money. However, using gifts to build social networks that may serve instrumental purposes may be part of large, current-day monetized societies as well. When this happens, it raises important questions about the line between a gift and a bribe. Good examples of this come from the countries of the former Soviet Union (though they certainly exist in our own society as well). In communist times (1917–1991), having at least some money was relatively common, but goods that could be bought with the money were scarce. In this condition, a system called *blat* pervaded many aspects of life. *Blat* referred to social connections, reinforced by gift giving, that allowed people to gain access to goods, services, employment, and often admission to universities. A proverb of the era said "better 100 friends than 100 rubles."

In the post-Soviet Union era, *blat* and other arrangements persist but they are increasingly complicated. Now, goods are widely available in most places in the former Soviet Union, but money to buy them is not. Abel Polese (2008) examines gift giving and corruption in Ukraine in the early 2000s, and finds a wide gray area between the two. The Ukrainian government was unable to adequately provide many services to its citizens. Salaries paid to government workers, including doctors and teachers, were inadequate to cover their living expenses. In this context, money and goods received by doctors and teachers from their patients and students were extremely important to their economic survival. However, are these gifts or bribes? From a U.S. perspective, they were bribes and evidence of corruption. From the perspective of the Ukrainian government, receiving gifts of any kind is illegal, but these practices were tolerated to avoid paying higher wages. The perspective of the participants themselves was nuanced. In at least some cases, people giving gifts and payments saw these as signs of gratitude rather than bribes. For many, the sequence of events was important: A payment received before taking an exam or undergoing surgery is a bribe, payment afterwards, a gift. The specific actions of the service provider also make a difference. Teachers may allow students to pass exams and doctors might provide services in expectation of receiving a gift, but they believe that is different from requiring an upfront payment. As one of Polese's informants expressed it: "If I receive it, it's a gift. If I demand it, then it is a bribe" (Polese 2008:53).

Neither gift givers nor gift receivers understand their actions as simple corruption. But neither do these transactions create the ongoing social ties typical of most gift giving. Such transactions are not exactly gifts and not exactly bribes, and Polese proposes the term *brift*, halfway between gift and bribe to describe them. He argues that brifting is a fundamental aspect of Ukrainian social life and that although brifts in some cases do harm Ukraine's social and economic structures, they are "complementary to an economic system that does not guarantee even distribution of welfare" (2008:57). However, as Ukraine's economic situation deteriorated through the first decade and a half of the 21st century, its problems with

Ukraine.

corruption increased. In 2015, the watchdog group Transparency International ranked Ukraine as 130 of 167 on its corruption index and, by far, the most corrupt nation in Europe (Transparency International 2016). Government corruption was a significant cause of the political events that led to the Russian military intervention that began in 2014 (Merry 2016).

▌▐ Redistribution

In **redistribution**, goods are collected from or contributed by members of a group and then given out to the group in a new pattern. Thus, redistribution involves a social center to which goods are brought and from which they are distributed. Redistribution occurs in many different contexts. In household food sharing, pooled resources are reallocated among family members. In state societies, redistribution is achieved through taxation.

Redistribution can be especially important in small-scale societies where political organization includes "bigmen," self-made leaders who gain power and authority through personal achievement. Such individuals collect goods and food from their supporters. Often these items are redistributed back in communal feasts, which the bigman sponsors to sustain his political power and raise his prestige.

Redistribution also occurred in some chiefdoms. In these cases, however, a distinct hierarchy was involved. Chiefs collected goods and staple foods from many communities to support their households and attendants as well as to finance large public feasts that helped solidify their power (Earle 1987).

Potlatch feasting among Native American groups of the Pacific Northwest, including the Kwakwaka'wakw (Kwakiutl), Haida, and Tlingit, is a good example of redistribution (see Figure 6.6). In these groups, potlatches were held to honor and to validate the rank of chiefs and other notables, usually in connection with births, deaths, and marriages (Rosman and Rubel 1971). A leader holding a potlatch called on his followers to supply food and other goods to be consumed and distributed during a feast to which he invited group members and rivals. The number of guests present and the amount of goods given away or destroyed revealed the wealth and prestige of the host chief. At a potlatch, the host publicly traced his line of descent

Redistribution: Exchange in which goods are collected and then distributed to members of a group.

Potlatch: A form of redistribution involving competitive feasting practiced among Northwest Coast Native Americans.

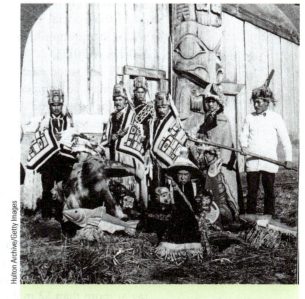

Hulton Archive/Getty Images

Figure 6.6 Potlatches are competitive feasts held among Native Americans of the Northwest Pacific coast. Here, a group of Haida people pose for a photo before a potlatch in Klinkwan, Alaska in 1901.

The Tlingit, Haida, and Kwakiutl of the Pacific Northwest Coast.

and claimed the right to certain titles and privileges. Each of these claims was accompanied by giving away, and sometimes destroying, large quantities of food and goods, such as blankets and carved wooden boxes. As these goods were given or destroyed, the individual and his supporters boasted of their wealth and power.

The feasting and gifts given at a potlatch demonstrated the host's right to the titles and rights he claimed, and created prestige for him and his followers. Guests either acknowledged the host's claims or refuted them by staging an even larger potlatch. Thus, potlatching involved not only friendship but also competition and rivalry.

Between 1884 and 1951, the Canadian government authorities outlawed potlatch, which they believed was wasteful and irrational (Bracken 1997). Since the 1950s, the potlatch has been revived as a symbol of tribal identity and cooperation rather than a major element in tribal economy.

From an economic perspective, feasts such as the potlatch encourage people to produce much more than they would otherwise. This increases not only the amount of work they do but also the amount of food and goods they produce and consume. Because this wealth is often given to people who traveled substantial distances to come to a feast, it was distributed to a fairly large population and ecological area.

Although the term *potlatch* (a Chinook word meaning "to give away") refers specifically to the feasting of Northwest Coast people, feasting is a widespread phenomenon. In many places, it plays an important role in establishing social identities, creating political power and inequalities as well as in accomplishing work and creating gender identities (Hayden and Villeneuve 2011).

We see some elements of competitive feasting in our own society. There may be competition within families or within communities to throw the largest and most elaborate holiday parties, weddings, or coming-of-age celebrations (such as confirmations, bar or bat mitzvahs, and quinceañeras). A couple married in a brief, low-cost wedding and a couple married in a lavish ceremony have the same legal standing, but the weddings make different statements about power and prestige. A poll of nearly 18,000 brides who got married in 2011 put the average cost of a wedding in the United States at more than $27,000 (Reaney 2012), an extraordinary amount in a nation where the average family income that year was just slightly over $50,000. However, high-prestige weddings in many cases cost very much more. When Chelsea Clinton married hedge fund manager Marc Mezvinsky in 2010, ABC News estimated the price tag at more than $2 million, with more than a quarter million spent on flowers alone (Mayerowitz 2010). And the 2004 wedding of Vanisha Mittal, daughter of Indian billionaire Lakshmi Mittal, cost an estimated $60 million (Barlow 2011).

Redistribution may either increase or decrease inequality within a society. A **leveling mechanism** is a form of redistribution that tends to decrease social inequality. Leveling mechanisms force accumulated resources or capital to be used in ways to ensure that social goals are considered along with economic ones. Leveling mechanisms take many different forms. For example, if generosity rather than the accumulation of wealth is the basis for prestige, those who desire power and prestige will distribute much of their wealth. Sometimes, as with the potlatch, this is accomplished through feasting. However, there are numerous other possibilities.

Manning Nash (1961) and June Nash (1970) described a number of leveling mechanisms that operate in the village of Amatenango, in the Chiapas district of Mexico. First was the organization of production by households. As mentioned earlier, economic expansion and accumulation of wealth are limited where households, rather than business firms, are the productive units. Second, the system of inheritance ensures that all children share equally in the estate of a parent. Thus, large estates are generally divided at the death of their owners and rarely persist over generations. Third, people who accumulate more wealth than their neighbors or have wealth but are not generous may face accusations of witchcraft, and those believed to be guilty may be killed.

Finally, in Amatenango, prosperous community members must hold religious and secular offices, called "cargos." Cargos are held for a year at a time and require their holders to perform civic duties and to pay for feasts and celebrations. Cargos are ranked, and those held by older, wealthier community members are more prestigious and more expensive. Such customs are common in southern Mexico and Central America and are referred to as **cargo systems**.

Anthropologists have shown that community obligations such as cargos help limit the economic gap between the relatively rich and the poor, but they do not eliminate it. In fact, they may help preserve social hierarchies (Chance and Taylor 1985). Wealthy individuals take expensive cargos that increase their prestige (or their recognition [Magazine 2012]) but do not severely impact their total wealth. They remain rich throughout their lives. The poor are generally unable to take cargos and remain poor throughout their lives. Thus, although some wealth is redistributed, in the long run, economic differences are reinforced rather than equalized (Cancian 1989:147).

▮▮ Market Exchange

Market exchange is the principal distribution mechanism in most of the world's societies today (see Figure 6.7). Goods and services are bought and sold at a monetary price determined, at least in theory, by impersonal

Leveling mechanism: A practice, value, or form of social organization that evens out wealth within a society.

Cargo system: A ritual system, common in Central and South America, in which wealthy people are required to hold a series of costly ceremonial offices.

Market exchange: An economic system in which goods and services are bought and sold at a money price determined primarily by the forces of supply and demand.

Figure 6.7 Market exchange is the principal distribution mechanism in most current day societies. Oshode market, outside of Lagos, Nigeria, pictured here, was one of the region's largest. It was demolished in 2016.

market forces. Buyers and sellers are usually not connected by webs of kinship, association, or, in many cases, even community residence.

The market involves cultural and moral assumptions that are well illustrated by the results of the ultimatum game. As we noted earlier, ultimatum players from market economies tended to offer relatively large shares of their money to their partners, and these partners tended to reject low offers, even though this penalized both players. They played this way because they shared a culturally based understanding of the market. For an impersonal market to run smoothly, most participants must believe that they will usually be treated fairly by people they do not know. People who take advantage of anonymity to enrich themselves at others' expense spoil the market and must be punished. Thus, ultimatum players from market economies are often willing to reject low offers, taking a loss to show the other player that anonymous partners must bargain and exchange fairly.

Of course, the ideal of fair and impersonal exchange is just that—an ideal. Real markets are full of conflicts, inequities, and outright cheats. In our own society, there are clearly areas of commerce in which people anticipate a certain amount of deceit. For example, merchants of used goods, particularly cars and machinery, often have reputations for shady practices.

The importance of fair play among relatively anonymous actors is illustrated by electronic marketplaces such as eBay or Amazon. In these cases, a sophisticated system of ratings gives knowledge about a participant's past transactions. This provides trading partners a degree of certainty that the terms of trade will be fair. But, anyone buying online knows that the fewer and worse the ratings of their trading partners, the greater the risk they are taking (and the greater the potential rewards must be). The phrase *caveat emptor* (let the buyer beware) neatly captures the notion that the rules of even trade are not always in force.

In principle, the primary factors that set prices and wages in a market are related to supply and demand, and individuals participate freely in a market, choosing what they buy and sell. However, the market is almost never truly free. Most markets occur in social and cultural contexts that limit or forbid certain kinds of transactions. As we have seen, people in many societies gain access to land, labor, and some goods through ties of kinship or obligations of reciprocity and redistribution. In such places, markets, if they exist at all, are limited to a small number of goods. In theory, in a society dominated by the market, everything can be bought or sold. In practice, however, all societies limit what can be purchased legally. For example, we live in a market-dominated society but, for moral, social, and political reasons, there are restrictions on the sale of drugs, guns, children, and college degrees.

Many other factors interfere with the market in almost all societies. In some cases, wealthy and powerful individuals, organizations, and industries fix prices or wages, forcing people into wage labor or the market at disadvantageous terms. In other cases, monopolies, secret knowledge, private deals, and hidden connections may distort the market. In yet other cases, cultural ideas about the proper or "just" price of a good or service are more important than supply and demand. Sometimes, governments control or influence the prices of commodities such as grain, setting them either high (to encourage farmers) or low (to feed often rebellious city dwellers cheaply).

Capitalism

Although some individuals probably act as capitalists in most monetized economies, societies organized primarily by capitalism are a late development in the history of humankind. Capitalist societies were not a natural and inevitable outcome of economic evolution. Rather, they owe their origin to the specific conditions of the Industrial Revolution in Europe in the 18th and 19th centuries and have become increasingly prevalent in the world in the past 150 years.

Capitalism expanded from northern Europe, North America, and Japan and has transformed economies worldwide, connecting them in a complex integrated international economy (Wallerstein 1995). We describe this historic process in Chapter 13, and we examine and analyze the problems and promises of the global economy in Chapter 14. Here we focus on describing capitalism and pointing out some of its most salient features.

In noncapitalist societies, most people produce goods to consume them, to trade them for other goods, or to pay rents and taxes. In capitalist societies, **firms** produce goods as a means to create wealth. For example, General Motors is not really in business to make cars. General Motors (GM) is in business to increase the wealth of its shareholders. Manufacturing automobiles is one (but only one) of the ways it achieves

Firm: An institution composed of kin and/or nonkin that is organized primarily for financial gain.

that end. GM is also heavily involved in banking (primarily through its auto finance business, GM Financial) and was historically involved in aviation, military contracting, and the production of consumer products such as refrigerators.

Productive resources become **capital** when they are used with the primary goal of increasing their owner's financial wealth. In capitalism, this becomes the most common (but not the only) use of such resources. **Capitalism** is further characterized by three fundamental attributes: First, most productive resources are owned by a small portion of the population. Banks, corporations, and wealthy individuals own the vast majority of farms, factories, and business of all kinds. Although many Americans invest in business through ownership of stocks, mutual funds, and retirement plans, ownership of substantial wealth is highly concentrated. For example, in the United States in 2015 about 55 percent of U.S. households had money invested in stocks or mutual funds and thus owned some share of a business (McCarthy 2015). However, the median value of all financial assets (bank accounts, retirement accounts, stocks, mutual funds, and so on) held by U.S. families in 2013 was only $21,200 (Bricker et al. 2014). According to G. William Domhoff (2013), in 2010, the wealthiest 10 percent of American households held over 90 percent of all stocks and mutual funds owned in the United States. Thus, although a great many people held some ownership of business, the vast majority was held by comparatively few.

The second attribute of capitalism is that most individuals' primary resource is their labor. To survive, people sell their labor for a salary or an hourly wage.

The third attribute is that the value of workers' contribution to production is always intended to be greater than the wages they receive. The difference between these two is the profit that accrues to those who own the production resources, generally the shareholders of a corporation (Plattner 1989:382–384). The extremely high wages of some professional athletes and entertainers provide a good illustration of this principle. For example, Cleveland Cavaliers player LeBron James signed a $23 million dollar a year contract in 2015 (Badenhausen 2016). For the team owner, Dan Gilbert his high salary was easily justified. Gilbert rightly believes that James's presence on the team increases his own wealth. When James returned to the Cavaliers in 2014, their arena revenue jumped more than 40 percent. Gilbert bought the Cavaliers for $375 million in 2005. In 2016 it was valued at $1.1 billion (Forbes 2016a). James's work accounts for a significant percentage of that increase. James's contract, along with more than $45 million in endorsement deals makes him a very wealthy man. His net worth is believed to be about $300 million (Isidore 2015). However, James's wealth pales before that of Gilbert,

Capital: Productive resources that are used with the primary goal of increasing their owner's financial wealth.

Capitalism: An economic system in which people work for wages, land and capital goods are privately owned, and capital is invested for profit.

believed to be about $5.4 billion, placing him at number 286 on Forbes's list of the planet's wealthiest people (2106b).

We should note here that in a capitalist society, the amount a person is paid has little to do with the value of their labor to society (a very difficult quantity to measure). Although we may be fans of Mr. James, we will not suffer terribly when he eventually retires. And life continued unchanged for most of us during the 161-day NBA lockout of 2011. However, if sanitation workers were to strike or be locked out and we had no trash pickup for more than 5 months, almost all of us would be deeply affected, and our lives would be far more difficult. By this measure, sanitation workers are much more socially useful than professional basketball players, but they shouldn't expect to make millions any time soon.

Modern capitalist economies are dominated by market exchange, but this does not mean that people always experience their economy in terms of buying and selling at whatever price the market will bear. Capitalism always occurs within the context of other social relationships, and sometimes these provide a mask behind which it can hide. In other words, capitalist relationships are sometimes camouflaged by family ties or social obligations. When this happens, entrepreneurs may be able to extract extra profits. The production of knitted sweaters in Turkey is a good example of this.

Turkey produces many goods and services used in wealthy capitalist nations. Most of the inhabitants of Istanbul, its largest city, are part of a capitalist economy, selling their labor in enterprises aimed at generating a profit. However, as Jenny B. White (1994) reports, many of them, particularly women, understand their work in terms of reciprocity and kin obligations rather than capitalism and the marketplace.

Turkey is a patrilineal and patriarchal society. Turkish women live in complex social networks characterized by social obligations and relations of reciprocity. To a great degree, they measure their worth by the work they do for family members. Being a good woman means laboring for family and relatives.

Married women live with their husbands' families and are expected to manage the households and to keep their hands busy with knitting and other skilled tasks (see Figure 6.8). Such tasks are

Yaacov Dagan/Alamy

Figure 6.8 For many Turkish women, knitting is a social obligation. This is one factor that leads them to accept very low wages for sweaters they knit. However, these sweaters enter a capitalist trade system and are sold for high prices in wealthy nations.

Turkey.

not considered work (in the sense of work outside of the home) but are rather understood as necessary obligations of married life.

In the neighborhood White (1994:13) investigated, almost everyone believed that women should not work for money, yet about two-thirds of women earned money by knitting garments that were sold in wealthy nations. How is this contradiction explained? The women who do it see their production as a way for them to keep their hands busy and thus part of their duty as wives rather than as a form of paid labor. Their work forms part of their obligation to their husband's family and to organizers who are often relatives, neighbors, and friends. They consider their work a gift of labor and understand the payments they receive to be gifts from someone with whom they have an established social relationship. Because the women's work is set within a context of global capitalism, though work organizers may be relatives and friends, they are also capitalist entrepreneurs hoping to make money. Since the women produce goods for the capitalist marketplace, their wages should be set by that market. However, the capitalist aspect of their work is masked by social relations they have with the labor organizer. Because they understand their work in terms of a social obligation, they rarely think about how much they are earning per hour or how they might use their time and talents to make more money. Thus, they are willing to accept far lower wages than might otherwise be the case.

In some ways, the system serves the women well. They are able to fill their roles as wives and in-laws, and their social connections with labor organizers may give them some degree of security from the ravages of the marketplace. This is important in a country such as Turkey, where most people have little money and social services are few. However, it is clear that the greatest beneficiaries of this system are firms and consumers in wealthy nations. The fact that social relations mask capitalism for poor women in Turkey allows rich consumers to buy hand-knitted sweaters at very low prices, and the firms that sell the sweaters to make windfall profits.

It would be difficult to find any people in the world today not affected by capitalist markets. For the most part, members of traditional societies enter the market as low-wage laborers. The wealth they produce accrues to elites within poor nations as well as to owners and consumers in wealthy nations (Wolf 1982). The case of the Turkish women illustrates some of the ways in which this process takes place. Not all societies are able to make such accommodations, however, and the expansion of capitalism and political power has been accompanied by the wide-scale destruction of traditional societies. Chapter 13 examines this process in some detail.

▌▌▌ Resistance to Capitalism

Capitalism is a powerful economic system. It undoubtedly provides a greater number of goods and services to larger populations than do other ways of organizing an economy, but at a cost. When some individuals or groups own or control basic resources, others must inevitably be denied access to them. This results in permanently differentiated economic and social classes. Capitalism dictates that there will always be rich and poor. Often, part of the population lives in extreme poverty, without access to basic resources. In American society, this includes the homeless, the landless rural poor, and the permanently unemployed.

Although the capitalist economy has expanded in every part of the world, there probably are no countries where all of the population is directly involved in it. Noncapitalist groups, often indigenous people, remain. These people are often pushed to areas such as the jungles of Brazil or the border between Pakistan and Afghanistan, where the terrain or climate make agriculture unprofitable and military control expensive and difficult. However, mass-produced goods, media, and fashions from capitalist societies are easily found, even in these locations. In other places, issues of race, gender, and ethnicity prevent people from fully participating in the capitalist economy.

Despite the international success of capitalism, it has from its origins encountered frequent and sometimes violent resistance. In the early 19th century, Luddites smashed the weaving machines of early capitalists in an attempt to preserve skilled labor and cottage industries. By the late 19th and early 20th centuries, radical unions such as the Industrial Workers of the World campaigned for the abolition of capitalism and wage labor. In the 1960s anticapitalist protests broke out across Europe, Japan, and the United States. Protests in France in 1968 were particularly widespread, with workers joining student protesters and bringing the nation to the brink of revolution. Protests continued in the late 1990s and early 2000s with riots and mass arrests accompanying meetings of major capitalist institutions such as the World Bank and World Trade Organization. In the wake of the 2008 financial crisis, protests broke out again in many places. The best known of these was the Occupy movement of 2011, which began in New York but rapidly became global with rallies held in more than 900 cities throughout the world (Adam 2011). Although support for the movement eventually diminished, resistance to the current distribution of wealth continues. In 2015, a Gallup Poll reported that 63 percent of Americans believe that wealth should be distributed more evenly (Newport 2015a).

In addition to taking to the street in protest, people resist capitalism in other, more subtle ways. The fundamental social arrangement of capitalism is that most people sell their labor for wages to capitalists who reinvest profit to create greater wealth. However, many people in the United States and throughout the world neither work for wages nor hire workers and make investments to increase their wealth. In the United States, they often get by using a combination of techniques that include subsistence gardening, garage sales, and trading their labor with others (see Figure 6.9). They work for others only when they absolutely must, taking part-time jobs or leaving full-time employment as soon as they have enough cash for an immediate need (Halperin 1990; Hansen 1995). And this is not only an American phenomenon: Wilson (2003:303) found that people who drove horse carriages (jarveys) in Ireland were often fleeing wage labor. Other members of their families worked in factories and they had previous experience of wage labor themselves but had given it up. One said that even if they paid him twice as much to work in a factory, he'd rather drive a carriage.

In the United States, individuals are often very proud of their ability to support themselves outside the boundaries of wage labor. However, the fact that they resist principal elements of capitalism (perhaps unknowingly) in so doing reminds us that economic systems are not natural and inevitable. The ways in which we organize our economy are the result of history, politics, economics, and individual choices—a creation of culture, not natural law.

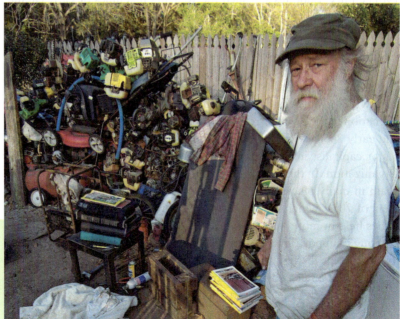

Figure 6.9 Garage sales, gardening, raising livestock, and doing odd jobs help many Americans avoid full participation in the capitalist economy.

© imac/Alamy Stock Photo

BRINGING IT BACK HOME:
UX (USER EXPERIENCE)

In the past several decades, greater numbers of anthropologists have sought employment in business and have been involved in designing some well-known consumer products. For example, ethnographic research conducted by Susan Squires and Bryan Byrne was instrumental in the development of Go-Gurt, a popular sweetened yogurt product marketed to parents of young children.

More recently, technology companies are among the biggest consumers of anthropology. Microsoft is reportedly the world's second largest employer of anthropologists (Baer 2014) and Women in Technology International Hall of Fame member and anthropologist Genevive Bell is a Vice President and Fellow at Intel as well as director of the company's Corporate Sensing and Insights group. Bell (2016) says her job is "to make sense of what makes people tick, what delights and frustrates them, and to use those insights to help shape the next generation of technology insights."

George Anders (2015) notes that "Throughout the major U.S. tech hubs...software companies are discovering that liberal arts thinking makes them stronger." There is a good reason for this. As technology progresses, many jobs on the technical side such as software engineering become automated. Fewer (but very highly skilled) people are needed to fill them. On the other hand, jobs related to how people use technology and how to market technology increase. For example, in the spring of 2015, Facebook was advertising 146 jobs for software developers but 225 for sales and business development specialists.

A key intersection of anthropology and business is the development of the field of UX or user experience. UX refers to the ways in which people interact with products, services, and companies; the ways end users feel about the systems and objects they use and how these fit into their lives. Part of this is simply ease of use. However, a lot of it has to do with context, expectations, past experiences, and the ways people actually use things in their lives. Anthropological techniques such as participant observation are particularly useful in studying UX.

For Christian Madsbjerg and Mikkel Rasmussen (2014), two of the principals of the anthropological consulting company ReD, the core of UX is sensemaking, the ways in which people bring "the complex interplay between their interior lives and their social, cultural, and physical worlds" to bear on the ways in which they understand and use goods and services. They give the example of their work with the toymaker Lego. In the mid-2000s Lego was failing in its attempt to move into new markets such as video games and action figures. They produced products that looked cool but were not popular. To find out what parents and children wanted from Lego, the company did ethnographic research. Researchers spent time with families, interviewed parents and children, shopped with families and took pictures. They found that what kids wanted from Legos was to escape from their overly structured lives and hone their skills. The new, more structured products didn't allow kids to reach these goals in the ways that the old ones did. To survive, Lego needed to focus on their core business and make products that allowed kids greater freedom to play.

Anthropologists have made products more friendly and businesses more money. However, UX also raises some ethical problems. For example, anthropologists mine information from their informants. If corporations then profit from this information, is payment owed to the informants? Most anthropologists publish their research findings, but corporate research is usually private. Should it be? Some key consumers of anthropological research are beverage and packaged-food companies, but should anthropologists be promoting the sale of sugary drinks and junk food? Should anthropology be a way to help corporations make more money?

YOU DECIDE:

1. Historically, the introduction of cheap, mass-produced manufactured goods has undercut existing economies and drawn people into the capitalist economy, generally as consumers of low-quality merchandise and low-paid wage earners. Given this, should anthropologists be involved in the design and marketing of products to groups about which they have expertise?

2. With or without anthropology the advance of capitalism into all areas of the world has been relentless. With the aid of anthropologists, corporations can produce products that meet local needs and are marketed in culturally appropriate ways. The alternative often is inappropriate, poorly designed, and poorly marketed products. Given this, can anthropologists justifiably refuse to work with corporations?

3. Perhaps the previous two questions present a false dichotomy. What are some positions that anthropologists might take between these two? Are they practicable in the real world without the security of a university appointment?

CHAPTER SUMMARY

1. What cultural economic principles are demonstrated by the dictator and ultimatum games? The games show that people's economic behavior differs from culture to culture. Some of this variation is systematic. People from market-oriented societies tend to play differently from those from societies with other forms of economic organization.

2. What is economics, and how is it related to culture? Economics is the study of the ways people use their scarce resources to produce and distribute goods and services. However, such choices are always set within a cultural context. People in different societies are motivated by different values and achieve their desired ends in different ways.

3. Give examples of productive resources and how access to them changes at different levels of social complexity. In every society, certain goods are productive resources. Such resources generally include land, labor, and knowledge. Societies have systems by which such resources are allocated to their members. As social complexity increases, access to productive resources becomes more restricted.

4. How is labor organized in most small-scale, preindustrial, and peasant societies? In most small-scale societies, labor is organized by the household or kin group. Work that people both perform and receive locates them with respect to their social network and often is integral to their identity.

5. How is labor organized in large-scale and industrial societies? As societies become more populous, the number of specialized jobs found in them increases. Current-day wealthy societies have extremely high degrees of specialization. This creates great efficiency but involves changing notions of identity and often has heavy human costs.

6. What three general mechanisms for the distribution of goods and services are described in this chapter? In all societies, there are systems for distributing and consuming goods and services. Every society uses some combination of reciprocity, redistribution, and the market to redistribute goods and services and to provide patterns and standards for their consumption.

7. What is reciprocity and what are three different types of reciprocity? Exchange among people of similar status is characterized by reciprocity. As social distance among individuals increases, the characteristic form of reciprocity tends to change from generalized, to

balanced, and, sometimes, to negative. The kula trade in the South Pacific provides an example of balanced reciprocity.

8. What is redistribution, and in what kinds of societies is it commonly found? In redistribution, goods are collected by a central individual or office and then distributed in a new pattern. Redistribution is characteristic of exchange in chiefdoms as well as parts of state-level economies. Potlatch among Pacific Northwest coastal Native Americans provides an example of redistribution.

9. What are the chief characteristics of market exchange, and where is market exchange found? In market exchange, goods and services are bought and sold at a money price determined, at least in theory, by the impersonal forces of supply and demand. Market exchange is found in most societies but is the main economic mechanism of current-day states.

10. What are the defining characteristics of capitalism? In capitalism, the owners of productive resources use them to increase their financial wealth. In capitalist societies, a small percentage of the population primarily hold productive resources, most people sell their labor for wages, and the value of people's labor is always more than the wages they receive. Capitalism can be masked by other relationships such as reciprocity.

11. Where is resistance to capitalism found, and what forms does it take? Although capitalism is ubiquitous around the world, many people resist it, sometimes protesting violently against it. People also resist capitalism by avoiding wage labor and, to some degree, participation in the market.

KEY TERMS

Balanced reciprocity	Kin group
Capital	Kula ring
Capitalism	Leveling mechanism
Cargo system	Market exchange
Division of labor	Negative reciprocity
Economic system	Potlatch
Economics	Prestige
Firm	Productive resources
Generalized reciprocity	Reciprocity
Household	Redistribution

Jake KY Anderson/Alamy

This photo of an Asante chief of Ghana illustrates the point that as societies become more complex, specialized positions of authority, such as kings and chiefs, develop as centers of power and control.

7

POLITICAL ORGANIZATION

AFTER YOU HAVE READ THIS CHAPTER, YOU WILL BE ABLE TO:

△ Define different aspects of the political process, including the relationship between wealth and power and apply these to the distribution of power in the Asante state.

△ Contrast egalitarian, rank, and stratified societies, illustrating the key features of each.

△ List the major features of leadership in band, tribal, chiefdom, and state-level societies.

△ Assess the role that warfare plays in different forms of political organization.

△ Compare the Asante and the United States to explain how political ideology helps maintain social stratification in state-level societies.

△ Describe some factors that support nationalism in nation-states.

△ Explain how anthropology contributes to our understanding of the roles of ethnic and indigenous groups in the maintenance of nation-states.

WEALTH AND POWER IN THE ASANTE STATE

T he precolonial Asante state in West Africa is a good example of how the integration of power and wealth operates in the structure of the state (McCaskie 1995). The highly productive Asante economy supported a complex social hierarchy ruled by the Asantehene, or king. The urban elite mainly transacted government business, performed elaborate state ceremonies, and produced luxury goods for the wealthy. The Asantehene's household daily consumed large quantities of locally grown food, along with imported delicacies such as mutton, turkey, duck, wild game, rice, European biscuits, tea, sugar, and wine, reflecting the association between elite status and material well-being.

Precolonial Asante society was composed of slaves, peasant commoners, urban specialists, and government officials, with the Asantehene and his royal family at the top of the hierarchy. Social stratification was based on achievement, competition, and especially accumulation of wealth, with many opportunities for social competition and social mobility. Though the state did use coercive force—espionage, detention, fines, confiscation of property, exile, and execution—a key factor in its stability for over 150 years was the government's success in promoting the core Asante values that wealth and power went hand in hand and that the accumulation of wealth by an individual was of benefit to the whole society. Accumulating wealth resulted in high office, and holding high office was justified by the accumulation and display of wealth, especially gold, and control of the rituals in which wealth was displayed.

The state accepted only gold for payment of fines, tributes, taxes, and levies. Those who could not pay had to provide land and laborers instead, enriching the state coffers. The state also permitted an individual to buy himself out of a mandatory death sentence with a payment of gold to the state and enacted various "estate taxes," which prevented the emergence of a class of hereditary property owners that might be a threat to its own power. The state controlled the opportunities to accumulate wealth on the largest scale: Commanding the state's armies, conducting the state's trade, holding state office, or being a favored beneficiary of the state's laws were themselves gifts of the state.

The state also controlled "symbolic capital." Only the state could bestow titles or other symbols of high status, or organize the complex rituals and ceremonies that glorified the state, emphasizing the role of public officials as providers for and protectors of the people. Although the Asante state became a British colony in the late 19th century and an ethnic group within the Republic of Ghana when the British left in 1957, the Asantehene today retains his high traditional position as a ritual, spiritual, and cultural leader of the Asante people.

▌▌▌ POLITICAL PROCESSES

Political processes—the ways in which individuals and groups organize to use power and authority to achieve public goals—are complex in all societies and must be understood in their cultural, historical, economic, and political contexts. Political organization and the uses of power grow out of specific situations and change as these situations change. A good example is the so-called Arab Spring.

On December 17, 2010, Mohamed Bouazizi, a young man who lived in a remote town in Tunisia, burned himself to death to protest against police corruption and brutality after the police confiscated his unlicensed vegetable cart, which was his only source of income. This act led to widespread, initially peaceful protests and also riots throughout Tunisia; by April 2011, the "Arab Spring" in which protesters successfully overthrew the police states of Tunisia, Egypt, and Libya, among others, as well as the leaders who ruled them, was well under way. Through the widespread use of social media, and the desperation of the many unemployed young people, the public protests gathered momentum and many people began to believe that these "old, rotten regimes" could be brought down by a "revolution" of ordinary people (Lynch 2012). The aftermath of the Arab Spring demonstrates how complicated political processes are. While the result of the Arab Spring was a partly successful revolution because it deposed totalitarian governments and instituted the writing of new, more democratically influenced constitutions in some nations, it also resulted in often violent conflict between different tribal groups, between different Islamic religious factions, and between Islamists and secularists (Agha and Malley 2012); in many places little real change occurred (Cambanis 2015), while in others, like Libya, the death of the dictator resulted in the disintegration of the state (Pelham 2015; Shane and Becker 2016).

Rebellion, which is the attempt of one group in a society to reallocate power and resources within an existing political structure, and **revolution**, which is an attempt to overthrow the existing political structure and put another type of political structure in its place, are both examples of the political process—how groups and individuals organize to use power and authority to achieve various public goals. These goals may benefit the larger society or they may benefit only smaller groups

Rebellion: The attempt of a group within society to force a redistribution of resources and power.

Revolution: An attempt to overthrow an existing form of political organization and put another type of political structure in its place.

or individuals. Political decisions and activities by groups and individuals may be motivated by material profit, prestige, altruism, survival, or any combination of motives, but are usually justified by reference to the public good.

The Arab Spring—and other protest movements, such as Occupy Wall Street, which occurred in 2011, and its spin-offs—demonstrate the fine line between rebellion and revolution; how some rebellions and uprisings may end up as revolutions and why many revolutions fail. History demonstrates the importance of outside help in this regard, much as the success of the American Revolution was aided by France, and also how nonviolent protests, such as in British-ruled India, may also be successful in changing the face of government and the distribution of power (Roberts and Ash 2009).

The study of political processes illustrates how new kinds of political organization and ideologies develop and how power changes hands, as well as how political structures and political organization may be used to stabilize a social order, avoid or resolve conflicts, and promote the general welfare, but how they may also be used to contest prevailing political ideologies and change or even destroy existing political systems. **Factions**—informal alliances within a group or society, as well as governments—use diverse means to gain their ends. These may include violence and terror, behind-the-scenes manipulation, peaceful protest, the ballot box, and political lobbying, propaganda, or bribery.

Factions: informal alliances within well-defined political units such as lineages, villages, or organizations.

▌▌▌ POLITICAL ORGANIZATION

Political organization: The patterned ways in which power is legitimately used in a society to regulate behavior, maintain social order, make collective decisions, and deal with social disorder.

Political organization is about how societies use power to address the universal problem of maintaining themselves over time with a minimum of social disorder and social discontent. This means that every society must make and implement decisions affecting the whole society; provide a means of managing conflicts, dissent, and deviance; and generally regulate behavior so that it is consistent with social order.

▌▌▌ Power and Authority

Power: The ability to impose one's will on others.
Authority: The ability to cause others to act based on characteristics such as honor, status, knowledge, ability, respect, or the holding of formal public office.

Power is the ability to exercise one's will over others: Sources of power are ultimately based on the control of resources that people need or desire. Anthropologists examine the sources and uses of power and analyze how political organization is related to other cultural patterns and social institutions. Power differs from **authority**, which is the socially approved, or legitimate, use of power. An individual's authority may be based on personal characteristics, such as knowledge, ability, social status, and respect. Political leaders have authority based on their legitimate occupation of public office, but they may also wield power through their control of resources and/or control over the use of force or knowledge. Power can exist without authority: An armed robber has power, but no authority. Authority can also exist without power. The Dalai Lama has great authority, but no real power.

The shared values and beliefs that legitimate the distribution and uses of power and authority in a particular society are called its **political ideology**. A political ideology may be widely, though not universally shared; the sources of power may be coercive (based on force or the threat of force), consensual, or more likely, both. Types of political organizations differ in the degree to which they use coercion or consensus—a generally agreed-upon political ideology—to achieve and maintain social order.

Political ideology: The shared beliefs and values that legitimize the distribution and use of power in a particular society.

Social Control and Conflict Management

Because all societies contain conflict, all societies must manage conflict and persuade individuals to conform to (at least most of) society's norms if they are to survive. In small-scale societies, organized through kinship, conformity results mainly from the internalization of norms and values as part of enculturation and from many informal processes and sanctions. Internalization of norms also regulates behavior in complex, socially stratified state societies, but the control of the state over many social institutions and regulatory processes, including the mobilization of force, is also crucial.

Transgression of society's rules are handled differently in different types of societies (see Figure 7.1). In small-scale societies, informal mechanisms of social interaction such as ridicule, avoidance, or gossip are effective means of social control because most people value the esteem of (at least some) others, and because marginalized people may also be restricted from access to resources. These mechanisms may also be effective when used against society's leaders (Besnier 2009).

Courtesy of Andrew Arno

Figure 7.1 The informal kava drinking circle is an important means of resolving disputes in Fiji and other Pacific Islands. Unlike the adversarial process of Western law, informal processes attempt to reconcile the disputants.

Informal sanctions, such as gossip or ridicule, are also effective in small groups in complex and industrialized societies. Bullying, which combines gossip and ridicule, both in face-to-face encounters and on social media, is an important sanction among teenagers in American schools, leading some of those "picked on" even to commit suicide. In some small-scale societies, fear of witchcraft accusations or other supernatural interventions is widely used to ensure social control of "deviants," those who try to stand above the group, are malicious, have a nasty temper, or refuse to share according to group norms (Evans-Prichard 1958/1937). Avoidance works in small-scale groups and societies because where cooperative action is necessary to succeed or even to survive, a person shunned by others is at a great psychological and economic disadvantage. In almost all societies today, widespread media availability also has a great impact on how ordinary people think about events and people, particularly those that involve conflict (Arno 2009).

Law refers to the systematic application of force by a constituted authority in society (Moore 1978:220). Law is applied when a social norm is so important that its violation authorizes the community, or some part of it, to punish an offender, resolve a conflict, or redress a wrong. In every society, some offenses are considered so disruptive that force or the threat of force is applied. In this sense, law is universal, although in small-scale societies it is most often embedded in other social institutions, like kinship relations or religion, and is most often directed at maintaining existing social relationships. In more complex, stratified societies, law's functions belong to separate legal institutions, such as a police force, courts, and a prison system, and punishment is aimed at asserting society's control over the individual, rather than repairing damaged social relationships (Moore 1978:168).

TYPES OF POLITICAL ORGANIZATION

Systems of political organization are related to social complexity and the degree to which political roles, institutions, and processes are centralized and differentiated from other aspects of social organization or embedded within other social institutions. Anthropologists identify four main types of social complexity: **bands**, **tribes**, **chiefdoms**, and **states**. Each of these types of societies is associated with characteristic forms of leadership and social control; and different systems of **social differentiation**, or social hierarchy (Service 1962). Inequalities exist in all societies, but not all societies formally recognize these differences, nor do these inequalities necessarily affect access to important resources.

Law: A means of social control and dispute management through the systematic application of force by a politically constituted authority.
Band: A small group of people related by blood or marriage, who live together and are loosely associated with a territory in which they forage.
Tribe: A culturally distinct population whose members consider themselves to have descended from the same ancestor.
Chiefdom: A society with social ranking in which political integration is achieved through an office of centralized leadership called the chief.
State: A hierarchical, centralized form of political organization in which a central government has a legal monopoly over the use of force.
Social differentiation: The relative access individuals and groups have to basic material resources, wealth, power, and prestige.

In smaller-scale nonindustrial societies such as bands, tribes, and chiefdoms, the uses of power and authority, decision making, and the coordination and regulation of human behavior are highly integrated. Power and authority do not operate independently but are embedded in other social institutions such as kinship, economics, and religion. In these societies, **leadership**, the ability to direct an enterprise, may be based on political office or individual authority, but it may also be based on an individual's position as the head of a kinship group; on supernatural connections and interventions; or on the relative access and control individuals and groups have over basic material resources, wealth, power, and prestige.

Anthropologists define three ideal types of social differentiation: *egalitarian societies, rank societies,* and *stratified societies.* In **egalitarian societies**, individual (as well as age and gender) distinctions are recognized, but no individual or group is barred from access to material resources or has power over others. There are no rules of inheritance by which some individuals accumulate material goods or prestige passed down over generations. Unlike egalitarian societies, **rank societies** recognize formal differences among individuals and groups in prestige and symbolic resources, and these may be passed on through inheritance. However, there are no important restrictions on access to basic resources, and all individuals can obtain the material necessities for survival through their membership in kinship groups.

In **stratified societies**, there are formal and permanent social and economic inequalities. Wealth, prestige, and office are frequently passed down over generations, establishing relatively permanent elites. **Elites** are those who have maximum access to all culturally valued resources, whether power, wealth, or prestige, and possessively protect their control over these resources. In stratified societies, some individuals and groups are also systemically denied access to the basic material resources needed to survive. Thus, stratified societies are characterized by permanent and wide differences among groups and individuals in their standard of living, security, prestige, political power, and the opportunity to fulfill one's potential. All contemporary industrialized nations are stratified societies, even those such as the United States or socialist societies like Cuba, which proclaim equality as a dominant value.

Political organization, social differentiation, and social complexity can be analyzed separately, but in reality, they intersect with each other in significant ways. The following types of societies described are ideal types; the reality is much more complex, as history, geography, culture, and other factors all affect the specific characteristics of any particular society. Although many anthropologists reject the evolutionary implications of these typologies (the idea that societies develop on a single trajectory from simpler bands to more complex states), the typologies are useful in grasping some of the varieties of political organization.

Leadership: The ability to direct an enterprise or action.

Egalitarian society: A society in which no individual or group has more privileged access to resources, power, or prestige than any other.

Rank society: A society characterized by institutionalized differences in prestige but no important restrictions on access to basic resources.

Stratified society: A society characterized by formal, permanent social and economic inequality in which some people are denied access to basic resources.

Elites: The social strata that has differential access to all culturally valued resources, whether power, wealth, or prestige, and possessively protects its control over these resources.

▌▌▌ Band Societies

A band is a small group of people (usually 20 to 50) belonging to extended families who live together and are loosely associated with a territory in which they make a living. Foragers generally live in bands, which tend to be egalitarian and mainly use generalized or balanced reciprocity as mechanisms of exchange. Band societies have minimal role specialization or differences of wealth, prestige, or power. Bands are fairly independent of one another, with few higher levels of social integration or centralized mechanisms of leadership. Ties between bands are mainly established by marriage and kinship, and also by trading relations. Band membership is flexible, with individuals easily changing residence from one band to another. The flexibility of band organization is particularly adaptive for a foraging way of life and low population density.

Band societies have no formal leadership; decision making is by consensus. Leaders in foraging bands are usually the elders, whose experience, knowledge of group traditions, special skills or success in foraging, and generosity are sources of prestige. Leaders cannot enforce their decisions; they can only persuade, attracting others to their leadership on the basis of past performance. Among some Inuit, for example, a local leader is called "The One to Whom All Listen," "He Who Thinks," or "He Who Knows Everything Best." Social order in band societies is primarily maintained through informal sanctions such as gossip, ridicule, and avoidance. It is also maintained by supernatural interventions and sanctions, such as the public confessions directed by a shaman among the Inuit (Balikci 1970). This pattern may not serve them well in contemporary U.S. courts, where they may too freely admit guilt, which penalizes them in the adversarial legal system of the United States. Inuit bands sometimes resolve disputes through public contests that involve physical action, such as head butting or boxing, or verbal contests, like song duels, where the weapons are words—"little, sharp words like the wooden splinters which I hack off with my ax" (Hoebel 1974:93).

Individual violence, such as the frequent fights over women among the Ju/'hoansi hunters of the Kalahari Desert in Africa, does occur in band societies, but because of the low level of technology, lack of formal leadership, and other ecological factors, organized warfare is largely absent. Bands have no warriors and no cultural or social support for sustained armed conflict (Lee 2003). When conflict gets too disruptive, bands may break up into smaller units, which separates people who are in extended conflict and prevents prolonged hostilities (Turnbull 1968).

Tribal Societies

A tribe is a culturally distinct population whose members view themselves as descended from the same ancestor. Tribes are mainly found among pastoralists and horticulturalists; they are generally egalitarian and exchange goods through reciprocity and redistribution. Like bands, most tribes do not have distinct or centralized political institutions or roles, and power and social control are embedded in other institutions, such as kinship or religion. Tribes are usually organized into unilineal kin groups (p. 236), who "own" the basic economic resources and are the units of political activity. These large unilineal kin groups are consistent with the larger populations in horticultural and pastoral societies relative to foraging band societies.

The effective political unit in tribal societies may occasionally shift from independently operating local units of a tribe to higher-level unity. These units may even have been in a state of ongoing violent conflict among themselves; higher-level unity most often occurs in response to the threat of attack from another tribe or the opportunity to attack another tribe. Among the Nuer of East Africa, lineages at different levels join each other to attack a common enemy (Evans-Pritchard 1968/1940), a process that steers competition away from close kin and helps stronger tribes who want to expand into nearby territories held by weaker tribes.

Organizations based on age, also help integrate tribal societies beyond kinship. In these organizations individuals move through life's stages together in an organized progression. Age-based groups are mainly male and have political and military functions. Because their members come from different kinship groups, age-based groups are an important basis for wider social integration throughout a tribal society. Other kinds of associations, such as the military societies among some Plains Indian tribes in North America, and the secret societies found in West Africa, also help integrate tribal societies.

Tribal societies have leaders but no centralized government and few formal positions of authority. In New Guinea, for example, the typical leader is a "bigman"—a self-made man who gains power and authority through personal achievements rather than through holding office. A bigman begins as the leader of a small, localized kin group. He builds up his capital, mainly in the form of pigs, and attracts followers through generous loans, sponsoring feasts, purchasing high ranks in secret societies, helping his military allies, paying bridewealth for young men seeking wives, and other initiatives. These actions increase his reputation and put other people under obligation to him, thus further extending his alliances and influence.

The bigman is a fragile mechanism of tribal integration above the local level, however, because it does not create a permanent office but

Judith Pearson

Figure 7.2 This New Guinea man is a bigman, an informal leader in Melanesian tribal societies. His influence mainly depends on his ability to distribute resources, among which pigs are the most important.

Mediation: A form of managing disputes that uses the offices of a third party to achieve voluntary agreement between the disputing parties.

rather depends on the constant striving of an individual. Bigmen rise and fall, and their support disperses when they die. Big men are vulnerable because they must spur their local group on to ever greater production if they are to hold their own against other bigmen in the tribe. To maintain prestige, a bigman must give his competitors more than they can give him. Excessive giving to competitors means a bigman must begin to withhold gifts to his followers. The resulting discontent may lead to defection among his followers, or even to the murder of the bigman. Bigman status cannot be inherited, so each aspiring bigman must begin anew to amass the wealth and forge the internal and external social relationships on which bigman status depends (Sahlins 1971) (see Figure 7.2).

Tribes mainly use informal mechanisms for controlling deviant behavior and settling conflicts. Payments demanded by an aggrieved party to compensate for damage are important in New Guinea, among other places. The amount of compensation is based on the severity of the act that precipitated a dispute, and the individual's kin group shares in the payment. Payment of compensation implies acceptance of responsibility by the donors and acceptance of compensation implies a willingness to terminate the dispute by the recipients (Scaglion 1981). Demands for excessive compensation, however, may not resolve conflicts, but rather become the basis for further disputes (Ottley and Zorn 1983).

Mediation, a common form of tribal conflict management, aims to resolve disputes through consensus rather than adversarial interactions so that the prior social relationship between the disputants is maintained and harmony is restored to the social order. Mediation involves a third party, either a go-between, or even the whole community, in resolving conflict between the disputants. Among the Kpelle of Liberia, a moot, or form of mediation, takes place before an assembled group of kinsmen and neighbors (Gibbs 1988). After an opening ritual, the mediator reminds the audience of its common interests and close ties. All participants, both disputants and the audience, can question each other directly. After everyone has been heard, the mediator proposes a solution that expresses the consensus between the audience and the disputing parties. The party found to be at fault apologizes to the other, food and drink are ritually distributed, and reconciliation is achieved. Through the work of anthropologist James Gibbs, Kpelle mediation became a model for the emerging mediation movement now widely used in the United States to help settle conflict ranging from labor disputes to divorce proceedings (Fry and Bjorkqvist 1997).

Warfare in Tribal Societies

Despite mainly using nonviolent methods of conflict resolution, tribal societies seem prone to a high degree of **war (warfare)**. Perhaps, in the absence of strong mechanisms for tribal integration through peaceful means, and few strong motivations to produce food beyond immediate needs, warfare may help regulate the balance between population and resources. With slash-and-burn horticulture, for example, it is much harder to clear forest for cultivation than to work land that has already been used. Thus, a local group may prefer to take land from other groups, by force if necessary, rather than expand into virgin forest (Vayda 1976).

War (warfare): A formally organized and culturally recognized pattern of collective violence directed toward other societies or between segments within a larger society.

Tribal warfare may also be linked to patrilineality and patrilocality, which promote male solidarity. This enables the use of force to resolve both local conflicts and warfare carried out over long distances, as occurred among the Iroquois of North America (Ember and Ember 1971). Most anthropologists generally agree that warfare is grounded in historical, material, cultural, social, and ecological conditions, and not in any biologically based human instinct for aggression.

The classic ethnography of intratribal violence and warfare describes the Yanomamo of the Amazon areas of Venezuela and Brazil. According to their ethnographer, Napoleon Chagnon (2013), the frequent and intense warfare among the Yanomamo is motivated mainly by revenge, which then becomes part of an ongoing cycle of intervillage hostility. Each village tries to preserve its autonomy by defeating its enemies in warfare, or in warlike aggressive raids and rituals such as chest pounding or club fighting. The cycle of hostility may initially grow out of sorcery accusations in a village where a death has occurred, or revenge for the abductions or rape of women, which then perpetuate more violence.

There is an ongoing debate in anthropology about the best way to explain Yanomamo warfare: Chagnon suggested a biological theory; this is rejected by many anthropologists, who emphasize functional or historical factors. For example, Yanomamo warfare may function as a means of population control—not due to deaths in battle, but indirectly through female infanticide in this warlike society where aggressive males are more highly valued than females. The shortage of women resulting from female infanticide becomes a motivation for war as villages compete for women (Divale and Harris 1976).

The Yanomamo of Brazil.

Extreme intervillage Yanomamo violence may also have resulted from European contact, which caused severe depopulation as a result of European disease epidemics, fatal malnutrition, and intensified competition over European goods. Metal machetes, axes, and knives are very useful for horticulturalists, and the introduction of firearms substantially increased warfare fatalities. By the 1960s, Yanomamo increasingly settled around European outposts such as missionary stations to more easily acquire these goods, and this population concentration led to the depletion of game. The decline of the availability of meat undermined cultural norms of reciprocity, and this also increased conflict within and between villages. These historical factors complement other explanations of Yanomamo "fierceness" and raise questions about how fierce the Yanomamo actually are (Ferguson 1992).

▌▐ Chiefdoms

Although there is a great diversity among chiefdoms (Earle 1987), a chiefdom may be defined as "an autonomous political unit comprising a number of villages or communities under the permanent control of a paramount chief" (Carneiro 1981:45). Chiefdoms are different from tribes because, unlike tribes, in which all social segments are structurally and functionally similar, chiefdoms are made up of social parts that are structurally and functionally different from one another. Chiefdoms may be the first step in integrating villages as units within multilevel forms of political organization (Carneiro 1981).

Chiefdoms vary greatly in their social complexity (Peoples 1990), ranging from simpler tribal structures to those with elaborate systems of social stratification. They may consist of large settlements that function as administrative centers, surrounded by smaller villages. Each geographical unit within a chiefdom may also have its own chief or council. Chiefdoms, like tribes, are also organized through kinship; unlike tribes, however, chiefdoms have centralized leadership vested in the political office of the chief. Chiefs are born to the office and are often sustained in it by religious authority and genealogical records.

Chiefdoms are rank societies, generally based on highly productive horticulture or pastoralism (highly productive foragers on the northwest coast of North America are exceptions), which permit sufficient accumulation of food so that chiefs can appropriate surpluses to redistribute throughout the society. Redistribution is the main mode of exchange in rank societies, though balanced reciprocity is also important.

Anthropologists generally agree that the rise of chiefdoms is related to redistributive exchange and the ability to deploy labor. Goods are appropriated by the chief and then redistributed to the rest of society in feasts and rituals. Although redistribution is a primary support of the chief's power and prestige, chiefs may also control their communities by coercion or despotism (Earle 1987). Internal violence within chiefdoms is lower than in tribes because the chief has the authority to resolve conflict and punish deviant individuals.

Complex chiefdoms are characteristic of Polynesia. Tahitian society was divided into the ariki, or chiefly families and important lineages; the raatira, who were the heads of less important families and lineages; and the manahune, the rest of the population. Social rank in Tahiti had economic, political, and religious aspects. Mana, a spiritual power, was possessed by all people, but in different degrees depending on rank. The ariki had the most mana because they were closest to the ancestral gods who are the source of mana. Elaborate taboos separated those with more mana from those with less and also regulated social relations among the three ranks. Higher-ranked people could not eat with those of lower rank, and men, who ranked higher than women and children, could not eat with them. The highest-ranking ariki was so sacred that anything he touched became poison for those below him. In some Polynesian islands, the highest chief was kept completely away from other people and even used a special vocabulary that no one else was allowed to use.

Although a chief's authority is backed by his control of symbolic, supernatural, administrative, economic, and military power, violent competition for the office of chief does sometimes occur. Chiefdoms may also be rendered unstable if the burdens the chief imposes on the people greatly exceed the services they receive from him. Chiefs generally suppress any attempt at rebellion or threats from competitors and deal harshly with those who try to take their power. To emphasize the importance of this office for the society, offenses against a chief are often punished by death.

Chieftainships, like other forms of political structure, have significantly changed in the past 200 years, as a result of Western colonialism, wider participation in consumer economies, the spread of Christianity, and other aspects of globalization. These changes may build, however, on traditional structures and provide continuity. In the mid-19th century, the traditional Polynesian society of Tonga, for example, was a typically loose confederation of autonomous chiefdoms. Supported by British missionaries, however, an ambitious minor chief consolidated his power and became a King, founding a dynasty that continues to rule to this day (Besnier 2011).

State Societies

A state is a socially stratified, centralized form of political organization in which a central government has a legal monopoly over the use of force. Generally speaking, states are based on agriculture and industrialism, but some, like the Asante state, were based on horticulture. In states, law rather than kinship regulates social relations between the different social strata and defines a person's rights and duties. Units based on territory are central to state organization, and individuals belong to states by virtue of being born in a specific locale (or of parents from that locale), though states may also limit rights of residents. The state can incorporate a variety of political units, classes, and ethnic groups without disintegrating, making states more populous, heterogeneous, and powerful than any other kind of political organization.

Government: An interrelated set of status roles that become separate from other aspects of social organization, such as kinship, in exercising control over a population.

Bureaucracy: Administrative hierarchy characterized by specialization of function and fixed rules.

States are characterized by **government**, an interrelated set of status roles that become separate from other aspects of social organization, such as kinship. **Bureaucracy**, an administrative hierarchy characterized by specialization of function and fixed rules, is essential to state functioning. The administrative divisions of a state are territorial units, like cities or districts. Each unit has its own government specifically concerned with making and enforcing public policy, although these governments are not independent of the central government.

State organization helps maintain society in many ways. States use taxation to redistribute wealth. They may subsidize or penalize various sorts of production. States can order people to work on roads and buildings and to serve in armies, thus affecting the workforce available for other occupations. States protect the exchange and distribution of goods by making travel safe for traders as they move from one place to another, by keeping peace in the marketplace, and by backing contracts. The many economic, coordinating, and controlling functions of states, in peace and war, require extensive record keeping, which gave rise to writing and systems of weights and measures. Urbanization developed in states, where cities arose as administrative, religious, and economic centers. These centers then stimulated important cultural achievements in science, art, architecture, and philosophy.

A key characteristic of state societies is the government's monopoly over the use of force. Most modern states use a code of law to make clear how and when force will be used and forbid individuals or groups to use force except under its authorization. Laws (usually written) are passed by authorized legislative bodies and enforced by formal and specialized institutions. Courts and police forces have the authority to punish deviants through fines, confiscation of property, imprisonment, and even death. In practice, in authoritarian states, rulers may "become the law," implementing and enforcing laws that suit their own purposes. States frequently engage in warfare, which both increases and centralizes their power. Warfare enables states to extend the regulation of daily life, resolve internal conflict, and more stringently control information and communication channels.

Anthropologists explain the origin of the state in several ways. As historical and ecological situations change, a state may change its political structures, subdue a competing group, or establish regional dominance through trade. These initial shifts set off a chain reaction that may lead eventually to state formation. Ecological factors appear to have been dominant in the emergence of the Inca Empire in what is now Peru (Figure 7.3) (Carneiro 1970). In this area, independent, dispersed farming villages were confined to narrow valleys bounded by the sea, the desert, or mountains. As the population grew, villages split and populations dispersed until all the available land was used up. At this point, more intensive methods of agriculture were applied to land already being farmed, and previously unusable land was brought under cultivation by terracing and irrigation. As the population continued to increase, pressure for land intensified, resulting in war.

Because of the constraints of the environment, villages that lost wars had nowhere to go. To remain on their land, they had to accept a politically subordinate role. As more villages were defeated, the political organization of the area became more complex, and chiefdoms developed. The warring units were now larger, and as conquest of larger areas continued, centralization of authority increased. Finally, the entire area was brought under the control of one chief. The next step was the conquest of weaker valley chiefdoms by stronger ones until powerful empires emerged, most notably that of the Inca. States may also emerge out of violent rivalry

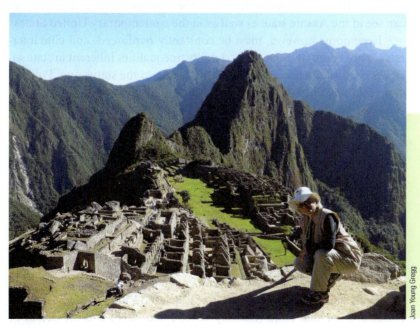

Figure 7.3 The rise of the state is a key event in human political organization. This photograph illustrates Machu Picchu, the center of the Inca Empire, which emerged as a result of specific ecological conditions. It was destroyed by the Spanish conquistadors and is now a global destination for archeologists, tourists and students.

Joan Young Gregg

between kinship groups, during which the winners become the rulers, leading to early state formation as perhaps occurred in Mesopotamia, China, and Mexico (Otterbein 2010). The rulers controlled the population by repressive sanctions and waged war through their control of elite military organizations. As war between mature states declined, these states may have waged defensive war against other, early state aggressors.

▊▊ The State and Social Stratification

Intensive cultivation enables a state's government to appropriate an economic surplus through taxation. This surplus supports the development of cities, economic and occupational specialization, and extensive trade. As specialized, non–food-producing elites emerge, economic and social inequalities become a key element in social structure. In state societies, unlike most chiefdoms, only a part of the surplus goes back to the people directly. The rest supports the activities of the state itself: maintaining administrative bureaucracies, standing armies, artists and craftworkers, and a priesthood, as well as supporting a ruling class in a luxurious lifestyle.

Hegemony: The dominance of a political elite based on a close identification between their own goals and those of the larger society.

With elites almost always a numerical minority, the question arises of how they manage to dominate. One means is through **hegemony** (Gramsci 1971), a process whereby the state succeeds in promoting elite values among ordinary people in the larger society (Durrenberger and Doukas 2008:214). Although primarily serving elite interests, hegemonic cultural ideologies explain the existing social order as benefitting the society as a whole, repressing the greater benefits to the elite, a process we can see in the Asante state as well as in the contemporary United States.

Hegemony, however, must be constantly reinforced, and elite interests cannot count on permanent stability; inequalities inherent in state societies continually pose substantial challenges to the status quo. Political and economic elites thus use many and varied economic, political, and symbolic means to ward off efforts to depose the government or to disrupt the privileges of vested interests. To the extent that elites provide reasonably effective protection of some basic economic and political rights, hegemony works to maintain the state, and the constant use of force may not be necessary. In all societies, perhaps especially in totalitarian and authoritarian states, it is always there in the background, however, as a potential instrument of social control (Nagengast 1994:116). Furthermore, states may control their populations by withholding the granting of citizenship to their residents; for example, the Burmese (Myanmar) refusal to grant citizenship to Muslim Rohingyas (Perlez 2014)), the penalties imposed by the Chinese government on families with a second child (which is against the "one child law") including the possible denial of citizenship for that child (Buckley 2015; Zhao 2016) and the denial of citizenship to the tens of thousands of Syrian children living as refugees outside Syria (Sengupta and Saad 2015). People denied citizenship may lose rights such as the right to vote, the right to enroll in school, the right to a driver's license, the right to remain in a country, and also a right to papers that would permit them to leave a country.

Anthropological theories of the rise of the state tend to emphasize either conflict (Fried 1967) or integration (Service 1971), though these are not mutually exclusive. Integration, or functional, theories emphasize the benefits of the state to its members: its ability to provide the stability needed for growth and technological development, protection of the rights of its citizens, effective mechanisms for the peaceful settlement of disputes, protection of trade and financial arrangements, defense against external enemies, and an ability to expand. Conflict theories emphasize the emergence of the state as centrally related to protecting the power and privileges of an elite class through management of political ideology, when necessary, and force.

▌▌▌ THE EMERGENCE OF THE NATION-STATE

Although empires are states that expand to incorporate a wide variety of ethnic groups and cultures, **nation-states** are governments and territories that are identified with (relatively) culturally homogeneous populations and national histories (see Figure 7.4). A nation is popularly felt

Nation-state: A sovereign, geographically based state that identifies itself as having a distinctive national culture and historical experience.

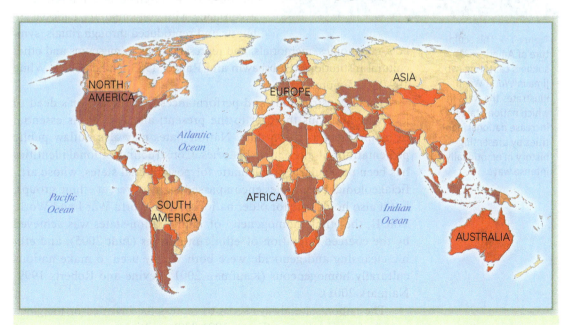

Figure 7.4 Contemporary world maps reinforce the importance of the nation-state as a territorial unit.

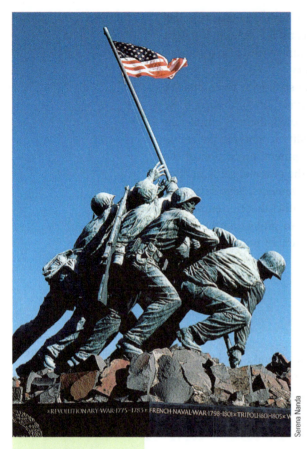

Serena Nanda

Figure 7.5 This sculpture of American soldiers capturing Iwo Jima in World War II illustrates the ways in which nation-states increase national identities by presenting history in emotionally intense ways.

by its members to be a natural entity based on bonds of common descent, language, culture, history, and territory. In fact, all modern nation-states are composed of many ethnic (and other) groups; Benedict Anderson (1991) calls nation-states "imagined communities," because an act of imagination is needed to weld the many disparate groups that actually make up the state into a coherent national community.

In addition to constructing national identities by drawing boundaries between spatially defined insiders and outsiders, nation-states are constructed by attaching people to time as well as to space. A common interpretation of the past is essential in creating national identities. As different groups within a nation may have different interpretations of its history, the creation of national histories often is marked by struggles over which version of history will prevail (Deák 2002; Friedman 1992). "Tradition," "the past," "history," and "social memory" all are actively invented and reinvented in accordance with contemporary national interests and reproduced through rituals, symbols, ceremonies, memorials, and representations in museums and other cultural institutions (Hobsbawm and Ranger 1983; Nanda 2004; White 1997) (see Figure 7.5).

These constructions and performances link the nation's dead to its living and thus the past to the present; all of which is essential to maintaining a nation-state. Nation-states may also outlaw public presentations of alternative histories. Constructing national identities has been particularly problematic for postcolonial states, whose artificial colonial boundaries encompassed many different ethnic groups, but it also holds true for older nations. After World War I and World War II, the ethnic homogeneity of many nation-states was achieved by the coerced migration of ethnic minorities (Judt 2005), and ethnic cleansing and genocide were both widely used to make nations culturally homogeneous (Kaufman 2001; Levine and Roberts 1999; Naimark 2001).

The nation-state always seeks to repress the invented or imagined nature of national unity (Foster 1991:238), and it has many sources of power in fostering some group identities and marginalizing or disparaging others. States use media, politics, educational institutions, and the law, among other things, to create a national culture and identity that becomes the only authorized representations of society and suppresses subcultural variations.

▌▌▌ The Nation-State and Ethnicity

Ethnicity, like nationality, is an imagined identity, which is based on the *perceived* "natural" ties—such as culture, religion, language, and national origin largely unchanged from generation to generation (Geertz 1973b:277)—by which groups of people distinguish themselves and are distinguished from others in the same social environment. Ethnic groups view themselves as sharing an ethnic identity that differentiates them from other groups or from the larger society as a whole. Ethnic boundaries are the claimed cultural attributes by which ethnic groups distinguish themselves from others. But although ethnicity does have cultural content, ethnic group identity is constructed: The perception that one belongs to a particular ethnic group and the emergence of particular ethnic groups and identities evolves from the *interaction* of a group with other groups and with the larger society, significantly shaped by competition and conflict over resources (Barth 1998/1969). This view of ethnicity leads anthropologists to ask questions about how ethnic groups and ethnic identities emerge, change, and disappear in responses to economic and social environments, especially as related to political and economic inequality (De Vos and Romanucci-Ross 1995).

The popular media often explain ethnic conflict and violence, including genocide, as natural eruptions of age-old ethnic and tribal hatreds and culture clashes between different groups within newly formed nation-states; a contemporary example is the violent civil war and clashes between the Nuer and the Dinka in the recently created nation of South Sudan (Gettleman 2016; Kristoff 2016). Anthropologist Sharon Hutchinson's title of her ethnography of the Nuer, *Nuer Dilemmas: Coping with Money, War, and the State* (1996), highlights how many ethnic and tribal conflicts may be better explained as contemporary struggles for political and economic power. Building on cultural and community differences, each tribe attempted to control the new state government (Gladstone and Cowell 2013). Tribal identities became ethnic identities in the new nation-state, in the competition for power and resources, like oil, violence and starvation became part of the attempt of the tribes to adapt to modern processes like money economies, shared political power, and the multicultural nature of the modern nation-state.

Ethnicity: Perceived differences in culture, national origin, and historical experience by which groups of people are distinguished from others in the same social environment.

◼◼▮ The Nation-State and Indigenous Peoples

Indigenous people: Small-scale societies designated as bands, tribes, or chiefdoms that occupied their land prior to European contact.

In much of the world today, particularly in North and South America and Australia, indigenous peoples are an important part of the multicultural landscape in nation-states. **Indigenous peoples** are those small-scale societies designated as bands, tribes, and chiefdoms that occupied their land prior to European contact. Generally, indigenous people are closely identified with their land, are relatively egalitarian, manage resources at the community level, and (previously) had high levels of economic self-sufficiency. They consider themselves distinct from other sectors of society now living in their territories and today function as nondominant sectors of the larger nation-states of which they are a part. Indigenous societies today are determined to preserve and transmit their lands and culture to future generations in order to continue their existence as a people, which frequently brings them into conflict with the nation-state (Lee 2000).

As a result of European expansion, especially to the New World, beginning in the 15th century, many indigenous societies completely disappeared, or survived only as remnants in marginal geographic areas (see Chapter 13). The destruction of indigenous peoples intensified rapidly by the mid-19th century as new frontiers were opened up in nations such as the United States, Australia, and Brazil. Although there was much resistance, indigenous peoples in most places were no match for the military and economic power of nation-states. After World War II, many indigenous peoples were incorporated into new postcolonial states, such as in Indonesia, Malaysia, and India, and few independent, self-sufficient indigenous societies remained (Maybury-Lewis 1997).

National policies of neglect or hostility toward indigenous peoples were often based on the expectation that indigenous peoples eventually would disappear as they were assimilated into national cultures and participated in national and global economic programs. International financial organizations, such as the World Bank and the International Monetary Fund—whose lending practices supported economic "development" programs that adversely affected the subsistence economies of indigenous peoples (Bodley 2000:378)—were also based on this assumption.

Policies of cultural assimilation, designed to foster a national identity, also contributed to the cultural loss among indigenous peoples, as in the United States. In many Central and South American societies, indigenous Indian cultures may not be totally repressed, but Indians may be identified with a fossilized past as a folkloric irrelevance, a tourist commodity, or a backward culture standing in the way of national development (Alonso 1994:398). Only a few nations have raised indigenous Indian ethnicity to a central place in national identity and political leadership, such as the election of Evo Morales as president of Bolivia in 2006 (Guillermoprieto 2006).

The incorporation of indigenous peoples into modern nation-states involved at least partial destruction of their political and economic autonomy. Because indigenous peoples must maintain control over their land base and subsistence resources to remain self-sufficient and politically autonomous, their political defeat was usually accompanied by their economic marginalization. Europeans—and others—appropriated their land; without their land base, indigenous peoples were forced into participation in the global market economy and forced to give up their traditional livelihoods or were pulled into national economies by their desire for Western goods. The colonial agenda was also imposed on indigenous peoples through the imposition and enforcement of Western law.

After World War II, the United Nations provided an international framework within which the concept of human rights and self-determination was expanded to include indigenous peoples. Because the United Nations policy worked within the framework of the nation-state, however, it did little to support indigenous rights in any substantial way. Some of this changed with the passage of the Declaration on the Rights of Indigenous Peoples in 2007, although several industrialized societies such as Canada, fearful of indigenous land claims, did not sign the declaration.

▮▮▮ USING ANTHROPOLOGY: ADVOCATING FOR THE CHAGOSSIANS

Forty years ago, 1,500 Chagossians, an indigenous group on the island of Diego Garcia, an island in the Indian Ocean, were forcibly removed from their homes when the island became a military base for the United States during the Cold War. Diego Garcia continues its military role today; it is used as a storehouse for military weaponry and was used as a takeoff point for American bombing of Iraq and Afghanistan during the Gulf War.

In the late 18th century, the French had created coconut plantations on these previously uninhabited islands, using imported slave and indentured laborers from Madagascar, Mozambique, and India. Called Ilois, these people created a distinct culture and society, almost totally isolated from the rest of the world. They constructed a viable subsistence economy based on vegetable gardens, fishing, chickens, and ducks, a life that provided security, with universal employment and free housing, education, pensions, and basic health care, as well as small salaries the plantation owners and the Mauritian government provided. Later, the French colonial government added schools, refuse removal, small dirt roads, and some modern technology like motorbikes, trucks, and tractors to the island.

The Chagossians of Diego Garcia.

In 1965, through secret arrangements, the American and British governments took complete military and political control of the islands, deciding that "the Chagossians must go." Government benefits began winding down, mail service was suspended, and hundreds of Chagossians found themselves stranded in Mauritius. "Life turned completely upside down," one Chagossian told anthropologist David Vine, "[we were] in the fire with our feet burning." Most Chagossians were sent to Mauritius, where they were promised compensation in the form of land, housing, employment, and money.

Vine's ethnography of the Chagossians, *Island of Shame* (2009), is based on archival research of British and American documents, fieldwork among the displaced Chagossians on Mauritius, and interviews with military and congressional representatives instrumental in the island's transformation. The Chagossians, as a displaced people, are entitled to compensation under United Nations laws protecting the rights of indigenous cultures. After their eviction, they formed the Chagos Refugees Group, which is waging an ongoing struggle both to receive just compensation and to return to their island; they seek, in fact, to work for the U.S. military, not to remove it. By 1997, the group had brought lawsuits against the British government and planned one against the United States.

Vine, along with several lawyers, documented the Chagossians' status as indigenous peoples, how they have been harmed as a result of their displacement, and what would be fair compensation as a result of their displacement. Vine's advocacy for the Chagossians is just one example of how anthropology makes a difference for indigenous peoples.

BRINGING IT BACK HOME:
DO GOOD FENCES MAKE GOOD NEIGHBORS?

State governments view a fixed and secure border as essential to sovereignty and national security (see Figure 7.6), with a corresponding right and responsibility to control immigration. This is an increasingly contentious issue in contemporary society, where migration has expanded enormously, as a result of economic inequalities and extreme violence, often within states themselves. In the United States, immigration debates importantly center around the Mexican border, which has become highly militarized in an effort to keep out undocumented migrants.

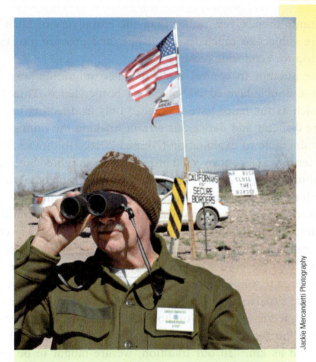

Jackie Mercandetti Photography

Figure 7.6 Protecting borders is an urgent concern for nation-states as they try to hold back undocumented immigrants who are increasingly crossing borders for economic and political purposes.

The need for strong border controls in the United States has been justified by the need to protect the domestic labor market, to protect the nation from terrorism, to prevent undocumented immigrants from entering the country, and to restrain criminal activity, such as human smuggling or the importation of illegal guns and drugs. In spite of fencing, lighting, the use of infrared scopes, underground sensors, increased law enforcement, and vigilante groups, hundreds of thousands of undocumented Mexicans and more recently, immigrants from Central America, many of them children, who cross the border to escape from the extreme gang violence in their home countries such as Guatemala, El Salvador, and Honduras are attempting to enter the United States (Bacon 2014; Nazario 2014). To some extent the United States itself is partly responsible for this violence, as it endorsed public policies that led to the hollowing out of Central American states by supporting oppressive dictators (Holtzman 2016; Martinez 2014). Although the debate over undocumented immigration generates much heat, most of it is aimed at the undocumented immigrants themselves, rather than the employers of such workers who are subject to much less vigilance, and provide motivation for migration for economic reasons.

One attempt to control undocumented migration was the erection of a double-layered 700-mile-long border fence. Thus far, measures such as the fence have succeeded only in directing immigration to more difficult and dangerous terrain, making the immigrants even more vulnerable to exploitation (Ahmed 2016; Holthouse 2005). The border fence was a controversial project that highlighted both economic and cultural clashes in the American Southwest, including undermining the long-term cultural adaptation of Mexican immigrants in border cities, such as Laredo, Texas (Cave 2014), and the opposition of the Tohono O'odham Native Americans whose reservation was closed off by the wall near Tucson, Arizona. The Tohono O'odham claim a need to freely cross the border to visit friends and relatives in Mexico, take their children to school, gather traditional foods, and visit religious sites to perform rituals, all of which they have been doing for years. Their cultural concerns also focus on how the wall restricts the free range of deer, wild horses, coyotes, jackrabbits, and other animals they revere and regard as kin. "In our tradition, we are taught to be concerned about every living thing as if they were people. We don't want that wall," said one tribal council member.

The Tohono O'odham cooperate extensively with the U.S. border patrol and the Department of Homeland Security in patrolling the border. Because the federal government is the trustee of all Indian lands, it could build the fence through the reservation without tribal permission, but that would jeopardize the valuable help the Tohono O'odham now gives the government (Archibold 2006).

YOU DECIDE:

1. Do you think human movement between states should be free and unrestricted? Why or why not? If you believe that there should be restriction of immigration to the United States, what criteria would you use for admitting immigrants?

2. What kinds of solutions would you suggest to the problem of undocumented immigration? Do you think that border fences and walls make a substantial contribution in addressing this problem? Why or why not?

3. Decisions made by states often pit groups in society against each other. In this case, do you think the need to prevent undocumented immigrants crossing the border justifies overriding the cultural

values of the Tohono O'odham? How would you mediate the conflict between the U.S. government and the Tohono O'odham over fencing off the border on their reservation?

CHAPTER SUMMARY

1. How does political organization relate to power? Anthropologists try to understand political organization by focusing on power: Who has it? What are its sources? How is it related to other aspects of culture, especially political ideology? And how is it used in achieving public goals?

2. How is social control maintained in different kinds of societies? In all societies, social control is effected through formal sanctions such as exile, death, and punishments meted out by courts, judges, police, and other institutionalized forms of regulation. Conformity is also achieved through informal means such as gossip, ridicule, and ostracism.

3. What is the relationship between political organization and social differentiation? Political organization is closely related to social differentiation, which is in turn related to the dominant pattern of making a living and exchanging goods and services. Band societies, which are characteristic of foragers, are egalitarian and dominated by generalized reciprocity.

4. What are the main characteristics of tribal societies? Tribal societies, found among pastoralists and horticulturalists, also tend to be egalitarian and operate through generalized reciprocity as well as balanced reciprocity. Though tribal societies have many different nonviolent means of resolving conflicts within the society, they also have a high degree of warfare.

5. What are the main characteristics of chiefdoms? Chiefdoms, which are found in highly productive horticultural societies and among pastoralists, are called rank societies. Though kinship integrates the society, social units are socially ranked, and social position may be inherited. The chief is a central office, supported by his position as one who redistributes goods within the society.

6. What are the main characteristics of state societies? The most complex form of political organization is the state; it is found mainly in agricultural and industrial societies and is associated with social stratification. Social, political, and economic inequality are institutionalized and maintained through a combination of internalized controls (hegemony) and force. Kinship ties between the upper and

lower classes no longer serve to integrate the society, and there is a wide gap in standards of living.

7. What are the main characteristics of a nation-state, and what role does ethnicity play in the construction of nationalism? The nation-state is a state that identifies itself with a culturally homogeneous group and a shared history and geographic territory, and uses various social and cultural institutions to foster nationalism. Many nation-states are in fact multicultural, incorporating ethnic groups who also define themselves as culturally homogeneous. Sometimes ethnic conflict occurs between various ethnic groups within a nation or between ethnic groups and the nation itself.

8. What are indigenous groups and how do they relate to the construction of nation-states? Many nation-states today incorporate indigenous peoples, whose cultures, economies, and social institutions are constrained by the need to live within these complex societies and their regulatory systems.

9. How are national borders implicated in contemporary political issues? With the large numbers of migrants crossing borders, many borders are now militantly policed and guarded by walls or fences, both of which often promote protests and violent conflict.

KEY TERMS

Authority	Mediation
Bureaucracy	Nation-state
Band	Political ideology
Chiefdom	Political organization
Egalitarian society	Power
Elites	Rank society
Ethnicity	Rebellion
Factions	Revolution
Government	Social differentiation
Hegemony	State
Indigenous people	Stratified society
Law	Tribe
Leadership	War (warfare)

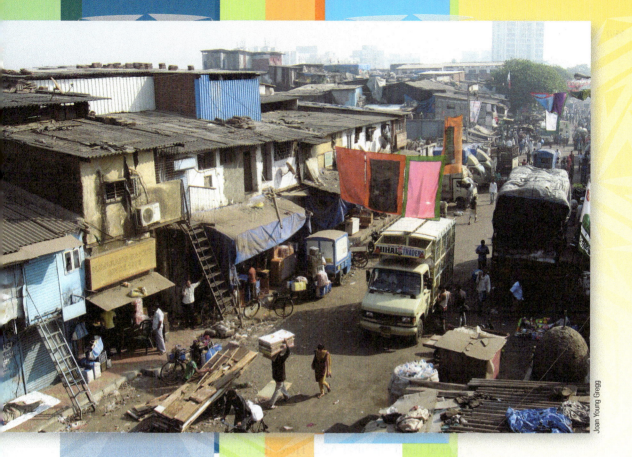

Joan Young Gregg

Dharavi Slum in Mumbai, India, is typical of urban slums in all parts of the underdeveloped world. Like many slum dwellers, most of the inhabitants are rural migrants, struggling to survive, depending on their children to help contribute to their meager income, which is hardly sufficient to feed the family. A widespread indication of universal social stratification is that these urban slums are often invisible to the upper classes and the elites.

8

STRATIFICATION: CLASS, CASTE, RACE, AND ETHNICITY

AFTER YOU HAVE READ THIS CHAPTER, YOU WILL BE ABLE TO:

△ Describe global and local aspects of social stratification and economic inequality.

△ Summarize the strengths and weaknesses of the functionalist and conflict analyses of inequality.

△ Discuss the relationship between wealth, power, and prestige.

△ Explain the differences between a class and a caste system, giving examples of each.

△ Analyze the ideal and the realities of the social class system in the United States.

△ Explain the intersection of race and class in the United States with examples.

△ Compare the construct of race in the United States with that in Brazil.

△ Describe the American immigration narrative and how it relates to social stratification in the United States.

WEALTH AND POVERTY: GLOBAL PERSPECTIVES

E CONOMIC inequality is a global phenomenon and is also central to the culture and society of the United States. Consider, for example, a middle-class family in North America: the four family members have a combined income of more than $50,000; they live in a comfortable home or apartment and have one or two cars. Each child has a separate bedroom. The family's many consumer goods are mostly manufactured outside North America. They eat three meals a day, and much of their diet is based on imported foods. The children are healthy and attend a good school, which will prepare them for college and allow them to choose among a variety of professional careers. On average they will live to be around 80 years old. This middle-class family faces increasing problems, however. Strong competitive pressures for both parents at work and for the children at school, rising medical costs, annually increasing college tuition, economic recession leading to job layoffs and insecurity, increasing debt, and fear of losing their homes threaten their way of life, and many people are pessimistic about the future. Still, millions of people throughout the world are aspiring to this family's lifestyle and economic status.

We can understand these aspirations by comparing this family with a typical family in rural Asia. Here, the household averages ten or more people, including parents, children, and other relatives, and has a combined annual income of less than $500. The family lives in a one-room house, working as tenant farmers on a large agricultural estate owned by an absentee landlord. The adults and older children work all day on the land. None of the adults can read or write. Only two of the five school-age children regularly attend school, and they will get only a basic primary education. The family often eats only one meal a day, which rarely changes and leaves the children hungry. The house has no electricity or fresh water supply. There is much illness but very few medical practitioners. The work is hard, the sun is hot, and the aspirations for a better life are continually being snuffed out (Todaro and Smith 2003).

This extreme poverty drives many of these peasants to look for better opportunities in cities, but while opportunities may improve somewhat, life in urban slums, like Dharavi, in India, pictured in the chapter opener, is also very difficult. To a great extent the family's survival depends on their children's economic contributions (Boo 2012). While most of us would agree that children should be "protected from economic exploitation and from performing any work that is likely to be hazardous or to interfere with the child's education, or to be harmful to . . . [their] development," as stated in the United Nations charter on the rights of children, in fact, perhaps as many as a billion children worldwide live in just these conditions. Over 100 million of these children live on the streets, though they are largely invisible to people from richer countries in the West and to the well-off residents in their own nations.

⁣⁣⁣ EXPLAINING SOCIAL STRATIFICATION

Social stratification results from unequal access to the goods and services in state societies. No state has ever successfully organized a large and diverse population without stratification and economic inequalities.

Two major explanations of social stratification are functional and conflict theories. **Functionalism** holds that social stratification generally benefits the whole society, by rewarding people socially and economically for working harder, taking risks, doing difficult jobs, or spending more time in school or occupational training. Medical doctors, for example, whose work is essential to society, are rewarded for their long years in school by both high income and high prestige.

Although functionalism explains some aspects of contemporary social stratification, it does not explain everything; sanitation workers are essential for society but not among the most highly rewarded. Nor does social stratification necessarily result in the most qualified people getting the most demanding or elite positions in society. In addition, though getting rich is a powerful motivator, other considerations also count in people's life choices. And even in the most open class systems, resentment of economic and social inequality may eventually explode into open conflict and even violence, especially when the inequality is based on factors that an individual is born with and cannot change, such as family background, social connections, gender, ethnicity, race, and inherited wealth (Berreman 1988; Stiglitz 2012).

In contrast to functionalism, **conflict theory** holds that social stratification results from the constant struggle for scarce goods and services in all stratified societies. Inequalities exist because the elites use their wealth, power, and prestige to control the system of production and the apparatus of the state. When political ideologies falter and elite dominance is challenged, elites may fall back on the threat or use of force to maintain the status quo. Conflict and change are thus inherent in systems of social stratification.

Conflict theory is associated with Karl Marx and his followers, who focus on the economic aspect of social stratification. For Marxists, the relationship of individuals to the means of production is critical in

Social stratification: A social hierarchy resulting from the relatively permanent unequal distribution of goods and services in a society.

Functionalism (functionalist perspective): A theoretical position in anthropology that focuses on finding general laws that identify different elements of society, showing how they relate to each other, and demonstrating their role in maintaining social order.

Conflict theory: A perspective on social stratification that focuses on economic inequality as a source of conflict and change.

determining their power and prestige. Marx differentiated two main social classes in capitalist society: the capitalists, who own the means of production, and the workers, who must sell their labor to survive. Marx predicted that the inherent conflict between the workers and the owners of the means of production would eventually lead to capitalism's downfall. Although Marxist predictions have not been fully realized, conflict theory is useful in explaining some aspects of social stratification. However, just as functional theorists may ignore structural conflict, conflict theorists may sometimes ignore the solidarity across class, caste, racial, ethnic, and gender lines, which also bring about change.

▆▍▎ Criteria of Stratification: Power, Wealth, and Prestige

Power: The ability to impose one's will on others.

All social stratification systems depend on the complex interaction of the three main dimensions of stratification: power, wealth, and prestige. Anthropologists analyze **power** by examining its sources, the channels through which it is exercised, and the goals it is deployed to achieve. For example, in the United States, we might analyze the different sources, uses, and goals of power among corporate CEOs, elected public officials, entertainment celebrities, heads of organized crime families, or information technology entrepreneurs. Cross-culturally, we might compare the sources, uses, and goals of power among an American president, the prime minister in a parliamentary system of government such as France, the chairman of the Communist Party in the People's Republic of China, the Ayatollah (Supreme Leader) in the Islamic Republic of Iran, or the King of Jordan.

Wealth: The accumulation of material resources or access to the means of producing these resources.

Wealth is the accumulation of material resources or access to the means of producing these resources. Although wealth is not the sole criterion of social status even in capitalist societies, it can eventually translate into high social position and power. Wealth enables people to send their children to the most prestigious schools, buy homes in the best residential locations, and join the right social clubs. It enables access to political power through large campaign contributions to politicians or permits people to run for political office themselves.

Prestige: Social honor or respect.

The bases of **prestige**, or social honor, vary cross-culturally. Prestige may be based on race and ethnicity, income, accumulated wealth, power, personal characteristics such as integrity or charisma, family history, and/or the display of material goods. Not all wealth is equally a source of prestige; illegally earned incomes generally carry less prestige than legitimate enterprises. Compare the prestige, for example, between a drug czar making billions of dollars and winners of Nobel Prizes, or between political leaders who live in highly publicized luxury with leaders like

Mahatma Gandhi of India or Nelson Mandela of South Africa, who led austerely simple lives or who languished in prison for decades.

Occupation is a key source of prestige in all societies, both for its relation to income and for the cultural values attached to it, though different societies rank occupations differently (see the section on the Hindu caste system below). Cultural rankings of occupations may change over time. In 18th-century Europe, surgery was a lower-class occupation performed by barbers; in contemporary North America, surgeons rank very high in prestige because of their very high income, their prodigious skills and training, and their importance to society's health.

In China, the evaluation of occupations has changed radically. Before the Communist revolution, a Confucian value system dominated and scholars had the highest prestige. After the revolution, workers were honored and scholars often explicitly ridiculed and despised. Today, with China's increasing economic role in globalization, free-market enterprises are now valued, and businesspeople, previously a target of socialist contempt and even violence, are highly regarded, or at least highly rewarded financially. As a result, a large and growing middle class has emerged, but inequality has also increased, particularly between rural and urban areas. Even as the new economy has benefited the Chinese in general, millions of urban migrants remain poverty-stricken and exploited; this suggests that rapidly increased prosperity tends to result in increased class stratification (Wong 2008).

There has long been a debate over whether prestige or economic factors are most important in explaining behavior and identity in stratified societies. In contrast to Marx's argument for the primacy of economic or class interests, Max Weber, a late 19th-century German sociologist, argued for the dominance of social status, dress, speech, and other external behavior patterns; indeed, it is sometimes argued that anxiety about social status is the animating force in modern societies. Weber argued that even political action can be motivated by a group's desire to defend its social position, sometimes in opposition to its economic self-interest, a position Marx called "false consciousness." For example, in the American South, whites were more committed to the prestige based on their white racial identity than in joining with blacks to improve their economic conditions.

CLASS SYSTEMS

Two main types of social stratification systems are "open class systems," in which social position is based on **achieved status**, that is, a person's individual efforts, and "closed class systems," where social position is based on **ascribed status**, or birth, using criteria such as race, ethnicity,

Achieved status: A social position that a person chooses or achieves on his or her own.

Ascribed status: A social position into which a person is born.

Class: A category of people who all have about the same opportunity to obtain economic resources, power, and prestige and who are ranked relative to other categories.
Class system: A form of social stratification in which the different strata form a continuum and social mobility is possible.
Social mobility: Movement from one social stratum to another.

family heritage, or biological sex. In fact, in modern complex societies, both achievement and ascription play a role in the social stratification system, though to different degrees.

A **class** is a category of people who generally share similar economic resources, power, and prestige and who are ranked in relation to other class categories. A **class system** has possibilities for **social mobility**, or movement between the classes that is (ideally) based on individual achievement rather than on ascribed status. Even in the most open class systems, however, ascribed statuses always play a role in moving from one class to another. Closed stratification systems, or caste systems, in which there is little or no possibility of social mobility, are discussed later.

The American Class System

The nature of class in the United States is hotly debated. Some analysts insist that the United States is a society without classes. In fact, the sociologist Paul Blumberg (1980) called the notion that the United States is a class-based society "America's forbidden thought." At the same time, American ideology praises social mobility, and links it closely to The American Dream, the idea that a person can move from one class to another through education, hard work, self-reliance, and taking risks. America has also understood itself as a middle class nation. In a 2015 Gallup poll, 51 percent of Americans said they were members of the middle or upper middle class. Although this number is down from earlier surveys, it still represents the majority of Americans. Thirty-three percent of Americans say they are working class, and only 15 percent lower class (Newport 2015b).

Class differences in America are strongly reflected in differences in lifestyle, occupational roles, values, social affiliations, leisure activities, religious beliefs, and political views (see Table 8.1). Many of these are directly related to residential segregation. Members of the wealthier classes are able to live in neighborhoods that have good access to excellent schools, grocery stores that carry high-quality foods, hospitals, professional facilities, and opportunities for leisure such as health clubs and parks. The poor, on the other hand, often live in neighborhoods where the schools are failing, where good-quality grocery stores are so rare that these neighborhoods are sometimes called "food deserts," and where access to medical care and places for leisure-time activities are scarce. Poor neighborhoods and poor cities are also often subject to the worst effects of environmental pollution. A 2012 study by Michelle Bell and Keita Ebisu showed that in the United States, hazardous air pollution was worst in non-white low income communities. In 2015, the water supply in Flint Michigan, one of the nation's poorest cities (Kennedy 2016), was

Table 8.1 U.S. Class Structure

Class	Annual Income	Education	Occupation	Approx. %
Privileged Classes				
Capitalist	$1,000,000 +	Prestigious universities	CEOs, investors, heirs	1
Upper-middle	$100,000 +	Top colleges/ postgraduate	Upper managers, professionals	14
Majority Classes				
Middle	$55,000	High school/some college	Lower managers, teachers, civil servants	30
Working class	$35,000	High school	Clerical, sales, factory	30
Lower Classes				
Working poor	$22,000	Some high school	Service jobs, laborers	13
Underclass	$10,000 or less	Some high school	Unemployed	12

Adapted from Gilbert (2011:244).

shown to be contaminated with lead. Lead poisoning particularly affects children, leading to developmental delays and learning disabilities and numerous other problems. Thus, Flint's future is likely to be blighted.

The historical phenomenon of social mobility has been very real for at least some Americans. Particularly in the 19th and 20th centuries, millions of deeply impoverished people, mostly from southern and eastern Europe came to America. The descendants of these immigrants make up the majority of today's middle, upper middle, and upper class. They are some of the world's wealthiest people.

The promise of social mobility through education and hard work continues to draw immigrants and inspire their children. Consider the case of Gloria Castillo. In 2006, Castillo, 22, a child of undocumented immigrants, was married, with two children, and living in a tough neighborhood in Dallas, Texas. She worked the night shift at a fast-food chain store, 10:30 p.m. to 6:30 a.m., for $252 a week before taxes, and received no health care benefits. To help make ends meet, she worked a second job, earning $150 a night for the hour and a half it took her to clean three bathrooms in a local bar. Her husband worked at an auto parts shop during the day, so Gloria took the children, age 7 and 8, for a fast-food breakfast before dropping them at school, returned home, slept until 2 p.m., picked up the kids, prepared their frozen-food dinners, put them to bed at 7 p.m., spent a few hours with her husband, and left for work. On Saturdays she attended a community college, working toward a degree as a paralegal. "I got dreams," she said (LeDuff 2006).

It is important to remember, however, that mobility in the United States has always been significantly correlated with race, ethnicity, gender, and class (DeParle 2012a). Throughout much of American history, African Americans and Latinos were systematically denied pathways for social mobility. Sometimes this was directly coded into law (e.g., the Jim Crow laws prevalent throughout the first half of the 20th century in many Southern States). At other times it was more informal (e.g., the refusal of banks to make loans to people of color).

In addition to inequality of opportunity, the American class system faces challenges from the persistence of deep poverty, the stagnation and decline in wages for many jobs, particularly those available to people without education, increasing inequality, and relatively low possibilities for social mobility (see Figure 8.1).

Extreme poverty, which affects millions of Americans in places ranging from Appalachia to Indian reservations to the Florida tomato fields and to inner cities, has been a constant part of American life and has increased in recent years (Hedges and Sacco 2012). In many places in America, jobs of any kind, let alone well-paying jobs, are almost impossible to find. Consider the case of "Evie" a 40-year-old African American woman interviewed by Serena Nanda in 2014. Evie lived with her grandchild near Lake Okeechobee, just 50 miles West of Palm Beach Florida, one of America's wealthiest communities. When Nanda asked her what people in her community do, she replied, "Folks don't do anything out here. There are no jobs; all the young people leave and I don't blame them.

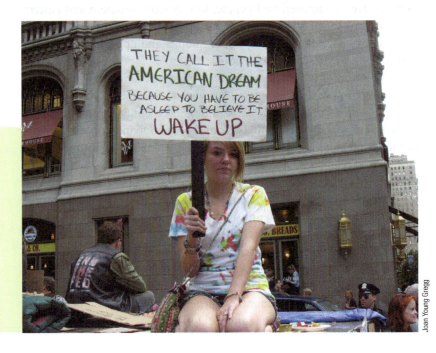

Figure 8.1 Occupy Wall Street, a resistance movement in 2011 and 2012 raised important questions about social mobility and the concentration of wealth and power in the US. The movement spread across the world. Anthropologist David Graeber played an important role as a spokesperson for the movement.

Joan Young Gregg

The sugar is all done by machines now, no jobs at all, folks fish here so they can eat." Evie told Nanda that she used to work in Palm Beach, but quit her job. Between low wages, high expenses for gas and car maintenance, as well as police harassment, it just wasn't worth it (Nanda 2014).

Problems of American poverty have been augmented by both the decline of manufacturing jobs and the Great Recession of 2007–2009. There has been substantial economic recovery since the depths of that recession, and in February 2016 the official government unemployment rate stood at 4.9 percent, lower than its historical average between 1947 and 2015 (U.S. Bureau of Labor Statistics 2016). However, this low unemployment rate camouflages the fact that many people earn far less than they did before the recession and have slim hopes for high-paying jobs. In 2007, David Loechner earned $65,000 a year managing a truck rental company, and his wife earned $24,000 working two part-time jobs. They lived in a $1,000-a-month furnished apartment and thought of themselves as solid, middle-class citizens. When the Great Recession hit, Loechner lost his job, and it took over a year to find another—working as a janitor in a supermarket, earning $8.60 an hour. His wife became too depressed to work. The Loechners eat a lot of soup, and shop online at free thrift sites. "We're no longer middle class," Brenda says (Brubaker 2012).

At the same time that middle-class jobs disappeared, inequality sky-rocketed. Between the end of the 1940s and the early 1970s, incomes grew at about the same pace for all members of American society. However, beginning in the 1970s, the wealth for America's richest began to increase more rapidly than that for others. Between 1979 and 2011, the after-tax income of the poorest 20 percent of the population increased by 48 percent, but the after-tax income of the wealthiest quadrupled (see Table 8.2)

Table 8.2 Total Net Worth of U.S. Households, 2007

Share of Wealth Held By	Percentage
Top 1 percent	34.6
Next 4 percent	27.3
Next 5 percent	11.2
Next 10 percent	12.0
Highest quintile combined	85.0
Fourth quintile	10.9
Third quintile	4.0
Lowest two quintiles combined	0.2

From Wolff 2010 (p. 44).

(Stone et al. 2015). According to a Pew Center report, in 1983, upper-income families had three times as much wealth as middle-income families. By 2013, they had seven times as much wealth. The Pew report notes that the Great Recession had by far the harshest effect on the poorest people, who lost, on average, 41 percent of their wealth while the wealthiest lost only 17 percent (Pew Research Center 2015b). The wealth of the richest Americans is truly astonishing. The wealth of America's 20 richest people is the same as the combined wealth of the poorest half of the nation (Collins and Hoxie 2015). Because money buys access to power, the extremely wealthy are often able to pressure lawmakers to enact policies that increase their wealth still further.

Finally, the effects of inequality are worsened by the relative lack of social mobility in America. Although people certainly do change social classes, the odds of achieving wealth are heavily biased by the families of their births. For example, a child born into a family with an income in the poorest 20 percent of the nation has less than a 1 in 12 chance of making it into the wealthiest 20 percent of Americans, compared with a 1 in 3 chance of remaining where she or he started. Conversely, a child born into a family from the wealthiest 20 percent of the nation has better than a 1 in 3 chance of remaining there (Chetty et al. 2014). Americans often think their country has a high rate of social mobility as compared with others. However, numerous studies have shown both that Americans overestimate how much mobility there is in the United States and that the United States has less social mobility than most other wealthy nations, particularly Western European nations and Canada (DeParle 2012a).

Using Anthropology: Homelessness and Social Activism

Having a livable home, central to the American Dream, also differs among social classes. The maintenance of one's home is a critical issue for poor urban residents, most of whom live in rental apartments, often owned by exploitative or uncaring landlords. Many poor urban renters have no understanding of how to achieve their legal rights to have their apartments maintained by their landlords, who have much greater access to the legal system. Some local urban governments are trying different approaches to this problem using the latest information technology, hiring tech-savvy college graduates to increase the chances of success for poor people in housing courts. In New York City, for example, Dan Kass, an IT graduate from a prestigious college developed a mobile app, JustFix.nyc, which provides practical information for urban tenants on how to use housing courts to achieve justice against negligent landlords who don't make their legally required repairs (Soria 2015).

One critical aspect of the economic downturn and housing crises in both urban and rural America is the huge increase in homelessness (Desmond 2016; Johnson 2016; Senior 2014). Almost 50 years ago, anthropologist Elliot Liebow's ethnography on "street corner men" in Washington, D.C., made homelessness, largely ignored by the media, visible (1967). But contemporary engaged cultural anthropologists go further: according to Vincent Lyon-Callo (2004), engaging in political action must accompany educating the public in order to change the lives of homeless people. Lyon-Callo rejects the American view that the problem of homelessness in the United States can best be solved by a free capitalist market, private initiative, and a "social services" orientation, which aim at reforming homeless people themselves. This orientation obscures the importance of unemployment, declining wages, the exploitation of workers, the power of landlords, and the lack of affordable housing, as the root of homelessness. For Lyon-Callo, promoting political and social change is slow and discouraging work, but it is a necessary beginning. Working in collaboration with community members and homeless people in Northampton, Massachusetts, Lyon-Callo helped create a winter cot program in community churches, a living-wage campaign, and new job opportunities for homeless people, efforts that helped improve "life on the ground" for homeless people in this one small American community.

▌▌▌ CASTE

In contrast to open class systems, a **caste system** is based on birth, or ascribed status. Individual movement between castes or marriage between individuals from different castes is theoretically not possible. Castes are socially ranked and characteristically associated with traditional occupations, which carry different degrees of purity or spiritual pollution and may exhibit subcultural differences. A caste system, then, consists of ranked, culturally distinct, interdependent, endogamous groups, with rigidly maintained boundaries between the castes. Castelike systems exist in several cultures, but caste is mainly identified with India, where it is deeply culturally and historically embedded and plays a central role in social stratification.

Caste system: Social stratification based on birth in which social mobility between castes is not possible.

▌▌▌ The Caste System in India

The Indian caste system is unique in its complexity, its relation to Hindu religious beliefs and rituals, and the degree to which the castes (or, more accurately, subcastes) are cohesive and self-regulating groups. The four main castes (*varnas*), ranked according to the ritual purity of their

India.

traditional occupations, are the Brahmins, who are priests and scholars; the Kshatriyas, who are rulers and warriors; the Vaisyas, or merchants; and the Shudras, or menial workers and artisans. Below these four varnas is a fifth group, previously called untouchables, now called Dalits, who perform spiritually polluting work such as cleaning latrines or tanning leather. Traditionally, the mere touch, or even shadow, of a Dalit, contaminated higher caste purity (hence the term, untouchables).

Caste boundaries are maintained by rules against intercaste marriage, eating together, and spatial segregation: Traditionally, the lowest castes in Indian villages were prohibited from using high-caste wells and temples. In its rural setting, the caste system involved traditional exchanges of goods and services between higher and lower castes. Families of artisan and serving castes—carpenters, potters, blacksmiths, water carriers, and leather workers—performed services for high-caste landowning families, and in return received, among other things, grain, clothing, animal fodder, animal products, or small amounts of cash. These relationships, which continued over several generations, were viewed by the higher castes as the benefits of the caste system: Landowners gained a steady supply of available workers while the serving castes gained a relatively reliable source of subsistence. The lower castes, however, viewed themselves as exploited; these different perceptions are examples of the ongoing debate over functional versus conflict explanations of social stratification.

Although Indian castes are ranked on the basis of prestige rather than wealth, higher castes benefit materially—and politically—as well as symbolically from their higher status. They use their considerable political power to maintain these material benefits and resist any efforts at lower castes' attempts to change the system. Although the lower castes *appear* to accept their position, their conformity often hinges on their awareness that economic sanctions and physical force often results from resistance; indeed, violent intercaste conflict occurs frequently in rural India. Traditional Hindu religious belief holds that individuals occupy their social position based on the virtue of their actions in a previous life, a convenient justification for elite caste hegemony, which functions like the dominant American ideology that holds that one's class status is a result only of individual effort.

▮▮▮ CHANGES IN THE CASTE SYSTEM

The caste system in India, like any social stratification system, continues to change. When India became independent of British rule, untouchability was outlawed and affirmative action programs in education and government jobs for lower castes, tribal peoples, and untouchables were incorporated into the constitution, a process that generates political conflicts, much as affirmative action does in the United States. A low caste may also try to raise its social position by requiring its members to follow the rules and rituals of higher castes and constructing a new story of high-caste origin for itself. Dr. B. R. Ambedkar, a follower of Mahatma Gandhi, urged those of lower caste to convert to Buddhism, to put them outside the caste system altogether.

Today, partly as a result of increasing differentiation of wealth and power *within* castes, caste ranking appears less sharply defined than formerly, in both rural and urban areas, and especially among those in higher castes. In cities and in public spaces, caste boundaries such as interdining have also weakened, though many caste-related boundaries, particularly regarding marriage, remain in intimate settings and rural areas. The traditional connection between caste and occupation is also weakening, as new occupations, such as factory work and information technology, which are not caste-related, open up opportunities for those in both lower and middle castes (Kapur 2012) (see Figure 8.2). Even people who live in slums have improved their lives through such occupations as recycling trash (Boo 2012). Still, people in higher castes continue to be the primary beneficiaries of India's recent economic growth, through their previous accumulation of capital, their higher education, their business and social contacts, and their ability to speak English.

Figure 8.2 Sonu, a low-caste village woman moved to the city for better economic opportunities and now works as a maid for an upper-class family. Here she proudly poses in her best sari, in front of her flat-screen television set.

Courtesy of Serena Nanda

⦙⦙⦙ RACE: A CULTURAL CONSTRUCT

When traveling in Malaysia, Nanda asked a friend to explain this exceptionally diverse society. He began by saying, "The Indians are the black people," referring to the dark skin color of the Indians in Malaysia who are mainly from South India. Joking with him a little, Nanda asked, "If the Indians are the black people, who are the white people?" "Oh," he answered, without missing a beat, "the Portuguese used to be the white people but now the Chinese are the white people."

This conversation makes sense in terms of Malaysia's economic history, where its main ethnic groups—the Chinese, Indians, indigenous Malays, and the small population of Portuguese descended from 16th-century traders who politically dominated Malay society for 100 years—occupied different economic niches. The Portuguese were later defeated by the British, who colonized Malaysia (then called Malaya) and replaced the Portuguese in the most important political and economic positions. After Malaysia's independence, the British left, and the Chinese moved into many commercial and professional positions and now dominate the Malaysian economy. Having taken over the economic position formerly occupied by the Portuguese and then the British, the Chinese are now defined as having taken over their racial category as well.

Race: A culturally constructed category based on *perceived* physical differences.

The term **race** is used to define people based on *perceived* physical differences that imply hereditary differences. Anthropologists emphasize that race is not a natural category, but is rather a significant cultural and social factor used to justify differential treatment of people based on appearance and presumed ancestry. Even in the absence of physical differences among groups of people, class, ethnicity, and caste are often conceptualized in racial terms. The 19th-century English theologian Charles Kingsley described the Irish as "human chimpanzees . . . a race of utter savages, truly barbarous and brutish," noting unhappily, that "[their] skins are as white as ours" (in Curtis 1968:84). The British used the idea of a "degenerate Irish race" to justify their control over Ireland, just as people in the United States used racist stereotypes of Africans to justify slavery.

Conceptualizing group differences as "racial" implies differences in culture, character, morality, intelligence, personality, and purity that are seen as natural, inherited, and unalterable, in a word, ascribed. Differences in outward physical appearance make it easier to distinguish "races" socially, but as the English perceptions of the Irish indicate, a lack of observable physical differences does not prohibit the implementation of racial stratification.

▌▌▌ Racial Classification in Brazil

In much of Brazil, as in the American South, a plantation system whose core was African slave labor formed an important part of the economy, especially in the Northeast. After 1888, when Brazil abolished slavery, the government attempted to "whiten" its population by implementing policies encouraging European immigration and teaching only Euro-Brazilian history and culture. At the same time, however, unlike the United States, where interracial marriages were outlawed in many states, racial distinctions and racial discrimination in Brazil were not encoded in law, and interracial marriage and sexual relations were common (Goldstein 1999; Sheriff 2001).

In contemporary Brazil, individuals of African descent account for about 45 percent of the total population, yet only about 15 percent of these people identify themselves as *preta* (black) in the census. The rest mainly self-identify as *parda* (brown, of partial African ancestry), though claims to indigenous Indian ancestry are growing, both as a way to secure material gains, such as land rights, and as a way to avoid the stigma of blackness (French 2010) (see Figure 8.3).

Although Brazilian understandings of race are flexible and complex, race is implicated in a profoundly unequal class system: whites at the top, blacks at the bottom, and *parda* somewhere in between. Anthropologist Conrad Kottak (1992:67) studied a village where the villagers were of African slave ancestry, but almost half identified themselves as *mulatto,* a commonly used intermediate category between black and white. Brothers and sisters were often classified as belonging to different races, depending on multiple criteria such as skin color, nose length and shape, eye color and shape, hair type and color, and shape of the lips. The villagers used more than ten different racial terms to describe people, such as mulatto, *mulatto claro* (light mulatto), or *sarara,* meaning a person with reddish skin and light curly hair. These terms were applied inconsistently, and there was wide disagreement among villagers in placing individuals into racially defined categories, with such placement frequently mediated by class and social status. Indeed, as many as 133 shades of blackness have been identified in Brazil (Bailey 2009; Gates 2011).

In Brazil, as in much of Latin America, multiracialism is viewed as central to a positive national identity (see Daniel 2006). In the 1940s, influential Brazilian anthropologist and politician Gilberto

Figure 8.3 These girls represent a small part of the great racial diversity in Brazil.

Joan Young Gregg

Freyre promoted the idea that "Brazilianness" resulted from mixing among people of European, African, and indigenous ancestry (Bailey and Telles 2006; Freyre 1946). Brazilian politicians and some social scientists used Freyre's work to promote the idea of Brazil as a racial democracy. In the 1970 census, the military government declined to ask people's race, based on the argument that there was no race issue in Brazil (Bailey and Telles 2006:77). The official denial of race in Brazil has had both positive and negative effects. On the one hand, the linkage between Brazilian identity and multiracialism makes it easier for Brazilians to negotiate their own identity. It has also resulted in a society where, in theory, opportunity is open to people of diverse physical characteristics. On the other hand, the persistent denial that race is a social issue has led to a widespread refusal to take discrimination and racial stratification seriously in spite of the fact that racial inequality exacts a high toll. On every measure of social and economic well-being, Brazilians who self-identify as having African ancestry are far worse off than are those who self-identify as white: their illiteracy rates are far higher and their wages are far lower, with higher education almost exclusively found among white Brazilians. As one Brazilian told a reporter, "Black is Beautiful, but White—White is just easier." (Nolen 2015). The United Nations Human Development Index (HDI) ranks Brazil 74th in the world; if white and African-descended populations were measured separately, the white population would rank 48th and the African-descended population would rank 108th (Roland 2001).

Because the American government is committed to providing public education to all its citizens, educational disparities between whites and nonwhites are much greater in Brazil, where this commitment was instituted only after World War II. Thus, the general level of education in Brazil for both whites and nonwhites is much lower than in the United States. Brazil has a high rate of illiteracy, and higher education is almost entirely the province of white elites (Berman, in Danaher and Shellenberger 1995:91). In attempting to deal with this inequality, the Brazilian government passed a new law requiring public universities to reserve half their seats for the mostly poor students in Brazil's public schools; this will considerably raise the number of Brazilians of African descent in higher education (Romero 2012). A comparison of Brazilian and American racial stratification systems thus indicates that racial inequality exists in societies with very different cultural constructs of race.

Race and Racial Stratification in the United States

In the United States, the cultural construct of race primarily divides people into white and black, based on presumed ancestry, a dichotomy that has its roots in slavery (Nesbitt 2007). Some exceptions are regional variations such as the Anglo-Hispanic distinction in the American Southwest, the complex racial/ethnic system in Hawai'i, and the legal designations of Native Americans. The predominant black/white dichotomy ignores the reality that widespread racial mixing occurred historically and continues into the present (Basson 2008). This denial is changing however. In the United States Census of 2010, people were permitted to self-identify as more than one race, and nine million people—an increase of 32 percent over the 2000 Census—chose to do so (U.S. Census Bureau 2012).

Anthropologists also note that while culturally race is identified with minorities, white is also a racial identity, but because white has been the cultural norm, the privileges and advantages that go with it are unconsciously assumed and largely invisible. Ethnographer Alice Goffman, for example, a white woman, describes how she was treated with civility, dignity, and helpfulness in boarding an airplane, while a young brown man was stopped and treated with suspicion and his tote bag very carefully searched (Lewis-Kraus 2016). This difference is even more apparent when it comes to shopping, buying or renting a place to live, or using a credit card.

In the United States, race, class, and ethnicity interact in complex ways to produce a culturally unique social stratification system, which impacts every aspect of life, and indeed, the very potential of life itself. African Americans have a higher mortality rate for both infants and mothers (Stolberg 1999), unequal access to health care, and unequal health care outcomes. Cancer survival rates, death rates for heart disease and HIV/AIDS, and complications from diseases like diabetes, such as loss of a limb or kidney disease, are all substantially higher for African Americans than for whites. Black children are six times more likely to be adversely impacted by elevated lead poisoning, which has both physical and psychological effects, than are white children, a fact that is partially a result of substandard housing (Markowitz and Rosner 2013). Racial health disparities are also linked to unequal access to medical insurance; in New York City, for example, 30 percent of African Americans, Latinos, and members of other minority groups are uninsured, as compared with 17 percent of whites (though insurance through "Obamacare" has somewhat improved this disparity).

Racial stratification negatively affects job and educational opportunities, access to fair credit, salary levels, accumulation of wealth, and home ownership. Blacks are increasingly subject to high mortgage rates and widespread home foreclosures—black and Latino homeowners were nearly twice as likely to lose their homes to foreclosure than their white counterparts—all of which negatively affects minority social mobility. Blacks are also subject to higher debt, partly as a result of interactions with the criminal justice system, as they often cannot pay fines for

Figure 8.4 Black Lives Matter is a nationwide protest movement that calls attention to the many injustices experienced by blacks in American society, especially fatal encounters with the police. Video recordings of these encounters indicate that in many cases these men had their hands up; were shot in the back while running away, or had no weapons, and contrary to official reports posed no physical threats to police officers.

Chip Somodevilla/Getty Images

low-level crimes, which then multiply or result in their being jailed. Debt caused by fines heightens tension between the population and the police and has resulted in police violence against blacks, for example, the case of the death of Michael Brown in Ferguson, Missouri, which led to the emergence of the protest group, Black Lives Matter (Figure 8.4).

The intersection of race, class and the ensuing decrease in chances for social mobility is indicated by long-standing inequalities in income and wealth between blacks and whites. In 2005, the median per capita income for blacks was $16,629 and $28,946 for whites. This economic gap—made worse by the meltdown in the Detroit auto industry, where employment was an important route to African American mobility (Chapman 2008)—is even more obvious in asset accumulation. In 2004, African American families' median net worth was $20,600, and that of Latinos was $18,600, only 14.6 percent and 13.2 percent, respectively, of the $140,700 median net worth for whites (Muhammad 2008).

Although most Americans, white and black, are literate, and most are high school graduates, educational disparities between blacks and whites are still a major aspect of our social stratification system. Most anthropologists hold that unequal educational access, differential economic position, and high unemployment do not result from a "culture of poverty" but rather reflect the oppression of racial stratification. Anthropologist John Ogbu argued, for example, that immigration status is key: "involuntary minorities" such as African Americans, Mexican Americans, and Native Americans perceive social stratification in the United States as unfair, permanent, and systemically discriminatory, and they develop behaviors that hinder their success, while "voluntary minorities," or immigrants, empha-size education as the main route to economic success and accordingly at-tain higher degrees of educational achievement (Gibson and Ogbu 1991). Asian Americans, for example, largely credit their traditional cultural val-ues of family support and educational achievement for their success in American society, which is indeed impressive (Spencer 2012).

Other anthropologists, while acknowledging the negative effect of the "oppositional cultures" of involuntary minorities in urban schools, hold that these cultural patterns have their source in the poverty of inner-city neighborhoods—discriminatory educational policies such as low ex-pectations of minority students, overcrowded and underfunded schools, and less-qualified teachers (Mateu-Gelabert and Lune 2007)—and that the problem of educational inequity is not a problem of minority culture, but rather one of an unequal distribution of resources.

Racial stratification also defines the use of public spaces and levels and types of criminalized behavior and violence. As noted in Alice Goffman's 2014 ethnography of a black neighborhood in Philadelphia, *On The Run,* the huge unemployment rate of young black males in the urban black neighborhoods leads to widespread criminal behavior, such as drug dealing, which affects interactions with law enforcement and the criminal justice system, further increasing the prejudice of potential employers against hiring black males (Jencks 2014). Incarceration of mi-norities is one of the most important aspects of racial stratification in the United States. Although African Americans and Latinos comprise only 25 percent of the national population, they make up more than 60 percent of those in prison. Black women are also overrepresented in prison, con-victed at rates 10 to 35 times higher than white women, which has highly negative effects on black families and their children. Historian Michelle Alexander characterizes the American prison system as "The New Jim Crow" (2010), detailing the context, responses, and social results, of the racially discriminatory incarceration patterns characteristic of our society.

This incarceration disparity has its roots in the disappearance of work resulting from deindustrialization and globalization, which re-sulted in a huge spike in African American crime rates. The political response was to devote a huge increase in government spending to the construction of prisons (largely privately run) and to increasing law en-forcement staff. Disproportionate sentences for drug offenses committed by blacks similar to those committed by whites also illustrated the dis-criminatory effects of laws that so impoverished urban black communi-ties. Because government statistics do not normally include incarcerated individuals, much of this discrepancy never made its way into the media and public consciousness, again, pushing American class stratification to the social margins.

ETHNICITY AND STRATIFICATION

Ethnicity, like the nation, is a constructed narrative that focuses primarily on cultural differences, though it may also incorporate racial differences. In many nation-states different ethnic groups have differential access to political and economic resources, and different symbolic roles in the national narrative (see Figure 8.5).

Ethnic Stratification in the United States

The dominant narrative of ethnicity in the United States is that we are a nation of immigrants who are welcomed into this country to pursue freedom from fear and the American Dream. In fact, this narrative is rife with contradictions, and it conflicts with the ongoing project of creating an American national identity based on a common culture and language. Historically, the vision of the American nation was largely restricted to immigrants from northern and western Europe. The Constitution originally limited citizenship to those who were "free and white (and male)," excluding Native Americans, Mexican Americans, and African Americans. With increasing immigration from southern and eastern Europe in the late 19th century, by the 1920s, immigration was restricted for Asians, Latin Americans, southern and eastern Europeans, and people from the Middle East. These restrictions were based on a widely shared American view that these people were "undesirable elements"—racially inferior and from cultures that would prevent their assimilation into the larger American society.

Figure 8.5 The election of the first African American president, Barack Obama, and his appointment of the first Hispanic Supreme Court Justice, Sonia Sotomayor, represent a historic moment in the intersection of race, class, ethnicity, and gender in the United States.

Saul Loeb/AFP/Getty Images

By the 1950s, concerns over immigrant assimilation abated, and the United States celebrated itself as a "melting pot," in which all ethnicities were blended to produce a unique American identity (Glazer and Moynihan 1970). In fact, many important ethnic cultural patterns, like language, had faded for those of European descent, although more subtle ethnic patterns, such as food preferences; verbal and nonverbal means of communication; the experience of health, illness, and pain; occupational choices; and voting patterns continued (Cerroni-Long 1993; Schensul 1997). The melting pot analogy always had excluded Mexican Americans, African Americans, Native Americans, and people from Asia and the Middle East.

By the 1960s, a new model of ethnic relations, called multiculturalism, emerged. Supported by the civil rights movement, multiculturalism embraced cultural diversity as a positive value. In 1965, a new Immigration and Nationality Act explicitly aimed at reversing the discriminatory basis of earlier immigration laws. This greatly expanded the numbers of immigrants from nations previously discriminated against, and resulted in substantially increased immigration from the Middle East, the Indian subcontinent, China, Korea, the Caribbean, parts of Central and South America, including Mexico, and Africa (Abdo 2006; Ewing 2008a; Pew Research 2007; Wong 2008), greatly increasing ethnic diversity. In 2012, the U.S. Census reported that by 2042 no single ethnic group will be big enough to be a majority (Preston 2015).

▌▌▌ Muslim Immigrants after 9/11 in the United States

Anthropologists studying immigration consider how its changing contexts are shaped by changing local, national, and global economies and political conditions (Brettell 2003), such as the rise of international terrorism; the cyclical nature of global, national, and regional economies; the increase of illegal immigration; and the violence that accompanies global political instability. With the rise of terrorism, both domestically and internationally, the commitment to multiculturalism is declining, particularly regarding South Asians, Arabs, and Muslims but also other nationalities (Iyer 2015).

For more than 200 years, immigrants from the Middle East were mainly Christians from Muslim-dominated countries like Syria and Lebanon, who constructed a common ethnic identity as Arab (Ewing 2008a). The 1965 immigration laws opened the United States to Muslim immigrants from South Asia as well as from the Middle East, many of whom were skilled and highly educated. These new immigrants began organizing as Muslims, focusing on maintaining Islamic religious practices rather than ethnically identifying with their nations of origin. This led to a more public presence for Islam, with expanded construction of mosques and Islamic schools (Abdo 2006); the expansion of a Koranically acceptable banking system that rejects charging interest on loans; a renewed emphasis on Muslim identity practices such as wearing the hijab, especially among the younger generation and particularly after 9/11; and the emergence of Muslim institutions providing information about Islam to the American public (Goodstein 2009).

After 9/11, research on immigrants indicated increasing American hostility toward Muslims (see Abdo 2006; Ewing 2008a; see also, Bayoumi 2012; Strum and Tarantolo 2003). In spite of this hostility, American Muslims express almost as much satisfaction with their lives as other Americans, and on many socioeconomic indicators, such as annual income, compare favorably with non-Muslims (Pew Research 2007). Fifty percent of American foreign-born Muslims have attended college, and most believe that they can fulfill their American Dream with hard work; this is a higher percentage than among African American Muslims. Sixty-three percent of American foreign-born Muslims see no conflict between being a devout Muslim and living in a modern society, although some younger Muslims do identify with extreme fundamentalism. Compared with Europe, however, the Muslim presence in the United States has engendered little extreme conflict and violence (see the Chapter 12 Bringing It Home feature).

▌▌▌ Ethnic Stratification and Latinos in the United States

The approximately 55 million Latinos in the United States share Spanish as a common language, but are in fact a culturally diverse group, including Mexican Americans, Puerto Ricans, Cuban Americans, and other Latin Americans, mostly from Central America. Legal immigration of Latinos sharply increased subsequent to the 1965 immigration law, so a larger proportion of Latinos, particularly Mexican Americans, are first-generation immigrants. As of 2002, Mexicans accounted for about 20 percent of the total legal immigration to the United States. It is also estimated that they constitute approximately three-fifths of the almost 12 million undocumented immigrant population (Strum and Selee 2004).

Much of the Mexican American population of the United States originated in the populations of the Southwest and California, whose settlement predated the 1846–1848 Mexican–American War. Originally rural agricultural workers, since the 1950s, Mexican Americans have become about 90 percent urban, concentrated in California, Texas, New Mexico, and Arizona. Puerto Ricans and Cubans, in contrast, initially migrated to urban areas, especially East Coast cities, with Cubans mainly concentrated in South Florida. Political upheavals and increasing violence in Central America led to increasing numbers of both documented and undocumented immigrants from Guatemala, Nicaragua, Honduras, and El Salvador.

Although Mexican immigrants are still largely concentrated in the Southwest, since 1990, they have been drawn, primarily by low-wage meatpacking factory and construction employment, to other parts of the country that had not previously experienced Latino immigration, such as Arkansas, Georgia, Colorado, and North Carolina. Much of the work Latino immigrants perform, as in the meat-processing plants in the Midwest, is difficult, dirty, and hazardous, with few health benefits (Preston 2009). With the downturn in the American economy and a crackdown on undocumented immigrants through raids on their places of employment, stricter scrutiny of Social Security cards, the withdrawal of social services, local laws prohibiting driving licenses, and greater cooperation between local police forces and federal immigration agents, the already low economic position of Latinos is under increasing threat. And although many Americans losing their jobs can turn to the government for a safety net of unemployment insurance and job assistance, this is not available to undocumented immigrants, who are working longer hours for less pay, at any job they can get (see Figure 8.6). As a result, there is an exodus of Mexican immigrants, both legal and undocumented, from the Southwest. As one sociologist pointed out, many factories in rural parts of the country are only able to hang on because of immigrant workers taking jobs other Americans won't take. As wages fall, employers tend to move from white employees, to black employees, to Latino employees, and in many cases, ultimately to closing their businesses (Preston 2009).

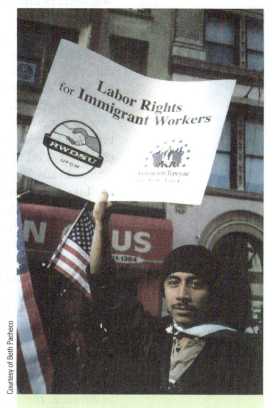

Courtesy of Beth Pacheco

Figure 8.6 Latinos, who make up the largest number of immigrants in the United States, are often economically exploited by employers. In recent years, they have become more active in pressing for immigration reform and for fair labor practices for workers.

BRINGING IT BACK HOME:
THE VOICES OF NEW IMMIGRANTS

In addition to the economic motivations of many immigrants, the spread of near starvation, ethnic conflict, civil wars, and human rights abuses in many contemporary societies has increased the number of immigrants to the United States. Many of these new immigrants are from places like Sudan, Somalia, El Salvador, Kurdistan, Vietnam, and Iraq: These places are familiar to Americans only because of U.S. political or military interventions, but most Americans have little knowledge of these cultures. In addition, unlike migrants from the late 19th and early 20th centuries, these contemporary migrants are as—or more—likely to be found in rural Wisconsin or Georgia, in small cities in the Southwest, or the far reaches of Maine or Minnesota than in ethnically diverse urban centers.

Putting a human face on the lives of different ethnic groups helps us understand how the lives of these migrants have been shaped by the difficulties they face in trying to understand and fit into American society. Ping Chong, director of a brilliant and innovative theater company, uses anthropological techniques of individuals telling their own stories to introduce these immigrants to diverse American audiences. In using the title "Undesirable Elements" for his theater pieces on migrants, Chong (2012) plays on the term used in the American political culture of the 19th and early 20th centuries about non-European immigrants.

Like an anthropologist, Ping Chong has the double vision of an insider/outsider. He was born into a family of Chinese opera stars who were forced to migrate from China because of their dissident political beliefs, and he grew up in the ethnic enclave of New York City's Chinatown. He describes himself as a "young man sitting on a cultural fence."

The stories told by the immigrants in Ping's plays frequently emphasize the comparisons they see between the diverse ethnic and racial stratification system in the United States and their own societies, as well as the contrast between American ideals and the reality of ethnic and racial stratification.

One migrant from Kurdistan says, "everyone we watched on American TV shows was blond-haired and blue-eyed, but when we arrive in America, they are not. This [diversity] is the *real* America." Another Kurdish migrant says, "I don't speak English. It's hard. I look different. I have black eyes and black hair. The kids in my class think I'm weird." Another migrant teenager, fleeing the violence accompanying the fall of the shah in Iran, who was a strong American ally, couldn't understand the anti-Iranian bumper stickers she saw on cars or the restaurant signs saying Iranians would not be served. "I am very confused," she said, "I thought

I was an American." Saul, a teenaged Mexican immigrant, is shopping in a mall in Atlanta, Georgia. He sees there is a white salesperson following him. Now, when Saul enters a shop he tells the salesperson, "Yeah, I'm Mexican, but don't worry. I'm not going to steal anything. I have money."

Perhaps the most telling comment on American stratification comes from a migrant now applying for college: "I had to check a box: Caucasian, black, Hispanic, Asian, other. I don't know which one to check. The administrator tells me, you are from Venezuela, check Hispanic. I say, but Hispanic is someone from Spain. I'm half Lebanese, half Venezuelan, half Catholic, half Druze from the Middle East. People here talk about race and color, but that doesn't happen in Venezuela or Lebanon. What does it have to do with what people are?" What indeed? That is a major question in this chapter.

YOU DECIDE:

1. How have you experienced American class, race, and ethnic stratification in the United States? How does your experience relate to the ideal of the American Dream?
2. The historical narrative in the United States emphasizes both the assimilation of American immigrants and multiculturalism, a respect for cultural differences. Which narrative do you think best describes the contemporary United States and why?
3. How would you check the box on your racial and ethnic identity? What does this "have to do with what people are?" Or with "being American?"

CHAPTER SUMMARY

1. What are the differences between functionalist and conflict theories of social stratification? Functionalist theory holds that social stratification benefits the whole society because it motivates people to undertake all the jobs necessary for the society to survive. Conflict theory emphasizes the conflicts within stratified societies as different social strata, with opposing interests, clash with one another over goals and resources.
2. Define the major dimensions of social stratification, and explain how they relate to other aspects of culture and society. The major dimensions of social stratification are power, wealth, and prestige, which are closely tied to occupation, which is closely tied to income. The particular value system of a culture shapes how these factors interact to determine where a person is placed in the stratification system.

3. What are the main features of the class system in the United States? The culture of the United States emphasizes "the American Dream," the idea that one can and should improve one's life chances and material wealth. Although many Americans dismiss the importance of class in the United States, there are important material and life-change differences in the different social classes. Inequality between social classes is increasing, as is downward mobility.

4. What are the main differences between a class system and a caste system? In a class system, social position is ideally achieved, rather than ascribed, although class status in reality is also ascribed. People can move between the social classes. Classes are largely based on differences of income and wealth, but also are characterized by different lifestyles and cultural differences. In the Indian caste system, based on Hindu ideas of ritual purity, social position (caste) is largely ascribed (based on birth), and caste boundaries are sharply defined by prohibitions on intercaste marriage and intercaste food sharing, which tend to reinforce class as well as caste differences.

5. How do the Brazilian and American racial stratification systems differ from each other? In the United States, race is mainly conceived as a dichotomy between white and black and is based on presumed ancestry. In Brazil, race is constructed as a continuum, though race and class in both societies interact and benefit members of the racial elites.

6. What is the major narrative of ethnicity in the United States? The cultural diversity of the United States has largely been framed in terms of ethnicity based on the national origins of immigrants who came seeking the American Dream. African Americans, Native Americans, and Mexican Americans were ignored in this narrative, but today's immigrants come from a wider historical and geographical background than previously.

KEY TERMS

Achieved status
Ascribed status
Caste system
Class
Class system
Conflict theory
Functionalism

Power
Prestige
Race
Social mobility
Social stratification
Wealth

Sara Gouveia

The matrilineal family, which centers on a core of women, and includes brothers and sons, but not husbands and fathers, is the most important kinship group among the Na and allied ethnic groups in China.

9
MARRIAGE, FAMILY, AND KINSHIP

AFTER YOU HAVE READ THIS CHAPTER YOU WILL BE ABLE TO:

△ Describe some of the roles and functions that marriage and family have in society.

△ Define the incest taboo and present two different explanations for it.

△ Define endogamy and exogamy and give examples of each.

△ Summarize the differences between polygamy, polygyny, polyandry, and monogamy and some of their important functions in different societies.

△ Explain the difference between bride service, bridewealth, and dowry, and their different functions in different social contexts.

△ Discuss how the American family has changed in the past half century and some reasons for these changes.

△ Explain how kinship systems are related to culture and why they are culturally important.

△ Explain how extended families differ from nuclear families and how patrilineal families differ from matrilineal families.

A Society Without Marriage: The Na of China

I N the 1950s, Frank Sinatra sang, "love and marriage . . . go together like a horse and carriage." But this is not true in all cultures (Blumenfield 2004:15; Cai Hua 2001). Among the Na and some other societies of Southwest China, the culturally normative institution that joins men and women in sexual and reproductive partnerships is called *sese*. Except historically among the elites, the Na do not practice marriage, and do not even have a word for it. In the sese relationship, a man passes a night in a lover's household and returns to his own family in the morning. All sexual (and potentially reproductive) activity takes place during this concealed visit of a Na male to the house of a woman who has agreed beforehand to lie with him. As lovers, their relationship involves affection, respect, and intimacy, but does not include notions of fidelity, permanence, or paternal responsibility for children. There is no coercion in the relationship: Either party may offer, accept, or decline an invitation for a visit. To spare the other's feelings, one may say: "Tonight is not possible. I already have one for tonight," and a woman may even turn away an invited lover at the door if she chooses. But although either the woman or the man may initiate the visit, it is always the man who comes secretly to the woman's household. Concealment is necessary because of a Na taboo forbidding a household's male members to hear or see any sexual talk or activities involving household females. Males will never answer the door after dark lest they encounter a woman's lover, and the lover himself makes every effort to avoid detection, often bringing food to prevent the guard dog's barking, speaking only in whispers during intercourse, and leaving quietly before daybreak.

Both women and men have multiple partners, serially or simultaneously, and no records are kept of visits to ascertain the paternity of children. The Na do not have a word for incest, illegitimate child, infidelity, or promiscuity. The Na are matrilineal, and children by a variety of fathers stay with the mother's household for their entire lives. When a generation lacks females, a household may adopt a relative's child or encourage a son to bring his lover into the household. The only males in a Na household are relatives of different generations, who are brothers, uncles, and granduncles. There are no husbands or fathers. Where males are in short supply in a family, a woman may bring her lover home.

The Na visit, which has been part of Na culture for more than a thousand years, is treated as a mutually enjoyable but singular occurrence that entails no future conditions. The Chinese state has periodically tried to change what they call this "barbarous practice," but without success so far.

Location of the Na.

But as the Na adapt to the new conditions of the nation-state and the globalizing economy, they are increasingly subjected to state-sponsored public school education and media, which reflect mainstream Han mores and lifestyles and stigmatize Na practices. This, as well as their inability to name a father on official documents, may spell the end of Na visits. At the same time, however, the Na culture has attracted tourists, whose presence has benefited the Na economy; this has given them an impetus to retain the *sese* system that distinguishes them from the larger Chinese culture (Qin 2015).

▌▌▌ FORMS AND FUNCTIONS OF MARRIAGE

All human societies face certain problems for which marriage, the creation of families, and kinship systems offer solutions. Every society must regulate sexual access between males and females, find satisfactory ways to organize labor, assign responsibility for child care, provide a clear framework for organizing an individual's rights and responsibilities, and provide for the transfer of property and social position between generations. The many human solutions to these challenges are guided by cultural rules, accounting for a wide variety of kinship and family systems. These systems tend to be adaptive to subsistence patterns and other realities: When these change, rules about kinship and family also tend to change.

The need to regulate sexual access stems from the potentially continuous receptivity of human males and females to sexual activity. If sexual competition was not regulated and channeled into stable relationships that were given social approval, it could cause societal conflict. These relationships need not be permanent. However, in most societies—though not all—they are relatively stable; we refer to these relationships as marriage. **Marriage**, which refers to the customs, rules, and obligations that establish a socially endorsed relationship between adults and children, and between the married couple's kin groups, is a very widespread, though not a universal social institution, as the Na illustrate (see Figure 9.1). But in the absence of safe and dependable contraception throughout most of human history and with the near certainty that children would be born, marriage, as a relatively stable union between a male and female that involves responsibility for children as well as economic exchange, became the basis for most human adaptations.

In addition to forming bonds between a couple, marriage extends social alliances by linking together different families and kin groups,

Marriage: The customs, rules, and obligations that establish a special relationship between sexually cohabiting adults, between them and any children they take responsibility for, and between the kin of the married couple.

Figure 9.1 Marriage rituals in India, as elsewhere, contain many symbolic elements. The color red symbolizes fertility and the bride's gold jewelry indicates her family's social status and is considered auspicious for a long married life.

Chander Dembla

leading to cooperation among groups of people related to the married couple. This expansion of the social group within which people can work together and share resources is a great advantage for the survival of the human species.

Although marriage and the subsequent formation of families in most societies rests on the biological complementarity of males and females in reproduction, both marriage and family are cultural patterns. Thus, they differ in form and function both among and within human societies and change over time with changing political and economic circumstances and the life stages of individuals.

Heterosexual, monogamous marriage, dominant in the United States, is only one of many culturally acceptable kinds of marriages worldwide. Marriages involving plural spouses or same-sex relationships also fulfill the functions of marriage in satisfactory ways. This cultural variation makes it difficult to give one universally applicable definition of marriage.

Among some African societies, woman–woman marriage is an alternative to heterosexual marriages. This allows a barren woman to divorce her husband, take another woman as her wife, and arrange for a surrogate to impregnate this woman. Children born from this arrangement become members of the barren woman's natal lineage and refer to her as their father. A similar pattern is found among the Azande in East Africa, where royal power is sustained by multiple wives. Where there was a shortage of marriageable women, a man might take a young man for his wife and the couple would be recognized as a married couple (Kilbride 2004).

Like marriage, the concept of the family also varies among cultures. In many societies, the most important family bond is between lineal blood relations (father and children or mother and children) or between brothers and sisters rather than between husband and wife. In these societies, the lineage or the clan rather than the immediate family confers legitimacy on children.

▌▌▌ MARRIAGE RULES

Every society has culturally defined rules concerning sexual relations and marriage. These rules may determine how spouses are chosen, limit marriage to certain groups, dictate the number of spouses and how they are chosen, allow for dissolving marriages, determine rules for remarriage, specify the kinds of exchanges and rituals that legitimate marriage, and determine the rights and obligations established by marriage. Among the most universal of these rules is the incest taboo.

▌▌▌ Incest Taboos

Incest taboos are rules that prohibit sexual relationships with specific categories of kin. Incest taboos are universal, though they apply to different categories of kin in different societies. Because sexual access is a key right of marriage, incest taboos restrict who are considered acceptable marriage partners.

Except for brother–sister marriage in some ancient empires like Egypt, Peru, Rome, and Hawai'i, probably to keep power and wealth within royal families, incest taboos banning sex between parents and their children and between brothers and sisters are universal. In many societies, people beyond the immediate family, such as lineage or clan members, or certain categories of cousins may be covered by the incest taboo. These rules demonstrate that kinship, although based on biological relationships, is in fact, a cultural construct. For example, although an individual's parallel and cross-cousins both stand in the same biological relationship to an individual, in some societies, the incest taboo may cover one category but not the other.

Different explanations have been proposed for the universality of the incest taboo. Biologically based theories argue that the incest taboo prevents inbreeding that would have a deleterious effect on humanity. Although sex between close biological relatives does lead to increased birth defects, it is questionable whether this connection would be perceived in premodern societies, which have extremely high infant mortality rates. And, as we noted, the incest taboo may apply to people who are not close biological relatives.

Psychologically based theories argue either that humans have an innate aversion to those with whom they are raised, or that sexual competition

Incest taboo: A prohibition on sexual relations between relatives.

among siblings or parents and children would create disruption and kin role confusion in the family. However, these theories do not account for all the incest taboos and avoidance patterns in different societies. In addition, if aversion to intimate kin is innate, what is the need for a rule against it?

Alliance theory argues that incest taboos force people to marry outside their group, creating wider social bonds that are useful in helping these groups survive. When Margaret Mead asked a man in New Guinea if he was allowed to marry his sister, he was astonished. If a man married his sister, he replied, he would have no brother-in-law with whom to hunt, to garden, or to visit (in Lévi-Strauss 1969/1949:485). Creating wider alliances is a very powerful argument for the incest taboo.

Endogamy: A rule prescribing that a person must marry within a particular group.

Endogamy rules require people to marry within their own group, however that group is defined. As noted previously, blood relations among royalty may be encouraged or required to marry each other. In India, castes and subcastes are endogamous; in the United States, although there are no named endogamous groups, racial groups, religious groups, and social classes tend to be endogamous, based on opportunities to meet, cultural norms, and similarities in lifestyle.

▮▮▮ Preferential Marriages

Some societies have preferential marriage rules, usually involving cousin marriage. In **cross-cousin marriage** the preferred partners are the children of one's parents' siblings of the opposite sex—mother's brother or father's sister. Preferred cross-cousin marriage reinforces ties between kin groups established in the preceding generation, preserving the relationship between two intermarrying kin groups across generations (see Figure 9.2)

Cross-cousin marriage: Marriage between an individual and the child of his or her mother's brother or father's sister.

Parallel-cousin marriage: Marriage between the children of a parent's same-sex siblings (mother's sister or father's brother).

Parallel-cousin marriage involves children of the parents' same-sex siblings—mother's sister or father's brother—and is found in some Arab and North African Muslim societies. Because descent and inheritance are in the male line in Muslim Arab societies, parallel-cousin marriage helps prevent the fragmentation of family property and keeps economic resources within the family. Parallel-cousin marriage reinforces the solidarity of brothers, but by socially isolating groups of brothers from each other, it adds to factional disputes and disunity within the larger social system. This illustrates that

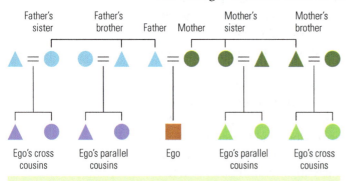

Figure 9.2 This diagram indicates the relationships of cross-cousins and parallel cousins. In many cultures, people are forbidden to marry either cross or parallel cousins, but not both.

although different kinship and family structures may contribute to solidarity and stability at one level of society, they may be socially disruptive at another level. Again, because cross-cousin and parallel-cousin marriage differentiate kin who are equally biologically close (see Figure 9.2), preferred cousin marriage rules demonstrate the important cultural dimension of kinship systems.

The **levirate** and the **sororate** are two types of marriage rules that demonstrate the importance of marriage as an alliance between two groups rather than between individuals. These rules allow a marriage to survive the death of one of the partners with the continuance of group alliances and fulfillment of the marriage contract. Under the levirate, a man marries the widow of his dead brother, and in some cases the children born to this union are considered children of the deceased man. Thus, the levirate enables the children to remain within the dead husband's descent group.

In the sororate, when a woman dies, her kin group supplies a sister as a wife for the widower. The sororate also allows the husband of a barren woman to marry her sister, and at least some of the children of this marriage are considered those of the first wife. If no qualifying relative is available to fulfill the levirate or the sororate, other appropriately classified kin may be substituted, or these marriages may not take place.

Levirate: The custom whereby a man marries the widow of a deceased brother.
Sororate: The custom whereby, when a man's wife dies, her sister is given to him as a wife.

▌▌▌ Number of Spouses

All societies have rules about how many spouses a person may have at one time. **Monogamy**, which permits each individual to have only one spouse at any given time, is the rule in Europe and North America, but not in most of the world's cultures. **Polygamy**, or plural marriage, includes **polygyny**, the marriage of one man to several women, and **polyandry**, the marriage of one woman to several men. About 75 percent of the world's cultures permit (and prefer) polygyny (Murdock 1949:28), but even in these cultures, the male/female ratio and the requirements of a brideprice, which many men cannot afford, inhibit its actual occurrence.

Monogamy: A rule that permits a person to be married to only one spouse at a time.
Polygamy: A rule allowing more than one spouse.
Polygyny: A rule permitting a man to have more than one wife at a time.
Polyandry: A rule permitting a woman to have more than one husband at a time.

▌▌▌ Polygyny

Polygyny has important economic and political functions in some societies. Where women are economically important, polygyny increases a man's wealth and therefore his social position. Because marriage links groups together, having several wives from different groups within a society also extends a man's alliances. Thus, chiefs, headmen, and state leaders may take wives from many different groups or villages to increase their political power.

Polygyny is found primarily in societies where plural wives—and their children—increase both a family's labor supply and its productivity. For example, among the Tiwi of Australia, a foraging group, women's food collecting makes a very important contribution to the food supply. Thus, the more wives a man has, the better his family's standard of living (Goodale 1971). Although Western cultural stereotypes criticize polygyny as oppressing women, the status of females in polygynous societies is not uniformly low and may even, as among the Tiwi, be relatively high and accord women a high degree of sexual and economic freedom. Where women's work is hard and monotonous, as it often is, women may welcome the addition of a co-wife because it eases their own workload and provides daily companionship. Conflict among co-wives does occur in polygynous societies and is sometimes mitigated by sororal polygyny, a preference for a man to marry sisters. In many polygynous societies, co-wives live in separate dwellings, and cultural norms requiring a man to distribute his economic resources and sexual attentions evenly among his wives also mitigate family conflict. Like all other cultural patterns, marriage rules adapt to changing economic and social circumstances. Thus, with declining amounts of available agricultural land, increasing expenses in educating children, and the social pressures of Western and Christian condemnation of polygyny, this form of marriage has to some extent declined or been driven underground in parts of Africa (Kilbride 2006).

▌▌ Polyandry

Polyandry is relatively rare, found mainly in Tibet, Nepal, and some indigenous groups in India, like the Toda. In Tibet, as in other polyandrous societies, polyandry is related to a shortage of land. If brothers marry a single wife, their father's land can be kept intact within the family rather than fragmented over the generations. Polyandry is also functional in societies where men are away from home for long periods of time, in that a woman has more than one husband to provide for her. Among the Toda, polyandry was related to a shortage of women, but because they no longer practice female infanticide, and under the influence of Christian missionaries, the Toda today are largely monogamous (Queen and Haberstein 1974).

▌▌ Choosing a Mate

The cultural context of marriage includes how mates are chosen. In most societies, kin-group interests—rather than individual desires—are the bases of mate selection, and the families of the bride and groom take an important, even determinative, role in selecting their children's spouses, often through a go-between. This practice of arranged marriage strongly contrasts with marriage in the United States, where individuals ideally select their own mates on the basis of sexual compatibility, emotional needs, physical attractiveness, and personality, a cluster of patterns called "romantic love."

Arranged marriage is related to other cultural patterns. In India, for example, its dominance is aligned with the patrilineal, patriarchal, and patrilocal ideals of Indian society. Even in contemporary India, where women are increasingly working outside the home, most people prefer arranged marriage, although patterns are changing. Among the urban middle class, the bride and groom are more likely to meet, perhaps even outside family visits, before they marry; traditionally, potential spouses did not see each other before the wedding ceremony (Nanda 2000a; Nanda and Gregg 2009). Economic and cultural globalization has also had an impact. In South India, young, lower-class women are working in garment factories, earning salaries that are becoming essential to family subsistence. In the past, these families paid the dowries of their daughters in arranged marriages (even if they had to borrow much of the dowry), but now many of these women save for their own dowries. This has led to greater independence for young, unmarried women who now demand greater rights to choose their own mates rather than accepting the matches their families arrange. These "love matches" have, however, disrupted the kin support networks that traditionally accompany arranged marriages and put these women at greater risk for abuse and infidelity (Lessinger 2013). Increasingly, women all over India, including rural India, are participating in paid work, trying to supplement the meager incomes of their families. This has often subjected them to sanctions and even violence, but the income is critical and many women are defying even their husbands in their determination to work (Barry 2016).

▮▮▮ THE EXCHANGE OF GOODS AND RIGHTS IN MARRIAGE

Almost everywhere, the public rituals and ceremonies that accompany marriage distinguish it from other, similar kinds of unions. Marriage involves the transfer of certain rights and obligations, primarily involving sexual access of the partners to each other, rights over any children born to the marriage, obligations by one or both parents to care for children born to the union, and rights of the marriage partners to the economic services of the other.

Figure 9.3 Displaying bridewealth in Africa. Bridewealth often includes the presentation of goods from the family of the husband to the family of the wife, as depicted here among the Fulani of Guinea-Bissau in West Africa.

Ami Vitale/Alamy

Almost universally, marriage requires an exchange of goods or services between the families of the bride and groom (see Figure 9.3). Although sometimes called "gifts," these exchanges are obligatory for the transfer of marital rights, and if the exchanges are not completed, the rights in marriage can be forfeited. Although certain exchanges are dominant in a society, any particular society may have several legitimate forms of exchange (Huber, Danaher, and Breedlove 2011).

Bride Service and Bridewealth

Bride service, bridewealth, and dowry are three main kinds of marriage exchanges. In addition, other less-common forms include groom service, where a potential bride spends a week or two at the groom's house to demonstrate her domestic skills (Huber et al. 2011).

In bride service, most commonly found in foraging societies where few material goods are accumulated, the husband must work for a specified number of years for his wife's family in exchange for his marital rights (Marlowe 2004). Among the Ju/'hoansi of the Kalahari Desert in Africa, this may be as long as 15 years or until the birth of the third child.

Bridewealth: Goods presented by the groom's kin to the bride's kin to legitimize a marriage (formerly called "bride-price").

The most common form of marriage exchange is **bridewealth**, where cash or goods are given by the groom's kin to the bride's kin to seal the marriage. Bridewealth previously was called *bride-price*, but this falsely conveys the idea that the marriage is merely an economic exchange (Ogbu 1978) and that women's status in such societies is devalued. In fact, in these societies, daughters are valuable to their families because their bridewealth finances males' marriages.

In societies with bridewealth, a person can claim compensation for a violation of conjugal rights only if the bridewealth has been paid. Furthermore, bridewealth paid at marriage is returned (subject to specified conditions) if a marriage is terminated. Although many studies of bridewealth emphasize its role in entitling a husband to domestic, economic, sexual, and reproductive rights, bridewealth also confers rights on the wife, as it allows wives to hold their husbands accountable for violations of conjugal rights. In sanctioning these mutual rights and obligations, bridewealth helps stabilize marriage by giving both families a vested interest in keeping the couple together.

Although globally widespread, bridewealth transactions are particularly characteristic of Africa. Among the Kipsigis, a pastoralist/horticultural society of East Africa, the traditional bridewealth payment was livestock, but it now includes cash (Borgerhoff Mulder 1995:576). Formerly, when agricultural land was available and crop prices were high, bridewealth was high because of the importance of women's agricultural labor. Now, however, land is scarce, crop prices are low, and women's agricultural labor has lost its value, so bridewealth has declined. On the other hand, Kipsigis parents of educated girls often demand high bridewealth as compensation for their daughters' school fees because their daughters' education will both increase their earning potential and benefit their marital home.

Dowry

Dowry, which is less widespread than bridewealth, refers to goods given by a bride's family to the groom's family and is associated with private ownership of property. Today, dowry is mainly associated with India, and although it is illegal, it remains central to arranged marriage. One explanation of Indian dowry is that it is a voluntary gift, symbolizing affection for a daughter leaving home and compensating her for her traditional exclusion from the inheritance of land or property. Dowry is also sometimes explained as a source of a married woman's security because it always includes jewelry, which is—theoretically—her property (in practice, her husband's family usually keeps control of it). Dowry is also sometimes explained as compensation to the groom's family, who must now take on the economic burden of a wife, who traditionally did not work outside the home. In contemporary India, with its new emphasis on consumerism and social-class mobility, dowry is increasingly perceived by the husband's family as a way to improve their financial and social standing. As such, insufficient dowry is sometimes used as emotional blackmail of a woman's family and is linked to wife abuse and even wife murder (Nanda and Gregg 2009; Stone and James 2005). Historically, dowry was also a pattern in Europe and the United States; perhaps the custom of the bride's family paying for the wedding is a survival of dowry.

Dowry: Presentation of goods by the bride's kin to the family of the groom or to the couple.

▌▌▌ USING ANTHROPOLOGY: DOMESTIC VIOLENCE AND THE CULTURAL DEFENSE

Kinship relationships, especially in patriarchal cultures, are a frequent context of violence. When the government of Kazakhstan invited anthropologist Edward Snajdr (2007) to analyze and address the high increase in domestic violence in this officially multicultural society, one female colonel from a domestic violence law enforcement unit told him, "From early childhood, Kazakh males are the bosses. It is normal for a husband to beat his wife."

It may be normal, but in the United States and many other societies, including Kazakhstan, it is illegal. Although some multicultural societies like Kazakhstan do consider "culture" in responding to domestic violence, courts in the United States do not generally recognize culture as a defense. The "cultural defense" of domestic violence in court has mainly been used to defend men who come from immigrant cultures where domestic violence is normal. These cases have sometimes even involved anthropologists as expert witnesses, testifying to violence as a culturally appropriate response to a wife who has dishonored her family through sexual transgressions (Norgren and Nanda 2006; Renteln 2004), and judges have used this as a mitigating circumstance and reduced the sentence (Winkelman 1996).

Most anthropologists have criticized this position. Along with women's groups and legal scholars, they protest that there should be only one standard of justice, which should not be affected by a defendant's cultural background. In this view, a court's decision to allow a cultural defense sends out the dangerous message that immigrant women cannot be fully protected by U.S. law.

In addition, the cultural defense distorts the anthropological concept of culture as varied and changing; lawyers, judges, and the popular media tend to have a static and generalizing perspective on culture, which is inaccurate (Demian 2008). Anthropology does not accept the idea that "culture made me do it," but anthropology has been helpful in raising awareness of the need for culturally and linguistically sensitive responses to victims of domestic violence. Ethnographies that illuminate the diverse cultural contexts of domestic violence (Nanda and Gregg 2009) and groups like Sakhi, a charitable organization in New York City dedicated to eradicating domestic violence among the city's many families of South Asian descent, show how culturally relevant interventions make an important difference in serving victims of domestic violence in both our own and other societies.

FAMILY STRUCTURES, HOUSEHOLDS, AND RULES OF RESIDENCE

Two basic types of families are the elementary, or nuclear, family and the extended family. **Nuclear families** are organized around the relationship between husband and wife (the conjugal tie). The **extended family** is based on **consanguinity**, or blood ties between relations extending over three or more generations.

A household, or domestic group, is different from a family (see Chapter 6). Although most households contain people related by blood or marriage, nonkin may be included; conversely, members of a family may be spread out over several households. Household composition is affected by the cultural rules about residence after marriage. Under neolocal residence rules, married couples create their own households. Under patrilocal residence rules, a newly married couple lives with the husband's family, whereas under matrilocal residence rules, the couple lives with the wife's family. Under avunculocal residence rules, the couple lives with the wife's uncle's family (usually the husband's mother's brother); this rule permits the geographical concentration of male lineage mates and the preservation of male control of lineage wealth in a matrilineal system. Bilocal residence rules permit a couple to choose between living with the wife's family or the husband's family. Each of these residence rules is associated with a different type of kinship system.

Nuclear families: Organized around the relationship between husband and wife (conjugal tie).
Extended family: Family based on blood relations extending over three or more generations.
Consanguinity: Blood ties between people.

Nuclear Families

A nuclear family, consisting of a married couple and their children, is mainly associated with neolocal households. Only 5 percent of the world's societies are traditionally neolocal. The nuclear, neolocal family is well adapted to industrialized capitalism, where jobs are not generally dependent on family connections and where employment and promotion often require geographical mobility. Independence and flexibility are also requirements in foraging societies, and nuclear families predominate in more than 75 percent of all foraging groups.

The Changing American Family

American culture still generally extols the independent, nuclear, neolocal family, although the diversity of American family structures is far from this ideal. This is a result of the high divorce rate, legal same-sex marriage (see Figure 9.4), the increasing number of working mothers and single-parent households, the growing number of unmarried couples living

Figure 9.4 Families based on gay and lesbian relationships are increasingly a part of the American family culture. Here, the two fathers of the boy and girl have been together for over 20 years. Their mothers have been in a relationship for over 15 years. Together, they form a happy and successful family unit. The children divide their time between their mothers' home and their fathers' home, which are very near to each other.

© Billie L. Porter

together in long-term relationships, surrogate reproduction and of childless couples, the greater number of people who never marry, the increasing number of people who remarry after divorce or widowhood, and the increasing number of three-generation households.

The high rates of divorce and remarriage enmesh nuclear families in larger and more complicated kinship networks. Sometimes called "blended families," these networks include previously divorced spouses and their new marriage partners; sometimes children from previous marriages; or multiple sets of grandparents and other similar relations. Although blended families may function in some ways like traditional two-parent families, in fact, only one child in six averages a weekly visit with a divorced father, and only one in four sees him once a month. Almost half of the children of divorced parents have not seen their biological fathers for more than a year, and more than two-thirds have lost contact with him ten years later (Hacker 2002:22). Another change in the American family is the growing number of multigenerational families, which has increased substantially since 1970, caused both by the increase of immigrants who live in such families (Kramer 2011) and by an increase in the number of adult children moving back to their parental home because they cannot find employment. At the same time, the number of Americans living alone is also rising, including young people, middle-aged people, and even the elderly (Klinenberg 2012a; 2012b).

In 2009, single-parent households, mainly single-mother households, accounted for about 27 percent of all households with children, and 3.1 million American children lived with neither of their parents (Kreider and Ellis 2011). One study estimates that about half the children in the

United States will spend at least some of their childhood in a single-parent family, either as the result of divorce or separation, or because their mothers never married (Luker 1996).

An important and increasing trend in the United States is children being born to unmarried mothers; today, that figure is over 40 percent, reaching to over 50 percent for children born to women under 30. This trend occurs in other wealthy countries as well: In Sweden, over 55 percent of births are to unmarried mothers, and France and the United Kingdom both have higher rates than the United States (Ventura 2009). In the past, children being born to unmarried mothers were associated with teenage pregnancies; today, most unmarried mothers are between the ages of 20 and 30. Although rates of birth to unmarried mothers are up for all ethnic groups in the United States, they have risen particularly sharply among Hispanic and black women; these groups account for 53 percent and 73 percent, respectively, of all births to unmarried women (Wildsmith, Steward-Streng, and Manlove 2011; see also, Banks 2011). As a group, single-mother families are far poorer than other families (DeParle 2012b; Mather 2010). One exception to the trend of single motherhood is college graduates, for whom marriage makes more sense economically than it does for poor women whose mates are less likely to have well-paying jobs or even to be employed (Cherlin 2014; Coontz 2014; Miller and Alderman 2014).

▌▊▎ Composite Families

Composite (compound) families are aggregates of nuclear families linked by a common spouse, most often the husband. The typical composite family is a polygynist household, consisting of one man with several wives and their respective children, with each wife and her children normally occupying a separate residence. In composite families, the tie between a mother and her children is particularly strong. The dynamics of the composite family typically involves the interaction of the husband with several wives, interaction between co-wives, and competition among the children of different wives over inheritance and succession.

Composite (compound) family: An aggregate of nuclear families linked by a common spouse.

▌▊▎ Extended Families

The extended (consanguineal) family consists of two or more generations of male or female kin and their spouses and offspring, occupying a single household under the authority of a household head. An extended family is not just a collection of nuclear families; in an extended family system, lineal ties—the blood ties between generations (such as father and son)—are more important than the ties of marriage.

Extended families are particularly adaptive among cultivators as they provide more workers than nuclear families, which is adaptive both in food production and in the production and marketing of handicrafts. In peasant agricultural societies where land ownership is important for both prestige and power, the extended family helps keep land intact over generations rather than parceling it out into ever smaller and more unproductive pieces among male descendants. Although the extended family is the ideal in more than half of the world's societies, it is found most often among the landlord and prosperous merchant classes.

The patrilineal extended family is organized around the male line: a man, his sons, and the sons' wives and children. Societies with patrilineal extended families also tend to have patrilocal residence rules. A matrilineal family is organized around the female line: a woman, her daughters, and the daughters' husbands and children. Matrilineal families may have matrilocal residence rules or avunculocal residence rules.

KINSHIP SYSTEMS: RELATIONSHIPS THROUGH BLOOD AND MARRIAGE

Kinship: A culturally defined relationship established on the basis of blood ties or through marriage.

Kinship system: The totality of kin relations, kin groups, and terms for classifying kin in a society.

Kinship includes relationships described through the idiom of blood and relationships through marriage. Kinship determines the formation of social groups (like families), is the basis for classification of people in relation to each other, structures individual rights and obligations, and regulates behavior. Because all of these elements of social life are entwined, anthropologists refer to kinship as a system. Although a **kinship system** always rests on some kind of biological relationship, kinship systems are cultural phenomena, as indicated earlier by the differential classification of parallel and cross-cousins. Kinship classification may or may not reflect a scientifically accurate assessment of biological ties.

In small-scale, nonindustrial societies, kinship is the most important social bond. It is the basis of group formation, and norms of kinship govern the most important relationships, rights, and responsibilities between individuals and groups. The extension of kinship ties is the main way of linking groups to one another and of incorporating strangers into a group. Even in modern industrialized societies, where citizenship is an important basis of rights and obligations, kinship has many important functions. It is the major context within which wealth is inherited. Kinship is important on many ritual occasions, and there is a strong sentiment that "blood is thicker than water."

Kinship systems have several functions necessary to the continuation of a society: They provide continuity between generations and provide for the orderly transmission of property and social position between generations. Kinship systems define a universe of others on whom a person can depend for aid. The adaptiveness of social groups larger than the nuclear family accounts for the fact that expanded kin groups are found in so many human societies.

Kinship systems grow out of a group's history as well as its relationship to the environment and its subsistence strategies. Once in place, however, kinship systems take on a life of their own, although as economic and historical circumstances change, kinship ideologies may be manipulated and negotiated to fit the new realities.

Rules of Descent and the Formation of Descent Groups

In anthropological terminology, **descent** is a culturally established affiliation with one or both parents. Descent is an important basis of social group formation in many societies. A **descent group** is a group of consanguineal (blood-related) kin who are lineal descendants of a common ancestor extending beyond two generations. In nonindustrial societies, descent groups organize domestic life, enculturate children, determine the use and transfer of property and political and ritual offices, carry out religious rituals, settle disputes, engage in warfare, and structure the use of political power.

Descent: The culturally established affiliation between a child and one or both parents.

Descent group: A group of kin who are descendants of a common ancestor, extending beyond two generations.

Unilineal Descent

The rules for establishing descent may be unilineal or bilateral. Under **unilineal descent**, descent group membership is based on links through *either* the paternal line or the maternal line, but not both. Unilineal descent rules are either patrilineal, in which a person belongs to the descent group of the father, or matrilineal, in which a person belongs to the descent group of the mother. One important adaptive advantage of unilineal descent systems is that kin groups do not overlap, thus binding their members more tightly to one another. Also, unilineal descent rules provide a clearly defined group membership for everyone in the society. This allows people to more easily understand their rights of ownership, social duties, and social roles, and allows them to relate to a large number of known and unknown people in the society.

Unilineal descent: Descent group membership based on links through either the maternal or the paternal line, but not both.

Unilineal descent groups can perpetuate themselves over time even though their membership changes. Like modern corporations, unilineal descent groups are permanent units that have an existence beyond the individuals who are members at any given time. Old members die and new ones are admitted through birth, but the integrity of the corporate group persists. Such groups can own property and manage resources, also like modern corporations.

▊ Types of Unilineal Descent Groups: Lineages and Clans

Lineage: A group of kin whose members trace descent from a known common ancestor.

Patrilineage: A lineage formed by descent in the male line.

Matrilineage: A lineage formed by descent in the female line.

A **lineage** is a kin group whose members trace descent from a common ancestor and who can demonstrate those genealogical links among themselves. **Patrilineages** are lineages formed by descent through the male line; **matrilineages** are formed by descent through the female line. Lineages may vary in size, from three generations upward. Related lineages may form clans. The common clan ancestor may be a mythological figure; sometimes, no specific ancestor is known or named.

Clans and lineages have different functions in different societies. The lineage often is a local residential or domestic group whose members cooperate on a daily basis. Clans are generally not residential units but tend to spread out over many villages. Therefore, clans often have political and religious functions rather than primarily domestic and economic ones. Clans are important in regulating marriage. In most societies, clans are exogamous, which strengthens their unilineal character. **Exogamy** is a rule specifying that a person must marry outside a particular group. If a person married within the clan, his or her children would find it difficult to make sharp distinctions between maternal and paternal relatives. This person would not know how to act toward others, and others would not know how to act toward him or her. Clan exogamy also extends the network of peaceful social relations within a society as different clans are allied through marriage.

Exogamy: A rule specifying that a person must marry outside a particular group.

Patrilineal descent: A rule that affiliates a person to kin of both sexes related through males only.

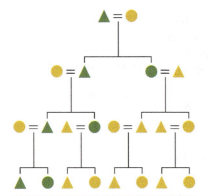

Figure 9.5 Membership in a patrilineal descent group is based on links through the father only. Sons and daughters belong to their father's descent group (shown in dark green), as do the children of sons but not of daughters.

▊ Patrilineal Descent: The Nuer

In societies with **patrilineal descent** groups, both males and females belong to the descent group of the father, the father's father, and so on (see Figure 9.5). Thus, a man, his sisters and brothers, his own children, his brother's children (but not his sister's children), and his son's children (but not his daughter's children) all belong to the same descent group. Inheritance and succession to office move from father to son.

Although the status of women varies in patrilineal systems, in general, the husband is guaranteed rights and control over his wife (or wives) and children because the continuity of the descent group depends on this. Patrilineal systems most often have patrilocal rules of residence, so a wife may find herself living among strangers, which tends to undermine female solidarity and support.

The Nuer, an East African pastoral people, are a patrilineal society. All rights, privileges, obligations, and interpersonal relationships are regulated by kinship. A man, his father, his brothers, and their children are considered the closest kin. Patrilineal membership confers rights to land, requires participation in certain religious ceremonies, and determines political and judicial obligations, such as making alliances in feuds and warfare.

Lineage membership may spread over several villages, helping to create alliances between members of otherwise independent villages that contain members of several different lineages. Each Nuer clan, which is viewed as being composed of related lineages, not individuals, is also spread over several villages. Because one's own lineage or clan and one's mother's lineage and clan are exogamous, kinship relations are widely extended throughout the tribe. In the absence of a centralized system of political control, these kinship-based alliances are an important mechanism of governance. The Nuer believe that close kin should not fight with one another, so interlineage or interclan disputes are kept small and are settled rapidly (Evans-Pritchard 1968/1940). But nonkin are perceived as potential enemies, so an attack by outsiders on one lineage segment may cause all clan members to join in warfare against a common enemy and their clan brothers (Sahlins 1961).

▇ Matrilineal Descent: The Hopi

In matrilineal societies the most important ties are between a woman, her mother, and her siblings. Because children belong to the mother's descent group, the membership of a **matrilineal descent** group (see Figure 9.6) consists of a woman, her brothers and sisters, her sisters' (but not her brothers') children, her own children, and the children of her daughters (but not of her sons).

In matrilineal societies, the rights and responsibilities of the father in a patrilineal society fall to a woman's brother, not her husband. Marriage gives a man sexual and economic rights over his wife, but not rights over their children. After marriage, a man usually goes to live with or near his wife's kin; he is thus an outsider in his wife's household, while she is surrounded by her kin. Because a husband's role in a matrilineal society is less important than in a patrilineal one, marriages in matrilineal societies tend to be less stable.

In matrilineal societies, like the Hopi of the American Southwest, the rights and responsibilities vested in male elders fall to a woman's brother rather than her husband. This decreases conflict between fathers and sons, but also means that a man must pass on his knowledge, property, and offices

Matrilineal descent: A rule that affiliates a person to kin of both sexes related through females only.

Figure 9.6 Membership in a matrilineal descent group is defined by links through the mother. Sons and daughters are members of their mother's descent group (shown in dark green), as are the children of daughters but not of sons.

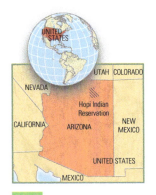

Location of the Hopi.

to the sons of his sister, not his own sons. This may engender conflicts between a man and his nephews, who are subject to his control. Thus, in a matrilineal system, a man's loyalties are split between his own sons and his sisters' sons, a tension that does not occur in patrilineal systems.

Among the Hopi, the strongest tie is between sisters, who, with their mother, form the foundation of the household group. If one sister dies, another sister looks after her children; sisters cooperate in all domestic tasks, and the few quarrels that arise are settled by the mother's brother or by their own brothers.

Husbands are peripheral in their wife's household. Their mother's place is their home, to which they return for rituals and ceremonials and upon separation or divorce. A son belongs to his mother's lineage, keeps his personal and ritual property in her home, and consults his mother for all important decisions.

A boy's relationship with his maternal uncle is characterized by reserve, respect, and even fear, while his relationship with his father is affectionate and involves little discipline. He has a few ritual and economic obligations to his father's family but engages in little direct cooperation and does not come under their authority. A Hopi man teaches his sons the subsistence tasks of farming and sheepherding, and sons support their father in his old age. A man's relationship with his daughter is affectionate but not close, and he has few specific duties regarding her upbringing.

Hopi matrilineal clans extend over many villages, as both his own clan, his father's clan, and his mother's father's clan are exogamous. Through matrilineal clan membership and through marriage, a Hopi man acquires a wide range of relatives, all of whom are called by kinship terms. This relates a Hopi man to almost everyone in his village, in other villages, and to similar clans in other Pueblo societies (Eggan 1950).

▌▌Double Descent

Double descent: The tracing of descent through both matrilineal and patrilineal links, each of which is used for different purposes.

About 5 percent of the world's cultures practice **double descent**. In this system, a person belongs both to the patrilineal group of the father and to the matrilineal group of the mother. However, these descent groups operate in different areas of life. Among the Yako of Nigeria, for example, rights to farmland, forest products, as well as some religious offices derive from membership in a patrilineal group, while matrilineal relations govern the transfer of accumulated wealth, such as currency, livestock, tools, weapons, and household goods.

Bilateral Kinship Systems

About 40 percent of the world's societies do not have lineages and are bilateral; in a few cases, they are ambilineal. Under rules of **bilateral descent**, both maternal and paternal lines are used equally as the basis for reckoning descent and for establishing the rights and obligations of kinship. Bilateral systems do not have clear-cut descent groups. Rather, they have networks of kin, called kindreds, which are defined only in their relation to a particular individual. Except for brothers and sisters, every individual's kindred is unique. Kindreds are actually overlapping categories of kin rather than social groups, and thus are more difficult to organize as cooperative, kin-based collectivities. For example, because a kindred is not a group, it cannot own land or have continuity over time.

Bilateral descent: Both maternal and paternal lines are used as a basis for reckoning descent.

American Bilateral Family

Bilateral kinship systems seem particularly adaptive in societies where mobility and independence are important. They are basic to Western culture, including the United States, and predominate among foraging societies as well (see Figure 9.7).

In some Pacific Island societies, the kinship system is ambilineal: Individuals may choose to affiliate with either their mother's or their father's descent group, but not simultaneously with both. Upon marriage, the new couple can live with either spouse's descent group, a decision most often based on access to land, although friendship and politics also play a role.

Figure 9.7 Kinship ties through descent and marriage are important, even in societies like the United States. This family reunion of the Tracys, with nuclear families wearing shirts of the same color, indicates the importance of both the nuclear family and the kindred.

Courtesy of Tom Curtin

THE CLASSIFICATION OF KIN

In all societies, kin are referred to by special terms. The total system of kinship terms and the rules for using these terms make up a kinship classification system. Every kinship classification system groups some relatives together (referred to by the same kinship term) and differentiates them from other relatives (called by different terms). Some kinship systems have only a small number of kinship terms, whereas others have a different term for almost every relative.

The classification of kin is related to the roles they play in society. In a kinship diagram, Ego is the person from whose perspective the chart is drawn and viewed. If, for example, Ego refers to his father and his father's brothers by the same term, his relationship with them tends to be similar. By the same token, if Ego's father and father's brothers are referred to by different terms, it is expected that Ego will act differently toward each of them and that they will act differently toward him. These ideals are modified (within limits) by the relationships and personalities of particular individuals.

Kinship classification is one of the most important regulators of behavior in most societies. It defines how each person must act toward others and how others must act toward him or her. Kinship classification systems are related to other aspects of culture, such as the types of social groups that are formed and the systems of marriage and inheritance.

Understanding the variety of kinship systems makes the crucial anthropological point that although each society considers its own kinship classification system natural and normal, the logic underlying all kinship systems is cultural, not biological. For example, in the United States, the brothers and sisters of one's parents and their spouses are called "aunt" and "uncle," and the children of these relatives are called "cousin." Have you ever asked yourself why the same term is used for mother's sister, a relative by blood, and mother's brother's wife, a relative by marriage? Or why there are no separate terms for male and female cousins, but gender does differentiate nieces from nephews?

Principles for the Classification of Kin

Lineal kin: Blood relations linked through descent, such as Ego, Ego's mother, Ego's grandmother, and Ego's daughter.

Societies use a combination of some, but not all, of seven important principles of kinship classification in their kinship terminology: (1) *generation*, which distinguishes ascending and descending generations from Ego; (2) *relative age*, where seniority counts, for example, in distinguishing an older from a younger brother; (3) *lineality* versus *collaterality*, where **lineal kin** are related in a single line, such as grandfather–father–son, whereas collateral kin are descended from a common ancestor with Ego but are not Ego's direct ascendants or descendants, for example, siblings or cousins; (4) *gender*, which differentiates relatives according to whether they are male or female (in English, for example, gender distinguishes between aunt and uncle, but not cousins); (5) *consanguineal* versus *affinal* kin, which differentiates relatives by blood in contrast to relatives by marriage; whereas the principle of (6) *sex of linking relative* operates, for example, to differentiate cross-cousins from parallel cousins; and (7) *bifurcation*, which distinguishes relatives from the mother's side of the family from those of the father's side and is used by societies that distinguish the mother's brother from the father's brother. These seven principles combine in different ways to form different types of kinship systems.

In making sense out of kinship systems, anthropologists attempt to understand the relationship of terminologies, rules of descent, and kinship groups to the ecological, economic, and political conditions under which different kinship systems emerge.

BRINGING IT BACK HOME:
CARING FOR THE ELDERLY

Aging is a universal biological aspect of being human that must be understood within a cultural context (Sokolofsky 2009). One essential question every society must address is who will care for the aged. This question is particularly important today: With the advent of modern medicine, particularly in wealthy Western nations, old age has become associated with a long dying process and such potentially incapacitating diseases as hypertension, cancer, coronary heart disease, and Alzheimer's disease, resulting in the emergence of many forms of institutionalized care, such as assisted living facilities, nursing homes, and in-home care (Nanda and Gregg 2011).

Even in societies with extended family systems, like India and China, where family care for the aged at home is embedded in traditional cultural values, such institutions now have an expanded role in elder care (Lamb 2009). In China, as the young migrate to cities, old people are left in the villages and the traditional obligations for a son to provide for his parents in their old age are breaking down (French 2006; Jacobs and Century 2012). Indeed, girls may now be favored over boys as they are emotionally closer to their families and take their family care obligations more assiduously (Greenhalgh 2007). Still, some urban communities, in an effort to shame people who neglect their elderly parents, post their names on public bulletin boards; in others, local homes for the elderly fine children who miss weekend parental visits.

And in societies like Japan, where integration and group harmony are valued over competitive independence, the Japanese elderly are frequently anxious about becoming a burden to their children and anxious about their inability to ever pay back the obligations they incur toward family members who care for them (Traphagan 1998). With Japan's smaller families, new death rituals have been constructed so that those left behind will be less burdened by elaborate—and expensive—mortuary rites (Kawano 2010).

American Muslims are also finding that the realities of modern life may conflict with the Koranic interpretation to care for one's elderly relatives at home. For many American Muslims, the idea of nursing homes is unthinkable, but some working Muslim families have no other options. In response, some Muslims are designing institutions for the elderly that make these more acceptable—by adjoining the nursing homes to mosques or providing communal prayer rooms, serving halal food, providing same-sex medical and nursing care, and adding multilingual staff (Clemetson 2006).

In the United States, the importance of independence as a cultural value and the anxiety surrounding "becoming a burden" help explain the increasing numbers of elderly people who prefer to live alone if financially able to do so. This varies by gender: Elderly widowed or divorced males are twice as interested in dating and remarriage as elderly women (Klinenberg 2012a). There is also variation among subcultures: Among Italian Americans, elderly parents have a high expectation that they will be taken care of by and will live with their children. Unlike the Indian diaspora, in which sons are mainly responsible for elder care, this responsibility among Italian Americans tends to fall more on daughters than on sons. This can lead to difficulties, especially if the parent is widowed or in poor health, if family finances are tight, or if daughters are working professionals, as is increasingly the case. As in other aspects of family structure, economics, culture, public policy, and personal family factors all play a role in who cares for the elderly.

YOU DECIDE:

1. Who do you think should bear the major burden for caring for the elderly in American society? How do various options reinforce or conflict with important American values, such as individualism, economic success, or privacy?

2. What options would you choose for caring for the elders in your own family? How are these choices shaped by your own current life situation or the future you envision for yourself? What private or government services do you think could ease this responsibility for elder care in a way consistent with American values?

3. How does gender affect the experience of elder care, for example, the differences between caring for a widowed father or a widowed mother, or whether this responsibility should fall more on sons or daughters? Explain your response.

CHAPTER SUMMARY

1. What are some major functions of marriage and the family? Three major functions of marriage and the family are regulating sexual access between males and females, arranging for the exchange of services between males and females, and assigning responsibility for child care.

2. Define the incest taboo and give some explanations for its universality. Incest taboos are prohibitions on mating between people classified as relatives. It may function to prevent disruption based on sexual competition within the family and force people to marry out of their immediate families, thus extending their social alliances.

3. What are some universal or widespread marriage rules? Exogamy and endogamy are almost universal. Cousin marriage, the number of spouses, the exchange of goods and services, the degree of control a kin group has over spousal choice, and the responsibilities for elders are all embedded in marriage rules.

4. What are the two basic types of families, and how are these related to other social or economic conditions? The *nuclear* family is found mainly in contemporary industrial and foraging societies. The *extended* family is found predominantly in agricultural societies.

5. What defines a household, and how does household composition relate to other rules about marriage and family? A household is usually made up of family members, but may include others. Household composition is shaped by postmarital residence rules, which are most commonly patrilocal, but may also be matrilocal, or least frequently, neolocal, as in the United States.

6. What are kinship systems, and what are their functions in society? Kinship systems are cultural creations that define and organize relatives by blood and marriage. They include groups formed by kinship

and the terms used to classify different kin. Kinship systems provide continuity between generations and define a group of people who can depend on one another for mutual aid.

7. How are lineages different from clans in structure and functions? Lineage members can trace their descent from a common ancestor while clan members believe they have a common ancestor but cannot trace the relationship genealogically. Lineages mainly have domestic functions, while clans mainly have political and religious functions. Both lineages and clans are important in regulating marriage.

8. What is the difference between patrilineal and matrilineal systems? In patrilineal systems, a man's children and his sons' children, but not his daughters' children, belong to his lineage. In matrilineal systems, a woman's children belong to her lineage, not their father's lineage. In matrilineal systems, the mother's brother has authority over his sisters' children, and relations between husband and wife are more fragile than in patrilineal systems.

9. What are some of the important categories of kinship terminology? Kinship terminology categorizes people according to generation, relative age, lineality or collaterality, gender, consanguinity or affinity, bifurcation, and sex of the linking relative.

KEY TERMS

Bilateral descent
Bridewealth
Composite (compound)
   family
Consanguinity
Cross-cousin marriage
Descent
Descent group
Double descent
Dowry
Endogamy
Exogamy
Extended family
Incest taboos
Kinship
Kinship system

Levirate
Lineal kin
Lineage
Marriage
Matrilineage
Matrilineal descent
Monogamy
Nuclear family
Parallel-cousin marriage
Patrilineage
Patrilineal descent
Polyandry
Polygamy
Polygyny
Sororate
Unilineal descent

Serena Nanda

The hijras of India are an alternative gender, neither men nor women. They exhibit exaggerated female gestures, wear women's clothing, keep their hair long, and perform at weddings and childbirths.

10

SEX AND GENDER

AFTER YOU HAVE READ THIS CHAPTER, YOU WILL BE ABLE TO:

Δ Differentiate between sex and gender.

Δ Illustrate some diverse ways in which gender is culturally constructed, with at least two examples.

Δ Describe some alternative gender roles using examples from different cultures.

Δ Compare sexuality practices in different societies.

Δ Explain some functions of gender-related initiation rites for males and females.

Δ Summarize different theories that attempt to explain gender hierarchy.

Δ Compare gender relations typical of foraging, horticultural, pastoral, agricultural, and industrial societies.

THE HIJRAS: AN ALTERNATIVE GENDER IN INDIA

Hijra: An alternative gender role in India conceptualized as neither man nor woman.

THE **hijras** are an ambiguous gender role in India. Although born male, they are considered neither man nor woman. Hijras undergo an operation in which their genitals are surgically removed. This procedure accounts for the popular designation of hijras as eunuchs. Hijras consider this operation a rebirth, and it is carried out as an act of devotion to the Hindu mother goddess. After the operation, hijras are believed to incorporate the goddess's powers of procreation. Thus, their presence is required at weddings and at the birth of a child.

Hijra performances involve clapping, drumming, and the tinkling of ankle bells, which announce their arrival. Tossing their spangled scarves, flashing their heavy jewelry, and beating their drums, the hijras sing and dance, making comic, ribald gestures and striking sexually suggestive feminine poses, causing men to laugh and women to hide discreet, embarrassed giggling behind their hands. In celebrating the birth of a male child, the dancers take the infant from his mother's arms and bless him with wishes for prosperity and virility, meanwhile examining his genitals to confirm that he is a fully formed male infant. At the end of their performance, the hijras are given their traditional payment of money, cloth, and sweets, satisfied with having once again confirmed their importance in Indian society.

Because they are born male, hijras are mainly perceived as "not man," but they are also thought of as "man plus woman." They adopt women's clothing, gestures, and behaviors. They must wear their hair long, like women, and they have a special language that includes feminine expressions, intonations, and female kinship terms. But hijras are also "not woman," mainly because they cannot bear children.

Gender role: The cultural expectations of men and women in a particular society, including the division of labor.

As neither man nor woman, hijras identify with the many ambiguous **gender roles** and figures in Hindu mythology and Indian culture: male deities who change into or disguise themselves as females temporarily, deities who have both male and female characteristics, male religious devotees who dress and act as women in religious ceremonies, eunuchs who serve in the Muslim courts, and the ascetics, or holy men of India, whose renunciation of all sexuality paradoxically becomes the source of their power to bless others with fertility. Indian culture thus not only accommodates such androgynous figures as the hijras but also views them as meaningful, sacred, and even powerful (Nanda 1999; 2013).

▌▌▌ SEX AND GENDER AS CULTURAL CONSTRUCTS

India is only one of many societies throughout the world where cultural support is given to individuals who transcend or bridge the differences between male and female (Nanda 2014). Bangladesh also contains hijra communities (Hossain 2012); other alternative gender roles are the *mahu* of Polynesia (Besnier 1996; Matzner 2001), the *xanith* of Oman (Wikan 1977), the *two-spirit* found in many Native American tribes (Roscoe 1991; 1995; Whitehead 1981; Williams 1986), the *travesti* of Brazil (Kulick 1998), the *kathoey* of Thailand (Costa and Matzner 2007), the *bakla* of the Philippines (Johnson 1996; Manalansan 2003), the *waria* of Indonesia (Boellstorff 2004; Graham 2006), the *yan daudo* of Nigeria (Gaudio 2009), and the many gender alternatives in Malaysia (Peletz 2009). Most of these roles involve males who adopt women's work, dress, and behavior, but there are female alternative gender roles as well (Blackwood 1998).

Why do anthropologists study such esoteric subjects as alternative genders, and what we can learn from them? After all, the division of humans into two opposite sexes—male and female—appears to be natural and a basic aspect of human biology. Sex assignment, which takes place at birth, is assumed to be permanent for a person's lifetime. Many of us take for granted that sex is the same as gender and that people come in two opposing and unchangeable categories. But, although every culture acknowledges the biological differences between male and female, there is great cultural variety in the number of sexes and genders a society constructs and how sex and gender are defined. As Alexeyeff and Besnier (2013) point out in their study of alternative genders in Pacific Island societies, understanding marginal gender roles helps us explore the gender norm, as well as the relationships between gender and sexuality, local and global dynamics, and historical change and how those considered marginal subvert or reinforce larger cultural and social structures.

A basic anthropological concept is the distinction between the biological and cultural aspects of being male or female. **Sex** refers to the biological differences between male and female, particularly the visible differences in external genitalia and the related difference in the role each sex plays in the reproductive process. **Gender** is the cultural and social classification of masculine and feminine. In other words, *gender* refers to the social, cultural, and psychological constructs that different societies superimpose on the biological differences of sex (Worthman 1995:598). Every culture recognizes distinctions between male and female, but cultures differ in the meanings attached to these categories, the supposed sources of the differences between them, and the relationship of these categories to other cultural and social facts. As noted previously, gender

Sex: The biological difference between male and female.

Gender: A cultural construction that makes biological and physical differences into socially meaningful categories.

is not limited to masculine and feminine; neither in fact, is sex. In the United States in the 20th century, the parents of infants born biologically intersexed were persuaded by medical and psychological professionals to "fix" their sex through surgery and socialize such infants into the gender consistent with their new, altered sex. But more recent research indicates that there are many different kinds of biological intersex conditions and that the designation of intersexuality is, like the concepts of sex and gender, culturally constructed (Karkazis 2008; 2014; Nanda 2013; Bolin and Whelehan 2015).

Gender and gender relations are among the basic building blocks of culture and society, central to social relations of power; individual and group identities; formation of kinship and other groups; and attribution of meaning and value. This makes gender a central interest of contemporary anthropology. Understanding that gender roles are not biologically determined but rather are culturally constructed raises new questions about the culturally patterned nature of women's and men's lives in all cultures, including our own.

Cross-cultural ethnography demonstrates that not only do different cultures incorporate different genders beyond those of man and woman, but that concepts of masculine and feminine also vary among cultures. Thus, to grasp the potential and the limits of diversity in human life, we must look at the full range of human societies—particularly those outside Western historical, cultural, and economic traditions. When we broaden our perspective on sex and gender beyond our own society, we see that culture counts. Both sex and gender are culturally constructed and extraordinarily diverse, as are the relationships between sex and gender.

Cultural construction of gender: The idea that gender characteristics are the result of historical, economic, and political forces acting within each culture.

The work of anthropologist Margaret Mead was essential in developing the now central anthropological principle of the **cultural construction of gender**. In other words, gender characteristics are the result of historical, economic, and political forces acting within each culture. In the 1930s, Mead (1963/1935) began to question the biologically determined nature of gender. In her famous 1935 book, *Sex and Temperament in Three Primitive Cultures,* she examined the behavior of men and women in three New Guinea societies, the Arapesh, the Mundugumor, and the Tchambuli. Mead found that the whole repertoire of behaviors, emotions, and roles that go into being masculine and feminine is patterned by culture. Among the Arapesh, men and women both were expected to act in ways that Americans considered naturally feminine. Both sexes were concerned with taking care of children and nurturing. Neither sex was expected to be aggressive. In Mundugamor society, both sexes were what American culture would call masculine: aggressive, violent, and with little interest in children. Among the Tchambuli, the personalities of men and women were different from each other but opposite to American conceptions of masculine and feminine. Women had the major economic role and showed common sense and business shrewdness. Men were more interested in esthetics. They spent much time decorating themselves and gossiping. Their feelings were easily hurt, and they sulked a lot.

Although Mead's ethnographic descriptions of these societies were later criticized and superseded (di Leonardo 1998:213–215; 2003; Roscoe 2003), her work made a lasting contribution by raising the issue of the great diversity in cultural definitions of masculine and feminine and by calling attention to the ways in which gender and gender relations are cultural constructs. A society's **gender ideology**, that is, its totality of ideas about sex, gender, the natures of men and women, including their sexuality, and the relations between the genders, is significant not only in its own right but because it is a core element in a society's stratification system, which is also gendered.

Location of the Arapesh, the Mundugamor, and the Tchambuli.

Gender ideology: The totality of ideas about sex, gender, the natures of men and women, including their sexuality, and the relations between the genders.

CREATIVE EXPRESSIONS OF GENDER: DEEP PLAY AND MASCULINE IDENTITY

Every society includes many and varied cultural dimensions of gender ideology and gender identity. Games and sports such as football in the United States, cockfighting in Bali, rugby in Tonga, or bullfighting in Spain are all ways of both learning and reinforcing culturally constructed gender values. Clifford Geertz calls these activities "deep play" (Geertz 1973a), because they heighten emotions, display compelling aspects of social structure and culture, and reinforce culturally constructed gender identities.

A prime example of deep play in the construction of masculinity is the Spanish bullfight. Although many outsiders and a growing number of Spaniards, consider bullfighting a cruel assault on animals, bullfighting is traditionally an aesthetic ritual central in gender ideology, and most of the people who enjoy it do not view it as a form of violence or cruelty (Eller 2006:104). Despite their violent acts, bullfighters are culturally compelled to restrain any sign of anger or aggression; indeed, such signs contradict the essence of bullfighting as an art. In Spanish culture, bullfights involve a complex and elaborate process of ritualized violence that makes it not only acceptable but also beautiful. The point of a bullfight is not simply to kill a bull; that would be easy and would lack any cultural meaning. Rather, it is the skill, grace, and courage of the bullfighter that is essential to the performance. The bullfight embodies the values of male competition in defense of the male self-image of honor. For the audience, the maximum vindication of honor is in the physical showdown, in

Figure 10.1 The Spanish bullfight is one of the many diverse ways in which masculine gender identities and roles are expressed in the deep play of sports.

public, between two men. The matador symbolizes the role of the honorable male; he is not a fighter or a man with a reputation for violence, nor is he an athlete, personally aggressive, or necessarily big or muscular. In a bullfight, the bull is the angry and ferocious male, whereas the matador is skilled, self-controlled, and calm—he is able to master the violent situation without becoming violent himself.

For the matador and the spectators, it is not the suffering of the bull but the style and aesthetic performance of the matador that is central. At the kill, the most dangerous part of the performance for the matador, the matador cannot use his sword to weaken the bull or defend himself. Any prolonged suffering of the bull is strongly disapproved of by the spectators, and a matador who performs a sloppy kill is called a murderer. For the Spanish, a bullfight is not an example of indulging in man's animal nature (which is how they view a North American boxing match), but a performance that allows man to transcend his animal nature as it distinguishes a man of honor from a man of anger. Honor is a central concept in Spanish masculine identity—and indeed in much of Mediterranean culture (Gilmore 1996). The art of the bullfight is one of the ways in which this cultural value is expressed, for both the performers and the audience.

In spite of the well-established connection between bullfighting and masculinity in Spain, this cultural construct of gender is slowly changing. Over the past century, women in Andalusia, in southern Spain, have been fighting to enter the bullring. Many Andalusians, however, including male bullfighters, reject this attempt to overturn traditional gender roles.

Some male bullfighters refuse to fight in the ring with women; parents discourage their daughters from pursuing a bullfighting career, trainers refuse to train women bullfighters, and some spectators refuse to attend bullfights in which female bullfighters participate. But the women bullfighters themselves are persisting. And some Andalusians support the women's efforts: In contrast to those who reject women participating in this most masculine example of Spanish "deep play," some male Andalusians view the women as supremely courageous and professional, and find them, in their tight costumes, supremely sexy. But, however one views women bullfighters, they certainly stretch the traditional notion of what it means to be a woman in Spain (Gottlieb 2002:167–189).

On the Pacific Island of Tonga, rugby is the form of deep play central to the construction of masculinity (Besnier 2012). Rugby is of English origin and was introduced to Tonga in the early 20th century. Today almost all Tongan boys play rugby from early childhood. Girls, in contrast, play netball, a watered-down version of basketball, which is of practically no public interest. Rugby is essential in male socialization: All Tongan villages and boys' schools have rugby clubs, and boys and many men play rugby informally almost every day. Rugby gives boys the chance to learn resourcefulness and skills to confound opponents, central to the male gender role. For Tongans, rugby expresses ideals of virility, fortitude, and controlled aggression, and it favors the large, heavily muscular bodies of Tongan men, also central to masculine identity and pride.

Ironically, because of a shortage of outstanding rugby players in Japan, where rugby is an elite but marginal sport, Tongan players have been recruited to beef up rugby teams. The Tongan players are viewed as both physically and socially unattractive, however. Their corpulence, hairiness, crude manners, hard drinking, and chain smoking are identified as "gorilla macho," the very antithesis of the contemporary Japanese masculine ideal of "slim macho," which incorporates a slim and well-groomed look. Such is the diversity of constructions of masculinity from a cross-cultural perspective (Besnier 2012).

CULTURAL VARIATION IN SEXUAL BEHAVIOR

Understanding gender systems as culturally constructed also helps explain the cultural variations in definitions of appropriate sexual behavior. Although sexual activity is most often—and for most people—viewed as "doing what comes naturally," a cross-cultural perspective demonstrates that human sexual activity is patterned by a culture's gender ideology and influenced by learning.

Culture patterns the habitual responses of different peoples to different parts of the body. What is erotic in some cultures is considered disgusting in others. Kissing, for example, is not universal. The Tahitians learned to kiss from the Europeans; before this cultural contact, Tahitians began sexual intimacy by sniffing. Among the Alaskan Inuit, sniffing the hollow in another's cheek can be both a pattern of sexual as well as non-sexual behavior. When an adult asks a child to do this, it is affectionate and innocent, whereas among adults it is considered quite erotic. Like a kiss in our own culture, it is the social construct of behavior that counts.

Sexual foreplay is also culturally diverse. In the Trobriand Islands, a couple expresses affection by inspecting each other's hair for lice, a practice Westerners may find disgusting. To the Trobrianders, however, the European habit of a couple going on a picnic with a knapsack of prepared food is equally disgusting, although it is perfectly acceptable for a Trobriand boy and girl to gather wild foods together as a prelude to sexual activity (Malinowski 1929b:327, 335).

Who is considered an appropriate sexual partner also differs among cultures. In some societies, like the United States, same-sex practices may stigmatize men as homosexual, but same-sex intimacy may be a matter of indifference or even approval in other cultures. Among the Sambia of New Guinea, what Americans call homosexual practice is culturally central in the sex/gender system as a core ritual in male initiation. In Sambian culture, women are viewed as dangerous creatures that pollute men and deplete them of their masculinity substance. The Sambia believe that males do not naturally mature as fast or as competently as females. The Sambia believe that males cannot achieve reproductive competence without semen, which is not naturally produced but must be externally and artificially introduced into the body. Thus, an essential part of Sambia male initiation is for boys to consume semen from adult men through repeated homosexual fellatio. Only in this way can boys become "strong men" capable of becoming fathers and vigorous warriors (Herdt 1981; 1996:431–436).

Among ancient Greeks, homosexual relationships were considered superior to heterosexual relations, and in many contemporary cultures, such as India (Seabrook 1999) or Brazil (Kulick 1998), the male who takes the dominant (inserter) role in same-sex relationships is not considered homosexual and his behavior is not stigmatized. In Thailand, as long as a man fulfills his family obligations to marry, his homosexual practice does not become a source of discrimination or dishonor (Jackson 1999). The many cultures in which same-sex relationships are viewed as normal variants of human sexuality contrast strongly with the prevailing view in 19th- and 20th-century Europe and the United States, where consistent male heterosexuality was considered essential to masculine identity.

The ages at which sexual response is believed to begin and end, the ways in which people make themselves attractive, the importance of sexual activity in human life, and its variation according to gender—all these are patterned and regulated by culture and affect sexual response and behavior. Two classic ethnographies that highlight the role of culture in impacting sexuality are that of the Irish of Inis Beag and that of the Polynesians of Mangaia.

Anthropologist John Messenger (1971:15) describes Inis Beag as "one of the most sexually naive of the world's societies." Sex is never discussed at home when children are near, and parents provide practically no sexual instruction to children. Adults believe that "after marriage nature takes its course." (As we shall see, "nature" takes a very different course in Inis Beag than it does in Polynesia!) Women are expected to endure but not enjoy sexual relations; to refuse to have intercourse is considered a mortal sin among these Roman Catholic people. There appears to be widespread ignorance in Inis Beag of the female capacity for orgasm, which is considered deviant behavior in any case. Nudity is abhorred, and there is no tradition of dirty jokes. The main style of dancing allows little bodily contact among the participants; even so, some girls refuse to dance because it means touching a boy. The separation of the sexes begins very early in Inis Beag and lasts into adulthood. In sexual relations, there is a virtual absence of sexual foreplay, almost no premarital sex, and a high percentage of celibate males. In explaining the extraordinarily late age of marriage, one female informant told the anthropologist, "Men can wait a long time before wanting 'it' but we [women] can wait a lot longer" (Messenger 1971:16).

The extreme sexual repression in Inis Beag is usefully compared to sexual ideology among Polynesians of Mangaia, described by Donald Marshall (1971). Fantasies of complete sexual freedom in the "South Seas" have long been a part of Western culture. In fact, no society has complete sexual freedom, but compared to the traditional Puritan culture of the West, Polynesia perhaps comes closest. In Mangaia, sexual intercourse is one of life's major interests. Sex is not discussed at home, but Mangaia elders teach sexual information to boys and girls at puberty. For adolescent boys, this formal instruction about the techniques of intercourse is followed by a culturally approved experience with a mature woman in the village. After this, the boy is considered a man. This contrasts with Inis Beag, where a man is considered a "lad" until he is about 40. In Mangaia, there is continual public reference to sexual activity: Sexual jokes, expressions, and references are expected as part of the preliminaries to public meetings. And yet, in public, sex segregation is the norm. Boys and girls should not be seen together in public, but practically every girl and boy has had intercourse before marriage. The act of sexual intercourse itself is the focus of sexual activity. Both men and women are expected to take pleasure in the sexual act and to reach orgasm. Celibacy is practically unknown. The contrast between Inis Beag and Mangaia indicates clearly that societies' different attitudes pattern the sexual responsiveness of males and females in each society.

▮▮▮ Gender Ideology and Women's Sexuality

A culture's gender ideology always includes ideas about sexuality, and most societies view males and females as different in this respect. In societies where women are considered more sexually voracious than men, such as both Muslim and Hindu India—a clear contrast with the traditionally dominant Western view—this ideology is often used to justify men's control over women. This control becomes a basis for gender stratification, constraints on women's lives, and discrimination against women who work, go to school, or appear outside their homes without a male escort. It also may include control over women's dress, marriage, divorce, and laws regarding adultery and abortion. Male control over women in many societies, ranging from the horticultural Yanomamo to contemporary postindustrial societies, is often expressed in widespread violence against women, including beatings, rape, forced suicide, and even murder. Society's control of female sexuality may also be inscribed on female bodies, as in female circumcision (Barnes-Dean 1989); Chinese foot binding (Anagnost 1989); and in the West, anorexia and eating disorders motivated by the cultural ideal of model-like slimness (Rhode 2010).

In many cultures, male control of female sexuality is central to notions of honor and shame, and thus to cultural understandings of masculinity (Gilmore 1996; Wikan 2008). Violence against women today is also a political tool, illustrated by widespread rape in warfare in the Congo, the Sudan, and the Islamic state in Iraq and Syria, among other places; as an expression of social stratification, as in the recent gang rape of a lower-caste young woman by the high-caste men in a north Indian village (Yardley 2012); or part of the male culture at a high-status college like Amherst, in the United States, where college administrators look the other way and try to persuade rape victims not to bring charges (Perez-Pena 2012). During the period of military rule in Myanmar (formerly Burma), for example, the state demonized revered political activist and opposition leader, Aung San Suu Kyi, in gendered and sexualized terms, holding that like all women, she used female guile and manipulation to achieve her political goals. The government's propaganda held that, also like other women, she was driven by lust and thus was unfit for any leadership roles (Peletz 2012).

Although some cultural anthropologists emphasize the universality of certain gender ideologies, anthropology also emphasizes the significant diversity regarding women's sexuality both within and among cultures, as affected by history, geography, economics, politics, and the impact of globalization. The issue of female modesty and control of sexuality in Islam provides a useful example (El-Feki 2013). Although Islam is a global religion, Muslim gender ideologies and practices regarding women's sexuality and requirements for modest dress vary in different Islamic societies. This is illustrated by the debates over the wearing of the hijab, or headscarf (see Figure 10.2). For some Muslims, as well as for many non-Muslim Westerners, the hijab is a sign of the oppression of women, making them invisible and restricting their freedom of choice. But some young Muslim women in Europe and the United States view the hijab as a liberating garment that forces the world to see them as more than sexual objects and establishes their identity as Muslims (Bowen 2007).

The Qur'anic injunction requiring modest dress for Muslim women (Qur'an 24:30–31) does not command any specific style, nor specifically mention hijab, making room for much local variation and interpretation. The varying practices regarding female modesty are shaped by history, culture, religious politics, and the degree of male dominance in a society. Factors influencing modest female dress vary among religious sects, among social classes, between rural and urban populations, and among the generations, ranging from the total restrictions on women's autonomy

Joan Young Gregg

Figure 10.2 The hijab, or headscarf, worn by these Malaysian girls, is one means by which some Muslims accommodate the Islamic requirement for women to dress modestly. Wearing the hijab has become a political issue in some Muslim and European societies.

in Saudi Arabia, to the "split personality" of cosmopolitan Dubai. In some societies, most Muslim women only wear a hijab that loosely covers their hair and neck; in others, like Yemen, women wear full head and body coverings as well as a face veil. In the airlines of the United Arab Emirates, a compromise is reached between fashion and religion as air hostesses wear "jaunty little caps with attached gauzy scarves that hint at hijab" (Zoepf 2008). In Afghanistan, under the Islamic State, women were required to wear a burqa, or full body and face covering; these restrictions weakened with the defeat of the Taliban.

In all of these countries, some women resist these laws and customs (Ali 2006; Manji 2003), with varying responses from both the public and public officials. In Tunisia, with the support of international nongovernmental organizations, the great increase in women working outside the home, and important socioeconomic changes impacted by globalization, particularly the tourist industry, wearing the veil and various religion-based laws regarding polygyny, child custody, divorce, and unequal inheritance have become issues for debate in this still patriarchal society. And in Turkey, although women commonly wear the headscarf in public, until recently, they were previously not permitted to wear it in government offices or universities. Wearing the hijab is part of a heated public debate about what should be the secular versus religious character of this largely Muslim state (Tavernise 2008).

Cultural anthropologist Pardis Mahdavi makes an important contribution to this discussion through her ethnography in the Islamic Republic of Iran. In Iran, women are required to wear the hijab, and wearing a chador (outer garment or cloak) is increasingly common because of government and some public pressure. Mahdavi's ethnography of sexuality in Iran (2009), however, describes the widespread breach of many Muslim sexual restrictions, such as premarital chastity, marital fidelity, and the wearing of modest dress among educated, upper-class Iranians. Dating, fashion, nail polish, makeup, and immodest dress are outlawed in Iran, but the formerly widespread policing of these practices in public places has diminished greatly, and girls wear layers of makeup in private. Women's more modern headscarfs are often so transparent and fashionable that they actually look sexy.

The relation between gender practice and culture particularly impacts men in the Muslim diaspora. As anthropologist Katherine Ewing (2008b) demonstrates, German society demonizes Turkish Muslim men as the "other," bearers of Islamic "barbarism," who are associated with the repression and abuse of women as victims of patriarchal oppression. These German assumptions about Turkish masculinity play a central role in the construct of German national identity, reinforced by the popular media, films, social work policies, and public policy, assumptions that Ewing points out are based on long-standing European fantasies about Middle

Eastern gender relations that are contrasted with European enlightenment. This deep study of cross-cultural variation is one of anthropology's most important contributions, and it also helps us reflect more deeply on our own cultural values in the intensely emotional area of gender.

▌▌▌ MALE AND FEMALE RITES OF PASSAGE

In all cultures, the role expectations of individuals change at different points in life, and the individual must learn what is necessary for these new roles. In many societies, the transition from one social status to another is formalized by special **rites of passage**, which move individuals publicly and ceremonially from one stage of life to the next. One widespread rite of passage signals the transition from childhood to adult gender roles (van Gennep 1960/1909).

Rite of passage: A ritual that moves an individual from one social status to another.

Male rites of passage have important psychological and sociological functions. They reinforce the social order by dramatizing cultural values in a public context; they express and affirm male relationships, male solidarity, and, sometimes, male dominance; they publicly validate a change of status from child to adult; and they transmit the cultural knowledge necessary to being a responsible adult male in the society.

These initiation rites often involve an extended period during which boys are separated from the larger society, which emphasizes the importance of an individual's responsibility to his kinship group as well as to the larger community (Hart 1967). The rites often include painful practices such as scarification or circumcision that symbolize the formal transition from child to adult. Such rites may also include difficult and dangerous tasks, such as killing a large animal, which test a boy's preparation for the obligations of male adulthood.

Among the Maasai, a herding society in Kenya, male initiation rites are part of an age-graded social system. Males follow a well-ordered progression through a series of age grades, entry into which requires a formalized rite of passage. After childhood, boys are initiated as warriors, and they remain in that stage for about 15 years. Warriorhood is a period of training in social, political, and military skills and is traditionally geared to warfare and cattle raiding. The warriors then graduate ceremonially to a less active stage, during which they can marry, and then finally, to elderhood in a great ceremony.

Male rites of passage have been interpreted as a means of psychologically separating boys from identification with their mothers (Whiting, Kluckhohn, and Anthony 1967); as the symbolic appropriation of the fertility related to female reproductive capacities; and as a fertility cult in which men celebrate and ritually reproduce their control over the fertility of crops, animals, and humans. These rites also have important social functions. They bring together boys from different parts of the tribe and serve as a lifetime source of solidarity and political integration in social systems that have little formal or central government.

Although masculinity does take different forms in different cultures (Conway-Long 1994; Gutmann 1996; Kimmel 1996), a very widespread cultural pattern is one in which men must prove themselves to be virile, successful in competition with other men, daring, heroic, and aggressive, "proving their manhood" in formal rites, or more informally, on the streets, in bars, or in warfare (Gilmore 1990). In Chuuk, Micronesia (formerly the U.S. territory of Truk), for example, male adolescents engage in excessive drinking and violent brawling, an expression of a cultural concept of masculinity that is defined by competitiveness, assertiveness, risk taking in the face of danger, physical strength, and physical violence (Marshall 1979). Recently, the Chinese government has put out the call for more male teachers in order to "make boys men" through boys-only martial arts classes or teaching stories of heroic Chinese men (Hernandez 2016).

Anthropologist David Gilmore (1990) calls this widespread male need to publicly test and prove one's manhood the "manhood puzzle." To the question of why manhood needs to be proved, why it is regarded as so uncertain or precarious that manhood requires trials of skill, endurance, or special rituals, Gilmore suggests that cultural patterns of "proving manhood" help ensure that men will fulfill their roles as procreators, providers, and protectors of their families. This essential contribution to society, he argues, is at the heart of the "macho" masculine role and accounts for its intensity, near universality, and persistence.

Figure 10.3 In Tamilnadu, India, a girl's coming of age ceremony, pictured here, marks her entry into womanhood. The ritual celebrates her first menstruation and her first sari, and signifies that she is eligible for marriage. Because menstruation is seen as polluting, after three days of seclusion the ceremony ends by a cleansing effected by pouring water over her body.

Serena Nanda/ImagesofAnthropology.com

Female Rites of Passage

Female rites of passage are more widespread than male rites, although generally less spectacular and intense (See Figure 10.3). Female initiation into adulthood is often performed at menarche (first menstruation), but there is much cross-cultural variability (Lutkehaus and Roscoe 1995). Sometimes the initiate is isolated from society; sometimes she is the center of attention. Some rituals are elaborate and take years to perform; others are performed with little ceremony.

As with male rites, female initiation rites also have multiple interpretations. In matrilocal societies, in which the young girl continues her childhood tasks in her mother's home, an important function of the rite is to publicly announce a girl's status change, as she will now carry out these tasks as a responsible adult (Brown 1965), and to teach girls what they need to know to be effective adults. Female rites of passage also channel sexuality into adult reproduction, and in some rituals, the rites emphasize the connections between beauty, sexuality, and power. These rites, in New Guinea, for example, motivate girls to bear and rear children, strengthen their fortitude, and provide them with the capacity for the hard work necessary to assist their husbands in gathering wealth.

POWER AND PRESTIGE: GENDER STRATIFICATION

A central concern in anthropology is **gender stratification**. Anthropologists have long debated whether male dominance is universal and, if so, why it is so. In the interest of addressing these questions, anthropologists look at the social and cultural significance of women's roles as mothers, sisters, wives, and daughters; women's economic contributions in different types of societies; informal as well as formal sources of women's power and influence; development of women's identities; and changes in all these dimensions as a result of historical factors, particularly colonialism, technological and economic change, and globalization.

One early anthropological theory that addresses the widespread, some say universal, subordination of women to men is called the **private/public dichotomy**. This theory holds that female subordination is based on women's universal role as mothers and homemakers, occupying a domestic (private) world that is less prestigious than the public world dominated by men (Rosaldo and Lamphere 1974). But a closer look indicates that the private/public dichotomy is not universal but rather characterizes the highly gender-stratified 19th-century capitalist societies, such as those of Victorian Europe and the United States: In these societies, productive relationships moved out of the household, and middle-class women (but not working-class women) retreated into the home, where they were supposed to concern themselves solely with domestic affairs, repress their sexuality, bear children, and accept a subordinate and dependent role (Martin 1987; for a reevaluation of this theory, see Lamphere 2005). The private/public dichotomy seems less applicable to smaller-scale, non-Western societies where home, family, economics, and politics were not so easily separated, and where women played an important though perhaps not as easily observable role in economic production and

Gender stratification: The ways in which gendered activities and attributes are differentially valued and related to the distribution of resources, prestige, and power in a society.

Private/public dichotomy: A gender system in which women's status is lowered by their almost exclusive cultural identification with the home and children, whereas men are identified with public, prestigious, economic, and political roles.

distribution (Friedl 1975). With increasing Western influence on these societies, through capitalism, Christian missionaries, and colonialism, the public/private dichotomy became a more relevant context for gender stratification (Leacock 1981; Lockwood 2005:504).

Other anthropologists have used controlled cross-cultural comparisons to understand male dominance. Sanday (1981), for example, concluded that male dominance was *not* universal but occurred in connection with ecological stress and warfare: Where the survival of the group rests more on male actions, such as warfare, women accept male dominance for the sake of social and cultural survival.

▌▌▌ Gender Relations: Complex and Variable

Patriarchy: A male-dominated society in which most important public and private power is held by men.

Anthropological debates in earlier gender studies focused on which gender dominated a society. Structural male dominance, called **patriarchy**, was considered universal, or nearly so, although matriarchy, or female dominance, was held to exist in some societies. Although anthropologists generally do not find matriarchies where women hold power equal to that of men in patriarchies, there is more recognition today that female power does find a place in many societies. With a greater understanding of the complexity and variability in gender stratification systems, anthropologists today have moved from the question of whether male dominance is universal to explanations of gender stratification in particular societies. This has led to a closer examination of the sexual division of labor in different types of societies and of the informal as well as formal bases of female power.

▌▌ Gender Relations in Foraging Societies

Earlier anthropological descriptions of foraging societies viewed hunting, a largely male activity, as the major source of the food supply, providing the basis of male dominance in these societies. Later ethnographic studies have modified this view. In many foraging societies, such as the Tiwi of Australia and the Ju/'hoansi of the Kalahari Desert in Namibia, women make very significant contributions to the food supply by gathering vegetables (Hart and Pilling 1960; Lee 2003). In other societies, like the Agta of the Philippines, women also substantially contributed to the food supply by hunting (Estioko-Griffin 1986), although in different ways and for different kinds of animals than men hunted. These contributions by women to the society's food supply were an important source of female power.

The Tlingit of the northwest coast of North America is a foraging society in which women traditionally had equal power and prestige with men. Important Tlingit social roles are based on individual ability,

The Tlingit, on the Northwest Coast of North America.

training, and personality rather than on gender (Klein 1995). Both Tlingit women and men achieve prestige through their own efforts and their own kin relationships. Women may be heads of clans or tribes, and Tlingit aristocrats are both male and female. Titles of high rank are used for both men and women, and the ideal marriage is between a man and woman of equal rank. The prestige the Tlingit achieved through extensive trade with other coastal societies is open to both men and women. Although long-distance trade centered on men in the past, women often accompanied the men, acting as negotiators and handling the money, and both girls and boys were—and are today—expected to "work, save, get wealth and goods" (Klein 1995:35).

Gender egalitarianism continues to be a core Tlingit cultural value. Today, women occupy the highest offices of the native corporations administering Tlingit land and are employed in government, social action groups, business and cultural organizations, and voluntary associations (Klein 1976). Tlingit women take advantage of educational opportunities and easily enter modern professions. Unlike many non-Western societies, where European contact diminished women's economic roles and influence, modernization expanded Tlingit women's roles, and modern gender egalitarianism is not experienced as diminishing men, who encourage their wives and daughters to go into public life.

■■ Gender Relations in Horticultural Societies

Generally speaking, women have more autonomy and power in egalitarian foraging societies than in horticultural, pastoral, or agricultural societies, but again, there is great cross-cultural variation (see Figure 10.4). For example, the Iroquois of the eastern United States are highly egalitarian (Brown 1975), whereas the Yanomamo of Venezuela and Brazil are highly sex-segregated and male-dominated (Chagnon 1997), as are most societies in highland New Guinea (Strathern 1995; but see Lepowsky 1993).

A high degree of sex segregation, paralleled by the importance of males in ritual, is

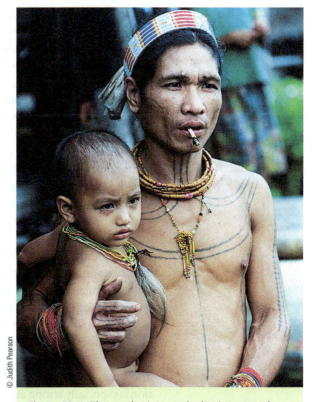

Figure 10.4 The emphasis on male dominance and aggression in horticultural societies overlooks the elements of affection and nurturance that males show as fathers, as in the Iban society of Indonesia.

associated with male dominance in some horticultural societies. Among the Mundurucu of South America, for example, adolescent boys are initiated into the men's cult and thereafter spend most of their lives in the men's house, only visiting their wives, who live with the children in their own huts in the village. The men's cults exclude women and are surrounded by great secrecy. The men's house itself usually is the most imposing structure in the village and houses the cult paraphernalia and sacred musical instruments, which are flutelike in shape (like male genitals) and are the symbolic expressions of male dominance, just as the men's house is an institution of male solidarity (Murphy and Murphy 1974).

The solidarity of women in horticultural societies usually is not formalized in associations but is based on the cooperation of domestic life and strong interpersonal bonds among female kin. In sub-Saharan Africa, for example, the most important economic and emotional ties for both men and women are more likely to be between generations (consanguineal ties) than between spouses (conjugal ties). Women's most important ties are with their children, particularly their sons, on whom women depend for emotional support and security in old age (Potash 1989:199). Women, like men, also use kinship ties with their natal groups to gain access to land, gain support in marital disputes, and participate in ritual activities (Sacks 1982). In many parts of West Africa, women's power is expressed through political office (Kaplan 1997) and also through formally organized secret societies, such as the Sande society of Sierra Leone (MacCormack 1974). Contemporary ethnography demonstrates that women's power and influence sometimes go beyond their economic contributions, their significant roles within households and families, and even beyond formal political offices sometimes occupied by women. An important dimension of female power may rest on female alliances and participation in networks and groups outside the household that provide arenas for entertainment, prestige, influence, and self-esteem. Anthropologist Annette Weiner (1976), for example, demonstrated the important exchanges among women in the Trobriand Islands, where the emphasis on male kula exchanges had excluded any anthropological attention to women's participation in exchange networks.

In some societies, like the Yoruba of West Africa, power is conceptualized as a vital force present in all living things. Personal power may be projected through certain body parts, for example, the eyes, mouth, hands and fingers, and genitals. Power associated with sexuality and reproduction is especially strong and potentially dangerous and polluting, especially female genital power. Indeed, the universal covering of the female genitals may well be related to the power of these body parts (Stevens 2006).

The impact of European expansion on women in horticultural societies varied. Generally, women's roles declined as indigenous economies shifted from subsistence horticulture to cash crops sold in the world market. Among the Nukumanu, a Pacific island society, women's primary responsibilities were domestic, whereas men contributed food acquired at longer distances from the home through fishing, collecting shellfish, and collecting and husking coconuts. Men also made canoes and constructed new buildings, whereas women cooked food and collected and prepared leaves for thatch. Both women's and men's roles were highly valued in traditional Nukumanu society. Women exclusively controlled and cultivated swamp taro lands, which were inherited matrilineally. Matrilocality added to women's status, whereas men's power came from their economic contribution and their exclusive occupation of formal positions of power in the chiefly hierarchy.

With the advent of German colonial occupation in the 1880s, most of Nukumanu was turned over to the production of copra (dried coconut meat). Wage laborers were brought in from nearby islands, commercially marketed foods such as wheat flour and rice supplanted taro, and men's wages were needed to buy coffee, tea, and sugar (once luxury items). As a result, women's traditional sphere of influence and their status declined, while men's spheres of power expanded (Feinberg 1986). The traditional segregation of men's and women's activities also intensified. Kareve (a potent alcoholic beverage made from fermented coconut sap) was introduced in the 1950s, and men's economic activities, such as canoe building, took on a social aspect involving drinking. Because kareve production and consumption takes up much of men's leisure time and excludes women, sexual segregation increased.

As taro declined in importance, women's collective activities became more individualized, leaving them more isolated and dependent on their husbands and brothers than previously. Male–female tensions also increased partly as a result of kareve drinking, which many women vehemently oppose. The traditional tendency for men to travel off the island more than women also lowered women's status, and even today men primarily go overseas for wage labor and higher education. More recently, however, more women are leaving the island to take advantage of educational and career opportunities, and the prestige, money, and social influence of such women may move Nukumanu back toward its tradition of sexual egalitarianism.

▮▮ Gender Relations in Pastoral and Agricultural Societies

Pastoral and agricultural societies tend to be male-dominated, although there is some variation. In pastoral societies, women's status depends on the degree to which the society combines herding with cultivation, its specific historical situation, and the diffusion of cultural ideas, such as

Islam. Generally speaking, women's contribution to the food supply in pastoral societies is small (Martin and Voorhies 1975). Men do almost all the herding and most of the dairy work as well. Male dominance in pastoral society is partly based on the required strength to handle large animals, but females sometimes do handle smaller animals, engage in dairy work, carry water, and process animal by-products such as milk, wool, and hides (O'Kelly and Carney 1986). Pastoral societies generally do not have the rigid distinction between public and domestic roles of agricultural societies. Herders' camps typically are divided into male and female spaces, but both men and women work in public, somewhat blurring the private/public dichotomy.

In pastoral societies, men predominantly own and have control over the disposition of livestock, which is an important source of power and prestige. However, the disposition of herds is always subject to kinship rules and responsibilities, and men and women may jointly hold animals. Still, the male economic dominance in pastoral societies seems to give rise to general social and cultural male dominance, reinforced by patricentric kinship systems and the need for defense through warfare (Sanday 1981).

Again, this generalization is subject to variation. Among the Tuareg of the central Sahara, for example, which is a matrilineal society, women generally have high prestige and substantial influence (Rasmussen 2005). Tuareg women do not veil their faces, they have social and economic independence and can own property, including herd animals, and they have freedom of movement. There is minimal sex segregation, and women organize many social events as singers and musicians. Although the traditionally high status of Tuareg women, and matrilineality itself, is undermined today by the migration of men to cities, where they work for wages, and by the incorporation of the Tuareg into larger nation-states, with their patrilineal cultures, cities may also provide increasing opportunities and freedom for Tuareg women.

In agricultural societies, with the use of plows, the direct female contribution in food production generally drops drastically, though this varies. Women, for example, play important productive roles in wet rice agriculture. As women's economic contribution declines, they lose status, and this is also generally accompanied by their increasing isolation in domestic work in the home and increasing numbers of children (Ember 1983). Machine technology reduces the overall labor force, and this also particularly affects women, who are disproportionately excluded from mechanized agriculture. Women are also paid lower wages as agricultural laborers and are concentrated in such labor-intensive agricultural tasks as weeding, transplanting, and harvesting. Also, as men more easily enter a cash economy, selling crops and animals, transition to this economic system in most cases also lowers women's status and makes them more dependent on men.

Women's status in modern stratified societies varies greatly and is affected by economic development, political ideology, and globalization. Women have been highly involved in the global economy, primarily through the expansion of industrial production by multinational corporations in Latin America, Asia, and Africa. As urban lifestyles and industrial production replace rural lifestyles and agriculture, women may even benefit relative to men. For example, in Mata Chico, Peru, in the 1930s, the only way for women to get land, a critical resource, was to marry. But by the 1980s, as Peru became increasingly urban, many occupations were available to both men and women. Because women could support themselves and their children through employment in urban areas, they began to remain single longer and in some cases chose to not marry at all (Vincent 1998).

▮▮ Using Anthropology: Economic Development for Women

As with colonialism, foreign aid and development programs often fail because while they increase male productivity, they neglect the economic role of women (Kristoff and WuDunn 2009). Indeed, development programs may actually increase gender inequality (Moser 1993; Warren and Bourque 1989). Where anthropologists are involved in development projects, however, more attention may be paid to women's roles. Ann Dunham,* an anthropologist, craftsperson, and weaver, did her fieldwork in Indonesia, and was particularly interested in craft marketing, an important potential source of income for village Indonesians (Dunham et al. 2009). Dunham became particularly interested in the economic possibilities of marketing and later worked for the Ford Foundation and the U.S. Agency for International Development (USAID) development projects in Indonesia and Pakistan. Her fieldwork findings challenged the then-common notion that the culture of the poor themselves created the roots of poverty, a view portrayed by one of anthropology's most prominent anthropologists, Clifford Geertz, who worked in Indonesia 25 years before Dunham. In contrast to Geertz, Dunham observed that underdevelopment in these village communities largely resulted from a scarcity of capital. As a development anthropologist, Dunham—who also worked with international organizations like the World Bank and the Ford Foundation—set up credit cooperatives for Indonesian women

---

*Ann Dunham (1942–1995) was the mother of President Barak Obama.

street food sellers, factory workers, hand-loom weavers, shop girls, and scavengers. Women mainly work in Indonesian markets and form an essential part of the economy and the family. The success of the Grameen Bank project of microlending for women, which results in their increasing prestige, income, and autonomy, confirmed Dunham's anthropological insights about the potential of village woman. The global marketing of women's textiles and pottery from Mexico and Guatemala has also proven economically successful, although here it has sometimes led to greater tension and even violence between men and women (Nash 1993; 1994:15). As anthropologists increasingly point out, the impact of development projects on women is a result of the interplay of specific economic and cultural conditions in a particular society (Lockwood 2005).

GENDER HIERARCHIES IN WEALTHY NATIONS

In spite of gender egalitarian ideologies, even in the wealthy nations of Europe, Asia, and North America, the status of women is not equal to that of men. In the United States, for example, the view that women should be excluded from all but domestic and child-rearing roles has historically been culturally dominant and remains so among many Americans today. Although American women have made great strides in professions such as law, medicine, and academe, there is still much stereotyping and discrimination. More women than men may go to medical school, but they tend to take on less prestigious medical specializations after graduation. Even in academic anthropology, where women like Margaret Mead and Ruth Benedict are among our most influential and celebrated elders, women's rates of promotion to full professor lag behind the rates of men.

Until the 20th century, women in the United States were denied many rights granted to men. They could not vote until 1920 and in many places could not serve on juries until the mid-20th century. Even today, the numbers of women in Congress are decidedly small, and, as of this writing, there has yet to be a female president or vice president. Domestic violence, sexual harassment, and continued attempts to constrain women's reproductive rights are other significant problems still being fought over in the United States. Gender identities and gender stratification are taught from infancy. In some progressive societies like Sweden, a real effort is made to blur gender differences. Teachers avoid the pronouns "him" and "her" and avoid gender nouns like boy and girl. The library contains few classic fairy tales, such as Cinderella or Snow White, which are laden with gender stereotypes. Boys as well as girls are allowed to cry, and neither sex is admonished for engaging in activities typically associated with the other gender, though there appears to be less opposition to girls taking on boys' roles than the opposite. The Swedish government and the public realize that erasing gender stratification must begin early (Tagliabue 2012).

Contemporary societies, such as Vietnam, for example, are also transforming gender ideology and practice in the transition from state socialism to partly neoliberal market economies (Leshkowich 2011). Early socialist ideology proudly announced its support for gender equality, but today has tweaked that notion, as it encourages women to participate in the new economy (see Figure 10.5). Previously, socialism had denigrated petty traders, most of whom were women, as part of an unpatriotic and antirevolutionary class motivated by personal monetary gain. But to capitalize on the growing economic importance of these markets, especially for the increasing international tourist trade since the end of the Vietnam War, the Vietnamese government currently emphasizes how market trade is particularly suited to women's innate gendered personalities. Women realize the advantage of this gender construct themselves and encourage it by denigrating their status in relation to their customers, engaging in flattery and "sweet talk" with their customers, and perhaps most importantly, defining men as innately incapable of successfully engaging in such trade. For the government, this new feminine gender construct also turns women into a productive class in the socialist system. Thus do economics, politics, and gender construction interact in the contemporary world.

Figure 10.5 In socialist Vietnam, both culture and state ideology have constructed women's gender identity as especially suitable for managing small-scale markets. Men are considered too impatient and lazy for this work.

Joan Young Gregg

BRINGING IT BACK HOME:
DISCRIMINATION AGAINST TRANS PEOPLE IN THE UNITED STATES

The availability of sex-change operations since the mid-20th century led to the gender identity role of the transsexual. The emergence of this role helped sustain the Euro-American binary sex/gender system: male and female, man and woman, and reinforced the Western view that genitals and biological sex at birth are the defining criteria of gender, a position still upheld by many American judges (Nanda 2014; Norgren and Nanda 2006). In contemporary societies, however, prominently including the United States, **transgenderism** is emerging as the dominant concept used to characterize ambiguous or alternative sex/gender identities. Transgenderism includes a wide range of individuals who identify with gender roles different from those indicated by their biological sex at birth. It incorporates both transsexuals and those who have not had sex-reassignment surgery. In the United States, the transgender movement is centered on androgyny and nonpermanent gender transformations and identities and is both an individual and a collective phenomenon. Demands for equal treatment for transpeople is now part of an activist movement, with implications in law, sports, employment, health care, the military, prison life, schools, and the use of public toilet facilities (Currah and Stryker 2014; *New York Times* Editorial Board 2015).

Transgenderism occurs in all social classes (Nutt 2015), but poor and minority transwomen suffer most from intimidation and physical abuse, and the expense of transsexual surgery has been a tremendous obstacle in their achieving a new gender identity (Terry 2015). This is now somewhat less oppressive, as many health plans have overturned their long-held exclusion of transitional surgery and in some states the surgery is paid for by Medicare (Sontag 2015).

Incarceration also disproportionately victimizes transpeople: they are subject to harassment, humiliation, and even violence both by other prisoners and by guards. Some prisons have transferred transgender prisoners to isolation cells, which provides some physical protection, but can cause great emotional distress.

One acrimonious contemporary debate concerns whether transwomen (this term refers to individuals born biologically as males who have transitioned to a female gender identity) should be allowed to use women's bathrooms, locker rooms, and shower facilities, particularly in schools. In 2014, the city government in Houston, Texas, passed an ordinance stating that denial of such access was discriminatory and

Transgenderism: Transgenderism includes a wide range of individuals who identify with gender roles different from that of their biological sex at birth. It incorporates both transsexuals and those who have not had sex-reassignment surgery.

prohibited. However, the law was vigorously protested by residents, who viewed it as opening the gates of sexual predation by men using women's restrooms, and it was repealed in 2015 (Fernandez 2015). "This law... permits biological males and even registered sex offenders to enter female showers, bathrooms or locker rooms," said one of the protestors. While some defenders of transpeoples' rights suggest a compromise in assigning transwomen private changing and showering facilities, transpeople view this as a violation of their civil rights. Clearly this is a new, contentious issue in the "culture wars" (Smith and Davey 2015).

YOU DECIDE:

1. Give reasons to support your view as to whether prisons should house transwomen inmates in men's prisons, women's prisons, isolation cells, or provide separate transgender residential units?
2. Should transpeople be eligible for subsidized health benefits, such as surgery or hormone treatments, to further their sex/gender change? Why or why not?
3. Defend or criticize the right of transwomen to play on girls' sports teams and use girls' bathrooms or locker rooms and showers, in elementary and high schools, using political, cultural, or equal rights arguments.

CHAPTER SUMMARY

1. What is the difference between sex and gender? *Sex* refers to biological differences between male and female; *gender* refers to the social classification of masculine and feminine and the roles that people assume.
2. What is the evidence that gender is culturally constructed? An important anthropological principle is that gender, including sexuality, is not biologically determined but is culturally constructed. This is demonstrated by the presence of alternative genders in different societies and by the culturally variable definitions of femininity and masculinity in different cultures.
3. Are sexual behavior and sexual desire "doing what comes naturally"? Views about the nature of male and female sexuality are part of gender ideologies. Attempts to control female sexuality, for example, in constraints on women's dress in Islam, are embedded in gender hierarchies and culture.

4. How do gender-based initiation rites function in different societies? Many societies have rites of passage for males and females, in which boys and girls are transformed into adult men and women. These rites have many social and psychological functions, such as the transmission of cultural knowledge, the public acceptance of the obligations of adulthood, and the reaffirmation of cultural values, including gender hierarchies.

5. What are some of the theories anthropologists have developed to explain the universality or near universality of male dominance? A male-dominated gender-stratification system is one in which men are dominant, reap most of the social and material rewards of society, and control the autonomy of women. Two important theories used to explain male dominance are male control over economic resources and women's association with the domestic rather than the public sphere.

6. What are some of the differences in gender stratification systems in foraging, horticultural, agricultural, and industrial societies? Gender stratification is interrelated with the economy. Foraging societies appear to be mostly egalitarian, but women also have sources of power—through marketing or specialized economic niches in more complex societies. There is great variety, however; European colonialism and contemporary globalization, including development projects, have brought both positive and negative changes to gender stratification systems.

KEY TERMS

Cultural construct of gender	Patriarchy
Gender	Private/public dichotomy
Gender ideology	Rite of passage
Gender role	Transgenderism
Gender stratification	Sex
Hijra	

Thierry Falise/LightRocket/Getty Images

On Vanuatu, the John Frum movement is a classic example of what anthropologists call a cargo cult. Here, John Frum worshippers celebrate by marching in military formation. The letters USA are painted in red on their chests.

11

RELIGION

AFTER YOU HAVE READ THIS CHAPTER, YOU WILL BE ABLE TO:

△ Summarize the basic characteristics shared by all religions.

△ Analyze the roles of sacred narratives and symbols in religion.

△ Discuss widespread religious rituals, with examples of rites of passage and rites of intensification.

△ Explain the differences between priests and shamans, and give examples of the kinds of societies in which each is found.

△ Define prayer, magic, and sacrifice, and give examples of their uses.

△ Examine the roles that accusations of witchcraft or sorcery play in society.

△ Summarize the role of religion in social change, including in personal and community identities.

CARGO CULTS

IGH on a mountaintop in New Guinea, a group of men are performing a ritual around the body of a small plane that crashed there years ago. Their ritual is aimed at ensuring the arrival of *cargo*, their word for the trade goods of Western culture that are the focus of their desires, stimulated by their encounters with Europeans, Americans, and Japanese over the past hundred years. Outsiders frequently promised wealth and political equality, but members of these groups soon realized that their words did not match reality. Not only did Melanesians fail to gain riches and power, but, in many cases, they grew poorer and were more deeply oppressed under colonial rule.

Melanesians observed that these outsiders did not seem to work but instead made "secret signs" on scraps of paper, built strange structures, and behaved in odd ways. For example, they built airports and seaports with towers and wires, and they drilled soldiers to march in formation. When they did these things, planes and ships arrived, disgorging a seemingly endless supply of material goods. Melanesians, who did so much hard physical labor, got nothing.

In Melanesian culture, secret knowledge was the source of power and wealth. Plainly, the outsiders knew the secrets of cargo and were keeping them from the islanders. Many Melanesians believed that if they could learn the hidden knowledge and rituals of cargo, they could rid their societies of oppressive colonial governments and gain access to immense wealth for themselves.

In this context, Melanesians made numerous attempts to discover the knowledge and rituals of cargo. Cargo cults usually began with a local prophet who claimed such knowledge and announced that the world was about to end in a terrible catastrophe, after which God (or the ancestors or a local culture hero) would appear, and a paradise on Earth would begin. The end of the world could be caused or hastened by the performance of rituals that copied what Melanesians had observed the outsiders doing. In some places, the faithful sat around tables dressed in European clothes, making signs on paper. In others, they drilled with wooden rifles and built wharves, storehouses, airfields, and lookout towers in the hope that such ritual would cause planes to land or ships to dock and disgorge cargo.

Cargo cults are not limited to Melanesia. In the United States and Latin America, millions of followers of prosperity theology and the Word-Faith movement believe that God wants Christians to be wealthy (Van Biema and Chu 2006). Promoted by Oral Roberts and other televangelists, the movement teaches their adherents that if they give money (the more, the better) to movement churches and pray with sincerity, devotion, and frequency, God will reward them with cash and other material wealth, such as cars and houses. In other words, if they perform the correct rituals, they will receive cargo. If they remain poor, it is because they failed to properly ask God for wealth.

Cargo is not merely a cult in the United States; it is central to our culture. Westerners do seem obsessed with cargo: many have an endless desire for consumer goods and the belief that buying specific brands of cars, drinks, or clothing will make them forever young, sexy, and powerful (Lindstrom 1993). Some might say that this is as likely to happen as it is for cargo to descend from the skies in Melanesia.

CHARACTERISTICS OF RELIGION

Recent research links religious experience to specific capacities of the right temporal and right parietal lobes of the brain (Chan et al. 2009; Johnstone and Glass 2008). Because religiosity is a biologically based capacity of humans, it is unsurprising that all societies have spiritual beliefs and practices that anthropologists refer to as *religion*. Yet because of the great diversity of these beliefs and practices, defining religion is surprisingly difficult. Most definitions focus on the supernatural. However, for most Westerners, the natural is easily equated with the normal, logical, and rational, and the supernatural with the unusual, illogical, and irrational. However, religious believers generally understand their own beliefs and experiences as normal, logical, and rational as well.

From an anthropological perspective, all religions share six common characteristics. First, religions are composed of sacred stories that members believe are important. Second, religions make extensive use of symbols and symbolism. Third, religions propose the existence of beings, powers, states, places, and qualities that cannot be measured by any agreed-upon scientific means—they are nonempirical (sometimes referred to as supernatural). Fourth, religions include rituals and specific means of addressing the supernatural. Fifth, all societies include individuals who are particularly expert in the practice of religion. Sixth, all religions claim that at least some people have or have had direct contact with the supernatural. Thus, we might define **religion** as a social institution characterized by sacred stories; symbols and symbolism; the proposed existence of supernatural beings, powers, states, places, and qualities; rituals and means of addressing the supernatural; and specific practitioners.

Early anthropologists were primarily interested in the development of religion. They argued that religion had evolved from **animism**, the belief

Religion: A social institution characterized by sacred stories, symbols, and symbolism; the proposed existence of immeasurable beings, powers, states, places, and qualities; rituals and means of addressing the supernatural; specific practitioners; and change.

Animism: The notion that all objects, living and nonliving, are imbued with spirits.

that all living and nonliving objects are imbued with spirits, passed through a stage of polytheism and finally arrived at monotheism. They held that this evolutionary process was characterized by increasing levels of logic and rationality. However, this view has been discredited. Today, anthropologists understand that there is no orderly process of religious evolution and that no one religion can be considered any more logical or evolved than any other. Anthropologists today are interested in exploring religion in terms of its functions, its symbolism, and its relation to both social stability and change.

Religion may provide meaning and order in people's lives, and it may reduce social anxiety and give people a sense of control over their destinies. It may promote and reinforce the status quo. But religion may also make people anxious or fearful. It may serve to resist the status quo, and it may catalyze radical politics and even murderous violence. This chapter illustrates how the defining characteristics of religion work in society, how religion affects the individual lives of society members, and how religion can motivate social change.

▮▍▎ Sacred Narratives

Sacred narratives (myths): Stories of historical events, heroes, gods, spirits, and creation that members of a religious tradition hold to be holy and true.

Cosmology: A system of beliefs that deals with fundamental questions in the religious and social order.

Fundamentally, all religions consist of stories told by members of a group. These **sacred narratives** are powerful ways of communicating ideas. Sometimes, such stories are held to have a sacred power that is evoked when they are told. Sacred narratives may recall historic events, although these are often clothed in poetic language.

Sacred narratives may be called myths, as they often include stories of heroes, explanations of origins, and distortions of reality. Although the word *myth* often denotes a false belief (or one we do not share), all peoples—whether ancient Greeks or contemporary Americans—are convinced that the central stories of their own religions are true. By explaining the central role of sacred beings in creating the world we live in, sacred narratives legitimize beliefs, values, and customs. The origin narrative of the Hopi, an agricultural people of Arizona, provides an example. The Hopi subsist mainly on blue corn, which is more difficult to grow than other varieties of corn but is stronger and more resistant to damage. The Hopi believe that before their ancestors appeared on Earth, they were given their choice of subsistence activities. The ancestors chose blue corn and were taught the techniques for growing it by the god Maasaw. Thus, the Hopi live their religious understanding of the world by growing this crop. The stories that accompany this action reinforce social customs and enhance solidarity.

Religious narratives provide **cosmologies**, or frameworks for interpreting events and experiences. These are visible in religious symbols and rituals as well. A cosmology may include principles or beliefs about the nature of life and death, the creation of the universe, the origin of society,

The Hopi.

the relationship of individuals and groups to one another, and the relationship of humankind to nature.

Cosmologies give meaning to the lives of believers. By defining the place of the individual in society and establishing moral codes, they provide people with a sense of personal identity, a sense of belonging, and a standard of behavior. When people suffer a profound personal loss, when life loses meaning because of radically changed circumstances or catastrophic events, or when people are perceived negatively and marginalized by their societies, religion can supply a new identity or new responses that become the basis for personal and cultural survival.

▮▮▮ Symbols and Symbolism

Religious stories depend on symbolism, which may be expressed in words, in material objects such as masks and statues, in body decorations, by objects in the physical environment, or through performance. Some religious symbols are understood to have power in and of themselves, such as the masks used in African ceremonies. Part of the power of religious symbols is that they pack many different and sometimes contradictory meanings into a single word, idea, object, or performance. The Christian cross, for example, includes the meanings of death, love, sacrifice, identity, history, power, weakness, wealth, poverty, and many more.

Because they carry so many meanings, religious symbols often have great emotional and intellectual power. As a result, they can be used in leadership. For example, since the first centuries of Christianity, the cross has been used as a military symbol and to rally people to political causes. Desecration of the cross may inflame passions and provoke very strong reactions as well.

Symbolic representation allows people to grasp the often complex and abstract ideas of a religion without much knowledge of the underlying theology. In Hinduism, for example, the abstract idea of communion with God, is represented in plays, paintings, and sculptures as the love between the divine Krishna, in the form of a cowherd, and the milkmaids, particularly Radha, who are devoted to him. Dramatic reenactments, songs, and artwork about the love of Krishna and Radha offer paths to communion with God that ordinary people can understand and participate in.

▮▮▮ Supernatural Beings, Powers, States, and Qualities

Although many religions do not separate the natural from the supernatural, all religions propose that there are important beings, powers, emotional states, or qualities that exist apart from human beings, even

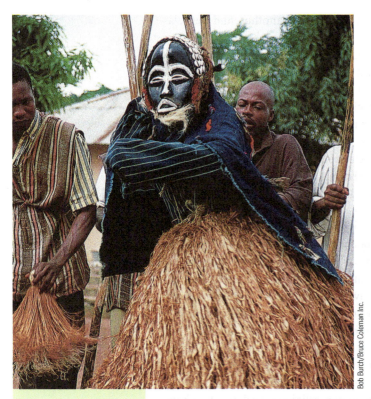

Bob Burch/Bruce Coleman Inc.

Figure 11.1 In religious ritual, humans may be transformed into supernatural beings. This masked dancer from Cote d'Ivoire is not just a person wearing a mask, but a person who has become a supernatural being.

God (deity): A named spirit who is believed to have created or to have control of some aspect of the world.
Polytheism: Belief in many gods.
Monotheism: Belief in a single god.
Mana: Religious power or energy that is concentrated in individuals or objects.

if they acknowledge that there is no scientifically agreed-upon way to measure them. For example, although many people claim to see proof of God's existence, there is nothing that members of all religions, as well as those who do not believe in any religion, could agree upon to measure that would demonstrate the existence of God. Thus, science, which depends upon such empirical measurement, can neither prove nor disprove the existence of God.

Most religions populate the world with spiritual beings (see Figure 11.1) who incorporate diverse qualities, as illustrated, for example, in the understandings of spirits and souls of animals among the Netsilik Inuit. The Netsilik depend on hunting and believe that if the soul of an animal they kill receives proper religious attention, it will be pleased and reincarnate itself in another animal and let itself be killed again. An animal soul that does not receive the proper attention, however, will be angered and will not let itself be killed a second time and the hunter may go hungry. Particularly offended animal souls might become bloodthirsty monsters and terrorize people (Balikci 1970:200–201).

The term **god** (or **deity**) is generally used for a named spirit believed to have created or to have control of some aspect of the world. Only about half of all societies have this belief (Levinson 1996:229). **Polytheism** refers to a belief in many gods and **monotheism** to a belief in a single god, but this distinction is not absolute. In some polytheistic religions, like Hinduism, for example, the many gods are viewed as different aspects of one god, or one divine essence. Conversely, in monotheistic religions, the one god may have several aspects, as in the Christian belief in God the Father, God the Son, and God the Holy Spirit.

In addition to supernatural beings, religions posit the existence of supernatural states, qualities, or powers, such as the enlightenment of Buddhist tradition, the saintliness of Catholicism, or the nirvana of the Hindus. In Polynesia, the impersonal spiritual force is called **mana**. Specific places, objects, or individuals, such as Tahitian chiefs (see Chapter 7), have more mana than ordinary people. Mana is powerful but dangerous if not approached with caution. That is why a belief in mana is often associated with an elaborate system of taboos, or prohibitions.

◼️◼️ Addressing the Supernatural: Rituals

People enact their religion through **ritual**: ceremonial acts or repeated stylized gesture used for specific occasions and involving the use of religious symbols (Cunningham et al. 1995). Religious rituals may involve telling or acting out sacred stories; the repetition of words considered to be sacred; the use of music, dance, drugs, or pain that sometimes moves worshippers to a state of trance; and the use of ritual objects to convey religious messages.

Ritual: A ceremonial act or repeated stylized gestures used for specific occasions involving the use of religious symbols.

The stories, symbols, and objects of worship that make up the content of religious rituals are exceedingly diverse, yet there are commonalities. Many religious practices are aimed at ensuring success in human activities. Prayers, sacrifice, and magic are often used in the hope that they will aid a particular person or community. Further, despite great diversity, some types of rituals, including rites of passage and rites of intensification, are extremely widespread, if not universal.

◼️ The Power of the Liminal

The word **liminal** refers to those objects, places, people, and statuses that are understood as existing in an indeterminate state, between clear-cut categories. Objects that are liminal often play important roles in religious ritual.

Liminal: The stage of a ritual, particularly a rite of passage, in which one has passed out of an old status but has not yet entered a new one.

Anthropologist Victor Turner (1969) wrote that rituals frequently generate liminal states, in which the structured and hierarchical classifications that normally separate people into groups such as castes, classes, or genders are dissolved. Thus, in ritual, people can behave in ways that would be unacceptable under other circumstances. In some cases, this includes role reversals. For example, many Japanese festivals included ritual transvestism, where community members dance in the clothing of the opposite sex (Norbeck 1974:51). In the Wubwang'u ritual among the Ndembu of Zambia, men and women publicly insult each other's sexual abilities and extol their own, but no one is allowed to take offense (Turner 1969:78–79). Ritual role reversals include class as well as gender. In Holi, the Hindu harvest festival, members of the lower class and castes throw colored powder (and in the old days, excrement and urine) at males of the middle and upper classes.

More controversially, Turner argued that in liminal states people experienced a state of equality and oneness he called **communitas**. In the wake of natural disasters such as hurricanes and earthquakes or human-made ones such as terrorist attacks, social distinctions may be repressed.

Communitas: A state of perceived solidarity, equality, and unity among people sharing a religious ritual, often characterized by intense emotion.

The wealthy and the poor, the powerful and the powerless may have strong experiences of unity and community identity. But Turner's ideas are controversial: the wealthy and powerful may talk about the unity they feel with the poor and powerless, but the reverse is not necessarily true. Poor people claiming the same social status as the rich are likely to face harsh penalties. The powerless may also use liminal symbols and rituals of reversal to subvert the social order (even if temporarily), expressing feelings not of oneness, but of conflict with the powerful.

Institutionalized liminal statuses sometimes emerge in state-level societies, such as monasteries and convents where people live permanently as members of a religious community. Members of particular occupational groups, such as nuns and priests, people with certain diseases, or people in ambiguous social statuses are also liminal. While liminal groups often have low status, paradoxically, this may be the source of their power, such as the hijras of India (see Chapter 10) whose sexual ambiguity contains the power both to bless and to curse.

Antistructure: The socially sanctioned use of behavior that radically violates social norms; frequently found in religious ritual.

Anthropologists often refer to the status reversals and carnival atmosphere of some rituals involving liminality as **antistructure**. Although all societies must have structure to provide order and meaning, antistructure—the temporary ritual dissolution of the established order—is also important, helping people to more fully realize the oneness of the self and the other (Turner 1969:131).

▌▌Rites of Passage

Rite of passage: A ritual that moves an individual from one social status to another.

Rites of passage are public events that mark the transition of a person from one social status to another, such as birth, puberty, marriage, and death, and may include other transitions as well. Rites of passage involve three phases (van Gennep 1960/1909): first, separation, in which the person or group is detached from a former status. The second phase, transition, is often characterized by liminality, where individuals have been detached from their old statuses but not yet attached to a new one. The third stage is reincorporation, in which the passage from one status to another is symbolically completed. After reincorporation, the person takes on the rights and obligations of his or her new social status.

Initiation rites for boys and girls are good examples of rites of passage (Figure 11.2). Before these rituals, boys and girls have the public status of children; afterward, they have the public status of adult men and women, in which dating or marriage is now possible. In the case of baptisms or other birth ceremonies, a newly born child is moved from the status of non–community member to community member. Funerals mediate between the living and the dead.

Basic training for military service is a rite of passage familiar to many Americans: recruits are separated from their friends and families

Figure 11.2 In Judaism, 13-year-old boys are initiated into adult religious responsibilities through the ritual of *bar mitzvah*. Here, a boy holds the sacred Torah scrolls at a bar mitzvah ceremony in Jerusalem.

and taken to military posts where they are given identical haircuts and identical uniforms. All signs of differences among them are minimized; their position in life before joining the military does not matter. Ideally, they are treated identically during training. Training itself involves a wide variety of rigorous exercises and tasks designed to impart knowledge and build trust and camaraderie. In this state, recruits experience communitas, a shared identity along with the breaking down of barriers between individuals. Training ends with a large ceremony that reintegrates the recruits, now soldiers, into society with a new identity.

▌▌Rites of Intensification

Rites of intensification are rituals directed toward reinforcing the values and norms of the community and strengthening group identity and well-being. Through these rituals, the community maintains continuity with the past, enhances the feeling of social unity in the present, and renews the sentiments on which social cohesion depends (Elkin 1967).

Rite of intensification: A ritual structured to reinforce the values and norms of a community and to strengthen group identity.

In some groups, rites of intensification are connected with totems. A **totem** is an object, an animal species, or a feature of the natural world that is associated with a particular descent group. Totemism is a prominent feature of the religions of the Australian aborigines. Groups of related individuals are linked with particular totemic species that they are usually prohibited from eating (see Verdon and Jorion 1981). In their religious rituals, members of each group assemble to celebrate their totem. The ceremonies explain the origin of the totem (and hence, of the group) and reenact the time of the ancestors. Through singing and dancing, both

Totem: An object, an animal species, or a feature of the natural world that is associated with a particular descent group.

performers and onlookers are transported to an ecstatic state in which they no longer recognize themselves and feel as though they are being carried away to a special world (Durkheim 1961/1915:247–251).

Emile Durkheim, a pioneer in the anthropological study of religion, believed that totems were symbols of common social identity. When people worshipped totems, they were worshipping that common identity and at the same time reinforcing the moral and social order of their society. The ecstatic religious experience of their shared identity helped to bind them together.

The religious rituals of the Australian aborigines may seem exotic, but Americans participate in similar observances, some religious but many secular, to the same effect. The rallies associated with college football games are a good example. If the game is "good" or the school has "spirit," these gatherings produce enormous excitement among their fans and transport them to "a special world," increasing collective identity and intensifying loyalty to the school (and hopefully motivating financial donations from them as alumni). Schools, like Australian descent groups, also have totems, usually in the form of animal mascots.

▌▌Prayer, Sacrifice, and Magic

Prayer, sacrifices, and magic are found in most religious traditions. Although theoretically differentiated by the degree of control that humans believe these acts exert over the spirit world, the distinctions between them are mainly a matter of degree.

Prayer: Any conversation held with spirits and gods in which people petition, invoke, praise, give thanks, dedicate, supplicate, intercede, confess, repent, and bless.

Prayer is any conversation held with spirits and gods in which people petition, invoke, praise, give thanks, dedicate, supplicate, intercede, confess, repent, and bless (Levinson 1996). A defining feature of prayer is that people believe the results depend on the will of the spirit world rather than on actions humans perform. When prayer involves requests, the failure of a spirit to respond to a request is understood as resulting from its disinclination rather than from improper human action. Prayer may be done without any expectation of a particular response from the beings or forces prayed to. There are many forms of prayer. In the West, prayer mainly involves words recited aloud or silently, but in Buddhist tradition, people may pray by hoisting flags or spinning wheels with prayers written inside them.

Sacrifice: An offering made to increase the efficacy of a prayer or the religious purity of an individual.

Sacrifice occurs when people make offerings to gods or spirits to increase their spiritual purity or the efficacy of their prayers. People may sacrifice the first fruits of a harvest, animal lives, or, on occasion, human lives. Changes in behavior are often offered as sacrifices, as in the Muslim practice of fasting during daylight hours for Ramadan, the Catholic practice of giving up something desirable for Lent, or the Hindu practice of women fasting once a year for their husband's welfare. In many religions, people make a vow to carry out a certain kind of behavior, such as going on a pilgrimage or building a place of worship, if a prayer is answered.

Magic is an attempt to mechanistically control supernatural forces. When people do magic, they believe that their words and actions *compel* the spirit world to behave in certain ways. Failure of a magical request is understood to result from incorrect performance of the ritual rather than the refusal of spirits to act, as in prayer.

Magic: A religious ritual believed to produce a mechanical effect by supernatural means.

Imitation and contagion are two of the most common magical practices. In **imitative magic**, the procedure performed resembles the result desired. Infant baptism is an example: water washes away dirt, holy water washes away sin, a kind of spiritual dirt; a classic anthropological example is hunting magic, where people imitate the hunt through dance in order to be successful.

Imitative magic: The belief that imitating an action in a religious ritual will cause the action to happen in the material world.

Contagious magic is based on the idea that an object that has been in contact with a person retains a magical connection with that person. For example, people may use an individual's hair or fingernails to magically cause harm to others. People in the United States often attribute special power and meaning to objects that have come in contact with famous or notorious people. Signed baseballs, bits of costumes worn by movie stars, pens used to sign famous documents and, sometimes, bits of the stars themselves all become collectors' items and are imbued with special power and importance.

Contagious magic: The belief that things once in contact with a person or object retain an invisible connection with that person or object.

In many cultures, magical practices accompany most human activities. Among the people who live along the upper Asaro River in Papua New Guinea, when a child is born, its umbilical cord is buried so that it cannot later be used by a sorcerer to cause harm. To prevent an infant from crying at night, a bundle of sweet-smelling grass is placed on the mother's head, and her wish for uninterrupted sleep is blown into the grass. The grass then is crushed over the head of the child who, in breathing its aroma, also breathes in the mother's command not to cry (Newman 1977:413).

Divination is a widespread ritual practice directed toward obtaining useful, hidden, or unknown information from a supernatural authority. Divination may be used to predict the future, diagnose disease, find hidden objects, or discover something about the past. In many cultures, divination is used to discover who committed a crime. Many Americans are familiar with divination techniques such as tarot cards, palmistry, flipping coins, reading auras, and the Magic 8 Ball.

Divination: A religious ritual performed to find hidden objects or information.

Divination makes people more confident in their choices when they do not have all the information they need or when several alternative courses of action appear equal. It may be practiced when a group must decide on something about which there is disagreement. If the choice is made by divination, no member of the group feels rejected.

Prayer, sacrifice, magic, and divination are frequently related to risk. The less predictable an outcome is, the greater the likelihood these will be used. For example, professional baseball players in the United States rarely use magical practices in outfielding, for which there is little uncertainty, but often use magic for hitting and pitching, the least predictable aspects of the game. Detroit Tigers infielder Tim Maring wore the same clothes and put them on exactly in the same order each day during a batting streak (Gmelch 2000). Many of us do similar things. If you have studied for a test and know the material well, you are unlikely to spend much time praying for success. You are more likely to pray if you have not studied, and you may even bring your lucky pencil or another charm to the test.

Experimental studies show that praying or doing magic to help or hurt an individual has no effect if that person does not know about your prayers or magical activities (see Flamm 2002; Tessman and Tessman 2000). However, when such attempts are known, they may have a profound effect, altering the emotional state of the individuals involved. Bringing your lucky pencil to an exam may give you added confidence and improve your performance, but with sorcery, the individual against whom the sorcery is to be used must know about it to be affected. In a study of these phenomena, Walter Cannon (1942) argued that an individual who was aware that he or she was being attacked by sorcery could exhibit increased anxiety and sometimes an extreme stress reaction that might lead to death. Much work in biomedicine in the past 60 years confirms Cannon's ideas and details the specific biochemical pathways through which such reactions may occur (Sternberg 2002).

▋▐ Religious Practitioners

Every society includes people who are believed to have a special relationship with the religious world, such as shamans, priests, witches, and sorcerers. These and other religious practitioners organize and lead major ritual events, engage in supernatural practices to heal, gain power, and pursue other objectives for themselves or others.

▋▍ Shamans

Shaman: An individual socially recognized as being able to mediate between the world of humanity and the world of gods or spirits but who is not a recognized official of any religious organization.

A **shaman** is a part-time religious practitioner who is otherwise like an average member of his or her community. Learning to be a shaman may involve arduous training, and many are deeply learned in ritual, herbalism, and magical technique, but such study is never sufficient. The distinctive characteristic of shamans is direct personal experiences of the supernatural that other members of the community accept as authentic. Shamans use prayer, meditation, song, dance, pain, drugs, or any combination of these techniques to achieve trance states in which they understand themselves (and are understood by their followers) to be entering the real world of the supernatural. They may use such contact to search for guidance for themselves or for their group, to heal the sick, or to divine the future (see Figure 11.3). Almost all societies have some shamans, but in foraging and tribal societies, shamans are likely to be the only religious practitioners.

In some cultures, almost every adult is expected to achieve direct contact with the supernatural. In some Native American societies, this is achieved through a vision quest, in which individuals develop a special relationship with a particular spirit from whom they receive special kinds of power and knowledge and who act as a personal protector or guardian. The vision seeker might fast, isolate himself or herself at a lonely spot, or use self-mutilation to intensify his or her emotional state to receive the vision.

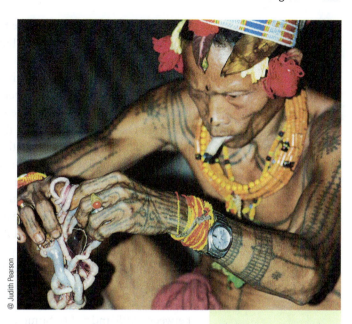

© Judith Pearson

Figure 11.3 Among the Mentawai of Indonesia, shamans practice divination by reading the entrails of chickens and pigs to diagnose and cure illness.

Particularly before the advent of modern medicine, many societies treated illness by means that today would be considered primarily spiritual rather than medical. Illnesses were thought to be caused by broken taboos, sorcery, witchcraft, or spiritual imbalance, and shamans had an important role in curing. The shaman, usually in a trance, would travel into the supernatural world to discover the source of illness and how to cure it.

In the modern world, shamanic curing often exists alongside modern technological medicine. People go to shamans for healing when they have diseases that are not recognized by modern medicine, they lack money to pay for modern medical treatment, or they have tried such treatment and it has failed. Shamanistic curing can have important therapeutic effects. Shamans frequently treat their patients with drugs from the culture's traditional pharmacopoeia, and some (but not all) of these have been shown to be scientifically effective (Fábrega 1997:144). Shamanic curing ritual also uses symbolism and dramatic action to bring together cultural beliefs and religious practices in a way that enables patients to understand the source of their illness. Such rituals present a coherent model of sickness and health, explaining how patients got ill and how they may become well again, and these models can exert a powerful curative force (Roberts et al. 1993).

Mwanza Region, Tanzania.

Although scientific medicine has made great advances in the past one hundred years, magical beliefs about health are still common throughout the world (Morton 2009).

As the HIV/AIDS epidemic swept through parts of Africa in the 1990s and 2000s, many of the beliefs about the causes and cures for the disease involved witchcraft or the violation of taboos (see Rödlach 2006). Hansjörg Dilger (2008) reported that among the Luo in Tanzania, people often think that the violation of the religious regulations that cover many aspects of social and sexual life results in *chira*, a disease with symptoms similar to AIDS. In Mwanza in northeastern Tanzania, people understood the medical causes of sexually transmitted diseases such as syphilis or gonorrhea and usually considered these to have natural, biological causes. People also accepted that AIDS was a biological, naturally caused disease, but believed that most people who were alleged to have AIDS were victims of a form of witchcraft called *lusumbo* (Mshana et al. 2006). Yamba (1997) reports that witchcraft accusations related to HIV/AIDS in Zimbabwe led to the deaths of 16 accused witches in a 4-month period between 1995 and 1996. Some people might go to Western-trained doctors to treat AIDS, but they are far more likely to go to traditional healers to treat diseases they believe to be caused by witchcraft.

▐ Priests

Priest: One who is formally elected, appointed, or hired to a full-time religious office.

In most state societies, religion is a formally established institution consisting of a series of ranked offices that exist independently of the people who fill them (a *bureaucracy*). Anthropologically, a **priest** is a person who is formally elected, appointed, or hired to a full-time religious office. Priests are responsible for performing certain rituals on behalf of individuals, groups, or the entire community. Jewish rabbis, Muslim imams, Christian ministers, and Hindu *purohits* all fit the definition of priests. Priests are most often associated with powerful gods and they are distinguished from laypersons. Laypeople participate in ritual largely as passive respondents or as an audience rather than as managers or performers. People generally become priests through training and apprenticeship and are certified by their religious hierarchy. Although priests need not have ecstatic religious experiences in mainstream religious denominations in the United States, this is not the case in all priestly religions. Ultimately, the priest's authority derives from a priestly office. However, in some cultures, like the ancient Maya, such office may also give a person the right to seek direct ecstatic contact with gods and spirits.

State societies generally attempt to suppress independent shamans or bring them under bureaucratic control. Shamans claim the ability to directly contact the supernatural without certification by any institutionalized religion, and this challenges the authority of church and state.

▚ Witches and Sorcerers

The idea of witchcraft in American society is complicated by movies, cartoons, and other media that portray witches in a wide variety of imaginative ways. It is important to understand, however, that throughout the world and throughout history, belief in the existence of witches and sorcerers is widespread, and they are usually viewed as evil and a source of social problems. Even when people go to witches or sorcerers for healing or to solve problems, their attitude is at best ambivalent: The person who can magically heal or resolve a problem can also magically cause illness and create a problem.

While most Americans (including anthropologists) use the words *witch* and *sorcerer* interchangeably, some societies make a clear distinction between the two. In these cases, **witchcraft** is understood as a physical aspect of a person. People are witches because their bodies contain a magical witchcraft substance, generally acquired through inheritance. If a person's body contains the witchcraft substance, his or her malevolent thoughts will result in misfortune among those around him or her. Sorcerers, on the other hand, are those who do physical magic by manipulating words and objects.

Witchcraft: The ability to harm others by harboring malevolent thoughts about them; the practice of sorcery.

The Azande of East Africa, a classic example, believe that witches' bodies contain a substance called *mangu*, which allows them to cause misfortune and death to others (Evans-Pritchard 1958/1937). People who have the witchcraft substance may not be aware that they are witches and are believed to be unable to prevent themselves from causing evil. The Azande believe that when witches experience jealousy, anger, envy, or other negative feelings, they cause evil to befall those around them, particularly family members. They also believe in the existence of sorcerers who manipulate magical poisons to cause illness and misfortune. Similar beliefs about the unconscious or involuntary practice of magic are widespread. For example, in northern Mexican and Mexican American tradition, mal ojo (evil eye) directed at children can be intentional, but often it is not. The envy and jealousy that an adult might consciously or unconsciously feel while looking at a child can harm the child.

The idea that some people can perform magical acts through the conscious manipulation of words and ritual objects with the intent of causing harm or good is widespread. People who believe in a witchcraft substance almost always also believe in the ability of certain people to do physical magic as well.

Although people practice magic, a principal social effect of witchcraft comes through people accusing others of witchcraft. Leveling witchcraft accusations against friends and neighbors is common in many cultures and serves various purposes. The most common form of witchcraft accusation serves to stigmatize differences. People who do not fit into conventional social categories are often suspected of witchcraft. Although men were sometimes accused of witchcraft, women were far more frequently accused. Often, these accusations were related to the failure of such women to subscribe to the social and sexual mores of their communities. For example, in a study of a community in Spain, Heidi Kelley (1991) found that although many women were occasionally accused of using witchcraft, villagers agreed that two must be witches. These were a pair of sisters living together without husbands but with the illegitimate child of one. Although such witches were sometimes killed, they were usually allowed to remain in a community, serving as negative role models, examples of what not to be.

Witchcraft and sorcery accusations may be used to scapegoat. In times of great social change when war, disease, calamity, or technological change undermines the social order, people's lives lose meaning. Under such circumstances, a community may turn to witchcraft accusations, blaming their misfortunes on the presence of evildoers—witches and sorcerers who must be found and destroyed to reassert normality. In 16th- and 17th-century Europe, for example, the witch craze, which resulted in the death of thousands of men and women, was a time not only of great artistic and technological achievement but also of great social disasters (Hester 1988). Plague swept repeatedly through Europe, and the medieval social and religious order collapsed in war and chaos. Where governments and religious institutions remained strong, witchcraft accusations were relatively scarce. However, where these institutions collapsed, accusations were frequent (Behringer 2004). Under these circumstances, people were willing to believe that witches were the cause of their misery and to pursue reprisals against people they suspected of being witches. Much more recently, between 1992 and 1994, 57 alleged witches were killed in Gusii, in southwestern Kenya. This included three incidents in which sons killed their mothers and were exonerated by their communities. Ogembo (2001) relates these killings to economic stress, political upheaval including ethnic attacks, and the specifics of Gusii kinship and ideology.

▌▌▌ RELIGION AND CHANGE

Religion is generally a force that preserves the social order. This is particularly evident in stratified societies, where the elite invoke religious authority to control the poor. In these situations religion helps maintain social, economic, and political inequality. However, even when religion does not support social stratification, it is usually a conservative force promoting the idea that the way that society has historically been ordered is right and proper.

Most religions contain implicit or explicit visions of the ideal society—images of the way a correct, just social order should look. No society actually achieves its vision; people never live exactly the way they are supposed to. Because most of the time religion validates society, most people feel that the society they live in is reasonably good.

However, if societies undergo rapid change, for example, as a result of colonization, disease, or technological change, or if some groups are systematically oppressed, the vision of the ideal world painted by people's religious beliefs may be far removed from their daily experience. People may feel lost, that their vision of the ideal cannot be attained, or that it is simply wrong. Under these conditions, prophets may emerge and new religions may be created. Religious movements vary in the effectiveness with which they bring social and political change. Even those that fail in these respects may create powerful new identities among their members. This applies to the Rastafarians, discussed below.

Religion offers a series of principles, encapsulated in story, symbol, and interpretation that can serve as a charter for political action. Thus, religion can be a powerful force for social change, providing people with the rationale and motivation for political involvement and personal renewal. From the U.S. civil rights movement to the Iranian Revolution, the Taliban and the Tea Party, and the so-called Islamic State religious leaders can have a powerful political impact.

▌▌▌ Varieties of Religious Prophecy

To begin a new religion or substantially modify an existing one, prophets must identify what is wrong with the world, present a vision of what a better world looks like, and describe a method of transition from the existing world to the better world. Religious movements can, to some degree, be characterized by what they believe about this better world and the ways to achieve it.

Religious movements may be nativistic or vitalistic. A nativistic movement aims to restore what its followers believe is a past golden age. The nativistic message is generally that things have degenerated because the people have fallen away from the ways of the ancestors. The glorious past may be regained if certain practices are followed.

The Ghost Dance is a good example of a nativistic religious movement. It arose in the late 19th century among the Plains Indians of the United States as a response to the disastrous effects of European invasion. As disease, warfare, and technological change undermined native cultures, prophets emerged who taught that a past golden age would reemerge if Indians returned to traditional practices and performed specific rituals, including the Ghost Dance. The prophecy spread widely among

Native Americans, especially the Sioux, for whom the conditions of conquest and reservation life were particularly oppressive. U.S. government agents, frightened that the Ghost Dance movement would lead to new wars against the whites, ordered the Sioux to stop the dance. Some Sioux did, but others fled and continued to perform the Ghost Dance. In December 1890, the 7th Cavalry captured the last remaining band of Ghost Dancers at Wounded Knee. In the ensuing battle, about 350 Sioux Ghost Dancers, including many women and children, were killed. This battle effectively ended the Ghost Dance, although it continued among small groups up until the 1960s.

▌▌▌ Using Anthropology: Religion and Change— The Rastafarians

A vitalistic religion looks to the future rather than the past and believes that a golden age can be achieved by following the teachings of a prophet. The Rastafarian religion is a vitalist religious movement. It originated in Jamaica in the 1930s and had its roots in a commitment to overcoming the negative images of blackness experienced by the poor and oppressed Jamaican peasantry under British colonial rule. This rule was originally based on a plantation economy worked by African slaves. However, after the end of slavery in the 1830s, plantations were replaced by small farms and a peasant society organized around a system of localized, small-scale exchanges involving interpersonal networks of extended kin and a strong sense of communitas. In the 1890s, this system began to be replaced by a capitalist economy which incorporated peasants as wage laborers. Capitalism exacerbated both poverty and racial stratification as the largely white and biracial middle and upper classes accumulated wealth at the expense of the black peasantry.

In 1930, Ras Tafari was crowned Emperor Haile Selassie I of Ethiopia and was proclaimed "King of Kings" and the "Lion of Judah." This coronation of a black King received enormous publicity in Jamaica. One result was a prophetic revelation by Leonard Howell, who, returning to Jamaica after serving in the U.S. Army, declared that the coronation of Haile Selassie fulfilled biblical prophecies: Haile Selassie was a new messiah and the hope of freedom for all black people (Lewis 1993). Howell and other Rasta leaders founded communities in and around Kingston, celebrating what they understood as traditional African values such as cooperative work efforts, respect for life, and the unity of all peoples of African descent. Haile Selassie was their central symbol (Figure 11.4).

Rastafarians are actually quite diverse in their religious beliefs and practices. But the core of the religion is a rejection of the values of capitalist society and the competitive marketplace. Rastafarians emphasize

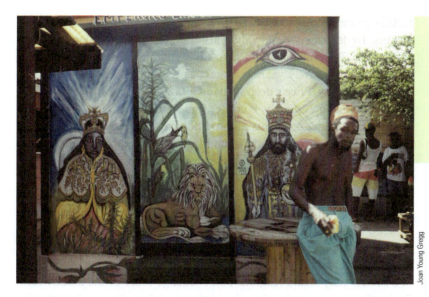

Joan Young Gregg

Joan Young Gregg

Figure 11.4 Haile Selassie I, symbolized as the Lion of Judah, is the messiah of the Rastafarian religion. Here he is shown with his wife as a way of noting the inclusion of both women and men in the religious community.

the repatriation of blacks to Africa, a concept mainly understood symbolically, as a call to live what Rastafarians believe are African lifestyles in whichever country they find themselves.

Rastafarians use marijuana at "reasoning sessions," where they interpret biblical passages and share beliefs about freedom, slavery, colonialism, and racism. The sale of marijuana also allows them a way to earn a living, although in the United States, it has subjected them to arrest and incarceration (Norgren and Nanda 2006). Rastas reject much of the social and psychological orientation of modern society and their religion and culture allows them to survive in a manner consistent with their own worldview.

Anthropologist Charles Price is a Rastafarian who has carried out extensive engaged ethnography on Rastafarians in Jamaica and the United States (2009). Price focused on the history of the Rastafarian religion in Jamaica through the narratives of individual Rastafarians as they explain how they develop and maintain their Rastafarian identity. As Price points out, these personalized Rasta narratives contribute to a wider understanding of how stigmatized identities like Rastafari and blackness are given positive value through a new religious ideology and corresponding rituals.

The first Rastafarians, who saw Haile Selassie I as a Messiah, promoted a positive conception of Black identity and culture. This positive view contrasted with the dominant White, European ideology that identified the good, the worthy, and the normal in Jamaica with European and white history, culture, and experience. Price shows how the development of Rastafarian identity is part of a long, historical, racialized dialogue challenging white oppression as reinforced by culture, religion, and education. The growth of Rastafarianism illustrates how efforts by blacks to develop racially grounded cultural alternatives developed into a durable cultural identity. By focusing on individual histories, as well as the larger historical context, Price movingly illustrates how poor, black, denigrated peasants came to positively value blackness as central to their individual and collective identity. Price's deep individual oral histories also contribute to understanding how ethnicity is created and sustained in the modern world.

Price actively applies his anthropological understandings of Rastafarianism by advising prison chaplains on the Rastafarian culture—their dietary codes, major rituals, necessary garments and ritual implements, such as drums and the Bible—so that interactions between correctional officers and Rasta prisoners can be more positive and less aggressive. In conjunction with his interest in black identity, Price is also engaged in an action-oriented study of how black men in North Carolina negotiate challenges and obstacles in their daily lives.

The Rastafarians are one example of how the poor and powerless in a society may create religions that challenge those of the mainstream. Such religions may rationalize their lower social position and emphasize an afterlife in which their suffering will be rewarded. In some cases, these religions have a **messianic** outlook; they focus on the coming of a special individual who will usher in a utopian world. Other religions are **millenarian**; they look to a future disaster that will destroy the current world and establish a world characterized by their version of justice. In many messianic and millenarian religions, members participate in rituals that give individuals direct access to supernatural power.

Messianic: Focusing on the coming of an individual who will usher in a utopian world.

Millenarian: Belief that a coming catastrophe will signal the beginning of a new age and the eventual establishment of paradise.

▮▮ Religions, Change, and Social Stratification

The holiness churches common among coal miners and the rural poor in Appalachia are also a good example of a religion that has emerged in response to poverty and hardship. In church services, loud music, singing, and dancing cause some members to experience "being filled with the Holy Spirit." In this ecstatic state, they handle poisonous snakes (see Figure 11.5). Snake handlers are frequently bitten and sometimes die. However, for members, snake handling proves that "Jesus has the power to deliver them from death here and now" (Daugherty 1976:234). For them, such ecstatic practices demonstrate their ability to gain access to God's power. The fact that social elites are rarely members of such groups is proof that holiness members have access to forms of power that social elites lack (Burton 1993; Covington 1995).

Religious **syncretism** is often found among deeply oppressed people. In syncretism, people merge two or more religious traditions, hiding the beliefs, symbols, and practices of one behind similar attributes of the other. Santeria, an African-based religion originating in Cuba, is a good example (Murphy 1989). Santeria emerged from slave society. Europeans

Syncretism: The merging of elements of two or more religious traditions to produce a new religion.

Figure 11.5 In states of religious ecstasy, members of holiness churches in Appalachia handle poisonous snakes. For church members, such practices demonstrate their ability to gain access to God's power, but may also be fatal. Pastor Mack Wolford, seen here, died of a rattlesnake bite received during a service in 2012.

epa european pressphoto agency b.v./Alamy

attempted to suppress African religions, but the slaves resisted by combining African religion, Catholicism, and French spiritualism to create a new religion (Lefever 1996). They identified African deities, called orichas, with Catholic saints and used them for traditional purposes such as curing and casting spells, and influencing other aspects of the worshipper's life. In this way, they could appear to practice Catholicism as they continued to practice their own religions.

Fundamentalism: A proclamation of reclaimed authority over a sacred tradition that is to be reinstated as an antidote for a society that is believed to have strayed from its cultural moorings.

BRINGING IT BACK HOME:
FUNDAMENTALISM
AND RELIGIOUS CHANGE

As the pace of social change has increased, it has been accompanied by increases in what is often called religious **fundamentalism**. Membership in American Christian denominations that describe themselves as fundamentalist has ballooned. Jewish orthodox groups such as Lubavitch Hasidim have also grown, as have groups like the Hindu nationalist Bharatiya Janata Party in India. Strains in Islam that are frequently described as fundamentalist are implicated in numerous conflicts around the world.

There is much debate surrounding the use of the term *fundamentalist*, which originated in American Christianity. Characteristics such as biblical literalism that serve to define Christian fundamentalism are not necessarily relevant to other religions. However, we preserve the term as a way to describe a wide variety of religious groups that claim exclusive rights to interpret sacred traditions, interpret these traditions in absolutist ways, and argue that their interpretations are antidotes for societies that they say have strayed from their cultural moorings.

Although members of fundamentalist groups sometimes see their religious beliefs as unchanging, the rise of fundamentalism is an important religious change. Further, fundamentalist movements tend to have specific founders and locations of origin. For example, much of the American fundamentalist movement began with *The Fundamentals: A Testimony to the Truth*, a series of books published between 1910 and 1915. Modern Islamic fundamentalism is associated with the work of Sayyid Qutb (born in the Egyptian village of Musha described in Chapter 5) and the Muslim Brotherhood.

Scholars have shown that fundamentalisms have similar properties. Fundamentalists tend to see religion as the basis for both personal and communal identity. They tend to believe that there is a single unified truth that they can possess and understand. They tend to envision themselves as fighting in a cosmic struggle of good against evil. Fundamentalists tend to perceive themselves as a persecuted minority even when this is not the case. They are selective about which parts of their tradition they emphasize and which parts of modernity they accept and reject (Almond, Sivan, and Appleby 1995; Hadden and Shupe 1989).

The pattern of the emergence of fundamentalism largely fits the model of religious change described in this chapter. In the past century, the world has faced truly revolutionary changes. The forces of technology and global capitalism have permeated societies and brought people of disparate cultures together in a vast global network. However, this process has not been peaceful and has not produced equity. Traditional livelihoods have been undermined, and the gap between the wealthy and the poor has grown. Governments have been discredited. Faced with profound change, people look for stability and certainty. For some, fundamentalism seems to offer a solution. Much (but not all) fundamentalism is nativistic, calling for a return to the society and values of an earlier time, a time that believers understand to have been better than the current era. However, specific local histories also play an extremely important role in the emergence of fundamentalisms. It would be impossible, for example, to explain the appearance of the fundamentalist group Hamas without reference to the Israeli–Palestinian conflict. Similarly, the development of the Taliban is directly related to the events surrounding the Russian invasion of Afghanistan.

The forces that create rich ground for fundamentalism do not seem likely to abate any time soon. Because rapid political, technological, and economic change is likely to continue, fundamentalisms will probably continue to experience strong growth. This poses an extraordinarily difficult problem. On the one hand, people are surely entitled to their religious beliefs. The vast majority of people who might be classified as fundamentalist are innocent of any wrongdoing; they neither promote nor condone violence. They live peacefully with neighbors of different religious beliefs. On the other hand, fundamentalist beliefs have been repeatedly implicated in murderous violence: from the bombings of abortion clinics and the Olympic Games in Atlanta to the 9/11 attacks on the United States to the repeated anti-Muslim and anti-Sikh violence perpetrated by Hindu fundamentalists in India.

There is no doubt that much violence is inflamed by the harsh political and economic conditions of life and by the subversion of long-standing cultural practices. Promoting prosperity, more equitable distribution of resources, greater cultural sensitivity, and more responsive and honest government will certainly reduce popular support for violence. However, a small percentage of believers in all fundamentalist traditions understand the world in absolutist terms and see violence as a divinely ordained response. For these, nothing short of the total victory of their ideas is acceptable.

YOU DECIDE:

1. The rise of fundamentalism raises important questions. First, clearly, the people we call fundamentalist have greatly varying beliefs, but are there commonalities despite these differences? What are these? Give examples.
2. Using specific examples, describe some local and global forces that have encouraged the development of fundamentalism in many different locations throughout the world.
3. Do you see fundamentalism as a problem? If so, why, and what do you think could or should be done about it? If you think it is a problem, can you propose some partial solutions?

CHAPTER SUMMARY

1. What characteristics do all religions have in common? The great diversity in beliefs and practices worldwide makes religion difficult to define. However, all religions include sacred stories, ideas about

the supernatural (or nonempirical), rituals, symbols, and specialized practitioners.

2. What are sacred narratives, and what roles do they play in religion? Sacred narratives, sometimes called myths, are stories that express religious ideas. Sacred narratives explain and validate beliefs, values, and customs.

3. What is the importance of symbols in religion? Religious ideas are often expressed in symbols that have multiple meanings and frequently great emotional power. Symbols allow people to grasp the complexities of religion without much knowledge of the underlying theology.

4. What roles do supernatural beings and powers play in religion? Religions assume that there are nonmeasurable beings, powers, emotional states, and qualities that exist apart from humans but are important to them. Frequently people, objects, and places are understood as imbued with spiritual power or mana.

5. What is ritual, and how is it related to liminality? Ritual is behavior that enacts religion. Many rituals involve liminality or "between-ness." In states of liminality, normal social rules may be overturned and people may experience temporary states of equality and oneness or communitas.

6. What are rites of passage and rites of intensification? Rites of passage are public rituals that mark a person's transition from one status to another. Examples include marriage and funerals. Rites of intensification are rituals that strengthen group identity.

7. What are prayer, sacrifice, and magic? What are critical differences among them? Prayer, sacrifice, and magic are rituals individuals and groups use to interact with the world of the supernatural. Most religions include examples of all three. The key difference between them is the degree to which people believe that their own actions determine outcomes. Also common is the use of divination, a religious technique to discover the hidden.

8. What are shamans and priests, and what is the difference between them? Shamans and priests are two kinds of religions practitioners. Shamans receive power through claims of direct contact with the supernatural and are found in almost all societies. Priests are members of bureaucracies and are appointed, elected, or hired to their positions. They are most common in state-level societies.

9. What are witches and sorcerers, and how do accusations of witchcraft usually operate in society? In most societies, witches and sorcerers are people who are considered to use nonempirical means to harm those around them (modern-day Wiccans are an exception to this).

Accusations of witchcraft stigmatize certain kinds of behavior or scapegoat individuals for social or medical problems. In some parts of Africa, AIDS symptoms are understood to be evidence of witchcraft.

10. When is religious prophecy likely to be heard, and what are common types of prophecy? Religious prophecy is generally heard when there is rapid social, economic, technological, and political change. Prophecy may be nativistic, calling for a return to a past golden age, or vitalistic, looking to a future golden age. It may emphasize the coming of a savior or a period of destruction after which a new world will emerge.

11. What is the basis of the growth of the Rastafarians? The growth of Rastafarianism stems from its contribution to an individual and communal identity that positively values blackness as a counter to the stigmatization and oppression of blacks.

12. Under what conditions does fundamentalism occur, and what are its characteristics? Fundamentalism tends to occur in times of rapid change. Fundamentalists often view religion as a basis of identity, believe in a single truth, understand life as a battle between good and evil, and believe they are a persecuted minority. They are selective in their acceptance of modernity.

KEY TERMS

Animism	Monotheism
Antistructure	Polytheism
Communitas	Prayer
Contagious magic	Priest
Cosmology	Religion
Divination	Rite of intensification
Fundamentalism	Rite of passage
God (or deity)	Ritual
Imitative magic	Sacred narratives (myths)
Liminal	Sacrifice
Magic	Shaman
Mana	Syncretism
Messianic	Totem
Millenarian	Witchcraft

Jeff Morgan 01/Alamy

12

CREATIVE EXPRESSION: ANTHROPOLOGY AND THE ARTS

AFTER YOU HAVE READ THIS CHAPTER, YOU WILL BE ABLE TO:

Δ Summarize some of the functions of art in political and ritual contexts.

Δ Describe the ways art can symbolize key cultural concepts and themes, using examples.

Δ Analyze the roles that art can play in politics. Give examples of the use of art to promote political ends.

Δ Discuss how art is used to express cultural and personal identity, using examples from different societies.

Δ Describe the relationship between art made for use within a particular culture and the international art market.

World music combines elements of the local and the global. Africa is an especially important source of world music. Here, the Nigerian popular singer Queen Salawa Abeni performs at the Brecon Jazz festival in Wales. Abeni sings "waka," a Yoruba musical style heavily influenced by Islamic music.

World Music: The Local Goes Global

DESPITE the close connection between the arts and particular cultural themes, the arts today have a global reach. One of the fastest-growing global phenomena is the emergence of world music. **World music** incorporates different musical styles from cultures throughout the world. It includes not only Caribbean music like reggae and salsa but also Celtic folk songs, Louisiana blues and Cajun, and songs from Africa, the Middle East, and Asia.

World music: World music incorporates different musical styles from cultures throughout the world.

World music is based on local musical traditions, produced for local occasions, in local languages. Communications technology and migrations have spread these musical traditions around the world. Reggae, a Jamaican musical style linked to the religious resistance of the Rastas and widely popularized by Bob Marley (Jelly-Schapiro 2009), is today performed by Africans, Asians, and Europeans as well as Jamaicans. World music combines Western styles with local instruments. For example, Mory Kanté, an African musician who plays traditional African instruments like the balafon and the kora, is backed by a band of Western drums, guitars, basses, and keyboards. The reverse is also true. The recordings of Shakira, Black Eyed Peas, Vampire Weekend, and Beyonce have all been influenced by indigenous musical traditions.

The influence of Africa and African-derived music stands out in world music, for example, by creating endless variations from shared foundations in call-and-response and polyrhythm. The music of African religious ceremonies was preserved by slaves and adapted into the sacred and secular music of the New World (Pareles 1996). From the polyrhythmic basis of North American ragtime and early New Orleans jazz, through the African-Cuban percussionist influence of Mongo Santamaria, to the performance combination of Youssou N'Dour of Senegal, to the contemporary albums of singers from West Africa such as Salif Keita, Africa has influenced world music. The music of African Americans also has worldwide popularity: Hip-hop music of urban African American culture is popular in Japan, Cambodia (Mydans 2008; Sterling 2010), and China (Wang 2009), as well as in Europe. In Marseille, in Southern France, hip-hop helps transcend differences between its diverse populations of Muslims, Jews, and other immigrants, helping to prevent the interethnic violence found in other French cities (Kimmelman 2007).

Bhangra, which originated in the folk music of Punjab, India and eastern Pakistan, was originally performed at harvest festivals. Today, bhangra beats are mixed with British pop music and reggae. The amalgam of

Bhangra: A musical form originating in the folk music of Punjab in northern India and eastern Pakistan that is mixing with British pop music and reggae to become a popular form of world music.

contemporary **bhangra** with rock, pop, reggae, and hip-hop styles has spread from London, where it particularly involves members of the South Asian diaspora, to the urban United States, Canada, and other nations with substantial South Asian populations. It is also now popular in India and Pakistan.

Bhangra means different things to different people. To the young, urban, British-born South Asians who created it, bhangra was a music of resistance, with its lyrics—in Punjabi and English—articulating the problems of racism and the balancing of tradition and modernity among this South Asian diaspora (Lipsitz 1994). In smaller British towns, South Asians understood bhangra as a traditional art form, using bhangra parties as occasions to dress in traditional Indian clothing and bring back their traditional cultural memories (Bennett 1997). Many South Asian elders, however, consider modern bhangra to be a Western pollution of tradition and particularly object to its dance styles that involve close contact between men and women (Katrak 2002). Like all music, bhangra retains its links with its local identities but has also changed as it has diffused around the world.

THE ARTS

Creative expression, like religion, is universal; the arts serve many of the same functions as religion and are similar in using symbols to convey their meanings. **Art** refers to the ways people in every society express themselves using characteristic forms of creativity that are guided by aesthetic principles involving imagination, beauty, skill, and style. Through art, people interpret the world with images and symbols that express the basic themes, values, and perceptions of reality in ways that are culturally meaningful.

Art: Forms of creative expression that are guided by aesthetic principles and involve imagination, skill, and style.

Each culture has specific artistic symbols that stand for things or events in nature and human society or are associated with particular emotions. Because these symbols are culturally specific, art must be understood in its cultural context. Anthropologists are interested in both the more obvious meanings and the deeper meanings of symbols, and the ways in which they are connected to other elements in a culture. But in some cultures, the power of art is not merely symbolic: Artistic creations may be viewed as reality itself. For example, mask dancing in many African cultures is both symbolic and real. The costumes and their different elements have symbolic meanings, but mask dancing is also real in the sense that the masked dancer does not just *represent* the supernatural being but has *become* the supernatural being. In our own culture, the original of a famous artwork also carries the kind of power that a replica does not have.

Cultures differ in their artistic emphases: Some cultures use visual media, others use verbal skills, such as storytelling, and still others use dance and music to convey their central aesthetic values. Calligraphy, for example, is an important art form in both China and the Islamic Middle East, but for different reasons. In China, written language is a central defining attribute of Chinese civilization and a key source of Chinese cultural identity and unity. In Islam, calligraphy is the most respected of the graphic arts because it is the visual representation of the Koran. Because of the Muslim prohibition on the visual representation of graven human images (often extended to animal representations), calligraphy and representations of flowers and geometric designs have an important place in Islamic aesthetics.

Art embodies an artistic style, which refers to a characteristic manner of expression. Different cultures as well as different artists have different artistic styles. Although artistic styles do change, they are often very stable, lasting hundreds, and in some cases thousands, of years. Where art is closely tied to religion, artistic styles tend to be more stable than where art and religion are independent of each other.

▌▌▌ THE FUNCTIONS OF ART

Art has many functions: It is a vehicle for the display of cultural themes; it validates social hierarchies by making visible the power of the state or a ruling elite; and it is an important way to express personal, social, and individual identities. Art, whether in artifact, movement, or sound, is often central to ritual. Art can be used to support a society's social structure and the importance of its elites. Artistic displays may express the divine source of the ruler's power; the social and ethnic divisions of society, as in totemic symbols; and the political structure through which the society is governed, for example, in the building of temples and monuments. Both the totem poles and the artistic products and performances associated with the potlatch of the Northwest coast of North America are art forms that reflect and send powerful messages about the importance of social hierarchy in these societies (Jonaitis 1991). Art can also be used to resist social hierarchy, providing powerful ways to express disunity and conflict, to resist state authority, and to give voice to members of oppressed or marginalized groups. The Br'er Rabbit folktales of the American South illustrate how stories can undercut the powerful: The trickster, a weak but clever hero resists those in power through wit rather than force. These African American folktales, which ridicule and question social order, have an obvious relationship to slavery and oppression (Friedheim and Jackson 1996:24).

However, as society changes so does art. As possibilities of open protest against the racial caste system increased in the United States, African American oral traditions also changed. The "badman," who openly displays his arrogance and virility, came to supplant the trickster as hero (Abrahams 1970), an image diffused into the blaxploitation films of the 1970s and into the gangsta figure in hip-hop and gangsta rap.

Creative expression is also important in constructing and intensifying personal and group identities, generating intense emotions that foster cultural and social unity. Thus, art forms do not merely reflect a society and its culture, but also heighten cultural integration by displaying and confirming the values a society holds in common. The powerful artistic symbols of a society express universal themes—death, pride, gender relations, aggression, solidarity, and identity—in ways that are culturally particular and therefore culturally compelling, even when (some might say particularly when) their content is not consciously articulated. The arts make dominant cultural themes visible, tangible, and thus more real. In Western music, for example, the use of the minor scale conveys the emotion of sadness. Various other musical forms are traditionally associated with other emotions. These artistic conventions can be used to evoke emotions because people in that culture have been taught the association. Similarly, in the United States, a story that begins "Once upon a time" signals that it is not about real events and people. This knowledge sets the stage for the audience to respond to the story emotionally in certain ways.

The arts are particularly useful in expressing the more unconscious, repressed aspects of a culture, as described later for the Japanese popular art of anime. Broadly understood, games, sports, and performance, or what Clifford Geertz calls "deep play" (1973a), like Spanish bullfighting, or soccer in Tonga, are also art forms that express unconscious cultural themes. Like other creative forms, they intensify emotions, display compelling aspects of social structure and culture, and reinforce cultural and personal identities.

In the West, some media art, for example, so-called reality shows or TV travelogues, are sometimes used to dramatically represent outsiders in either negative or fantastical ways. An example of this is the TV show that appeared on both the Travel Channel and BBC, *Mark & Olly: Living with the Machigenga* (sic), in which several Indiana Jones–type Westerners travel to remote locales to "get accepted" by exotic tribes (2009). In this case, the shows misrepresented the Amazonian tribes they filmed as mean and savage. They mistranslated native words and presented rituals that they had scripted as authentic. In addition, FENAMAD, an organization representing the indigenous people of the region where they filmed, accused them of responsibility for a flu epidemic that caused several deaths. The show's producers denied this accusation (Shepard 2011).

Western media representations of indigenous people, which now reach wide, global audiences, often breach ethical principles that are central to anthropological representations of indigenous peoples and other non-Western societies.

Franz Boaz called "the seeing eye ... an organ of tradition," and Marshall Sahlins once quipped that "There is no such thing as an immaculate perception" (Price 1989:19, 22). Both these anthropologists were emphasizing that art is not only produced, but also viewed, through the lens of culture, which shapes the response of audiences to specific artistic products. The high value that the modern West places on art for art's sake is not universal: In most societies, art is not produced or performed to express an artist's individuality, provide pleasure, or provide social commentary but rather is inseparable from other activities such as religious or political ritual or the production of utilitarian objects. Although some people in all societies are recognized as more competent in these skills than others, this competence does not necessarily translate into the specialized role of artist.

Furthermore, although producing art in all cultures is recognized as a creative process, it is not necessarily an innovative one (Price 1989). Many cultures do not prize originality—the creation of something entirely new—in their arts, but rather value improvisation, that is, creating interesting and endless variations on already established artistic themes (Vogel 1991:20); indeed, this characterized Western art from the fall of Rome to the Renaissance. Where the arts are allied with religion, as in Navajo songs, there is only one right way to sing a song, with no improvisation permitted. The Navajo believe that "foreign music is dangerous and not for Navajo" (McAllester 1954). Though anthropologists primarily view art through the lens of specific local cultures, globalization—which integrates the arts of many cultures, as in world music—complicates the relationships between art and culture.

▌▌▌ Art and Ritual: Paleolithic Cave Art

The spectacular Paleolithic cave art made by early *Homo sapiens* in Europe, which is about 10,000 to 32,000 years old, demonstrates the connection between art and ritual. The Altamira caves in Spain, and the Lascaux and Grotte Chauvet caves in France, contain elaborate and realistic images of the abundant and diverse plants and animals that existed in these areas (see Figure 12.1). In addition to painting, these early humans also made jewelry, carved and engraved human figures, made ritual and ceremonial objects, placed elaborate grave goods in burial sites, and made patterned notations that may indicate some form of record keeping.

Courtesy of the Peabody Museum of Archeology and Ethnology, Harvard University, 2005.16.351.2

Figure 12.1 The spots and handprints seen in this 15,000-year-old painting of a horse, found in Pech Merle Cave in France, support the argument that these prehistoric paintings had ritual significance for their creators.

Many of the images indicate the sexual and seasonal characteristics or behavior of various animal species, for example, stags baying in the autumn rut, a bellowing bison bull and butting mammoth bulls in the autumn, a bison licking a summer insect bite, and a bison with molting fur in the summer. Archeologists speculate that these images played a role in ritual, religion, and storytelling and were possibly used in curing ceremonies or rites of passage.

Because many of the images are of animals that were commonly eaten, some anthropologists argue that they were drawn as part of ceremonies intended to magically increase the chances of a successful hunt and that they contain encoded information about hunting techniques and other information useful for survival in the harsh conditions of the Ice Age (Strauss 1991). But the paintings also include images of animals, such as lions, that were not commonly eaten, but were associated with varying signs and symbols such as handprints or abstract signs. This suggests that many of the images were made for ritual use. Because these paintings were made over 20,000 years in different places, they are likely to have had diverse functions, and no one theory explains them all.

ART AND THE REPRESENTATION OF CULTURAL THEMES

A characteristic of all art is the conscious or unconscious expression of cultural themes, as illustrated for example, in the importance of World War II in postwar Japanese art.

Manga and Anime in Japan

Anime: Animation, as in the popular culture of Japan; usually refers to animation of manga, or comic book graphic art.

Manga: Japanese comic book art.

Important aspects of post–World War II popular culture in Japan are **anime** (animation) and **manga** (comic book art). Anime, the animation of manga, is now familiar throughout the world, displayed in animation films, video games, children's toys, the Internet, commercial products, and museum and art gallery displays in Japan and abroad. They have also spawned a subculture in Japan, called *otaku* (the closest translation is "nerd" or "geek"), whose darker side includes an obsession with themes of war and violence, including nuclear catastrophes, mutant monsters, robots, and science fiction. On the apocalyptic side of this popular culture are monsters like Godzilla, who was awakened from eons of submarine sleep by a hydrogen bomb explosion. Godzilla exhibits radiation-induced physical deformities and engages in nightly attacks on Tokyo, which reduce the city and its screaming population to ashes.

Takashi Murakami, a successful designer for Louis Vuitton, curated a manga and anime museum show in the United States in 2005 called "Little Boy: The Arts of Japan's Exploding Subculture," after the name given to the atomic bomb dropped by the United States on Hiroshima. Murakami interprets anime and manga, and its otaku subculture, as growing out of the repercussions of the Japanese defeat by the United States in World War II, the dropping of the atomic bomb, and the democratization and demilitarization the American military imposed on postwar Japan. In Murakami's view, Japan has not really examined its responsibility for these traumatic historical events. He claims that denying these traumas created repressed emotions such as anxiety, shame, and a pervasive sense of impotence, which find their outlets in the popular culture of manga and anime (Smith 2005). In calling his museum show "Little Boy," Murakami asserts that Japan's postwar dependence on the United States has kept it from growing up. This infantilism is reflected in the popular fascination in Japan with fantasies of violence and power, such as the Godzilla-like monsters and mushroom-cloud explosions that are so frequently used in Japanese animation.

Paradoxically, these anime and manga themes are sometimes joined with another major pop culture theme, an obsession with *kawaii*, or "cuteness." Cuteness is particularly displayed in images of Lolita-like preadolescent, seemingly innocent, schoolgirls, who nevertheless also convey a sexual knowingness that belies their appearance. One major cuteness image is Hello Kitty, a big-eyed, beribboned, expressionless pussycat character (without a mouth to express emotion), whose image—on clocks, stuffed toys, purses, music boxes, and wallpaper—fuels over $750 million a year in domestic and international sales (Fitzpatrick 2014).

Although anime and manga display cultural and psychological themes that are particularly Japanese, they have huge worldwide popularity, and there has been a rich cross-fertilization between American and Japanese manga and anime in popular culture. In the United States, Japanese-style cartoons are represented in the widely popular My Little Pony, Friendship is Magical, and Transformers Animated, among others. Takashi Okazaki's *Afro Samurai* manga relies heavily on elements of hip-hop and other aspects of American culture, leading to an anime series, a TV movie, and a video game. *Tenjho Tenge, Infinite Ryvius*, and *Samurai Champloo* also include American elements, particularly hip-hop dance and music. As Condry (2005) notes, the intense interchange between Japanese and American youth culture is often ahead of commercialization. The Internet, television, and other media allow almost instant access to events and fashion in New York, Los Angeles, and Tokyo. Members of different cultures pick up styles and statements that appeal to them, recasting culture to give it meaning within their own context. The deep roots of hip-hop culture in the African American urban experience have not prevented Japanese artists from making it their own as well.

▍▍▍ ART AND POLITICS

An important function of the arts is to legitimate social hierarchy and power, thus contributing to political stability, especially useful in times of political transition. Imperial China and the Inca and Spanish in Peru provide good examples. Inca royalty commissioned indigenous artists to paint portraits of their kings to keep alive the memory of Inca rulers for those claiming royal descent and noble status. The native elite of Peru thus asserted their claims to high status and power within the colonial hierarchy by depicting their own illustrious forebears in paintings, the visual language of European culture. In imperial China, also, the arts were central in legitimizing the ruling class, especially the emperor (Hearn 1996).

The Chinese believed that only those with knowledge of the past could have a vision of the future. Thus, it was essential for the imperial courts to possess historical writings and paintings in order to display that knowledge. Throughout Chinese imperial history, figure painting was directed toward commemorating the emperor. Life-size portraits of the emperor had to incorporate the two main Chinese ideals of imperial rule: moral authority and the power of the emperor's central role in a controlled bureaucratic administration. Thus, paintings of the emperor had to show him with individualized features representing the humanistic Confucian values of compassion and virtue while conveying the imposing demeanor of the absolute ruler, the Son of Heaven. Another artistic representation that conveyed imperial power was a series of almost life-size portraits of Chinese cultural heroes, commissioned by some emperors in the 12th century. By displaying these paintings in the court, the emperor demonstrated his identification with a mythologized past and his rightful place in the lineage of Confucian rulers.

But while the arts can help stabilize a society, they also provide powerful ways to express disunity and conflict within a society, to resist state authority, to give voice to members of oppressed or marginalized classes or social groups, and to send political messages (Figure 12.2). Folktales and other oral traditions are also used to reverse, ridicule, or question the social order and, in doing so, may provide ways of expressing resistance to conflicts that arise out of domination and control.

Using Anthropology: The Multiple Roles of Museums

Museums are central institutions in connecting cultures. Particularly in Europe and the United States, museums are a major point of contact between Westerners and indigenous peoples. One of the most famous museums in the world is the American Museum of Natural History (AMNH) in New York City. Originally created in the late 19th century for the entertainment and education of schoolchildren and the city's "working classes," the AMNH first established exhibits in natural history, such as paleontology and archaeology, which play important roles in understanding evolution and the human past.

Gradually, the museum incorporated ethnographic exhibits, sending expeditions around the world to collect artifacts from British Columbia, Siberia, Peru, and other remote places, where it was feared that indigenous peoples would soon disappear under the impact of a changing world. By the turn of the 20th century, the AMNH began its own anthropology program, and with the addition of Franz Boas and Clark Wissler to the staff, cultural anthropology exhibits were a central feature in the museum. These became a major attraction for New Yorkers and tourists alike. Under Boas, scientific research was added to entertainment and education as a central goal of museum anthropology.

In a fascinating history of the AMNH anthropology department, Stanley Freed—chair of the department for 7 years and the curator of North American Ethnology for 40—illuminates the importance of the relationship between anthropology and museums (Freed 2012). Many of the most famous U.S. anthropologists, like Clark Wissler, Margaret Mead, and Colin Turnbull, were associated with the AMNH, and Freed's stories provide a more personal look at anthropological history, as well as the ways in which international and urban politics affected both museums and museum anthropology.

Joan Young Gregg

Figure 12.2 Creative expression can be used to send political messages. The dress pictured here, created by an American middle school student, is made of candy wrappers and bottle caps to emphasize how Americans eat unhealthy food and pollute the environment.

A central anthropological role of Western museums is exhibiting non-Western art; before the expansion of world tourism, this was the major way Westerners learned about indigenous peoples. In the 19th century, indigenous arts, particularly the arts of Africa, were mainly exhibited as anonymous ethnographic artifacts. In the early 20th century, however, Western fine art underwent a modernist revolution and Pablo Picasso, among other European artists began to incorporate features of African and Oceanic art—much of which had a modernist and abstract look—into their own artistic creations. Artists and art historians at this time were not interested in understanding the cultural meanings of this art for the people who made it, however, or in discovering the actual artists. Rather, consistent with their own view of art, European artists and art historians mainly responded to the art in terms of its aesthetic principles.

Cultural anthropology, in contrast, emphasizes that art must be understood in its cultural context. This approach to understanding art, including attempts to discover the identity of the individual artists, now predominates in the exhibit of indigenous arts in both art and ethnographic/natural history museums (Cotter 2009; 2012; Price 1989; 2007; Steiner 1994; 1995; 2002). For anthropologists, cultural and functionalist perspectives on this art are central. In analyzing the way the arts contribute to the functioning of society, anthropologists are particularly interested in the social or symbolic worlds in which indigenous art was originally seen or used, such as religious ritual or social relationships. Though it took almost a half century for the anthropological approach to be widely adopted, it has made a real difference in enriching Western understandings of indigenous art and indigenous peoples. The anthropological perspective on indigenous art includes indigenous narratives framing the exhibition of this art, labeling objects to emphasize ethnographic context, and collaborating with indigenous peoples in curating exhibits of their arts.

Native Americans, for example, have long contested museum exhibits of their material culture, claiming that such exhibits misleadingly represent their societies as timeless rather than dynamic; excluded Native American voices, consultation, or collaboration; neglected contemporary Native American artists; displayed sacred objects that should not be seen by the nonnative public; and ignored any representation of contemporary political issues involving Native Americans. This has changed significantly: Native American cultural revitalization, remembrance, and political struggle are now prominent in exhibitions of Native American art, for example, in an exhibit on the Kwakiutl potlatch at the AMNH (Jonaitis 1991), which involved Kwakiutl Indians in all aspects of the exhibition's curation. Native American perspectives and involvement have also importantly shaped the new Smithsonian National Museum of the American Indian in our nation's capital.

As these anthropological perspectives gained influence, many art and ethnographic museums began to consider how both culture and power are implicated in displays of indigenous art (Hochschild 2005); indeed, today, museum exhibits themselves have become the subject of ethnographic inquiry, for what they tell us about the indigenous arts they exhibit, the culture of the people who arrange and promote such exhibits, and the cultural perceptions of museum visitors (Price 2007; 2009).

▮▮▮ Art and Historical Narratives

One important and widespread function of creative expression is to construct, display, and sustain narratives of a people's cultural identity, or create new national narratives through depictions of the past (Nanda 2004). Museums play an important role in this goal, aimed at both local and international audiences. Because they display cultural identity and history in ways that are visible, tangible, and emotionally compelling, the arts are an important way of recording, interpreting, and remembering both an actual and a legendary past.

These records, whether material or oral, embody the effort of a people to define, explain, and amuse themselves and to keep alive their cultural identity. Many of the old stories told by Native American groups incorporate jokes and demonstrate the resilience of people who have experienced great hardship. The ledger drawings of some Native American groups are an example of the use of art to record history and preserve cultural identity (Berlo 1996; Greene 2001; Powers 2005). Native American ledger drawings also provide a readable historical record, a way for people to anchor themselves in the real world and locate themselves in history beyond myths and legends.

Ledger drawings got their name from the ledger books obtained from trading posts in which the Native Americans drew their records. The ledger drawings were made only by men and initially served mainly to record the lost life of warfare, hunting, and tribal identity. At the turn of the 19th century, Native Americans were already using drawings—on skin shirts, robes, and teepee covers—to record personal histories. By the 1860s, these drawings had become more elaborate, colored, and carefully composed, and the original material of war deeds had expanded to include social customs and communal history. Ledger drawing flourished as an art form from about the 1870s to about the 1920s, during the early reservation period, a time of profound cultural change. It expanded when about 70 Native Americans, mostly southern Cheyenne, were imprisoned for a time at Fort Marion, in St. Augustine, Florida. They produced scores of ledger drawings, for personal pleasure, for sale to tourists, and as gifts for the whites with whom they interacted. This period was a time of profound cultural trauma as Native Americans left the old free life of the buffalo-hunting days for a new life as semiprisoners living on government rations, under official pressure to abandon their religion, traditional ceremonies, and the old ways of communal living. Ledger drawings serve not only as an important expression of Native American arts, but also as important documents in the recording of actual events that can be used to expand knowledge about the past.

ART AND THE EXPRESSION OF IDENTITIES

In all cultures, the creative process is used to express both individual and cultural identity.

Body Art and Cultural Identity

For thousands of years, people all over the world have been marking and adorning their bodies. Almost all cultures alter their members' bodies. Circumcision and other genital operations, scarification, piercing, and tattooing are common throughout the world's cultures. These are used to announce identification with particular groups and to mark social position. Tattooing, scarification, and genital operations are ways of permanently engraving group membership on the body. Applying tattoos or facial scars marks one as a member of a group in a visible way that cannot be easily denied. Such body changes may carry elements of particular status as well as membership. For example, body marking has been used in Western Europe since ancient times; tattoos and body painting have been used to mark outlaw status, nobility, soldiers, slaves, and various kinds of religious observance and status (Schildkrout 2004). In a study of tattooing in Polynesia, Gell (1993) argues that tattooing both creates and reinforces status hierarchy differences among people and also is critical in the relationship of humans to the sacred. But Gell's work also shows enormous variation in the meanings of tattoos in different Polynesian island societies.

In many cultures, body art is associated with enhancing beauty, and thus related to gender. In India and the Middle East, henna, an orange-red dye made from the leaves of a small shrub, is used to dye fingernails and other parts of the hands and feet to enhance a woman's beauty, especially on ceremonial occasions such as religious holidays or marriage (Messina 1988). In Morocco, where anthropologist Maria Messina studied the body art of henna application, a young girl is first decorated with henna at age 3 or 4, in preparation for the important

Muslim holiday of Ramadan. But the cultural importance of henna is primarily related to marriage, and marks the transition of a girl to a woman. The "night of henna" is the first night in the 3-day marriage celebration; a girl is also decorated with henna at a "henna party" toward the end of her pregnancy. The month of Muharram, which marks the Muslim New Year, is another occasion for decorating married women with henna.

Henna parties are also viewed as a way of preventing illness or misfortune by placating malevolent spirits, called jinn. Sometimes women hire specialists to apply henna designs on the skin, but a member of the woman's family may also do this. Although certain designs are traditional in certain regions, henna specialists also innovate in styles, and designs change according to the occasion and also according to fashion. Most of the designs have no explicit meaning, as representational art (art depicting any figures or forms found in nature or culture) is forbidden in Islam.

In addition to the cosmetic function of henna, and the prevention of illness, henna parties are celebrations during which friends visit and possibly sing and dance. They also provide occasions during which women are the center of attention. The application of henna designs has diffused from its original home (probably in India), and is now common also among non-Indians in the United States, functioning less as a display of a group identity than as an expression of an individual's assertion of choice and personal preference.

Art and Personal Identity: Fritz Scholder, Indian and Not Indian

For people in European-based cultures, one of the more obvious functions of the arts is the expression of personal identity. Indeed, in these cultures, personal identity is assumed to be deeply connected to an artist's body of work. However, such art must also deal with and reflect broader cultural themes. Fritz Scholder (1937–2005) was a controversial artist whose work reflects both deep issues of individual and cultural identity. Scholder's father was half Indian and half German, and his family did not live on an Indian reservation. Although enrolled in his father's tribe (the Luiseño), he often said he was not Indian. Until Scholder's work in the 1960s, much Native American painting, by both native and nonnative artists, romanticized native life and the natural world and reflected popular clichés about the lives of native peoples. In contrast, Scholder's works combined historical images with abstract expressionism and pop art and presented a provocative challenge to these clichés. He directly addressed some uncomfortable truths about contemporary Native American life, such as alcoholism, poverty, and injustice. Scholder's painting, "Indian with Beer Can," generated especially outraged responses among both native and nonnative viewers because it broke the taboo on talking about the ways that alcoholism devastated so many Indian lives. Another of his powerful and controversial paintings is that of a Buffalo Dancer with an ice cream cone. While many viewers found this image disrespectful, for Scholder it cast a realistic look at the contact between the traditional and the modern in contemporary native life.

Scholder's ambivalence about his Indian identity, reflected in his art, and his frequent statements that he was not Indian, led other native artists to criticize what they saw as his denial of the very source of his artistic success. Scholder's powerful art illustrates both his own shifting identities and new perspectives on his culture and how the two are intertwined (Ringlero 2008).

▮▮▮ Art and Personal Identity: Frida Kahlo

The work of Frida Kahlo, a 20th-century Mexican painter, is another example of how art combines elements of the artist's personality, life experiences, political ideology, and national identity. Kahlo was born to an ethnically mixed middle-class family. Her father was a German Jew and her mother half Mexican and half Native American. In her childhood, she contracted polio, and a subsequent bus accident left her leg deformed and her body in great pain. Her marriage to the great Mexican muralist Diego Rivera was filled with conflict, and her attempts to have a child ended in a miscarriage. All of these cultural and personal issues are reflected in her painting, the subjects of which deal with issues of illness and health, female sexuality and gender identity, marginality, cultural identity, power, and pain.

Kahlo was profoundly influenced by the Mexican Revolution. Although she was born in 1907, she claimed she was born in 1910, the year of the Revolution, to demonstrate her identification with the poor and the peasants, in whose name the Revolution was carried out. The Revolution ushered in a time of political freedom that led to a new pride in Mexico. This fostered the awareness of indigenous, pre-Columbian, Mexican art, craft, and native traditions, among European influenced painters such as Kahlo and her husband Diego Rivera.

In her paintings Kahlo drew on many elements of Mexican culture, such as *retablos* (votive paintings of Christian saints and martyrs); the Mexican folklore image of La Llorona, the archetypal, sexually voracious predator and evil woman who stands in contrast to the saintly wife and mother; and the indigenous Mexican Tehuana costume, with its long embroidered skirts and blouses, which expressed her solidarity with Mexican peasants. Kahlo also wore this Mexican dress herself to demonstrate the cultural independence of Mexico; the dress had the added benefit of hiding her deformed leg. Kahlo's self-portraits also evidenced dualistic principles, like contrasts of dark and light and night and day, which originated in pre-Columbian myth. Kahlo's paintings also examine the imbalance of power between Mexico and the United States, and the images of her broken body reflect the shattered dreams of the Mexican Revolution (see Figure 12.3).

Although Kahlo was well known in Mexico, it was mainly since the 1990s that she attracted great interest beyond Mexico; she has now become an international cult figure. Her art particularly speaks to women, especially women's experiences of physical pain, of childbirth, and of the emotional pain of love, which is symbolized by the many broken hearts in her self-portraits. In Kahlo's art, we clearly see the important role of art in expressing the many strands—cultural, political, physical, and familial—that make up an artist's personal identity—and through their expression in art, speak to a world wider than the artist's own.

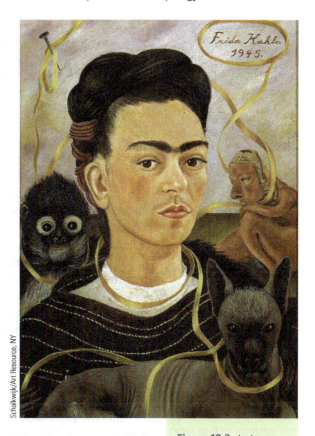

Schalkwijk/Art Resource, NY

Figure 12.3 An important function of art is the expression of personal and national identities. Frida Kahlo incorporated Mexican cultural elements in her self-portraits to assert her identification with the Mexican peasantry and their revolutionary ideals.

▌▌▌ART AND REPRESENTATIONS OF THE OTHER

In representing cultural identities, art depicts not only the "we"—that is, the cultural in-group—but also the "other"—the alien, the foreigner, the outsider. Indeed, artistic forms are important aspects of cultural ideologies of difference, communicating in subtle but significant ways the nature of we/they distinctions.

The rendering of the other appears in art all over the world. Artistic products may reflect the subjects of the art, but they are also a source of insight into the mind-set of the artist, reflecting, perhaps, the cultural fantasies one group of people entertains about another (Bassani and Fagg 1988). Artistic images of outsiders may be useful as historical documents, portraying details of behavior and costume, but the unknown aspects of foreigners also act as an invitation to the imagination in which the reality of the observed becomes subordinate to the fantasies of the observers (Tsuruta 1989).

▌▌▌ Orientalism in European Art: Picturing the Middle East

One result of the encounters between Europeans and other peoples was a profound rethinking of European cultural identity (Schwartz 1994). Although these encounters were experienced differently in different times and places, Europeans most often responded by creating opposite categories of "them" and "us" (Bitterli 1986). These dichotomies take many forms: East and West; primitive, or barbarian, and civilized; traditional and modern; developed and undeveloped. As we noted earlier, the differences in museum exhibits of Western and non-Western art implicitly distinguished between the "civilized" us of the West and the non-Western "primitive" other.

In the 19th century, Europeans explored, conquered, and then wrote about and painted North Africa, Arabia, the Levant, and the Ottoman Empire. This region, today called the Middle East, was then called the Orient. European artists of the 19th and 20th centuries offered armchair travelers a vividly graphic image of the Islamic, largely Arabic cultures inhabiting this world. One important impetus for these representations, particularly in France, was the Napoleonic campaigns in Egypt (1798 to 1799). By the mid-19th century, the Egyptian experience had become part of the French cultural spirit and was found in a wide range of artistic representations in a style called **Orientalism** (Hauptman 1985:48).

Orientalism: Scholarship and art generated by Europeans, representing their views of the Middle East.

Creative expressions representing the Middle East are particularly interesting. In the 19th century, the Middle East was depicted in European art as an enchanting land of mystery, fairy tales, and exotic beauty, yet also threatening in its opposition to European culture. Artists sought out the picturesque and the awesome (fabled ruins, biblical sites, deserts, and mountains). They emphasized the exoticism and glamour of Oriental markets, camel caravans, and snake charmers. Above all, European artists depicted their fantasies of "Oriental" women, hidden behind the veil or revealed in a harem or in slave markets (Alloula 1986; Thornton 1994). Such images were more a reflection of European romanticism than an accurate depiction of Middle Eastern culture. However, they have helped shape our understandings of the Middle East (particularly of gender relations) and, as a result, have had important political ramifications (Said 1978). Europeans saw the Oriental "other" as threatening because they perceived it as the opposite of European civilization. They viewed Europe as democratic, dynamic, and rational and viewed the Orient as despotic, static, and irrational. This perception of the Orient was reflected in and reinforced by European paintings (see Figure 12.4). Islam was captured not in its religious experience (to which Europeans were generally hostile) but in the architecture of its mosques and its practice of prayer, all portrayed in lavish, opulent detail. Although many Europeans traveled to the

Juan Gimenez-Martin/Dahesh Museum of Art

Figure 12.4 The enigma of the Middle Eastern woman, whether hidden behind a veil or revealed in a harem, was a core image of Orientalist painting. In many cases, these were purely works of the imagination, as in this painting, Juan Gimenez Martin's "In the Harem," painted in the artist's studio in Rome.

Orient, painters generally worked from secondhand sources or, in some cases, purely from imagination. However, their works were rendered in exquisite detail, which gave viewers a sense of historical accuracy.

Gender roles and relationships were a central theme in Orientalist painting. Men were shown as clearly dominant and pictured in public places, where women were mostly absent. The Arab warrior was the most common symbol of Oriental masculinity, but men were also painted in more relaxed poses, drinking coffee or smoking a hookah. But Oriental women were central to European fantasies of the period (Thornton 1994). The difficulty of finding women to pose in no way inhibited their depiction. Indeed, this gave free rein to artists' imaginations.

Harems and slave markets, painted for male patrons by male artists, offered a convenient way of feeding European lust by displaying the dominant men and vulnerable women of another culture, far removed from home. Pornographic scenes disguised as either documentation or art were integral to the European market for Orientalist painting (Thubron 2009). These images were not confined to fine art but found frequent expression in other elements of culture such as the picture postcard, a genre that the poet Malek Alloula calls the "comic strip of colonial morality." The postcards reveal the preoccupation of Europeans with the veiled female body. The native models for these postcards were photographed in studios reenacting exotic rituals in costumes photographers provided. The models represent the French fantasy of the inaccessible Oriental female, more tempting because she is behind the veil in the forbidden harem.

Alloula connects these Orientalist fantasies to colonial reality, noting that the raiding of women has always been the dream and the obsession of the total victor: "These raided bodies are the spoils of victory, the warrior's reward." The postcards are an "enterprise in seduction directed to the troops, the leering wink in the encampment" (1986:122).

Orientalist representations of women also reflected the long-standing conflict between Christian Europeans and Middle Eastern Muslims. Since the Middle Ages, Europeans had criticized Muslims for their practice of polygyny, which Europeans associate with promiscuity. Thus, popular images of slave girls, harems, and concubines provided a continual source of horror and titillation for Western critics of the Muslim world. Even today, much Western thinking about the contemporary Middle East is concerned with the veiling, segregation, and oppression of women (Hale 1989).

▌▌▌ WORLD ART

The diffusion of the art of indigenous peoples has today become an important part of a global economy. For Western tourists, the art of traditional and authentic indigenous peoples is a deep and unchanging aspect of their cultures, and purchasing this art is an important part of their experience. In fact, however, traditional art changes as do other aspects of culture, under the impact of globalization, the emergence of art markets, and the expansion of global tourism. Ritually and socially significant creative expressions in indigenous societies are transformed as they become part of a global market. Anthropologists are particularly interested in examining how art becomes functionally and stylistically reconceptualized to meet a global demand and how this "traffic in culture" affects both the art and the cultural identities of the people who create it (Cotter 2012; Price 1989; Steiner 1994; Venbrux, Rosi, and Welsch 2006). In addition to providing new sources of income, objects and performances that originated in traditional indigenous ritual and social life become artistic *products* around which modern cultural identities are constructed, both by outsiders and by members of the societies themselves. As a result of this global context, anthropologists and art historians now speak of **world art**, in which the arts of indigenous peoples are increasingly circulated, and in which the role of the artist is no longer anonymous, but increasingly known, as is typical of Western society. Previously, even when an individual artist could be tracked down, dealers and collectors were generally not interested in doing so; anonymity was often exploited by art middlemen who learned that objects were worth more to buyers from Europe and the United States if they were portrayed as coming from unknown, preferably long-deceased artists in remote villages. The middlemen are quite willing to manipulate both the art objects and the information about their production to meet these demands (Steiner 1995:157). Today, however, this is changing, and the identification of native artists has now become an important factor in both understanding and marketing their arts.

World art: The contemporary visual arts and cultural performances of non-Western peoples.

Outsider interest in developing and marketing indigenous arts in the United States helped create the status of artist where it did not previously exist, as happened in the life and work of the Pueblo Indian potter Maria Martinez (1887–1980) of San Ildefonso (Babcock 1995). In 1908 and 1909, archaeologist and museum director Edgar Lee Hewett asked Martinez to make pottery modeled on the ancient designs he had uncovered near her village. Martinez, with her husband Julian, elaborated their techniques and designs, producing a new black on black pottery style. Maria and Julian actively popularized and promoted their work outside their community, demonstrating their technique and wares at several world fairs and expositions. By the 1930s, the profile of northern New Mexico, in which San Ildefonso is located, was substantially raised among art collectors as well-known artists like Georgia O'Keeffe and Ansel Adams, among others, came to work and live in the area. After Julian's death in 1943, Maria began to work with younger family members; her son Popovi Da (1922–1971) was not only a talented artist but also a talented promoter who toured nationally promoting Martinez pottery.

The community of San Ildefonso now became identified with fine pottery, and Maria Martinez became a star of the art world, her signed pottery now selling for thousands of dollars. Ironically, because of her connections to the national and global art market, she also became a romanticized image of the authentic Native American woman potter.

▌▌▌ Tourism and World Art

The arts have always been important in marking cultural boundaries. They retain that importance in the contemporary world, particularly with regard to the construction of ethnic identities of indigenous peoples and their relation to tourism (Graburn 1976). The linking of the arts to cultural identity is promoted by popular television shows about non-Western cultures, the worldwide sale of ethnic arts (including on the Internet), traveling museum shows in which indigenous peoples are represented through their arts, the circulation of tribal arts among Western art collectors, and particularly, tourism. Artistic objects and performances that have their origin in ritual and social life may become, through tourism, a core around which modern cultural identities are constructed and an important source of income as well (see Figure 12.5).

Tourism can transform indigenous, culturally authentic, and creative art into mass-produced souvenirs and performances lacking any cultural meaning. On the other hand, it can also support and reaffirm cultural identities by reviving respect for traditional art forms. These are not necessarily mutually exclusive results. In the American Southwest, as we have seen, the 20th century brought a resurgence of wide interest in Native

Figure 12.5 Many traditional arts have been given new life by the tourist industry. Here an artist in Bali paints traditional designs on a cloth hanging designed for sale to tourists.

Joan Young Gregg

American arts, and this has resulted in the production of a great deal of outstanding art in both traditional and new media. This continues today, and both older and more recent native artworks fetch high prices on the international market. But, as anyone who has traveled in the area knows, the Southwest is also awash with cheap bric-a-brac often mass-produced in Asia. Also, in Bali, the interest of tourists in cultural performances has given such events an economic boost and allowed local troupes to buy new instruments for their musical ensembles and new costumes. It also has encouraged the opening of schools and institutes throughout Indonesia for training people in creating traditional art forms. An expert and professional group of Indonesian artists has maintained tight control over performances to conserve the quality of the arts. Similarly, interest in the Inuit arts and their sale to tourists has been an extremely important alternative source of income for them, especially as hunting declines. The connection between art, tourism, and the strengthening of cultural identity is also seen in the weaving of Native American women in Guatemala and Mexico (Nash 1986).

Ritually and socially significant cultural elements change meaning as they become part of staged performances for tourists or move from their original cultural contexts into the world art market. This is part of a larger process in which culture itself has become a marketable commodity, reshaped and packaged in part in response to the demands of globalization. Among the more recent anthropological interests in art are the ways in which the artworks of nonindustrial societies have become commodities in the process of globalization and the ways in which they have been reconceptualized functionally and stylistically to meet a worldwide demand. It is still unclear whether this marketing of culture will move the world inevitably toward cultural homogenization or whether the global economy and the global village will always leave room for the emergence of meaningful local artistic expressions of cultural identity.

■▊ Marketing Indigenous Arts

Anthropologist Kathleen Adams describes how indigenous arts and identities change under the impact of global tourism and commodification (Adams 2006). Among the Toraja, subsistence cultivators in South Sulawesi, Indonesia, two spiritually important artistic productions are tongkonan, spectacularly carved ancestral houses, and tau taus, wooden effigies of nobles carved in connection with mortuary rituals. Although the Toraja today are predominantly Christian, their traditional art and elaborate rituals connected with the tongkonan and the tau taus are still a major component of contemporary Toraja cultural identity. Tourism has been essential in the maintenance of these traditional aspects of Toraja culture.

By the late 1960s, the expansion of organized tourism to the Toraja area was focused on viewing Toraja mortuary rituals of animal sacrifice; the tongkonan and the tau tau became important parts of Indonesia's tourist development program, aimed at increasing the flow of Western capital (Volkman 1984:162). Tourist interest in the tongkonan led to a ban by the Indonesian government on altering them. The question was even raised as to whether the Toraja should be permitted to live in them, lest they damage these "tourist objects" (Adams 1990:33). Reflecting the worldwide tourist demand for "portable art," the Toraja soon began carving miniature tongkonan and selling them in souvenir shops.

The tau taus also changed under the tourist gaze and the global art market. Traditionally, tau taus, commissioned by the family, represented the spirit of a dead person, considered the vessel of the Torajan soul. When the mortuary rites are completed, the tau tau is placed with its relatives on platforms chiseled into limestone cliffs, where it becomes a visual link between the community of the living and the community of the dead.

Today, tau taus may incorporate Western cultural elements, such as digital watches, eyeglasses, Western clothing, Bibles, and crosses. And while tau taus were traditionally carved only for the wealthiest nobility and were therefore a symbol of aristocratic status among the Toraja, the tau taus are symbolic of a generalized Torajan identity for tourists today. Miniature tau taus are sold in tourist markets, along with large carvings of the burial cliffs. Thus, tourism began a process by which ritually significant objects have been transformed into art objects of economic significance.

The Toraja.

As traditional tau taus were transformed into artistic commodities in a global art market, hundreds of them were stolen and sold to American, European, and Asian art collectors. Redesignated by Western curators and collectors as archaic Indonesian art, some effigies have also found a home in Western museums. A stolen tau tau is irreplaceable; its theft is tantamount to the abduction of an ancestor, and the loss must be redressed by ritual propitiation. However, legal, political, and economic obstacles stand in the way of repatriation, and tau taus today are openly sold for thousands of dollars in international galleries. The Toraja realize that without the tau taus, tourism will decline, depriving them of an important source of income and prestige. The Indonesian government, more to maintain tourist interest than to address Torajan concerns, has replaced stolen tau taus with newly made ones, but the Torajans reject these not only as clumsily made but also as having no spiritual significance because they were not made under ritual conditions (Adams 2006).

Paradox and pathos thus attend the tau tau today. Their meaning has changed from ritual object to art commodity: Whereas the tau tau once served as a protection for the family of the deceased, today the family of the deceased must protect the tau tau.

BRINGING IT BACK HOME:
RELIGION, ART, AND CENSORSHIP

"[T]his show is disgusting," said New York City's then Mayor Rudolph Giuliani, commenting on *Sensation*, a 1999 art exhibit at the Brooklyn Museum of Art. He was referring specifically to a painting by the African artist Chris Ofili called "The Holy Virgin Mary." The painting depicted a black Madonna in a colorful flowing robe, dabbed with a clump of elephant dung and surrounded with images of women's buttocks and genitals clipped from pornographic magazines (Steiner 2002). The Giuliani administration attempted to cut the museum's funding and evict it from its building unless it removed the offending works. They were prevented from doing so by a court decision (*The Brooklyn Institute of Arts and Sciences v. the City of New York and Rudolph W. Giuliani*, 64 F.Supp2d 184 [F.D.N.Y. 1999], Opinion and Order 99 CV 6071), which argued that these actions violated freedom of speech.

In 2009, Sony released the video game *Hanuman: Boy Warrior* to worldwide protest by Hindu groups (Hanuman is a Hindu deity and a central figure in one of the epics of Hinduism). Rajan Zed, a leader of the protest and president of the Nevada-based Universal Society of Hinduism, said that controlling Hanuman with a joystick was denigrating. "Lord Hanuman was not meant to be reduced to such a 'character' in a video game and be in the company of *America's 10 Most Wanted, Bad Boys, Jackass,* and *Killer7*" (Das 2009).

In spring 2010, an episode of *South Park* depicted Muhammad as being inside a bear suit (presumably to avoid showing his image). Following the airing of the episode, a radical Islamic website warned the show's creators that they could be killed. In the following episode, Muhammad was replaced by Santa Claus, and Comedy Central, which airs the show, censored numerous scenes (Pilkington 2010).

Incidents such as this are not limited to the United States. In 2001, the Taliban government of Afghanistan destroyed the 1,500-year-old Buddhas of Bamiyan, the largest Buddha sculptures in the world at the time. The Buddhas and artwork in the caves associated with them had been the object of numerous earlier attacks, some dating back to the Genghis Kahn (Higuchi and Barnes 1995). In 2012, rebel forces destroyed ancient tombs in the city of Timbuktu, and when forced from the city by French troops in 2013, they attempted, largely unsuccessfully, to burn manuscripts and artifacts they considered un-Islamic (Balter 2013). And the satirical depictions of the prophet Muhammad in the French magazine, Charlie Hebdo, resulted in terrorist attacks on January 7, 2015, by Islamist gunmen who forced their way into the magazine's office, killing 12 people. The Islamic State has also destroyed much of the ancient site of Palmyra and numerous other ancient sites in Syria.

In the United States, religious freedom and freedom of speech are both deeply held cultural values. Yet, Americans also believe, as Supreme Court Justice Oliver Wendell Holmes Jr. (1841–1935) said, "the right to swing my fist ends where the other man's nose begins" (Trachtman 2009:87). In an age of complexity, diversity, and instant global communication, someone's nose seems always to be in the way.

YOU DECIDE:

1. Have you experienced artistic portrayals of your own beliefs that you found offensive? If so, did you think they should be censored? What role did your culture play in your opinion?
2. If the majority in a community finds an artistic representation of their religion offensive, should it be censored? Why or why not?

Does it make a difference if censorship comes from the government or from a corporation like Sony or Viacom (the company that owns Comedy Central)?

3. Art offensive to religion has sometimes led to violence and death (consider deaths resulting from protests over the Danish cartoon depictions of Muhammad or the Nazi's use of anti-Semitic art). Is fear of violence sufficient justification for artistic censorship?

CHAPTER SUMMARY

1. What are the basic differences between the anthropology of art and art history? Anthropologists examine the cultural and functional contexts of art, local standards of beauty, and the relation of art to ritual and social relations. Art historians, in contrast, emphasize what they call the intrinsic aesthetic value of art objects with little attention to function and cultural contexts.

2. In what ways do the arts of various cultures differ from each other? The forms of creative expression differ in different societies, as do the rules by which art is created, the importance of originality in art, the interactions of the artist with the audience, the purposes for which art is made, the roles of the artist, and the relation of art to other aspects of culture.

3. What are some aspects of the power of art? The power of art may lie in its emotional expression of important cultural themes, or the art itself may be regarded as inherently powerful, as when art is performed as part of a ritual, an example being when prehistoric hunters painted pictures of animals to achieve control over hunting.

4. Using one example, describe the relationship between art and cultural themes. The symbolic nature of art, with multilayered levels of meaning, functions to communicate cultural themes. In Japan, for example, anime and manga display the repressed themes of Japanese militarism in World War II, the trauma of the atomic bombing of Hiroshima and Nagasaki, and the postwar dependence of the Japanese on the United States and resulting feelings of powerlessness.

5. What are some of the relationships between art and history, art and social structure, art and social justice? The arts may be used to validate a political structure, as in memorials to ruling powers; challenge existing social and political structures by mocking those in power or questioning society's rules; or to record history and commemorate past events.

6. What are some of the connections between the arts and personal identities? Body art can express a cultural identity, a social status, or a personal identity. In Morocco, for example, henna painting of women's hands is intimately related to celebrating a marriage. Native American artist Fritz Scholder used his paintings to question his own Indian/not Indian identity, while Frida Kahlo's paintings reflect her gender and multicultural identities.

7. How does art express boundaries between the cultural in-group and the cultural other? Art can not only express the cultural identity of an in-group, but also reinforce that identity by depicting the "other," as in European Orientalism, which represented European fantasies of the Middle East.

8. How does art become an important factor in the cultural identities of indigenous peoples as they interact with others in a globalized context? Today, many indigenous societies, such as the Toraja of Indonesia, are known throughout the world because of their art forms. The global context for indigenous art around the world includes the Internet, international art collections, museum exhibits, and particularly, tourism. Although tourism may confer economic benefits, it also sometimes results in artistic objects, performances, and rituals that had spiritual meanings becoming transformed into staged displays or commodities in international art markets.

KEY TERMS

Anime

Art

Bhangra

Manga

Orientalism

World art

World music

Richard Warms

13

POWER, CONQUEST, AND A WORLD SYSTEM

Man with a painting of his father, a veteran of the *Tirailleurs Sénégalais*—an army the French drafted and recruited from their colonial possessions in West Africa between 1857 and 1960.

AFTER YOU HAVE READ THIS CHAPTER, YOU WILL BE ABLE TO:

⊿ Identify some of the critical reasons for the European expansion of the 16th century.

⊿ Summarize the key methods Europeans used to gain wealth from their global expansion.

⊿ Assess the roles of joint stock companies and monoculture plantations in creating European wealth.

⊿ Compare and contrast the era of colonization between 1500 and 1800 with colonizing in the 19th century.

⊿ Outline the role of disease in European expansion and compare its effects in the Americas and in Africa and Asia.

⊿ Analyze the ways in which Europeans attempted to extract wealth from their colonies in the 19th and 20th centuries.

⊿ Discuss the reasons why almost all colonies achieved independence by the end of the 1960s.

VETERANS OF COLONIAL ARMIES

HEN I (Rich Warms) was young, I was a Peace Corps volunteer. I lived in a town called Ouahigouya in a country that was then called Upper Volta (now Burkina Faso) in West Africa. I spent most of my time working in small villages, but I'd also wander around the town. Frequently on my wanderings, I'd be stopped by a grizzled-looking old man who would start yelling at me in German. Then in French (the language of government and education in Upper Volta), he'd inform me that he'd been a prisoner of the Germans in World War II. At first I took him to be a drunk and a crazy person (the place where he always stopped me was near a bar). But as I got to know him and other residents of the town better, I learned that what he told me was true. He had been a German prisoner. That, of course, left me wondering how it was possible. After all, I didn't think that this particular individual could have been visiting Europe when the war broke out.

As I spoke to him and to many others like him over the 15 years that followed, I learned a story that had been left out of my high school and college history lessons. I learned that, starting in the second half of the 19th century, France began to create a black African army called the *Tirailleurs Senegalais* or Senegalese Riflemen. In the early years, the French bought slaves to fill the army ranks. But after a time, they turned to levying a draft on their colonies and then, after World War II, to a volunteer force. First, they used this army to conquer the areas that became French colonies in Africa. Later, they used these troops to fight in the trenches in World War I and to suppress rebellion in various colonial possessions. In World War II, African troops were essential to the conquest of North Africa and Italy and to taking back France itself. When people think of Charles De Gaulle's Free French forces of that war, they generally summon up a Hollywood image of a white guy in a beret. In fact, before the last phase of the liberation of France in 1944, most Free French forces were black Africans and were more likely to be called Mahamadou than Pierre. In the late years of French colonialism, it was African troops, among others, who fought at the Battle of Dien Bien Phu, which ended the French colonial venture in Vietnam in 1954.

In the 1990s, I interviewed more than 50 surviving members of the **Tirailleurs Senegalais** in Mali. The stories they told were fantastic, even unbelievable. Dragged out of small African villages and sent to fight in Europe and elsewhere around the globe, they faced horrors and culture shock that nothing could have prepared them for. Some cracked under the strain, responding with violent outbursts and, when they made it home, with

Burkina Faso & Mali.

Tirailleurs Senegalais: Senegalese riflemen. An army that existed from 1857 to 1960, composed largely of soldiers from French African colonies led by officers from metropolitan France.

drunkenness and insanity. However, most learned to adapt. When they got home, they sometimes put their language skills, organizational skills, and bravery to new uses, playing important roles in their communities. But many were also deeply aggrieved. They felt neglected by history and by France. In 1991, Mory Samake, a veteran of World War II, told me:

> Look, when you work for someone, he's got to recognize your efforts. They treat us like their dogs. They are white, we are black but we are all equal. If someone cuts my hand and someone cuts one of their hands, the blood is just the same. When we were there fighting the war, no one said "this one is white, this one is black." We didn't go to fight with ill will. We gave our blood and our bodies so that France could be liberated. But now, since they have their freedom, they have thrown us away, forgotten us. If you eat the meat, you throw away the bone. France has done just that to us.

The story of the Tirailleurs Senegalais and Mory Samake's anger with the French remind us of several extremely important points. A cliché has it that history is written by the winners. It might be more accurate to say that history is written by the powerful and usually presented as a narrative of their inevitable triumph. But such a history ignores inconvenient truths or relegates them to footnotes and appendices. The relation between wealth and poverty and between the powerful and the powerless, or, in this case, between the colonized and the colonizer, are among the most important of these truths.

We tend to assume that the social arrangements we see today, the distribution of wealth and poverty, of power and powerlessness, are of great historical depth. However, our world is the current result of large-scale historic processes that involved the ebb and flow of wealth and power among nations and among different areas of the world. These processes have had a particularly important impact on the kinds of small-scale societies that anthropologists often study.

The patterns of political, social, and economic change over the past several centuries are complex and diverse. However, a central theme of this history is the expansion of the power of places that are now wealthy. This occurred in thousands of locations and had many different effects. Sometimes cultural contact was accidentally genocidal, sometimes intentionally so. Many traditional cultures have been destroyed, but others have prospered, although in altered forms. Members of different cultures often confronted each other through a veil of ignorance, suspicion, and accusations of savagery. But sometimes, common interests, common enemies, mutual curiosity, and occasional friendships among people overrode their differences.

In this chapter, we describe the overall pattern of change during the past several hundred years. In the broadest sense, this involved the incorporation of relatively separate cultures and economies into a vast, chaotic, yet integrated world economic system. Understanding this history is critical for anthropologists.

People sometimes think of anthropologists as people who study small, isolated groups relatively unaffected by outside political, economic, and technological forces. Anthropologists themselves have sometimes made this mistake. However, work in the past several decades has shown that the changing patterns of global trade, politics, information, and technology have had deep impacts on seemingly isolated groups for hundreds of years. These patterns have helped shape their cultures, influencing critical practices such as family and political structure, the conditions under which people labor, and what they produce. To understand the ways in which individual cultures throughout the world have developed, anthropologists need to understand the larger patterns of history that have affected them.

These historical patterns have resulted in enormous inequalities both within and among societies and nations as wealth and labor flowed from one area of the world to another. They created the financial accumulation necessary for the Industrial Revolution and the development of capitalism. The Ottoman Empire as well as Russia and Japan played critical roles in the story. However, the expanding influence and power of western European states and the colonies settled by their subjects and citizens probably had the greatest impact worldwide. For that reason, this chapter focuses on them. We begin with a bird's-eye view of Europe and the rest of the world as it might have appeared in 1400.

■■■ MAKING THE MODERN WORLD

As surprising as it may seem now, a visitor touring the world on the eve of European expansion in 1400 might well have been amused by the notion that European societies would soon become enormously wealthy and powerful. Other areas of the globe would have seemed much more likely prospects for power. Europeans had devised oceangoing vessels, but Arab and Chinese ships regularly made much longer voyages. The cities of India and China made those of Europe look like mere villages (e.g., the population of London in 1400 was less than 40,000 [Williams 1970], about the size of today's Culver City, CA or East Lansing, MI). Almost no European states could effectively administer more than a few hundred square kilometers. Certainly, there was nothing that could compare to China's vast wealth and centralized bureaucracy. Europeans were masters of cathedral and castle construction, but other than that, their technology was backward. War, plague, and economic depression were the order of the day (Scammell 1989). Moreover, other areas of the world seemed to be growing in wealth and power. Despite occasional setbacks, the Islamic powers had expanded steadily in the five centuries leading up to 1400, and Muslim societies stretched from Spain to Indonesia. Not only had these empires preserved the scholarship of India and the ancient Mediterranean civilizations, but they also had greatly increased knowledge in astronomy, mathematics, medicine, chemistry, zoology, mineralogy, and meteorology (Lapidus 1988:96, 241–252).

In the Americas, populations were probably far larger than is commonly thought. In 1934, the anthropologist A. L. Kroeber estimated that the population before Columbus was about 8.4 million. However, more recent work and new discoveries have led to a reevaluation of this number. Some estimates of the pre-Columbian population place the number high as 100 million. A good current estimate is about 57 million inhabitants (Keen and Haynes 2013:12). Jerry Moore (2014: 417) conservatively estimates the population of the Inca Empire in 1500 as between 6 million and 14 million people. Morris and von Hagen (2011:113) estimate the population of Cuzco, the capital of the Inca Empire, at 100,000. The Incas administered an empire that was more than 2,400 miles long (about the same as the distance from New York to Los Angeles).

China had an extraordinarily ancient and powerful civilization. In 1400, the population of Nanjing, its capital, was over 1 million (about 25 times larger than London) (Modelski 2004). As late as 1793, Emperor Ch'ien Lung, believing China to be the most powerful state in the world (or perhaps showing bravado in the face of foreign traders), responded to a British delegation's attempt to open trade by writing to King George III: "Our dynasty's majestic virtue has penetrated into every country under heaven and kings of all nations have offered their costly tribute by land and sea. As your Ambassador can see for himself, we possess all things. . . . [W]e have never valued ingenious articles, nor do we have the slightest need of your country's manufacturers" (Peyrefitte 1992:288–92). Unfortunately for the Chinese, by the time the emperor wrote this letter, it was no longer accurate. Within a half century, at the end of the First Opium War, Britain virtually controlled China.

▎▎▎ EUROPEAN EXPANSION: MOTIVES AND METHODS

From slow beginnings in the 15th century, European power grew rapidly from the 16th to the 20th centuries. Many theories have been suggested to account for the causes and motives of European expansion. Although it was often a cover for more worldly aims, the desire of the pious to

Christianize the world was certainly a motivating factor. The archives of the Jesuit order include more than 15,000 letters, written between 1550 and 1771, from people who wanted to be missionaries (Scammell 1989:60). The desire to find a wide variety of wonders, both real and imagined, was also important. The Portuguese looked for routes to the very real wealth of Eastern empires, such as China, and also for the mythical kingdom of Prester John, a powerful but hidden Christian monarch, the fountain of youth, and the Seven Cities of Cibola.

Beyond this, there was always the desire for wealth. Nations and nobles quickly invested in exploration as gold and diamonds were discovered. The poor and oppressed of Europe saw opportunities for wealth and respect in the colonies. There, they sometimes fulfilled their dreams of wealth by re-creating the very social order they had fled.

Various social and technological developments aided European expansion. These included the rise of a banking and merchant class, a growing population, and the development of the caravel, a new ship that was better at sailing into the wind. Two other developments, the **monoculture plantation** and the **joint stock company**, were to have critical impacts on the world's people.

In many cases, however, the key advantage that Europeans had over other people was the diseases they carried. Almost every time Europeans encountered populations in the Americas or on islands, they brought death and cultural destruction in the form of microbes.

The European search for wealth depended on tactics that, in their basic form, were ancient. Two of the quickest ways to accumulate wealth are to steal it from others and to get other people to work for you for free. State societies have always practiced these methods. War, slavery, exploitation, and inequality had been present in most of the world since ancient times, so there was nothing fundamentally new about their use by Europeans. However, no earlier empire had been able to practice these tactics on the scale that the European nations would. All previous empires, however large, were regional affairs. European expansion, for the first time in history, linked the entire world into an economic system. This system created much wealth but made impoverishment and slavery possible on a scale never before seen.

▮▮▮ Pillage

One of the most important means of wealth transfer was **pillage**. In the early years of expansion, Europeans were driven by the search for precious metals, particularly gold and silver. When they found such valuables, they moved quickly to seize them. Metals belonging to indigenous peoples were soon sent back to Europe, and mines were placed under

Monoculture plantation: An agricultural plantation specializing in the large-scale production of a single crop to be sold on the market.

Joint stock company: A firm that is managed by a centralized board of directors but is owned by shareholders.

Pillage: To strip an area of money, goods, or raw materials through the threat or use of physical violence.

Figure 13.1 Europeans often took art, artifacts, and human remains from the areas they colonized. In this 2012 picture, members of a repatriation team carry 20 Maori mummified heads that were taken to Europe in the 18th and 19th centuries. The heads were returned to New Zealand after a four year political struggle.

MARTY MELVILLE/Getty Images

European control. The profits of these enterprises were enormous. For example, in 1531, Pizarro captured the Inca Emperor Atahualpa and received between 11 and 24 tons of silver and gold as his ransom. A gang of Indian smiths worked nine forges day and night to melt down this treasure, which was then shipped back to Spain (Duncan 1995:158). In the early 17th century, 58,000 Indian workers were forced into silver mining in the town of Potosi in the Peruvian Andes (Wolf 1982:136). Between 1500 and 1660, Spanish colonies in the Americas exported 300 tons of gold and 25,000 tons of silver (Scammell 1989:133).

Such looting was not limited to the New World. After the British East India Company came to power in India, it plundered the treasury of Bengal, sending wealth back to investors in England (Wolf 1982:244). In addition, art, artifacts, curiosities, and occasionally human bodies were stolen around the world and sent to museums and private collections in Europe (see Figure 13.1).

Forced Labor

Forced labor was another key element of European expansion. Although Europeans acquired forced laborers through debt servitude as well as by requiring labor from the people they governed, the most notorious example of forced labor was African slavery. Europeans did not invent slavery in general or African slavery in particular. Slavery had long been practiced in both Europe and Africa. Non-Europeans probably exported more than 7 million African slaves to the Islamic world between 650 and 1600 (Lovejoy 1983). However, Europeans did practice African slavery on a larger scale than any people before them. Between the end of the

15th century and the end of the 19th century, approximately 11.7 million slaves were exported from Africa to the Americas. More than 6 million left Africa in the 19th century alone (Coquery-Vidrovitch 1988). No one really knows how many died in the process of capturing and transferring slaves within Africa. Estimates vary from one to five individuals dead for every slave successfully landed in the Americas.

The massive transport of people had two important economic effects: First, the use of slave labor was extremely profitable for both slave shippers and plantation owners. Second, slave labor created continuous warfare and impoverishment in the areas from which slaves were drawn. In these places, some undoubtedly grew rich on the profits of slavery but the loss of so many people and the violence and political instability resulting from the capture and transport of slaves radically altered African societies (Coquery-Vidrovitch 1988).

The demand for slaves was created by monoculture plantations—farms devoted to the production of a single crop for sale to distant consumers. Sugar, tobacco, and cotton produced this way in the Americas and spices produced on monoculture plantations in Asia were sold to consumers located primarily in Europe. Through the 19th century, sugar was the most important monoculture crop. British consumption of sugar increased some 2,500 percent between 1650 and 1800. Between 1800 and 1890, sugar production grew another 2,500 percent, from 245,000 tons to more than 6 million tons per year (Mintz 1985:73). Today, the world consumes more than 381 billion pounds of sugar each year, about 54 pounds for every person on the planet (USDA 2015). Until the 19th century, the massive amount of labor required for growing and processing sugar was largely provided by slaves. Between 1701 and 1810, for example, Barbados, a small island given over almost entirely to sugar production, imported 252,500 slaves, almost all of whom were involved in growing and processing sugar (Mintz 1985:53).

Joint Stock Companies

The joint stock company was another innovation that allowed extremely rapid European expansion and led to enormous abuses of power. Most early European exploration was financed and supported by aristocratic governments or small private firms. By the turn of the 17th century, however, the British and Dutch had established joint stock companies. The French, Swedes, Danes, Germans, and Portuguese followed by midcentury. The best known of these companies include the Dutch East India Company (founded in 1602), the British East India Company (founded in 1600), the Massachusetts Bay Company (founded in 1628), and the Hudson's Bay Company (founded in 1670).

Joint stock companies were the predecessors of today's publicly held corporations. The idea was simple. To raise the capital necessary for large-scale ventures, companies would sell shares. Each share gave its purchaser a small percentage of the ownership of the company and entitled him or her to a portion of the profits (or losses) from the company's business. Exploration and trade by joint stock companies had critical advantages over earlier forms. First, a great deal of capital could be raised rapidly, so business ventures could be much larger than had previously been possible. Second, although the motives of aristocratic governments often included the search for prestige and missionary zeal, joint stock companies existed to provide profits to their shareholders and were relatively single-minded in pursuit of that goal. Because they were frequently empowered to raise armies and conduct wars, they could have devastating effects on the societies they penetrated.

Dutch East India Company (VOC): A joint stock company chartered by the Dutch government to control all Dutch trade in the Indian and Pacific oceans. Also known by its Dutch initials VOC for Verenigde Oostendische Compagnie.

The **Dutch East India Company** (also called **VOC**, after its initials in Dutch) is an example of a joint stock company. Based on money raised from the sale of shares, the VOC was chartered by the Dutch government to hold the monopoly on all Dutch trade with the societies of the Indian and Pacific Oceans. Shares in the VOC were available on reasonable terms and were held by a wide cross section of Dutch society (Scammell 1989:101).

Heeren XVII: The Lords Seventeen, members of the board of directors of the Dutch East India Company.

In many ways, the company functioned as a government in the places in which it was chartered to operate. Led by a board of directors called the **Heeren XVII** (the Lords Seventeen), it was empowered to make treaties with local rulers in the name of the Dutch Republic, occupy lands, levy taxes, raise armies, and declare war. However, although governments are to some degree beholden to those they govern, the VOC was interested solely in returning dividends to its shareholders. This it did very successfully. Through the 17th and early 18th centuries, the VOC distributed annual dividends of 15.5 to 50 percent. It returned dividends of 40 percent per year for 6 consecutive years from 1715 to 1720 (Boxer 1965:46). By comparison, the average annual dividend paid by a Standard and Poor's 500 stock index between 1960 and 2007 was between 2 and 5 percent.

Through the 17th century, the VOC used its powers to seize control of many of the Indian Ocean islands. Among these were Java, including the port of Jakarta (which became their headquarters, renamed Batavia), Sri Lanka (Ceylon), and Malacca (see Figure 13.2). In addition, the VOC acquired the right to control the production and trade of the most valuable spices of the area (cloves, nutmeg, and mace) and took brutal steps to maintain this monopoly. For example, during the 1620s, virtually the entire population of the nutmeg-producing island of Banda was deported, driven away, starved to death, or massacred. They were replaced with Dutch colonists using slave labor (Ricklefs 2008). By the 1670s, the

Figure 13.2 Principal holdings of the Dutch East India Company in the Pacific in the 1660s.

Dutch had gained complete control of all spice production in what is now Indonesia (Wolf 1982).

Natives did not submit passively to VOC control, and the company did not have a clear-cut military advantage. Instead, the VOC rapidly (and ultimately, disastrously) became embroiled in the area's wars. For example, in the 17th century, the Mataram dynasty controlled most of central Java. In 1677, when the dynasty faced rebellion, the VOC intervened on its behalf in hopes of cash payments and trade concessions. In a bloody campaign, the combined VOC and dynasty forces crushed the rebellion and established Emperor Amangkurat II on the throne. Trouble ensued when the VOC received neither payments nor concessions. An armed force that the VOC sent to make its demands was defeated by Amangkurat II's forces in 1686. The company was unable to recoup its losses or to claim its trading privileges (Ricklefs 2008). This was just the beginning of a series of extremely brutal wars pitting different factions of Javanese kingdoms against each other and against the VOC. Kingdoms alternately allied with and fought against the VOC as their interests dictated. These conflicts lasted until 1757.

The company often acted with extraordinary violence. The treatment of the Chinese in Batavia is a good example. The Chinese had come to Batavia as traders, skilled artisans, sugar millers, and shopkeepers. Despite harsh measures against them, roughly 15,000 lived there by 1740. VOC officials believed they were plotting rebellion, and after an incident in which several Europeans were killed, VOC Governor General Adriaan

Valckenier hinted that a massacre would not be unwelcome. In the melee that followed, Europeans and their slaves killed 10,000 Chinese. The Chinese quarter of the city burned for several days, and the VOC was able to stop the looting only by paying its soldiers a premium to return to duty (Ricklefs 2008:113).

The burden of continual warfare, as well as corruption and inefficiency, forced the VOC into serious financial difficulties. By the last quarter of the 18th century, large areas of coastal Java had been depopulated by years of warfare, but the VOC had not succeeded in controlling the principal kingdoms of the island. The Heeren XVII were dismissed by the Netherlands government in 1796, after an investigation revealed deep corruption and mismanagement. On December 31, 1799, the VOC was formally dissolved, and its possessions were turned over to the Batavian Republic, a Dutch client state of France.

The story of the VOC was, in large measure, repeated by other mercantilist trading firms organized by the British, French, Germans, Portuguese, Danes, and Swedes. In each case, companies generated enormous profits but eventually fell into disarray and either were dissolved or were taken over by their national governments.

Despite their eventual failure, the trading companies placed fantastic riches in the hands of European elites. Europeans invested this wealth in many different ways: in the arts, in luxury goods, in architecture, and also in science and industry. This supply of wealth became one of the sources for the Industrial Revolution and the rise of capitalism itself.

The effects were far less pleasant for the regions in which the trading companies operated. The VOC and other trading companies left poverty and chaos in their wakes. In every case, Europeans fundamentally altered the communities with which they came into contact. Frequently, brutal policies and disease destroyed entire cultures. However, in most cases, societies were not simply overrun. Before the 19th century, Europeans did not have a truly decisive technological advantage over others. Instead, Europeans collaborated with local elites, which often were able to use their contact with the foreigners to increase their own wealth and power. However, as a whole, their societies suffered.

▌▌▌ THE ERA OF COLONIALISM

Colonialism: The active possession of a foreign territory and the maintenance of political domination over that territory.

Colony: A foreign territory under the immediate political control of a nation-state.

Colonialism differs in important ways from the earlier expansion of European power. Whereas much of the initial phase of European expansion was carried out by private companies and often took the form of raiding and pillaging, colonialism involved the active possession of foreign territory by European governments. **Colonies** were created when nations established and maintained political domination over geographically separate areas and political units (Kohn 1958).

There were several different types of European colonies. Some, as in Africa, existed primarily to exploit native people and resources. In other areas, such as North America and Australia, the key goal was the settlement of surplus European population. Still other locales, such as Yemen, which borders the Red Sea and thus controlled shipping through the Suez Canal, were seized because they occupied strategic locations.

At one time or another, much of the world came under direct European colonization, but the timing of colonialism varied from place to place. The Americas were colonized in the 1500s and 1600s, but most other areas of the world did not come under colonial control until the 19th century.

As long as Europeans confronted others with broadly similar weaponry and military tactics, the result was indecisive, and local governments were able to retain autonomy and power. By the 19th century, however, the Industrial Revolution gave Europeans (and their North American descendants) decisive advantages in both technological sophistication and quantity of arms. Although European colonizers faced frequent rebellions and proved unable to entirely subdue guerrilla activity in all places, no non-European government or army could defeat them.

Colonization, 1500 to 1800

As we have seen, before the 1800s, very little of Africa or Asia was colonized. In these places, Europeans established small coastal settlements, but these existed largely because they were profitable for both Europeans and at least some local elites. In most cases, local powers had the ability to expel Europeans or to strictly limit their activities. Relatively few Europeans settled permanently in such colonies.

In the Americas, the situation was radically different. There, Europeans quickly established colonies and immigrated in large numbers. For example, between 1492 and 1600, more than 55,000 Spaniards immigrated to the New World. In the 50 years that followed, another quarter million joined them (Boyd-Bowman 1975). By comparison, in the first half of the 19th century, the total Dutch population of Indonesia, Holland's most important colonial possession, was about 2,100 (Zeegers et al. 2004).

Although there was stiff resistance to European expansion in the Americas, and Indian wars continued until the late 19th century, Europeans were victorious almost everywhere they wanted to expand. Technology aided European expansion, but the main reason for rapid European success was probably disease. In the wake of contact, up to 95 percent of

Figure 13.3 In the wake of conquest, up to 95 percent of the population of the Americas died. This colonial-era woodcut shows the Wampanoags of what is now Massachusetts grieving for those who died from smallpox.

North Wind/North Wind Picture Archives

the total population of the New World died (see Figure 13.3). Although Europeans also died of diseases, they did so in far smaller numbers (Diamond 1998; Karlen 1995; Newson 1999; Palkovich 1994). It is hard for us to fully comprehend the impact of death on such a large scale. Only the worst of 20th-century genocides can begin to compare. But, even in these cases, it was particular subgroups within populations that suffered, not entire populations.

Although epidemics may have occasionally been caused intentionally, neither Europeans nor natives had any knowledge of contagion or germs. The vast majority of deaths were not premeditated. However, Europeans came to see the handiwork of God in the epidemics that decimated Native Americans. God, they believed, clearly intended them to populate the Americas and was removing others to make that possible.

New World natives lacked immunity to European diseases. Most of the diseases that killed the indigenous population—including diphtheria, influenza, measles, mumps, smallpox, and tuberculosis—originated in domesticated animals (Wolfe, Dunavan, and Diamond 2012), which were largely absent from the Americas. Rodent species that were confined to Europe, Africa, and Asia were another disease source. In addition, many diseases—including smallpox, influenza, and tuberculosis—require large reservoirs of populations, in some cases up to a half million individuals (Diamond 1992). Although populations this large existed south of the Rio Grande, many North American groups were too small to sustain such crowd diseases and, therefore, lacked immunity to them.

Cortés's conquest of Mexico is a good example of the political effects of disease. When Cortés first appeared in 1519, the Aztec leader Montezuma, following his tradition, gave Cortés gifts and opened the city of Tenochtitlán to the Spanish. When it became clear that the Spanish were their enemies, the Aztecs expelled them from the city in a fierce battle that cost the Spanish and their allies perhaps two-thirds of their total army. By the time Cortés returned in 1521, a smallpox epidemic had killed up to half the Aztecs. Even after such crushing losses to disease, the Spanish conquest of Tenochtitlán took more than 4 months to accomplish (Berdan 1982; Clendinnen 1991; Karlen 1995). Had the Aztecs not been devastated by disease, they might have again defeated Cortés.

The deaths of Native Americans had dire effects throughout the Americas. The increasing population of Europeans and the diminishing population of natives ensured that resistance to European domination could not be very effective. When John Winthrop, the first governor of Massachusetts, declared that the settlers had fair title to the land because it was *vacuum domicilium* (empty land), he was creating a legal fiction (he was well aware of the natives and their need for agricultural and hunting land), but he also knew that the native population was declining rapidly.

The massive loss of human population may also have changed the ecology of America. The enormous flocks of passenger pigeons and endless herds of buffalo reported in the 18th and 19th centuries may have resulted from the deaths of the human population that previously preyed on these animals and controlled their populations (Mann 2011; Neumann 1985).

If not for disease, the European experience in the Americas probably would have been very similar to its experience in Asia and Africa. Rather than establishing control over vast amounts of territory, Europeans probably would have been confined to small coastal settlements and would have been involved in protracted battles with powerful local kingdoms.

Colonizing in the 19th Century

By the beginning of the 19th century, the Industrial Revolution was underway in Europe and North America. This had two immediate consequences. First, it enabled Europeans and Americans to produce weapons in greater quantity and quality than any other people. Second, it created an enormous demand for raw materials that could not be satisfied in Europe. In addition, discoveries in medicine, particularly vaccines and antimalarial drugs, improved the odds of survival for Europeans in places previously considered pestilential. Thus, Europeans had both motives and means to colonize (see Figure 13.4).

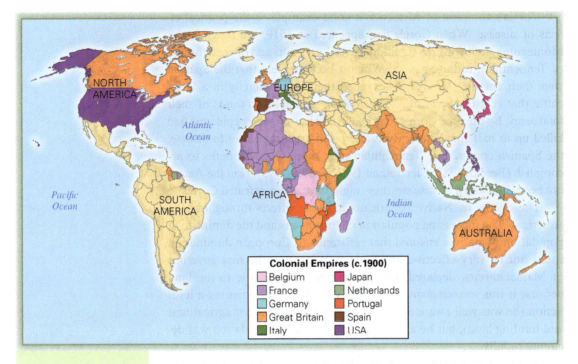

Figure 13.4 By 1900, most nations in the Americas had achieved independence. However, much of the rest of the world was under colonial rule. Many areas not formally colonized, such as China, were dominated by European powers.

Acting in their own self-interest, Europeans and Americans generally did not move rapidly to place other areas under their colonial control. The primary goal of European expansion was the pursuit of wealth and plunder. Mercantilist firms were rapid cost-effective ways to get them. The financial burden of establishing companies such as the VOC was borne by their shareholders. However, colonizing an area required some level of government expenditure. At the very least, this included administrative officials and the troops to back them, all of whom had to be equipped and paid out of the national treasury. In most cases, infrastructure such as roads, bridges, and railways had to be built. These were expensive undertakings, and European taxpayers and governments were generally not enthusiastic about funding them.

Most often, European governments felt forced to assume colonial control either because of the scandals surrounding the collapse of mercantile companies or out of fear that their national commercial interests were threatened, generally by other European nations. This fear led to the Berlin Conference, which partitioned Africa among European powers in the late 19th century.

After European governments had established colonies, they had to convince both their own populations and those they colonized that this action was proper. They defended colonization by cloaking it in the ideology of social betterment. In Britain, citizens were encouraged, in the words of the poet Rudyard Kipling, "to take up the white man's burden" of bringing civilization to the "savage." In France, the population was told that it had a *mission civilisatrice*, a civilizing mission that would both help the savages in the colonized areas and increase French political and cultural power throughout the world. The government portrayed its colonial practices as *rayonnement*, lighting the way for others (Cole and Raymond 2006:158–59). In the colonies, as we will see next, subjects were taught that they were colonized for their own good and that their societies would advance as a result.

▮▮ Making Colonialism Pay

Once colonies were seized, they had to be administered and they had to be made profitable. Colonizing powers hoped that tax revenues from colonial subjects would support the cost of colonial government as well as the construction of various public works. However, in many cases, taxes were insufficient, and taxpayers in the colonizing country were required to make up the difference between colonial income and expenses. Despite this situation, colonies were extremely profitable (see, for example, Bagchi 2002).

Colonies gave businesses based in the colonizing country places in which they could operate free of competition. This was particularly important for Britain and France, two of the most important colonial powers. In the late 1700s, the Industrial Revolution began in Britain, but by the end of the 19th century, its factories were aging. New, more efficient industrial processes developed in the United States and Germany enabled these countries to produce cheaper manufactured goods (Allitt 2002). France came to industrialization relatively late and had a fairly weak road and rail network. As a result, it had difficulty competing with the United States, Germany, and Britain. Colonies created a zone of protection for older British industry and newer French manufacturers, thus enabling high profits for firms in these nations.

The costs of the colonies were borne (unequally) by subject colonial populations and by colonizing country taxpayers. The windfall profits from colonialism went to shareholders of companies operating in the colonies.

Finding ways to extract taxes and create the conditions in which corporations could make money often meant the systematic undermining of indigenous ways of life. Although the newly colonized societies had for centuries traded with others, frequently including Europeans, external trade usually accounted for only a small percentage of their economy. For the most part, their economic relations were drawn along kinship lines, and most of their production was for their own consumption. For colonialism to be profitable, these patterns had to change. Colonial subjects had to produce the goods that colonizing societies wanted and to labor in ways that would be profitable to the colonizers. From the colonizers' perspective, the key problem was finding ways to cause these changes. Some of the methods they used were control of local leaders, forced labor, forced production of particular commodities, taxation, and direct propaganda through education.

Sometimes colonial powers seized direct control of the political leadership, placing their own nationals in most powerful positions, but this was expensive, and foreign colonial leaders often lacked sufficient knowledge of local language and culture to govern effectively. More often, colonialists ruled indirectly through native leaders. These were recruited through promises of power and wealth as well as their realization that colonial governments held the reins of power and were unlikely to lose them any time soon. In some cases, colonial powers offered education, employment, and improved status to people who were oppressed or outcast in precolonial society; these individuals were particularly likely to support the colonizers.

A well-organized chain of command was needed for colonial powers to rule effectively. In hierarchical societies where kings or chiefs already existed, this did not pose a difficult problem. Most often, local elites sympathetic to the colonizers were able to retain a degree of power, although they became answerable to the colonial authorities. Those elites who resisted colonial rule were rapidly replaced. Regions where precolonial relationships were largely egalitarian posed a more difficult problem. If there was no chief or there were many co-chiefs, establishing colonial authority was far harder. Colonizers tried to solve this problem by creating new chiefly offices. Sometimes colonialists and missionaries forged entire new ethnic groups, lumping together people with different traditions and even different languages (Harries 1987). For example, the Bété, an ethnic group of the central Ivory Coast in Africa, did not exist before the era of colonialism but was created by the actions of colonial and postcolonial governments (Dozon 1985).

In the long run, policies of indirect rule created the preconditions for instability and violence. Political leaders were compromised by their close connections with colonial authorities, and often lost the confidence and respect of those they purported to lead. Ethnic groups created for the purposes of colonial rule tended to fragment when that rule diminished.

One of the most direct ways that European governments tried to make their colonies profitable was through **corvée labor**—unpaid work demanded of native populations. Until World War II, most colonial governments insisted on substantial labor from their subjects. The British often compelled subjects to work for up to 1 month a year. The Dutch required 2 months. In 1926, the French enacted a law that permitted an annual draft of labor for their West African colonies. Conscripts were

Corvée labor: Unpaid labor required by a governing authority.

compelled to work for 3 years on bridge and road building, irrigation projects, and other public works. Mortality rates during the 3 years of forced labor often were very high, making corvée labor one of the most hated institutions of colonialism. Natives resisted colonial demands by concealing workers or by fleeing from authorities when such work was demanded (Evans 2000; Ishemo 1995).

Even when subject populations were not forced into labor gangs, economic and social policies of colonial regimes required them to radically alter their cultures. For example, Portuguese colonial policy in Mozambique forced almost 1 million peasants to grow cotton. The colonial government controlled what these growers produced, where they lived, with whom they traded, and how they organized their labor. Although a few growers prospered, the great majority became impoverished and struggled to survive in the face of famine and hardship (Isaacman 1996). By the 1960s, the brutality and terror used by the colonial regime resulted in a civil war that continued into the 1990s.

Conditions were perhaps worst in the Congo, ruled between 1885 and 1908 as the personal property of King Leopold II of Belgium. There, each native owed the government 40 hours of labor each month in exchange for a token wage (Bodley 1999:116). Failure to work sufficiently or to produce the proper quantities of goods (particularly rubber) was met with extreme measures. Leopold's subjects were held hostage, were beaten or whipped, had their hands cut off, and, in many cases, were killed outright (see Figure 13.5). By the time the Belgian government stripped Leopold of his control of Congo, between 4 million and 8 million Congolese had been killed or had starved to death (Hochschild 1998).

In addition to forced labor and forced production, the British and French both drafted natives into their armed forces. They used these armies to capture and control their colonies, fight colonial wars, and augment their regular armies wherever needed. The *Tirailleurs Senegalais,* drafted from France's West African colonies, were described at the opening of this chapter. Additional *Tirailleurs* units included groups from Algeria, Morocco, Madagascar, Vietnam, Cambodia, and other French colonial possessions. In East Africa, the British drafted and recruited the King's African Rifles. In India, the British created an entire army led by British officers but consisting almost entirely of colonial subjects drawn primarily from ethnic groups the

Universal Images Group/SuperStock

Figure 13.5 From 1885 to 1908, Congo was the property of King Leopold II of Belgium. Atrocities committed during that era cost the lives of 4 million to 8 million Congolese. Punishments for disobedience or failure to meet payment quotas included chopping off children's hands.

British considered particularly warlike. About 1.3 million members of the Indian Army served in World War I, primarily on the Western Front and also in the Middle East (Nayar and Paul 2003:66).

Although particular projects might use forced labor, to make a colony truly profitable, colonial masters also used other methods to encourage the population to work for them voluntarily or to produce the goods they desired. Taxation was a critical one of these. Taxation was needed to support the colonial government, but because colonizers knew that colonial economies were small and their tax receipts low, they rarely expected taxes to provide the full cost of governing. However, taxing colonial subjects had another purpose: to force them into the market system. Taxes generally had to be paid in colonial money, which native subjects could obtain only by working for a colonist or by producing something that the colonists wanted to buy. This participation in the market and wage labor was viewed as the essential precondition for "civilizing" the natives.

Taxation often forced colonial subjects into a vicious cycle of dependency on the market system. To raise money for taxes, subjects had to work directly for the colonizers or produce things that colonizers desired. But spending time on these tasks meant that less time could be spent making goods or raising crops for one's own consumption. This in turn meant that food and goods increasingly had to be purchased from the market, which was dominated by companies colonialists owned.

In addition to policies aimed at forcing subjects to take part in an economy centered in the industrial world, colonial governments took more direct aim at cultures through educational policies. Colonial education was often designed to convince subjects that they were the cultural, moral, and intellectual inferiors of those who ruled them. For example, education in 19th-century India encouraged children to aspire to be like the ideal Englishman (Viswanathan 1988). In France's African colonies, children were directly taught to obey their colonial masters, as illustrated in this passage from a turn-of-the-century reader designed to teach French to schoolchildren and used in the colonies:

> It is . . . an advantage for a native to work for a white man, because the Whites are better educated, more advanced in civilization than the natives, and because, thanks to them, the natives will make more rapid progress . . . and become one day really useful men. . . . You who are intelligent and industrious, my children, always help the Whites in their task. (cited in Bodley 1999:104)

Education was often aimed at the children of elites. These children were taught that, although they might never reach the level of the colonists, they were considerably more advanced than their uneducated countrymen. In France's African colonies, individuals who were educated and assimilated to French culture were known both by the French and by themselves as *evolues*, or evolved people. This increased the perception of the uneducated and unassimilated as being backward and primitive. Thus, schooling both reinforced the colonizers' position and created a subservient educated class convinced that was superior to other colonial subjects (Kelly 1986).

Using Anthropology: Unpleasant History

Students are often taught history in ways that celebrate unity and the triumph of local, regional, or national causes. Museums and historic sites frequently gloss over unpleasant aspects of history. For example, the Jefferson National Expansion National Memorial in St. Louis is best known for Gateway Arch but also includes the Old Courthouse, the site of litigation in the Dred Scott case of 1847. That case, eventually decided by the Supreme Court in 1857, denied U.S. citizenship to African Americans, prevented the U.S. Congress from regulating slavery, and was a critical step leading to the Civil War. It is probably the most famous thing that happened at the courthouse. However, although the courthouse became a national monument in 1935, it did not devote an exhibit to Dred Scott until 2007 (Baumann et al. 2011:41).

Telling unhappy stories is often deeply problematic. People usually want their history and their heroes portrayed in the best possible light, especially when negative information might reinforce stereotypes. Many issues of community representation were evident in the interactions between the Scott Joplin House State Historic Site in St. Louis, Missouri, and its surrounding community.

Scott Joplin (1867–1917) is probably the best-known ragtime composer (see Figure 13.6). Joplin was profoundly gifted and driven to succeed but he was also an African American living in a deeply racist United States. Many aspects of his life reflected this. Joplin moved to St. Louis in 1901, at a time when large numbers of African Americans were migrating from the rural South to northern and midwestern cities. In St. Louis, blacks faced hard conditions of segregation and discrimination. Joplin's neighborhood included the highest density of African American population in the city as well as some of the city's deepest poverty and worst living conditions. Although Joplin's first successful music publication "Maple Leaf Rag" appeared in 1899 and would eventually sell millions of copies, he made very little from it in these years,

MPI/Stringer/Archive Photos/Getty Images

Figure 13.6 Ragtime composer Scott Joplin (1867–1917) lived in St. Louis, Missouri, between 1901 and 1903.

and his living conditions were similar to those of other impoverished African Americans. You can hear a recording of Joplin playing "Maple Leaf Rag" at http://bit.ly/1WSKjGE).

The Joplin House Historic Site includes the apartment block where Joplin lived from 1901 to 1903 as well as other surrounding buildings and open spaces. Anthropologists and historians Timothy Baumann, Andrew Hurley, and Valerie Altizer and site administrator Victoria Love worked with local residents, including businesspeople, religious leaders, and educators to increase community involvement with the historic site and decide how to represent some less pleasant aspects of Joplin's life.

Baumann and his colleagues discovered three areas of community sensitivity: the facts that Joplin's apartment lacked an indoor toilet, that there were almost certainly numerous brothels nearby, and that Joplin died of syphilis. Community members feared that exhibits that mentioned these aspects of Joplin's life would encourage negative stereotypes about their neighborhood and St. Louis's African American community. The anthropologists helped historic site officials and local community members find ways to address these concerns. In each case, the solution was to place Joplin's life in a broader social and economic context. In the case of sanitation, it was important to note that many of St. Louis's older neighborhoods lacked indoor plumbing in this era and that failures to modernize plumbing were the result of poverty and segregation, not the desires of people living in the neighborhood. A discussion of brothels led to an understanding of the very limited wage-earning options open to women in the early 20th century and the extremely low wages they were paid. And this led to a movement to open a women's shelter and a children's safe house on the grounds of the historic site. The issue of Joplin's death from syphilis was sensitive but committee members thought it was critical because syphilis was common in Joplin's era and, today, St. Louis has one of the highest syphilis rates in the nation. The response was to set age-appropriate guidelines for how and when tour guides and docents should discuss Joplin's death.

Work on the Joplin House Historic Site shows how careful attention to context, community concerns, and historical research can help us explore, understand, and come to terms with difficult aspects of our own history.

Colonialism and Anthropology

The origins and practice of modern anthropology are bound up with the colonial era. Both anthropology and 19th-century colonialism are products of the 18th-century age of European enlightenment, the Industrial Revolution, the birth of modern science, and other historical and

St. Louis, MO.

philosophical forces. For example, the evolutionary theories of 19th-century anthropologists described a world in which all societies were evolving toward perfection. This idea shows elements of enlightenment rationality (they were systematizing knowledge and trying to discover laws of social development) and 19th-century romanticism (nations were moving toward perfection). It was very clearly influenced by the scientific theories of Charles Darwin and the social Darwinism of Herbert Spencer. It was also a convenient philosophy that could be pressed into service as a rationale for colonization: Colonization could help "primitive" societies evolve (Ghosh 1991; Godelier 1993).

One of the most important impacts colonialism had on anthropology was in determining the locations of fieldwork. British Commonwealth anthropologists tended to work in British colonies, French anthropologists in their colonies, and Americans within U.S. borders, in areas "protected" by the Monroe Doctrine (a policy stating that the United States would consider European "interference" in Latin America to be aggression) or in areas of American influence and control in the Pacific. In some cases, colonialism may have played a role in determining the topics of anthropological research. Studies of indigenous political systems or law were of particular interest to colonial governments. Colonialism and, more importantly, the discourse of rationalism and science also tended to promote a kind of anthropology in which the anthropologist speaks as an active authority claiming to objectively describe essentially passive subjects.

In the first half of the 20th century, colonial governments faced with the practical problems of governing their possessions sometimes relied on information provided by anthropologists. Anthropologists, anxious to find funding for their research, argued that their studies had practical value to colonial administrators (see, for example, Malinowski 1929a). However, anthropology did not come into being to promote or enable colonialism, which would have gone on with or without it (Burton 1992).

Anthropologists did not generally question the political reality of colonialism, but they often self-consciously tried to advance the interests of the people they studied. Most anthropological research was financed by private charitable organizations with reformist agendas and not by governments (Goody 1995). The result was that colonial officials generally mistrusted anthropologists, believing they were much too sympathetic to colonial subjects (Prah 1990). Sometimes they were banned from continuing their research. For example, the great South African anthropologist and apartheid opponent Max Gluckman was declared a "Prohibited Immigrant" in Northern Rhodesia (today's Zambia), an area where he had done much research (Gordon and Wesson 2013).

▌▌▌ DECOLONIZATION, NEOCOLONIALISM, AND POSTCOLONIALISM

The eras of Western expansion and colonization radically and permanently changed the world. By the time of World War II, all peoples had been affected by Western expansion and their cultures altered by this experience. Some, attempting to resist foreign influences and protect their ways of life, had moved as far away from outsiders as possible (see, for example, Breusers 1999). However, most people lived in societies where the presence and influence of outsiders, as well as their demands for goods and labor and their attempts to change culture were fundamental facts of life.

Most of the nations of the Americas had gained their independence in the 18th and 19th centuries. In Africa and Asia, independence from European colonialism was not achieved until after World War II (see Figure 13.7). Many nations that were part of the Soviet Union did not achieve independence until the late 1980s and early 1990s. Some colonies persist today, although usually with the consent of the majority of their residents. For example, Britain has some 14 "overseas territories," including Bermuda, Gibraltar, and the Pitcairn Islands. French "overseas departments" include Martinique and French Guiana. The United States "organized unincorporated territories" include American Samoa and Guam. Many consider the U.S. relationship with Puerto Rico colonial as well (Grosfoguel 2003; Melendez 1993).

There were as many reasons for granting independence as there were for exploration and colonialism, but three are of particular importance: civil disobedience, changing political alignments, and changing economic structures.

Figure 13.7 Kwame Nkrumah, Ghana's first president, proclaims independence on March 6, 1957.

National Archives Photo No. 306-RNT-57-18116

Governing colonies was never a simple affair, and from the beginning, there was rebellion against colonial rule. Strikes, acts of terrorism, and guerrilla warfare were common throughout the colonial era. However, there was a substantial upsurge in these actions following World War II. One reason for this was the return of combat veterans. Veterans knew how to fight European-style warfare. Moreover, they and their supporters felt that the colonizing countries owed them a deep debt for their service, a debt to be paid partially by increased political liberties.

In some places, resistance took the form of agitation and demonstrations, but in others, bitter anticolonial wars broke out. In Madagascar, for example, almost 90,000 died in a rebellion between 1947 and 1948. In Algeria, between 1954 and 1962, France fought a protracted war that left at least one-quarter of a million dead (Kepel 2005). Anticolonial wars also broke out in Vietnam, Mozambique, Angola, and numerous other places.

The end of World War II also created a fundamentally different balance of world power. European nations, which held the largest number of colonies, were greatly weakened, which left the United States and the Soviet Union as the dominant superpowers. They quickly engaged in a cold war that was to last for more than four decades, but neither nation had a strong interest in preserving the colonial status quo. Based on the belief that they could bring former colonies into their own economic and political orbit, both promoted rapid independence for colonial possessions and supplied money and weaponry to their supporters within the colonies.

Finally, international economics was also changing. In many cases, colonies had been created to allow European corporations access to areas where they could operate free of competition from those based in other nations. However, in the wake of World War II, corporate ownership began to become multinational, and corporations were less tied to their nations of origin, a move that continues today. This process undercut an important economic rationale of colonialism.

By December 1960, when the United Nations declared that "all peoples have the right to self determination" and that "immediate steps shall be taken . . . to transfer all powers to the peoples of [countries that have not yet achieved independence]" (UN Resolution 1514), the process of decolonization was already well underway. At that time, recently decolonized nations included India and Pakistan (1947), Cambodia (1953), Vietnam (1954), Ghana (1957), Guinea (1958), and many others.

By the late 1970s, almost all colonies held by western European nations had achieved independence. With the formal end of the Soviet Union in 1991 and the collapse of South African apartheid in 1994, almost all areas of the world had some form of home rule. Colonized areas became independent under a variety of circumstances and with many different levels of preparedness. In some, like Ghana, the transition to independence was reasonably orderly, and a sizable (but still inade-quate) number of individuals trained as administrators. In others, like Congo, the transition was profoundly violent, and very few colonial subjects had any experience with running a government. But although there were great differences among colonies, all came to independence as relatively poor nations in a world that was increasingly divided into the wealthy and the poor rather than the independent and the colonized.

In the half century since most former colonies achieved independence, debate about the nature of that achievement has raged among scholars, politicians, and activists. Some scholars point to the continuing relations of dependence that often characterize former colonies and former colonizing countries. They argue that this *neocolonialism* retained the fundamental structure of the colonial world, but allowed wealthy and powerful corporations an ever greater range in which to operate. Others point to the postcolonial predicament in which many ex-colonies find themselves. Despite formal independence, colonial ways of thinking and understanding remain. Institutions, practices, and conceptual categories do not simply depart with the colonizers. Instead, they may still be impediments to achieving stable and prosperous nations.

▌▌▌ AN INTERCONNECTED BUT UNSTABLE WORLD

The European expansion and the era of colonization were historic processes that changed the world from a collection of relatively independent economies and societies to a complex world system. The UN resolution declaring that all people had the right to self-determination was intended to end colonialism but exposed critical fault lines in this system. As we saw in Chapter 7 on political systems, nation-states are imagined communities composed of members of different groups. The late 20th and early 21st centuries have been characterized by frequent intense conflicts within and among nation-states as groups fought both for self-determination and to impose their vision of the state on others. Several nations have disintegrated under this pressure, including Czechoslovakia (split into the Czech Republic and Slovakia in 1992), Yugoslavia (dissolved 1992–2008), Ethiopia (split, creating the nation of Eritrea in 1993), and Sudan (split, creating the nation of Southern Sudan in 2011). In other places such as Iraq, Chechnya, Syria, and Ukraine bitter wars were (and in many cases still are) being fought over ethnic and state identity. In still other places such as Belgium, the United Kingdom, Canada, and Spain there is little risk of large-scale violence, but political and economic disputes are often increased by ethnic tensions.

Despite the violence and instability of the world, the interconnections among societies have only increased. Our world is characterized by enormous disparities in wealth and power and by an increasingly dense fabric of interwoven technology, finance, communication, and politics. There is no doubt that modernity has spread to virtually all places in the world. This process of extreme globalization interacts with and may replace both neocolonialism and postcolonialism. However, for the foreseeable future, societies promise enormous hope for their people but face enormous problems and inequities as well. We turn to some of those hopes and problems in the next chapter.

BRINGING IT BACK HOME:
THE LIMITS OF TOLERANCE

One of the impacts of colonialism has been migration from colonized countries to colonizing countries. In Europe, millions of Muslims from the Middle East, North Africa, and South Asia have migrated to Britain, France, Holland, and other nations. In 2015, more than 1.3 million refugees, mostly from Syria claimed political asylum in Europe; over 400,000 in Germany alone.

The flow of refugees and economic migrants has sometimes resulted in cultural conflict. On January 31, 2015, a crowd of refugees and migrants attacked women in the square outside Cologne Cathedral in Germany. Throughout late 2015 and early 2016 there was unrest at refugee camps in Northern France. Tensions have been heightened further by a series of terrorist attacks in France and Belgium.

Many non-Muslim Europeans associate Islam with backwardness, homophobia, and oppression of women, all values that contrast with the ways Europeans generally like to see themselves. These ideas about Islam, frequently exploited by right-wing political parties (Spiegel 2010), are associated with a sharp rise in anti-Muslim sentiment as well as laws that limit the public face of Islam. In March 2016, an event memorializing those killed and injured in the Brussels terror attack of March 22, 2016, was disrupted by right-wing protesters giving Nazi salutes and chanting "Death to Arabs" (CBS/AP 2016). Several European countries, including France and Belgium, have restricted Muslim dress, and Switzerland has banned the construction of minarets. Anti-Muslim violence has erupted in several places. The most notorious example is the 2011 murder of 77 non-Muslim Norwegians—mostly children—by Anders Breivik, a deeply disturbed individual who said he was motivated by anti-Muslim prejudice. However, the problem is far greater than a single insane person. Muslims have faced attacks and harassment in Germany, France, Ireland, and many other countries (Theodorou 2015).

The idea that Muslims should assimilate to preexisting European norms dominates much of the conversation on this issue. Some analysts have argued that Muslim immigrants are poorly integrated into European societies and do not wish to adopt European traditions or ideas (see, for example, Wasif 2011). In fact, the data show little difference between Muslim and non-Muslim Europeans on many issues. For example, Jackson and Doerschiler (2012:126–127) used large-scale survey techniques to show that Muslim youth in France and Britain are as supportive of European values such as individualism, equality, and secular society as their non-Muslim counterparts and are not much different from non-Muslims on measures of isolation or alienation. Muslims did join riots Britain in 2011, but most of the rioters were not Muslims. Half of Dutch Muslims report they "hardly ever" go to religious services (Schmeets 2012). Thus, the issue may be as much non-Muslim European attitudes toward Muslims as it is Muslims' failure to accept European values or assimilate to European culture.

The United States has a longer history of multiculturalism than Europe, and Americans frequently consider theirs to be a nation of immigrant communities. However, it is not clear how tolerant of difference they actually are. For example, in 2014 voters in Alabama approved an amendment to the state constitution aimed at banning Islamic law. Oklahoma voters had done the same in 2010. In both states, the Muslim population is minuscule. In 2016, leading Republican candidates for the presidency called for bans on Muslim immigration and special policing of Muslim neighborhoods. As of spring 2016, the United States has offered to resettle only 0.25 percent of the 4 million refugees who have fled Syria. The U.S. Congress and numerous state governors have staunchly opposed accepting even this tiny number. Germany has already accepted more than 40 times as many.

Muslims comprise about 7.5 percent of France's population, 5.8 percent of the population of Germany and 4.8 percent of the population of the United Kingdom (Hackett 2015). In the United States, they make up about 1 percent of the population. However, polls in late 2015, after the rise of ISIS and several European terror attacks, showed that people in Britain, France, and Germany had more favorable views of Muslims than people in the United States (Lipka 2015; Telhami 2015).

YOU DECIDE:

1. Do residents of the countries to which immigrants come have the right to demand that new arrivals adopt specific national customs?
2. Do immigrants have the right to insist that the countries in which they now live allow them practices and customs to which many members of the host culture object?
3. Are there limits to tolerance? What practices, no matter how well accepted they are in foreign cultures, do you think should not be permitted in the United States? What is the rational basis for your decision?

CHAPTER SUMMARY

1. Compare the current distribution of wealth and power in the world to their distribution in the 15th century. The world as we see it is the result of historical processes that have moved wealth and power from one area to another. In the 15th century, the centers of world power lay primarily in the Middle East and Asia. However, Europe was poised on the brink of a great expansion. The rise of today's wealthy nations was connected with the creation of poverty in other places in the world.
2. What were the primary motivations for European expansion? A combination of religious faith, greed, new social arrangements, and new technologies drove European expansion.
3. In what parts of the world were Europeans most successful at capturing and controlling new lands, and why? Europeans were most successful in controlling lands in the Americas because Native Americans lacked resistance to European diseases. As a result, native societies were depopulated and succumbed to European military pressure.
4. What is colonialism, and when were the main eras of European colonialism? Colonialism is the active possession of a foreign territory and the maintenance of political dominance over that territory. Europeans first colonized the Americas in the 16th century. However, elsewhere in the world, European colonization did not happen until the 19th century.
5. What were the key mechanisms Europeans used to make their control of foreign territory pay? Plunder of precious metals, the use of slave labor on monocultural plantations, and the joint stock company were all instrumental in creating wealth for Europeans. In addition, military and diplomatic maneuvering helped draw wealth from around the world into Europe.

6. Why did Europeans colonize in the 19th century, and how did they justify taking colonial possessions? Europeans colonized because of the collapse of earlier mercantilist firms or to protect their national companies from competition from other Europeans. They wished to increase their wealth and protect their trade. They justified colonialism by calling it a civilizing mission.

7. What methods did Europeans use to try to make colonialism pay? Europeans pressed colonial subjects into forced labor on roads and other projects. They used taxation in colonial money to fund the government and force natives to participate in the European-dominated cash economy. They used education programs to discredit local culture and create a class of people who could help with colonial administration.

8. When did the colonies taken in the 19th century gain their independence, and what key factors were responsible for this? Most colonies gained their independence between the end of World War II and 1965. Civil unrest in the colonies, the emergence of the United States and the Soviet Union as superpowers, and changes in the structure of international economics played critical roles in the timing of independence.

9. What problems did newly independent nations face? Many new nations lacked trained administrators, and had little infrastructure such as roads and railroads. Economic relationships favoring the former colonizing power often persisted as did the ways of thinking and behaving associated with colonialism.

KEY TERMS

Colonialism	Heeren XVII
Colonies	Joint stock company
Corvée labor	Monoculture plantation
Dutch East India Company	Pillage
(VOC)	Tirailleurs Senegalais

マクドナルド
ハンバーガー

月見バーガー
¥339

NEW きのこ月見
¥399

ton koene/Alamy

Multinational corpora-
tions such as McDonalds,
pictured here in Tokyo,
have profound economic
and cultural impacts
around the world.

14

CULTURE, CHANGE, AND GLOBALIZATION

AFTER YOU HAVE READ THIS CHAPTER, YOU WILL BE ABLE TO:

Δ Give examples of the types and degrees of economic inequality today.

Δ Compare and contrast the different models of economic development that have been popular in the past half century.

Δ Assess the role of multinational corporations in the world, and give examples of the advantages and problems that attend them.

Δ Summarize the role and importance of urbanization in the world, and give examples of urbanization in poor nations.

Δ Evaluate the significance of population growth, and analyze the effect of government policy and economics in controlling population growth.

Δ Discuss how family and kinship structures are adapting to globalization.

Δ Examine some of the key environmental challenges facing the world, and describe the differences between pollution in wealthy and poor nations.

Δ Analyze the role that political instability has played in culture change.

Δ Examine the relationship of globalization, migration, and refugees.

THE CONTRADICTIONS OF GLOBALIZATION

LTHOUGH the historical processes described in Chapter 13 have created a global economic network, the world is not a global village. A global village suggests a relatively small place, with easily visited spaces—a place where differences are minimized, a world of screen doors, broad porches, and friendly neighbors. But we live in a world of privilege and exclusion, of rapid change and of shocking inequality. In this globalized world, some areas are hubs that are easy to reach, are wealthy and powerful, and are in constant communication with each other. Other places are more remote, less in contact with the rest of the world, and reached only with real difficulty. Inequality creates differences beyond those of mere distance. For example, a technology or financial specialist working in Manhattan is likely to have close ties and communicate frequently with colleagues, relatives, and friends living and working thousands of miles away, while having almost no social connections with the urban poor living within sight of his or her office.

Our contemporary, globalized world is a contradictory place. All around us, we see increasing cultural homogeneity: a can of soda, a CD player, cell phones and Internet access, and fast food chains, like McDonalds, pictured in the chapter opening photo. At the same time, the world is increasingly divided, with great disparities in both quality and quantity of life. More than 1.2 billion of the world's population lives on less than $1 a day, while a meal for two at a good restaurant in any American city can easily top $100. In late 2015, the life expectancy in Japan was 83.7 years; in Sierra Leone it was 50 years and in Nigeria 54.5 years (World Health Organization n.d.). In addition, although many contemporary economic forces favor cultural homogeneity, people in many places are insisting, sometimes violently, on their right to preserve their cultural identity or to create new identities intentionally separating themselves from the dominant global culture. Globalization results in many challenges, some of which we examine in this chapter.

As we noted in Chapter 8, sharp contrasts in wealth and power operate both between countries and within countries. Imagine, for example, that you are in eastern Africa, where many small clusters of tiny huts dot a dry and barren land. Each cluster contains a group of extended families, all participating in and sharing the work. They have very little money because the people make and consume most of their food, shelter, and other goods themselves. They have few roads and no schools, hospitals, electricity, or water supply. But roads pass by the village bringing news of the outside world. Before long, tropical fruits will be grown here for export; these may end up on the dinner table of a rich family in South America or Europe. Radios made in Southeast Asia playing music performed by African bands recorded in northern Europe are prized possessions. And more and more people have cell phones and use them regularly. Communication links between remote villages and the rest of the world is increasing, a process that will greatly intensify in the future.

DEVELOPMENT

At the end of colonial rule, many newly independent nations were mired in poverty, uncontrolled urbanization, population growth, expanded immigration and emigration, ecological disaster, war, and political instability. The **gross national income (GNI)** of a nation—the total value of all its production—provides a rough estimate of national prosperity, which shows great worldwide disparities. In 2014, the GNI for the United States was $55,230, but 73 of the 208 nations listed by the World Bank had a per capita GNI of less than $5,000. For 52 of these nations, the figure was less than $2,500 (World Bank 2016a). In 2012, a total of 896 million people were living on less than $1.90 a day and over 2.1 billion on less than $3.10 a day (World Bank 2016b).

In the postcolonial period, during the Cold War, both the Eastern and Western blocs saw economic development in poor countries as an opportunity to spread their political ideologies and advance their economic systems. Thus, both these political blocs provided financial and military aid to poor nations with the goals of creating political allies and stable trading partners and also to secure sources of raw materials. In addition, some international agencies, wealthy nation governments, and thousands of private organizations involved in development projects truly hoped to bring a better life to the world's poor. The end of colonialism did not mean the end of forced cultural change, foreign intervention, or foreign influence. Instead, nations were brought into ever closer contact and the pace of change, both cultural and economic, increased.

Modernization Theory

The model of progress promoted by Western nations from the end of World War II until the 1970s was called **modernization theory**. It assumed that countries were poor because they had underdeveloped, backward economies and were dominated by traditional cultures that opposed the rational thinking demanded by modern society. Modernization theory held that poor countries needed to repeat the historic experience

Gross national income (GNI): The total value of all goods and services produced in a country.

Modernization theory: A model of development that predicts that nonindustrial societies will move in the social and technological direction of industrialized nations.

of wealthy countries to become wealthy themselves. Foreign aid from wealthy countries was aimed at building new roads and factories to support rural industrialization; introducing new farming techniques to enable peasants to cultivate cash crops; replacing traditional exchange mechanisms of obligation and reciprocity with a market system; and increasing education to undermine irrational, culturally influenced behavior.

But poor countries were also encouraged to take large loans from governments and banks in wealthy nations. The ability of poor nations to repay these loans was based on expectations of success for the development programs they funded. This kind of development served the interests of both donors in wealthy nations and elites in poor nations. It spread the influence of wealthy nations and made new markets for their products. In poor nations, money from development aid was often used to support an elite lifestyle of exaggerated conspicuous consumption and opened many possibilities for political patronage and corruption. Most of this money did little to improve conditions for ordinary people; indeed in many cases, their poverty increased. Part of the reason for the failure of development was modernization theory itself; it not only ignored the roles that colonialism and exploitation had played in creating wealthy nations, but also ignored the complexities in moving in a single pathway from "tradition to modernity" (Besnier 2011).

Human Needs Approaches

Basic human needs approach: Projects aimed at providing access to clean water, education, and health care for the poorest of the world's people.

The failure of most economic development plans in the 1960s, and the persistence of poverty, sickness, hunger, and illiteracy in poor nations, led to the emergence of a new approach to development: the **basic human needs approach**. Supporters of this approach argued that development could succeed only if people had access to basic necessities, such as education, pure water, and health and sanitation facilities, which were particularly urgent in isolated rural communities. Basic human needs projects continue to play an important role in foreign aid, particularly aid by nongovernmental organizations (NGOs). But human needs projects lost some prominence by the end of the 1980s, first, because although the projects did provide benefits to some communities, they did not create large economic growth, and second, because these projects had high overhead expenses and did not generate very much publicity for their donors. Recipient governments disliked them because they disbursed less money than more traditional modernization projects and because the groups being aided had relatively little political power. Perhaps most importantly, beginning in the 1980s, political changes in both the West and developing countries resulted in yet another approach to development.

Structural Adjustment

When the loans to poor-nation governments for financing modernization failed to produce wealth, these governments found themselves deeply in debt. At the same time, **neoliberalism**, a philosophy that holds that free markets, free trade, the free flow of capital, and minimum government regulation of the economy is the best way to increase economic and social development, was gaining strength in the United States and Europe. Neoliberals opposed state control or support of industries, and supported only the most minimal aid to impoverished individual nations. Those opposed to neoliberalism claimed it benefited only economic elites and made the poor poorer, both in developing countries and in the United States (Harvey 2005).

Neoliberalism created a new approach to development called **structural adjustment**. Under this regime, before wealthy nations would loan money for development to poorer nations, they demanded that recipients sell off state-owned enterprises; reduce subsidies to local businesses and industries; reduce spending on education, health, and social programs; and open their markets to free trade. Most poor nations protested these policies, but they were often forced to accept them because they were in debt and needed new money to operate their governments or increase their security. This was even, or perhaps especially, the case with countries discovered to be rich in oil and natural gas like Indonesia, Venezuela, Chad, Equatorial Guinea, and Nigeria, in West Africa (Coll 2012).

The evidence indicates that the results of structural adjustment are, at best, uneven. For example, a World Bank study of Africa showed that although countries adopting structural adjustment did better than those that did not, the differences were small and probably related more to political than economic factors (World Bank 2005:277). So far, structural adjustment policies have increased inequality within nations, and poverty remains an intractable problem (Greenberg 1997; Kim 2000; SAPRIN 2004).

One important organization in various modernization and development efforts is the **World Bank**. Officially called the International Bank for Reconstruction and Development, the World Bank is an international agency that provides technical assistance and loans to promote international trade and economic development, especially to poor nations. World Bank policy has changed since its creation in 1944, embracing at various times modernization theory, basic human needs projects, and structural adjustment policies. One current focus of the World Bank is poverty reduction in the poorest countries, with an emphasis on investment for economic growth that will uplift the poor.

Like development aid in general, World Bank efforts have been widely criticized for, among other things, the failure of many of its projects.

Neoliberalism: Political and economic policies that promote free trade, individual initiative, and minimal government regulation of the economy, and oppose state control or subsidy to industries and all but minimal aid to impoverished individuals.

Structural adjustment: A development policy promoted by Western nations, particularly the United States, that requires poor nations to pursue free-market reforms in order to get new loans from the International Monetary Fund and World Bank.

World Bank: The International Bank for Reconstruction and Development, an international agency that provides technical assistance and loans to promote international trade and economic development, especially to poor nations. The World Bank has often been criticized for interfering in the affairs of these nations.

The Bank's current neoliberal emphasis has often increased poverty in poor countries, as conditions for loans insisted on reducing money spent for government social services and raising food prices. Because many World Bank projects have been bad for the environment and for public health, such as its coordination with international oil companies (see Coll 2012), they have been the target of several worldwide protests.

▎▎▎ Development Anthropology and the Anthropology of Development

As development projects aimed more directly at improving the welfare of the poor, particularly in rural areas, the involvement of anthropologists increased, because they saw such projects as both desirable and necessary. This resulted in a new specialty: development anthropology. Development anthropologists are trained to act as intermediaries between development organizations and the recipients of aid. With their interest in the local aspects of globalization, their ethnographically based knowledge of remote communities, and their ability to provide cogent analysis and assessment, they make important contributions to development projects. In 1974, the U.S. Agency for International Development (USAID) employed one full-time anthropologist; by 1980, it employed more than 50 (Escobar 1997). In Haiti, for example, anthropologist and aid worker Timothy Schwartz (2008) focused on the way Haitians actually live, how they spend, and how they actually think about such issues as the family—topics not well understood by NGOs. This lack of understanding resulted in significant waste and failure in international aid donated to Haiti, including the millions donated in response to the horrific 2010 earthquake.

The World Bank has also employed anthropologists. Its current president (as of 2016) is Jim Yong Kim, a medical anthropologist who is a global health expert and a cofounder with Paul Farmer of Partners In Health, which focuses on improving health in the poorest nations through HIV/AIDS and tuberculosis reduction (Hodge 2011). Responding to criticism that the World Bank prioritizes Western cultural solutions and marginalizes local cultural approaches to development, Kim emphasizes the anthropologist's view to "amplif[y] the voices of developing countries and draw[s] on the expertise and experience of the people [being] serve[d]" (Lowrey 2012). But although Kim's previous public health projects have saved many lives, he has not generally opposed or called into question the neoliberal economic policies and structures that impede solutions to improving health among the very poorest countries. And herein lies the tension in development anthropology: While engaged anthropologists strongly favor development aid, they note that development may actually reinforce the structures of inequality that create poverty in the first place, and they call for programs that empower the oppressed (see Crush 1995; Pigg 2001). This may require a direct and pragmatic engagement with existing structures of power that may not appeal to all anthropologists, and perhaps explains why applied anthropology has not made the impact one would have hoped for.

There are successes, however. In 2008, anthropologists investigating dam construction in Laos, Turkey, and Uganda documented significant failures in the environmental and social programs that accompanied these projects; these discoveries resulted in some substantial changes to the programs (Checker 2009:165). Applied anthropologists help governments and other groups find solutions that are sensitive to local cultural traditions and respond to people's needs and aspirations (Paiement 2007). The poverty, disease, and other problems of the poor nations are social facts, aspects of human culture and human society, and thus can be changed. Anthropology can play an important role in this process.

As noted previously, Kim and Farmer's work, one of the more successful anthropological efforts, has involved medical anthropologists responding to the AIDS epidemic, which is especially severe in Africa (Timberg and Halperin 2012). Unlike in the West, where most cases of AIDS are the result of same-sex relationships (Feldman 2009) and infected needles used by heroin addicts, ethnographic research indicates that AIDS in Africa is mainly due to heterosexual relationships (Feldman 2008; Lee and Susser 2008). This requires taking different approaches to the spread of HIV/AIDS, particularly in Africa, for example, with the prevention of AIDS through education, abstinence, and condom use (see Figure 14.1).

Multinational corporation (MNC): A corporation that owns business enterprises or plants in more than one nation.

And although many development projects do not succeed, some do. Child mortality before the age of 5 has decreased by 50 percent from a generation ago; life expectancy has increased 20 percent; and literacy has increased 25 percent in the past generation.

Businesses that own enterprises and seek to market their goods and services in more than one nation are known as **multinational corporations (MNCs)**. MNCs bring employment opportunities as well as goods and services to people who otherwise would not have them. At the same time, they create major and controversial changes in the natural, economic, social, and political

Figure 14.1 Medical anthropologist Douglas Feldman doing field research aimed at HIV/AIDS prevention in Africa through changing normative behavior among Zambian adolescents.

environments. Poor nations are particularly vulnerable to MNCs, many of which have yearly budgets greater than those of poor-nation governments. For example, in 2014, each of the world's 20 largest MNCs had gross revenues of more than $161 billion, larger than all but about 50 of the 208 countries tracked by the World Bank (World Bank 2016c). The financial power of these corporations enables them to exert enormous influence on poor nations and makes it extremely difficult for these nations to regulate them. In addition, like all capitalist corporations, the fundamental goal of MNCs is to return wealth to their shareholders, the vast majority of whom live in wealthy nations. Thus, most MNC profits in poor nations contribute to the economy of wealthy nations.

■ Sweatshop Labor

Sweatshop: Generally, a pejorative term for a factory with working conditions that may include low wages, long hours, inadequate ventilation, and physical, mental, or sexual abuse.

The profits of MNCs are related to sweatshop production. **Sweatshops** are factories where workers, particularly women and children, are employed for long hours under difficult conditions at low pay. South and East Asia—a sweatshop belt, which includes China, South Korea, Indonesia, Malaysia, India, and Bangladesh—account for about one-quarter of the global economy (Kristoff and WuDunn 2009). Much sweatshop production is funneled into the United States in the form of cheap consumer goods. Major brands sold in the United States as well as in Europe, including Gap, Marks & Spencer (a popular British store), H&M, and Adidas produce clothes in places such as Cambodia, where workers are paid $0.50 an hour, conditions are so severe that they have resulted in mass fainting episodes, and worker protest is often met with lethal violence (Win 2015; Human Rights Watch 2015). The issue of sweatshop safety standards was again brought into the spotlight when, in April 2013, a textile factory in Bangladesh collapsed, killing 1129 factory workers, mainly women and children (Yardley 2013). Workers, manufacturers, building owners and government officials are conflicted about implementing safety standards; although most people understand the need for them, they impose an economic price many do not want to pay (Greenhouse and Manik 2014). The alternatives to unsafe factory conditions and exploitation for many workers may create worse conditions. Most of the workers are drawn from the ranks of the landless poor, and the wages they earn, however small, are often the main support for their families. Furthermore, although public protests and import restrictions aimed at sweatshops may improve conditions and wages, they may also cause a drop in sales, throwing people out of work.

Sweatshops are not limited to poor nations; the garment industry in Los Angeles employs about 45,000 workers, many under difficult conditions and at very low pay. A 2015 survey by the Garment Worker Center showed that more than 20 percent experienced on-the-job violence or harassment, almost half work 10 hours a day or more without overtime, and, because they are paid by the piece rather than by the hour, more than half receive less than the minimum wage (Garment Workers Center 2015). The sweatshops of MNCs are often pointed to as the cause for the economic decline in the United States as more goods are imported from factories elsewhere. Indeed, this has been a major focus of the 2016 presidential campaign. However, the facts suggest some skepticism: manufacturing jobs are on the decline around the world in a shifting global economy in which service, retail, and other kinds of employment are edging out the employment in factories, which are depending more on machines than on increasing labor for high productivity (Porter 2016).

▌▌▌ Electronics, Apple, and Foxconn

Many Westerners, including Americans, depend on computers, cell phones, and other electronics, but are unaware of the conditions under which they are made. Foxconn, a Taiwanese company whose main production facilities are in China, assembles about 40 percent of the world's electronics, employing nearly 1.2 million workers under the poorest conditions. Workers often work 7 days a week; they live in crowded dorms—sometimes with 20 people in a three-room apartment—and work on assembly lines that run 24 hours a day while workers stand, crouch, or sit on backless chairs all day. Some stand for so long that their legs swell and they cannot walk. Employees who arrive late are punished, and workers sometimes have to do two shifts in a row. Even with overtime, a worker earns only about $22 a day (Duhigg and Barboza 2012).

Workers who operate machines that polish iPad cases work in an area where the air is filled with aluminum particles that result from the polishing practice. Although Apple and Foxconn knew about the problem of excessive airborne aluminum dust, they did nothing to eliminate it; rather, with the high demand for iPads, the pace of work became frantic. Airborne dust can be explosive, and one day at the Chengdu factory a series of explosions shook the building, killing 3 and injuring 15.

Electronics made for many different companies are produced under harsh conditions, but Apple, as the world's largest electronics company, is involved in many of these issues. Apple outsources 100 percent of its manufacturing, and though it claims to hold the companies with which it does business to the highest safety standards and respect for rights of workers, yearly audits indicate that these patterns are consistently violated (Chen 2012; Duhigg and Greenhouse 2012). Because of Apple's enormous economic power, it can negotiate very low prices from its suppliers. This often means that suppliers cut corners and push their workers harder.

Figure 14.2 Foxconn, a huge Chinese company that produces electronics for companies such as Apple, has been accused of extreme sweatshop labor abuse. Here, Foxconn workers take part in a "Treasure Your life" rally, after a Foxconn worker's suicide.

Bobby Yip/Reuters

Thus far, despite substantial publicity about working conditions, Apple has successfully avoided major consumer resistance, both in the United States and in China (Apple's second largest market, and one in which it is currently expanding). It has done so partly by deflecting blame from itself to its production companies like Foxconn. Under continuing pressure, however, especially by the continuing investigations of the *New York Times* (see Figure 14.2) Apple agreed to be more active in correcting some of the abuses in its production facilities (Bradsher and Duhigg 2012).

MNCs that produce very popular products like Apple devices, raise questions about how such products can be produced at a price American and other Western consumers will find acceptable without exploiting workers. Some MNCs, like Nike, have improved working conditions, and are also making commitments of social responsibility to the regions in which they are located.

▐▐▐ URBANIZATION

In 1950, only about 16 percent of the total population of nonindustrialized nations lived in large cities. By 2000, this figure had reached 40 percent, and by 2008, more than half of the world's population lived in cities. By 2050, the world's urban population is expected to be about 6.4 billion, equal to the world's total population in 2004 (United Nations 2008:3). In 1950, seven of the world's ten largest cities (urban agglomerations) were located in Europe, Russia, Japan, and the United States, with an average population of about 6.7 million people. In 2015, only two

Blaine Harrington III/Alamy

John Seaton Callahan/Getty Images

cities in these nations made the top ten list: Tokyo and New York (ABC News Point 2015). The average population of the world's ten largest cities is now 20.5 million (United Nations 2012). Almost all the urban population growth between now and 2050 is expected to occur in the world's poor nations (United Nations 2008:4) (Figure 14.3). Some of the cities that will result will be truly enormous: By 2025, the population of Dhaka in Bangladesh will be almost 23 million, Lagos, Nigeria, almost 19 million, and Kinshasa, Democratic Republic of the Congo 14.5 million (United Nations 2012). They truly will be megacities presenting an enormous challenge in providing basic services to their populations.

Urban growth is significantly affected by rural people who come to cities seeking jobs and other social, material, and cultural advantages. They are forced out of the countryside by high population levels, inability to acquire land, environmental degradation, and, sometimes, violence. When new migrants arrive in urban areas, they often find dismal living conditions. In places such as Bogota, Casablanca, Cairo, and Kolkata (Calcutta), more than half of the urban population lives in slums and squatter settlements (Todaro and Smith 2003). However, in most cases, they also have access to more amenities in these places than in the rural communities they left. As bad as life can be in places like the slums of Mumbai, for example, most people are there because they believe their lives and prospects are better than in the places they left behind.

Urban life can be extremely difficult. Many of the urban poor face hunger, unsafe drinking water, inadequate or practically nonexistent sanitation facilities, substandard shelter, and environments teeming with trash. Disease and early death are rampant in the slums of the world's large cities. Also, the experience of the urban poor is not necessarily characterized by the association and solidarity that was typical of, for example, poor immigrant enclaves in 19th-century America. Survival on the margins of

Figure 14.3 More than half of the world's largest cities are in poor nations. These photos of Rio de Janeiro, Brazil, show the enormous contrast between the living conditions of the elite (left), and those of its many citizens who live in poverty. About 22 percent of Rio's residents live in *favelas* (right), with little access to clean water or sanitation.

the urban environment is often ruthlessly competitive. As Katherine Boo illustrates for India, in *Behind the Beautiful Forevers* (2012), in-fighting, crime, and violence are common in deeply impoverished urban communities. People struggle for any advantage that might allow them and their children to escape deep poverty. They face laws that protect the interests of the wealthy and powerful and often force them into illegal activities merely to survive. Frequently, police, justice systems, and even religious NGOs do not provide protection and services but rather extort what little money people have. Yet, despite these difficulties, cities continue to grow. This is an indication of both the truly deep poverty and desperation that characterizes so much of the rural areas of poor nations and the fervent desire of hundreds of millions of the world's poor for economic advancement. Development projects must provide adequate services, including water, sewage, education, and health care to both rural and urban populations. However, unless life chances and opportunities are improved in rural areas, urban development will only draw more migrants who will quickly overwhelm any improvements in services and increased economic opportunities.

POPULATION PRESSURE

The rate of population growth provides a dramatic index of the increasing speed of social change. About 2 million years ago, our remote ancestors numbered perhaps 100,000. By the time the first agricultural societies were developing 10,000 years ago, world population had reached 5 million to 10 million. Two thousand years ago, there were about 250 million people in the world. By 1750, this number had tripled to 750 million. Then population growth really began to accelerate. Fifty years later, in 1800, there were 1 billion people; by 1930, there were 2 billion. Since then, the world population has tripled, passing the 6 billion mark in the summer of 1999 (Fetto 1999). In spring 2016, the world population stood at over 7.3 billion (U.S. Census 2016). The world population continues to increase and is expected to rise to more than 10 billion by 2050 (see Figure 14.4). In the past 50 years, much of the world's population growth has taken place in poor nations. In 1950 about 1.7 billion people lived in poor nations. By 2050, that number is expected to rise to more than 8 billion, or about 86 percent of the world's population (Population Reference Bureau 2012).

Families Adapting to Globalization

In some cases, high population levels mean that the subsistence strategies people have used for years can no longer provide enough food. In parts of East Africa, for example, the amount of arable land per person declined 40 percent between 1965 and 1987 (World Bank 1992). This has resulted in important cultural changes, including land shortage and privatization of land ownership. In Tanzania, for example, up until about 1950, the Waluguru people gained access to land through their lineage, and the lineage head was a powerful figure. Now land must be purchased; this has resulted in the disappearance of the role of the lineage head and that role is hardly even remembered today. As land has become scarce, women in this matrilineal society have tightened their hold over it, weakening the position of men in marriage to the point where many prefer to migrate to the cities to marry. More than 37 percent of women over 20 are now unmarried, as compared with 15 percent of men (Van Donge 1992).

Population explosion and the search for land and wealth have also pushed people onto land previously occupied only by indigenous groups. For example, between 1955 and 1993, the Agta, a foraging group in the Philippines, was increasingly encroached upon by loggers and migrant farmers. By 1993,

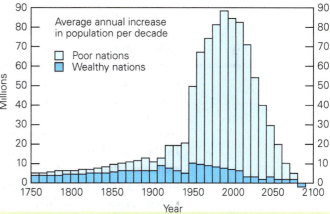

Figure 14.4 If current trends continue, world population will increase to about 10 billion by 2050 before leveling off. Most of this increase will be in poor nations.

the Agta had become landless migrant workers living at the lowest rung of Philippine society (Early and Headland 1998). Although nations like China have succeeded in reducing fertility through extreme population-control policies, such as the one-child policy, this so skewed the population in favor of boys that many poor, rural men cannot find brides. This has led to the importation of women from poorer countries such as Myanmar and Vietnam and often the physical and emotional abuse of women who are virtually captives in their husband's homes.

The functional, cross-cultural, and holistic perspectives of anthropology help us understand the impact of globalization on social institutions such as the family. Residence rules and family type are economically and politically adaptive. Thus, patrilocality is functional in traditional hunting and agricultural societies where men work cooperatively and is also functional where males cooperate in warfare (Ember and Ember 1971).

But family structures adapted to traditional subsistence patterns or forms of political organization may no longer be adaptive under the emerging industrial and postindustrial economies of the 21st century. New economies, along with population increase, the spread of global capitalism, changing technology, and women's new economic roles, have greatly affected family patterns. As more women enter the paid workforce, the value of marriage has declined. People everywhere marry later, and more people remain unmarried. In Japan, Taiwan, South Korea, and Hong Kong, the average age for marriage is now between 29 and 30 years for women and between 31 and 33 years for men. In 2010, a third of Japanese women entering their 30s were unmarried, and many of these will never marry (*Economist* 2011). A 2015 Japanese government survey showed that nearly 40 percent of single Japanese in their 20s and 30s do not want a romantic partner (*Japan Times* 2015).

Childbearing is also decreasing. In agricultural and herding societies, children are a good economic investment: The cost of raising them is relatively low and they provide a strong economic boost to the family. But both of these subsistence patterns are shrinking: In urban settings based on an information and service economy, economic benefits go to those who have technical training. The costs of raising and educating children become very high and the economic benefit of children to their families shrinks. In the United States, for example, the U.S. Department of Agriculture estimates that a middle-income family will spend almost $250,000 to raise a child born in 2013 from birth to age 18 years, not including college expenses (Vo 2015). Costs in other wealthy countries are comparable. Families in wealthy nations derive many benefits from their children, but only rarely are these economic.

Costs of raising children in poor nations are lower, but in the urban areas in which people increasingly live, they are still high, and this has driven family size down dramatically. For example, in Ethiopia, families in the capital city have, on average, four fewer children than families in rural areas (Mace 2008).

To replace the population, women must have between 2.1 and 2.5 children on average. However, in the European Union, women average only 1.6 children and, in some countries, fewer than this (Eurostat 2012). The number is comparable for wealthy Asian nations. In the United States, the number hovers near 2.1, the replacement value. Even in poor countries, fertility is declining rapidly. Government policies and technological changes also affect family size. Since the late 1970s, China has used a variety of incentives and punishments to encourage families to have only a single child. Many other countries now also promote family planning. In countries like China and India, where male children are more prestigious than female children, the combination of policies promoting family planning, the high cost of child rearing, and the increasing availability of ultrasound technology that allows people to determine the sex of their children, have resulted in many more boys than girls being born. This imbalance is strengthened by abortion, infanticide, and neglect of girls. The holistic approach of anthropology highlights the interconnectedness between political, economic, technological, and cultural factors in analyzing globalization and cultural change.

ENVIRONMENTAL CHALLENGES: POLLUTION

Ironically, even though the world's poor consume only a small fraction of the earth's resources, they also face some of the world's worst problems of pollution and environmental deterioration (Figure 14.5). The recent agreement of a climate pact in Paris and its signing at the United Nations in New York suggests that perhaps the countries of the world are now taking seriously the level of dangerous greenhouse gas emissions. But great challenges remain in all these societies as well as some skepticism about reaching its goals in an expeditious manner (Gillis and Davenport 2016).

The energy consumption of the United States alone is more than 14 times the energy consumption of the entire African continent (excluding South Africa) (Harrison and Pearce 2000). Given that consumption creates pollution, one might expect that people in the United States would live in a far dirtier environment than those in Africa. But this is not the case. Consider the city of Bamako, the capital of Mali, on any late afternoon in the dry season. Most streets are unpaved, and automobiles, trucks, carts, bicycles, and foot traffic have been stirring up dust all day. Because most of the city lacks regular trash pickup or sewage, waste from humans and animals has been churned into the air. People are beginning to cook their evening meal. Many, perhaps the majority, of the city's 1.6 million residents cook on either charcoal or wood fires that consume about 1 million tons of wood a year (Cissé 2007), and the smoke from cook fires joins the dust in the air. The combined effect of smoke and dust is like a thick, hot, dry fog. Because most houses are relatively open, lacking glass windows or doors that seal, the dust permeates indoors as well as the outdoors.

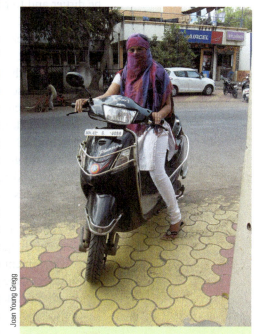

Joan Young Gregg

Figure 14.5 In Indian cities, the growth of industry and motor vehicles has given birth to a new fashion to protect local residents from dust and pollution.

And Bamako's population suffers. Pollution contributes to respiratory ailments, malaria, many diseases borne by sewage-contaminated water and air, and high childhood mortality.

Compare this with an American city of similar size, say San Antonio, Texas, a city of about 1.4 million. In San Antonio, most streets are paved and almost all homes have access to safe, publicly maintained water and sewage systems. Meals are cooked on appliances powered by electricity or gas. There is a huge amount of vehicular traffic, but cars and trucks are equipped with pollution-controlling devices. Although San Antonio is not one of the United State's wealthier cities, its population consumes many times the resources than does the population of Bamako. But almost all of San Antonio's population lives in environments that are healthier and far less polluted than Bamako.

Pollution is closely related to industrialization and globalization. Poor nations, desperate to provide some degree of prosperity to their citizens with limited amounts of capital to invest and limited means of attracting investment from abroad, use less expensive production technologies that generally produce more pollution than more expensive, higher-technology processes. Therefore, industry in poor nations tends to be dirtier and to pollute more than similar industries in wealthy nations. For example, China has experienced enormous economic growth but has relied extensively on lower-cost, more highly polluting industries, and at least 20 percent of the Chinese population lives in severely polluted areas. Ameliorating this problem by installing adequate pollution control in existing Chinese industries would cost $135 billion (Bremner 2006).

The financial power of MNCs may allow them to circumvent national laws designed to control pollution. A good example is oil production in the Niger Delta in Nigeria, where gas flaring (the burning off of the natural gas that is a by-product of oil production) releases toxins into the air and releases more carbon dioxide than all the automobiles and other industry in the rest of Africa combined. Gas flaring has been illegal in Nigeria since the 1980s, but continues today because strong and wealthy corporations, using techniques that include bribery and intimidation, are able to ignore or circumvent regulations enacted by the relatively weak government (Adetunji 2006; Walker 2009). In the Niger Delta, pollution has created an environmental disaster that has been instrumental in fomenting violence and civil unrest.

Global Warming

Global warming is another important aspect of ecological change caused by human activity (Intergovernmental Panel on Climate Change 2007; Oreskes 2004). Although there are some possible benefits to global warming in places like northern Europe and Russia, where it may extend the growing season through increased rainfall and reduce fuel consumption for heating, most impacts of warming are expected to be largely negative and to fall disproportionately on the poor. Many of the world's poor live in the tropics, where the effects of climate change are expected to be particularly severe. Warming may cut the growing season and reduce crop yields. The intensity of tropical storms is also expected to increase, with devastating effects. Wealthy nations have the resources to respond to climate change: They can build levees to control flooding, move their populations and their industries, and open new land to cultivation. Poor nations simply do not have the means at their disposal to do such things. Where survival is precarious today, climate change is likely to precipitate disaster (Intergovernmental Panel on Climate Change 2007).

POLITICAL INSTABILITY

Political instability has had dire consequences for cultures worldwide. Although violent confrontations often occurred in traditional societies, and Western expansion was accompanied by great loss of life and culture, people in the past hundred years have unleashed more brutality on each other than at any time in earlier human history. Industrialized and wealthy societies are primarily responsible for this savagery, having created the trenches of World War I, the death camps of World War II, nuclear weapons, and the Gulag.

The era since the end of World War II has been particularly devastating for poor nations. In some, such as French Indochina (now Vietnam), World War II faded into wars of independence that persisted until the 1970s. In many cases, traditional people became involved in networks of warfare that drew them into competition between the great powers. Both the United States and the Soviet Union furnished guerrilla movements, impoverished governments, and rebel armies with vast amounts of weaponry.

Although the end of the Cold War brought relief to some poor nations as wars fueled by great power rivalries such as those in Namibia and El Salvador came to a rapid end, rivalries that had been muted by the Cold War reemerged in new violent forms in other nations. In many places, aid from the United States, the Soviet Union, and other nations supported strong, centralized, and frequently repressive governments. When the Cold War ended, this support diminished, and governments that relied on it often fell apart. Nations such as Yugoslavia, Somalia, Liberia, and Sudan disintegrated as different groups within them fought for wealth, power, and control.

The events in Central Africa, such as Rwanda, Burundi, and the Democratic Republic of the Congo, have been particularly brutal. By the early 2000s, much of Central Africa was engulfed in what Gerard Prunier called Africa's World War. By the late 2000s, this war was believed to have cost over 4 million lives (Prunier 2008), and no end is in sight.

The widespread increase in violence has led to increasing numbers of people fleeing their homes in search of new, safe places. People seeking to leave their home countries are defined in different ways and this affects their acceptance in countries they wish to move to. A **refugee** is a person outside their home country who is unwilling or unable to return to their homeland due to a well-founded fear of persecution based on race, religion, nationality, a particular social group membership or political opinion. The migration crises in the world today is based on both those migrating for better lives elsewhere and those claiming refugee status because of violent conflict in their home countries (Eakin 2015). Syria today is one of the most violent places in the world and the largest source of refugees today, though refugees also come from Afghanistan, Yemen and other places (Ignatieff 2015).

Refugees: People forcibly displaced from their homes by either conflict or persecution.

▌▌▌ Using Anthropology: Helping Refugees

One by-product of contemporary political conflicts, human rights violations, and genocides has been the forced migration of people seeking safety from the conflicts in their home countries. Today, some 60 million people are seeking refugee status after having to leave their homes, the largest number since World War II (Human Rights Watch 2016). Although we assume that wealthier industrialized nations are the most important refugee havens, in fact, 80 percent of refugees are sheltered in poorer countries, such as Pakistan and Iran. Germany is the industrialized nation with the highest refugee population, about 500,000 (Brothers 2011), and appears most willing to absorb the millions of migrants from the contemporary Syrian war, compared to other European countries and the United States.

Anthropologists are actively involved with helping and advocating for refugee populations, both in the United States and elsewhere. The film, *Well-Founded Fear*, made by anthropologists Michael Camerini and Shari Robertson, highlights the process by which refugees are granted political asylum in the United States if they can prove a "well-founded fear of persecution based on race, religion, nationality, membership in a particular social group, or political opinion." Any foreigner who comes to the United States may apply for political asylum. In 1998, immigration officers who make the decision to approve or deny political asylum applications approved 13,000 of the 41,000 applications they received.

Those seeking refugee status request asylum based on the one-child policy in China; the rule that women must be veiled in Algeria; the suppression of political dissent in Romania and Nigeria; the oppression of gays in many countries; and forced female genital mutilation in West Africa. Iraqis are one of the newest refugee populations in the United States, driven here by the violence resulting from the U.S. invasion of Iraq in March 2003. Unlike the 900,000 Vietnamese refugees accepted in the United States after the Vietnam War, as of 2012, the number of Iraqi refugees resettled in the United States was only 84,902 (U.S. Citizenship and Immigration Services 2013). This is a very tiny number compared with the almost 4 million who have become refugees in countries in the Middle East. Many Iraqi refugees have settled in Detroit, where RefugeeWorks, an organization launched by anthropologists, tries to improve their chances for employment.

Another refugee group accepted into the United States, in flight from the civil wars in Sudan, are approximately 25,000 Nuer; even with the creation of the new nation of South Sudan, politically motivated violence continues, creating a disastrous humanitarian crisis (Hutchison 1996; Shandy 2007). More than 60,000 Bhutanese of Nepali ancestry have also become refugees as a result of ethnic cleansing by the king of Bhutan in the 1990s (Bird 2012).

Anthropologist Catherine Besterman, who carried out ethnography in southern Somalia, now collaborates with and acts as an advocate for the more than 10,000 Somali refugees who have been relocated in Lewiston, Maine, as part of an American resettlement plan for 10,000 Somali between 2004 and 2006 (Hepner 2011). Besterman teaches at Colby College and designed collaborative projects between Somali refugees and her students, creating videos and digital sites where the Somali talk about their lives and their transition to the United States. Besterman and her students also collaborate in making presentations to dispel anti-Somali and anti-refugee bias in Maine and nationally.

Other anthropologists, like Carole McGranahan (2012a; 2012b; Good 2007) testify for asylum seekers in court. McGranahan, who worked in Nepal, provides expert testimony on the current political conditions in Nepal and the cultural aspects of political conflict, on behalf of Nepalis seeking refuge in the United States. Anthropologist Mike McGovern uses his ethnographic experience in West Africa to write for the public explaining that although it is true that some refugees construct fictional narratives to gain U.S. approval, this comes out of a true desperation to flee the dire poverty and systemic violence in their home countries (2011). And anthropologist Jason de Leon writes on the inhumane conditions forced on the thousands of migrants, mostly women and children, seeking refuge in the United States from the perpetual gang violence in Central America (2015). Advocating for refugees is one of the very important ways anthropology makes a difference in the lives of real people.

▌▌▌ MIGRATION

Migrant is an inclusive term, applied to any foreigner entering, residing in, or leaving a country for any reason. Widespread political, economic, and social instability combined with relatively inexpensive air travel and economic opportunity has led to a huge increase in international migration, particularly of people from poor nations. In 2015 almost 244 million people, about 3.3 percent of the world's population, lived outside of the countries of their birth (United Nations Population Fund n.d.). These migrants have enormous influence both on the countries they leave and on those where they settle.

When migrants leave, they often make their home communities poorer by depriving these areas of their skills and labor. High-skilled workers can earn many times their local wages through migration. It is difficult to convince people to remain in poor, unstable countries when the salaries paid for their skills may be 30 or more times higher in wealthy nations. This has led to a "brain drain" from poor nations to rich nations.

But migrants' home communities may gain as well: Migrants provide their communities of origin with connections to the rest of the world, creating a broad network of support for community members. These connections bring information, ideas, products, and, perhaps most importantly, money. In 2015, the World Bank estimated that migrants sent $581.6 billion to people in their home countries (see Figure 14.6). Of this sum, $430 billion was sent to poor countries. India alone received $69 billion (World Bank 2016d). In some nations, remittances from migrants constitute a substantial percentage of the national economy. For example, remittances account for 35 percent of the gross domestic product in Tajikistan, 25 percent in Lesotho, and 23 percent in Nepal (World Bank 2011). By comparison, the United States spent a total of

Figure 14.6 Migrant Remittance Graph: Top Remittance-Receiving Countries, 2009.

Source: World Bank 2011, p. 14.

$6.43 billion on humanitarian aid in 2015, and total US foreign aid of all kinds was about $34 billion and accounted for less than 1 percent of the U.S. government budget (Foreignassistance.gov).

Migrants may profoundly change the countries in which they arrive, increasing the cultural complexity of the places where they settle, sometimes challenging cultural norms and values, and providing a pool of inexpensive labor that creates large profits for businesses in wealthy countries and low prices for consumers. However, the availability of immigrant labor may also suppress wages in their host countries.

Illegal immigrants are particularly vulnerable to exploitation. Further, although people in host countries may create programs to attract migrants in times of economic prosperity, they frequently turn against migrants in hard economic times, as happened when the world economy faltered in 2008 and 2009 and is happening to some extent today. Undocumented immigrants are particularly vulnerable to exploitation and deportation, but some nations have offered payment to legal immigrants to return to their home countries. The contemporary anti-immigration trend is illustrated by the increase in xenophobia in both Europe and the United States, the success of right wing political parties, and calls in many nations for increasing restrictions on immigration.

BRINGING IT BACK HOME:
AMERICA AS A FOREIGN CULTURE

A central contribution of anthropology is developing an understanding of others, which increases our ability to reflect more deeply on our own culture. Thus, we began our text with the outsider's look at American culture in the classic article on The Nacirema (and see p. 2). With a similar goal, anthropologists Philip DeVita and James Armstrong introduce us to the responses of foreign anthropologists working in the United States, in their book, aptly called *Distant Mirrors: America as a Foreign Culture* (2016).

Perhaps because of their emphasis on individualism, Americans seem more reluctant than others to acknowledge the influence of culture on their behavior and values, believing these to be solely a matter of individual choice; indeed, many deny that there is an American culture (Cerroni-Long 2016). Outsiders see it differently. Although recognizing the diversity of the United States, foreigners appear to agree on many aspects of American culture. This consensus derives partly from contrasts between the United States and others' culture of origin, just as our perceptions of others' cultures are derived from our own. The pragmatism, optimism, self-reliance, and voluntarism of Americans are perhaps the most widely noted, and often praised, aspects of American culture, patterns that perhaps derived from our history as both a frontier and an immigrant society (Nanda 2016) (Figure 14.7).

American egalitarianism is also frequently noted, but some perceptive outsiders see subtle class differences: When the leader of the Russian Moiseyev Folk Dance Company came to the United States in the late 1950s, Sol Hurok, who organized the tour, asked the troupe's leader "What surprised you most on your American tour?" Moiseyev replied, "In America, the workers are fat and the millionaires are thin" (Robinson 1994:355). This relationship between social class and body size still largely holds true in the United States, in contrast not just to Russia but to many other cultures; in India, for example, obesity was traditionally viewed as a sign of affluence.

For Asian visitors, the independence of even American toddlers is an eye opener. One anthropologist from the Philippines was amazed that American children choose their own food when the family goes

Joan Young Gregg

Figure 14.7 Volunteering: It's the American way. Volunteers from many communities in New York City reached out to help the victims of Hurricane Sandy. Unlike Hurricane Katrina, the storm damage affected people from all social classes and drew volunteers from across the social spectrum.

out to eat in a restaurant (Ojeda 2016). A Portuguese anthropologist expressed shock at the independence of American youth: "Is it true," he asked, "that the great ambition of an 18-year-old youngster is to leave his parents' house?" Jay Sokolofsky, an American ethnographer working in a Mexican village, reports that his informants were both puzzled and repelled by the American custom of young children having their own room, with a door they can close (2015). A Russian visitor expressed the view that this American emphasis on freedom and autonomy "destroys families," and that Americans lack the "close . . . relationships that surround a Russian from birth." Unlike in Russia, he emphasized, "instead of spending their 50s and 60s [caring for their grandchildren] American women are busy with their own lives" (Barry 2012). And as we noted in Chapter 9, even very elderly Americans value their independence greatly. This often means living alone or in a residential institution, without children or other relatives nearby, a situation unheard of in many cultures.

Almost all early visitors from Europe noted the importance of both independence and conformity in American culture, a contradiction that remains central in American life today. On the one hand, the United States is hailed as a land of freedom of thought, speech, and expression; on the other hand, many Europeans see Americans as politically passive, lacking the activist orientation of their own countries. But this depends on where you come from: Chinese students in American colleges note that Chinese culture "teaches us to be good listeners, American values teach us to be a good speaker" (Levin 2010).

Seeing ourselves through the eyes of others helps moderate our ethnocentrism as an exceptionalist society. "Americans are very patriotic," one visiting anthropologist noted, but they also have "a . . . blinding conviction that their ways are much better than the ways of other people . . . they do not [try] to understand the ways of other peoples. . . ." (Mucha 2016).

Many foreigners express awe at the material abundance of even ordinary Americans, and the desire to improve one's economic status is a main attraction for many immigrants. As one Mexican migrant explains to her son, "I am going to the United States because you can make lots of money there." An El Salvadoran agrees, "If you work hard [in the United States], you can have anything you want" (Chong 2012). And a child from Sudan joining his father was amazed that "he has glass in his windows, a refrigerator, a telephone, running water and I sleep in a bed."

But some see a downside to this material abundance, claiming it results in a mania of consumerism, turning Americans into permanent adolescents concerned only about materialism and afraid of death and old age.

But for people from former Communist nations, with their inferior and scarce consumer goods, extreme consumerism is a positive aspect of American culture. One Albanian migrant considered that she achieved the American Dream when she married a plastic surgeon and acquired her own credit cards. "It's not like Communism," she remarks, "the shopping is better. The sex is worse" (Prose 2011).

Foreigners also frequently notice the friendliness and informality of Americans, especially in small towns. An Englishman writes that the first thing he ever heard about Americans was that they all carried guns but that when he actually had direct contact with this "ferocious sounding tribe," he found out they were quite friendly (Dyer 2010). A Polish anthropologist also notes how kind, helpful, and friendly Americans are: "When I make new acquaintances, including the dental hygienist, everyone calls me by my first name" (Mucha 2016). This practice also surprised a Japanese migrant who noted: "Only my mother calls me by my first name." In Japan, except for very close friends, you call people by their last name and add "san," a term of respect (Chong 2012).

American informality spurred an international incident when Gary Locke, the newly appointed American ambassador to China, was photographed carrying his own backpack and luggage while checking in at the airline counter for his flight to his new post and carried his own luggage at the Beijing airport (Wong 2011; LaFraniere 2011). Ambassador Locke's actions, surprised—and pleased—many ordinary Chinese people, but were considered a grave insult by the political elites in China, who often live secret and very privileged lives. American informality seems allied to another American behavior pattern many foreigners note, that of complete strangers telling them the most intimate details of their lives. And a Portuguese anthropologist finds it discomforting that American men at a urinal will chat with strangers—about the weather, football, or even politics (Ramos 2016).

Sometimes, foreigners notice what might seem trivial about American behavior, but in fact, may be based on deeper cultural patterns. A recent Congolese migrant expressed amazement that "in America, people stay with their dogs in the house! In my country you cannot see this," he said. But he was even more amazed that "in the winter I see dogs putting on clothes!" (Chong and Bass 2011). Is there a culture of pets in the United States? Does it have deeper meanings? Some outsiders think so: South African President Jacob Zuma recently commented about Westerners, saying that "people who loved dogs more than people had a lack of humanity" and that (black) South African dog owners were trying to "emulate whiteness."

YOU DECIDE:

1. Two important aspects of globalization are the increase of foreigners coming to America and the global spread of American culture. Discuss how these different aspects of globalization affect the idea of American culture as unique.
2. Giving examples, discuss how the responses of foreigners to the United States are shaped by the histories and cultures of the places they come from.
3. Why is it important for Americans to hear how foreigners respond to American culture? If you are a foreigner yourself, what were some of your responses to American culture?

CHAPTER SUMMARY

1. Describe the level of inequality in the world, and explain how it affects wealthy and poor nations differently. Although all nations suffer inequality and poverty, these problems are particularly acute in poor nations, and have a profound effect on many of the people that anthropologists have historically studied.
2. What is development, and what different approaches have been taken to implement it? Development is the idea of creating wealth in poor nations that are considered poor because they have undeveloped economies. In the 1950s and 1960s, modernization approaches to development dominated; by the 1970s, basic human needs approaches emerged. Since the 1980s, structural adjustment programs dominate, focused on enforcing free markets as the means of development.
3. What are multinational corporations (MNCs), and how are they related to poverty? Multinational corporations own business enterprises in more than one nation. They are able to seek the most profitable venues to produce and market goods regardless of national boundaries. Because of their huge annual budgets as well as their mobility, they have gained vast economic and political power. Their Western shareholders benefit most from multinational corporations.
4. What are the major trends and problems associated with urbanization? More than half of the world's population currently lives in cities, a number expected to double in the next 40 years. In the future, most of the world's largest cities will be in poor countries; providing services to poor people in these cities is beyond the financial capacity of many nations.

5. What are the major problems associated with overpopulation? Overpopulation is an important problem when the rate of economic growth does not keep up with rising populations. But the appropriate level of human population for any area is significantly a political question involving judgments about how best to distribute resources and the necessity for healthy environments.

6. How are problems of environmental pollution different in poor versus wealthy nations? Even though poor nations produce only a small percentage of the world's pollution, environments in poor nations frequently are more polluted than those in rich nations. Global warming negatively affects poor countries because many of these are located in ecologically fragile zones and they have limited financial resources to cope with environmental change.

7. What role does political instability play in globalization, and how is this related to migration and the search for asylum? Political instability, caused by wars of independence, the Cold War, and ethnic rivalries have destroyed cultures and societies, causing a huge increase in global migration and refugees seeking asylum.

8. How has migration changed the relationships between cultures? Very high levels of migration create enormous flows of information and money between nations. Migrants change both the societies they leave and those in which they settle, frequently enriching both. Migrants often face discrimination, alienation, and isolation in the societies where they settle.

KEY TERMS

Basic human needs approach
Gross national income (GNI)
Migrant
Modernization theory
Multinational corporation
 (MNC)

Neoliberalism
Refugee
Structural adjustment
Sweatshop
World Bank

GLOSSARY

Achieved status: A social position that a person chooses or achieves on his or her own.

Adaptation: A change in the biological structure or lifeways of an individual or population by which it becomes better fitted to survive and reproduce in its environment.

Agriculture: A form of food production in which fields are in permanent cultivation using plows, animals, and techniques of soil and water control.

Anime: Animation, as in the popular culture of Japan; usually refers to animation of manga, or comic book graphic art.

Animism: The notion that all objects, living and nonliving, are imbued with spirits.

Anthropological theory: A set of propositions about which aspects of culture are critical, how they should be studied, and what the goal of studying them should be.

Anthropology: The scientific and humanistic study of human beings encompassing the evolutionary history of humanity, physical variation among humans, the study of past societies, and the comparative study of current-day human societies and cultures.

Antistructure: The socially sanctioned use of behavior that radically violates social norms; frequently found in religious ritual.

Applied anthropology: The application of anthropological knowledge to the solution of human problems.

Archaeology: The subdiscipline of anthropology that focuses on the study of past cultures based primarily on their material remains.

Art: Forms of creative expression that are guided by aesthetic principles and involve imagination, skill, and style.

Artifacts (in communications studies): Communication by clothing, jewelry, tattoos, piercings, and other visible body modifications.

Ascribed status: A social position into which a person is born.

Authority: The ability to cause others to act based on characteristics such as honor, status, knowledge, ability, respect, or the holding of formal public office.

Balanced reciprocity: The giving and receiving of goods of nearly equal value with a clear obligation of a return gift within a specified time limit.

Band: A small group of people related by blood or marriage, who live together and are loosely associated with a territory in which they forage.

Basic human needs approach: Projects aimed at providing access to clean water, education, and health care for the poorest of the world's people.

Bhangra: A musical form originating in the folk music of Punjab in northern India and eastern Pakistan that is mixing with British pop music and reggae to become a popular form of world music.

Bilateral descent: Both maternal and paternal lines are used as a basis for reckoning descent.

Biological (or physical) anthropology: The subdiscipline of anthropology that focuses on the study of people from a biological perspective, primarily on aspects of humankind that are genetically inherited.

Bridewealth: Goods presented by the groom's kin to the bride's kin to legitimize a marriage (formerly called "bride-price").

Bureaucracy: Administrative hierarchy characterized by specialization of function and fixed rules.

Call system: The form of communication among nonhuman primates composed of a limited number of sounds that are tied to specific stimuli in the environment.

Capital: Productive resources that are used with the primary goal of increasing their owner's financial wealth.

Capitalism: An economic system in which people work for wages, land and capital goods are privately owned, and capital is invested for profit.

Cargo system: A ritual system, common in Central and South America, in which wealthy people are required to hold a series of costly ceremonial offices.

Caste system: Social stratification based on birth in which social mobility between castes is not possible.

Chiefdom: A society with social ranking in which political integration is achieved through an office of centralized leadership called the chief.

Chronemics: The study of the different ways that cultures understand time and use it to communicate.

Class system: A form of social stratification in which the different strata form a continuum and social mobility is possible.

Class: A category of people who all have about the same opportunity to obtain economic resources, power, and prestige and who are ranked relative to other categories.

Code-switching: Moving seamlessly and appropriately between two different languages.

Cognitive anthropology: A theoretical position in anthropology that focuses on the relationship between the mind and society.

Collaborative ethnography: Anthropological work that gives priority to desires and interests of cultural consultants on the topic, methodology, and written results of fieldwork.

Colonialism: The active possession of a foreign territory and the maintenance of political domination over that territory.

Colony: A foreign territory under the immediate political control of a nation-state.

Communitas: A state of perceived solidarity, equality, and unity among people sharing a religious ritual, often characterized by intense emotion.

Comparative linguistics: The science of documenting the relationships between languages and grouping them into language families.

Composite (compound) family: An aggregate of nuclear families linked by a common spouse.

Conflict theory: A perspective on social stratification that focuses on economic inequality as a source of conflict and change.

Consanguinity: Blood ties between people.

Consultant/informant/interlocutor/ respondent/partner: A person from whom anthropologists gather data.

Contagious magic: The belief that things once in contact with a person or object retain an invisible connection with that person or object.

Conventionality: The notion that, in human language, words are only arbitrarily or conventionally connected to the things for which they stand.

Corvée labor: Unpaid labor required by a governing authority.

Cosmology: A system of beliefs that deals with fundamental questions in the religious and social order.

Cross-cousin marriage: Marriage between an individual and the child of his or her mother's brother or father's sister.

Cultural anthropology: The study of human thought, behavior, and lifeways that are learned rather than genetically transmitted and that are typical of groups of people.

Cultural construction of gender: The idea that gender characteristics are the result of historical, economic, and political forces acting within each culture.

Cultural ecology: A theoretical position in anthropology that focuses on the adaptive dimensions of culture.

Cultural relativism: The idea that cultures should be analyzed with reference to their own histories and values rather than according to the values of another culture.

Culture and personality: A theoretical position in anthropology that held that cultures could best be understood by examining the patterns of child rearing and considering their effect on social institutions and adult lives.

Culture shock: Feelings of alienation and helplessness that result from rapid immersion in a new and different culture.

Culture: The learned behaviors and symbols that allow people to live in groups; the primary means by which humans adapt to their environment; the ways of life characteristic of a particular human society.

Descent group: A group of kin who are descendants of a common ancestor, extending beyond two generations.

Descent: The culturally established affiliation between a child and one or both parents.

Diffusion: The spread of cultural elements from one society to another.

Displacement: The capacity of all human languages to describe things not happening in the present.

Divination: A religious ritual performed to find hidden objects or information.

Division of labor: The pattern of apportioning different tasks to different members of a society.

Dominant culture: The culture with the greatest wealth and power in a society that consists of many subcultures.

Double descent: The tracing of descent through both matrilineal and patrilineal links, each of which is used for different purposes.

Dowry: Presentation of goods by the bride's kin to the family of the groom or to the couple.

Dutch East India Company (VOC): A joint stock company chartered by the Dutch government to control all Dutch trade in the Indian and Pacific oceans. Also known by its Dutch initials VOC for Verenigde Oostendische Compagnie.

Ecological functionalism: A theoretical position in anthropology that focuses on the relationship between environment and society.

Economic system: The norms governing production, distribution, and consumption of goods and services within a society.

Economics: The study of the ways in which the choices people make combine to determine how their society uses its scarce resources to produce and distribute goods and services.

Efficiency (in food production): Yield per person per hour of labor invested.

Egalitarian society: A society in which no individual or group has more privileged access to resources, power, or prestige than any other.

Elites: The social strata that has differential access to all culturally valued resources, whether power, wealth, or prestige, and possessively protects its control over these resources.

Emic: Examination of societies using concepts, categories, and distinctions that are meaningful to members of those societies.

Enculturation: The process of learning to be a member of a particular group.

Endogamy: A rule prescribing that a person must marry within a particular group.

Ethnicity: Perceived differences in culture, national origin, and historical experience by which groups of people are distinguished from others in the same social environment.

Ethnocentrism (ethnocentric): Judging other cultures from the perspective of one's own culture. The notion that one's own culture is more beautiful, rational, and nearer to perfection than any other.

Ethnocentrism: Judging other cultures from the perspective on one's own culture. The notion that one's own culture is more beautiful, rational, and nearer to perfection than any other.

Ethnography: The major research tool of cultural anthropology, including both fieldwork among people in a society and the written results of such fieldwork.

Ethnology: The attempt to find general principles or laws that govern cultural phenomena through the comparison of cultures.

Ethnoscience: A theoretical position in anthropology that focuses on recording and examining the ways in which members of a culture use language to classify and organize their cognitive world.

Etic: Examination of societies using concepts, categories, and rules derived from science; an outsider's perspective.

Exogamy: A rule specifying that a person must marry outside a particular group.

Extended family: Family based on blood relations extending over three or more generations.

Factions: informal alliances within well-defined political units such as lineages, villages, or organizations.

Firm: An institution composed of kin and/or nonkin that is organized primarily for financial gain.

Foraging (hunting and gathering): Fishing, hunting, and collecting vegetable foods.

Functionalism: A theoretical position in anthropology that focuses on finding general laws that identify different elements of society, showing how they relate to each other, and demonstrating their role in maintaining social order.

Fundamentalism: A proclamation of reclaimed authority over a sacred tradition that is to be reinstated as an antidote for a society that is believed to have strayed from its cultural moorings.

Gender ideology: The totality of ideas about sex, gender, the natures of men and women, including their sexuality, and the relations between the genders.

Gender role: The cultural expectations of men and women in a particular society, including the division of labor.

Gender stratification: The ways in which gendered activities and attributes are differentially valued and related to the distribution of resources, prestige, and power in a society.

Gender: A cultural construction that makes biological and physical differences into socially meaningful categories.

Generalized reciprocity: Giving and receiving goods with no immediate or specific return expected.

Globalization: The integration of resources, labor, and capital into a global network.

God (deity): A named spirit who is believed to have created or to have control of some aspect of the world.

Government: An interrelated set of status roles that become separate from other aspects of social organization, such as kinship, in exercising control over a population.

Great vowel shift: A change in the pronunciation of English language that took place between 1400 and 1600.

Gross national income (GNI): The total value of all goods and services produced in a country.

Haptics: The analysis and study of touch.

Heeren XVII: The Lords Seventeen, members of the board of directors of the Dutch East India Company.

Hegemony: The dominance of a political elite based on a close identification between their own goals and those of the larger society.

Hijra: An alternative gender role in India conceptualized as neither man nor woman.

Historical particularism: A theoretical position in anthropology associated with American anthropologists of the early 20th century that focuses on providing objective descriptions of cultures within their historical and environmental contexts.

Holism (holistic): In anthropology, an approach that considers the study of culture, history, language, and biology essential to a complete understanding of human society.

Horticulture: Production of plants using a simple, nonmechanized technology and where the fertility of gardens and fields is maintained through long periods of fallow.

Household: A group of people united by kinship or other links who share a residence and organize production, consumption, and distribution among themselves.

Human Relations Area Files (HRAF): An ethnographic database that includes cultural descriptions of more than 300 societies.

Imitative magic: The belief that imitating an action in a religious ritual will cause the action to happen in the material world.

Incest taboo: A prohibition on sexual relations between relatives.

Indigenous people: Small-scale societies designated as bands, tribes, or chiefdoms that occupied their land prior to European contact.

Industrialism: The process of the mechanization of production.

Informant: See *Consultant*.

Innovation: An object or way of thinking that is based upon but is qualitatively different from existing forms.

Interpretive anthropology: A theoretical position in anthropology that focuses on using humanistic methods, such as those found in the analysis of literature, to analyze cultures and discover the meanings of culture to its participants.

Joint stock company: A firm that is managed by a centralized board of directors but is owned by shareholders.

Kin group: a group of people who understand themselves to be related by either blood or marriage.

Kinesics: The study of body position, movement, facial expressions, and gaze.

Kinship system: The totality of kin relations, kin groups, and terms for classifying kin in a society.

Kinship: A culturally defined relationship established on the basis of blood ties or through marriage.

Kula ring: A pattern of exchange among trading partners in the South Pacific Islands.

Law: A means of social control and dispute management through the systematic application of force by a politically constituted authority.

Leadership: The ability to direct an enterprise or action.

Leveling mechanism: A practice, value, or form of social organization that evens out wealth within a society.

Levirate: The custom whereby a man marries the widow of a deceased brother.

Lexicon: The total stock of words in a language.

Liminal: The stage of a ritual, particularly a rite of passage, in which one has passed out of an old status but has not yet entered a new one.

Lineage: A group of kin whose members trace descent from a known common ancestor.

Lineal kin: Blood relations linked through descent, such as Ego, Ego's mother, Ego's grandmother, and Ego's daughter.

Linguistic anthropology: The study of language and its relation to culture.

Magic: A religious ritual believed to produce a mechanical effect by supernatural means.

Mana: Religious power or energy that is concentrated in individuals or objects.

Manga: Japanese comic book art.

Market exchange: An economic system in which goods and services are bought and sold at a money price determined primarily by the forces of supply and demand.

Marriage: The customs, rules, and obligations that establish a special relationship between sexually cohabiting adults, between them and any children they take responsibility for, and between the kin of the married couple.

Matrilineage: A lineage formed by descent in the female line.

Matrilineal descent: A rule that affiliates a person to kin of both sexes related through females only.

Mediation: A form of managing disputes that uses the offices of a third party to achieve voluntary agreement between the disputing parties.

Messianic: Focusing on the coming of an individual who will usher in a utopian world.

Migrant: A broad inclusive term that can describe any foreigner entering, residing in, or leaving a country for any reason.

Millenarian: Belief that a coming catastrophe will signal the beginning of a new age and the eventual establishment of paradise.

Modernization theory: A model of development that predicts that nonindustrial societies will move in the social and technological direction of industrialized nations.

Monoculture plantation: An agricultural plantation specializing in the large-scale production of a single crop to be sold on the market.

Monogamy: A rule that permits a person to be married to only one spouse at a time.

Monotheism: Belief in a single god.

Morpheme: The smallest unit of language that has a meaning.

Morphology: A system for creating words from sounds.

Multinational corporation (MNC): A corporation that owns business enterprises or plants in more than one nation.

Nation-state: A sovereign, geographically based state that identifies itself as having a distinctive national culture and historical experience.

Negative reciprocity: Exchange conducted for the purpose of material advantage or the desire to get something for nothing.

Neoliberalism: Political and economic policies that promote free trade, individual initiative, and minimal government regulation of the economy, and oppose state control or subsidy to industries and all but minimal aid to impoverished individuals.

Nomadic pastoralism: A form of pastoralism in which the whole social group (men, women, children) and their animals move in search of pasture.

Norms: Shared ideas about the way things ought to be done; rules of behavior that reflect and enforce culture.

Nuclear families: Organized around the relationship between husband and wife (conjugal tie).

Organic analogy: The comparison of cultures to living organisms.

Orientalism: Scholarship and art generated by Europeans, representing their views of the Middle East.

Parallel-cousin marriage: Marriage between the children of a parent's same-sex siblings (mother's sister or father's brother).

Participant observation: The fieldwork technique that involves gathering cultural data by observing people's behavior and participating in their lives.

Partner: See *Consultant*.

Pastoralism: A food-getting strategy that depends on the care of domesticated herd animals.

Patriarchy: A male-dominated society in which most important public and private power is held by men.

Patrilineage: A lineage formed by descent in the male line.

Patrilineal descent: A rule that affiliates a person to kin of both sexes related through males only.

Peasants: Rural cultivators who produce for the subsistence of their households but are also integrated into larger, complex state societies.

Phone: Smallest identifiable unit of sound made by humans and used in any language.

Phoneme: The smallest unit of sound that serves to distinguish between meanings of words within a language.

Phonology: The sound system of a language.

Pillage: To strip an area of money, goods, or raw materials through the threat or use of physical violence.

Plasticity (in anthropology): The ability of humans to change their behavior in response to a wide range of environmental and social demands.

Political ideology: The shared beliefs and values that legitimize the distribution and use of power in a particular society.

Political organization: The patterned ways in which power is legitimately used in a society to regulate behavior, maintain social order, make collective decisions, and deal with social disorder.

Polyandry: A rule permitting a woman to have more than one husband at a time.

Polygamy: A rule allowing more than one spouse.

Polygyny: A rule permitting a man to have more than one wife at a time.

Polytheism: Belief in many gods.

Population density: The number of people inhabiting a unit of land (usually given as people per square mile or kilometer).

Postmodernism: A theoretical position in anthropology that focuses on issues of power and voice. Postmodernists hold that anthropological accounts are partial truths reflecting the backgrounds, training, and social positions of their authors.

Potlatch: A form of redistribution involving competitive feasting practiced among Northwest Coast Native Americans.

Power: The ability to impose one's will on others.

Prayer: Any conversation held with spirits and gods in which people petition, invoke, praise, give thanks, dedicate, supplicate, intercede, confess, repent, and bless.

Prestige: Social honor or respect.

Priest: One who is formally elected, appointed, or hired to a full-time religious office.

Private/public dichotomy: A gender system in which women's status is lowered by their almost exclusive cultural identification with the home and children, whereas men are identified with public, prestigious, economic, and political roles.

Productive resources: Material goods, natural resources, or information used to create other goods or information.

Productivity (food production): Yield per person per unit of land.

Productivity (linguistics): The idea that humans can combine words and sounds into new, meaningful utterances they have never before heard.

Proxemics: The study of the cultural use of interpersonal space.

Race: A culturally constructed category based on *perceived* physical differences.

Racism: The belief that some human populations are superior to others because of inherited, genetically transmitted characteristics.

Rank society: A society characterized by institutionalized differences in prestige but no important restrictions on access to basic resources.

Rebellion: The attempt of a group within society to force a redistribution of resources and power.

Reciprocity: A mutual give-and-take among people of equal status.

Redistribution: Exchange in which goods are collected and then distributed to members of a group.

Refugees: People forcibly displaced from their homes by either conflict or persecution.

Religion: A social institution characterized by sacred stories, symbols, and symbolism; the proposed existence of immeasurable beings, powers, states, places, and qualities; rituals and means of addressing the supernatural; specific practitioners; and change.

Respondents: See *Consultant*.

Revolution: An attempt to overthrow an existing form of political organization and put another type of political structure in its place.

Rite of intensification: A ritual structured to reinforce the values and norms of a community and to strengthen group identity.

Rite of passage: A ritual that moves an individual from one social status to another.

Ritual: A ceremonial act or repeated stylized gestures used for specific occasions involving the use of religious symbols.

Sacred narratives (myths): Stories of historical events, heroes, gods, spirits, and creation that members of a religious tradition hold to be holy and true.

Sacrifice: An offering made to increase the efficacy of a prayer or the religious purity of an individual.

Sapir–Whorf hypothesis: The hypothesis that perceptions and understandings of time, space, and matter are conditioned by the structure of a language.

Sedentary: Settled, living in one place.

Semantics: The subsystem of a language that relates words to meaning.

Sex: The biological difference between male and female.

Shaman: An individual socially recognized as being able to mediate between the world of humanity and the world of gods or spirits but who is not a recognized official of any religious organization.

Social differentiation: The relative access individuals and groups have to basic material resources, wealth, power, and prestige.

Social mobility: Movement from one social stratum to another.

Social stratification: A social hierarchy resulting from the relatively permanent unequal distribution of goods and services in a society.

Society: A group of people who depend on one another for survival or well-being as well as the relationships among such people, including their statuses and roles.

Sociolinguistics: The study of the relationship between language and culture and the ways language is used in varying social contexts.

Sororate: The custom whereby, when a man's wife dies, her sister is given to him as a wife.

State: A hierarchical, centralized form of political organization in which a central government has a legal monopoly over the use of force.

Stratified society: A society characterized by formal, permanent social and economic inequality in which some people are denied access to basic resources.

Structural adjustment: A development policy promoted by Western nations, particularly the United States, that requires poor nations to pursue free-market reforms in order to get new loans from the International Monetary Fund and World Bank.

Subculture: A group within a society that shares norms and values significantly different from those of the dominant culture.

Subsistence strategies: The pattern of behavior used by a society to obtain food in a particular environment.

Sweatshop: Generally, a pejorative term for a factory with working conditions that may include low wages, long hours, inadequate ventilation, and physical, mental, or sexual abuse.

Swidden (slash and burn) cultivation: A form of cultivation in which a field is cleared by felling trees and burning the brush.

Symbol: Something that stands for something else. Central to language and culture.

Symbolic anthropology: A theoretical position in anthropology that focuses on understanding cultures by discovering and analyzing the symbols that are most important to their members.

Syncretism: The merging of elements of two or more religious traditions to produce a new religion.

Syntax: A system of rules for combining words into meaningful sentences.

Tirailleurs Senegalais: Senegalese riflemen. An army that existed from 1857 to 1960, composed largely of soldiers from French African colonies led by officers from metropolitan France.

Totem: An object, an animal species, or a feature of the natural world that is associated with a particular descent group.

Transgenderism: Transgenderism includes a wide range of individuals who identify with gender roles different from that of their biological sex at birth. It incorporates both transsexuals and those who have not had sex-reassignment surgery.

Transhumant pastoralism: A form of pastoralism in which herd animals are moved regularly throughout the year to different areas as pasture becomes available.

Tribe: A culturally distinct population whose members consider themselves to have descended from the same ancestor.

Unilineal descent: Descent group membership based on links through either the maternal or the paternal line, but not both.

Universal grammar: A basic set of principles, conditions, and rules that form the foundation of all languages.

Values: Shared ideas about what is true, right, and beautiful.

War (warfare): A formally organized and culturally recognized pattern of collective violence directed toward other societies or between segments within a larger society.

Wealth: The accumulation of material resources or access to the means of producing these resources.

Witchcraft: The ability to harm others by harboring malevolent thoughts about them; the practice of sorcery.

World art: The contemporary visual arts and cultural performances of non-Western peoples.

World Bank: The International Bank for Reconstruction and Development, an international agency that provides technical assistance and loans to promote international trade and economic development, especially to poor nations. The World Bank has often been criticized for interfering in the affairs of these nations.

World music: World music incorporates different musical styles from cultures throughout the world.

REFERENCES

ABC News Point. 2015. "Top 10 List of Largest Cities in the World." Available at http://www.abcnewspoint.com/top-10-list-of-largest-cities-in-the-world, accessed August 11, 2016.

Abdo, Geneive. 2006. *Mecca and Main Street: Muslim Life in America after 9/11.* New York: Oxford University Press.

Abrahams, Roger D. 1970. *Deep Down in the Jungle.* Chicago: Aldine.

Adam, Nigel. 2007. "Lost Tribe Happy in Modern World." *Herald Sun,* February 3. Available at http://www.heraldsun.com.au/archive/news/lost-tribe-happy-in-modern-world/story-e6frf7l6-1111112932308, accessed July 14, 2016.

Adam, Karla. 2011. "Occupy Wall Street Protests Go Global." *Washington Post,* October 15.

Adams, Kathleen M. 1990. "Cultural Commoditization in Tana Toraja, Indonesia." *Cultural Survival Quarterly* 40(1):31–34.

Adams, Kathleen M. 1995. "Making-Up the Toraja? The Appropriation of Tourism, Anthropology, and Museums for Politics in Upland Sulawesi, Indonesia." *Ethnology* 34:143–152.

Adams, Kathleen M. 2006. *Art as Politics: Re-Crafting Identities, Tourism, and Power in Tana Toraja, Indonesia.* Honolulu: University of Hawai'i Press.

Adetunji, Jimoh I. 2006. "Nigeria: An End to Gas Flaring." *E Magazine: The Environmental Magazine* 17(4):38–39.

Agha, Hussein, and Robert Malley. "This Is Not a Revolution." *New York Review of Books,* November 8, 2012, pp. 42, 71.

Ahmed, Azam. 2016. "Step by Step on a Desperate Trek by Migrants Through Mexico." *New York Times,* February 8. Available at http://www.nytimes.com/2016/02/08/world/americas/mexico-migrants-central-america.html?_r=0, accessed July 18, 2016.

Aker, Jenny C., and Isaac M. Mbiti. 2010. "Mobile Phones and Economic Development in Africa." *Journal of Economic Perspectives* 24(3):207–232.

Alexander, Michelle. 2010. *The New Jim Crow: Mass Incarceration in the Age of Color Blindness.* New York: New York Press.

Alexeyeff, Kalissa, and Niko Besnier. 2013. "Gender on the Edge: Identities, Politics, Transformations." In Kalissa Alexeyeff and Niko Besnier (eds.), *Gender on the Edge: Transgender, Gay, and Other Pacific Islanders.* Honolulu: University of Hawai'i Press.

Ali, Hirsi Ayaan. 2006. *The Caged Virgin: An Emancipation Proclamation for Women and Islam.* New York: Free Press.

Allitt, Patrick N. 2002. *Victorian Britain.* Chantilly, VA: Teaching Co.

Alloula, Malek. 1986. *The Colonial Harem* (Myrna Godzich and Wlad Godzich, trans.). Minneapolis: University of Minnesota Press.

Almond, Gabriel, Emmanuel Sivan, and R. Scott Appleby. 1995. "Fundamentalism: Genus and Species." In E. Marty and R. Scott Appleby (eds.), *Fundamentalisms Comprehended* (pp. 399–424). Chicago: University of Chicago Press.

Alonso, Ana Maria. 1994. "The Politics of Space, Time and Substance: State Formation, Nationalism, and Ethnicity." In B. Siegel (ed.), *Annual Review of Anthropology* (vol. 23, pp. 379–405). Stanford, CA: Stanford University Press.

American Anthropological Association. 2007. *American Anthropological Association Executive Board Statement on the Human Terrain System Project.* Available at www.aaanet.org/about/Policies/statements/Human-Terrain-System-Statement.cfm.

American Anthropological Association *Code of Ethics* (2009). Available at http://s3.amazonaws.com/rdcms-aaa/files/production/public/FileDownloads/pdfs/issues/policy-advocacy/upload/AAA-Ethics-Code-2009.pdf.

Ammon, Paul R., and Mary S. Ammon. 1971. "Effects of Training Black Preschool Children in Vocabulary versus Sentence Construction." *Journal of Educational Psychology* 62(5):421–426.

Anagnost, Ana. 1989. "Transformations of Gender in Modern China." In S. Morgen (ed.), *Gender in Anthropology: Critical Reviews for Research and Teaching* (pp. 313–342). Washington DC: American Anthropological Association.

Anders, George. 2015. "That 'Useless' Liberal Arts Degree Has Become Tech's Hottest Ticket." *Forbes,* August 17. Available at http://www.forbes.com/sites/georgeanders/2015/07/29/liberal-arts-degree-tech/3/#59d0e8e86148, accessed April 21, 2016.

Anderson, Benedict. 1991. *Imagined Communities: Reflections on the Origin and Spread of Nationalism.* New York: Verso.

Anderson, Elijah. 1999. *Code of the Streets.* New York: Norton.

Archibold, Randal C. 2006. "Border Fence Must Skirt Objections from Arizona Tribe." *New York Times,* September 20, p. A24.

Artz, G., P. Orazem, and D. Otto. 2007. "Measuring the Impact of Meat Packing and Processing Facilities in the Nonmetropolitan Midwest: A Difference-in-Differences Approach." *American Journal of Agricultural Economics* 89(3):557–570.

Babcock, Barbara. 1995. "Marketing Maria: The Tribal Artist in the Age of Mechanical Reproduction." In Brenda Jo Bright and Liza Bakewell (eds.), *Looking High and Low: Art and Cultural Identity* (pp. 125–150). Tucson: University of Arizona Press.

Bacon, David. 2014. "Beyond Boundaries." *American Civil Liberties Union,* Summer, p. 21.

Badenhausen, Kurt. 2016. "LeBron James Tops The NBA's Highest-Paid Players 2016." *Forbes.* Available at http://www.forbes.com/sites /kurtbadenhausen/2016/01/20 /lebron-james-tops-the-nbas-highest -paid-players-2016/#285364d3486a, accessed April 21, 2016.

Baer, Drake. 2014. "Here's Why Companies Are Desperate to Hire Anthropologists." *Business Insider,* March 27. Available at http://www.businessinsider .com/heres-why-companies -aredesperateto-hireanthropologists- 2014-3, accessed April, 21, 2016.

Bagchi, Amiya Kumar. 2002. "The Other Side of Foreign Investment by Imperial Powers: Transfer of Surplus from Colonies." *Economic and Political Weekly* 37(23):2229–2238.

Bailey, Stanley. 2009. *Legacies of Race: Identities, Attitudes, and Politics in Brazil.* Stanford, CA: Stanford University Press.

Bailey, Stanley R., and Edward E. Telles. 2006. "Multiracial versus Collective Black Categories: Examining Census Classification Debates in Brazil." *Ethnicities* 6(1):74–101.

Baker, Lee D. 2000. "The First Measured Century." Hosted by Ben Wattenberg. PBS, July 19.

Baker, Lee D. 2007. "Columbia University's Franz Boas: He Led the Undoing of Scientific Racism." *Journal of Blacks in Higher Education* 22:89–96.

Balikci, Asen. 1970. *The Netsilik Eskimo.* Prospect Heights, IL: Waveland.

Balter, Michael. 2010. "Anthropologist Brings Worlds Together." *Science* 329:743–745.

Balter, Michael. 2013. "Timbucktu Manuscripts Apparently Escaped Burning." *ScienceInsider,* January 30. Available at http://news.sciencemag.org /scienceinsider/2013/01/timbuktu -manuscripts-apparently-.html, accessed April 23, 2013.

Banks, Ralph Richard. 2011. *Is Marriage for White People: How the African American Marriage Decline Affects Everyone.* New York: Dutton.

Barfield, Thomas J. 1993. *The Nomadic Alternative.* Englewood Cliffs, NJ: Prentice Hall.

Barker, Randolph, Robert W. Herdt, and Beth Rose. 1985. *The Rice Economy of Asia.* Washington DC: Resources for the Future.

Barlow, Tom. 2011. "The Most Extravagant Weddings." *Forbes.com.* Available at www.forbes.com/2011/04/06 /kate-middleton-prince-william-royal -weddings.html, accessed April 23, 2013.

Barnes-Dean, Virginia Lee. 1989. "Clitoridectomy and Infibulation." *Cultural Survival Quarterly* 9(2):26–30.

Barnett, Homer. 1953. *Innovation: The Basis of Cultural Change.* New York: McGraw-Hill.

Barry, Ellen. 2012. "Moscow Journal: A Hunger for Tales of Life in the American Cul-de-Sac." *New York Times,* December 11, p. A12.

Barry, Ellen. 2016. "Battling Tradition with Defiance." *New York Times,* January 31, p. 1A.

Barth, Fredrik. 1998/1969. *Ethnic Groups and Boundaries: The Social Organization of Culture Difference.* Prospect Heights, IL: Waveland.

Bassani, Ezio, and William Fagg. 1988. *Africa and the Renaissance: Art in Ivory.* New York: Center for African Art.

Basso, Keith. 1979. *Portraits of "The Whitemen."* New York: Cambridge University Press.

Basson, Lauren L. 2008. *White Enough to Be an American? Race Mixing, Indigenous People, and the Boundaries of State and Nation.* Chapel Hill: University of North Carolina Press.

Baumann, Timothy, Andrew Hurley, Valerie Altizer, and Victoria Love. 2011. "Interpreting Uncomfortable History at the Scott Joplin House State Historic Site in St. Louis, Missouri." *Public Historian* 33(2):37–66.

Bayoumi, Moustafa. 2012. "Fear and Loathing of Islam." *The Nation,* July 2–9.

BBC. 2015. "China Pollution: First Ever Red Alert in Effect in Beijing." *BBC.* December 8. Available at http://www .bbc.com/news/world-asia-china -35026363, accessed July 14, 2016.

Behar, Ruth, and Deborah A. Gordon. 1995. *Women Writing Culture.* Berkeley: University of California Press.

Behringer, Wolfgang. 2004. *Witches and Witch Hunts: A Global History.* Cambridge, MA: Polity.

Bell, Genevieve. 2016. "Genevieve Bell." *LinkedIn.* Available at https://www .linkedin.com/in/genevievebell, accessed April 21, 2016.

Bell, Michelle L., and Keita Ebisu. 2012. "Environmental Inequality in Exposures to Airborne Particulate Matter Components in the United States." *Environmental Health Perspectives* 120:1699–1704.

Bellah, Robert N., Richard Madsen, William M. Sullivan, Ann Swidler, and Steven M. Tipton. 1985. *Habits of the Heart: Individualism and Commitment in American Life.* Berkeley: University of California Press.

Bennett, Andrew. 1997. "Bhangra in Newcastle: Music, Ethnic Identity and the Role of Local Knowledge." *Innovation: The European Journal of Social Sciences* 10(1):107–117.

Benzaquén, Adriana S. 2006. *Encounters with Wild Children: Temptation and Disappointment in the Study of Human Nature.* Montreal: McGill-Queen's University Press.

Berdan, Frances F. 1982. *The Aztecs of Central Mexico: An Imperial Society.* New York: Holt, Rinehart, and Winston.

Bereiter, Carl, and Siegfried Engelmann. 1966. *Teaching Disadvantaged Children in Preschool.* Englewood Cliffs, NJ: Prentice Hall.

Berezovikova, I. P., and F. R. Mamleeva. 2001. "Traditional Foods in the Diet of Chukota Natives." *International Journal of Circumpolar Health* 60(2):138–142.

Berlo, Janet C. (ed.). 1996. *Plains Indian Drawings, 1865–1935: Pages from a Visual History.* New York: Abrams.

Berreman, Gerald D. 1988. "Race, Caste, and Other Invidious Distinctions in Social Stratification." In J. Cole (ed.), *Anthropology for the Nineties: Introductory Readings* (pp. 485–518). New York: Free Press.

Besnier, Niko. 1996. "Polynesian Gender Liminality through Time and Space." In G. Herdt (ed.), *Third Sex, Third Gender: Beyond Sexual Dimorphism in Culture and History* (pp. 285–328). New York: Zone.

Besnier, Niko. 2009. *Gossip and the Everyday Production of Politics.* Honolulu: University of Hawai'i Press.

Besnier, Niko 2011. *On the Edge of the Global: Modern Anxieties in a Pacific Island Nation.* Stanford, CA: Stanford University Press.

Besnier, Niko. 2012. "The Athlete's Body and the Global Condition: Tongan Rugby Players in Japan." *American Ethnologist* 39(3):491–510.

Bickerton, Derek. 1998. "Catastrophic Evolution: The Case for a Single Step from Protolanguage to Full Human Language." In James Hurford, M. Studdert-Kennedy, and C. Knight (eds.), *The Evolutionary Emergence of Language: Social Function and the Origins of Linguistic Form* (pp. 341–358). Cambridge, UK: Cambridge University Press.

Bill and Melinda Gates Foundation. n.d. "Who We Are, Foundation Fact Sheet." Available at www .gatesfoundation.org/Who -We-Are/General-Information /Foundation-Factsheet.

Bitterli, Urs. 1986. *Cultures in Conflict: Encounters between European and Non-European Cultures, 1432–1800.* Stanford, CA: Stanford University Press.

Bittman, Mark. 2008. "The Meat of the Matter." *Dallas Morning News*, February 10, 2008.

Blackwood, Evelyn. 1998. *Female Desires: Same-Sex Relations and Transgender Practices across Cultures.* New York: Columbia University Press.

Blumberg, Paul. 1980. *Inequality in an Age of Decline.* New York: Oxford University Press.

Blumenfield, Tami. 2004. "Walking Marriages." *Anthropology Newsletter* 45(5).

Bodley, John H. 1999. *Victims of Progress* (4th ed.). Mountain View, CA: Mayfield.

Bodley, John H. 2000. *Cultural Anthropology: Tribes, States, and the Global System* (3rd ed.). Mountain View, CA: Mayfield.

Boellstorff, Tom. 2004. "Playing Back the Nation: *Waria,* Indonesian Transvestites." *Cultural Anthropology* 19:159–195.

Bolin, Anne, and Patricia Whelehan (eds.). 2015. *International Encyclopedia of Human Sexuality.* West Sussex, UK: Wiley/Blackwell.

Boo, Katherine. 2012 *Behind the Beautiful Forevers: Life, Death, and Hope in a Mumbai Undercity.* New York: Random House.

Borgerhoff Mulder, Monique. 1995. "Bridewealth and Its Correlates: Quantifying Changes over Time." *Current Anthropology* 36:573–603.

Borofsky, Robert. 1994. "On the Knowledge and Knowing of Cultural Activities." In R. Borofsky (ed.), *Assessing Cultural Anthropology* (pp. 331–347). New York: McGraw-Hill.

Borofsky, Robert. 2005. *Yanomami: The Fierce Controversy and What We Might Learn From It.* Berkeley: University of California.

Bourgois, Philippe, and Jeff Schonberg. 2009. *Righteous Dopefiend.* Berkeley: University of California Press.

Bowen, John Richard. 2007. *Why the French Don't Like Headscarves: Islam, the State, and Public Space.* Princeton, NJ: Princeton University Press.

Boxer, C. R. 1965. *The Dutch Seaborne Empire 1600–1800.* New York: Knopf.

Boyd-Bowman, Peter. 1975. "A Sample of Sixteenth Century 'Caribbean' Spanish Phonology." In William Milan, John Staczek, and Juan Zamora (eds.), *1974 Colloquium on Spanish and Portuguese Linguistics* (pp. 1–11). Washington, DC: Georgetown University Press.

Bracken, Christopher. 1997. *The Potlatch Papers: A Colonial Case History.* Chicago: University of Chicago Press.

Brandt, Deborah. 2008. *Tangled Routes: Women, Work, and Globalization on the Tomato Trail* (2nd ed.). Lanham, MD: Rowman and Littlefield.

Bremner, Brian. 2006. "What's It Going to Cost to Clean Up China?" *Business Week.* Available at www.businessweek .com/stories/2006-09-26/whats-it -going-to-cost-to-clean-up-china.

Brettell, Caroline B. 2003. *Anthropology and Migration: Essays on Transnationalism, Ethnicity, and Identity.* Walnut Creek, CA: Altamira.

Breusers, Mark. 1999. *On the Move: Mobility, Land Use and Livelihood Practices on the Central Plateau in Burkina Faso.* London: LIT.

Bricker, Jesse et al. 2014. "Changes in U.S. Family Finances from 2010 to 2013: Evidence from the Survey of Consumer Finances." *Federal Reserve Bulletin* 100(4).

Briggs, Jean L. 1991. "Expecting the Unexpected: Canadian Inuit Training for an Experimental Lifestyle." *Ethos* 19(3):259–287.

Briggs, Jean L. 2005. "Emotions Have Many Faces: Inuit Lessons." *Anthropologica* 42(2):157–164.

Broadway, Michael J., and Donald D. Stull. 2008. "'I'll Do Whatever You Want, But It Hurts': Worker Safety and Community Health in Modern Meatpacking." *Labor Studies in Working-Class History of the Americas.* 5(2):27–37.

Brothers, Caroline. 2011. "U.N. Reports Steady Rise of Refugees. *New York Times,* June 20, p. A6.

Brown, Judith. 1965. "A Cross Cultural Study of Female Initiation Rites." *American Anthropologist* 65:837–855.

Brown, Judith. 1975. "Iroquois Women: An Ethnohistoric Note." In R. R. Reiter (ed.), *Toward an Anthropology of Women* (pp. 235–251). New York: Monthly Review.

Brown, Karen McCarthy. 1991. *Mama Lola: A Vodou Priestess in Brooklyn.* Berkeley: University of California Press.

Brubaker, Jack. 2012. "Falling Out of the Middle Class: When Bad Breaks Keep Piling Up." Lancaster Online. Available at http://lancasteronline.com /article/local/736404_Falling-out -of-the-middle-class--When-bad-breaks -keep-piling-up.html#ixzz2SX7pnhmp.

Brumfiel, Elizabeth. 1991. "Weaving and Cooking: Women's Production in Aztec Mexico." In J. M. Gero and M. W. Conkey (eds.), *Engendering Archaeology: Women and Prehistory* (pp. 224–251). Cambridge, MA: Basil Blackwell.

Brumfiel, Elizabeth M. 2006. "Cloth, Gender, Continuity, and Change: Fabricating Unity in Anthropology." *American Anthropologist* 108(4):862–877.

Bruun, Thilde Bech, Andreas de Neergaard, Deborah Lawrence, and Alan D. Ziegler. 2009. "Environmental Consequences of the Demise in Swidden Cultivation in Southeast Asia: Carbon Storage and Soil Quality." *Human Ecology* 37(3):375–388.

Bryant, Vaughn M. 2003. "Archaeology: Invisible Clues to New World Plant Domestication." *Science* 299(5609):1029–1030.

Buckley, Chris. 2015. "In One-Child China, Second Children, 'Outside Plan,' Often Live in Limbo. *New York Times,* November 1, p. A12.

Burton, John W. 1992. "Representing Africa: Colonial Anthropology Revisited." *Journal of Asian and African Studies* 27:181–201.

Burton, Thomas G. 1993. *Serpent-Handling Believers.* Knoxville: University of Tennessee Press.

Cambanis, Thanassis. 2015. *Once Upon a Revolution: An Egyptian Story.* New York: Simon & Schuster.

Cancian, Frank. 1989. "Economic Behavior in Peasant Communities." In Stuart Plattner (ed.), *Economic Anthropology* (pp. 127–170). Stanford, CA: Stanford University Press.

Cannon, Walter B. 1942. "The 'Voodoo' Death." *American Anthropologist* 44:169–180.

Carneiro, Robert. 1970. "A Theory of the Origin of the State." *Science* 169:733–738.

Carneiro, Robert. 1981. "The Chiefdom: Precursor of the State." In Grant Jones and Robert Kautz (eds.), *The Transition to Statehood in the New World* (pp. 37–79). Cambridge, UK: Cambridge University Press.

Carroll, Joseph. 2005. "Who Supports Marijuana Legalization?" *Gallup Poll Tuesday Briefing,* November 1.

Casasanto, Daniel. 2008. "Who's Afraid of the Big Bad Whorf? Crosslinguistic Differences in Temporal Language and Thought." *Language Learning* 58(Suppl 1):63–79.

Cashdan, Elizabeth. 1989. "Hunters and Gatherers: Economic Behavior in Bands." In S. Plattner (ed.), *Economic Anthropology* (pp. 21–48). Stanford, CA: Stanford University Press.

CBS. 2016. "State Department: 2 More Americans Identified as Killed in Brussels Attacks." *CBS,* March 28. Available at: http://www.cbsnews.com/news/state-department-2-more-americans-identified-as-killed-in-brussels, accessed April 21, 2016.

Cerroni-Long, E. L. 1993. "Teaching Ethnicity in the USA: An Anthropological Model." *Journal of Ethno-Development* 2(1):106–112.

Cerroni-Long, E. L. 2016. "Life and Cultures: The Test of Real Participant Observation." In Philip DeVita (ed.), *Distant Mirrors: America as a Foreign Culture* (4th ed., pp. 89–106). Long Grove, IL: Waveland.

Chagnon, Napoleon. 1997. *Yanomamo* (5th ed.). Fort Worth: Harcourt Brace Jovanovich.

Chagnon, Napoleon A. 2013. *Yanomamo: Legacy* (6th ed.). Belmont, CA: Wadsworth/Cengage.

Chan, Dennis, Valerie Anderson, Yolande Pijnenburg, Jennifer Whitwell, Jo Barnes, Rachael Scahill, John M. Stevens, Frederik Barkhof, Philip Scheltens, Martin Rossor, and Nick C. Fox. 2009. "The Clinical Profile of Right Temporal Lobe Atrophy." *Brain* 132:1287–1298.

Chance, John K., and William B. Taylor. 1985. "Cofradias and Cargos: An Historical Perspective on the Mesoamerican Civil-Religious Hierarchy." *American Ethnologist* 12(1):1–26.

Chance, Norman. 1990. *The Inupiat and Arctic Alaska: An Ethnography of Development.* Fort Worth: Holt, Rinehart and Winston.

Chapman, Mary M. 2008. "Black Workers in Auto Plants Losing Ground." *New York Times,* December 30, p. A1.

Checker, Melissa. 2009. "Anthropology in the Public Sphere: 2008. Emerging Trends and Significant Impacts." *American Anthropologist* 111(2):162–169.

Chen, Hanqing. 2012. "Interview: Richard Brubaker on Why Apple's Problems Go Beyond Foxconn." *Asia Society.* Available at http://asiasociety.org/blog/asia/interview-richard-brubaker-why-apples-problems-go-beyond-foxconn, accessed June 8, 2012.

Cherlin, Andrew J. 2014. "The Real Reason Richer People Marry." *New York Times,* December 7, p. SR3.

Chetty, Raj, et. al. 2014. "Where Is the Land of Opportunity? The Geography of Intergenerational Mobility in the United States." National Bureau of Economic Research working paper 19843. Available at http://www.nber.org/papers/w19843, accessed April 21, 2016.

Chibnik, Michael. 2005. "Experimental Economics in Anthropology: A Critical Assessment." *American Ethnologist* 32(2):198–209.

Chomsky, Noam. 1965. *Syntactic Structures.* London: Mouton.

Chong, Ping. 2012. *Undesirable Elements: Real People, Real Lives, Real Theater.* New York: Theatre Communications Group.

Chong, Ping, and Kyle Bass with Sara Zatz. 2010. "Cry for Peace: Voices from the Congo." Syracuse, NY: Syracuse Stage. [Stage play.]

Cissé, Almahady. 2007. "Mali: Wood—The Gift That Can't Keep On Giving." *Inter Press Service (Johannesburg),* April 13. Available at ipsnews.net/news.asp?idnews=37339.

Clark, Lauren, and Ann Kingsolver. n.d. "Briefing Paper on Informed Consent." *AAA Committee on Ethics.* Available at www.aaanet.org/committees/ethics/bp5.htm.

Cleaveland, A. A., J. Craven, and M. Dadfelser. 1979. *Universals of Culture.* New York: Global Perspectives in Education.

Clemetson, Lynette. 2006. "U.S. Muslims Confront Taboo on Nursing Homes." *New York Times,* June 13, p. A1.

Clendinnen, Inga. 1991. *Aztecs: An Interpretation.* Cambridge, UK: Cambridge University Press.

Clifford, James, and George E. Marcus. 1986. *Writing Culture: The Poetics and Politics of Ethnography.* Berkeley: University of California.

Cohen, Yehudi. 1971. *Man in Adaptation: The Institutional Framework.* Chicago: Aldine.

Cole, Alistair, and Gino Raymond. 2006. *Redefining the French Republic.* Manchester, UK: Manchester University Press.

Coleman, Michael C. 1999. "The Responses of American Indian Children and Irish Children to the School, 1850s–1920s: A Comparative Study in Cross-Cultural Education." *American Indian Quarterly* 23(3/4):83–112.

Coll, Steve. 2012. *Private Empire: Exxon-Mobil and American Power.* New York: Penguin.

Collins, Chuck, and Josh Hoxie. 2015. "Billionaire Bonanza. The Forbes 400 and the Rest of Us." Institute for Policy Studies, December 1. Available at http://www.ips-dc.org/billionaire-bonanza, accessed April 21, 2016.

Condon, Richard G., with Julia Ogina and the Holman Elders. 1996. *The Northern Copper Inuit: A History.* Toronto: University of Toronto Press.

Condry, Ian. 2005. "Must-Download TV and Cool Japan." *Anthropology Newsletter* 53 (January).

Conklin, Beth A. 1995. "'Thus Are Our Bodies, Thus Was Our Custom': Mortuary Cannibalism in an Amazonian Society." *American Ethnologist* 22(1):75–101.

Connolly, Bob, and Robin Anderson. 1987. *First Contact: New Guinea's Highlanders Encounter the Outside World.* New York: Penguin.

Conway-Long, Don. 1994. "Ethnographies and Masculinities." In Harry Brod and Michael Kaufman (eds.), *Theorizing Masculinities* (pp. 61–81). Thousand Oaks, CA: Sage.

Coquery-Vidrovitch, Catherine. 1988. *Africa: Endurance and Change South of the Sahara.* Berkeley: University of California Press.

Corbett, Greville G. 2008. "Number of Genders." In Martin Haspelmath, Matthew S. Dryer, David Gil, and Bernard Comrie (eds.), *The World Atlas of Language Structures Online.* Munich: Max Planck Digital Library, Chapter 30. Available at wals.info/feature/30, accessed on August 19, 2010.

Costa, LeeRay, and Andrew Matzner. 2007. *Male Bodies, Women's Souls: Personal Narratives of Thailand's Transgendered Youth.* Binghamton, NY: Haworth.

Cotter, Holland. 2009. "Putting 'Primitive' to Rest." *New York Times*, June 5, p. C1.

Cotter, Holland. 2012. "Imperiled Legacy." *New York Times*, August 5, p. AR1.

Covington, Dennis. 1995. *Salvation on Sand Mountain: Snake Handling and Redemption in Southern Appalachia.* Reading, MA: Addison-Wesley.

Crespin, Pamela. 2005. "The Global Transformation of Work." *Anthropology News* 46(3):20–21.

Crush, Jonathan. 1995. *The Power of Development.* New York: Routledge.

Culotta, Elizabeth. 2012. "Turning from War to Peace in Papua New Guinea." *Science* 337:1593–1594.

Currah, Paisley, and Susan Stryker (eds.). 2014. *TSQ: Transgender Studies Quarterly.* Durham, NC: Duke University Press.

Curtis, Lewis P. 1968. *Anglo-Saxons and Celts: A Study of Anti-Irish Prejudice in Victorian England.* Bridgeport, CT: University of Bridgeport.

Dahl, Dick. 2008. "Forensic Linguists Make a Science of Syntax." *Massachusetts Lawyers Weekly,* April 7.

Danaher, Kevin, and Michael Shellenberger (eds.). 1995. *Fighting for the Soul of Brazil.* New York: Monthly Review.

Danfulani, Umar Habila Dadem. 1999. "Exorcising Witchcraft: The Return of the Gods in New Religious Movements on the Jos Plateau and the Benue Regions of Nigeria." *African Affairs* 98(391):167–193.

Daniel, G. Reginald. 2006. *Race and Multiraciality in Brazil and the United States: Converging Paths?* University Park: Pennsylvania State University Press.

Das, Raju. 1998. "The Green Revolution, Agrarian Productivity and Labor." *International Journal of Urban and Regional Research* 22(1):122–135.

Das, Subhamoy. 2009. "Hindus Protest Sony's Hanuman Game." *Subhamoy's Hinduism Blog.* About.com: Hinduism. Available at hinduism.about.com/b/2009/04/22/hindus-protest-sonys-hanuman-game.htm, accessed August 20, 2010.

Daugherty, Mary L. 1976. "Serpent-Handling as Sacrament." *Theology Today* 33:232–243.

Deák, Istvan. 2002. "The Crime of the Century," *New York Review of Books*, September 26, p. 48.

Defoe, Daniel. 1726. *Mere Nature Delineated.* London: Warner.

Delcore, Henry D. 2007. "The Racial Distribution of Privilege in a Thai National Park." *Journal of Southeast Asian Studies.* 38(1):83–105.

de Leon, Jason. 2016. *The Land of Open Graves Living and Dying on the Migrant Trail.* Oakland: University of California Press.

Demian, Melissa. 2008. "Fictions of Intention in the 'Cultural Defense.'" *American Anthropologist* 110(4):432–442.

DeNavas-Walt, Carmen, and Bernadette D. Proctor. 2015. "Income and Poverty in the United States: 2014." *Current Population Reports.* Available at https://www.census.gov/content/dam/Census/library/publications/2015/demo/p60-252.pdf, accessed April 21, 2016.

DeParle, Jason. 2012a. Harder for Americans to Rise from Lower Rungs. *New York Times,* January 5. A1.

DeParle, Jason. 2012b. "Two Classes, Divided by 'I Do.': Marriage for Richer; Single Motherhood, for Poorer." *New York Times,* July 15, p. A7.

Desmond, Matthew. 2016. *Evicted: Poverty and Profit in the American City.* New York: Crown.

DeVita, Philip R. (ed.). 2016. *Distant Mirrors: America as a Foreign Culture* (4th ed.). Long Grove, IL: Waveland.

De Vos, George, and Lola Romanucci-Ross. 1995. "Ethnic Identity: A Psychocultural Perspective." In Lola Romanucci-Ross and George A. De Vos (eds.), *Ethnic Identity: Creation, Conflict, and Accommodation* (3rd ed., pp. 349–380). London: Sage.

Dickson, D. Bruce, Jeffrey Olsen, P. Fred Daum, and Mitchell S. Wachtel. 2005. "Where Do You Go When You Die? A Cross-Cultural Test of the Hypothesis That Infrastructure Predicts Individual Eschatology." *Journal of Anthropological Research* 61(1):53–79.

di Leonardo, Micaela. 1998. *Exotics at Home: Anthropologies, Others, American Modernity.* Chicago: University of Chicago Press.

di Leonardo, Micaela. 2003. "Margaret Mead and the Culture of Forgetting." *American Anthropologist* 105(3):592–595.

Dilger, Hansjörg. 2008. "'We Are All Going to Die': Kinship Belonging, and the Morality of HIV/AIDS-Related Illness and Deaths in Rural Tanzania." *Anthropological Quarterly* 81(1): 207–232.

Diamond, Jared. 1992. "The Arrow of Disease." *Discover* 13(10):64–73.

Diamond, Jared. 1998. *Guns, Germs, and Steel: The Fate of Human Societies.* New York: Norton.

Divale, William Tulio, and Marvin Harris. 1976. "Population, Warfare and the Male Supremacist Complex." *American Anthropologist* 78:521–538.

Domhoff, G. William. 2013. "Power in America: Wealth, Income, and Power." *Who Rules America?* (blog). Available at www2.ucsc.edu/whorulesamerica /power/wealth.html, accessed April 23, 2013.

Dominguez Martin, and Pasko Rakic. 2009. "Language Evolution: The Importance of Being Human." *Nature* 462:169–170.

Dozon, Jean-Pierre. 1985. "Les Bété: une creation coloniale." In J. L. Amselle and E. M'bokolo (eds.), *Au Coeur de l'ethnie* (pp. 49–85). Paris: Editions La Decouverte.

Drybread, Kristen. Drybread, Kristen. 2006. "Sleeping with One Eye Open: The Perils of Fieldwork in a Brazilian Juvenile Prison." In Andrew Gardner and David M. Hoffman (eds.), *Dispatches from the Field* (pp. 33–52). Long Grove, IL: Waveland.

Duhigg, Charles, and David Barboza. 2012. "Pressure, Chinese and Foreign, Drives Changes at Foxconn." *New York Times,* February 20, p. B1.

Duhigg, Charles, and Steven Greenhouse. 2012. "Electronic Giant Vowing Reforms in China Plant." *New York Times,* March 29, p. 1A.

Duncan, David Ewing. 1995. *Hernando de Soto: A Savage Quest in the Americas.* New York: Crown.

Dunham, S. Ann, Alice G. Dewey, Nancy I. Cooper, and Maya Soetoro-Ng. 2009. *Surviving against the Odds: Village Industry in Indonesia.* Durham, NC: Duke University Press.

Durkheim, Émile. 1961/1915. *The Elementary Forms of the Religious Life.* New York: Collier.

Durrenberger, E. Paul, and Dimitra Doukas. 2008. "Gospel of Wealth, Gospel of Work: Counterhegemony in the U.S. Working Class." *American Anthropologist* 110(2): 214–224.

Dyer, Geoff. 2010. "My American Friends." *New York Times Book Review,* p. 23.

Eakin, Hugh. 2015. "The Terrible Flight from the Killing." *New York Review of Books,* October 22. Available at http:// www.nybooks.com/articles/2015/10 /22/terrible-flight-killing, accessed August 22, 2016.

Early, John D., and Thomas N. Headland. 1998. *Population Dynamics of a Philippine Rain Forest People: The San Ildefonso Agta.* Gainesville: University Press of Florida.

Eckert, Penelope. 1989. *Jocks and Burnouts: Social Categories and Identity in the High School.* New York: Teacher's College Press.

Eckert, Penelope. 2000. *Linguistic Variation as Social Practice.* Oxford, UK: Blackwell.

Eckert, Penelope. 2004. "Language and Gender in Adolescence." In Janet Holmes and Miriam Meyerhoff (eds.), *The Handbook of Language and Gender. Blackwell Reference Online.* Available at http:// is.muni.cz/el/1423/podzim2012 /SAN230/um/the_handbook_of _language _and_gender.pdf, accessed May 28, 2010.

Economist, The. 2008. "The Good Consumer." *The Economist,* January 17.

Economist, The. 2011. "The Flight from Marriage." August 20. Available at www.economist.com/node/21526329, accessed June 8, 2012.

Economist, The. 2013. "Beijing's Air Pollution: Blackest Day." *The Economist,* January 14

Eggan, Fred. 1950. *The Social Organization of Western Pueblos.* Chicago: University of Chicago Press.

El-Feki. 2013. *Sex and the Citadel: Intimate Life in a Changing Arab World.* New York: Pantheon.

Eller, Jack David. 2006. *Violence and Culture: A Cross-Cultural and Interdisciplinary Approach.* Belmont, CA: Wadsworth.

Elkin, A. P. 1967. "The Nature of Australian Totemism." In J. Middleton (ed.), *Gods and Rituals* (pp. 159–176). Garden City, NY: Natural History.

Ember, Carol. 1983. "The Relative Decline in Women's Contribution to Agriculture with Intensification." *American Anthropologist* 85(2): 285–304.

Ember, Melvin, and Carol R. Ember. 1971. "The Conditions Favoring Matrilocal vs. Patrilocal Residence." *American Anthropologist* 73:571–594.

Engelmann, Siegfried, and Therese Engelmann. 1966. *Give Your Child a Superior Mind: A Program for the Preschool Child.* New York: Simon & Schuster.

Ensminger, Jean. 2002. "Experimental Economics: A Powerful New Method for Theory Testing in Anthropology." In Jean Ensminger (ed.), *Theory in Economic Anthropology* (pp. 59–78). Walnut Creek, CA: Altamira.

Ensminger, Jean, and Joseph Henrich. 2014. *Experimenting with Social Norms.* New York: Russell Sage Foundation.

Escobar, Arturo. 1997. "The Making and Unmaking of the Third World through Development." In M. Rahnema and V. Bawtree (eds.). *The Post-Development Reader* (pp. 263–273). Atlantic Highlands, NJ: Zed.

Estioko-Griffin, Agnes. 1986. "Daughters of the Forest." *Natural History* 5:37–42.

Eurostat. 2012. "Total Fertility Rate." Available at http://epp.eurostat.ec .europa.eu/tgm/table.do?tab =table&plugin=1&language =en&pcode=tsdde220, accessed June 8, 2012.

Evans, Peter. 2000. "Fighting Marginalization with Transnational Networks: Counter Hegemonic Globalization." *Contemporary Sociology* 29:230–241.

Evans-Pritchard, E. E. 1958/1937. *Witchcraft, Oracles, and Magic among the Azande.* Oxford, UK: Clarendon.

Evans-Pritchard, E. E. 1968/1940. *The Nuer.* Oxford, UK: Clarendon.

Ewing, Katherine Pratt (ed.). 2008a. *Being and Belonging: Muslims in the United States since 9/11.* New York: Russell Sage Foundation.

Ewing, Katherine Pratt. 2008b. *Stolen Honor: Stigmatizing Muslim Men in Berlin.* Stanford, CA: Stanford University Press.

Fábrega, Horacio. 1997. *Evolution of Sickness and Healing.* Berkeley: University of California Press.

Fadiman, Anne. 1997. *The Spirit Catches You and You Fall Down: A Hmong Child, Her American Doctors, and the Collision of Two Cultures.* New York: Farrar, Straus, and Giroux.

Fadiman, Anne. 2012. "Lia Lee: A Disabled Life that Changed the Face of Western Medicine." Produced by Joyce Hackel, *The World,* Public Radio International, December 21.

Feinberg, Richard. 1986. "Market Economy and Changing Sex-Roles on a Polynesian Atoll." *Ethnology* 25:271–282.

Feinberg, Richard. 1994. "Contested Worlds: Politics of Culture and the Politics of Anthropology." *Anthropology and Humanism* 19:20–35.

Feldman, Douglas A. (ed.). 2009. *AIDS, Culture, and Gay Men.* Gainesville: University Press of Florida.

Ferguson, R. Brian. 1992. "A Savage Encounter: Western Contact and the Yanomamo War Complex." In R. B. Ferguson and N. L. Whitehead (eds.), *War in the Tribal Zone: Expanding States and Indigenous Warfare* (pp. 199–227). Santa Fe: School of American Research.

Fernandez, Manny. 2015. "Tactics and Antagonists Draw Attention to Houston Vote on Rights Law." *New York Times,* November 1, p. 16A.

Ferraro, Gary P. 1994. *The Cultural Dimension of International Business* (2nd ed.). Englewood Cliffs, NJ: Prentice-Hall.

Fetto, John. 1999. "Six Billion Served." *Advertising Age,* June 1. Available at http://adage.com/article/american-demographics/billion-served/42474, accessed August 14, 2016.

Fitzpatrick, Michael. 2014. "Hello Kitty at 40: The Cat That Conquered the World." *BBC.* August 18. Available at http://www.bbc.com/culture/story/20140815-how-hello-kitty-invaded-the-world, accessed October 25, 2016.

Flamm, Bruce L. 2002. "Faith Healing by Prayer: Review of Cha, KY, Wirth, DP, Lobo, RA. Does Prayer Influence the Success of In Vitro Fertilization-Embryo Transfer?" *Scientific Review of Alternative Medicine* 6(1):47–50.

Fluehr-Lobban, Carolyn. 2005. "Cultural Relativism and Universal Rights in Islamic Law." *Anthropology News* 46(9):23.

Fondacaro, Steve, and Montgomery McFate. 2008. "In Memoriam— Michael Bhatia." Available at http://humanterrainsystem.army.mil/bhatia.html.

Fondebrider, Luis, and Richard A. Wilson. 2015. "Forensic Anthropology and the Investigation of Political Violence: Lessons Learned from Latin America and the Balkans." In Francisco Ferrandiz and Antonius Robben (eds.), *Necropolitics: Mass Graves and Exhumations in the Age of Human Rights* (pp. 41–52). Philadelphia: University of Pennsylvania Press.

Forbes. 2016a. "Cleveland Cavaliers." Available at http://www.forbes.com/teams/cleveland-cavaliers, accessed April 21, 2016.

Forbes. 2016b. "#286 Daniel Gilbert." Available at http://www.forbes.com/profile/daniel-gilbert, accessed April 21, 2016.

Ford, James D., Barry Smit, and Johanna Wandel. 2006. "Vulnerability to Climate Change in the Arctic: A Case Study from Arctic Bay, Canada." *Global Environmental Change* 16:145–60.

Fordham, Signithia. 1999. "Dissin' 'the Standard': Ebonics and Guerrilla Warfare at Capital High." *Anthropology & Education Quarterly* 30(3):272–293.

Foster, Don. 2003. "The Message in the Anthrax." *Vanity Fair,* October.

Foster, Robert J. 1991. "Making National Cultures in the Global Ecumene." *Annual Reviews of Anthropology* 20:235–260.

Fox, Margalit. 2012. "Lia Lee Dies: Life Went On around Her, Redefining Care." *New York Times,* September 14.

Freed, David. 2010. "The Wrong Man." *The Atlantic,* May.

Freed, Stanley. 2012. *Anthropology Unmasked: Museums, Science, and Politics in New York City.* Vols. I and II. Wilmington, OH: Orange Frazer.

French, Howard W. 2006. "Rush for Wealth in China's Cities Shatters the Ancient Assurance of Care in Old Age." *New York Times,* November 3, p. A8.

French, Jan Hoffman. 2010. "Book Review of *Legacies of Race: Identities, Attitudes, and Politics in Brazil.*" *American Anthropologist* 112(3):447.

Freyre, Gilberto. 1946. *The Masters and the Slaves: A Study in the Development of Brazilian Civilization.* New York: Knopf.

Fried, Morton. 1967. *The Evolution of Political Society.* New York: Random House.

Friedheim, William, with Ronald Jackson (eds.). 1996. *Freedom's Unfinished Revolution: An Inquiry into the Civil War and Reconstruction.* New York: New Press.

Friedl, Ernestine. 1975. *Women and Men: An Anthropologist's View.* New York: Holt, Rinehart and Winston.

Friedman, Jonathan. 1992. "The Past in the Future: History and the Politics of Identity." *American Anthropologist* 94:837–859.

Fry, Douglas P., and Kaj Bjorkqvist (eds.). 1997. *Cultural Variation and Conflict Resolution: Alternatives to Violence.* Mahwah, NJ: Erlbaum.

Garment Workers Center. 2015. Health and Safety in LA Sweatshops. Available at http://garmentworkercenter.org/wp-content/uploads/2015/09/StateofLAGarmentIndustry.pdf, accessed May 20, 2016.

Gates, Henry Louis, Jr. 2011. *Black in Latin America.* New York: New York University Press.

Gaudio, Rudolf Pell. 2009. *Allah Made Us: Sexual Outlaws in an Islamic African City.* West Sussex, UK: Wiley-Blackwell.

Geertz, Clifford. 1973a. "Deep Play: Notes on the Balinese Cockfight." In C. Geertz (ed.), *The Interpretation of Cultures* (pp. 412–453). New York: Basic Books.

Geertz, Clifford (ed.). 1973b. *The Interpretation of Cultures.* New York: Basic Books.

Geertz, Clifford. 2008/1973. "Deep Play: Notes on a Balinese Cockfight." In R. Jon McGee and Richard L. Warms (eds.), *Anthropological Theory: An Introductory History.* Boston: McGraw Hill.

Gell, Alfred. 1993. *Wrapping in Images: Tatooing in Polynesia.* Oxford, UK: Clarendon.

Gertel, Jorg, and Richard Le Heron. 2011. *Economic Spaces of Pastoral Production and Commodity Systems: Markets and Livelihoods.* Burlington, VT: Ashgate.

Gettleman, Jeffrey. 2016. "Onetime City of Hope in South Sudan Is Now City of Fear." *New York Times,* March 12, p. A1.

Ghosh, Anjan. 1991. "The Structure of Structure, or Appropriation of Anthropological Theory." *Review* 14(1):55–77.

Giancola, Jennifer, and Richard D. Kahlenberg. 2016. *True Merit: Ensuring Our Brightest Students Have Access to Our Best Colleges and Universities.* Lansdowne VA: Jack Kent Cooke Foundation.

Gibbs, James L., Jr. 1988. "The Kpelle Moot: A Therapeutic Model for the Informal Settlement of Disputes." In J. B. Cole (ed.), *Anthropology of the Nineties* (pp. 347–359). New York: Free Press.

Gibbs, W. Wayt. 2002. "Saving Dying Languages." *Scientific American* 287:78–86.

Gibson, Margaret A., and John Ogbu. 1991. *Minority Status and Schooling: A Comparative Study of Immigrant and Involuntary Minorities.* New York: Garland.

Gilbert, Dennis. 2011. *The American Class Structure in an Age of Growing Inequality* (8th ed.). Thousand Oaks, CA: Pine Forge.

Gilbert, Matthew. 2007. "Farewell, Sweet Ice." *The Nation,* May 7, pp. 26–27.

Gilbert, Matthew. 2012. Gwich'in Elders and Youth Speak on Climate Change in Arctic Village. *Cultural Survival.* April 6. Available at https://www.culturalsurvival.org/news/gwichin-elders-and-youth-speak-climate-change-arctic-village-alaska, accessed July 14, 2016.

Gilbert, Aubrey L., Terry Regier, Paul Kay, and Richard B. Ivry. 2006. "Whorf Hypothesis Is Supported in the Right Visual Field but Not the Left." *Proc Natl Acad Sci USA* 103(2):489–494.

Gill, Victoria. 2015. Evidence of 4300,000 year old human violence found. *BBC News.* May 28. Available at: http://www.bbc.com/news/science-environment-32890697, accessed April 22, 2016.

Gillis, Justin, and Coral Davenport. 2016. "Leaders Roll Up Sleeves on Climate, but Experts Say Plans Don't Pack a Wallop." *New York Times,* April 21. Available at http://www.nytimes.com/2016/04/22/science/united-nations-paris-climate-change-document.html, accessed August, 22, 2016.

Gilmore, David D. 1990. *Manhood in the Making: Cultural Concepts of Masculinity.* New Haven, CT: Yale University Press.

Gilmore, David D. 1996. "Above and Below: Toward a Social Geometry of Gender." *American Anthropologist* 98:54–66.

Glazer, Nathan, and Daniel P. Moynihan. 1970. *Beyond the Melting Pot* (2nd ed.). Cambridge, MA: MIT Press.

Gmelch, George. 2000. "Baseball Magic." In James Spradley and David McCurdy (eds.), *Conformity and Conflict* (pp. 322–331). Boston: Allyn and Bacon.

Godelier, Maurice. 1993. "L'Occident, miroir brisé: une evaluation partielle de l'anthropologie sociale assortie de quelques perspectives." *Annales* 48:1183–1207.

Goldschmidt, Walter R. 1986. *The Sebei: A Study in Adaptation.* New York: Holt, Reinhart and Winston.

Goldstein, Donna. 1999. "'Interracial' Sex and Racial Democracy in Brazil: Twin Concepts?" *American Anthropologist* 101:563–578.

Good, Anthony. 2007. *Anthropology and Expertise in the Asylum Courts.* New York: Routlege-Cavendish.

Goodale, J. 1971. *Tiwi Wives.* Seattle: University of Washington Press.

Goodstein, Laurie. 2009. "Poll Finds US Muslims Thriving but Not Content." *New York Times,* March 1, p. 11.

Goody, Jack. 1995. *The Expansive Moment: Anthropology in Britain and Africa 1918–1970.* Cambridge, UK: Cambridge University Press.

Gordon, Peter. 2004. "Numerical Cognition without Words: Evidence from Amazonia." *Science* 306(5695):496–499.

Gordon, Robert, and Cameron Wesson. 2013. "Max Gluckman." In R. Jon McGee and Richard L. Warms (eds.), *Theory in Social and Cultural Anthropology.* (vol. 1, pp. 336–341). Los Angeles: Sage.

Gottlieb, Anna. 2002. "Interpreting Gender and Sexuality: Approaches from Cultural Anthropology." In Jeremy MacClancey (ed.), *Exotic No More: Anthropology on the Front Lines* (pp. 167–189). Chicago: University of Chicago Press.

Graburn, Nelson H. H. (ed.). 1976. *Ethnic and Tourist Arts: Cultural Expressions from the Fourth World.* Berkeley: University of California Press.

Graham, Laura R. 2006. "Anthropologists Are Obligated to Promote Human Rights and Social Justice: Especially among Vulnerable Communities." *Anthropology News* 47(7):4–5.

Graham, Laura, Alexandra Jaffe, Bonnie Urciuoli, and David Valentine. 2007. "Why Anthropologists Should Oppose English Only Legislation in the U.S." *Anthropology News* 48(1):32–33.

Gramsci, Antonio. 1971. *Selections from the Prison Notebook (*ed. and trans. by Quentin Hoare and Geoffry Nowell-Smith). London: Lawrence and Wishart.

Green, Lisa J. 2002. *African American English: A Linguistic Introduction.* Cambridge, UK: Cambridge University Press.

Greenberg, James B. 1997. "A Political Ecology of Structural-Adjustment Policies: The Case of the Dominican Republic." *Culture & Agriculture* 19(3):85–93.

Greene, Candace W. 2001. *Silver Horn: Master Illustrator of the Kiowas.* Norman: University of Oklahoma.

Greenhalgh, Susan. 2007. "China's Future with Fewer Females." *China from the Inside.* Washington, DC: Public Broadcasting Service. Available at www.pbs.org/kqed/chinainside/women/population.html.

Greenhouse, Steven, and Julfikar Ali Manik. 2014. "Stalemate over Safety in Bangladesh." *New York Times,* June 26, p. B1. Available at http://www.nytimes.com/2014/06/26/business/international/stalemate-over-garment-factory-safety-in-bangladesh.html?_r=0, accessed August 22, 2016.

Grosfoguel, Ramon. 2003. *Colonial Subjects: Puerto Ricans in a Global Perspective.* Berkeley: University of California Press.

Gruschke, Andreas. 2011. "Nomads and Their Market Relations in Eastern Tibet's Yushu Region: The Impact of Caterpillar Fungus." In Jorg Gertel and Richard Le Heron (eds.), *Economic Spaces of Pastoral Production and Commodity Systems* (pp. 211–229). Burlington VT: Ashgate.

Guillermoprieto, Alma. 2006. "A New Bolivia?" *New York Review of Books* 53(13):36.

Gutmann, Matthew C. 1996. *The Meanings of Macho: Being a Man in Mexico City.* Berkeley: University of California Press.

Hacker, Jacob. 2002. *The Divided Welfare State: The Battle over Public and Private Social Benefits in the United States.* New York: Cambridge University Press.

Hackett, Conrad. 2015. "5 Facts about the Muslim Population in Europe." Pew Research Center. Available at http://www.pewresearch.org/fact -tank/2015/11/17/5-facts-about-the -muslim-population-in-europe. accessed April 22, 2016.

Hadden, Jeffrey K., and Anson Shupe. 1989. "Is There Such a Thing as Global Fundamentalism?" In Jeffrey K. Hadden and Anson Shupe (eds.), *Secularization and Fundamentalism Reconsidered* (pp. 109–122). New York: Paragon House.

Hakimzadeh, Shirin, and D'Vera Cohn. 2007. *English Usage Among Hispanics in the United States.* Washington, DC: Pew Hispanic Center.

Hale, Sondra. 1989. "The Politics of Gender in the Middle East." In S. Morgen (ed.), *Gender and Anthropology: Critical Reviews for Research and Teaching* (pp. 246–267). Washington, DC: American Anthropological Association.

Hall, Edward T. 1959. *The Silent Language.* Greenwich CT: Fawcett.

Hall, Edward T. 1966. *The Hidden Dimension.* New York: Doubleday.

Hall, Edward T. 1968. Proxemics. *Current Anthropology.* 9:83–109.

Hall, Edward T. 1983. *The Dance of Life: The Other Dimension of Time.* New York: Anchor/Doubleday.

Halperin, Rhoda H. 1990. *The Livelihood of Kin: Making Ends Meet "The Kentucky Way."* Austin: University of Texas Press.

Hansen, Edward C. 1995. "The Great Bambi War: Tocquevillians versus Keynesians in an Upstate New York County." In J. Schneider and R. Rapp (eds.), *Articulating Hidden Histories: Exploring the Influence of Eric R. Wolf* (pp. 142–155). Berkeley: University of California Press.

Harries, Patrick. 1987. "The Roots of Ethnicity: Discourse and the Politics of Language Construction in South-East Africa." *African Affairs* 87:25–52.

Harris, Marvin. 1966. "The Cultural Ecology of India's Sacred Cattle." *Current Anthropology* 7:51–66.

Harris, Marvin. 1989. *Our Kind: Who We Are, Where We Came From, Where We Are Going.* New York: Harper Perennial.

Harrison, Paul, and Fred Pearce. 2000. *AAAS Atlas of Population and Environment,* Victoria Dompka Markham (ed.). Berkeley: American Association for the Advancement of Science and the University of California Press. Available at atlas.aaas.org.

Hart, C. W. M. 1967. "Contrasts between Pre-Pubertal and Post-Pubertal Education." In R. Endelman (ed.), *Personality and Social Life* (pp. 275–290). New York: Random House.

Hart, C. W. M., and Arnold R. Pilling. 1960. *The Tiwi of North Australia.* New York: Holt, Rinehart and Winston.

Harvey, David. 2005. *A Brief History of Neoliberalism.* New York: Oxford University Press.

Hauptman, William. 1985. "Renoir's Master." *EMR* 15:48–66.

Hayden, Brian, and Suzanne Villeneuve. 2011. "A Century of Feasting Studies." *Annual Review of Anthropology* 40:433–449.

Hays, Kelly E. 2011. *Holy Harlots: Femininity, Sexuality, and Black Magic in Brazil.* Berkeley: University of California Press.

Hearn, Maxwell K. 1996. *Splendors of Imperial China: Treasures from the National Palace Museum, Taipei.* New York: Metropolitan Museum of Art.

Hedges, Chris, and Joe Sacco. 2012. *Days of Destruction, Days of Revolt.* New York: Nation Books.

Hepner, Tricia Redeker. 2011. "Collaborative Anthropology Comes to Life: Catherine Besteman and the Somali Bantu Experience." *AA* 13(2):346.

Henrich, Joseph, Robert Boyd, Samuel Bowles, Colin Camerer, Ernst Fehr, and Herbert Gintis. 2004. *Foundations of Human Sociality: Economic Experiments and Ethnographic Evidence from 15 Small-Scale Societies.* Oxford, UK: Oxford University Press.

Herdt, Gilbert H. 1981. *Guardians of the Flutes: Idioms of Masculinity.* New York: McGraw-Hill.

Herdt, Gilbert H. 1987. *The Sambia.* New York: Holt, Rinehart and Winston.

Herdt, Gilbert H. (ed.). 1996. *Third Sex, Third Gender: Beyond Sexual Dimorphism in Culture and History.* New York: Zone.

Hester, Marianne. 1988. "Who Were the Witches?" *Studies in Sexual Politics* 26–27:1–22.

Higuchi, Takayasu, and Gina Barnes. 1995. "Buddhist Cave Temples in Afghanistan." *World Archaeology* 27(2):282–302.

Hitt, Jack. 2012. "Words on Trial: Can Linguistics Solve Crimes that Stump Police?" *New Yorker,* July 23.

Hobsbawm, Eric, and Terence Ranger (eds.). 1983. *The Invention of Tradition.* Cambridge, UK: Cambridge University Press.

Hochschild, Adam. 1998. *King Leopold's Ghost.* New York: Houghton Mifflin.

Hochschild, Adam. 2005. "In the Heart of Darkness." *New York Review of Books,* October 6, pp. 39–42.

Hodge, G. Derrick. 2011. "Walking the Line between Accommodation and Transformation: Evaluating the Continuing Career of Jim Yong Kim." *AA.* 113(1):l48.

Hoebel, E. Adamson. 1960. *The Cheyennes: Indians of the Great Plains.* New York: Holt.

Hoebel, E. Adamson. 1974. *The Law of Primitive Man.* New York: Holt.

Hollenberg, K. 2006. "Vascular Action of Cocoa Flavanols in Humans: The Roots of the Story. *Journal of Cardiovascular Pharmacology* 47(Suppl 2:s99–102):119–121.

Holthouse, David. 2005. "Arizona Showdown." *Southern Poverty Law Center Intelligence Report,* Summer.

Holtzman, Elizabeth. 2016. "The US Has Its Own Refugee Crisis—One We Created and Now Must Solve." *The Nation,* February 11. Available at https:// www.thenation.com/article/the-us -has-its-own-refugee-crisis-one-we -created-and-now-must-solve, accessed July 18, 2016.

Horowitz, Irving L. (ed.). 1967. *The Rise and Fall of Project Camelot.* Cambridge, MA: MIT Press.

Horst, Heather A., and Daniel Miller. 2006. *The Cell Phone: An Anthropology of Communication.* New York: Berg.

Howe, James. 2012. "Chocolate and Cardiovascular Health: The Kuna Case Reconsidered." *Gastronomica 12(1):43–52.*

Howell, Signe. 1989. "To Be Angry Is Not to Be Human but to Be Fearful Is: Chewong Concepts of Human Nature." In Signe Howell and Roy Willis (eds.), *Societies at Peace: Anthropological Perspectives* (pp. 45–59). London: Routledge.

Hua, Cai. 2001. *A Society without Fathers or Husbands: The Na of China.* Cambridge, MA: Zone.

Huber, Brad, William F. Danaher, and William Breedlove. 2011. "New Cross-Cultural Perspectives on Marriage Transactions." *Cross-Cultural Research* 45(4):339–375.

Hughey, Matthew W. 2009. "Cinethetic Racism: White Redemption and Black Stereotypes in 'Magical Negro' Films." *Social Problems* 56(3):543–577.

Human Rights Watch. 2004. *Blood, Sweat, and Fear: Worker's Rights in U.S. Meat and Poultry Plants.* New York: Human Rights Watch.

Human Rights Watch 2015. "Work Faster or Get Out: Labor Rights Abuses in Cambodia's Garment Industry." Available at https://www.hrw.org/report/2015/03/11/work-faster-or-get-out/labor-rights-abuses-cambodias-garment-industry, accessed May 20, 2016.

Human Rights Watch. 2016. "World Report." Available at https://www.hrw.org/sites/default/files/world_report_download/wr2016_web.pdf, accessed August 22, 2016.

Hutchinson, Sharon E. 1996. *Nuer Dilemmas: Coping with Money, War, and the State.* Berkeley: University of California Press.

Ignatieff, Michael. 2015. "The Refugees and the New War." *New York Review of Books,* December 17.

Intergovernmental Panel on Climate Change. 2007. "Summary for Policymakers." In Solomon, S., D. Qin, M. Maning, Z. Chen, M. Marquis, K. B. Averyt, M Tignor, and H. L. Miller (eds.), *Climate Change 2007: The Physical Science Basis. Contributions of Working Group I to the Fourth Assessment Report of the Intergovernmental Panel on Climate Change.* Cambridge, UK: Cambridge University Press.

Isaacman, Allen. 1996. *Cotton Is the Mother of Poverty: Peasants, Work, and Rural Struggle in Colonial Mozambique (1938–1961).* Portsmouth, NH: Heinemann.

Ishemo, Shubi L. 1995. "Cultural Response to Forced Labour and Commodity Production in Portugal's African Colonies." *Social Identities* 1(1):95–110.

Isidore, Chris. 2015. "LeBron Shoots for Billionaire Status." *CNNMoney,* December 9. Available at http://money.cnn.com/2015/12/09/news/companies/lebron-james-endorsement-billionaire, accessed April 22, 2016.

Iyer, Deepa. 2015. *We Too Sing America: South Asian, Arab, Muslim, and Sikh Immigrants Shape Our Multiracial Future.* New York: New Press.

Jackson, P. 1999. *Lady Boys, Tom Boys, Rent Boys: Male and Female Homosexualities in Contemporary Thailand.* Binghamton, NY: Haworth.

Jackson, Pamela I., and Peter Doerschler. 2012. *Benchmarking Muslim Well-Being in Europe: Reducing Disparities and Polarizations.* Bristol, UK: Policy Press.

Jacobs, Andrew, and Adam Century. 2012. "As China Ages, Beijing Turns to Morality Tales to Spur Filial Devotion." *New York Times,* September 6, p. A11.

Japan Times. 2015. "Nearly 40% of Single Japanese Not Interested in Romance: Survey. *Japan Times,* June 22. Available at http://www.japantimes.co.jp/news/2015/06/22/national/social-issues/nearly-40-of-single-japanese-not-interested-in-romance-survey/#.Vz8hfvmDFBd, accessed May 20, 2016.

Jelly-Schapiro, Joshua. 2009. "The Bob Marley Story." *New York Review of Books,* April, pp. 34–37.

Jencks, Christopher. 2014. "On America's Front Lines." *New York Review of Books,* October 9, p. 34.

Jennings, Ken. 2013. "Is Your Electric Fan Trying to Kill You?" *Slate.com,* January 22.

Johnson, Mark. 1996. "Negotiating Style and Mediating Beauty: Transvestite (Gay-Bantut) Beauty Contests in the Southern Philippines." In Colleen Cohen, Richard Wilk, and Beverly Steoltje (eds.), *Beauty Queens on the Global Stage: Gender, Contests, and Power* (pp. 89–104). London: Routledge.

Johnson, Kirk. 2016. "Violence at a Homeless Camp Exposes Seattle's Underbelly." *New York Times,* March 2, p. 14.

Johnstone, Brick, and Bret A. Glass. 2008. "Support for a Neuropsychological Model of Spirituality in Persons with Traumatic Brain Injury." *Zygon* 43(4):861–74.

Jonaitis, Aldona (ed.). 1991. *Chiefly Feasts: The Enduring Kwakiutl Potlatch.* Seattle: University of Washington Press.

Jones, Maggie. 2012. "Postville, Iowa, Is Up For Grabs." *New York Times,* July 11.

Judt, Tony. 2005. *Postwar: A History of Europe since 1945.* New York: Penguin.

Kaplan, Flora E. S. (ed.). 1997. *Queens, Queen Mothers, Priestesses, and Power: Case Studies in African Gender.* New York: New York Academy of Sciences.

Kapur, Akash. 2012. *India Becoming: A Portrait of Life in Modern India.* New York: Riverhead.

Karkazis, Katrina. 2008. *Fixing Sex: Intersex, Medical Authority, and Lived Experience.* Durham, NC: Duke University Press.

Karlen, Arno. 1995. *Man and Microbes: Disease and Plagues in History and Modern Times.* New York: Putnam.

Katrak, Ketu H. 2002. "Changing Traditions: South Asian Americans and Cultural/Communal Politics." *Massachusetts Review* 43(1):75–88.

Kaufman, Stuart. 2001. *Modern Hatreds: The Symbolic Politics of Ethnic War.* New York: Cornell University Press.

Kawano, Satsuki. 2010. *Nature's Embrace: Japan's Aging Urbanites and New Death Rites.* Honolulu: University of Hawai'i Press.

Keen, Benjamin, and Keith Haynes. 2013. *A History of Latin America* (9th ed.). Belmont CA: Cengage.

Kelly, Gail P. 1986. "Learning to Be Marginal: Schooling in Interwar French West Africa." *Journal of Asian and African Studies* 21:171–184.

Kelley, Heidi. 1991. "Unwed Mothers and Household Reputation in a Spanish Galician Community." *American Ethnologist* 18(3):565–580.

Kennedy, Maev. 2011. "Peter the Wild Boy's Condition Revealed 200 Years after His Death." *The Guardian,* March 20.

Kennedy, Merrit. 2016. "Lead-Laced Water in Flint: A Step-by-Step Look at the Makings of a Crisis." National Public Radio, April 20. Available at http://www.npr.org/sections/thetwo-way/2016/04/20/465545378/lead-laced-water-in-flint-a-step-by-step-look-at-the-makings-of-a-crisis, accessed July 15, 2016.

Kepel, Gilles. 2005. *The Roots of Radical Islam.* London: Saqi.

Kilbride, Philip L. 2004. "Plural and Same Sex Marriage." *Anthropology News* 45(5):17.

Kilbride, Philip L. 2006. "African Polygyny: Family Values and Contemporary Changes." In Aaron Podolefsky and Peter J. Brown (eds.), *Applying Cultural Anthropology: An Introductory Reader* (5th ed., pp. 201–208). Mountain View, CA: Mayfield.

Kimmel, Michael. 1996. *Manhood in America: A Cultural History.* New York: Free Press.

Kimmelman, Michael. 2007. "In Marseille, Rap Helps Keep the Peace." *New York Times,* December 19, p. C1.

Klein, Laura F. 1976. "'She's One of Us, You Know': The Public Life of Tlingit Women: Traditional, Historical, and Contemporary Perspectives." *Western Canadian Journal of Anthropology* 6(3):164–183.

Klein, Laura F. 1995. "Mother as Clanswoman: Rank and Gender in Tlingit Society." In L. F. Klein and L. A. Ackerman (eds.), *Women and Power in Native North America* (pp. 28–45). Norman: University of Oklahoma Press.

Kleinman, Arthur. 1988. *The Illness Narratives: Suffering, Healing and the Human Condition.* New York: Basic Books.

Klinenberg, Eric. 2012a. *Going Solo: The Extraordinary Rise and Surprising Appeal of Living Alone.* New York: Penguin.

Klinenberg, Eric. 2012b. "One's a Crowd." *New York Times,* February 5, p. SR4.

Kluckhohn, Clyde. 1959. "The Philosophy of the Navaho Indians." In M. H. Fried (ed.), *Readings in Anthropology* (vol. 2). New York: Crowell.

Kluckhohn, Clyde, and Florence Kluckhohn. 1947. "American Culture: Generalized Organization and Class Patterns." In LymanBryson, Louis Finkelstein, and R. M. Maciver (eds.), *Conflicts of Power in Modern Culture: Symposium Conference in Science Philosophy and Religion* (pp. 106–128). New York: Harper.

Kofinas, Gary. 2007. *Subsistence Hunting in a Global Economy.* Available at http://arcticcircle.uconn.edu/NatResources/subsistglobal.html, accessed June 12, 2007.

Kohn, Hans. 1958. "Reflections on Colonialism." In R. Strausz-Hupe and H. W. Hazard (eds.), *The Idea of Colonialism* (pp. 2–16). New York: Praeger.

Kottak, Conrad P. 1992. *Assault on Paradise: Social Change in a Brazilian Village* (2nd ed.). New York: McGraw-Hill.

Kramer, Sarah. 2011. "Three Generations, One Roof." *New York Times,* September 25, p. MB1.

Krause, J., C. Lalueza-Fox, L. Orlando, W. Enard, R. E. Green, H. A. Burbano, J. J. Hublin, C. Hanni, J. Fortea, M. de la Rasilla, J. Bertranpetit, A. Rosas, and S. Paabo. 2007. "The Derived FOXP2 Variant of Modern Humans Was Shared with Neandertals." *Current Biology* 17(21):1908–1912.

Krauss, Michael E. 1992. "The World's Languages in Crisis." *Language* 68(1):6–10.

Kreider, Rose M., and Renee Ellis. 2011. "Living Arrangements of Children: 2009." *Current Population Reports,* no. P70-126. Washington, DC: U.S. Census Bureau.

Kristoff, Nicholas, and Sheryl WuDunn. 2000. "Two Cheers for Sweatshops." *New York Times,* September 24.

Kristof, Nicholas D., and Sheryl WuDunn. 2009. *Half the Sky: Turning Oppression into Opportunity for Women Worldwide.* New York: Knopf.

Kulick, Don. 1998. *Travesti: Sex, Gender, and Culture among Brazilian Transgendered Prostitutes.* Chicago: University of Chicago Press.

Kumar, G. Stanley Jaya. 1995. *Tribals from Tradition to Transition: A Study of Yanadi Tribes of Andhra Pradesh.* New Delhi: M D Publications.

Labov, William. 1972. *Language in the Inner City.* Philadelphia: University of Pennsylvania Press.

Labov, William, Sharon Ash, and Charles Boburg. 2005. *Atlas of North American English: Phonetics, Phonology and Sound Change.* Berlin: Mouton de Gruyter.

LaFraniere, Sharon. 2011. "Chinese Flock to U.S. Envoy, but Leaders Are Ruffled." *New York Times,* November 12, p. A5.

Lamb, Sarah. 2009. *Aging and the Indian Diaspora: Cosmopolitan Families in India and Abroad.* Bloomington: Indiana University Press.

Lamphere, Louise. 2005. "The Domestic Sphere of Women and the Public World of Men: The Strength and Limitations of an Anthropological Dichotomy." In Caroline B. Brettell and Carolyn F. Sargent (eds.), *Gender in Cross-Cultural Perspective* (4th ed., pp. 86–94). Upper Saddle River, NJ: Pearson/Prentice Hall.

Language in Society. 1997. A Language Is a Dialect with an Army and a Navy. *Language in Society* 26(3):469.

Lapidus, Ira M. 1988. *A History of Islamic Societies.* Cambridge, UK: Cambridge University Press.

Lareau, Annette. 2003. *Unequal Childhoods: Class, Race, and Family Life.* Berkeley: University of California Press.

Lassiter, Luke Eric. 2004. "Collaborative Ethnography." *AnthroNotes* 25(1):1–9.

Leacock, Eleanor Burke. 1981. *Myths of Male Dominance.* New York: Monthly Review.

Leathers, Dale G. 1997. *Successful Nonverbal Communication* (3rd ed.). Boston: Allyn and Bacon.

LeDuff, Charlie. 2006. "Dreams in the Dark at the Drive-Through Window." *New York Times,* November 27, p. A12.

Lee, Richard. 1984. The Dobe !Kung. New York: Holt, Rinehart, and Winston.

Lee, Richard B. 2000. "Indigenism and Its Discontents: Anthropology and the Small Peoples at the Millennium." Keynote address at the annual meeting of the American Ethnological Society, Tampa, Florida, March 2000.

Lee, Richard B. 2003. *The Dobe Ju/'hoansi* (3rd ed.). Belmont, CA: Wadsworth.

Lee, Richard B., and Ida Susser. 2008. "Confounding Conventional Wisdom: The Ju/'hoansi and HIV/AIDS." In Douglas A. Feldman (ed.), *AIDS, Culture, and Africa.* Gainesville: University Press of Florida.

Lefever, Harry G. 1996. "When the Saints Go Riding In: Santeria in Cuba and the United States." *Journal for the Scientific Study of Religion* 35:318–330.

Lepowsky, Maria. 1993. *Fruit of the Motherland: Gender in an Egalitarian Society.* New York: Columbia University Press.

Leshkowich, Ann Marie. 2011. "Making Class and Gender: (Market) Socialist Enframing of Traders in Ho Chi Minh City." *American Anthropologist* 113(2):277–290.

Lessinger, Johanna. 2013. "'Love' in the Shadow of the Sewing Machine: A Study of Marriage in the Garment Industry of Chennai, South India." In Shalini Grover, Ravinder Kaur, and Rajni Paltriwalla (eds.), *Marriage in Globalizing Contexts: Exploring Change and Continuity in South Asia.* Delhi: Orient Blackswan.

Levin, Dan. 2010. "The China Boom." *New York Times,* November 7, p. 16.

Levine, Mark, and Penny Roberts (eds.). 1999. *The Massacre in History.* New York: Berghahn.

Levine, Mary Ann, and Rita Wright. 1999. "COSWA Corner." *Society for American Archaeology Bulletin* 17(2).

Levinson, David. 1989. "Family Violence in Cross-Cultural Perspective." *Frontiers of Anthropology* (vol. 1). Newbury Park, CA: Sage.

Levinson, David. 1996. *Religion: A Cross-cultural Dictionary.* New York: Oxford University Press.

Lévi-Strauss, Claude. 1969/1949. *The Elementary Structures of Kinship.* Boston: Beacon.

Lewchuk, Wayne A. 1993. "Men and Monotony: Fraternalism as a Managerial Strategy at the Ford Motor Company." *Journal of Economic History* 53(4):824–856.

Lewis, Herbert S. 2001. "The Passion of Franz Boas." *American Anthropologist* 103(2):447–467.

Lewis, Richard D. 1996. *When Cultures Collide: Managing Successfully across Cultures.* London: Nicholas Brealey.

Lewis, Tom. 1991. *Empire of the Air: The Men Who Made Radio.* New York: Harper Perennial.

Lewis-Kraus, Gideon. 2016. "The Trials of Alice Goffman." *New York Times Magazine,* January 12. Available at http://www.nytimes.com/2016/01/17/magazine/the-trials-of-alice-goffman.html, accessed July 15, 2016.

Liebow, Elliot. 1967. *Talley's Corner: A Study of Negro Street Corner Men.* Boston: Little, Brown.

Lindstrom, Lamont. 1993. *Cargo Cult: Strange Stories of Desire from Melanesia and Beyond.* Honolulu: University of Hawai'i Press.

Lindquist, Danille Christensen. 2006. "'Locating' the Nation: Football Game Day and American Dreams in Central Ohio." *Journal of American Folklore* 119(4):444–488.

Lipka, Michael. 2015. "Muslims and Islam: Key Findings in the U.S. and Around the World. Pew Research Center, December 7. Available at http://www.pewresearch.org/fact-tank/2015/12/07/muslims-and-islam-key-findings-in-the-u-s-and-around-the-world, accessed April 22, 2016.

Lipsitz, George. 1994. *Dangerous Crossroads: Popular Music, Postmodernism, and the Poetics of Place.* London: Verso.

Lobao, Linda, and Katherine Meyer. 2001. "The Great Agricultural Transition: Crisis, Change, and Social Consequences of Twentieth Century U.S. Farming." *Annual Review of Sociology* 27:103–124.

Lockwood, Victoria. 2005. "The Impact of Development on Women: The Interplay of Material Conditions and Gender Ideology." In Caroline B. Brettell and Carolyn F. Sargent (eds.), *Gender in Cross Cultural Perspective* (4th ed., pp. 500–514). Upper Saddle River, NJ: Prentice Hall.

Lovejoy, Paul E. 1983. *Transformations in Slavery: A History of Slavery in Africa.* Cambridge, UK: Cambridge University Press.

Lowrey, Annie. 2012. "U.S. Candidate Is Chosen to Lead the World Bank." *New York Times,* April 17.

Luker, Kristin. 1996. *Dubious Conceptions: The Politics of Teenage Pregnancy.* Cambridge, MA: Harvard University Press.

Lutkehaus, Nancy C., and Paul B. Roscoe (eds.). 1995. *Gender Rituals: Female Initiation in Melanesia.* New York: Routledge.

Lyon-Callo, Vincent. 2004. *Inequality, Poverty, and Neoliberal Governance: Activist Ethnography in the Homeless Sheltering Industry.* Orchard Park, NY: Broadview.

MacCormack, Carol P. Hoffer. 1974. "Madam Yoko: Ruler of the Kpa Mende Confederacy." In Michele Z. Rosaldo and Louise Lamphere (eds.), *Woman, Culture and Society* (pp. 171–187). Stanford, CA: Stanford University Press.

Mace, Ruth. 2008. "Reproducing in China." *Science* 319:764–766.

Madsbjerg, Christian, and Mikkel B. Rasmussen. 2014. "An Anthropologist Walks into a Bar... ." *Harvard Business Review.* March. Available at https://hbr.org/2014/03/an-anthropologist-walks-into-a-bar, accessed April 22, 2016.

Magazine, Roger. 2012. *The Village Is Like a Wheel.* Tucson: University of Arizona Press.

Mahdavi, Pardis. 2009. *Passionate Uprisings: Iran's Sexual Revolution.* Stanford, CA: Stanford University Press.

Maine Rural Health Research Center. 2007. "Substance Abuse Among Rural Youth: A Little Meth and a Lot of Booze." Muskie School of Public Service Research and Policy Brief. Available at http://muskie.usm.maine.edu/Publications/rural/pb35a.pdf, accessed July 14, 2016.

Malinowski, Bronislaw. 1929a. "Practical Anthropology." *Africa* 2:22–38.

Malinowski, Bronislaw. 1929b. *The Sexual Life of Savages.* New York: Harcourt, Brace and World.

Malinowski, Bronislaw. 1948. *Magic, Science, and Religion and Other Essays.* New York: Free Press.

Malinowski, Bronislaw. 1984/1922. *Argonauts of the Western Pacific.* Prospect Heights, IL: Waveland.

Manalansan, Martin F. IV. 2003. *Global Divas.* Durham, NC: Duke University Press.

Manji, Irshad. 2003. *The Trouble with Islam: A Wakeup Call for Honesty and Change.* Toronto, ON: Random House Canada.

Mann, Charles. 2011. *1491: New Revelations of the Americas before Columbus* (2nd ed.). New York: Knopf.

Marcus, George E., and Michael M. J. Fischer. 1986. *Anthropology as Culture Critique: An Experimental Moment in the Human Sciences.* Chicago: University of Chicago Press.

Markowitz, Gerald, and David Rosen. 2013. *Lead Wars: The Politics of Science and the Fate of America's Children.* Berkeley: University of California.

Marlowe, Frank W. 2004. "Marital Residence among Foragers." *Current Anthropology* 45(2):277–284.

Marshall, Donald. 1971. "Sexual Behavior on Mangaia." In D. S. Marshall and R. C. Suggs (eds.), *Human Sexual Behavior: Variations in the Ethnographic Spectrum* (pp. 163–172). New York: Basic Books.

Marshall, Mac. 1979. *Weekend Warriors.* Palo Alto, CA: Mayfield.

Martin, Douglas. 2013. "Nevin S. Scrimshaw, Pioneer Nutritionist, Dies at 95." *New York Times,* February 12.

Martin, Emily. 1987. *The Woman in the Body.* New York: Beacon.

Martin, M. K., and Barbara Voorhies. 1975. *Female of the Species.* New York: Columbia University Press.

Martinez, Oscar. 2014. "The Children Will Keep Coming." *The Nation,* August 18/25, p. 11.

Mateu-Gelabert, Pedro, and Howard Lune. 2007. "Street Codes in High School: School as an Educational Deterrent." *City & Community* 6(3):173–191.

Mather, Mark. 2010. "U.S. Children in Single-Mother Families." *PRB Data Brief,* May 2010. Available at www.prb.org/Publications/PolicyBriefs/singlemotherfamilies.aspx, accessed June 11, 2012.

Matsumoto, David, and Tsutomu Kudoh. 1993. "American-Japanese Cultural Differences in Attributions of Personality Based on Smiles." *Journal of Nonverbal Communication* 17(4):231–243.

Matthiessen, Peter. 2007. "Alaska: Big Oil and the Whales." *New York Review of Books,* November 22, pp. 57–64.

Matzner, Andrew. 2001. *'O Au No Keia: Voices from Hawai'i's Mahu and Transgender Communities.* Philadelphia: XLibris.

Mauss, Marcel. 1990/1924. *The Gift: Form and Reason of Exchange in Archaic Societies* (W. D. Halls, trans.). New York: Norton.

Mayerowitz, Scott. 2010. "Chelsea Clinton Wedding Price Tag: $2 Million." *ABC News,* July 22. Available at http://abcnews.go.com/Travel/chelsea-clinton-marc-mezvinsky-rhinebeck-wedding-price-tag/story?id=11210739#.UXbV_2wo6Uk, accessed April 23, 2013.

Maybury-Lewis, David. 1997. *Indigenous Peoples, Ethnic Groups, and the State.* Boston: Allyn and Bacon.

McAllester, David. 1954. *Enemy Way Music.* Cambridge, MA: Harvard University Peabody Museum.

McCarthy, Justin. 2015. "Little Change in Percentage of Americans Who Own Stocks." *Gallup,* April 22. Available at http://www.gallup.com/poll/182816/little-change-percentage-americans-invested-market.aspx, accessed April 22, 2016.

McCaskie, T. C. 1995. *State and Society in Pre-Colonial Asante.* Cambridge, UK: Cambridge University Press.

McGee, R. Jon. 1990. *Life, Ritual, and Religion among the Lacandon Maya.* Belmont, CA: Wadsworth.

Mcgee, R. Jon, and Richard L. Warms. 2012. *Anthropological Theory: An Introductory History.* New York: McGraw-Hill.

McGranahan, Carole. 2012a. "An Anthropologist in Political Asylum Court, Part I." *Anthropology News,* March.

McGranahan, Carole. 2012b (April). "Anthropology and the Truths of Political Asylum, Part II." *Anthropology News,* p. 20.

McGovern, Mike. 2011. "Before You Judge, Stand in Her Shoes." *New York Times,* July 6, p. 21.

Mead, Margaret. 1963/1935. *Sex and Temperament in Three Primitive Societies.* New York: Dell.

Mead, Margaret. 1971/1928. *Coming of Age in Samoa.* New York: Morrow.

Melendez, Edwin. 1993. *Colonial Subjects: Critical Perspectives on Contemporary Puerto Ricans.* Boston: South End.

Merry, E. Wayne. 2016. "The Origins of Russia' War in Ukraine: The Clash of Russian and European 'Civilizational Choices' for Ukraine." In Elizabeth A. Wood et. al. (eds.), *Roots of Russia's War in Ukraine.* New York: Columbia University Press.

Messenger, John C. 1971. "Sex and Repression in an Irish Folk Community." In D. S. Marshall and R. C. Suggs (eds.), *Human Sexual Behavior: Variations in the Ethnographic Spectrum* (pp. 3–37). New York: Basic Books.

Messina, Maria. 1988. "Henna Party." *Natural History* 97(9):40.

Meyer, Stephen. 2004. "The Degradation of Work Revisited: Workers and Technology in the American Auto Industry, 1900–2000." *Automobile in American Life and Society.* Available at www.autolife.umd.umich.edu/Labor/L_Overview/L_Overview3.htm.

Miller, Claire Cain and Liz Alderman. 2014. "The Flexibility Gap." *New York Times,* December 14, p. B1.

Minor, Horace. 1956. "Body Ritual among the Nacirema." *American Anthropologist.* (new series) 58(3):503–507.

Mintz, Sidney W. 1985. *Sweetness and Power: The Place of Sugar in Modern History.* New York: Penguin.

Modelski, George. 2004. World Cities, Empires, and World System Evolution. Paper presented at the "Globalization and World System Dynamics" panel, annual conference of the International Studies Association, Montreal, March 18.

Montagu, Ashley. 1978. *Touching: The Human Significance of the Skin* (2nd ed.). New York: Harper and Row.

Moore, Jerry D. 2014. *A Prehistory of South America.* Denver: University of Colorado.

Moore, Robert. 2011. "If I Actually Talked Like That I'd Pull a Gun on Myself: Accent, Avoidance, and Moral Panic in Irish English." *Anthropological Quarterly* 84(1):41–64.

Moore, Sally Falk. 1978. *Law as Process: An Anthropological Approach.* London: Routledge and Kegan Paul.

Morgan, Marcyliena. 2004. "Speech Community." In Alassandro Duranti (ed.), *A Companion to Linguistic Anthropology* (pp. 3–33). Malden, MA: Blackwell.

Morris, Craig, and Adriana Von Hagen. 2011. *The Incas: Lords of the Four Quarters.* London: Thames and Hudson.

Morton, Mark. 2009. "The Shape of Food to Come." *Gastronomica: The Journal of Food and Culture* 9(4):6–7.

Moser, Caroline. 1993. *Gender Planning and Development: Theory, Practice, and Training.* New York: Routledge.

Mshana, Gerry, M. L. Plummer, J. Wamoyi, Z. S. Shigongo, D. A. Ross, and D. Wight. 2006. "She Was Bewitched and Caught an Illness Similar to AIDS: AIDS and Sexually Transmitted Infection Causation Beliefs in Rural Northern Tanzania." *Culture, Health, and Sexuality* 8(1):45–58.

Mucha, Janusz L. 2016. "An Outsider's View of American Culture." In Philip DeVita (ed.), *Distant Mirrors: America as a Foreign Culture* (4th ed., pp. 136–144). Long Grove, IL: Waveland.

Muhammad, Dedrick. 2008. "Race and Extreme Inequality." *The Nation,* June 30, p. 26.

Munn, Nancy D. 1990. "Constructing Regional Worlds in Experience: Kula Exchange, Witchcraft and Gawan Local Events." *Man* 25:1–17.

Murdock, George Peter. 1949. *Social Structure.* New York: Free Press.

Murphy, Joseph M. 1989. *Santeria: An African Religion in America.* Boston: Beacon.

Murphy, Robert. 1964. "Social Distance and the Veil." *American Anthropologist* 66:1257–1273.

Murphy, Yolanda, and Robert Murphy. 1974. *Women of the Forest.* New York: Columbia University Press.

Muskie School of Public Service. 2007. Substance Abuse Among Rural Youth: A little meth and a lot of booze. *Main Rural Health Research Center.* Available at: https://muskie.usm.maine.edu /Publications/rural/pb35a.pdf, accessed April 22, 2016.

Mydans, Seth. 2008. "U.S. Deportee Brings Street Dance to Street Boys of Cambodia." *New York Times,* November 30, p. A6.

Myerhoff, Barbara G. 1974. *Peyote Hunt: The Sacred Journey of the Huichol Indians.* Ithaca, NY: Cornell University Press.

Myerhoff, Barbara. 1978. *Number Our Days.* New York: Simon & Schuster.

Myers, Fred. 1986. *Pintupi Country, Pintupi Self: Sentiment, Place, and Politics among Western Desert Aborigines.* Washington, DC: Smithsonian Institution Press.

Myers, Steven Lee, Andrew C. Revkin, Simon Romero, and Clifford Krauss. 2005. "Old Ways of Life Are Fading as the Arctic Thaws." *New York Times,* October 20, p. A1.

Nader, Laura. 2006. "Human Rights and Moral Imperialism: A Double-Edged Story." *Anthropology News* 47(7):6.

Nagashima, Kenji, and James A. Schellenberg. 1997. "Situational Differences in Intentional Smiling: A Cross-Cultural Exploration." *Journal of Social Psychology* 137:297–301.

Nagengast, Carole. 1994. "Violence, Terror, and the Crisis of the State." In B. J. Siegel (ed.), *Annual Review of Anthropology* (vol. 23, pp. 109–136). Stanford, CA: Stanford University Press.

Naimark, Norman. 2001. *Fires of Hatred: Ethnic Cleansing in Twentieth-Century Europe.* Cambridge, MA: Harvard University Press.

Nanda, Serena. 1999. *Neither Man nor Woman: The Hijras of India* (2nd ed.). Belmont, CA: Wadsworth.

Nanda, Serena. 2000a. "Arranging a Marriage in India." In P. R. DeVita (ed.), *Stumbling towards Truth: Anthropologists at Work* (pp. 196–204). Prospect Heights, IL: Waveland.

Nanda, Serena. 2004. "South African Museums and the Creation of a New National Identity." *American Anthropologist* 106(2):379–385.

Nanda, Serena. 2013. "The Hijras: An Alternative Gender in India." In Elvio Angeloni (ed.), *Annual Editions, Anthropology (pp. 102–109).* New York: McGraw-Hill.

Nanda, Serena. 2014. "The Other Side of Paradise." *The Indypendent,* May 14. Available at https://indypendent .org/2014/05/14/other-side-paradise, accessed July 15, 2016.

Nanda, Serena. 2016. "Reflections on American Culture." In Philip DeVita (ed.). *Distant Mirrors: America as a Foreign Culture* (4th ed., pp. 5–22). Long Grove, IL: Waveland.

Nanda, Serena, and Joan Young Gregg. 2009. *The Gift of A Bride: A Tale of Anthropology, Matrimony, and Murder.* Lanham, MD: Rowman/Altamira.

Nanda, Serena, and Joan Gregg. 2011. *Assisted Dying: An Ethnographic Murder Mystery on Florida's Gold Coast.* Lanham, MD: Rowman Littlefield/Altamira.

Narayan, Kirin. 1993. "How Native Is a 'Native' Anthropologist?" *American Anthropologist* 95:671–686.

Narayanaswami, V. R. 2010. "Linguistics as an Identification Tool." *Livemint,* November 15. Available at www .livemint.com/Opinion /Oseful1LDWVtZkNPuXQACN /Linguistics-as-an-identification-tool .html, accessed April 23, 2013.

NASA. 2016. Arctic Sea Ice Minimum. *NASA Global Climate Change.* Available at http://climate.nasa.gov/vital-signs /arctic-sea-ice, accessed April 22, 2016.

Nash, June. 1970. *In the Eyes of the Ancestors: Belief and Behavior in a Mayan Community.* New Haven, CT: Yale University Press.

Nash, June. 1986. *Women and Change in Latin America.* South Hadley, MA: Bergin and Garvey.

Nash, June. 1993. "Introduction: Traditional Arts and Changing Markets in Middle America." In June Nash and Helen Safa (eds.), *Crafts in the World Market* (pp. 1–24). Albany: State University of New York Press.

Nash, June. 1994. "Global Integration and Subsistence Insecurity." *American Anthropologist* 96:7–30.

Nash, Maning. 1961. "The Social Context of Economic Choice in a Small Society." *Man* 219:186–191.

Nayar, Baldev Raj, and T. V. Paul. 2003. *India in the World Order: Searching for Major Power Status.* Cambridge, UK: Cambridge University Press.

Nelson, Edward William. 1983. *The Eskimo about Bering Strait.* Washington, DC: Smithsonian Institution.

Nesbitt, Richard. 2007. "All Brains Are the Same Color." *New York Times,* December 9, section 4, p 11.

Netting, Robert. 1977. *Cultural Ecology.* Menlo Park, CA: Cummings.

Neumann, Thomas W. 1985. "Human-Wildlife Competition and the Passenger Pigeon: Population Growth from System Destabilization." *Human Ecology* 13(4):389–410.

Newman, Philip L. 1977. "When Technology Fails: Magic and Religion in New Guinea." In James P. Spradley and David W. McCurdy (eds.), *Conformity and Conflict: Readings in Cultural Anthropology* (3rd ed.). Boston: Little Brown.

Newport, Frank. 2015a. "Americans Continue to Say U.S. Wealth Distribution Is Unfair." *Gallup,* May 4. Available at http://www.gallup.com/poll/182987/americans-continue-say-wealth-distribution-unfair.aspx, accessed April 22, 2016.

Newport, Frank. 2015b. "Fewer Americans Identify as Middle Class in Recent Years." April 28. http://www.gallup.com/poll/182918/fewer-americans-identify-middle-class-recent-years.aspx, accessed April 11, 2016.

Newson, L. 1999. "Disease and Immunity in the Pre-Spanish Philippines." *Social Science and Medicine* 48:1833–1850.

Newton, Michael. 2002. *Savage Girls and Wild Boys: A History of Feral Children.* London: Faber and Faber.

New York Times Editorial Board. 2015. "Transgender Today," May 4, 2015. http://www.nytimes.com/2015/05/04/opinion/the-quest-for-transgender-equality.html.

Nicolaisen, Ida. 2006. "Anthropology Should Actively Promote Human Rights." *Anthropology News* 47(7):6.

Nisbett, Richard E. 2007. "All Brains Are the Same Color." *New York Times,* December 9, section 4 (science), p. 11.

Nolen, Stephanie. 2015. "Black Is Beautiful, but White—White Is Just Easier." *Globe and Mail*, August 1, p. 1F.

Norbeck, Edward. 1974. *Religion in Human Life: Anthropological Views.* Prospect Heights, IL: Waveland.

Norgren, Jill, and Serena Nanda. 1996. *American Cultural Pluralism and Law* (2nd ed.). New York: Praeger.

Norgren, Jill, and Serena Nanda. 2006. *American Cultural Pluralism and Law* (3rd ed.). Westport, CT: Praeger.

Nutt, Amy Ellis. 2015. *Becoming Nicole: The Transformation of an American Family.* New York: Random House.

Offiong, Daniel A. 1983. "Witchcraft among the Ibibio of Nigeria." *African Studies Review* 26:107–124.

Ogbu, John. 1978. "African Bridewealth and Women's Status." *American Ethnologist* 5:241–260.

Ogembo, Justus M. 2001. "Cultural Narratives, Violence and Mother-Son Loyalty: An Exploration into Gusii Personification of Evil." *Ethos* 29(1):3–29.

Ojeda, Amparo B. 2016. "Growing Up American: Doing the Right Thing." In Philip DeVita (ed.), *Distant Mirrors: America as a Foreign Culture* (4th ed., pp. 145–151). Long Grove, IL: Waveland.

O'Kelly, Charlotte G., and Larry S. Carney. 1986. *Women and Men in Society: Cross-Cultural Perspectives on Gender Stratification.* Belmont, CA: Wadsworth.

Oliver, Mary Beth. 2003. "Race and Crime in the Media: Research from a Media Effects Tradition." In A. Valdivia (ed.), *A Companion to Media Studies* (pp. 421–436). London: Blackwell.

Oreskes, Naomi. 2004. "The Scientific Consensus on Climate Change." *Science* 306(5702):1686.

Oriard, Michael. 1993. *Reading Football: How the Popular Press Created an American Spectacle.* Chapel Hill: University of North Carolina Press.

Otterbein, Keith F. 2010. "Nobel Peace Prize—Passed Over Again." *General Anthropology: Bulletin of the General Anthropology Division*, Spring, p. 1.

Paiement, Jason J. 2007. "Anthropology and Development." *National Association for the Practice of Anthropology Bulletin* 27(1):196–223.

Palkovich, Anna M. 1994. "Historic Epidemics of the American Pueblos." In C. S. Larsen and G. R. Milner (eds.), *In the Wake of Contact: Biological Responses to Conquest* (pp. 87–95). New York: Wiley.

Pareles, Jon. 1996. "A Small World after All. But Is That Good?" *New York Times,* March 24, p. B34.

Peacock, Nadine R. 1991. "Rethinking the Sexual Division of Labor: Reproduction and Women's Work among the Efe." In M. di Leonardo (ed.), *Gender and the Crossroads of Knowledge: Feminist Anthropology in the Postmodern Era* (pp. 339–360). Berkeley: University of California Press.

Peletz, M. 2009. *Gender Pluralism: Southeast Asia Since Early Modern Times.* New York: Routledge.

Peletz, M. 2012. "Gender, Sexuality, and the State in Southeast Asia." *Journal of Asian Studies* 71(4):895–917.

Pelham, Nicolas. 2015. "Libya against Itself." *New York Review of Books,* February 19, p. 38.

Peoples, James G. 1990. "The Evolution of Complex Stratification in Eastern Micronesia." *Micronesia Supplement* 2:291–302.

Peregrine, Peter N., Carol R. Ember, and Melvin Ember. 2004. "Universal Patterns in Cultural Evolution: An Empirical Analysis Using Guttman Scaling." *American Anthropologist* 106(1):145–149.

Perez-Pena, Richard. 2012. "Student's Account Has Rape in Spotlight." *New York Times,* October 27, p. A15.

Perovich, D., et. al. 2015. "Sea Ice." *NOAA Arctic Report Card.* Available at http://arctic.noaa.gov/reportcard/sea_ice.html. accessed April 22, 2016.

Pew Research Center. 2007. "Muslim Americans: Middle Class and Mostly Mainstream." Available at http://pewsocialtrends.org/2007/05/22/muslim-americans-middle-class-and-mostly-mainstream, accessed November 15, 2010.

Pew Research Center. 2015a. "Cell Phones in Africa: Communication Lifeline." April 15. Available at http://www.pewglobal.org/2015/04/15/cell-phones-in-africa-communication-lifeline, accessed April 22, 2016.

Pew Research Center. 2015b. "Wealth Gap between Middle-Income and Upper-Income Families Reaches Record High." Available at http://www.bls.gov/news.release/pdf/empsit.pdf, accessed July 15, 2016.

Peyrefitte, Alain. 1992. *The Immobile Empire* (Jon Rothschild, trans.). New York: Knopf.

Pigg, Stacy Leigh. 2001. "Languages of Sex and AIDS in Nepal: Notes on the Social Production of Commensurability." *Current Anthropology* 16(4):481–541.

Pilkington, Ed. 2010. "South Park Censored after Threat of Fatwa over Muhammad Episode." Guardian.co.uk. Available at www.guardian.co.uk/tv-and-radio/2010/apr/22/south-park-censored-fatwa-muhammad, accessed August 20, 2010.

Pinker, Steven. 1994. *The Language Instinct.* New York: William Morrow.

Pinker, Steven. 2011. *The Better Angels of Our Nature.* New York: Viking.

Pitts, Leonard. 2007. "At Large, Replying to Those E-Mails about Vick." *Miami Herald,* September 12.

Plattner, Stuart. 1989. "Marxism." In S. Plattner (ed.), *Economic Anthropology* (pp. 379–396). Stanford, CA: Stanford University Press.

Polese, Abel. 2008. "'If I Receive It, It Is a Gift; If I Demand It, Then It Is a Bribe': On the Local Meaning of Economic Transactions in Post-Soviet Ukraine." *Anthropology in Action 15(3):47–60.*

Polyani, Karl. 1944. *The Great Transformation.* New York: Holt, Rinehart and Winston.

Population Reference Bureau. 2012. "2012 World Population Data Sheet." Available at http://www.prb.org/pdf12/2012-population-data-sheet_eng.pdf, accessed May 20, 2016.

Porter, Eduardo. 2016. "Contemplating the End of the Human Workhorse." *New York Times,* June 8, p. B1.

Potash, Betty. 1989. "Gender Relations in Sub-Saharan Africa." In S. Morgen (ed.), *Gender and Anthropology: Critical Reviews for Research and Teaching* (pp. 189–227). Washington, DC: American Anthropological Association.

Powers, Thomas. 2005. "The Indians' Own Story." *New York Review of Books,* April 7, p. 73.

Prah, Kwesi K. 1990. "Anthropologists, Colonial Administrators, and the Lotuko of Eastern Equatoria, Sudan: 1952–1953." *African Journal of Sociology* 3(2):70–86.

Preston, Julia. 2009. "A Slippery Place in the U.S. Work Force." *New York Times,* March 22, p. A1.

Price, Sally. 1989. *Primitive Art in Civilized Places.* Chicago: University of Chicago Press.

Price, Sally. 2007. *Paris Primitive: Jacques Chirac's Museum on the Quai Branly.* Chicago: University of Chicago Press.

Prose, Francine. 2011. *My New American Life.* New York: HarperCollins.

Prunier, Gerard. 2008. *Africa's World War: Congo, the Rwandan Genocide, and the Making of a Continental Catastrophe.* Oxford, UK: Oxford University Press.

Queen, Stuart, and Robert Haberstein. 1974. *The Family in Various Cultures.* New York: Lippincott.

Quinnipiac University. 2012. "American Voters Back Legalized Marijuana, Quinnipiac University National Poll Finds." December 5. Available at www.quinnipiac.edu/institutes--centers/polling-institute/national/release-detail?ReleaseID=1820, accessed April 23, 2013.

Radcliffe-Brown, A. R. 1965/1952. *Structure and Function in Primitive Society.* New York: Free Press.

Ramos, Francisco Martins. 2002. "My American Glasses." In Philip DeVita (ed.), *Distant Mirrors: America as a Foreign Culture* (4th ed., pp. 152–161). Long Grove, IL: Waveland.

Ranco, Darren J. 2006. "Toward a Native Anthropology: Hermeneutics, Hunting Stories, and Theorizing from Within." *Wicazo Sa Review* 21(2):61–78.

Rasmussen Reports. 2010. "87% Say English Should Be U.S. Official Language." *Rasmussen Reports,* May 11. Available at www.rasmussenreports.com/public_content/politics/general_politics/may_2010/87_say_english_should_be_u_s_official_language, accessed August 20, 2010.

Rasmussen Reports. 2014. "Americans Overwhelmingly Put English First." August 13. Available at http://www.rasmussenreports.com/public_content/lifestyle/general_lifestyle/august_2014/americans_overwhelmingly_put_english_first, accessed March 22, 2016.

Rasmussen, Susan. 2005. "Pastoral Nomadism and Gender: Status, Prestige, Economic Contribution, and Division of Labor among the Tuareg of Niger." In Caroline B. Brettell and Carolyn F. Sargent (eds.), *Gender in Cross Cultural Perspective* (4th ed., pp. 155–168). Upper Saddle River, NJ: Pearson/Prentice Hall.

Reaney, Patricia. 2012. "Average Cost of U.S. Wedding Hits $27,021." *Reuters,* March 23.

Renteln, Alison D. 2004. *The Culture Defense.* New York: Oxford University Press.

Republic of Indonesia. 1997. *Issues and Perspectives: A Solution to Java's Overcrowding.*

London: Embassy of the Republic of Indonesia. Available at www.indonesianembassy.org.uk/transmigration-7.htm, accessed March 3, 2010.

Rerkasem, Kanok, Deborah Lawrence, Christine Paddoch, Dietrich Schmidt-Vogt, Alan D. Ziegler, and Thilde Bech Bruun. 2009. "Consequences of Swidden Transitions for Crop and Fallow Biodiversity in Southeast Asia." *Human Ecology* 37:347–360.

Rhode, Deborah L. 2010. *The Beauty Bias: The Injustice of Appearance in Life and Law.* New York: Oxford University Press.

Ricklefs, Merle C. 1990. "Balance and Military Innovation in 17th Century Java." *History Today* 40(11):40–47.

Ricklefs, Merle. 2008. *A History of Modern Indonesia since 1200* (4th ed.). Stanford CA: Stanford University Press.

Ringlero, Aleta M. 2008. "Fritz Scholder: The Enigma." *Smithsonian National Museum of the American Indian,* Fall:16–24.

Robarchek, Clayton A., and Carole J. Robarchek. 1992. "Cultures of War and Peace: A Comparative Study of the Waorani and Semai." In James Silverberg and J. Patrick Gray (eds.), *Aggression and Peacefulness in Humans and Other Primates* (pp. 189–213). New York: Oxford University Press.

Roberts, Adam, and Timothy Garton Ash (eds.). 2009. *Civil Resistance and Power Politics: The Experience of Non-violent Action from Gandhi to the Present.* New York: Oxford University Press.

Roberts, Alan H., D. G. Kewman, L. Mercier, and M. Hovell. 1993. "The Power of Nonspecific Effects in Healing: Implications for Psychosocial and Biological Treatments." *Clinical Psychology Review* 13:375–391.

Robinson, Harlow. 1994. *The Last Impresario: The Life, Times, and Legacy of Sol Hurok.* New York: Viking.

Rödlach, Alexander. 2006. *Witches, Westerners and HIV: AIDS & Cultures of Blame in Africa.* Walnut Creek CA: Left Coast.

Rohde, Douglas, Steve Olson, and Joseph T. Chang. 2004. "Modelling the Recent Common Ancestry of All Living Humans." *Nature* 431:562–566.

Roland, Edna. 2001. "The Economics of Racism: People of African Descent in Brazil." Paper presented at the International Council on Human Rights Policy Seminar on the Economics of Racism, November 24–25, Geneva, Switzerland.

Romero, Simon. 2012. "Brazil Enacts Affirmative Action Law for Universities." *New York Times,* August 31, p. A4.

Rosaldo, Michelle Z., and Louise Lamphere. 1974. "Introduction." In M. Z. Rosaldo and L. Lamphere (eds.), *Women, Culture and Society* (pp. 1–16). Stanford, CA: Stanford University Press.

Roscoe, Paul. 2003. "Margaret Mead, Reo Fortune, and Mountain Arapesh Warfare." *American Anthropologist* 105(3):581–591.

Roscoe, Will. 1991. *The Zuni Man-Woman.* Albuquerque: University of New Mexico Press.

Roscoe, Will. 1995. "Strange Craft, Strange History, Strange Folks: Cultural Amnesia and the Case of Lesbian and Gay Studies." *American Anthropologist* 97:448–452.

Rosman, Abraham, and Paula G. Rubel. 1971. *Feasting with Mine Enemy: Rank and Exchange among Northwest Coast Societies.* Prospect Heights, IL: Waveland.

Roybal, Joe. 2007. "Big Beef Buyers." *Beef Magazine.* Available at http:// beefmagazine.com/mag/beef_big _beef_buyers/index. html.

Sacks, Karen Brodkin. 1982. *Sisters and Wives.* Westport, CT: Greenwood.

Sahlins, Marshall. 1961. "The Segmentary Lineage: An Organization of Predatory Expansion." *American Anthropologist* 63:332–345.

Sahlins, Marshall. 1971. "Poor Man, Rich Man, Big Man, Chief." In J. P. Spradley and D. W. McCurdy (eds.), *Conformity and Conflict* (pp. 362–376). Boston: Little, Brown.

Said, Edward. 1978. *Orientalism.* New York: Vintage.

Sala, Nohemi, et. al. 2015. "Lethal Interpersonal Violence in the Middle Pleistocene." *PLOS One* 10(5):e0126589.

Salzman, Philip. 1999. *The Anthropology of Real Life: Events in Human Experience.* Prospect Heights, IL: Waveland.

Salzman, Philip C. 2000. *Black Tents of Baluchistan.* Washington, DC: Smithsonian.

Salzmann, Zdenek. 1993. *Language, Culture and Society.* Boulder, CO: Westview.

Sanday, Peggy Reeves. 1981. *Female Power and Male Dominance.* New York: Cambridge University Press.

SAPRIN. 2004. *Structural Adjustment: The SAPRI Report.* London: Zed.

Scaglion, Richard. 1981. "Homicide Compensation in Papua New Guinea: Problems and Prospects." In *Law Reform Commission of Papua New Guinea Monograph 1.* Papua New Guinea: Office of Information.

Scammell, G. V. 1989. *The First Imperial Age.* London: HarperCollins Academic.

Schensul, Stephen L. 1997. "The Anthropologist in Medicine: Critical Perspectives on Cancer and Street Addicts." *Reviews in Anthropology* 26(1):57–69.

Schepartz, L. A. 1993. "Language and Modern Human Origins." *Yearbook of Physical Anthropology* 36:91–96.

Schildkrout, Enid. 2004. "Inscribing the Body." *Annual Review of Anthropology 33:319–344.*

Schmeets, Hans. 2012. "One in Six Go to Church or Mosque on a Regular Basis." *Statics Netherlands Web Magazine,* December 21.

Schmidt-Vogt, Dietrich, Stephen J. Leisz, Ole Mertz, Andreas Heinimann, Thiha Thiha, Peter Messerli, Michael Epprecht, Pham Van Cu, Vu Kim Chi, Martin Hardiono, and Truong M. Dao. 2009. "An Assessment of Trends in the Extent of Swidden in Southeast Asia." *Human Ecology* 37:269–80.

Schwartz, Richard D. 1990. "Human Rights Is an Evolving Culture." In Abdullahi Ahmed An Na'im and Francis M. Deng (eds.), *Human Rights in Africa: Cross-Cultural Perspectives* (pp. 368–381). Washington DC: Brookings.

Schwartz, Stuart B. 1994. *Implicit Understandings: Observing, Reporting, and Reflecting on the Encounters between Europeans and Other Peoples of the Early Modern Era.* Cambridge, UK: Cambridge University Press.

Science. 2012. "News and Analysis" 20 274–275.

Scott, Elizabeth M. 2001. "Food and Social Relations at Nina Plantation." *American Anthropologist* 103(3):671–691.

Scott, James. 1992. *Domination and the Arts of Resistance: Hidden Transcripts.* New Haven, CT: Yale University Press.

Scrimshaw, Nevin S. 2010. "The Origin and Development of INCAP." *Food and Nutrition Bulletin* 31(1):4–8.

Scrimshaw, Susan. 2012. "A 70-Year Marriage." *Timesunion.com,* February 14. Available at http://blog.timesunion .com/scrimshaw/a-70-year-marriage /632, accessed April 23, 2013.

Seabrook, Jeremy. 1999. *Love in a Different Climate: Men Who Have Sex with Men in India.* Brooklyn: Verso.

Sengupta, Somini, and Hawaida Saad. 2015. "As Refugees Flee, Thousands of Children Have No Country to Call Home." *New York Times,* November 6, p. A8.

Senior, Jennifer. 2014. "When Home Is an Elusive Objective." *New York Times,* February 22, p. Arts 1.

Service, Elman. 1962. *Primitive Social Organization.* New York: Random House.

Service, Elman. 1971. *Profiles in Ethnology.* New York: Harper and Row.

Shandy, Dianna J. 2007. *Nuer-American Passages: Globalizing Sudanese Migration.* Gainesville: University Press of Florida.

Shane, Scott, and Jo Becker. 2016. "A New Libya, with 'Very Little Time Left.'" *New York Times,* February 27, p. A1.

Sheehan, John. 1982. *The Enchanted Ring: The Untold Story of Penicillin.* Cambridge, MA: MIT Press.

Shepard, Glen H., Jr. 2011. "The Mark and Olly Follies." *Anthropology News,* May

Sheriff, Robin E. 2001. *Dreaming Equality: Color, Race and Racism in Urban Brazil.* East Brunswick, NJ: Rutgers University Press. 2001.

Silberbauer, George. 1982. "Political Process in G/wi Bands." In Eleanor Leacock and Richard Lee (eds.), *Politics and History in Band Societies* (pp. 23–35). New York: Cambridge University Press.

Smith, Adam. 1776. *An Inquiry into the Nature and Causes of the Wealth of Nations.* Dublin: Whitestone.

Smith, Mitch, and Monica Davey. 2015. "U.S. Says Transgender Student Has Rights in the Locker Room. *New York Times,* November 3, p. A1.

Smith, Roberta. 2005. "From a Mushroom Cloud, a Burst of Art Reflecting Japan's Psyche." *New York Times,* April 8, p. E33.

Snajdr, Edward. 2007. "Ethnicizing the Subject: Domestic Violence and the Politics of Primordialism in Kazakhstan." *Journal of the Royal Anthropological Institute (N.S.)* 13:603–620.

SOCPC. 2010. "Standard Occupational Classification." U.S. Bureau of Labor Statistics. Available at www.bls.gov /soc/major_groups.htm.

Sokolofsky, Jay. 2009. *The Cultural Context of Aging: Worldwide Perspective,*(3rd ed.). Westport, CT: Praeger.

Sokolofsky, Jay. 2015. *Mexico Engages the 21st Century: Never More Campesinos.* Belmont, CA: Cengage.

Sontag, Deborah. 2015. "'A Whole New Being': How Kricket Nimmons Seized the Transgender Moment." *New York Times,* December 13, p. 1A.

Soria, Chester. 2015. "NYC Turns toward Civic-Centered Tech." *Metro,* December 11–13, p. 4.

Southern Baptist Convention. 2006. Resolution 5 of the SBC Meeting, 2006, June 13–14: "On Alcohol Use in America." Available at www.sbc.net /resolutions/amResolution.asp?ID =1156.

Spencer, Kyle. 2012. "For Asians, School Tests Are Vital Steppingstones." *New York Times,* October 27, p. A20.

Spener, David. 2009. *Clandestine Crossings: Migrants and Coyotes on the Texas-Mexico Border.* Ithaca, NY: Cornell University Press.

Spiegel. 2010. "Continent of Fear: The Rise of Europe's Right-Wing Populists." *Spiegel Online,* September 28. Available at http://www.spiegel.de /international/europe/continent-of -fear-the-rise-of-europe-s-right-wing -populists-a-719842.html.

Sponsel, Leslie E. (ed.). 1995. *Indigenous Peoples and the Future of Amazonia: An Ecological Anthropology of an Endangered World.* Tucson: University of Arizona Press.

Spradley, James. 1970. *You Owe Yourself a Drunk.* Boston: Little, Brown.

Stanyon, Roscoe, Marco Sazzini, and Donata Luiselli. 2009. "Timing the First Human Migration into Eastern Asia." *Journal of Biology* 8:18.

Steiner, Christopher B. 1994. *African Art in Transit.* New York: Cambridge University Press.

Steiner, Christopher B. 1995. "The Art of the Trade: On the Creation of Value and Authenticity in the African Art Market." In G. E. Marcus and F. R. Myers (eds.), *The Traffic in Culture: Refiguring Art and Anthropology* (pp. 151–165). Berkeley: University of California Press.

Steiner, Christopher B. 2002. "Art/ Anthropology/Museums: Revulsions and Revolutions." In Jeremy MacClancy (ed.), *Exotic No More: Anthropology on the Front Lines* (pp. 400–17). Chicago: University of Chicago Press.

Sterling, Marvin D. 2010. *Babylon East: Performing Dancehall, Roots Reggae, and Rastafari in Japan.* Durham, NC: Duke University Press.

Stern, Pamela R. 1999. "Learning to Be Smart: An Exploration of the Culture of Intelligence in a Canadian Inuit Community." *American Anthropologist* 101:502–514.

Sternberg, Esther. 2002. "Walter B. Cannon and 'Voodoo' Death: A Perspective from 60 Years On." *American Journal of Public Health* 92:1564–1566.

Stevens, Phillips, Jr. 2006. "Women's Aggressive Use of Genital Power in Africa." *Transcultural Psychiatry* 43(4):592–599.

Stiglitz, Joseph E. 2012. *The Price of Inequality: How Today's Divided Society Endangers Our Future.* New York: Norton.

Stolberg, Sheryl Gay. 1999. "Black Mother's Mortality Rate Is Under Scrutiny." *New York Times,* August 8, p. A1.

Stone, Chad, et. al. 2015. "A Guide to Statistics on Historical Trends in Income Inequality." *Center on Budget and Policy Priorities.* October 26. Available at http://www.cbpp.org/research/poverty -and-inequality/a-guide-to-statistics-on -historical-trends-in-income-inequality, accessed July 15, 2016.

Stone, Glenn Davis. 1998. "Keeping the Home Fires Burning: The Changed Nature of Householding in the Kofyar Homeland." *Human Ecology* 26(2):239–265.

Stone, Linda, and Caroline James. 2005. "Dowry, Bride-Burning, and Female Power in India." In C. B. Brettell and C.

F. Sargent (eds.), *Gender in Cross-Cultural Perspective* (4th ed., pp. 312–320). Upper Saddle River, NJ: Prentice Hall.

Strathern, Marilyn. 1995. *Women in Between: Female Roles in a Male World: Mount Hagen, New Guinea.* Latham, MD: Rowman and Littlefield.

Strauss, Lawrence G. 1991. "Southwestern Europe at the Last Glacial Maximum." *Current Anthropology* 32:189–199.

Strum, Philippa, and Andrew Selee (eds.). 2004. *The Hispanic Challenge? What We Know about Latino Immigration.* Washington, DC: Woodrow Wilson International Center for Scholars.

Strum, Philippa, and Danielle Tarantolo (eds.). 2003. *Muslims in the United States: Demography, Beliefs, Institutions.* Washington, DC: Woodrow Wilson International Center for Scholars.

Stull, Donald D., and Michael J. Broadway. 2004. *Slaughterhouse Blues: The Meat and Poultry Industry in North America.* Belmont, CA: Wadsworth.

Tagliabue, John. 2012. "A School's Big Lesson Begins with Dropping Personal Pronouns." *New York Times,* November 14, p. A8.

Tavernise, Sabrina. 2008. "Putting a Dent in a Law against Insulting Turkishness." *New York Times,* January 25, p. A4.

Telhami, Shibley. 2015. "What Americans Really Think about Muslims and Islam." Brookings Middle East Politics and Policy, December 9. Available at http:// www.brookings.edu/blogs/markaz /posts/2015/12/09-what-americans -think-of-muslims-and-islam-telhami, accessed April 22, 2016.

Temple University. 2009. "Earliest Evidence of Domesticated Maize Discovered: Dates Back 8,700 Years." *Science Daily* 25(March): 3.

Terry, Don. 2015. "In the Crosshairs." *Intelligence Report.* Atlanta: Southern Poverty Law Center, p. 27.

Tessman, Irwin, and Jack Tessman. 2000. "Efficacy of Prayer: A Critical Examination of Claims." *Skeptical Inquirer* 24(2):31–33.

Theodorou, Angelina E. 2015. "5 Facts about Religious Hostilities in Europe." Pew Research Center. Available at http://www.pewresearch.org

/fact-tank/2015/02/27/5-facts-about-religious-hostilities-in-europe, accessed April 25, 2016.

Thornton, Lynne. 1994. *Women as Portrayed in Orientalist Painting.* Paris: PocheCouleur.

Thubron, Colin. 2009. "Madame Butterfly's Brothel." *New York Review of Books,* June 11, pp. 24–27.

Timberg, Craig, and Daniel Halperin. 2012. *Tinderbox: How the West Sparked the AIDS Epidemic and How the World Can Finally Overcome It.* New York: Penguin.

Todaro, Michael, and Stephen C. Smith. 2003. *Economic Development* (8th ed.). Harlow, UK: Pearson Addison Wesley.

Trachtman, Michael G. 2009. *The Supremes' Greatest Hit, Revised and Updated Edition: The 37 Supreme Court Cases That Most Directly Affect Your Life.* New York: Sterling.

Transparency International. 2016. Corruption Perceptions Index 2015. Available at http://www.transparency.org/cpi2015 accessed April 25, 2016.

Traphagan, John W. 1998. "Contesting the Transition to Old Age in Japan." *Ethnology* 37:333–350.

Tsuruta, Kinua. 1989. *The Walls Within: Images of Westerners in Japan and Images of the Japanese Abroad.* Vancouver, BC: Institute of Asian Research.

Turnbull, Colin. 1968. "The Importance of Flux in Two Hunting Societies." In R. B. Lee and I. DeVore (eds.), *Man the Hunter* (pp. 132–137). Chicago: Aldine.

Turner, Victor. 1967. *The Forest of Symbols: Aspects of Ndembu Ritual.* Ithaca, NY: Cornell University Press.

Turner, Victor. 1969. *The Ritual Process: Structure and Antistructure.* Chicago: Aldine.

UNEP/GRID-Arendal. 2008. "Population Distribution in the Circumpolar Arctic, by Country (Including Indigenous Population)." UNEP/GRID-Arendal Maps and Graphics Library. Available at http://maps.grida.no/go/graphic/population-distribution-in-the-circumpolar-arctic-by-country-including-indigenous-population1, accessed November 1, 2010.

United Nations. 2008. *World Urbanization Prospects.* Available at http://esa.un.org/unup.

United Nations. 2012. "World Urbanization Prospects: The 2011 Revision." United Nations Department of Economic and Social Affairs, Population Division. Available at http://esa.un.org/unpd/wup/index.htm, accessed June 18, 2012.

United Nations Population Fund. n.d. "Migration." Available at http://www.unfpa.org/migration, accessed May 20, 2016.

University of Virginia. 2008. "Choosing and Using Your Major." University Career Services. Available at http://www.career.virginia.edu/students/handouts/choosing_a _major.pdf, accessed April 24, 2013.

U.S. Bureau of Labor Statistics. 2016. "Employment Projections." Available at http://www.bls.gov/emp/ep_chart_001.htm, accessed October 25, 2016.

U.S. Bureau of Labor Statistics. 2016. "The Employment Situation June 2016." *Bureau of Labor Statistics.* Available at http://www.bls.gov/news.release/pdf/empsit.pdf, accessed July 15, 2016.

U.S. Census Bureau. 2012. "2010 Census Shows Multiple-Race Population Grew Faster than Single-Race Population." September 27. Available at http://www.census.gov/newsroom/releases/archives/race/cb12-182.html, accessed July 15, 2016.

U.S. Census Bureau. 2016. "World Population Clock." Available at http://www.census.gov/popclock, accessed May 20, 2016.

U.S. Citizenship and Immigration Services. 2013. "Iraqi Refugee Processing Fact Sheet." Available at: https://www.uscis.gov/humanitarian/refugees-asylum/refugees/iraqi-refugee-processing-fact-sheet, accessed May 20, 2016.

U.S. Department of Agriculture. 2012. "Fruit and Tree Nuts." Economic Research Service. Available at www.ers.usda.gov/topics/crops/fruit-tree-nuts.aspx.

U.S. Department of Agriculture. 2013a. "FSIS Recalls." Available at www.fsis.usda.gov/fsis_recalls/Recall_Summary_2012/, accessed April 24, 2013.

U.S. Department of Agriculture. 2013b. "U.S. Food Imports." Economic Research Service. Available at www.ers.usda.gov/data-products/us-food-imports.aspx#25416.

U.S. Department of Agriculture. 2014. "Preliminary Report Highlights: U.S. Farms and Farmers." Available at https://www.agcensus.usda.gov/Publications/2012/Preliminary_Report/Highlights.pdf, accessed July 14, 2016.

U.S. Department of Agriculture. 2015. "Sugar: World Markets and Trade." Available at https://apps.fas.usda.gov/psdonline/circulars/sugar.pdf, accessed April 25, 2016.

U.S. Department of Agriculture. 2016a. "Summary of Recall Cases in Calendar Year 2014." Available at: http://www.fsis.usda.gov/wps/portal/fsis/topics/recalls-and-public-health-alerts/recall-summaries, accessed April 25, 2016.

U.S. Department of Agriculture. 2016b. "U.S. Agricultural Trade Data Update." Available at http://www.ers.usda.gov/data-products/foreign-agricultural-trade-of-the-united-states-(fatus)/us-agricultural-trade-data-update.aspx, accessed March 11, 2016.

U.S. English. 2012. "Misconceptions about Official English." Available at www.us-english.org/view/15.

U.S. Environmental Protection Agency. n.d. "Pollutants and Sources." Available at www.epa.gov/ttnatw01/pollsour.html, accessed April 24, 2013.

Van Biema, David, and Jeff Chu. 2006. "Does God Want You to Be Rich?" *Time,* September 18.

van Donge, Jan Kees. 1992. "Agricultural Decline in Tanzania: The Case of the Uluguru Mountains." *African Affairs* 91:73–94.

van Gennep, Arnold. 1960/1909. *The Rites of Passage.* Chicago: University of Chicago Press.

Vayda, Andrew P. 1976. *War in Ecological Perspective.* New York: Plenum.

Venbrux, Eric, Pamela Sheffield Rosi, and Robert L. Welsch (eds.). 2006. *Exploring World Art.* Long Grove, IL: Waveland.

Ventura, Stephanie J. 2009. "Changing Patterns of Nonmarital Childbearing in the United States." *NCHS Data Brief* 18 (May).

Verdon, Michel, and Paul Jorion. 1981. "The Hordes of Discord: Australian Aboriginal Social Organization Reconsidered." *Man* 16(1):90–107.

Victor, David A. 1992. *International Business Communication*. New York: Harper Collins.

Vincent, Susan. 1998. "The Family in the Household: Women, Relationships, and Economic History in Peru." *Research in Economic Anthropology* 19:179–187.

Vine, David. 2009. *Island of Shame*. Princeton, NJ: Princeton University Press.

Viswanathan, Gauri. 1988. "Currying Favor: The Politics of British Educational and Cultural Policy in India 1813–1854." *Social Text* 19–20:85–104.

Vo, Lam Thuy. 2015. "How Much Does It Cost to Raise a Child?" *Wall Street Journal,* July 22. Available at http://blogs.wsj.com/economics/2016/06/22/how-much-does-it-cost-to-raise-a-child, accessed August 22, 2016.

Vogel, Susan. 1991. *Africa Explores: 20th Century African Art*. New York: Center for African Art.

Volkman, Toby Alice. 1984. "Great Performances: Toraja Cultural Identity in the 1970s." *American Ethnologist* 11(1):152–168.

Walker, Andrew. 2009. "Nigeria's Gas Profits 'Up in Smoke.'" *BBC News,* Nigeria, January 13. Available at http://news.bbc.co.uk/2/hi/africa/7820384.stm.

Wallerstein, Immanuel. 1995. *Historical Capitalism*. London: Verso.

Wang, Jimmy. 2009. "Now Hip-Hop, Too, Is Made in China." *New York Times,* January 24, p. C1.

Warren, Kay B., and Susan C. Bourque. 1989. "Women, Technology, and Development Ideologies: Frameworks and Findings." In S. Morgen (ed.), *Gender and Anthropology: Critical Reviews for Research and Teaching* (pp. 382–410). Washington, DC: American Anthropological Association.

Wasif, Sehrish. 2011. "European Muslims: Refusal to Integrate the Root of Most Problems." *Express Tribune,* July 22.

Waters, Mary C. 2011. "Debating Immigration: Are We Addressing the Right Issues?" In Marcelo M. Suarez Orozco, Vivian Louie, and Robert Suro (eds.), *Writing Immigration*. Berkeley: University of California Press.

Weiner, Annette B. 1976. *Women of Value, Men of Renown: New Perspectives on Trobriand Exchange*. Austin: University of Texas Press.

Wenzel, George W. 2009. "Canadian Inuit Subsistence and Ecological Instability—If the Climate Changes, Must the Inuit?" *Polar Research* 28:89–99.

White, Benjamin. 1980. "Rural Household Studies in Anthropological Perspective." In H. Binswanger, R. Evenson, C. Florencio, and B. White (eds.), *Rural Household Studies in Asia* (pp. 3–25). Singapore: Singapore University Press.

White, Geoffrey M. 1997. "Introduction: Public History and National Narrative." *Museum Anthropology* 21(1):3–6.

White, Jenny B. 1994. *Money Makes Us Relatives*. Austin: University of Texas Press.

Whitehead, Harriet. 1981. "The Bow and the Burden Strap: A New Look at Institutionalized Homosexuality in Native North America." In S. B. Ortner and H. Whitehead (eds.), *Sexual Meanings: The Cultural Construction of Gender and Sexuality* (pp. 80–115). Cambridge, UK: Cambridge University Press.

Whiting, John, Richard Kluckhohn, and Albert Anthony. 1967. "The Function of Male Initiation Ceremonies at Puberty." In R. Endelman (ed.), *Personality and Social Life* (pp. 294–308). New York: Random House.

Whorf, Benjamin L. 1941. "The Relation of Habitual Thought and Behavior to Language." In Leslie Spier (ed.), *Language, Culture and Personality* (pp. 75–93). Menasha, WI: Sapir Memorial Publication Fund.

Wiessner, Polly. 2009. Experimental Games and Games of Life among the Ju/'hoan Bushmen. *Current Anthropology* 50(1):133–138.

Wiessner, Polly, and Nitze Pupu. 2012. "Toward Peace: Foreign Arms and Indigenous Institutions in a Papua New Guinea Society." *Science* 337(6102): 1651–1654.

Wikan, Unni. 1977. "Man Becomes Woman: Transsexualism in Oman as a Key to Gender Roles." *Man* (new series) 12:304–319.

Wikan, Unni. 2008. *In Honor of Fadime: Murder and Shame*. Chicago: University of Chicago Press.

Wildsmith, Elizabeth, Nicole R. Steward-Streng, and Jennifer Manlove. 2011. "Childbearing Outside of Marriage: Estimates and Trends in the United States." *Child Trends Research Brief,* no. 2011-29.

Wilk, Richard (ed.). 2006. *Fast Food / Slow Food: The Cultural Economy of the Global Food System*. Lanham, MD: Altamira.

Williams, Gwyn A. 1970. *Medieval London: From Commune to Capital*. London: Athlone.

Williams, Trevor. 1984. *Howard Florey: Penicillin and After*. Oxford, UK: Oxford University Press.

Williams, Walter. 1986. *The Spirit and the Flesh* (2nd ed.). Boston: Beacon.

Wilson, Tamar Diana. 2003. "Is Semi-Informalized Self-Employment Counterhegemonic? A Comparison of Irish Jarveys and Mexicali Brickmakers." *Urban Anthropology* 32(3/4):281–309.

Win, Patrick. 2015. "The Slave Labor behind Your Favorite Clothing Brands: Gap, H&M and More Exposed." *Salon,* March 22. Available at http://www.salon.com/2015/03/22/the_slave_labor_behind_your_favorite_clothing_brands_gap_hm_and_more_exposed_partner, accessed May 20, 2016.

Wolf, Eric R. 1982. *Europe and the People without History*. Berkeley: University of California Press.

Wolfe, Nathan D., Claire P. Dunavan, and Jared F. Diamond. 2012. "Origins of Major Human Infectious Diseases. In Institute of Medicine (US), *Improving Food Safety Through a One Health Approach*. Washington DC: National Academies Press. Available at http://www.ncbi.nlm.nih.gov/books/NBK114494, accessed April 2, 2016.

Wolff, Edward N. 2010. "Recent Trends in Household Wealth in the United States: Rising Debt and the Middle Class Squeeze an Update to 2007." Levy Economics Institute of Bard College, working paper no. 589.

Wong, Edward. 2008. "Factories Shut, China Workers Are Suffering." *New York Times*, November 14, p. A1.

Wong, Edward. 2011. "Photo Turns U.S. Envoy into a Lesson for Chinese." *New York Times,* August 18, p. A14.

Wood, Graeme. 2013. "Anthropology Inc." *The Atlantic* 313(2):48–56.

Woodburn, James. 1968. "An Introduction to Hadza Ecology." In R. B. Lee and I. DeVore (eds.), *Man the Hunter* (pp. 49–55). Chicago: Aldine.

Woodburn, James. 1998. "Sharing Is Not a Form of Exchange: An Analysis of Property-Sharing in Immediate Return Hunter-Gatherer Societies." In C. M. Hann (ed.), *Property Relations: Renewing the Anthropological Tradition* (pp. 48–63). Cambridge, UK: Cambridge University Press.

World Bank. 1992. *Development and the Environment: World Development Report 1992.* New York: Oxford University Press.

World Bank. 2005. *African Development Indicators: From the World Bank Africa Database.* Washington, DC: World Bank.

World Bank. 2011. *Migration and Remittances Factbook 2011* (2nd ed.). Washington, DC: World Bank.

World Bank. 2016a. "GNI per Capita, Atlas Method: World Development Indicators." Available at http://data .worldbank.org/indicator/NY.GNP .PCAP.CD/countries/1W?order =wbapi_data_value_2014%20wbapi _data_value%20wbapi_data_value -last&sort=asc&display=default, accessed May 20, 2016.

World Bank. 2016b. "Poverty Overview." Available at http://www.worldbank. org/en/topic/poverty/overview, accessed May 20, 2016.

World Bank. 2016c. "GDP at Market Prices: World Development Indicators." Available at http://databank .worldbank.org/data/reports.aspx?sour ce=2&country=&series=NY.GDP .MKTP.CD&period, accessed May 20, 2016.

World Bank. 2016d. "Remittances to Developing Countries Edge Up Slightly in 2015." April 13. Available at http://www.worldbank.org/en /news/press-release/2016/04/13 /remittances-to-developing-countries -edge-up-slightly-in-2015, accessed May 20, 2016.

World Eskimo-Indian Olympics. 2016. "The WEIO Games." Available at http://www.weio.org/the_games.php, accessed February, 25, 2016.

World Health Organization. n.d. "Global Health Observatory Data Repository: Life Expectancy, Data by Country." Available at http://apps.who.int/gho /data/node.main.688, accessed May 20, 2016.

World Health Organization. 2004. "Pesticides and Health." Available at www .who.int/mental_health/prevention /suicide/en/PesticidesHealth2.pdf.

World Health Organization. 2008. "Children's Health and the Environment." Available at www.who.int/ceh/capacity /Pesticides.pdf.

Worthman, Carol M. 1995. "Hormones, Sex, and Gender." In William Durham, E. Valentine Daniel, and Bambi Schieffelin (eds.), *Annual Review of Anthropology* (vol. 24, pp. 593–618). Stanford, CA: Stanford University Press.

Wrangham, Richard. 2009. *Catching Fire: How Cooking Made Us Human.* New York: Basic.

Wright, Stephen. 2008. "Bali Murder: The Story Behind the Police Inspector's Evil Plot to Kill His Wife after She Asked for a Divorce." *Mail Online,* January 28. Available at www .dailymail.co.uk/news/article -508046, accessed April 24, 2013.

Yamba, Bawa. 1997. "Cosmologies in Turmoil: Witchfinding and AIDS in Chiawa, Zambia." *Africa* 67(2):200–223.

Yardley, Jim. 2012. "A Village Rape Shatters a Family, and India's Traditional Silence." *New York Times,* October 28, p. A1.

Yardley, Jim. 2013. "Report on Deadly Factory Collapse in Bangladesh Finds Widespread Blame." *New York Times,* May 23, p. A5.

Younger, S. M. 2012. *Calculating Chiefs: Simulating Leadership, Violence, and Warfare in Oceania.* Saarbrucken, Germany: LAP Lambert.

Zeegers, Maurice, Frans van Poppel, Robert Vlietinck, Liesbeth Spruijt, and Harry Ostrer. 2004. "Founder Mutations among the Dutch." *European Journal of Human Genetics* 12:591–600.

Zoepf, Katherine. 2008. "In Booming Gulf, Some Arab Women Find Freedom in the Skies." *New York Times*, December 22, p. A1.

INDEX